AIR WAR EUROPA

CHRONOLOGY

Books by Eric Hammel

76 Hours: The Invasion of Tarawa (with John E. Lane)
Chosin: Heroic Ordeal of the Korean War
The Root: The Marines in Beirut
Ace!: A Marine Night-Fighter Pilot in World War II
                                        (with R. Bruce Porter)
Duel for the Golan (with Jerry Asher)
Guadalcanal: Starvation Island
Guadalcanal: The Carrier Battles
Guadalcanal: Decision at Sea
Munda Trail: The New Georgia Campaign
Khe Sanh: Siege in the Clouds
First Across the Rhine (with David E. Pergrin)
Lima-6: A Marine Company Commander in Vietnam
                                        (with R. D. Camp, Jr.)
Ambush Valley
Fire in the Streets: The Battle for Hue
Aces Against Japan
Aces Against Germany
Six Days in June: How Israel Won the Six-Day War

AIR WAR EUROPA

AMERICA'S AIR WAR AGAINST GERMANY
IN EUROPE AND NORTH AFRICA
1942 – 1945

CHRONOLOGY

ERIC HAMMEL

Pacifica Press

Requests for permission to make copies of any part of the work should
be mailed to: Permissions, Pacifica Press, 1149 Grand Teton Drive,
Pacifica, California 94044.

Jacket illustration by Jim Laurier, Keene, New Hampshire
Jacket design and maps by Moody Graphics, Kansas City, Missouri

Manufactured in the United States of America

Trade Hardcover edition published in 1994

Library of Congress Cataloging-in-Publication Data

Hammel, Eric M.
　　Air war Europa : America's air war against Germany in Europe and north Africa, 1942–
1945 : chronology / Eric Hammel
　　572 p.　　　cm.
　　Includes bioliographical references (p.) and index.
　　ISBN 0-935553-25-8 (Trade Paperback edition)
　　1. World War, 1939–1945—Aerial operations, American. 2. World War, 1939–1945—
Campaigns—Western—Chronology. 3. World War, 1939–1945—Campaigns—Africa,
North—Chronology. I. Title.
D790.H2535　　1994
040.54'4973—dc20　　　　　　　　　　　　　　　　　　　　　　　94-4181
　　　　　　　　　　　　　　　　　　　　　　　　　　　　　　　　　　　CIP

*For All the American and Allied Airmen
Who Braved Those War-Torn Skies*

Table of Contents

Glossary & Guide to Abbreviations

1stLt: First Lieutenant
2dLt: Second Lieutenant

A-20: U.S. Douglas Havoc twin-engine light bomber
A-26: U.S. Douglas Invader twin-engine attack bomber
A-36: U.S. North American Apache fighter-bomber
AAFIB: Army Air Forces in Britain
AAFMTO: Army Air Forces, Mediterranean Theater of Operations
AEAF: Allied Expeditionary Air Force
Ar-96: German Arado advanced trainer
Ar-196: German Arado two-seat float plane
Ar-234: German Arado twin-engine jet bomber
Azon: Radio-guided azimuth bombs

B-17: U.S. Boeing Flying Fortress four-engine heavy bomber
B-24: U.S. Consolidated Liberator four-engine heavy bomber
B-25: U.S. North American Mitchell twin-engine medium bomber
B-26: U.S. Martin Marauder twin-engine medium bomber
Beaufighter: British-made Bristol 156 twin-engine fighter/night-fighter

benzol: German synthetic fuel
Bf-109: German Messerschmitt fighter
Bf-110: German Messerschmitt twin-engine fighter/night-fighter
Bisley: British Bristol 60 twin-engine light bomber
Boston: American-made British version of the Douglas A-20 twin-engine
　　　　　light bomber
BriGen: Brigadier General
Br.20: Italian Fiat twin-engine medium bomber
Bu-131: German Bücker two-place primary trainer

C-47: U.S. Douglas Skytrain twin-engine cargo/transport plane
C-54: U.S. Douglas Skymaster four-engine cargo/transport plane
Capt: Captain
CCS: Allied Combined Chiefs of Staff
Col: Colonel
CR.42: Italian Fiat biplane fighter

D.520: French Dewoitine fighter
DATF: Desert Air Task Force
Do-217: German Dornier twin-engine medium bomber
Droopsnoot: U.S. Lockheed P-38 variant with bombardier position

ETO: European Theater of Operations
ETOUSA: European Theater of Operations, U.S. Army
E-boat: German Navy torpedo boat

F-4: U.S. Lockheed P-38 reconnaissance variant
F-5: U.S. Lockheed P-38 reconnaissance variant
F-6: U.S. North American P-51 reconnaissance variant
F4F: U.S. Navy Grumman Wildcat carrier fighter
Fi-156: German Fieseler ground-cooperation/reconnaissance plane
Flak: Antiaircraft gun/fire (from FLieger Abwher Kannonen)
FO: Flight Officer (USAAF warrant officer)
FW-190: German Focke-Wulf fighter
FW-200: German Focke-Wulf Condor four-engine long-range
　　　　　reconnaissance bomber

G.50: Italian Fiat fighter
G.55: Italian Fiat fighter
GAF: German Air Force
GB-4: Allied guided bomb
GEE: Allied blind-bombing navigational system
Gen: General
GH: Allied blind-bombing system

H2S: Allied blind-bombing radar system
H2X: Allied blind-bombing radar system
HALPRO: USAAF Halverson Provisional bombardment detachment
He-111: German Heinkel twin-engine medium bomber
He-115: German Heinkel twin-engine reconnaissance float plane
He-177: German Heinkel twin-engine heavy bomber
Hs-126: German Henschel biplane reconnaissance plane

IAR.80: Romanian single-engine fighter

Ju-52: German Junkers tri-motor cargo/transport plane
Ju-87: German Junkers Stuka single-engine dive-bomber
Ju-88: German Junkers twin-engine medium bomber/dive-bomber

Lt: Lieutenant
LtCol: Lieutenant Colonel
LtGen: Lieutenant General

MAAF: Mediterranean Allied Air Forces
MAC: Mediterranean Air Command
MACAF: Mediterranean Allied Coastal Air Force
Maj: Major
MajGen: Major General
MASAF: Mediterranean Allied Strategic Air Force
MATAF: Mediterranean Allied Tactical Air Force
Mc.200: Italian Macchi interceptor fighter
Mc.202: Italian Macchi interceptor fighter
Mc.205: Italian Macchi interceptor fighter
Me-163: German Messerschmitt Komet rocket-propelled fighter

Me-210: German Messerschmitt twin-engine heavy fighter
Me-262: German Messerschmitt jet interceptor fighter
Me-323: German Messerschmitt six-engine heavy powered transport glider
Me-410: German Messerschmitt twin-engine heavy fighter
Micro-H: Allied blind-bombing system
Mistel: German Ju-88 flying bomb/FW-190 tandem
Mosquito: British de Havilland D.H.98 twin-engine fighter/reconnaissance
        plane
MTO: Mediterranean Theater of Operations

NAAF: Northwest African Air Forces
NAASC: Northwest African Air Service Command
NACAF: Northwest African Coastal Air Force
NASAF: Northwest African Strategic Air Force
NATAF: Northwest African Tactical Air Force
NATBF: Northwest African Tactical Bomber Force
NATC: Northwest African Training Command
NATCC: Northwest African Troop Carrier Command
NATOUSA: Northwest African Theater of Operations, U.S. Army

Oboe: Allied blind-bombing navigational system
OSS: U.S. Office of Strategic Services

P-38: U.S. Lockheed Lightning twin-engine fighter
P-39: U.S. Bell Airacobra fighter/fighter-bomber
P-40: U.S. Curtiss fighter/fighter-bomber
P-47: U.S. Republic Thunderbolt fighter/fighter-bomber
P-51: U.S. North American Mustang fighter/fighter-bomber
P-61: U.S. Northrop Black Widow twin-engine night-fighter
P-400: U.S. Bell Airacobra export fighter variant

R-boat: German Navy gunboat
RAF: Royal Air Force
Re.2000: Italian Reggiane fighter/fighter-bomber (also Re.2001 and
        Re.2005 variants)

SBD: U.S. Navy Douglas Dauntless carrier dive-bomber

Sgt: Sergeant
SHAEF: Supreme Headquarters, Allied Expeditionary Force
SM.79: Italian Savoia-Marchetti twin-engine medium bomber
SM.82: Italian Savoia-Marchetti twin-engine heavy bomber/transport
Spitfire: British Supermarine fighter
SS: Nazi military force (*Schutzstaffel*)
SSgt: Staff Sergeant

TAC: Tactical Air Command
TBF: U.S. Navy Grumman Avenger single-engine carrier torpedo bomber
TSgt: Technical Sergeant

U-boat: German Navy submarine
U.K.: United Kingdom (i.e., British Isles)
USAAC: U.S. Army Air Corps
USAAF: U.S. Army Air Force
USAAFNATO: U.S. Army Air Forces, North African Theater of
        Operations
USAAFUK: U.S. Army Air Forces in the United Kingdom
USAFBI: U.S. Army Forces in the British Isles
USAFIME: U.S. Army Forces in the Middle East
USAMEAF: U.S. Army, Middle East Air Forces
USSAFE: U.S. Strategic Air Forces in Europe (original designation)
USSTAF: U.S. Strategic Air Forces in Europe (final designation)

V-1: German flying bomb
V-2: German sub-orbital rocket bomb
V-weapon: Refers to German V-1 flying bomb

WDAF: Western Desert Air Force
Wellington: British Vickers twin-engine long-range night bomber

YB-40: U.S. Boeing B-17 gunship variant ("Y" prefix refers to in-service
        test model)

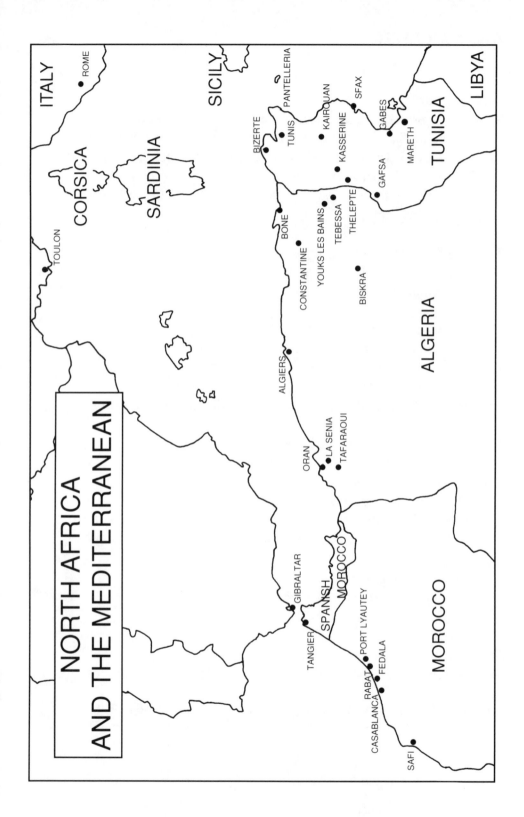

NORTH AFRICA
AND THE MEDITERRANEAN

ITALY
ROME

SICILY

CORSICA
SARDINIA

TOULON

PANTELLERIA
BIZERTE
TUNIS
KAIROUAN
SFAX
GABES
MARETH
KASSERINE
GAFSA
TUNISIA

BONE
YOUKS LES BAINS
TEBESSA
THELEPTE
CONSTANTINE
BISKRA

ALGIERS

ALGERIA

ORAN
LA SENIA
TAFARAOUI

GIBRALTAR
SPANISH
MOROCCO
TANGIER
PORT LYAUTEY
RABAT
FEDALA
CASABLANCA

MOROCCO

SAFI

LIBYA

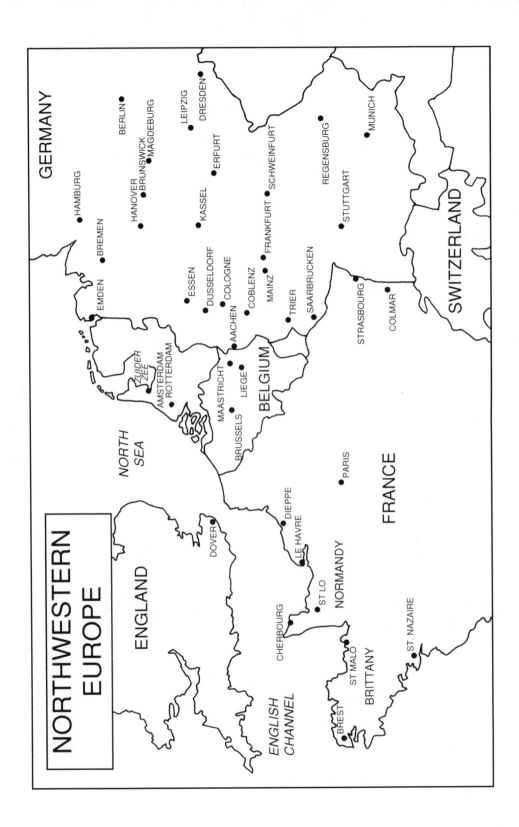

NORTHWESTERN EUROPE

GERMANY

SWITZERLAND

FRANCE

BELGIUM

ENGLAND

NORTH SEA

ENGLISH CHANNEL

NORMANDY

BRITTANY

HAMBURG

BREMEN

EMDEN

BERLIN

MAGDEBURG

BRUNSWICK

HANOVER

LEIPZIG

DRESDEN

ERFURT

KASSEL

ESSEN

DUSSELDORF

COLOGNE

AACHEN

COBLENZ

MAINZ

FRANKFURT

SCHWEINFURT

TRIER

SAARBRUCKEN

REGENSBURG

MUNICH

STUTTGART

STRASBOURG

COLMAR

ZUIDER ZEE

AMSTERDAM

ROTTERDAM

MAASTRICHT

LIEGE

BRUSSELS

PARIS

DIEPPE

LE HAVRE

DOVER

ST LO

CHERBOURG

ST MALO

BREST

ST. NAZAIRE

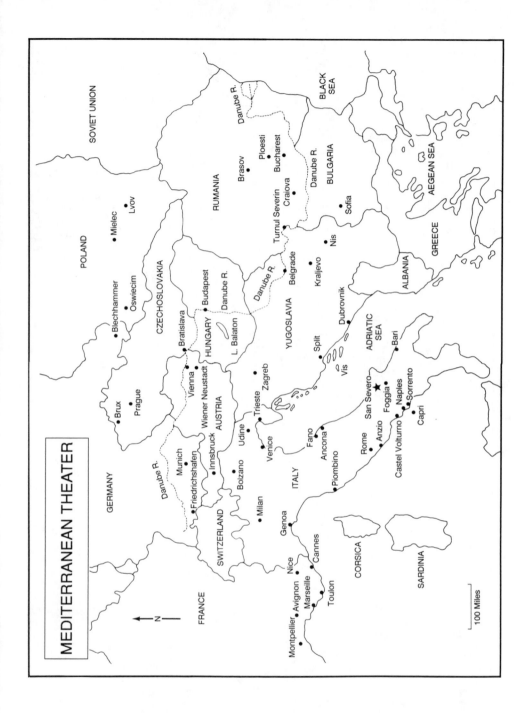

MEDITERRANEAN THEATER

INTRODUCTION

THE ROLE OF AMERICAN FIGHTERS IN NORTHERN EUROPE
A Narrative Overview

The popular conception of the struggle in the air over Europe during World War II is of pairs and quartets of sleek fighters racing over the German heartland to protect contrailed streams of lumbering bombers, stretching beyond sight. This is as it was late in America's air war against Germany, but it was as far from the truth as it is possible to get at the start of that great aerial crusade. In the beginning, the fighter was a short-legged creature whose role of protecting the bombers was quite far down the list, subordinate to role of guarding friendly territory and installations. The difference, which is crucial to understanding the course of the air war against Germany and her partners, was the product of technology—range and the power of aircraft engines—and intellect. Until surprisingly late in the war, the use of the fighter as an offensive weapon was stunted by the defensive mindset of even the leading "pursuit" acolytes of the interwar decades.

The pursuit airplane had evolved over the *fixed* battlefields of western Europe during World War I. The pursuit's sole duty at the start of that war— the reason the type was developed—was to prevent enemy observation airplanes from overflying friendly lines *and* to protect friendly observation airplanes from enemy pursuits while the observers overflew enemy lines. The pursuit was conceived as a *tactical* and a *defensive* weapon, and it was limited to these roles both by conception and by the technologies of the day.

Between the world wars, the development of the American pursuit aircraft was hobbled by budgetary restrictions that for many years slowed or obviated altogether the creation of new technologies or even methodical experimentation with new tactics. The U.S. Navy and, especially, the U.S. Marine Corps did advance the use of the single-engine pursuit as a close-support weapon to bolster the infantry, but the interests of various US. Army constituencies prevented similar advances in what had come to be called the Army Air Corps. To the degree that it developed at all, the Air Corps saw increasingly heavy and longer-ranged bombers in its future. And, as the limited available research-and-development dollars were expended on speedier bombers, the pursuits of the day were increasingly outranged and outrun. Inevitably, an ex post facto argument gave a voice to reality, and the American bombers of the late 1930s were designed to be "self-defending" because they could fly much farther and at least somewhat faster than could the pursuits of the day. The pursuits, which were being developed at a much slower pace, were relegated to a point-defense role—guarding cities, industrial targets, and air bases. When World War II began, the Air Corps—shortly to be renamed the Army Air Forces—was divided into two distinct combat arms: fighters and bombers. And, by virtue of the fighter's stunted development, there appeared little chance that the two would spend much time working together. (The combat radius of the B-17 heavy bomber was approximately 500 miles in late 1941, and the combat radius of the Army Air Corps' *best* fighter was around 200 miles. Put another way, the B-17 could stay aloft for more than five hours whereas the *best* American fighter could stay aloft for seventy to ninety minutes, at most.)

As soon as the Army Air Corps was pulled into World War II on December 7, 1941—right away, at Pearl Harbor and around Manila—it became focused on the defense of the U.S. East, West, and Gulf coasts; several Caribbean islands; bases in Greenland and Iceland; and on the strategically indispensable Panama Canal. There were few airplanes of any type to devote to these defensive missions, and those that were deployed defensively also had to serve as on-the-job trainers for hundreds of the raw young pilots who were beginning to emerge from the Air Corps' burgeoning flight schools.

The early attrition in training accidents—inexperienced pilots strapped into poorly designed or simply unforgiving high-performance airplanes—would have been scandalous if there had not been a war to be won.

Through the first half of 1942, all of the very few pilots and airplanes that could be spared from the defense of the U.S. coasts and sea lanes were rushed to defend Australia and the South Pacific. Dozens of these precious airplanes and pilots were lost in the pathetic defense of the Netherlands East Indies, and many more were lost in the early battles around Port Moresby, New Guinea. But, combined with other stop-gap measures—and a valiant effort by the U.S. Navy—the thin line managed to hold. However, the pressures exerted by the war against Japan continued to mount, and the Pacific and even China drew off the entirety of the Army Air Forces' slowly rising spare strength. Meantime, at home, the flight schools and several new operational training units were beginning to catch up with combat and training losses as well as with the heavy burden imposed by the formation of new fighter, bomber, and other-type groups. And fighter aircraft with a higher probability of survival were beginning to reach the Pacific and Asian war zones and coastal-defense air groups.

Fortunately, the United States could afford to be a bit late off the mark in her war against Germany. German efforts in 1940 to bring Great Britain to her knees all had failed miserably and, by the end of 1941, the bulk of Germany's air and land forces were mired in a frightful war of attrition deep inside Russia. For many months, the only point at which the United States and Germany met was at sea, where German submarines were beating the pants off American maritime power. The Army Air Forces helped marginally in the war against German submarines, but the main effort naturally fell to the U.S. Navy. In Great Britain, the British had the situation reasonably well in hand, although they would have collapsed had it not been for vast infusions of weapons and supplies from the United States. The land war in Egypt and Libya was teetering on the edge of collapse, but there was little the United States would be able to do for many months to influence the outcome—assuming the British held on that long.

So, while the Army Air Forces devoted the majority of its limited expendable resources to aiding China and Australia and to bolstering the U.S. Navy's early efforts in the Pacific—defensive programs, all—new air groups were being built up in the United States, and new and better bombers and fighters were rolling off scores of newly created assembly lines. As early as January

11, 1942, it was decided in high Army Air Forces circles to commit American air power in the United Kingdom. At first, however, the commitment would be more symbolic than real—little more than a meager show of interest that in fact masked an advanced combat-training program to be overseen by the Royal Air Force (RAF). Only later, when training bases and factories in the United States had caught up with the planning, would the U.S. Army Air Forces take on what its leaders had already billed as *the* decisive strategic campaign projected to be waged against the German industrial heartland.

As early as February 20, 1942, Brigadier General Ira Eaker arrived in England to establish the headquarters of the new Army Air Forces in Britain (AAFIB) Bomber Command. To the accompaniment of much public fanfare, Eaker formally opened his headquarters at High Wycombe, England, on February 23. However, AAFIB Bomber Command had no combat airplanes to its name; they would not be available for several months.

It fell to General Eaker to argue with his British hosts in favor of an independent role for the forthcoming Army Air Forces in Britain. Eaker knew going in that both the RAF and the British government wanted America's commitment to the air war in Europe to be subordinate to or an adjunct of the British theater air war. The Americans, however, wanted and felt they deserved an independent role, and it was Eaker's job to win the British to this viewpoint.

The American notion was strongly bolstered—in argument, at least—by the fact that the U.S. Army Air Forces had developed over many years a theoretical strategic air doctrine that was quite different from the RAF's experience-based strategic doctrine. The Americans favored and had equipped their bomber force to wage a precision daylight-bombing campaign against industrial targets hundreds of miles inside enemy territory. The RAF, on the other hand, was the only other air force in the world to have developed long-range four-engine heavy bombers, but its doctrine—the result of bloody experiences early in the war—had caused it to opt for "area" bombing at night. Doctrinal arguments aside, the British victims of the Nazi Blitz of 1940–41 were less squeamish than their American allies about bombing German civilians. Besides, the RAF had few long-range heavy bombers to its name and thus felt it needed to co-opt the promised infusion of American heavies. In any case, for whatever reason, the RAF commanders argued forcefully for the AAFIB Bomber Command heavy bombers, once they arrived, to join in the night-bombing curriculum.

For the time being, Eaker's arguments with the RAF hierarchy were moot. There would be no American air-combat units in the United Kingdom for several months, and then there would not be enough of them to make a dent in Hitler's Fortress Europa for many months more.

General Eaker's AAFIB Bomber Command was redesignated VIII Bomber Command (a component of the U.S. Eighth Air Force) on April 15, 1942. The first large contingent of USAAF headquarters personnel reached VIII Bomber Command headquarters on May 12, but no airplanes or aircrews had yet been dispatched from the United States.

Also arriving in England at this time was Brigadier General Frank O'D. "Monk" Hunter, who established the headquarters of his VIII Fighter Command, also at High Wycombe. Unlike Eaker, Hunter, a rather flamboyant World War I ace, quickly came to terms with British beliefs and aspirations regarding the employment of forthcoming American fighter groups. The RAF had opted for powerful short-range fighters that could defend friendly air bases and attack nearby enemy air bases, and their doctrine had more than proven itself during the Battle of Britain and the Blitz. Monk Hunter, who had spent most of his career arguing the point-defense case for the U.S. Army's fighters, was more than satisfied to augment the British fighter plan, at least until it came time for the Allies to prepare for the invasion of France in mid-1943 or mid-1944.

On June 10, 1942—a few days after the U.S. Navy won the great aerial victory in the Pacific, near Midway—ground personnel from two USAAF fighter groups, a USAAF transport group, and one USAAF heavy-bomber group squadrons arrived in the U.K.—but still no fighters, bombers, transports, pilots, or aircrewmen.

On June 15, Major General Carl "Tooey" Spaatz arrived to establish a headquarters for his Eighth Air Force at High Wycombe. A World War I combat commander with several German airplanes to his credit and decades of being at the leading edge of the growth of the Army Air Corps, Tooey Spaatz was one of the handful of Army Air Forces officers with the moral authority to win an independent role for American air units over the forceful arguments of Britain's top military and political leaders. Leaving the training of pilots and aircrews to Eaker and Hunter, Spaatz set out to forge an independent role for American air units. It was Spaatz's brief from his superiors to integrate and modulate the projected American daylight air offensive with—but not subordinate it to—Britain's night-bombing effort.

When pilots from the USAAF's 31st Fighter Group arrived in England shortly after General Spaatz, they did so with no airplanes; Spaatz had to arrange for the RAF to provide Spitfires for the American combat pilots.

Finally, on June 26, 1942, the advance flight echelon of the 97th Heavy Bombardment Group, which was equipped with Boeing B-17 Flying Fortress four-engine heavy bombers, left the United States to fly to England via Greenland. But this was another symbolic commitment, for the 97th had been activated in February 1942 and thus had not had time to be adequately trained to fly combat missions over heavily defended European targets. It would be several months, at minimum, before the 97th was prepared to take part in any real action.

The Army Air Forces' first combat mission against a German-held targets took place on July 4, 1942. It was an intentionally symbolic attack—note the date—but it was a poor symbol, for the six American-manned RAF-owned Douglas A-20 light attack bombers that accompanied six RAF-manned A-20s were emblazoned with RAF roundels, and not U.S. markings. In their attack on several German airfields in Holland, two of the American A-20s were shot down by flak—seven crewmen were killed and one was captured—two failed to reach the target, and a fifth A-20 was severely damaged. The U.S. Army Air Forces could not have asked for a less auspicious or more humiliating inauguration into what would become the greatest aerial offensive in the history of the world.

While half the world away the air battles for Port Moresby, New Guinea, continued, the very first U.S. Army Air Forces fighter mission over Occupied Europe took place on July 26, 1942. As part of their training syllabus, six 31st Fighter Group senior pilots took part in an RAF fighter sweep to Gravelines, a town on the English Channel 15 miles southwest of Dunkirk. German fighters challenged the American and RAF Spitfires, and the 31st Fighter Group's deputy commander was shot down and captured.

The 97th Heavy Bombardment Group had to wait a bit longer. Finally, on August 17, a dozen of the 97th's B-17s, with General Eaker along as an observer, conducted an afternoon raid against railroad marshalling yards near Rouen, France, 35 miles from the English Channel. Escort for the bombers was provided, not by American fighter groups, but by four RAF Spitfire squadrons. The results of the bombing were negligible—the target was hit, at least—and the RAF Spitfires held off all but two of the German fighters that came up to attack the American B-17s. One B-17 returned to base with a burning, smoking engine, but there were no losses and no injuries. Six other 97th Heavy Bombardment Group B-17s that conducted a diversionary flight over the French coast that afternoon were not molested.

Two days later, on August 19, the entire 31st Fighter Group joined with the RAF for a "big show" across the Channel, the tragic invasion rehearsal at Dieppe. While completing four twelve-plane missions over the beaches during the day, pilots from the 31st were officially awarded two confirmed and two probable victories.

The 31st Fighter Group continued to fly fighter-sweep missions over coastal France, but it was awarded only one probable and no confirmed victories before it was withdrawn from combat operations in October to prepare for its upcoming role in Operation TORCH, the invasion of French Northwest Africa. Meantime, on September 29, 1942, the RAF's three independent Eagle squadrons—fighter units composed entirely of American citizens who had enlisted in the Royal Air Force or Royal Canadian Air Force—were absorbed into the VIII Fighter Command as the newly commissioned 4th Fighter Group.

Thanks to the withdrawal and diversion of other VIII Fighter Command groups for the North African Campaign, the 4th Fighter Group, which was outfitted with Spitfires, was the only operational American fighter unit in northern Europe until May 1943. Already endowed with experienced combat pilots from its RAF days, including a number of aces, the 4th did about as well during its first six months of combat service as did RAF Spitfire units that were taking part in similar fighter-sweep missions over France. Between September 1942 and mid-April 1943, the 4th Fighter Group was awarded credit for fifteen confirmed victories over France, Belgium, and the Netherlands.

While the 4th Fighter Group alone was upholding the honor of American fighter units in England, nearly the full weight of the American air effort against Germany and her allies shifted southward, to French Northwest Africa.

The essence of the U.S. Army Air Forces campaign over northern Europe between October 1942 and the Spring of 1943 was that, for practical purposes, there was no air campaign. The diversion of most of the small Eighth Air Force—fighters *and* bombers—to battle over North Africa as part of the new U.S. Twelfth Air Force left the VIII Bomber Command and the VIII Fighter Command virtually no assets with which to wage any sort of offensive battle.

From October 1942 until May 1943, only the Spitfire-equipped 4th Fighter Group remained operational in the United Kingdom. The handful of other fighter groups that had reached the British Isles by October 1942 had been diverted or, in the case of the P-38–equipped 78th Fighter Group, stripped of its airplanes, which were needed as replacements by the Twelfth Air Force P-38 groups. Between the beginning of October 1942 and the end of April 1943, 4th Fighter Group pilots accounted for all of sixteen enemy airplanes. Between mid-March and April 8, the 4th was withdrawn from combat so it could transition from Spitfires to Republic P-47 Thunderbolts. The group's first aerial victories in the P-47—and the P-47's first victories ever—were scored on April 15 over the Belgian coast.

(It should be noted that a thriving business in aerial combat had developed in North Africa, from Algeria to the Western Desert, and that USAAF fighter pilots and bomber crews were engaged to the hilt, gaining experience and whittling away at the enemy air forces. By the time the first significant scores were being turned in over northern Europe, American bombers and fighters were ranging over Sardinia and Sicily. But theirs was a tactical war, waged upon a local stage. The utility of those victories and that experience in bringing about the fall of the Nazi empire was important but limited.)

As was to emerge in time, the paucity of aerial victories—even the paucity of aerial encounters—over northern Europe had less to do with the scarcity of American-manned fighters than it did with American fighter tactics. The 4th Fighter Group was as aggressive and aggressively led a fighter unit as ever fought in a war. In better times, with better tactics, it became one of America's premier fighter units. But during the period that it flew as the only American fighter unit in operation in northern Europe, and for several months beyond, it attained negligible results because it was hobbled by idiotic tactics.

The immediate culprit was Major General Monk Hunter, the commander of VIII Fighter Command, but it must be said that Hunter was a product of his training and, to a degree, poor technology. Both of these factors obliged him and his eager fighter pilots—Hunter was eager, too—to work apart, virtually in a separate war, from the Eighth Air Force's other combat arm, the VIII Bomber Command. Indeed, the doctrines that defined USAAF bomber and USAAF fighter operations were so far apart as to obviate direct cooperation.

The bombers had been built and the bomber crews had been trained to attack enemy targets without protection from fighters. In part, this was the fault of the high-order strategic thinking of the interwar decades. It was hoped by altruistic European survivors of the carnage of World War I to avoid the realities of ground combat by substituting the arms-length strategies of aerial bombardment. In 1942, air strategists honestly believed that the war could be won by bomber campaigns alone. Since the mid-1930s, the Americans who bought this argument had developed what they called the *self-defending* bomber. That innovation, however, had more to do with the fighter technology of the 1930s; fighters of the day possessed neither the range nor the speed of modern bombers. The fighter technology improved, but by mid-1942 the self-defending bomber had taken on a life of its own. It was believed that Germany could be bombed into submission by long-range self-defending bombers that were capable of flying unescorted to industrial targets anywhere in western or even central Europe.

As with most self-fulfilling prophecies, fact came to match belief. In 1942, American heavy bombers (and their British counterparts) had the range to strike targets in distant Berlin and beyond. The British had attempted daylight raids against Berlin early in the war, and they had been trounced by German fighter and antiaircraft-gun defenses. They had switched to night "area" raids, nominally against industrial targets but, in reality, against whomever or whatever their bombs happened to hit. The U.S. Army Air Forces, on the other hand, had developed qualms about "terror" bombings. And besides, America's leading bomber enthusiasts believed strongly in the efficacy of both their precision daylight-bombing doctrine and their self-defending heavy bombers. Moreover, American fighters of the day, though powerful and powerfully armed, still lacked the range to accompany the bombers all the way to Berlin and back. As improvements filtered to the frontline units, the bombers could eventually reach targets nearly 1,100 miles from their bases, but the fighters could still fly only 250 miles in one direction, and no farther.

Denied a role in escorting bombers to distant targets and blinded by an outmoded and actually quite silly doctrine he had helped develop in the 1930s, Monk Hunter opted to send his meager fighter assets on "fighter sweeps" over those areas of France, Belgium, and the Netherlands that were within the minimal operational range of any fighter type that could possibly have come into his hands by mid-1943. (This "operational" range was quite a bit less than 250 miles because the fighters needed some reserve for high-speed fighting, which consumed fuel by the barrel.) The longest-ranged operational fighter type the United States had during this period was the Lockheed P-38 Lightning, an airplane that had been designed as a medium-range bomber escort. But there were only two P-38 groups in action against Germany and her partners in mid-1943, and both of them were in North Africa. Other P-38 units were in the Pacific and more were training in the United States. Some of the new groups were bound to end up in England, but the most immediate need was in the Pacific because of the vast distances between island bases. For the foreseeable future, all that Monk Hunter's VIII Fighter Command could possibly get its hands on would be short-legged defensive fighters— some Bell P-39 Airacobras, perhaps, or, more likely, a few groups of new Republic P-47 Thunderbolts. The P-39 was an inadequate fighter by mid-1942, and the immensely heavy, seven-ton P-47 did not have much range.

It was not Hunter's fault that he had inadequate airplanes (forget that there was only one group flying!) and he was not alone in his misperception of the role of fighters in World War II. Hunter's failure to make a dent in the German fighter force—fourteen confirmed victories in seven months—also goes to the role to which the Army Air Forces both aspired and had been relegated by 1942.

The key to every decision Allied commanders made in 1942 and 1943 was the projected invasion of France. At first, when the United States entered the war it was hoped that the invasion would take place in mid-1943. By the late summer of 1942, however, the North African Campaign—and a huge number of other factors—made it clear that D day was going to take place in mid-1944. As the first symbolic raids and sweeps were undertaken over northwestern Europe by Eighth Air Force fighter and bomber units in mid-1942, there were two full years to achieve preinvasion goals from the air. North Africa threw the margin into a cocked hat. If luck held, it would be mid-1943 before the strategic-bombing campaign could be resumed, and then only one year would be left for cracking the German objectives.

The primary role of American and British air power in Europe from mid-1942 until the invasion was to be the defeat of the German Air Force (GAF). Operation POINTBLANK, the specific plan by which the Allies were to accomplish this feat, was promulgated in May 1943 following acceptance of the common goal by the RAF and the U.S. Army Air Forces. The defeat of the GAF was of primary concern to the Allies because, unlike the RAF or U.S. Army Air Forces, the GAF was a *tactical* air force, through and through. It had been developed in its entirety to support the German Army. Its bombers, for example, were light or medium models, and its bomber crews were trained to support ground troops at close or medium range. The GAF had *no* long-range capability, no strategic capability whatsoever. Its role was tactical and, at most, operational. As such, it was of enormous potential danger to an invasion fleet or a fledgling toehold on the soil of France. In order to ensure a safe landing by tens of thousands of Allied soldiers, two things had to happen in the air before the invasion began—or could begin: The GAF had to be seriously whittled down in strength *and* it had to be pushed as far back from the English Channel and North Sea coasts as possible. By forcing German tactical and operational air units to operate at the extremity of their range and in the smallest possible numbers—and *only* by doing so— could the mid-1944 invasion foreseen in mid-1942 be reasonably assured of success.

The goal of Operation POINTBLANK was to be accomplished in two ways: first, by simply shooting down German airplanes wherever they could be induced to fight and, second, by destroying Germany's ability to build new airplanes. To accomplish the latter, the destruction of the German aircraft industry, and related targets, the British and Americans opened the Combined Bomber Offensive. The RAF would undertake night "area" bombing raids against the German aircraft industry and the U.S. Army Air Forces would undertake daylight precision bombing raids against the same or similar targets. The simultaneous Anglo-American program of aggressive (but, alas, short-range) fighter sweeps over the French, Belgian, and Dutch coasts was aimed at engaging the GAF fighter wings in a battle of attrition that over time would destroy the bulk of whatever reduced numbers of fighters the shattered German aircraft industry managed to produce. Further, by destroying German fighters, the Allies hoped to induce the German aircraft industry to switch over from the production of tactical bombers to the increased production of replacement fighters.

Sadly, while American fighters were being ignored or, at best, assiduously avoided by the crack GAF fighter units within their meager range, the "self-defending" daylight heavy-bomber groups charged with attacking strategic targets deeper inside France, the Netherlands, and northwestern Germany were being butchered. While the German fighters were sidestepping needless and avoidable attrition simply by ignoring the American fighter sweeps, the bombers were locked in a one-sided form of attrition that did not bode well for their survival.

Beginning in April 1943, the 4th Fighter Group's new P-47 Thunderbolts were joined over the Channel and North Sea coasts by the Thunderbolts of the 78th Fighter Group; and another P-47 unit, the 56th Fighter Group, was in training in England. Despite the doubling of assets, the results remained abysmal. Meanwhile, losses of American heavy bombers continued to rise. Major General Ira Eaker, who had replaced Spaatz as Eighth Air Force commander when the latter went to North Africa, continued to believe in the efficacy of the self-defending bomber, but even he had to admit that there were not yet enough heavies available in northern Europe to make the strategy work. Eaker asked Monk Hunter to provide fighters for escort duty to the extremity of their range—going into the Continent (penetration), and coming out (withdrawal). The bombers would be on their own a good part of the way, but *some* protection at the margins apparently was deemed to be better than none at all. From May 4, 1943, onward, nearly all VIII Fighter Command sorties were devoted to escorting the bombers.

Seven German airplanes were downed by American fighters over northern Europe in May 1943, and eighteen fell in June (seven in one day, June 22). Action during the first three weeks of July was sluggish, but an extremely aggressive new commander, Major General Frederick Anderson, had just taken over the VIII Bomber Command on July 1, and he needed some time to make his aggressive new policies bite. On July 24, Anderson's VIII Bomber Command opened "Blitz Week" with the first of hopefully daily appearances over Germany. Weather shut down bomber operations on one of seven consecutive planned mission days, but the other six days saw strikes aggregating just over a thousand bomber sorties launched against fifteen targets all over northern and western Germany. Claims by bomber gunners were extravagant—330 victory credits were awarded—but there is no doubting that the German fighter forces were worn down somewhat, at least operationally, by the unrelenting appearances by the bombers.

The American day fighters put in fewer claims by far, but the fact that their claims were closer to reality made them startling in their own right. In July 1943, American fighter combat produced 38 victory credits, of which 33—9 and 24, respectively—were scored during just two Blitz Week missions. Not coincidentally, the two missions in question were not only bomber-escort missions—they were the first *long-range* bomber-escort missions ever flown by Eighth Air Force fighters.

On July 28, 1943, the 4th Fighter Group significantly increased the range of its P-47 fighters in an experiment with auxiliary fuel tanks. In so doing, its pilots took the Germans by surprise by flying much deeper into enemy territory than they ever had before. Nine German fighters were downed in what for the Germans was an unexpected melee around the American heavy-bomber stream. Two days later, on July 30, the P-47s of all three British-based P-47 groups were able to use for the first time what the pilots referred to as "bathtub" belly tanks. The 115-gallon tanks, which were designed for use in long-distance ferry flights, were not pressurized, and they gave the pilots a lot of problems, but they did add 150 to 200 miles to the Thunderbolt's operational range. Until then, the heavy fighter could reach no farther than the vicinity of Antwerp. With the tanks, the P-47s could make it well into the Netherlands. Thus, on July 30, when the target was the Focke-Wulf aircraft assembly plant in Kassel, Germany, more than two hundred B-17s and B-24s took part in a mission that was covered to the greatest depth ever by friendly fighters.

On the watershed July 30 mission, the 56th Fighter Group gave the bombers penetration support, the 78th Fighter Group provided early withdrawal support, and the 4th Fighter Group provided late withdrawal support. That meant that the 78th Fighter Group's P-47s would be with the bombers quite soon after the heavies came off the target. The overall tactical plan was simple: protect the bombers and drive away the German fighters.

The surprised German interceptor pilots either attempted to ignore the P-47s as they drove their own fighters into the bomber stream, or they were sucked into dogfights at the expense of attacking their primary targets, the bombers.

There it was—twenty-four confirmed victories in one day, on a single mission. The tactics and technology had changed, and American fighters had knocked down as many German airplanes in one mission as they had been able to knock down in dozens of fighter-sweep and even escort missions in the preceding two months. In a short time, the large numbers of sturdy, reliable, streamlined auxiliary fuel tanks that were shipped to or fabricated in England forever changed the tenor of the daytime air war in Europe. Indeed, the routine commitment of American long-range fighter escorts in mid-1943 changed the whole nature of war in the air as profoundly as the routine use of flimsy reconnaissance aircraft had transformed ground warfare in 1915.

The Germans knew there was no profit in attacking American fighters for the sake of engaging in dogfights that could go either way once they were joined. Fighters, per se, were no danger to the Third Reich. Bombers were. Bombers were a threat to everything—to home, to loved ones, and to German morale and equanimity. American bombers, if they were allowed to get through to their targets, were an especial danger to the GAF itself, for they had shown a propensity to concentrate on the German industries from which German fighters and bombers emerged—ball bearings, machine tools, and airplane factories themselves. German fighters would never attack American or British fighters unless there was an overwhelming opportunity to win. But bombers *had* to be attacked, no matter where or when they appeared over Germany or her satellites. And, so, if the American fighter enthusiasts wanted to destroy the GAF at least in part through a strategy of attrition, they had to tie their fortunes to those of the bombers. To do that, better or much-improved fighters needed to emerge from the American industrial behemoth, better escort tactics needed to evolve, and better operational ranges needed to be achieved by the fighters.

The VIII Fighter Command's three P-47 groups were credited with fifty-eight German airplanes in August 1943, all of them during bomber-escort duty. In stark contrast, the American P-47s flew 373 fighter-sweep sorties over France on August 15 and did not see a single German airplane.

Despite mounting pressure from his superiors in Washington to adopt changes, Monk Hunter continued to argue vehemently in favor of his ineffectual and discredited fighter-sweep tactic. In this, Hunter was supported by the Eighth Air Force commander, Major General Ira Eaker, who remained a vehement supporter in his own right of the self-defending bomber. Eaker was very close personally to the Army Air Forces chief, General Henry "Hap" Arnold, so his job was safe. But, though Hunter was also an old friend of Arnold's, he had become an annoying relic. Hunter was replaced as head of the VIII Fighter Command on August 29 by Major General William Kepner, formerly the commander of the U.S.-based Fourth Air Force. A fighter pilot's fighter pilot, Kepner was, in a word, aggressive. Moreover, his outlook was in full accord with the reality of the air war over northern Europe. He simply wanted to do whatever worked.

In September 1943, only thirty-nine victory credits were awarded to the American P-47 groups (including the newly committed 353d Fighter Group), but for various reasons, there were also few bomber missions flown that month. As if to confirm the lessons of the preceding months, the VIII Fighter Command mounted ninety-five fighter-sweep sorties on September 4 while RAF Spitfires escorted a large American B-26 medium-bomber mission over France.

The P-47s saw no German airplanes, but the Spitfires destroyed nineteen of the German fighters that rose to challenge the medium bombers. On September 22, when no bomber strikes were launched, the P-47s clocked 395 non-escort sorties over Occupied Europe, but only two German airplanes were downed. Five days later, however, twenty-one German fighters were shot down when the P-47s escorted a heavy-bomber mission to Emden, Germany.

By the end of September, it was obvious to everyone concerned—not least the Germans—that the Eighth Air Force had at last broken the code. The key to Allied air supremacy over northern Europe lay in the rigorous bombing of the German aircraft industry by heavy bombers, and of German fighter installations in France, Belgium, and the Netherlands by both heavy and medium bombers. (The latter was a function of an inexorable program aimed at pushing German tactical air units back from the proposed invasion beaches in France. Incessant bombing, which at the least disrupted flight operations, would eventually render the forward airfields untenable.)

The key role of the German day-fighter wings would be the destruction of the American bombers, and the key role of the American day fighters would be the destruction of the German day fighters that rose to challenge the bombers. As long as the bombers went out, the German fighters would attack, and thus the American fighters would have ample opportunity to *try* to destroy the GAF's tactical strength by means of attrition.

The American day-bomber offensive over northern Europe had tremendous but inconclusive and certainly indecisive results during the last quarter of 1943. On the plus side, six new Army Air Forces fighter groups got into action with the Eighth Air Force B-17s and B-24s between September 14 and December 28. Seven of the ten available groups were P-47 units; two of the new groups were equipped with very long range P-38s; and the last of the new fighter groups, the 354th, was the first in the world to go into action with the North American P-51B Mustang fighter.

In addition to the number of groups available, the Army Air Forces expanded the size of each group, and the groups themselves concentrated on breaking all records with respect to maintaining the highest possible number of battle-worthy airplanes. The higher numbers of fighters available for escort duty showed in the numbers of German fighters that were being reported as destroyed. And, within stringent guidelines set forth by the Eighth Air Force—stay with the bombers—many of the fighter groups were working on innovative tactics aimed at cutting deeper into the German fighter wings.

On November 4, 1943, the Eighth Air Force officially promulgated

Operation ARGUMENT, a limited air offensive specifically aimed at probing the limits and resilience of the GAF interceptor force over Germany. It consisted of official sanction and general guidelines for doing what was already being done. For the time being, the ARGUMENT operations plan was little more than a policy statement; it left the execution phase up to the commanders, based at any given time upon whatever was actually occurring in the aerial battlefields of northwestern Europe.

In October 1943, the American day fighters were awarded 75 confirmed victories, every one of them over German fighters. In November, VIII Fighter Command fighters were credited with 98 German fighters and 6 German bombers. And, in December, the American fighters downed 5 German bombers and 87 German fighters. (The scarcity of bomber kills stemmed only in part from the Americans' focus on German fighters; the GAF remained a tactical air force, so the vast bulk of its tactical bomber force was deployed on the Eastern Front, way beyond the range of the American fighters.)

The air battles over northern Europe became a race. Both sides were dedicating enormous resources to eking out incremental advantages by which they might counter the other. The Germans pulled the majority of their day fighters back, closer to or right into Germany, but that was only in part because the forward airfields became untenable as a result of unremitting Allied air attacks. The Germans had other, more compelling reasons to pull back their day fighters. If the short-legged German fighters remained based at the margins of the battle arena, they would have only one crack at the American bombers as the heavies flew toward Germany with their bombs. However, if the German fighters were deployed closer to the targets and had a large number of secondary airfields to fall into for fresh fuel and ammunition, they might get two cracks at the enormously long bomber streams before any bombs were dropped. And many of the German fighters would certainly have yet another crack at the heavies during the long trip back to England. So, the Germans built scores of little airfields and manned them with armorers and mechanics who only had to wait for the single- and twin-engine fighters to drop in for fuel, ammunition, and minor adjustments.

The Germans also adopted the mass head-on firing pass as their preferred anti-bomber tactic. By late 1943, they were often able to assemble as many as 150 single-engine fighters in one or two big formations ahead of the bomber stream, and these were often capable of initiating head-on attacks that damaged or downed many bombers, especially those in the lead, which were manned by skilled bomber leaders and the best bombardiers. Often, just before the single-engine German fighters attacked from dead ahead, twin-engine German fighters launched standoff attacks from the flanks, from beyond machine-gun range of the bombers. The twin-engine fighters lobbed heavy cannon shells or large rockets into the bomber formations to break up the formidable (but *not* "self-defending") bomber boxes. (It should be noted that most of the twin-engine GAF fighters were night fighters that could not be used to attack RAF night-bomber formations if they were drawn into combat against the USAAF day bombers—or, of course, if they were destroyed by USAAF day fighters. Some of the GAF's best-trained airmen died trying to lob rockets and cannon shells into USAAF heavy-bomber boxes.)

Even now, it is not clear what the original architects of the Allied strategic-bombing offensive against Germany really thought they might accomplish. The so-called "strategic" aerial offensive that was launched from bases in England in mid-1942 was at the time something new and untried, something theoretical. Was it to be aimed at terrorizing German civilians—a shock tactic the Germans had invented—or was it to be aimed at bringing German industry inexorably to its knees? Moral posturing aside, no one really knew what the end results of a successful strategic-bombing campaign might be; no one had ever thought through the goals of a sustained strategic-bombing offensive.

As events unfolded, the early architects of the strategic-bombing offensive against Germany had found themselves being drawn into a kind of warfare none had anticipated. Over time, due to the way the bombing offensive played out in the air over Occupied Europe, the actual focus of the campaign became the destruction of the German fighter force. At first, through most of 1943 the idea was to destroy the German fighters that were arrayed along the bomber routes—simply an end result of defending the bombers. But the bombing targets themselves quickly became the components of the German aircraft industry—airframe and air-engine factories, fighter assembly plants, ball-bearings works, and so forth. Although the strategic planners had not originally foreseen a program anything like this, Operation POINTBLANK evolved into a brilliant and elegant double-sided strategy.

By attacking the heart of the German aircraft industry, the strategic-bombing offensive killed German fighters two ways. First, and obviously, it killed German fighters while they were being built. But of greater importance was the way it made the Germans concentrate more and more of their raw materials, skilled workmen, and industrial capacity in order to make good the losses inflicted by the bombs. This shift in German industrial priorities had far-reaching effects. It kept vital and limited supplies from other programs— building tanks, for example, *or developing more-effective new fighters.* It destroyed valuable machine tools, or kept them occupied on aircraft production. It kept men from the fighting fronts, for the skilled workers involved in constantly rebuilding lost machine tools and aircraft components had to remain in industry rather than be inducted into the military services. It didn't actually matter, in the end, that German fighter production rose steadily as the Allied bombing offensives gained momentum, for the increased fighter production was entirely at the expense of other things the Germans needed to win the war. At some point, on a day unremarked by history, this maelstrom became the whirlwind.

Ultimately, an increase in German fighter production itself played into the evolving Allied strategy. More German fighters in the air meant more German fighter pilots to be shot down and killed. For that was the unanticipated but logical second goal of the Allied bombing offensive. The vast fleets of bombers that attracted the increased German fighter output became attritional traps. As the Germans concentrated more and more of their fighters against the bomber streams, more and more of those fighters *and their pilots* were destroyed by the vastly and increasingly superior American strategic fighter force. The only thing that might stop the bombers from destroying the German fighter industry was the German fighter force. But the German fighter force was inexorably chewed to bits by the superior American fighter force as it rose to challenge the American day bombers.

By the end of 1943, the defeat of the German fighter force, the destruction of the German aircraft industry, and the emergence of Allied air supremacy over northern Europe were all but foreordained. But achieving any of those goals, or all of them, required that relentless pressure be maintained upon all parts of the German aircraft industry and the German fighter force. Although ultimately the Allies could not lose the air war over Europe—America's unassailed, burgeoning industrial strength was too vast for that to *ever* happen—the day of victory could be put off, at terrible human costs, if the strategic-bombing offensive faltered or rested. The pressure on the German fighter force and the German aircraft industry had to remain constant or be increased.

As 1943 gave way to 1944, the American generals heading the daylight component of the Allied Combined Bomber Offensive were all sanguinary men who favored increasing the tempo, ratcheting up the violence, hastening Nazi Germany's Armageddon. And so it would be.

The trouble with the American fighter tactic of late 1943 was that it gave too much weight to the desires of the bomber crews. Naturally, as they had from the first mission onward, the bomber pilots and crewmen wanted the fighters to fly as close to the bomber streams as possible. The fighter pilots rejected this notion as a matter of course, but high and rising bomber losses seemed to argue in behalf of the close-in support. Thus, despite claims that they could do better on a longer leash, the fighters remained attached, limpet-like, to the bomber formations.

The close-in escort tactic made a certain sense when there were relatively few fighters flying at the extremity of their ranges. But the availability late in the year of many more fighters, and much longer ranged ones at that, slowly turned the old arguments on their ear. Either more fighters could accompany the bombers longer while remaining close in, or the fighters could exploit their added range to work farther out from the bombers—say, to engage the massed German fighters well before the bombers arrived on the scene. Realizing that the German fighters used much of their limited fuel getting into position and forming up ahead of the bombers, the fighter tacticians suggested that head-on attacks could be obviated altogether if the remaining fuel aboard the German fighters could be expended in life-and-death struggles with free-wheeling, aggressive, attack-oriented American fighters.

The VIII Fighter Command—Major General Bill Kepner—was willing to give the new idea a shot, but the Eighth Air Force—Major General Ira Eaker—shrank from the prospect. One reason for Eaker's demurrer might have been the highly inflated victory claims produced by gunners aboard the heavy bombers. While the awarding of confirmed victories to fighter pilots was controlled by several levels of confirmation, there were absolutely no limiting factors placed on claims by or credits awarded to bomber gunners. Perhaps this was a device to rescue the morale of sitting ducks, but, most likely, it was the work of wishful thinking. There was no gun-camera film, no requirement that victories be confirmed by fellow bomber crewmen, no requirement that an enemy airplane be seen as it crashed into the ground. Moreover, given the defensive arrangement of the bomber boxes and the sheer number of machine guns (thirteen .50-caliber machine guns per B-17, and ten per B-24), it was a rare German fighter that was not engaged by scores or even several hundred machine guns as it streaked through a bomber box. If the German fighter blew up—or if it didn't—everyone who fired a shot claimed a victory credit. So, while the fighters were turning in modest and highly regarded victory claims that numbered from one to fewer than fifty per mission, the bombers were "accounting" for scores and even a few hundred German fighters per mission. No wonder Eaker didn't want to end a good thing! With statistics like these to back him up, he *wanted* the German fighters to fly in close to the bombers—so the putatively effective bomber gunners could knock them down.

Once the loss of so many bombers and so many bomber crewmen could be rationalized in this manner, there was little incentive to change tactics. Nevertheless, the American day-fighter groups continued to advance their art. Their mechanics found ways to get more airplanes aloft per mission, everyone worked to eke out a few more minutes with the bomber formations, and tactics did change—because eager young fighter pilots simply didn't care as much about penalties imposed from above as they did about destroying German fighters.

The fact of the matter was that Ira Eaker misunderstood the purpose of the day-fighter program over northwestern Europe. His early and ongoing enthusiasm for the self-defending bomber created a blind spot with respect to the potential of the long-range fighter. Unlike his thirty-eight-year-old bomber commander, Major General Fred Anderson, Eaker did not realize that the bombers had, ipso facto, become bait for the German fighters and that the American fighters needed to be freer so they could exploit German vulner-abilities. Eaker's good friend, General Hap Arnold, kept Eaker on as the Eighth Air Force chief far longer than Eaker deserved, but Arnold had his limits.

On December 6, 1943, President Franklin Roosevelt ordered General Dwight Eisenhower to move from the Mediterranean Theater to England to head the new Supreme Headquarters, Allied Expeditionary Force (SHAEF). Within two days, Hap Arnold had closed a deal with Eisenhower over the establishment of a new U.S. Strategic Air Forces in Europe (USSAFE, but soon redesignated USSTAF), which was to coordinate the strategic-bombing efforts of the British-based Eighth and Italian-based Fifteenth strategic air forces against Germany. It was also agreed that Lieutenant

General Tooey Spaatz, who had served under Eisenhower in North Africa and the Mediterranean, would head USSAFE. On December 18, the Eighth Air Force's Ira Eaker was ordered to assume command of the Mediterranean Allied Air Forces as soon as his relief—the Fifteenth Air Force's Major General James Doolittle—could get to England.

Tooey Spaatz inaugurated his new USSAFE headquarters at Bushy Park, England, on January 1, 1944. On January 6, Jimmy Doolittle formally relieved Eaker as commander of the Eighth Air Force. The old Eighth Air Force headquarters was renamed on January 6 to serve as Spaatz's headquarters, and, on the same day, the old VIII Bomber Command headquarters was upgraded to serve as Doolittle's. Unfortunately, Major General Fred Anderson had to rebuild his bomber-command headquarters from scratch. (After January 6, 1944, there was no VIII Bomber Command, per se. However, Anderson functioned as Doolittle's deputy operations officer for bombing, and he had an adequate staff for the purpose.)

At the outset, Jimmy Doolittle was made to understand what Eaker had failed to grasp, and he gave Bill Kepner a reasonably free hand to unleash the escort fighters. At least, he gave Kepner an opportunity to move ahead *prudently* with the destruction of the German fighter force over Germany. And Kepner and his eager subordinates indeed moved ahead.

One of the most important new American innovations was "phased escort," in which each escort group was assigned to a particular section of the bombers' route to or from the target. How the fighters reached their rendezvous point was up to the individual groups, but emphasis was placed on economical routes and fuel settings, so the fighters could remain on station with the bombers for as long as possible. At the extremity of the assigned sector, a replacement escort group was to join up, and so forth. Among other advantages, phased support ended the effectiveness of a particularly maddening German tactic in which German fighters attacked the American fighters early in a mission to get them to drop their auxiliary fuel tanks long before the tanks were empty. This tactic often meant that American escorts had to turn for home before the main German attacks struck the bombers.

The first phased-escort mission was flown on January 7, 1944, and it made use of all eleven of the available escort groups. Three shorter-legged P-47 groups handled target penetration in rotation, the one P-51 and two P-38 groups traded off in sequence over the target, and the five remaining

P-47 groups handled target withdrawal. Although the American fighters downed only seven German fighters that day, the new tactic was deemed an overwhelming success and it was adopted on the spot as the standard.

At around the same time VIII Fighter Command was working out phased escort, the fighter jocks themselves were laying the groundwork for a new "freelance" tactic. It had started by accident on December 20, 1943, when the long-range P-38s of the 55th Fighter Group arrived at their rendezvous on time and the bombers arrived thirty minutes late. The fighter leader asked for permission to use the wait profitably, and he was allowed to do so. The 55th scored no victories that day, but it did manage to range far ahead of the bombers, and presumably its free-ranging presence had some effect on the ability of the German fighters to form up and deliver their attacks on the oncoming bomber stream. The experiment was repeated once or twice, when conditions allowed, but the tactic was not formally adopted for some time. However, by January 11, 1944, there were just enough fighter groups available for escort duties to allow the 56th Fighter Group to undertake a pair of planned freelance missions with the two small subgroups into which it divided itself.

Over the next few weeks, freelancing became a way of life for many of the American escort groups. And it paid off handsomely, just as its advocates had been declaring all along. German fighter losses—and pilot attrition—climbed.

The pressure was on from other quarters. There were two sets of dates in mid-1944 on which the right combination of moon and tides would make the invasion of France most likely. The first set of dates was in early May. If the GAF fighter force was going to be rendered moot before the invasion—a vital strategic imperative declared by the Allied ground commanders—then there were only four months left in which to do it. By mid-January, however, the American day fighters were still a long way from having their GAF counterparts on the run. A long way.

Despite the increasing tempo of bombings aimed at crippling the German aircraft industry, German fighter production was on the *rise* at the turn of the year. The Germans were producing more fighters eighteen months into the bomber offensive than they had been at the start. But, though there were more fighters, the point at which the Americans were defeating the German fighter force was in the attrition of German fighter pilots. Many of Germany's top fighter pilots already had been consumed in the aerial conflagration over

Germany's industrial heartland. Also, thanks to the ripple effect of the concentration by the American air forces on the Luftwaffe, the German pilot-training program was severely handicapped by a scarcity of training planes, instructors, and even fuel.

By late January 1944, the new team of American generals at the head of the daylight phase of the Anglo-American Combined Bomber Offensive was preparing to deal the GAF fighter force a series of death blows.

Although the American day bombers were "bombing hell" out of the German aircraft industry, the Germans had succeeded in dispersing the bulk of the interlinked aircraft-production factories into penny packets throughout Occupied Europe. Many of the new, smaller targets either had not yet been located by the Allies, or they were not worth the attention of a long-range bombing mission. The net result was a precipitous rise in German fighter production that would not abate until nearly the end of the war. Also, as the Germans abandoned some of their forward bases in northwestern Europe—and unengaged rear bases elsewhere—they enjoyed at least a temporary late-January surge in available fighters over Germany. And, of course, there were more fighters covering fewer and fewer square miles of contested airspace. All of these factors conspired against the bombers, which suffered greater losses, even though more-numerous German fighter-interceptors were being flown by an increasing percentage of inexperienced and even ill-trained inter-ceptor pilots.

The spiral of violence favored the American day fighters. There were growing numbers of American day fighters, and the range of the American fighters was improving. American pilots arriving in Europe were increasingly better trained, and the tactics they were employing were becoming more savvy and more aggressive by the day. Ironically, and unfortunately, the positive results of the campaign against the German interceptor force were partly masked by the appearance of many more American bombers in the skies over Germany. As a result of making more targets available to increasing numbers of German fighters, the real bomber losses rose even though the percentage of bomber losses went down.

The heavier bomber losses gave General Spaatz some pause in late January, but the total of claims for German fighters by American fighters was so high that Spaatz's aggressive subordinates—true believers, all, in the goals of Operation POINTBLANK—were able to talk the USSTAF commander into a redoubled effort. The result was Big Week, a master plan aimed at wearing down the German day-fighter force with a series of attacks against German aircraft and related factories on at least seven consecutive days in February.

The key to Big Week, which was formally dubbed Operation ARGUMENT, would be intentionally freeing the escort fighters as much as possible from close-escort work. Wherever possible, the escort fighters were to range ahead of the bombers to hit the German interceptors while they were still forming for their patented mass head-on attacks.

To conduct Big Week, the Eighth Air Force had at its disposal a daily in-commission force averaging 678 day fighters and approximately 1,000 heavy bombers. Spaatz and his subordinates were prepared to use every one of these aircraft as early as the first week of February—the bombers to goad the German fighters aloft and the fighters to knock the Germans down—but the weather was execrable. Almost-daily efforts well into the month resulted in total aborts or in very limited results. The Germans, however, were prime. They had an average daily in-service force of nearly 350 single-engine fighters and 100 twin-engine fighters with which to attack the bombers, and they had the desire to do so even in the face of the new and disturbing propensity of American escorts to range far ahead of the bombers. It is difficult to conceive of opposing forces more eager to get at one another, and both sides would have had the weather been more amenable to the process.

Finally, with days of clear weather ahead, the British kicked off the Big Week operation on the night of February 19–20 with a 730-sortie area attack against Leipzig. The Eighth Air Force day-bombing mission for February 20 was divided into three phases that went after aircraft-industry targets in Leipzig, Gotha, and Brunswick. The American day fighters claimed 61 confirmed victories that day, against American losses of 21 bombers and four fighters. The Germans acknowledged the loss of 58 fighters from all causes on February 20, including operational losses. (The German figures can be most accurately described as "writeoffs," for they include fighters that had to be scrapped after landing safely, usually because of damage inflicted by American machine guns.)

On February 21, 762 heavy bombers and 679 fighters went to Brunswick and several German airfields. The weather was marginal, however, and the German interceptors had a difficult time launching their attacks. Confirmed claims by American fighters amounted to 27 German fighters against losses of 16 bombers and 5 escorts. As usual, the German records show a different number of losses—in this case, 32 from all causes.

February 22 was to see the first joint mission by Eighth Air Force and the Italian-based Fifteenth Air Force. A total of 1,396 heavy bombers and 965 escorts were to strike aircraft factories or related facilities in six German cities.

Unfortunately, on February 22, deteriorating weather over most of Germany caused most of the bombers to return to base with their payloads. However, there was significant action through the day because several hundred bombers and hundreds of fighters pressed on to their primary or secondary targets despite the weather. VIII Fighter Command fighters turned in claims for 59 confirmed kills, and the bombers claimed 21. German sources admit to the loss of as many as 52 fighters over Germany from all causes.

The weather over northern Europe on February 23 was so bad that the Eighth Air Force was grounded. The Fifteenth Air Force put 102 B-24s over an aircraft assembly plant at Steyr, Austria, but there were not enough escorts on hand to beat back the German interceptors, and 17 of the B-24s were lost against a claim of just 1 Me-210 destroyed by a long-range P-38.

On February 24, U.K.-based Ninth Air Force light and medium bombers went in ahead of the Eighth Air Force heavy-bomber force and thoroughly disrupted the German forward airfields in the Netherlands. Then the heavy-bomber force went after aircraft factories at Gotha and the ball-bearing plants at Schweinfurt. The Fifteenth Air Force put a force of 83 B-24s and a group of P-38s over Steyr again. The Germans made their stand at Gotha and shot down a staggering 66 bombers and 12 escorts. The Americans claimed 155 German fighters downed for the day, but the German records indicate losses of 66 fighters from all causes.

Hounded from two flanks, the Germans were suckered on February 25 into looking south. The Fifteenth Air Force heavies went to Regensburg, Germany, early in the day, and there they lost 39 of 159 B-24s, plus 3 P-38s. The Eighth Air Force then followed up with its own mission to Regensburg and additional attacks against Augsburg, Furth, and Stuttgart—639 bomber sorties in all. What set the February 25 action apart was the sudden upsurge in the number of P-51 Mustang fighters the Americans were able to get over the various targets from bases in England. Nearly 140 Mustangs from three groups took part in the day's action.

There were signs on February 25 that the GAF fighter force had been worn down by the driving Big Week action. Despite the early opposition against the Fifteenth Air Force bombers over Regensburg, the total fighter-defense response was weak. The Americans claimed 59 victories in all for the day, and German sources show 49 losses from all causes.

Next day, February 26, Big Week was called on account of weather. Despite sanguinary hopes and mighty efforts, the Eighth Air Force heavy bombers were all but grounded for nearly a week. When the Americans came back in force, however, they would be looking to break the back of the German fighter force once and for all. In order to accomplish that feat, Spaatz, Doolittle, Kepner, and Fred Anderson thought their offensive forces were ready for the ultimate target—Berlin.

The first American day strike against the German capital was scheduled for March 3, 1944, but the weather that day was terrible. Of the entire Eighth Air Force, only the 4th Fighter Group and one of the P-38 groups flew all the way to the target, but they never even saw the ground. All the bombers were recalled or went after secondary targets.

On March 4, nearly 500 B-17s and more than 750 fighters were sent to Berlin, but there were only a few holes in the clouds, and only a few German fighters could find the attackers. In the end, just one combat wing composed of 38 bombers actually reached Berlin, and these bombers bombed the holes in the clouds without knowing what was underneath them—residential suburbs. There was almost no fighter action; 7 German airplanes were destroyed by American fighters over Germany.

On March 5, the fighter and bomber action took place over France, where the weather was good. In all, 16 German aircraft were destroyed, including several long-range patrol bombers that were caught on the ground at their base.

Berlin was put back on the boards on March 6. Despite marginal weather conditions, 730 Eighth Air Force heavy bombers and 803 American fighters took off from England to fight their way to the enemy capital. In all, the Germans responded with 328 fighter sorties. The result was the biggest, most-intense air battle of the war to that date. Eighty-one victory credits were awarded to American fighter pilots, but 69 heavy bombers fell to German guns, including ground-based antiaircraft weapons. For all the suffering, the bombers missed their industrial targets altogether and wound up killing approximately six hundred German citizens, mostly civilians. Moreover, the sum of German records shows that only 66 German fighters, at most, were written off from all causes on March 6.

The bomber force stood down on March 7 on account of weather, and then went back to Berlin on March 8. The ostensible target was a ball-bearing factory but, as always, the object was to wear down the German fighter force. This was accomplished insofar as American claims of 155 German fighters were matched by German records indicating 51 actual losses from all causes.

The weather over Berlin was bad on March 9, but the heavies were able to bomb through the undercast by using their supersecret on-board blind-bombing radar. The Germans barely put in an appearance, and only one German fighter was both claimed and actually destroyed.

For all practical purposes, the Allies could count themselves the victors of Operation ARGUMENT, the Big Week battle for superiority in the air over Germany. One note of self-congratulation and confidence was posted as early as March 10. On that day, Lieutenant General Lewis Brereton's Ninth Air Force—which so far had been lending its fighters and medium bombers to the offensive against Germany—was authorized to begin planning and executing its own program of preinvasion tactical strikes in France and the Low Countries.

The American fighter pilots and bomber crews were exhausted by March 9—they were given the day off on March 10—but the German interceptor force had been laid low. The proof came on March 11, when the heavies went in force to Munster, Germany, and *no* German fighters appeared.

From May 9 to May 14, 1944, Army Air Forces fighter pilots claimed *no* aerial victories over northern Europe. There was no action at all on March 12, 13, and 14 because the heavies were kept from going out by extreme icing conditions at altitude. The weather was merely "marginal" on March 15, and so the Eighth Air Force went out to see if the GAF had recovered from the many shocks it had sustained over the preceding three weeks. The reaction was middling. The GAF launched 165 effective interceptor sorties as the American heavies bored in toward Brunswick. Of these, American fighter pilots claimed 35 confirmed victories.

There was another big bomber mission against the German aircraft industry on March 16, and the American escorts claimed 75 German fighters. On the next mission, on March 18, the claims were for 38 German fighters. The bombers were grounded on March 20, but several fighter groups hopped over to France to beat up German airfields. They scored only 3 victories. The bombers flew to Bordeaux on March 21, and 10 German fighters were claimed. The German fighter force was ill, but it was alive, and it was capable of performing under circumstances advantageous to itself. Nothing much happened on the mission to Munster on March 22, but the Germans reacted on March 23, and the American fighters claimed 20 of them. Under the aegis of the Ninth Air Force, the Americans concentrated on targets in France on March 24, 25, and 26, and the American fighters claimed a total of 17 victories. A big bomber mission to Germany on March 29 resulted in 46 victory claims. This was to be the pattern for the remainder of the preinvasion daylight air offensive over northwestern Europe.

As early as February 13, 1944, the Anglo-American Combined Chiefs of Staff had issued an enabling directive aimed at the disruption of German lines of communication within reach of the Allied air forces based in England and Italy. The directive left it to the air force commanders to determine when it had become feasible to redirect significant operational forces against what came to be called "transportation targets." In late March, in light of what many analysts and senior air commanders perceived as the cumulative defeat of the GAF interceptor force over Germany in February and March, it became a matter of VIII Fighter Command policy—rather than individual group prerogative—to unleash the escort fighters that were returning home with full ammunition bays. The invasion of France was only a matter of weeks or, at most, two months away, and Occupied Europe was chock full of German military paraphernalia that could be scrapped from the air. In fact, ranked just behind escort duties, the destruction of transportation targets— locomotives, railroad cars, switching yards, barges, coastal vessels, bridges, and so forth—became the prime objective of the RAF fighter wings and U.S. Army Air Forces fighter groups based in Great Britain. As with many aspects of the air war in northern Europe, the formal plan for a campaign against transportation targets—set forth by the air commanders on March 25 and approved by General Eisenhower on March 26—codified and legitimatized what the fighter pilots had already been doing for some time under their own head of steam.

Beginning April 13, the two U.K.-based tactical air forces—the U.S. Ninth and the British Second—were turned loose against a vast array of tactical targets in France and the Low Countries. Many of the planned tactical sorties—as distinct from opportunistic attacks on ground targets by return-ing escort fighters—were aimed at coastal batteries in Normandy. However, to avoid giving away the invasion objective, these attacks had to be masked against a background of profitable attacks on every other kind of tactical target almost everywhere that the impending invasion *might* take place.

The RAF Bomber Command night offensive and the twin American daylight bomber offensives from the United Kingdom and Italy against strategic targets in Germany and Austria continued unabated during the spring run-up to the invasion. Vast fleets of heavy bombers were available to all three bomber forces, and the weather over the targets was clear far more often than it was not.

With many Army Air Forces fighter groups devoting more time to escorting medium bombers closer to the deck, or conducting their own destructive freewheeling hunting forays against ground targets of opportunity, the Germans and their Axis partners were pressed closer and closer to the wall. Somewhere, somehow, there were encounters in the air over the Axis nations and Occupied Europe nearly every day during the spring 1944 weeks leading up to the invasion.

On April 27, the Eighth Air Force was pulled off deep penetration over Germany for a day, and the heavies were sent to France to strike several transportation centers. The switch caught the Germans unprepared, and there was virtually no opposition. On May 9, the Eighth Air Force returned in strength to France and Belgium to pound seven GAF airdromes. By then, the date for the invasion of France—D day—has been firmly set for June 5 or June 6, and the various air forces based in the United Kingdom were working their way down target lists designed to cripple the GAF, the German Army, and the decision-making powers of the German high command. By May 11, the Ninth Air Force target list had reached the GAF airfields within fighter range of the Normandy beaches, but that included targets in eastern Belgium, Luxembourg, and even the Saar region of far western Germany.

By the middle of May 1944, the huge and growing Allied air forces in western and southern Europe had achieved air superiority. The GAF and other Axis air forces remained powers to be reckoned with in certain regions or under certain circumstances that demanded or favored strong defensive measures, but the air belonged to the Allied air forces. Where they went and when they flew had become largely a matter of convenience.

There is only one fair way to measure the success of Operation POINTBLANK and its many related phases and strategies: How much opposition was the GAF able to muster over the beaches and invasion fleet when the Americans, British, and Canadians invaded Normandy on D day, June 6, 1944?

On D day itself, two German fighters appeared over the invasion beaches. Two. No German fighters rose to challenge the hundreds of fighter-escorted transport aircraft that dropped several divisions of paratroopers behind the Normandy beaches, and no German airplanes attacked the huge invasion armada. On June 6, twenty-six German airplanes—fighters and light bombers—were destroyed over France by U.S. Army Air Forces fighters, but none of these came within sight of the Normandy coast. The GAF never contested the invasion in any meaningful form. On June 6, 1944, and on every day of the war that remained to be fought, operations by the GAF's tactical bomber force against the Allied armies in northwestern Europe was ineffectual nearly to the point of nonexistent.

By early July 1944, all the American and British Allied air forces in northern and southern Europe were ranging far and wide across the length and breadth of their area of responsibility, attacking whatever they were directed to attack, whenever they chose and wherever they needed to go. In doing so, they cumulatively destroyed a vast proportion of the Axis industrial base and what remained of the Axis air forces. The schedule was grueling; there were missions every day that the warplanes could get into the air. Over time, the pilots on the winning side started to wear out, though the supply of replacements never abated.

Almost from the outset of the invasion of France, Ninth Air Force tactical fighter groups were deployed in Normandy, both to protect and support the ground forces, and to allow these fighters to penetrate deeper or for more time into the enemy heartland. Following the British, Canadian, and American breakout from Normandy in late July and the lightning race across France and Belgium in August, British and American fighter groups advanced right behind the ground forces, as quickly as new fighter strips could be built or captured GAF facilities could be rehabilitated. The Third Reich was getting smaller by the week, Allied fighters were gaining range through technical advances, and pretty soon Allied fighters were able to range over nearly all that was left of Hitler's empire.

The GAF fighter force had been in decline since Operation ARGUMENT, the decisive Big Week battles over Germany in late February 1944. Strangely, although the Eighth and Fifteenth air forces had been trying to bomb the German aircraft industry to dust for two years, there seemed to be more German fighters aloft than ever. Perhaps there were; German single-engine fighter production had been *increasing* steadily through 1944. However, if there were more German fighters, the pilots manning them were raw, and the performance of the two main types—the Focke-Wulf FW-190 and utterly outmoded Messerschmitt Bf-109—had not been climbing appreciably, if at all. While Germans waited for "miracle" weapons, their ill-trained young men continued to die at the controls of their obsolete or obsolescent first-line fighters. In the meantime, American fighter pilots got better and better at what they did, and they had technologies at their disposal that made killing less sportsmanlike and more businesslike by the day.

The pressure on the German industrial base never let up; the strategic-bombing missions never abated. When there were no longer enough industrial targets for the vast Eighth Air Force bomber force, the B-17s and B-24s out of England simply laid waste to what remained of Germany's communications system. As long as the heavies appeared over Germany, the GAF interceptors rose to challenge them. The fighting and dying in the skies over Germany never subsided until the bitter end had been achieved.

The end game in northern Europe was pathetic. The German Army and GAF fought on, and tens of thousands of Germans died. The leading cause of death during the final months of the war against Germany was the Battle of the Bulge. In December 1944, thanks to a full-court press by both sides, particularly after the appalling weather over Belgium broke near the end of the month, Eighth and Ninth air force fighter pilots were officially credited with destroying an unbelievable 836 German airplanes of all types. The best single-day score was 135 German airplanes on December 23, the very day the weather broke. On the first day of 1945, alone, 66 German fighters and 3 German bombers were confirmed destroyed over eastern Belgium and western Germany by Eighth and Ninth air force fighters. The total number of victory credits awarded to Eighth and Ninth air force fighters in January 1945 was 301, of which a staggering 174 were awarded for combat on just one day, January 14. This, in some of the worst flying weather in recorded history! In February 1945, Eighth and Ninth air force fighters bagged—that's an apt description—199 German airplanes of all types. And they bagged an even 400 in March 1945, more by steady attrition than because of any one big air battle.

Aerial combat over Europe was still a deadly game for American fighter pilots, to be sure. During the final months of the war in Europe, bad luck and operational accidents claimed the lives of many American pilots, including a few high-scoring aces. But many a fighter pilot saw the period as the last best opportunity to become an ace or, in the case of aces, to set scoring records, and that tended to make some pilots reckless. Also, many American airmen died going after well-defended ground targets. Undoubtedly, strafing ground targets was a leading cause of death among USAAF fighter pilots.

At the end, there was some new spice added to the old air-combat recipe. German jet fighters and bombers began appearing over Europe in late 1944, and they were damn hard to knock down. American-made jets were at least a year away from becoming operational, so the only means at hand for downing a GAF jet—other than getting it to fly into the ground, which happened on occasion—was to out-think the pilot or simply get lucky. The jets caused some excitement and wonderment, but they were too little and too late.

The GAF never gave up. Its defense of Germany was unrelenting. In April 1945, the last full month of the war in Europe, 534 German airplanes were downed over the shrinking Third Reich by Eighth, Ninth, Twelfth, Fifteenth, and First Tactical air force fighters. But the bitter end was near.

The very last German airplane to fall to an American fighter based in Italy—a Twelfth Air Force P-47 Thunderbolt—was a fighter downed over northern Italy on April 26, 1945. It was the only aerial victory ever scored by 2d Lieutenant Roland Lee of the 57th Fighter Group's 66th Fighter Squadron. That was fitting, for the very *first* confirmed Army Air Forces aerial victory in what would become the Mediterranean Theater of Operations had been a German fighter downed on October 9, 1942, by 1st Lieutenant William Mount, a P-40 pilot flying with the 57th Fighter Group's 64th Fighter Squadron. In between Lieutenant Mount's and Lieutenant Lee's victories, American fighter pilots based in North Africa, Mediterranean islands, and Italy, and ranging over North Africa, the Mediterranean, and southern Europe—even as far away as the Soviet Union and Poland—were credited with destroying 3,764 Axis warplanes—German, Romanian, Italian, Hungarian, and even Vichy French.

The announcement on May 1 that Hitler had died the day before by his own hand took the wind out of every German sail, save those of the most ardent Nazis. Nevertheless, two German fighters were downed over Germany on May 1; there were three kills on May 2; one kill on May 3; five on May 4, one on May 7; and nine on May 8, 1945, the last day of the war in Europe.

The very last German airplane to be downed by an American fighter in World War II was a Siebel Si-204 twin-engine staff plane that was destroyed at 2005 hours on May 8, 1945. The lucky pilot of the American fighter, a

P-38, was 2d Lieutenant Kenneth Swift, of the 429th Fighter Squadron, an element of the Ninth Air Force's 474th Fighter Group. The Siebel was Lieutenant Swift's only combat victory in the war, but it was the 7,504th victory credit awarded to a U.S. Army Air Forces pilot in the European Theater of Operations. The very first had been for a Focke-Wulf FW-200 Condor four-engine reconnaissance bomber that two pilots—2d Lieutenant Elza Shahan and 2d Lieutenant Joseph Shaffer—shot down near Iceland on August 14, 1942.

Altogether, in the air war against Germany and her partners, U.S. Army Air Forces fighter pilots were officially credited with 11,268 aerial victories.

AIR WAR EUROPA

CHRONOLOGY

DECEMBER 1941

December 7, 1941

Japan attacks United States bases and military forces at Pearl Harbor, Midway, and, east of the International Dateline, in the Philippine Islands, and at Wake, and Guam.

December 8, 1941

The United States, Great Britain, and their allies declare war on Japan.

December 11, 1941

Germany and Italy declare war on the United States.

December 24, 1941

The ARCADIA Conference between the United States and Great Britain opens in Washington, D.C., to consider a joint global war strategy. Attending are U.S. President Franklin D. Roosevelt and British Prime Minister Sir Winston S. Churchill.

JANUARY 1942

January 11, 1942

UNITED STATES: The U.S. War Department approves a plan to dispatch U.S. troops, including an air contingent, to Northern Ireland.

January 13, 1942

UNITED STATES: The British and American chiefs of staff, attending the ARCADIA Conference in Washington, D.C., agree to move U.S. Army Air Corps (USAAC) units and contingents to bases in the U.K. as soon as possible.

January 14, 1942

UNITED STATES: The ARCADIA Conference ends in Washington, D.C., after taking decisions to form an Anglo-American Combined Chiefs of Staff (CCS) to direct the war effort, to exert the main effort against Germany and her European allies, and to occupy French Northwest Africa at the earliest opportunity.

Col Claude E. Duncan departs for the U.K. to establish facilities headquarters units that will oversee the USAAC's proposed heavy-bomber campaign against Germany.

January 18, 1944

UNITED STATES: In the first deployment of its kind in the war, 1,400 USAAC officers and men depart by ship to establish facilities in Northern Ireland.

January 26, 1942

UNITED KINGDOM: The first convoy of U.S. troops, including the advance USAAC air-base detachment, arrives in Northern Ireland.

UNITED STATES: LtGen Henry H. Arnold, USAAC chief of staff, recommends that the U.S. Army Air Forces in Britain (AAFIB) be composed of a base command, a fighter command, and an interceptor command.

January 28, 1942

UNITED STATES: The Eighth Air Force

is activated at Savannah, Georgia. It is initially designated to support a contemplated Allied invasion of French Northwest Africa.

January 31, 1942

UNITED STATES: BriGen Ira C. Eaker is designated to head the AAFIB Bomber Command and is ordered to proceed to the U.K..

FEBRUARY 1942

February 1, 1942

UNITED STATES: The new Eighth Air Force's VIII Bomber Command is activated at Langley Field, Virginia, and the VIII Interceptor Command is activated at Selfridge Field, Michigan.

February 6, 1942

UNITED STATES: The U.S. War Department announces the formal creation of the Anglo-American Combined Chiefs of Staff to coordinate worldwide war efforts of the two principal Allied partners.

February 12, 1942

UNITED STATES: LtGen Henry H. Arnold announces plans to deploy 16 heavy-bomber groups, three pursuit groups, and eight photographic squadrons to the U.K. during 1942.

February 15, 1942

UNITED KINGDOM: LtCol Townsend Griffiss becomes the first USAAC officer to die in Europe in World War II when the transport in which he is a passenger is mistakenly shot down by Royal Air Force (RAF) fighter pilots.

February 20, 1942

ENGLAND: BriGen Ira C. Eaker, commanding general–designate of the AAFIB Bomber Command, arrives by air with six staff officers in order to select a site and oversee the preparation of a headquarters.

February 22, 1942

ENGLAND: Under the direction of MajGen James E. Chaney, commanding general of U.S. Army Forces in the British Isles (USAFBI), BriGen Ira C. Eaker formally establishes the AAFIB Bomber Command on British soil.

February 23, 1943

ENGLAND: Headquarters, VIII Bomber Command, is officially established in the U.K. under the command of BriGen Ira C. Eaker.

MARCH 1942

March 3, 1942

UNITED STATES: The Eighth Air Force is formally released from responsibility for helping to plan an Allied invasion of French Northwest Africa.

March 9, 1942

UNITED STATES: As part of a major reorganization of the U.S. Army, the United States Army Air Forces (USAAF) is officially established under the command of LtGen Henry H. Arnold.

March 14, 1942

UNITED STATES: The U.S. Joint Chiefs of Staff (JCS) decides to build up U.S. ground and air forces in the U.K. for an eventual offensive against Germany.

March 20, 1942

UNITED STATES: The USAAF issues "Plan for Initiation of U.S. Army Bombardment Operations in the British Isles," an elaboration of earlier statements relating to a proposed strategic air offensive in Europe against Germany and her Axis partners.

March 25, 1942

FRANCE: Maj Cecil P. Lessig becomes the first USAAF pilot in the war to complete a combat mission over Occupied Europe when he pilots an RAF Spitfire fighter in a fighter sweep over France. However, when 50 German Air Force (GAF) fighters rise to challenge the 36 RAF Spitfires, the RAF aircraft return to their base without engaging.

March 27, 1942

UNITED STATES: The U.S. Army War Plans Division issues "Plan for Operations in Northwestern Europe," in which a tentative timetable for an invasion of France is offered. Following a buildup (Operation BOLERO), the plan envisages an invasion (Operation SLEDGEHAMMER)—as early as the autumn of 1942 in the event the Soviet Union is on the brink of collapse. If not, the main Anglo-American invasion of

France (Operation ROUNDUP) is foreseen as taking place in the spring of 1943.

March 30, 1942

SOUTH ATLANTIC: A detachment of U.S. soldiers is landed on Ascension Island, which is midway between South America and Africa. Engineers with the force are to begin building an airstrip contemplated for use by bombers and other long-range aircraft ferrying between the two continents.

March 31, 1942

UNITED STATES: MajGen Carl Spaatz, a senior USAAF officer, suggests that the missionless Eighth Air Force headquarters be shipped to the U.K. to assume operational control over the AAFIB commands already established there.

APRIL 1942

April 7, 1942

UNITED STATES: The U.S. War Department directs the USAAF to transfer Headquarters, Eighth Air Force, to the U.K. to oversee the various commands of the fledgling AAFIB.

April 8, 1942

ENGLAND: Gen George C. Marshall, U.S. Army chief of staff, and Mr. Harry Hopkins, special adviser to President Franklin D. Roosevelt, arrive to begin discussions over the implementation of Operation BOLERO, the buildup of American forces and materiel in the U.K.

April 9, 1942

CANADA: A USAAF detachment arrives in Labrador to begin preparations in support of Operation BOLERO.
UNITED STATES: Headquarters, Eighth Air Force, is redeployed to Bolling Field, D.C., to prepare for its contemplated move to the U.K.

April 12, 1942

ENGLAND: Gen George C. Marshall, attending the BOLERO conference, receives the BOLERO air plan from LtGen Henry H. Arnold, the USAAF chief of staff, who at the time is in Washington, D.C. Arnold also requests that Marshall arrange the transfer of Headquarters, Eighth Air Force, to the U.K.

April 14, 1942

ENGLAND: The British government and the CCS accept the BOLERO plan for the buildup of American military forces and supplies in the U.K. leading to an invasion of France and an all-out ground and air offensive against Germany.

April 15, 1942

ENGLAND: BriGen Ira C. Eaker establishes a headquarters for his VIII Bomber Command at Wycombe Abbey, in High Wycombe.
UNITED STATES: USAAF personnel

from the 15th Light Bombardment Squadron and the 2d Air Depot Group's 689th Quartermaster Company depart by ship for England. (The bomber crews, detached from their parent 27th Light Bombardment Group, are bound for England on a training mission in RAF night-bombing techniques employing searchlights—a program the RAF will soon terminate.)

April 27, 1942

UNITED STATES: Eighteen hundred fifty USAAF officers and enlisted men composed the advance echelons of Headquarters, Eighth Air Force; VIII Bomber Command; VIII Fighter Command; VIII Base Command; the 2d Air Depot Group; and a weather detachment depart by ship from Boston, bound for the U.K.

April 28, 1942

UNITED STATES: The VIII Ground Air Support Command is activated at Bolling Field, D.C., for eventual deployment to the U.K. as an element of the Eighth Air Force.

MAY 1942

May 5, 1942

UNITED STATES: MajGen Carl Spaatz replaces BriGen Asa N. Duncan as Eighth Air Force commanding general. Until Spaatz can reach the Eighth's nominal headquarters in England, BriGen Ira C. Eaker will serve as temporary commander in addition to his duties as VIII Bomber Command commanding general.

May 6, 1942

LIBERIA: An advance USAAF detachment arrives in Liberia to support the projected southern trans-Atlantic flight of USAAF aircraft to the war zone.

May 7, 1942

MALTA: The aircraft carriers USS *Wasp* and HMS *Eagle* launch Royal Air Force Spitfire fighters to reinforce the besieged island's British garrison.

May 11, 1942

ENGLAND: The 1,850 USAAF officers and men dispatched from Boston on April 27 arrive safely by ship in the U.K.

May 12, 1942

ENGLAND: The first large contingent of Eighth Air Force headquarters personnel, including the advance headquarters of the VIII Fighter Command, arrives at High Wycombe.

May 14, 1942

ENGLAND: BriGen Frank O'D. Hunter assumes command of the VIII Fighter Command at High Wycombe.

Personnel from the 15th Light Bombardment Squadron arrive by ship from the United States for RAF training in a special night-bombing techniques.

May 17, 1942

ENGLAND: As the Eighth Air Force advance headquarters detachments begin to plan for training and supplying tactical units preparing to ship over from the United States to the U.K., 50 USAAF intelligence

officers arrive in the U.K. to undergo training by RAF Bomber Command.

May 19, 1942

UNITED KINGDOM: The Eighth Air
Force advance headquarters assumes operational control of all USAAF personnel and
detachments in the British Isles.

May 23, 1942

ENGLAND: The British government
agrees to operate the RAF repair depot at
Burtonwood jointly with the USAAF for use
by the Eighth Air Force beginning in June
1942. Eventually, the facility will be fully
transferred to the Eighth Air Force.

May 26, 1942

ENGLAND: An Anglo-American conference opens in London to consider policy for
allocation of air assets and the establishment of USAAF forces in the U.K.

May 30, 1942

ENGLAND: During consultations begun
on May 26, LtGen Henry H. Arnold
presents his RAF counterpart with a
"Programme of Arrival of U.S. Army Air
Forces in the United Kingdom," in which
Arnold outlines the projected arrival of 66
combat air groups by March 1943.

JUNE 1942

June 4, 1942

UNITED STATES: The USAAF issues a report projecting the eventual deployment of 3,649 airplanes to the U.K.

June 5, 1942

UNITED STATES: The United States declares war on Romania, Hungary, and Bulgaria.

The VIII Base Command is officially redesignated VIII Service Command, and Col Harold A. McGinnes assumes command.

As part of a general redeployment of operational units to the U.S. West Coast to contest an anticipated Japanese naval attack, the 1st Fighter Group is ordered to stand down from preparations for redeployment to the U.K. and fly to California instead.

June 8, 1942

UNITED KINGDOM: U.S. Army Forces in the British Isles (USAFBI) is redesignated European Theater of Operations, U.S. Army (ETOUSA). MajGen James E. Chaney remains in command.

June 9, 1942

INTERNATIONAL: The United States and Great Britain agree to pool food and production resources.

June 10, 1942

ENGLAND: Service units and the advance ground echelons of the 1st Fighter Group, 31st Fighter Group, 60th Transport Group, 97th Heavy Bombardment Group, and 5th Air Depot Group arrive in the U.K.

UNITED STATES: The VIII Fighter Command, headquartered in Bangor, Maine, is formally assigned its first two fighter groups, the 1st (in P-38s) and the 31st (in P-39s).

June 11, 1942

ENGLAND: The ground personnel of the 31st Fighter Group, who arrived by ship a day earlier, are posted to Atcham Airdrome to begin training under RAF supervision with British-built Spitfire fighters. An advance ground detachment from the 1st Fighter Group, a P-38 unit, is assigned to Goxhill Airdrome.

June 12, 1942

ROMANIA: In the first USAAF combat engagement in Europe, HALPRO, an independent force of 13 (of 24) USAAF B-24 heavy bombers commanded by Col Harry A. Halverson and temporarily based at Fayid Airdrome, Egypt (while en route to China), attacks the Romanian oil fields at Ploesti in a daring low-level daylight mission. After taking off from Fayid individually between 2230 and 2300 hours on June 11, the B-24s arrive over the target area beginning at dawn. Ten B-24s attack the Astra Romana refinery at Ploesti, one B-24 attacks the port area at Constanta, and two B-24s attack unidentified targets. Three B-24s are interned in Turkey and the remainder land at friendly bases in Iraq (where one B-24 crash-lands owning to fuel depletion). Although damage to the targets is negligible, the attack is deemed an operational success.

June 15, 1942

ENGLAND: LtGen Carl Spaatz arrives in the U.K. to assume direct command of the Eighth Air Force. Also, the VIII Bomber Command establishes the 1st Provisional Heavy Bombardment Wing headquarters at Brampton Grange.
MEDITERRANEAN: During the morning, seven Egyptian-based HALPRO B-24s and two RAF Liberators attack Italian Navy units that are attempting to intercept a British supply convoy bound for Malta. The heavy bombers attack the Italian warships with 500-pound bombs and, among other damage, score a direct hit on the battleship *Littorio*. Although overall bomb damage is not severe, the Italian naval force withdraws from the area. (Despite Col Harry A. Halverson's best efforts to move his unit on to forward bases in China, HALPRO is detained in the Middle East, where, along

with an RAF Liberator squadron, it is the only Allied long-range bomber unit.)

June 17, 1942

EGYPT: Col Bonner Fellers, a U.S. Army military observer with British forces in the Middle East, cables the U.S. War Department with an assessment of the bleak British military outlook in Egypt and adds that all possible effort must be directed toward staging USAAF heavy bombers into the region for purposes of attacking Axis lines of supply across the Mediterranean. Fellers also notes his conviction that a British collapse in the Middle East will lead to the fall of India to Japanese forces.

June 18, 1942

ENGLAND: LtGen Carl Spaatz formally assumes command of the Eighth Air Force from BriGen Ira C. Eaker, who has been serving as its interim commanding general pending Spaatz's arrival.

The British Air Ministry publishes a list of 87 airfields in England that eventually will be turned over to the USAAF.
UNITED STATES: British Prime Minister Sir Winston S. Churchill arrives in Washington, D.C., to undertake a secret conference with President Franklin D. Roosevelt.

June 19, 1942

EGYPT: BriGen Russell L. Maxwell, head of the U.S. Military North African Mission, assumes command of the U.S. Army Forces in the Middle East (USAFIME).

June 20, 1942

ENGLAND: MajGen James E. Chaney, ETOUSA commanding general, is ordered to return to the United States as soon as he is relieved by his designated successor, MajGen Dwight D. Eisenhower. (In Washington, Eisenhower receives instructions from Gen George C. Marshall, U.S. Army chief of staff, to integrate all USAAF units deployed in the U.K. into the Eighth Air Force. Eisenhower is also told that the broad objective of the Eighth Air Force will be to attain air supremacy in the skies over northern Europe as a vital prerequisite for the contemplated invasion of Occupied Europe by Allied ground forces.)

LIBYA: The strategic port city of Tobruk falls to Axis ground forces.

UNITED STATES: In secret deliberations in Washington, D.C., President Franklin D. Roosevelt and Prime Minister Sir Winston S. Churchill decide to embark upon a fresh Anglo-American campaign to seize French Northwest Africa as a means for relieving pressure on the British Eighth Army in Libya and Egypt and to secure a possible staging area for an invasion of southern Europe. (A prior invasion plan had been early in 1942.)

June 21, 1942

LIBYA: During the night of June 21–22, nine HALPRO B-24s attack the harbor at Benghazi after the target is illuminated by RAF bombers carrying flares and incendiary bombs.

UNITED STATES: Policy agreements concerning air cooperation and Operation BOLERO are signed by the top U.S. and British air commanders, who are meeting in Washington, D.C.

June 23, 1942

LIBYA: During the night of June 23–24, ten HALPRO B-24s attack the harbor area at Benghazi.

MIDDLE EAST: Due to the British Army's loss of Tobruk, Libya, (on June 20) and the resulting German threat to Egypt—and thanks in large part to a June 17 cable to the U.S. War Department from Col Bonner Fellers—LtGen Lewis H. Brereton, then serving as commanding general of the Tenth U.S. Air Force in India, is ordered to proceed immediately to Egypt with all available air assets to establish a new U.S. combat air command. On the same day, HALPRO is formally commandeered to Brereton's control.

June 24, 1942

ENGLAND: MajGen Dwight D. Eisenhower arrives in the U.K. to assume the post of ETOUSA commanding general.

June 25, 1942

ENGLAND: Headquarters, Eighth Air Force, is officially established at Bushey Park.

LIBYA: During the night of June 25–26, HALPRO B-24s attack the harbor area at Tobruk.

UNITED STATES: The U.S. Joint Chiefs of Staff approves the plans for Operation BOLERO worked out by the British and American air chiefs.

June 26, 1942

CANADA: At 1625 hours, 15 97th Heavy Bombardment Group B-17s arrive at Goose Bay, Labrador, on the first leg of their trailblazing flight to the U.K. from Presque Island, Maine, via a newly established northern ferry route. These are the first Eighth Air Force combat aircraft to depart the United States. (After taking off again late in the afternoon on the next leg of the journey, three of these aircraft are lost in bad weather over Greenland, but all crewmen will be saved.)

INDIA: LtGen Lewis H. Brereton, several key Tenth Air Force staff officers, and a small headquarters detachment depart India to assume control of a nascent USAAF presence in the Middle East. Also departing India for the Middle East at this time are seven B-17s from the 7th Heavy Bombardment Group's 9th Heavy Bombardment Squadron.

LIBYA: During the night of June 26–27, HALPRO B-24s attack the harbor area at Tobruk.

June 28, 1942

EGYPT: HALPRO B-24s attack German Army tanks and motor vehicles along the Sollum-Matruh road.

As British ground forces prepare to defend Cairo along a line based at El Alamein, LtGen Lewis H. Brereton establishes the new U.S. Army Middle East Air Force (USAMEAF) in Cairo. At first, Brereton's command consists solely of the 20 remaining HALPRO B-24s and the seven B-17s of the 9th Heavy Bombardment Squadron (veterans of air action against the Japanese over Java and India). Also, the USAMEAF Air Support Command is activated in Cairo under the command of BriGen Elmer E. Adler.

ENGLAND: MajGen Dwight D. Eisenhower officially relieves MajGen James E. Chaney as ETOUSA commanding general.

LIBYA: HALPRO B-24s attack shipping and harbor facilities at Tobruk.

June 29, 1942

ENGLAND: 1stLt Alfred W. Giacomini becomes the Eighth Air Force's first warzone fatality when the 31st Fighter Group Spitfire he is piloting on a training flight crashes at Atcham Airdrome.

FRANCE: In the very first bombing attack over occupied Europe undertaken by a USAAF pilot, Capt Charles C. Kegelman, the commanding officer of the 15th Light Bombardment Squadron, pilots one of 12 RAF Boston (A-20) light attack bombers dispatched against the railroad marshalling yards at Hazebrouck, near Lille. (The 15th Light Bombardment Squadron arrived in England in May to train for a night-bombing role, but the RAF pilot program to which it was attached has been shut down, so the unit has resumed day training under the supervision of the RAF's 226 Squadron, which Capt Kegelman's crew accompanies to Hazebrouck.)

LIBYA: HALPRO B-24s attack Tobruk harbor during the night of June 29–30. One B-24 is lost and its ten crewmen become the first USAAF combat casualties in the Middle East.

June 30, 1942

ENGLAND: VIII Support Command assumes joint control, with the RAF, of the Burtonwood air depot.

PALESTINE: As Gen Erwin Rommel's *Afrika Korps* advances on Cairo and the Suez Canal, LtGen Lewis H. Brereton removes his USAMEAF headquarters from the threatened city to Palestine.

JULY 1942

July 1, 1942

EGYPT: The German Army advance on Cairo and the Suez Canal is halted by the British Eighth Army near El Alamein.

LIBYA: During the night of July 1–2, HALPRO B-24s attack the harbor at Tobruk.

SCOTLAND: The first USAAF B-17 to reach the U.K. as part of Operation BOLERO arrives at Prestwick Airdrome (the northern ferry route terminus) after flying in stages across the North Atlantic. This airplane belongs to the VIII Bomber Command's 97th Heavy Bombardment Group.

UNITED STATES: USAAF headquarters revises its Operation BOLERO estimate downward; instead of the projected 66 combat groups in the U.K. by March 1943, the new estimate projects only 54 groups by April 1943. The reason given is the demands being made to provide units to other theaters.

The 57th Fighter Group, with 72 P-40 fighters, departs Quonset, Rhode Island, aboard the USS *Ranger,* a U.S. Navy light aircraft carrier that will ferry the land-based fighter group to within 100 miles of Accra, Gold Coast. From Accra, the P-40s will cross Africa to Egypt for duty with USAMEAF.

July 2, 1942

EUROPEAN THEATER: The CCS approve the plan submitted by the U.S. and British air chiefs for Operation BOLERO.

LIBYA: During the night of July 2–3, HALPRO B-24s and 9th Heavy Bombardment Squadron B-17s attack the harbor and German Army supply dumps at Tobruk.

July 3, 1942

LIBYA: HALPRO B-24s attack the harbor at Tobruk.

July 4, 1942

LIBYA: During the night of July 4–5, HALPRO B-24s attack ships and port facilities at Benghazi.

MEDITERRANEAN: HALPRO B-24s attacking an Axis convoy at sea are credited with setting a tanker on fire.

NETHERLANDS: In an act more symbolic than prudent, 15th Light Bombardment Squadron crews are assigned to man six American-built, RAF-owned (and RAF-marked) Boston (A-20) light attack bombers for a low-level raid against four GAF airdromes in the Netherlands. Along with six RAF-manned Bostons and an escort of RAF fighters, the American-manned Bostons attack De Kooy, Bergen/Alkmaar, Haamstede, and Valkenberge airdromes. One of the USAAF-manned Bostons is downed over De Kooy, another is downed over Bergen/Alkmaar, one is so severely damaged by German antiaircraft (flak) fire that it is later written off, and a fourth is lightly damaged.

July 5, 1942

LIBYA: During the night of July 5–6, USAMEAF B-17s and B-24s attacking the harbor at Benghazi probably destroy an ammunition ship.

PALESTINE: Five B-17s from the 9th and 436th Heavy Bombardment squadrons arrive at Lydda Airdrome from India.

July 6, 1942

ENGLAND: VIII Air Force Service Command headquarters is established at Bushey Park under the command of MajGen Walter H. Frank.

July 8, 1942

LIBYA: During the night of July 8–9, USAMEAF B-24s attack harbor facilities and shipping at Benghazi, and 9th Heavy Bombardment Squadron B-17s attack Tobruk harbor.

July 9, 1942

MEDITERRANEAN: Six USAMEAF B-24s en route to attack shipping at sea are attacked by GAF fighters. One B-24 is downed with its crew, and the remaining B-24s abort the mission.

SCOTLAND: Seven 1st Fighter Group P-38s are the first USAAF fighters to arrive in the U.K. via the northern ferry route.

July 10, 1942

MIDDLE EAST: The 57th Fighter Group, en route to the Middle East by ship, is formally assigned to USAMEAF.

UNITED STATES: Operation BOLERO planners project estimates of 137 combat groups stationed in the U.K. by the end of 1943.

July 11, 1942

LIBYA: During the night of July 11–12, USAMEAF B-24s attack shipping and port facilities at Benghazi.

July 12, 1942

FRANCE: Six RAF-marked Bostons flown by 15th Light Bombardment Squadron crews attack the Abbeville/Drucat Airdrome from 8,500 feet. (Thereafter, the 15th Light Bombardment Squadron stands down to receive its own airplanes, which are to be former RAF A-20s.)

July 13, 1942

LIBYA: During the night of July 13–14, USAMEAF B-24s attack port facilities and shipping at Benghazi, and 9th Heavy Bombardment Squadron B-17s attack Tobruk harbor. One B-24 is downed by flak.

UNITED STATES: The 52d Fighter Group is assigned to the VIII Fighter Command.

July 14, 1942

UNITED STATES: The first air echelon of the 12th Medium Bombardment Group, in B-25s, departs Morrison Field, Florida, for service with USAMEAF.

July 15, 1942

ICELAND: Six 1st Fighter Group P-38s and two 97th Heavy Bombardment Group B-17s are forced by severe weather conditions to make emergency landings on the Greenland ice cap while transiting to England as part of Operation BOLERO.

LIBYA: During the night of July 15–16, USAMEAF B-24s attack port facilities and shipping at Benghazi.

July 16, 1942

UNITED STATES: The ground echelons of the 98th Heavy Bombardment Group (B-24s), 12th Medium Bombardment Group (B-25s), and 57th Fighter Group (P-40s) depart by ship for the Middle East.

July 17, 1942

LIBYA: USAMEAF B-24s attack Benghazi harbor, and USAMEAF B-17s attack Tobruk.

UNITED STATES: The first air echelon of the 98th Heavy Bombardment Group, in B-17s, departs Morrison Field, Florida, for Egypt via the southern ferry route (South America to central Africa via the Azores).

July 18, 1942

ENGLAND: The first planning conference for the invasion of French Northwest Africa is held under the direction of MajGen Dwight D. Eisenhower. The date for the invasion is tentatively set for October 7, 1942.

July 19, 1942

LIBYA: USAMEAF B-24s attack Benghazi harbor, and 9th Heavy Bombardment Squadron B-17s attack Tobruk harbor.

July 20, 1942

PALESTINE: All USAMEAF heavy bombers (19 B-24s and nine B-17s) are organized into the 1st Provisional Heavy Bombardment Group, commanded by Col Harry A. Halverson and with headquarters at Lydda Airdrome.

July 21, 1942

ENGLAND: LtGen Dwight D. Eisenhower officially assigns to the Eighth Air Force the mission of attaining air supremacy over western France by April 1, 1943—in time for the then-projected invasion of France, set for a few weeks later.

GREECE: 1st Provisional Heavy Bombardment Group B-24s attacking Axis shipping in Suda Bay claim hits on two vessels.

July 22, 1942

LIBYA: 1st Provisional Heavy Bombardment Group B-17s attack Tobruk.

UNITED STATES: The 14th Fighter Group air echelon, in P-38s, departs for England via the northern ferry route, but it will be held in Iceland for air defense.

July 23, 1942

EGYPT: The 98th Heavy Bombardment Group, in B-24s, is assigned to USAMEAF.

ENGLAND: Despite German penetrations deep inside Russia (between the Don and Volga rivers, toward Stalingrad), fear of a Soviet collapse, and ongoing pressure from the United States, the British government officially refuses to launch Operation SLEDGEHAMMER, the proposed 1942 invasion of France.

LIBYA: 1st Provisional Heavy Bombardment Group B-24s attack Benghazi harbor. One crewman is killed when the B-24 in which he is riding crashes upon return to its base.

UNITED STATES: The first air echelon of the 301st Heavy Bombardment Group, in B-17s, departs for England via the northern ferry route.

July 24, 1942

LIBYA: During the night of July 23–24, 1st Provisional Heavy Bombardment Group B-17s attack the harbor at Tobruk.

UNITED STATES: In view of the projected Allied invasion of French Northwest Africa, the U.S. JCS approves the shift of many medium- and heavy-bombardment groups from assignment to bases in the U.K. to commitment to the new theater. Also, 15 combat groups formerly assigned to the Eighth Air Force but not yet deployed there are reassigned to the Pacific Theater.

July 25, 1942

ENGLAND: The first USAAF C-47 transports—from the 60th Troop Carrier Group—arrive at Chelveston Airdrome following their flight from the United States.

LIBYA: During the night of July 25–26, USAMEAF B-17s and B-24s attack Tobruk harbor. One Axis ship is damaged.

PALESTINE: The 334th Heavy Bombardment Squadron becomes the first element of the fresh 98th Heavy Bombardment Group to arrive in service with USAMEAF. Upon their arrival from Florida via the southern ferry route, the squadron and two group headquarters B-17s are assigned to Ramat David Airdrome.

UNITED STATES: Plans for Operation TORCH, the combined Anglo-American invasion of French Northwest Africa, are advanced when the CCS agree to a command setup for the invasion force.

July 26, 1942

FRANCE: In the first operational mission undertaken by a USAAF fighter unit in Europe, the 31st Fighter Group dispatches six of its British-built Spitfire fighters to accompany an RAF fighter sweep in the vicinity of Gravelines. The group executive officer, LtCol Albert P. Clark, becomes the first Eighth Air Force fighter pilot to be shot down in the war, and he is taken prisoner by the Germans.

July 27, 1942

ENGLAND: Orders establishing the 1st and 2d Heavy Bombardment wings are issued by VIII Bomber Command.

RAF Fighter Command agrees to provide escort for USAAF high-altitude bombers with squadrons equipped with the new Spitfire IX fighters until such time as high-altitude USAAF fighter units are trained and ready to assume the escort assignment.

The last B-17s and P-38s of the 97th Heavy Bombardment Group and 1st Fighter Group, respectively, arrive in England via the northern ferry route. (The 1st Fighter Group's 27th Fighter Squadron is temporarily detached from the parent unit to bolster air defenses in Iceland.)

July 28, 1942

ENGLAND: VIII Fighter Command reopens its headquarters at Bushey Park and BriGen Frank O'D. Hunter officially assumes command. Also, BriGen Robert C. Candee officially assumes command of the VIII Ground Air Support Command.

The final air echelon of the 60th Troop Carrier Group arrives from the United States via the northern ferry route. The unit, consisting of 53 C-47 transports, is assigned to the VIII Ground Air Support Command.

LIBYA: During the night of July 28–29, 1st Provisional Heavy Bombardment Group B-17s attack Tobruk harbor.

MEDITERRANEAN: USAMEAF B-24s attacking an Axis convoy at sea claim hits on two merchant ships.

July 30, 1942

LIBYA: During the night of July 30-31, 1st Provisional Heavy Bombardment Group B-17s attack Tobruk harbor.

PALESTINE: Following its journey across Africa from Accra, Gold Coast, the 57th Fighter Group, in nearly 70 P-40s, arrives for duty with USAMEAF.

July 31, 1942

EGYPT: Following a journey along the southern ferry route from Florida, the first air echelon of the 12th Medium Bombardment Group, in B-25 medium bombers, arrives at Deversoir Airdrome, near the Nile Delta, for service with USAMEAF. Veteran South African Air Force bomber pilots and crewmen are assigned to the USAAF group to provide last-minute training.

ENGLAND: A Provisional Troop Carrier Command is organized from disparate USAAF transport units operating in the U.K.

GREECE: USAMEAF B-24s attacking an Axis convoy in Pylos Bay claim hits on two merchant ships.

AUGUST 1942

August 1, 1942

EGYPT: In their unit's combat debut, seven B-24s of the 98th Heavy Bombardment Group's 344th Heavy Bombardment Squadron based at the forward heavy-bomber field at Fayid, Egypt, attack a tank repair depot and port facilities at Mersa Matruh.

MEDITERRANEAN: USAMEAF B-24s attacking an Axis convoy at sea claim mortal hits on a large merchant ship. One B-24 is written off after crash-landing at its base.

August 4, 1942

MEDITERRANEAN: USAMEAF B-24s attacking an Axis convoy at sea during the night of August 4–5 claim hits on two merchant ships.

August 5, 1942

FRANCE: In the first mission overseen by VIII Fighter Command, 11 31st Fighter Group Spitfires undertake an uneventful sweep over the French coast.

August 6, 1942

LIBYA: USAMEAF B-24s attack the harbor at Tobruk.

August 7, 1942

PALESTINE: With the arrival of its third flight echelon via the southern ferry route, the entire 98th Heavy Bombardment Group air echelon is available for combat duty as part of USAMEAF.

August 8, 1942

ENGLAND: While on an RAF-supervised training flight near Shoreham, Maj Harrison R. Thyng, commanding officer of the 31st Fighter Group's 309th Fighter Squadron, becomes the first USAAF fighter pilot to fire bullets into a GAF warplane in World War II. The GAF FW-190 fighter escapes, however, and Maj Thyng is given only a "damaged" credit.

UNITED STATES: MajGen Dwight D. Eisenhower is selected by President

Franklin D. Roosevelt and Prime Minister Sir Winston S. Churchill to command Operation TORCH, the invasion of French Northwest Africa. Eisenhower will retain his post as ETOUSA commanding general.

August 9, 1942

EGYPT: Following a week of training under the supervision of RAF* combat veterans, USAMEAF's 57th Fighter Group, in P-40s, mounts its first operational sweep. No opposition is encountered.
ENGLAND: The 301st Heavy Bombardment Group, in B-17s, arrives at Chelveston Airdrome to begin advanced combat training for eventual operational duty with VIII Bomber Command.

August 10, 1942

MIDDLE EAST: LtGen Lewis H. Brereton reports that the USAMEAF bombing campaign against the Axis ports at Benghazi, Tobruk, and Matruh has reduced Axis supply intake at the three ports by an estimated 40 percent.

August 12, 1942

EGYPT: The 98th Heavy Bombardment Group's 345th Heavy Bombardment Squadron, in its combat debut, attacks Besa Matruh.
ENGLAND: The 31st Fighter Group is declared fully operational. Until more USAAF combat units become active, the unit will operate under RAF control.

August 14, 1942

EGYPT: Six 57th Fighter Group P-40s make their unit's combat debut when they escort RAF light bombers in an attack against El Fuka Airdrome. In a brief melee with five GAF Bf-109s, one P-40 is downed off the coast, but the pilot is rescued and returned to duty.
ICELAND: Credit for the destruction of the first German warplane downed by a USAAF

---

* "RAF" may be taken to mean any and all British and Commonwealth air commands, units, and personnel.

fighter in World War II is shared by two USAAF fighter pilots, 2dLt Joseph D. R. Shaffer, a P-40 pilot with the Iceland Air Command's 33d Fighter Squadron, and 2dLt Elza E. Shahan, a P-38 pilot with the 1st Fighter Group's 27th Fighter Squadron, which is en route to England. The victim is an FW-200 Condor reconnaissance-bomber, which crashes into the sea 9 miles off Grotta Point, Iceland.
LIBYA: 98th Heavy Bombardment Group B-24s attacking the harbor at Tobruk claim one ship damaged.

During the night of August 14–15, USAMEAF B-24s attack the harbor at Tobruk.

August 16, 1942

EGYPT: The 323d Service Group and the ground echelons of the 12th Medium Bombardment, 57th Fighter, and 98th Heavy Bombardment groups arrive by ship from New York to assume responsibility for supplying and maintaining USAAF combat units based in Egypt and Palestine.

During the evening, B-25s of the 12th Medium Bombardment Group's 81st Medium Bombardment Squadron undertake their unit's combat debut and USAMEAF's first bombing mission in direct support of the British Eighth Army—an attack on an Axis depot and tank-repair facility at Matruh.

August 17, 1942

EGYPT: BriGen Auby C. Strickland is designated to command the new IX Fighter Command, which will oversee USAMEAF fighter units.

The final air echelon of the 12th Medium Bombardment Group arrives at Ismailia Airdrome. In all, 57 B-25s have completed the journey from Florida via the southern ferry route.
ENGLAND: The VIII Ground Air Support Command headquarters is established at Membury.
FRANCE: In the first raid over western Europe undertaken by USAAF heavy bomb-

ers, a single mixed squadron of 12 B-17s from the 97th Heavy Bombardment Group, escorted by RAF Spitfire fighters, attack the Sotteville railroad marshalling yard at Rouen, France, with more than 18 tons of bombs between 1739 and 1746 hours. The mission leader is Col Frank Armstrong, commander of the 97th, and the pilot of the lead bomber (in which Armstrong is co-pilot) is Maj Paul Tibbets. Also along as an observer is BriGen Ira C. Eaker, the VIII Bomber Command commanding general. Flak bursts result in superficial damage to two B-17s, and there are no casualties.

Sgt Kent R. West, an aerial gunner, is the first member of the Eighth Air Force to be credited with downing a GAF airplane, in this case one of the GAF fighters that attacks the bomber formation.

August 18, 1942

ENGLAND: The first flight echelon of the 92d Heavy Bombardment Group, in B-17s, arrives from the United States via the northern ferry route and is assigned to the VIII Bomber Command's 1st Heavy Bombardment Wing. The 92d is the first USAAF bomber unit to fly nonstop from the United States to the United Kingdom.

UNITED STATES: Following more than a month's duty in Iceland, the 14th Fighter Group's 48th and 49th Fighter squadrons, in P-38s, proceed to bases in England, but the group's 50th Fighter Squadron is detached for what turns out to be permanent duty in Iceland. On arrival in England, the 48th and 49th Fighter squadrons are reunited with the 14th Fighter Group ground echelon, and the truncated group is assigned to the VIII Fighter Command's 6th Fighter Wing. It and the 1st Fighter Group, which arrived in England in July, will be the only USAAF fighter units to fly across the North Atlantic.

August 19, 1942

ENGLAND: The 1st Heavy Bombardment Wing is formally assigned to the Eighth Air Force to oversee the operations of several

B-17 groups already in the theater and others that are slated to arrive.

FRANCE: Approximately 5,000 British and Canadian troops conduct a raid-in-force against the German-held English Channel port of Dieppe. Throughout the day, in support of the RAF cover force, American-manned, British-built Spitfire fighters of the USAAF's 31st Fighter Group conduct interception missions over the beachhead. At approximately 0900 hours, 2dLt Samuel R. Junkin of the 309th Fighter Squadron becomes the first USAAF fighter pilot to single-handedly down a GAF warplane (an FW-190 fighter) in World War II. In 123 combat sorties, eight 31st Fighter Group Spitfires and four of their pilots are lost to German fire, but two confirmed victory credits are awarded to the group's pilots, and the official USAAF fighter baptism over Europe is counted as a success. The day's missions are the first ever mounted under the control of the VIII Fighter Command.

In bomber action, 22 97th Heavy Bombardment Group B-17s attack the Abbeville/Drucat Airdrome between 1032 and 1040 hours as a means of disrupting GAF operations against the Dieppe landing force. Three B-17s are damaged, but there are no casualties. Meantime, six B-17s sent out on a dry diversionary run are fired on, and two USAAF airmen are wounded.

IRELAND: The 52d Fighter Group mounts its first combat mission of the war, a scramble by four Spitfires against GAF aircraft reported to be off Northern Ireland. No enemy aircraft are sighted, and the Spitfires return to their base without incident.

August 20, 1942

ENGLAND: RAF and USAAF staffs agree in principle to mount a coordinated day-and-night strategic-bombing offensive against Germany from British soil.

FRANCE: Eleven 97th Heavy Bombardment Group B-17s, in a late-afternoon mission, attack a marshalling yard at Amiens. No casualties or damage result from the raid.

Assorted fighter sweeps and escort missions throughout the day by the 31st Fighter Group result in no action.

UNITED STATES: The Twelfth Air Force is formally activated at Bolling Field, D.C., for eventual service in French Northwest Africa.

August 21, 1942

ENGLAND: LtGen Carl Spaatz is formally named ETOUSA Air Officer, which will give him a role in influencing theater strategic planning in behalf of the USAAF.

ENGLISH CHANNEL: Twelve 97th Heavy Bombardment Group B-17s, while on their way to Rotterdam to bomb the shipyards, arrive late at their rendezvous with RAF fighters. Shortly, the fighters must return to their base for lack of fuel, thus leaving the bombers without escort. Just after the friendly fighters turn for home, the B-17s are attacked by 20-25 GAF fighters, of which two are claimed by bomber gunners. One B-17 is damaged, five crewmen (including the pilot) are wounded, and the co-pilot, 2dLt Donald A. Walter, is killed—VIII Bomber Command's first combat fatality of the war. The bombers are recalled as they arrive over the French coast, and the entire mission is aborted.

MEDITERRANEAN: USAMEAF B-24s attacking an Axis convoy southwest of Crete claim two ships probably sunk. However, GAF Bf-110 fighters force a straggling B-24 to crash-land at sea, and all aboard the bomber are declared missing.

August 22, 1942

EGYPT: 12th Medium Bombardment Group B-25s attack the German Army tank repair shops and depots at Matruh. One B-25 is mistakenly downed by an RAF fighter pilot.

SOUTH ATLANTIC: Brazil declares war on Germany, thus opening the way for use by USAAF bombers and transports of the shortest possible ferry route between South America and Africa.

UNITED STATES: The XII Air Force Service Command is activated.

August 23, 1942

LIBYA: Just before dusk, USAMEAF B-24s attack the harbor at Tobruk.

August 24, 1942

ENGLAND: Eighteen sorties mounted by the 31st Fighter Group, including a scramble to find a GAF daylight raider, result in no contacts.

The 6th Fighter Wing is assigned to Atcham Airdrome to train replacement pilots for Eighth Air Force combat fighter groups.

Having completed its advanced operational training at Goxhill Airdrome, the 1st Fighter Group, in P-38s, transfers to Ibsley Airdrome to prepare for operational combat duty as part of the 6th Fighter Wing.

FRANCE: Twelve 97th Heavy Bombardment Group B-17s attack the shipyard at Le Trait between 1616 and 1623 hours. There is no enemy response.

LIBYA: USAMEAF B-24s attack the harbor at Tobruk.

UNITED STATES: The XII Fighter Command is formally assigned to the Twelfth Air Force.

August 25, 1942

ENGLAND: Units of the Provisional Troop Carrier Command are transferred to the operational control of the VIII Ground Air Support Command.

GREECE: USAMEAF B-24s attack the Corinth Canal.

ICELAND: The 27th Fighter Squadon is relieved of its temporary assignment to Iceland air defenses and dispatched to England to rejoin the 1st Fighter Group.

MEDITERRANEAN: 12th Medium Bombardment Group B-25s attack Axis shipping at sea and Axis landing grounds.

August 27, 1942

ENGLAND: Forty-two sorties through the

day by 31st Fighter Group Spitfires result in no enemy action.

The 92d Heavy Bombardment Group air echelon, in B-17s, arrives in England via the northern ferry route.

The Eighth Air Force establishes a Combat Crew Replacement Center at Bovingdon.

MEDITERRANEAN: USAMEAF B-24s attacking an Axis convoy at sea report leaving one ship in sinking condition.

NETHERLANDS: Seven 97th Heavy Bombardment Group B-17s attack a shipyard at Rotterdam. Three of the B-17s are damaged by enemy fire and one crewman is wounded.

August 28, 1942

ENGLAND: Thirty-eight 31st Fighter Group sorties result in no contacts.

FRANCE: Eleven 97th Heavy Bombardment Group B-17s attack the aircraft factory and GAF repair depot at Meaulte. Three B-17s are damaged and one crewman is killed.

LIBYA: Two USAMEAF B-24 squadrons attack shipping and port facilities at Tobruk.

August 29, 1942

BELGIUM: Eleven 97th Heavy Bombardment Group B-17s attack the Courtrai/Wevelghem Airdrome and one B-17 attacks a nearby target of opportunity, Steene Airdrome. Three B-17s are damaged by enemy fire, but there are no casualties.

ENGLAND: Two two-plane scrambles to intercept enemy raiders marks the combat debut of the 1st Fighter Group, in P-38s. However, neither scramble results in a contact.

The 52d Fighter Group, in Spitfires, arrives at Goxhill Airdrome following the completion of a transition cycle in Northern Ireland.

FRANCE: In its first mission as a full group, the 31st Fighter Group dispatches 36 Spitfires on what turns out to be an uneventful sweep along the French coast. Similarly, 32 1st Fighter Group P-38s sent on a similar sweep make no contacts.

LIBYA: During the night of August 29–30, 12th Medium Bombardment Group B-25s attack an Axis landing ground, and USAMEAF B-24s attack the harbor at Tobruk.

MEDITERRANEAN: USAMEAF B-24s dispatched to attack an Axis convoy at sea fail to make contact and return to base with their bombs.

August 30, 1942

EGYPT: Feeling the pinch of USAAF and RAF bombing attacks against its main supply ports, the German Army's *Afrika Korps* mounts its long-awaited attack against Alexandria. All available USAMEAF aircraft are committed to stopping the German armored offensive.

LIBYA: USAMEAF B-24s attack Tobruk harbor.

August 31, 1942

EGYPT: 12th Medium Bombardment Group B-25s accompany RAF Bostons in an attack against German Army vehicles behind the main El Alamein battle line.

ENGLAND: The XII Bomber Command establishes a temporary headquarters at High Wycombe from which it will prepare for its role in the upcoming invasion of French Northwest Africa.

LIBYA: USAMEAF B-24s attack Tobruk harbor, and 12th Medium Bombardment Group B-25s attack aircraft parked on a GAF landing ground.

57th Fighter Group P-40s escort RAF bombers during an attack on Maryut.

SEPTEMBER 1942

September 1, 1942

CRETE: USAMEAF B-24s attacking the harbor at Candia claim hits on three ships.
EGYPT: 12th Medium Bombardment Group B-25s accompany RAF light bombers in attacks on German Army tanks and trucks around the Alam-el-Halfa battle area. Also, two 57th Fighter Group P-40 squadrons escort and support various RAF missions.
ENGLAND: The 97th Heavy Bombardment Group is taken off flight status for several days in order to transition completely to new B-17F bombers. The group's older B-17Es are turned over to the new Combat Crew Replacement Center.

Fighter sweeps and patrols by the 1st, 31st, and 52d Fighter groups, although the heaviest to date, achieve no results.

The 60th Troop Carrier Group is assigned to the VIII Ground Air Support Command's newly arrived 51st Troop Carrier Wing.
LIBYA: During the night of September 1–2, USAMEAF B-24s attack Tobruk Harbor.

September 2, 1942

EGYPT: 12th Medium Bombardment Group B-25s attack GAF landing grounds and, in support of the RAF, attack German Army troops and vehicles around Alam-el-Halfa. Also, 57th Fighter Group P-40s escort and support RAF missions against German Army positions.

By day's end, the German Army offensive toward Alexandria has been turned back by British Eighth Army ground forces supported in large measure by USAMEAF and RAF aircraft working together.
ENGLAND: Col Claude E. Duncan is appointeded XII Bomber Command commanding officer.
LIBYA: USAMEAF B-24s attack the port of Tobruk.

September 3, 1942

EGYPT: 12th Medium Bombardment Group B-25s attack GAF and German Army installations, vehicles, and troop concentrations in support of British Eighth Army ground units fighting around Alam-el-

Halfa; and 57th Fighter Group P-40s support numerous RAF missions in and around the battle area.

MEDITERRANEAN: USAMEAF B-24s attack an Axis convoy at sea with unknown results.

September 4, 1942

EGYPT: 12th Medium Bombardment Group B-25s, supporting RAF Bostons, help repel a German Army ground attack near Alam-el-Halfa.

In the 57th Fighter Group's first air-to-air action in North Africa, 2dLt Thomas T. Williams, a 66th Fighter Squadron P-40 pilot, is credited with a Messerchmitt Bf-109 single-engine fighter probably destroyed as he escorts RAF bombers near Alam-el-Halfa.

MEDITERRANEAN: USAMEAF B-24s join with the RAF and the Royal Navy in attacking an Axis convoy at sea. Two Axis ships are reported sunk and one is reported on fire.

September 5, 1942

CRETE: USAMEAF B-24s attack shipping and port facilities at Candia Bay.

EGYPT: 57th Fighter Group P-40s escort RAF bombers that help to repel the German Army attack on Alam-el-Halfa.

ENGLAND: A combined Anglo-American planning group confirms that the initial objectives of Operation TORCH will be Algiers and Oran (Algeria) and Casablanca (Morocco).

Responding to advice from MajGen Carl Spaatz, his ETOUSA Air Officer, MajGen Dwight D. Eisenhower agrees to leave at least a token force of bombers and fighters in the U.K. when the bulk of U.S. fighting power in the theater shifts focus to Operation TORCH.

The 67th Observation Group arrives by ship from the United States and is assigned without airplanes to the VIII Ground Air Support Command. Using cast-off RAF equipment, the unit will serve for more than a year as a reconnaissance training and demonstration unit.

FRANCE: In its first independent mission of the war, the 15th Light Bombardment Squadron, in 11 A-20s turned back to the USAAF by the RAF, attacks the Le Havre port area. This morning mission, which is escorted by 24 31st Fighter Group Spitfires, is not challenged.

The 301st Heavy Bombardment Group, in B-17s, conducts its first combat mission of the war, an attack on the Rouen/Sotteville marshalling yard. Altogether, 31 B-17s from the 97th and 301st Heavy Bombardment groups attack the target at around 1030 hours without sustaining damage or any crew injuries from enemy fire.

UNITED STATES: Headquarters and Headquarters Squadron, Twelfth Air Force, departs New York for England, where its personnel will take part in planning the aerial phase of Operation TORCH.

September 6, 1942

ENGLAND: The entire 93d Heavy Bombardment Group air echelon, in B-24s, arrives from the United States and is assigned to VIII Bomber Command's 1st Heavy Bombardment Wing. The 93d is the first heavy-bomber unit to arrive in the U.K. in a single formation. The unit's ground echelon also arrives by ship in Scotland.

FRANCE: Eleven 301st Heavy Bombardment Group B-17s attack the St.-Omer/Longuenesse Airdrome without loss or incident. Two 301st Heavy Bombardment Group B-17s that cannot find their group's primary target attack St.-Omer/Ft. Rouge Airdrome.

Thirty B-17s from the 97th Heavy Bombardment Group and the newly committed 92d Heavy Bombardment Group attack the aircraft repair facility and airdrome at Meaulte. One B-17 from each group is lost, and a total of seven are damaged. In all, casualties amount to one killed, five wounded, and 18 missing in action, the heaviest losses sustained to date by the Eighth Air Force on one mission.

Twelve 15th Light Bombardment

Squadron A-20s, escorted by 37 31st Fighter Group Spitfires, attack the Abbeville/Drucat Airdrome at 1700 hours without incident or loss.

September 7, 1942

ENGLAND: The 2d Heavy Bombardment Wing headquarters is formally assigned to the Eighth Air Force.

MEDITERRANEAN: USAMEAF B-24s attack Maleme Airdrome (Crete) and convoys at sea and in Suda Bay (Greece).

NETHERLANDS: Although the 97th and 301st Heavy Bombardment groups dispatch 15 and 14 B-17s, respectively, only four 97th Group bombers attack a Rotterdam shipyard at around 1020 hours, and only five 301st Group bombers attack targets in Utrecht at around 1115 hours. GAF fighters attack both formations and damage five B-17s in all, killing one and wounding four crewmen. USAAF gunners are credited with downing 12 GAF fighters.

September 8, 1942

ENGLAND: Virtually closing down Eighth Air Force operations over Occupied Europe, MajGen Carl Spaatz directs all USAAF headquarters and units based in the U.K. to provide support for the upcoming Operation TORCH. Several Eighth Air Force combat units immediately begin transferring to the Twelfth Air Force.

In another administrative action, MajGen Spaatz formally outlines the cooperative Eighth Air Force day-bombing role and RAF Bomber Command night-bombing role in the gathering strategic air offensive against Germany.

The 3d Photographic Group arrives by ship from the United States and is assigned to the VIII Ground Air Support Command.

GREECE: USAMEAF B-24s attack shipping and port facilities at Suda Bay.

September 9, 1942

LIBYA: USAMEAF B-24s attack port facilities and shipping at Tobruk.

September 10, 1942

ENGLAND: The newly arrived 303d Heavy Bombardment Group, in B-17s, is assigned to VIII Bomber Command's 1st Heavy Bombardment Wing.

September 11, 1942

UNITED KINGDOM: Headquarters and Headquarters Squadron, Twelfth Air Force, and the XII Air Force Service Command headquarters arrive by ship from New York to prepare for the upcoming invasion of French Northwest Africa. Also arriving by ship is the 91st Heavy Bombardment Group ground echelon, which is assigned to VIII Bomber Command's 1st Heavy Bombardment Wing.

September 12, 1942

LIBYA: During the night of September 12–13, USAMEAF B-24s attack shipping and port facilities at Benghazi and Tobruk.

UNITED KINGDOM: Headquarters, 3d Bombardment Wing, and Headquarters, 4th Bombardment Wing, arrive by ship from the United States, but personnel from the latter are immediately transferred to man open XII Bomber Command billets.

The 4th Fighter Group is formally activated on British soil. It will be manned by those U.S. citizens serving in the RAF who wish to transfer to the USAAF.

September 13, 1942

LIBYA: Working in coordination with a Royal Navy battle force, British Army ground observers, and RAF combat units, USAMEAF B-17s and B-24s mount 35 sorties and 12th Medium Bombardment Group B-25s mount 66 sorties against the harbor at Tobruk. Twenty assorted bomber sorties are also mounted against the harbor at Benghazi. Four B-25s are lost over Tobruk.

September 14, 1942

ENGLAND: As a means to facilitate preparations of the Twelfth Air Force for

Operation TORCH, the air force headquarters and commands are attached to corresponding Eighth Air Force headquarters and commands for familiarization purposes.

Large numbers of personnel and units (some only nominally attached to the Eighth Air Force) are formally transferred to the Twelfth Air Force, including two heavy bombardment groups (97th and 301st), three medium bombardment groups (310th, 319th, and 320th), a light bombardment group (47th), a light bombardment squadron (15th), four fighter groups (1st, 14th, 31st, and 52d), three troop carrier groups (60th, 62d, and 64th), an observation group (68th, ground echelon only), and various service units. Many of these units are completing training in the U.K. and have not yet attained operational status. All units involved in the transfer will continue to train or conduct operational missions under Eighth Air Force control until they are redeployed to North Africa.

GREECE: USAMEAF B-24s attacking Axis ships in Suda Bay are credited with setting a tanker afire.

LIBYA: USAMEAF heavy bombers attack Tobruk.

September 15, 1942

EGYPT: USAMEAF B-24s and 57th Fighter Group P-40s support RAF attacks on German Army facilities and troops west of El Alamein.

The 57th Fighter Group displaces forward from Palestine to the vicinity of Cairo.

GREECE: A lone B-24 dispatched to reconnoiter Suda Bay claims one hit for one bomb dropped on an Axis tanker.

September 16, 1942

EGYPT: For operational convenience, operational control of the 57th Fighter Group is assumed by the RAF's Western Desert Air Force (WDAF).

ENGLAND: As part of its training cycle for Operation TORCH, the 60th Troop Carrier Group drops an entire battalion of the U.S. 82d Airborne Division.

LIBYA: During the night of September 16–17, USAMEAF B-24s attack the harbor at Benghazi.

September 17, 1942

GREECE: USAMEAF B-24s attack shipping in Pylos Bay and the port facilities and shipping at Sphakia, Khalones, and Pylos Island.

September 18, 1942

ENGLAND: The VIII Ground Air Support Command is redesignated VIII Air Support Command.

Col Rosenham Beam is named XII Ground Air Support Command commanding officer, and a number of RAF support units are attached to XII Fighter Command because corresponding USAAF units are not available. (The RAF units include radar operators, signalmen, observers, and air-warning specialists.)

September 19, 1942

GREECE: During the night of September 19–20, USAMEAF B-24s attack Pylos Bay, Pylos Island, and Khalones.

September 20, 1942

EUROPEAN THEATER: The combined Anglo-American planning group sets November 8 as D day for Operation TORCH. Nearly all of the USAAF fighter and bomber groups that will have arrived in the U.K. by then are earmarked for a rapid transfer to airfields in French Northwest Africa as soon as they can fly direct or be staged in via RAF bases at Gibraltar.

September 22, 1942

ENGLAND: In the first fighter action in more than a month, two 31st Fighter Group Spitfires are scrambled to intercept a GAF Ju-88 medium bomber sighted off Selsey Bill. Maj Harrison R. Thyng is credited with a "probable."

BriGen John K. Cannon relieves Col Rosenham Beam as commander of the XII Ground Air Support Command.

LIBYA: USAMEAF B-24s attacking Axis shipping in Benghazi harbor claim hits on a large vessel and several smaller ships.

September 23, 1942

SCOTLAND: MajGen James H. Doolittle assumes command of the Twelfth Air Force, whose headquarters is now in Scotland, awaiting movement of the seaborne invasion force to French Northwest Africa.

September 24, 1942

ENGLAND: The XII Ground Air Support Command is redesignated XII Air Support Command.

September 25, 1942

CRETE: Failing to locate an Axis convoy south of Crete, USAMEAF B-24s return to base with their bombs aboard.

LIBYA: USAMEAF B-24s attack Benghazi.

September 26, 1942

FRANCE: Of 75 heavy bombers dispatched to attack GAF airdromes or conduct diversionary raids, only 16 reach their targets, and no bombs are dropped. The entire 301st Heavy Bombardment Group is recalled from the main attack because it cannot locate its fighter escort over the English Channel; the 97th Heavy Bombardment Group is prevented from bombing by thick cloud cover over its diversionary target, and it cannot divine its position until a tail wind has blown it all the way out to the Bay of Biscay; and bad weather also results in the failure of the 92d Heavy Bombardment Group to attack its diversionary targets.

Only days before most U.S. citizens serving as pilots in the RAF are to be transferred to the USAAF, 11 of them flying with the RAF's 133 "Eagle" Squadron are lost while escorting RAF bombers to targets in France.

MEDITERRANEAN: Three USAMEAF B-24 squadrons dispatched to undertake various strikes against Axis shipping return to base without having found any targets.

September 27, 1942

ENGLAND: Col Thomas W. Blackburn is named to head the XII Fighter Command.

LIBYA: USAMEAF B-24s attacking an 8,000-ton vessel unloading in Benghazi harbor fail to score any hits.

September 29, 1942

ENGLAND: At an official ceremony at Bushey Hall, most U.S. citizens serving in the RAF's three Eagle squadrons are formally released by the RAF for service in the USAAF, and all are assigned (with their Spitfire V and IX fighters) to the 4th Fighter Group, which was officially commissioned by the USAAF on British soil on August 22. The 4th Fighter Group is to operate from Debden Airdrome, in Essex. The group's ground echelon is formed from the 50th Fighter Squadron ground echelon (formerly a component of the 14th Fighter Group) and USAAF mechanics and armorers trained by the RAF to work on Spitfires. The new group is immediately put on full operational status.

GREECE: USAMEAF B-24s attack port facilities at Suda Bay.

September 30, 1942

ENGLAND: BriGen Delmar H. Dunton assumes command of the XII Air Force Service Command.

OCTOBER 1942

October 1, 1942

ENGLAND: The 350th Fighter Group is activated in England under special authority granted by USAAF Headquarters to the Eighth Air Force. The unit, which is initially destined for a ground-attack role with the Twelfth Air Force, is equipped with a mixture of spare P-39, P-400, and P-38 fighters available in the U.K. at the time.

GREECE: USAMEAF B-24s attacking Axis ships in Pylos Bay claim hits on a large vessel.

MEDITERRANEAN: USAMEAF B-24s dispatched to attack an Axis convoy at sea fail to locate the target.

October 2, 1942

FRANCE: The 4th Fighter Group, in Spitfires, undertakes its first combat mission as part of the Eighth Air Force. While escorting six 97th Heavy Bombardment Group B-17s on a diversionary bombing raid against St.-Omer/Longuenesse Airdrome, the RAF-trained American pilots (of which 22 are on the mission) down four FW-190s around Dunkirk, Nieuport, and Calais.

The 15th Light Bombardment Squadron, in A-20s, attacks a ship in the Le Havre port at 1420 hours.

Thirty-two 97th and 301st Heavy Bombardment group B-17s, escorted by 31 1st Fighter Group P-38s and approximately 350 RAF fighters, attack Albert/Meaulte Airdrome. Claims by 97th and 301st group gunners amount to nine GAF fighters downed and 13 probably downed. Six 301st Group B-17s are damaged by enemy fire and, on return, one of the B-17s, with three injured crewmen aboard, crash-lands.

October 3, 1942

GREECE: USAMEAF B-24s attacking Axis ships in Pylos Bay during the night of October 3–4 down two GAF fighters.

October 6, 1942

EGYPT: LtGen Bernard L. Montgomery issues a plan to the British Eighth Army for an offensive from the now-stable El Alamein front. It will begin on October 24, taking place two weeks ahead of the projected Anglo-American invasion of French Northwest Africa.

LIBYA: USAMEAF B-24s attack Benghazi harbor. Two B-24s are lost to attacks by Axis fighters.

October 7, 1942

GREECE: USAMEAF B-24s attacking shipping and port facilities at Suda Bay claim seven direct hits on a tanker and eight direct hits on a fuel installation.

October 8, 1942

ENGLAND: As a means of wearing down the enemy at times when heavy-bomber forces are grounded by bad weather over the Continent, MajGen Ira C. Eaker, commanding general of VIII Bomber Command, recommends the creation of a specially trained intruder force, capable of penetrating to Continental targets in any weather.
LIBYA: Two B-24 squadrons from USAMEAF's 98th Heavy Bombardment Group are turned back by bad weather while on their way to attack Benghazi, but the provisional independent Halverson Bombardment Squadron (formerly HALPRO) is able to attack shipping in Benghazi harbor.

October 9, 1942

ENGLAND: Upon its return from a mission to France, the 92d Heavy Bombardment Group is withdrawn from combat to undertake the training of B-17 replacement combat crews assigned to the VIII Bomber Command.
EGYPT: When reconnaissance aircraft discover that the Axis landing grounds at El Daba and Sidi Haneish are waterlogged, 16 12th Medium Bombardment Group B-25s join RAF bombers and fighter-bombers in exploitive attacks that destroy or damage as many as 26 Axis aircraft on the ground.
  1stLt William J. Mount, a P-40 57th Fighter Group P-40 pilot, scores the first USAAF air-to-air victory in North Africa against a GAF Bf-109 fighter in the vicinity of El Alamein.
FRANCE: In the Eighth Air Force's heaviest daylight-bombing mission to date, approximately 108 USAAF heavy bombers—

including 24 B-24s of the newly committed 93d Heavy Bombardment Group—are dispatched to attack a steel plant, an engineering works, and a locomotive and freight-car factory around Lille. Sixty-nine bombers attack the primary targets and ten attack various targets of opportunity, including the city of Roubaix and two GAF airdromes. Although 72 1st and 4th Fighter group escorts fail to down any GAF interceptors, the heavy bombers are credited with the destruction of 25 GAF fighters, plus 38 probables.* In all, three B-17s and one B-24 are lost, one each is damaged beyond repair, and 46 others sustain damage. Ten are wounded and 29 are counted as missing.
  Several "firsts" are accumulated this day by Eighth Air Force heavy bombers. On its first combat mission, the 93d Heavy Bombardment Group becomes the first B-24 unit to enter combat with the Eighth Air Force. The first mission-related midair collision sustained by Eighth Air Force heavy bombers occurs during the flight to France, when a pair of 92d Heavy Bombardment Group B-17s collide. (Both B-17s are forced into vertical dives but both escape and return to bases in England.) And a B-17 of the 301st Heavy Bombardment Group that has been damaged by enemy fire over the target becomes the first Eighth Air Force bomber ever to ditch at sea. Although the B-17 sinks in just over a minute, all of its occupants are saved.

---

* Even though claims by the bombers gunners were probably highly inaccurate, the tendency of analysts of the period to view the claims as credible   not to mention the tendency to draw erroneous conclusions when comparing the apparent performance of the gunners and the fighters   had immense ramifications upon the course of the USAAF bomber offensive for at least the whole of the following year, for the numbers and the comparisons gave credence to the flawed USAAF daylight-bombing strategy built around the myth of the "self-defending" bomber.

LIBYA: USAMEAF B-24s attack shipping and port facilities at Benghazi.

October 10, 1942

EGYPT: USAMEAF B-25s attack Axis landing grounds behind the El Alamein front.

ENGLAND: The 31st Fighter Group is removed from operational status with the Eighth Air Force so it can prepare for its role in Operation TORCH.

The first air echelon of the 44th Heavy Bombardment Group, in B-24s, arrives from the United States for service with VIII Bomber Command's 2d Heavy Bombardment Wing; and the first air echelon of the 91st Heavy Bombardment Group, in B-17s, arrives from the United States for service with VIII Bomber Command's 1st Heavy Bombardment Wing.

LIBYA: USAMEAF B-24s attack shipping and port facilities in Benghazi harbor.

October 11, 1942

MEDITERRANEAN: USAMEAF B-24s attack an Axis convoy at sea.

October 12, 1942

EGYPT: USAMEAF Bomber Command is organized in Cairo under the command of Col Patrick W. Timberlake. Effective RAF control of USAAF heavy-bomber units ceases as these units come under USAMEAF Bomber Command control.

ENGLAND: VIII Fighter Command is made responsible for overseeing the transfer of Twelfth Air Force air echelons to North Africa from the U.K.

LIBYA: USAMEAF B-17s attack the harbor at Tobruk.

October 13, 1942

EGYPT: 57th Fighter Group P-40 pilots are credited with downing two Bf-109s in an action approximately 10 miles south of El Alamein.

October 14, 1942

EGYPT: Thirty-four 12th Medium Bom-

bardment Group B-25s and part of the group ground echelon displace forward to a landing ground within 50 miles of the British Eighth Army battle line. For operational convenience, the group is placed under RAF control.

LIBYA: USAMEAF B-17s attacking shipping in Tobruk harbor claim hits on a large ship and the destruction of a small ship moored alongside.

October 15, 1942

FRANCE: The 14th Fighter Group, in P-38s, completes its first combat mission with the Eighth Air Force by escorting RAF Boston light bombers to France.

October 16, 1942

ENGLAND: By this date (having started on September 14), the following combat units have been assigned to the Twelfth Air Force for use in the upcoming campaign in French Northwest Africa: 97th and 301st Heavy Bombardment groups (B-17s); 1st, 14th, and 82d Fighter groups (P-38s); 31st and 52d Fighter groups (Spitfires); 81st and 350th Fighter groups (P-39s); 3d Photographic Group (B-17s, F-4s, and F-5s); 47th Light Bombardment Group (A-20s); 15th Light Bombardment Squadron (A-20s); and 60th, 62d, and 64th Troop Carrier groups (C-47s). Many of these units represented approximately half the former strength of the Eighth Air Force.

LIBYA: Although many USAMEAF B-17s and B-24s dispatched to attack Benghazi harbor must abort in the face of bad weather, several B-24s are able to attack the target.

October 17, 1942

SCOTLAND: Operation TORCH convoys begin to assemble in the Firth of Clyde.

October 19, 1942

EGYPT: USAMEAF B-25s join RAF units in an all-out three-day effort against Axis landing grounds behind the El Alamein front.

LIBYA: USAMEAF B-24s attacking

shipping at Tobruk harbor claim a direct hit on one vessel.

October 20, 1942

EGYPT: Allied air activity in Egypt intensifies precipitously as a means for achieving local air superiority in time for the October 24 start of the El Alamein offensive. USAMEAF B-25s support RAF bombers in attacking Axis landing grounds behind the El Alamein front.

ENGLAND: MajGen Dwight D. Eisenhower directs the Eighth Air Force, as its first priority, to ensure the safety of TORCH convoys by attacking German submarines and submarine bases within reach of USAAF airfields in the U.K. Also, of secondary importance, the Eighth Air Force is directed by Eisenhower to attack GAF airdromes within range of the convoy routes.

LIBYA: USAMEAF B-17s and B-24s dispatched against Tobruk fail to locate the target due to bad weather and poor visibility, but three B-17s attack the coastal highway near Bardia while returning to their bases.

October 21, 1942

EGYPT: USAMEAF B-25s support RAF bombers in attacking Axis landing grounds behind the El Alamein front.

FRANCE: Cloud cover prevents all but 15 of 90 B-17 and B-24s dispatched against the submarine base at Lorient from finding their targets. (The 97th Heavy Bombardment Group, which is the only unit to drop its bombs on the target, completes its final mission with the Eighth Air Force, as do the 92d and 301st groups.)

Eight of 17 B-17s dispatched by the 11th Combat Crew Replacement Command attack Cherbourg/Maupertus Airdrome and claim ten of 36 attacking GAF fighters downed, plus four probably downed. USAAF losses on this mission amount to three B-17s downed and six damaged plus five crewmen wounded and 30 missing.

LIBYA: Bad weather prevents USAMEAF

B-24s from locating Benghazi harbor, but German Army tent camps and Axis landing grounds near the coast in Egypt are attacked during the return flight.

October 22, 1942

CRETE: In an extension of the USAAF and RAF air offensive against Axis landing grounds and airdromes in Egypt and Libya, USAMEAF heavy bombers attack Maleme Airdrome.

EGYPT: USAMEAF B-25s attack Axis aircraft dispersed on the ground behind the El Alamein front; and 57th Fighter Group P-40s escorting the B-25s attack tent camps and vehicles along the coastal highway near El Hamma, reconnoiter the area west of El Daba, and attack German Army artillery positions.

A USAAF headquarters detachment that has been gaining experience under the RAF is redesignated as the headquarters of the new joint Anglo-American Desert Air Task Force (DATF), a tactical air command that is to provide direct support for the British Eighth Army during the imminent El Alamein offensive. LtGen Lewis H. Brereton is designated to head the new command in addition to his ongoing duties as the USAMEAF commanding general. Brereton's DATF deputies are BriGen Auby C. Strickland, who will be chief of staff, and BriGen Elmer E. Adler, who will head a new Air Force Service Command.

The 57th Fighter Group and 12th Medium Bombardment Group, which have been operating temporarily under RAF control, are transferred to the control of the new DATF.

GREECE: USAMEAF B-17s dispatched to attack Candia abort in the face of bad weather.

UNITED KINGDOM: The cargo echelon of the U.K.-based component of the TORCH invasion fleet sails from the Firth of Clyde, Scotland, and the first headquarters echelon of the Twelfth Air Force begins moving from England to North Africa.

October 23, 1942

EGYPT: The British Eighth Army's El Alamein offensive opens at 2140 hours with a massive artillery barrage.

GREECE: USAMEAF B-17s dispatched against Candia abort in the face of bad weather.

LIBYA: USAMEAF B-24s dispatched against Benghazi abort in the face of bad weather.

UNITED STATES: The first echelon of the Western Task Force component of the TORCH invasion fleet sails from Hampton Roads, Virginia.

October 24, 1942

EGYPT: As the British Eighth Army's El Alamein offensive begins, USAMEAF's 12th Medium Bombardment Group, in B-25s, mounts 50 combat sorties against German Army troop concentrations, vehicle traffic, artillery emplacements, and tent camps. 57th Fighter Group P-40s escorting RAF and British Commonwealth bombers attack targets of opportunity, including tanks and motor vehicles.

UNITED STATES: The second echelon of the Western Task Force component of the TORCH invasion fleet sails from Hampton Roads, Virginia.

October 25, 1942

BERMUDA: The small fleet aircraft carrier USS *Ranger* and three escort carriers (*Sangamon, Santee,* and *Suwanee*) whose U.S. Navy fighter and light-bomber squadrons will directly support the various amphibious assaults in French Northwest Africa sail to rendezvous with the Western Task Force. (The U.S. Navy light-bomber types are Douglas SBD-3 Dauntless dive-bombers and Grumman TBF-1 Avenger torpedo bombers, and the U.S. Navy fighters are all Grumman F4F-4 Wildcats.)

EGYPT: Continuing their support of the British Eighth Army's El Alamein offensive, 30 12th Medium Bombardment Group B-25s, escorted by 57th Fighter Group P-40s, attack a wide range of tactical targets. 57th Fighter Group P-40 escort pilots down four Bf-109s in a morning air action over a GAF landing ground.

ENGLAND: The 1st Fighter Group stands down from operational missions with the Eighth Air Force so it can prepare for its eventual role in Operation TORCH.

FRANCE: Thirty-five 4th Fighter Group Spitfires and 24 14th Fighter Group P-38s escort RAF bombers to France, but they encounter no enemy airplanes and return early due to bad weather. This is the 14th Fighter Group's final mission before being transferred to the Twelfth Air Force for the North Africa invasion. For the moment, only the 4th Fighter Group remains on operational status with VIII Fighter Command.

LIBYA: USAMEAF B-17s and B-24s dispatched against Benghazi abort in the face of bad weather.

SCOTLAND: The troop echelon of the U.K.-based component of the TORCH invasion fleet sails for North Africa from the Firth of Clyde.

October 26, 1942

EGYPT: Eighteen 12th Medium Bombardment Group B-25s, escorted by 57th Fighter Group P-40s, attack tactical targets in support of the British Eighth Army's El Alamein offensive.

Capt Thomas W. Clark, a P-40 pilot with the 57th Fighter Group's 65th Fighter Squadron, becomes the first USAAF fighter pilot flying in Europe or North Africa to score a double victory. Clark's victims are Italian Air Force Mc.202 fighters downed near El Dabr. In the same action, two other Mc.202s are downed by other members of the 65th Fighter Squadron. In all, the 57th Fighter Group mounts 72 effective combat sorties through the day.

ENGLAND: The final air echelon of the 62d Troop Carrier Group arrives from the United States via the northern ferry route and is assigned to the 51st Troop Carrier

Wing. The group is slated to take part in Operation TORCH.

LIBYA: After being grounded by bad weather for a week, more than 30 USAMEAF B-17s and B-24s attack Tobruk-bound Axis convoys at sea off the Libyan coast.

October 27, 1942

EGYPT: 57th Fighter Group P-40s mounting a surprise low-level dawn raid against the Fuka-Bagush landing ground destroy several parked aircraft, motor vehicles, and tents.

During the afternoon, while on their way to attack another Axis landing ground, eight bomb-laden 57th Fighter Group P-40s and eight P-40 escorts engage a formation composed of 20 Italian Air Force CR.42 biplane fighters, 20 GAF Ju-87 dive-bombers, and 20 GAF Bf-109 fighters. Four CR.42s and three GAF Bf-109s are downed, all of the latter by 1stLt Lyman Middleditch, Jr., of the 64th Fighter Squadron—the best showing so far in a single action by a USAAF pilot in Europe or North Africa. (Middleditch has already been credited with a Bf-109 downed on October 25, and is thus the high-scoring USAAF fighter pilot in Europe and North Africa.) No USAAF fighters are lost in achieving the best one-day score amassed so far in the war against Germany and Italy by USAAF fighter pilots.

12th Medium Bombardment Group B-25s, escorted by 57th Fighter Group P-40s, attack German Army tanks, motor vehicles, and other ground targets in and around Matruh.

ENGLAND: The air echelon of the 305th Heavy Bombardment Group is fully assembled after flying from the United States. The new unit is assigned to VIII Bomber Command's 1st Heavy Bombardment Wing.

October 28, 1942

EGYPT: Continuing their support of the British Eighth Army's El Alamein offensive, 122th Medium Bombardment Group

B-25s and 57th Fighter Group P-40s attack a wide range of tactical targets. While escorting USAAF and RAF light and medium bombers, 57th Fighter Group P-40 pilots down a total of five Bf-109s in three separate actions during the day.

MEDITERRANEAN: USAMEAF B-17s dispatched against an Axis convoy at sea fail to locate the target in the face of bad weather and poor visibility. However, the B-17s do find Axis warships in Pylos Bay, Greece, and these are attacked without known results.

October 29, 1942

CRETE: During the night of October 29–30, 1st Provisional Heavy Bombardment Group B-17s and B-24s attack Maleme Airdrome. One heavy bomber is lost.

EGYPT: Continuing their support of the British Eighth Army's El Alamein offensive, 12th Medium Bombardment Group B-25s and 57th Fighter Group P-40s attack a wide range of tactical targets.

October 30, 1942

EGYPT: One Bf-109 is downed and at least four others are damaged when the 57th Fighter Group's 64th Fighter Squadron mounts a morning attack at wave-top height against a GAF landing ground on the coast well behind the German lines at El Alamein. Also, 12th Medium Bombardment Group B-25s, escorted by 57th Fighter Group P-40s, attack the Axis landing grounds at El Daba and Fuka-Bagush.

ENGLAND: The final air echelon of the 64th Troop Carrier Group arrives from the United States via the northern ferry route and is   assigned to the 51st Troop Carrier Wing. The group is slated to take part in Operation TORCH.

October 31, 1942

CRETE: During the night of October 31–November 1, USAMEAF B-24s dispatched to attack Maleme Airdrome fail to find the target in the face of bad weather and poor visibility.

EGYPT: 12th Medium Bombardment Group B-25s attack an Axis landing ground, and escorting 57th Fighter Group P-40 pilots down three Bf-109s.

ENGLAND: In an assessment provided to Gen Henry H. Arnold, MajGen Carl Spaatz predicts that attacks upon German Navy submarine pens by the Eighth Air Force might prove to be very costly in terms of aircraft lost. Nevertheless, Spaatz affirms his intention to continue such attacks.

PALESTINE: The 376th Heavy Bombardment Group is activated at Lydda to absorb all the B-24s operating with the 1st Provisional Heavy Bombardment Group. Two squadrons comprise surviving HALPRO B-24s and, for the time being, one squadron is composed of B-17s that had been transferred from India in July (i.e., the 9th Heavy Bombardment Squadron). The RAF's only heavy-bomber unit in the region—160 Squadron, in Liberators—is also attached to the new group for operational and logistical purposes.

NOVEMBER 1942

November 1, 1942

CRETE: USAMEAF B-24s attack Maleme Airdrome.

EGYPT: 57th Fighter Group P-40s escort RAF bombers on tactical strikes and attack ground targets of opportunity behind the El Alamein front.

The USAMEAF ground echelon is reinforced by an air depot group and two service groups.

November 2, 1942

EGYPT: After fighting its way into and containing the German Army defensive positions before El Alamein, the British Eighth Army begins the breakout phase of its plan to sweep through Libya and Tunisia to link up with the Anglo-American TORCH invasion forces in French Northwest Africa.

Forty 12th Medium Bombardment Group B-25s directly support attacks by a British Eighth Army armored division as well as attacking German Army tanks and troops across a broad segment of the battle area. The 57th Fighter Group also directly supports British Eighth Army ground troops. In a dawn raid on a GAF landing ground, the P-40 pilots destroyed seven Axis aircraft on the ground.

The advance flight echelon of the 79th Fighter Group, a P-40 unit, arrives at Cairo/Heliopolis Airdrome following a transcontinental journey from Accra, Gold Coast, where its fighters had been assembled at a factory set up for the purpose. Shortly, 79th Fighter Group senior officers are attached to the 57th Fighter Group for combat familiarization.

LIBYA: 376th Heavy Bombardment Group B-17s attack shipping and port facilities at Tobruk. Hits are claimed on two Axis merchantmen, and fires are started ashore that will burn steadily for two days.

November 3, 1942

EGYPT: Allied aircraft supporting the British Eighth Army breakout attacks mount more than 300 sorties against Axis forces fleeing along the coastal highway. In 45 bomber sorties and 88 fighter sorties, 12th Medium Bombardment Group B-25s and 57th Fighter Group P-40s attack numerous tactical targets, including tanks, motor vehicles, road convoys, an Axis landing ground, ammunition and supply dumps, fuel installations, and troop concentrations.

November 4, 1942

EGYPT: With Axis forces in full retreat, 12th Medium Bombardment Group B-25s and 57th Fighter Group P-40s continue to attack ground targets in direct support of the British Eighth Army.

LtGen Frank M. Andrews replaces BriGen Russell L. Maxwell as commanding general of U.S. Army Forces in the Middle East (USAFIME).

LIBYA: Nine USAMEAF B-24s attacking Benghazi harbor claim direct hits on three ships and the downing of an Axis fighter.

November 5, 1942

EGYPT: Its breakout from El Alamein complete, the British Eighth Army regroups and opens the pursuit phase of the offensive beneath a wide-ranging and aggressive aerial umbrella that includes every available USAAF fighter and bomber based in Egypt. 12th Medium Bombardment Group B-25s contribute 42 effective sorties, and 57th Fighter Group P-40s mount a total of 68 escort and fighter-bomber sorties.

An advance air and ground echelon ("A" Party) comprising half of the 57th Fighter Group is ordered forward to a former Axis landing ground near El Daba. This is part of a two-platoon system adopted from the RAF. At the next opportunity, the El Daba force will remain in place, continuing to provide fighters and fighter-bombers, while the so-called "B" Party leapfrogs it to a base even nearer the receding battle front.

November 6, 1942

EGYPT: With half the group on the move,

the 57th Fighter Group's "B" Party mounts 34 effective combat sorties in support of the British Eighth Army pursuit of Axis forces. The P-40s are credited with destroying German Army motor vehicles around Mersa Matruh.

Six 79th Fighter Group senior pilots join the 57th Fighter Group for a strafing attack against an Axis motor convoy near the Egyptian coast. Although the attack is deemed a success, the 79th Fighter Group commanding officer, LtCol Peter McGoldrick, is killed when he force-lands his battle-damaged P-40 and detonates a land mine.

LIBYA: USAMEAF B-24s attacking the harbors at Tobruk and Benghazi claim hits on two Axis ships.

November 7, 1942

EGYPT: Bad weather grounds or hampers many 12th Medium Bombardment Group and 57th Fighter Group missions.

376th Heavy Bombardment Group B-24s begin to redeploy from bases in Palestine to bases in Egypt.

FRANCE: In the Eighth Air Force's first bombing mission since October 21, 23 B-17s of the 91st, 301st, and 306th Heavy Bombardment groups and 11 B-24s of the 93d Heavy Bombardment Group attack the Brest U-boat base with nearly 80 tons of bombs. This action marks the 91st Heavy Bombardment Group's combat debut. Against claims of four GAF fighters downed and three probably downed over Brest, the 91st Heavy Bombardment Group has 11 B-17s damaged and the 93d Heavy Bombardment Group has one B-24 damaged and one B-24 damaged beyond repair, plus three crewmen wounded.

In their unit's combat debut, 44th Heavy Bombardment Group B-24s mount an unchallenged diversionary flight over France.

UNITED KINGDOM: Movement of Twelfth Air Force air units from bases in the U.K. to North Africa begins—in some cases directly to bases in North Africa during the night of November 7–8, and in other cases via Gibraltar.

November 8, 1942

EGYPT: Although severely slowed by rain over the past four days, the pursuit phase of the El Alamein offensive continues. However, due to the weather, including severe flying conditions, large parts of the Axis force evade capture and outrace the pursuing British ground forces and Anglo-American air groups.

Mersa Matruh falls to the British Eighth Army.

376th Heavy Bombardment Group B-24s begin combat operations from a base near the Nile Delta.

ENGLAND: Following its mission to France, the 301st Heavy Bombardment Group stands down to prepare for its transfer to North Africa.

FRANCE: Eleven 91st Heavy Bombardment Group B-17s attack the Abbeville/Drucat Airdrome at the cost of five aircraft damaged and five crewmen wounded. Also, 42 B-17s of the 301st and 306th Heavy Bombardment groups attack an industrial area in Lille at the cost of eight B-17s damaged and three crewmen injured. The 4th Fighter Group, in Spitfires, provides withdrawal support for the Lille mission, but no enemy aircraft are engaged. Claims by bomber gunners amount to 11 GAF fighters downed and six probably downed.

FRENCH MOROCCO: XII Air Support Command headquarters is established ashore to oversee USAAF operations in support of U.S. Army ground troops. In an event for which he was later awarded a Medal of Honor, Col Demas T. Craw, a XII Air Support Command staff officer, volunteers to negotiate an armistice with commanders of the Vichy French forces in the region. However, as Col Craw is attempting to find passage to the French lines, he is killed by machine-gun fire.

FRENCH NORTHWEST AFRICA: Under an aggressive umbrella of carrier-based U.S. Navy fighters and light bombers, the Anglo-American invasion forces are landed at widely dispersed points along the Algerian and Moroccan coasts. Aerial opposition by obsolescent Vichy French Air Force fighters is easily overcome. Ten pilots flying F4F Wildcat fighters from the U.S. Navy's Fighting Squadron 41 (USS *Ranger*) down 13 aircraft in a fighter-versus-fighter battle over Cazes Airdrome, French Morocco, and five other Vichy warplanes are destroyed by pilots from other fighter squadrons in other action.

The 60th Troop Carrier Group, equipped with 39 C-47 transports, undertakes its first combat mission of the war by flying from England with a reinforced battalion of U.S. Army paratroopers. The plan is to land peacefully at the Oran/La Senia and Oran/Tafaraoui airdromes at 0100 hours, November 8, but due to aircraft becoming lost and separated during the long flight, and to unexpected antiaircraft fire at various Vichy French airdromes, the operation degenerates into a complete shambles. Many C-47s are forced down and many of their crewmen and passengers are taken prisoner by Vichy troops. Three C-47s with troops aboard—along with troops parachuting from a fourth C-47—land in Spanish Morocco and are interned. Three C-47s with troops aboard are shot down by Vichy fighters. It will be several days before all the 60th Troop Carrier Group's airplanes, crewmen, and passengers are accounted for, and only 14 of the original 39 aircraft will be available for use.

At about 1700 hours, the 31st Fighter Group's 308th and 309th Fighter squadrons arrive at Tafaraoui Airdrome, south of Oran, Algeria, after staging through Gibraltar from England. One 309th Fighter Squadron Spitfire is shot down in the landing pattern by Vichy French fighters, and its pilot is killed, but the survivors swiftly recover from the surprise attack and three of them each shoot one of the four Vichy Dewoitine D.520 fighters before the lone survivor flees.

Headquarters elements of MajGen James H. Doolittle's Twelfth Air Force land from ships at Arzieu, Algeria, as do the headquarters of BriGen Thomas W. Blackburn's XII Fighter Command and ground echelons of the 31st Fighter Group and 319th Medium Bombardment Group.

At 1730 hours, in an uncontested attack, GAF He-111 level bombers and Ju-88 torpedo bombers attack Allied ships offloading troops and supplies at Cape Matifou, near Algiers. The USS *Leedstown* is torpedoed.

VICHY FRANCE: Vichy France severs diplomatic relations with the United States.

November 9, 1942

ALGERIA: Spitfires of the 31st Fighter Group's 308th and 309th Fighter squadrons turn back a morning attempt by a French Foreign Legion motorized column to reinforce Oran from the south by way of the road running beside the squadrons's new home at Oran/Tafaraoui Airdrome. The Spitfires destroy at least five Vichy light tanks and many trucks before the column retreats to the south.

When Vichy French shore batteries are trained inland to bear on Oran/La Senia Airdrome, they are put out of action in a strafing attack mounted by 31st Fighter Group Spitfires from Tafaraoui.

GAF medium bombers attack Allied vessels off Algiers. In this attack, the USS *Leedstown,* which had been damaged by a GAF torpedo on November 8, is sunk by bombs during another uncontested GAF attack.

During the afternoon, most of the 52d Fighter Group, a USAAF Spitfire unit, arrives at Oran/Tafaraoui Airdrome from Gibraltar, but six of its Spitfires run out of gas and are forced down along the way. Also, advance elements of the 3d Photographic Group arrive in Algeria following a flight from England via Gibraltar.

At 1605 hours, MajGen James H. Doolittle and his staff land at Arzieu following a flight from Gibraltar in a B-17 escorted by 25 52d Fighter Group Spitfires. From Arzieu, Doolittle's B-17 and 12 of the Spitfires proceed to Oran/Tafaraoui.

EGYPT: As the British Eighth Army enters Sidi Barrani, the 57th Fighter Group's "B" Party moves forward to a former Axis landing ground at Sidi Haneish.

The 376th Heavy Bombardment Group moves to Abu Sueir Airdrome, near the Nile Delta.

FRANCE: Thirty-one VIII Bomber Command B-17s and 12 B-24s attack the St.-Nazaire U-boat base. While bombing from between 7,500 and 10,000 feet, three 306th Heavy Bombardment Group B-17s are downed by flak and 22 are damaged, with crew losses of one killed and 32 missing. Eleven aircraft from other groups are also damaged. It is decided that, hereafter, heavy-bombing attacks will take place only from high altitude.

FRENCH MOROCCO: U.S. Navy pilots from Fighting Squadron 9 (USS *Ranger*) are credited with the destruction of six Vichy French fighters in the air near Fedala during an early-morning battle.

U.S. Navy light bombers off the USS *Santee* attack the Marrakech Airdrome and destroy 20 Vichy French aircraft on the ground.

GIBRALTAR: Thirty-nine 64th Troop Carrier Group C-47s arrive from England with a British Army paratroop battalion.

TUNISIA: The German Army invades Tunisia without opposition and immediately begins staging troops and materiel from Italy through Tunis\El Aouina Airdrome.

November 10, 1942

ALGERIA: Thirty-four 64th Troop Carrier Group C-47s embarking a British Army paratroop battalion arrive from England after stopping over at Gibraltar on November 9.

CRETE: 376th Heavy Bombardment Group B-17s attack the harbor at Candia.

FRENCH MOROCCO: The 33d Fighter Group air echelon, in 72 P-40 fighters, is launched from the USS *Chenango* at noon to occupy the airport at Port Lyautey. However, the runway is pitted with bomb craters, resulting in many damaged fighters.

FRENCH NORTHWEST AFRICA: Most Vichy French units in Algeria and Morocco cease resistance. In all, six Spitfires and three C-47s are lost in action.

LIBYA: USAMEAF B-24s attack the harbor at Benghazi.

November 11, 1942

ALGERIA: 134 U.S. Army paratroopers are flown directly from England into Algiers/Maison Blanche Airport by 13 64th Troop Carrier Group C-47 transports. Later in the day, 34 64th Troop Carrier Group C-47s loaded with British Army paratroopers also arrive at Maison Blanche, direct from England.

An advance flight echelon of the 319th Medium Bombardment Group, in B-26s, arrives at St.-Leu Airdrome.

EGYPT: In the USAAF's best day so far against Germany and her allies, 57th Fighter Group P-40 pilots down eight Axis aircraft in two separate morning engagements.

The 98th Heavy Bombardment Group, in B-24s, begins combat operations from Fayid Airdrome.

The British Eighth Army captures Halfaya.

FRENCH NORTHWEST AFRICA: All remaining Vichy French resistance in Algeria and Morocco ceases at 0700 hours.

LIBYA: The British Eighth Army drives into Libya and captures Bardia.

MEDITERRANEAN: USAMEAF B-24s attacking Axis shipping at sea north of the Libyan coast claim four direct hits on one vessel.

VICHY FRANCE: The German Army occupies Vichy France.

November 12, 1942

ALGERIA: The Duzerville Airdrome at Bone, a city near the Algeria-Tunisia border, is captured by British commandos landing from the sea and 312 British paratroopers dropped at 0600 hours from 26 64th Troop Carrier Group C-47s out of Algiers/ Maison Blanche Airport.

EGYPT: The 57th Fighter Group's "A" Party moves forward to a former Axis landing ground at Sidi Azez.

USAMEAF is formally dissolved and replaced by LtGen Lewis H. Brereton's new Ninth Air Force, which immediately assumes responsibility for overseeing USAAF aircraft and operations in support of the British Eighth Army. The new Ninth Air Force components are: a provisional IX Bomber Command, under BriGen Patrick W. Timberlake; IX Fighter Command, under Col John C. Kilborn; and IX Air Support Command, under BriGen Elmer E. Adler.

The 79th Fighter Group ground echelon arrives by ship from the United States.

FRENCH MOROCCO: Fifty-eight of the 33d Fighter Group's 60 P-40s are finally assembled at the Port Lyautey Airdrome after taking two days to get off the USS *Chenango*. The two others have been lost, one in a crash at sea and one without a trace from an unknown cause. Seventeen of the group's P-40s have been damaged in landings because of runway damage resulting from attacks by U.S. Navy light bombers during the invasion.

November 13, 1942

ALGERIA: An advance element of the 1st Fighter Group, in P-38s, arrives at Oran/ Tafaraoui Airdrome from England by way of Gibraltar. Also, B-17s of the 97th Heavy Bombardment Group's 340th Heavy Bombardment Squadron arrive at Algiers/ Maison Blanche Airport from England by way of Gibraltar. (BriGen Asa N. Duncan, the Eighth Air Force's first commander, is killed when the 97th Heavy Bombardment Group B-17 in which he is a passenger goes down over the sea along the way to North Africa.)

Five 64th Troop Carrier Group C-47s out of Maison Blanche Airport land at noon at Bone's Duzerville Airdrome with fuel and antiaircraft guns for the British occupation force, which is under an unremitting Axis bombardment. After dark, five more supply-laden C-47s, escorted by five USAAF P-38 fighters, also land at Duzerville. These flights are considered decisive in bolstering the ability of the British Army troops to hold the airdrome.

EGYPT: The 98th Heavy Bombardment Group, in B-24s, redeploys from bases in Palestine to Fayid and El Kabrit airdromes, near the Nile Delta. The veteran group, which has been trained to undertake single-plane missions (and which has, in fact, conducted numerous missions in three-plane tactical formations) is ordered to retrain to undertake missions in which the entire group can fly and bomb effectively in squadron and group formations.

FRENCH MOROCCO: The 33d Fighter Group displaces to Casablanca from the bomb-cratered field at Port Lyautey.

LIBYA: As the British Eighth Army recaptures Tobruk, the 57th Fighter Group's "B" Party moves forward to the large former Axis base at Gambut, 30 miles east of the port city. Also, an advance 98th Heavy Bombardment Group ground detachment is established at Gambut Main Airdrome to facilitate long-range heavy-bomber missions originating in Egypt and staging through the forward base.

November 14, 1942

ALGERIA: Three fuel-laden 64th Troop Carrier Group C-47s brave Axis fire to land at Bone to resupply the British Army troops holding out there.

EGYPT: The 79th Fighter Group, in P-40s, and the 19th Heavy Bombardment Wing headquarters, which are both in the process of arriving from the United States, are formally attached to the Ninth Air Force.

FRANCE: Unable to locate the La Pallice U-boat base from above solid cloud cover, 15 VIII Bomber Command B-17s and nine B-24s divert to their secondary target, the St.-Nazaire port area, where they drop 57

tons of bombs at the cost of one B-24 damaged.

LIBYA: Of six IX Bomber Command B-24s dispatched to attack Benghazi harbor, only one locates the target.

November 15, 1942

ALGERIA: The entire 1st Fighter Group and the two-squadron 14th Fighter Group, both in P-38s, are reassembled at Oran/Tafaraoui Airdrome following flights from England by way of Gibraltar. Also fully assembled at Tafaraoui are the 62d Troop Carrier Group, in C-47s, and the 15th Light Bombardment Squadron, in A-20s, both of which have also staged through Gibraltar from England.

Flying from Algiers/Maison Blanche Airport, 20 60th Troop Carrier Group C-47s, escorted by 18 USAAF P-38s, drop 350 U.S. Army paratroopers on Youks-les-Bains, Algeria, from 400 feet at 0945 hours. A second force of 32 64th Troop Carrier Group C-47s laden with British Army paratroopers is dispatched to Souk el-Arba, but it is recalled due to bad weather.

LIBYA: Two small formations of IX Bomber Command B-24s dispatched to attack Tripoli are prevented from reaching the target by bad weather. However, one group attacks a motor convoy, an airdrome, and road traffic.

As soon as British Eighth Army ground troops capture Martuba Airdrome, the 57th Fighter Group "A" Party is ordered to redeploy to it. (To facilitate the new leapfrog tactic, an RAF squadron flying Lend-Lease P-40s, is attached to the 79th Fighter Group at Martuba; thereafter, as the "A" and "B" parties leapfrog to new bases in the wake of the British Eighth Army advance, they do so at equal and effective strength.

TUNISIA: Elements of the British First Army enter western Tunisia from Algeria.

November 16, 1942

FRANCE: Four 4th Fighter Group Spitfires are dispatched to strafe targets of opportunity along the French coast. Although one

Spitfire is severely damaged when it hits a tree, it returns to base and lands safely.

LIBYA: Allied aircraft from the newly captured airfield at Martuba, including the 57th Fighter Group "A" Party, are able to effectively cover a convoy from Port Said, Egypt, much of the way to Malta.

TUNISIA: Thirty-two 64th Troop Carrier Group C-47s, escorted by 12 P-38s, drop 384 British Army paratroopers on Souk el-Arba Airdrome, only 90 miles from Tunis.

Six B-17s from the 97th Heavy Bombardment Group's 340th Heavy Bombardment Squadron, mount the veteran group's first mission in North Africa, an attack on Bizerte's Sidi Ahmed Airdrome. This is the first heavy-bomber mission flown by a XII Bomber Command unit.

November 17, 1942

FRANCE: Of 63 VIII Bomber Command heavy bombers dispatched, 35 B-17s and B-24s attack the St.-Nazaire U-boat base with nearly 94 tons of bombs. Losses are 16 bombers damaged, one crewman killed, and three crewmen wounded against claims by bomber gunners of six GAF fighters downed and eight probably downed. The 303d Heavy Bombardment Group, in its combat debut with 16 B-17s, fails to find the target. Six 44th Heavy Bombardment Group B-24s also fail to find their target, the Cherbourg/Maupertus Airdrome, but in this case there is solid cloud cover over the GAF base.

The 305th Heavy Bombardment Group makes its combat debut when it dispatches ten B-17s on a diversionary flight.

TUNISIA: The battle for Tunisia effectively begins when elements of the British First Army probing toward Tunis contact German ground forces 70 miles west of the city. Meantime, a force of U.S. Army paratroopers dropped by USAAF C-47s captures Gafsa Airdrome, in west-central Tunisia.

November 18, 1942

FRANCE: Twenty-one 91st and 306th Heavy Bombardment group B-17s attack the La Pallice U-boat base, as planned, while 19 303d Heavy Bombardment Group B-17s mistake St.-Nazaire (more than 100 miles distant) for La Pallice and drop their bombs there. (The 303d Heavy Bombardment Group had failed to locate *any* target during its debut mission the day before.) In separate action, 13 93d Heavy Bombardment Group B-24s attack Lorient. Overall losses are one B-17 missing, one B-24 damaged beyond economical repair, three B-24s and 24 B-17s damaged, six crewmen killed, and 14 crewmen wounded. Also, two 4th Fighter Group Spitfires destroy a locomotive while on a strafing mission in France.

FRENCH MOROCCO: The 47th Light Bombardment Group, in A-20s, arrives at Mediouna following a flight from England in which one airplane is lost at sea. Also arriving at Mediouna is one B-25 squadron of the 310th Medium Bombardment Group.

LIBYA: 376th Heavy Bombardment Group B-17s attack the marshalling yard and port area at Benghazi.

November 19, 1942

ALGERIA: B-17s of the 97th Heavy Bombardment Group's 341st Heavy Bombardment Squadron arrive at Algiers/Maison Blanche Airport from England by way of Gibraltar.

EGYPT: The 79th Fighter Group moves to a former Axis landing ground well behind the battle front and begins an intensive period of advanced combat training. The group will also serve as a reserve fighter pool for the DATF, and its pilots will be given opportunities to fly in combat with the 57th Fighter Group.

ENGLAND: VIII Bomber Command adds the submarine yards at Bremen, Kiel, and Vegesack to its list of approved targets. These are the first USAAF targets in Germany.

NETHERLANDS: A 4th Fighter Group Spitfire pilot downs an FW-190 fighter off Flushing during a shipping patrol over the North Sea.

TUNISIA: B-17s of the 97th Heavy

Bombardment Group's 340th Heavy Bombardment Squadron, escorted by 14th Fighter Group P-38s, attack Tunis/El Aouina Airdrome, destroying eight Axis airplanes on the ground.

November 20, 1942

ALGERIA: During the night, approximately 30 GAF Ju-87 dive-bombers and Ju-88 medium bombers, apparently from bases in Sardinia, attack the Algiers/Maison Blanche Airport for two hours and destroy on the ground two P-38s, one B-17, four RAF reconnaissance Spitfires, and three RAF Beaufighters.
EGYPT: The British Eighth Army's advance across Egypt and on into Libya is so rapid that 12th Medium Bombardment Group B-25s are now out of range of the front line. The veteran group is therefore put on training status.
LIBYA: The strategically vital port city of Benghazi falls to the British Eighth Army.

November 21, 1942

ALGERIA: For the second consecutive night, GAF bombers based in Sardinia attack the Algiers/Maison Blanche Airport, this time destroying one B-17 and damaging 16 other Allied aircraft on the ground. This attack, and the one on the preceding night, leads to an immediate upgrading of night-fighter and night antiaircraft defenses.
BELGIUM: A 4th Fighter Group Spitfire pilots downs an Fi-156 observation plane near Furnes during a fighter sweep.
TUNISIA: Making use for the first time of the staging facilities at Gambut Main, near Tobruk, Libya, nine of 15 98th Heavy Bombardment Group B-24s dispatched from their bases in Egypt complete their attacks on the harbor at Tripoli. Later in the day, eight 376th Heavy Bombardment Group B-24s attack the harbor at Tripoli, also after staging through Gambut Main. The refueling stop at Gambut adds 300 miles to the effective combat radius of the Nile Delta–based B-24s.

The 14th Fighter Group's 48th Fighter Squadron, in P-38s, mounts a strafing attack against German Army units moving on the U.S. Army garrison at Gafsa. Six of the P-38s are lost as they attempt night landings at Youks-les-Bains Airdrome in Algeria.

November 22, 1942

ALGERIA: B-17s based at the Algiers/ Maison Blanche Airport are withdrawn to Oran/Tafaraoui Airdrome to prevent further damage or losses at the hands of GAF bombers operating from bases in Sardinia.

The 14th Fighter Group (two P-38 squadrons only) and the 15th Light Bombardment Group, in A-20s, move forward to Youks-les-Bains Airdrome and Tebessa Airdrome, respectively, to directly support U.S. and British ground forces fighting along the front.

The advance headquarters of Col Claude E. Duncan's XII Bomber Command arrives from England to begin overseeing bomber operations.
FRANCE: Although 76 VIII Bomber Command heavy bombers are dispatched against the Lorient U-boat base, only 11 303d Heavy Bombardment Group B-17s find a hole in the clouds and drop their bombs. The 305th Heavy Bombardment Group, in B-17s, makes its combat debut but drops no bombs.

November 23, 1942

ALGERIA: Headquarters, Twelfth Air Force, redeploys from Gibraltar to Algiers.

The 51st Troop Carrier Wing headquarters begins overseeing transport and cargo operations for the Twelfth Air Force.
EGYPT: Originally assigned to a dissolved Allied air command in the Caucusus region of the Soviet Union, the 316th Troop Carrier Group, comprising 52 C-47s, begins arriving at Deversoir Airdrome, near the Nile Delta, following a journey from the United States via the southern ferry route.
FRANCE: Thirty-six of 58 VIII Bomber Command B-17s and B-24s dispatched

attack the St.-Nazaire U-boat base with nearly 79 tons of bombs. Losses are four B-17s missing, 16 B-17s and one B-24 damaged, three crewmen killed, 43 crewmen missing, and 16 crewmen wounded. In addition, one damaged B-17 crashes on landing at the cost of two crewmen killed and eight injured. Claims against enemy aircraft amount to 16 destroyed and two probably destroyed. Bomber crews report that GAF fighters attack from head-on rather than, as in the past, from rear to front of the bomber formations. (The head-on attacks are indeed a new intentional tactic being tested for the first time by GAF fighter pilots.)

Despite few encouraging signs that the U-boat bases are being damaged, the British First Lord of the Admiralty, Admiral Sir Dudley Pound, writes to MajGen Ira C. Eaker that the cumulative effect of the USAAF heavy-bomber attacks is disrupting the servicing schedule of German Navy U-boats deploying to the Atlantic from bases in western France.

LIBYA: The El Alamein offensive grinds to a halt as Axis forces dig in at El Agheila. While the British Eighth Army begins an immediate logistical buildup in anticipation of renewing its eastward offensive in November, RAF and Ninth Air Force combat units open a campaign of attrition against the Axis ground defenses, air components, and lines of supply.

SARDINIA: XII Bomber Command B-17s on their way to attack Elmas Airdrome abort because of bad weather.

November 24, 1942

SARDINIA: In what was to have been their unit's combat debut in the theater, a small force of 319th Medium Bombardment Group B-26s, with fighter escort, is only 20 miles south of Sardinia when it is ordered to abort the mission.

TUNISIA: XII Bomber Command B-17s, escorted by P-38s, abort their mission against Bizerte harbor because of bad weather.

In the course of two fighter engagements, 14th Fighter Group P-38 pilots down 11 Axis aircraft, including nine Italian Air Force transports downed between Gabes and Sfax at 1355 hours. Five of the transports are claimed by the 49th Fighter Squadron's 1stLt Virgil M. Lusk. (Lusk is awarded official credit for only four of the transports. If he did in fact down all of the five claimed, he is the first USAAF ace in the war against Germany and her partners, and the first USAAF "ace in a day" in World War II.) 1stLt James E. Butler, also of the 49th Fighter Squadron, is credited with the other four Italian transports.

November 25, 1942

EGYPT: The 316th Troop Carrier Group air echelon, less one squadron, arrives in Egypt and immediately begins operational duties. The 316th is the first unit of its kind to operate in the Western Desert.

November 26, 1942

ALGERIA: The first air echelon of the 301st Heavy Bombardment Group, in B-17s, arrives at Oran/Tafaraoui Airdrome from England.

LIBYA: IX Bomber Command B-24s conducting three separate attacks on Tripoli claim direct hits on three Axis vessels.

TUNISIA: 14th Fighter Group P-38 pilots down seven GAF aircraft, including five Ju-52 transports, during two separate missions.

November 27, 1942

DODECANESE ISLANDS: 376th Heavy Bombardment Group B-17s attacking the harbor at Portolago Bay (Leros Island) claim hits on two Axis vessels.

This is the last mission undertaken by B-17s under the control of the 376th Heavy Bombardment Group, or, indeed, the Ninth Air Force. Hereafter, the only heavy bombers associated with the group and the air force are B-24s.

EGYPT: The hitherto provisional IX Bomber Command is formally established.

November 28, 1942

TUNISIA: Thirty-seven XII Bomber Command B-17s of the 97th and 301st Heavy Bombardment groups attack Bizerte Airdrome and port area. GAF fighters down two of the bombers.

In their unit's first completed mission of the campaign, several 319th Medium Bombardment Group B-26s attack the port facilities, oil tanks, and railway yard at Sfax. This is the first medium-bomber mission flown over North African soil by a Twelfth Air Force unit, and the first B-26 mission ever flown in the theater.

November 29, 1942

ENGLAND: The 78th Fighter Group, in P-38s, arrives by ship from the United States and is assigned to the VIII Fighter Command.

LIBYA: IX Bomber Command B-24s attacking Tripoli harbor at dusk claim hits of two vessels, an antiaircraft battery, docks, and warehouses.

TUNISIA: Forty-four C-47 transports of the 62d and 64th Troop Carrier groups drop 530 British Army paratroopers at Depienne, near Oudna Airdrome, 10 miles south of Tunis. However, although the paratroopers sustain no losses in a highly accurate jump, the subsequent ground attack fails despite concerted ground-support attacks by RAF and USAAF aircraft. (The British paratroopers, who are forced by a German Army counterattack to retreat, will reach Allied lines on December 2.) The failure of this and other ground attacks results in a months-long stalemate on the ground.

15th Light Bombardment Squadron A-20s, escorted by P-38s, attack Gabes Airdrome.

319th Medium Bombardment Group B-26s are ordered to return to Algiers/ Maison Blanche Airport when they reach a point only 30 miles from their target of the day, Bizerte.

1st and 14th Fighter group P-38 pilots down two GAF Bf-110 twin-engine fighters and two Ju-88 medium bombers during two separate actions.

November 30, 1944

ENGLAND: In an agreement reached between USAAF and RAF commanders, USAAF fighters based in England will devote themselves fully to escorting and supporting the Eighth Air Force heavy-bomber day offensive, leaving defense of air bases in the British Isles (including USAAF bases) to the RAF.

TUNISIA: At about noon, B-17s of the 97th Heavy Bombardment Group, escorted by 16 1st Fighter Group P-38s, attack port facilities in Bizerte. One Bf-109 is downed and another is damaged by one 27th Fighter Squadron pilot.

Nine 319th Medium Bombardment Group B-26s, escorted by P-38s, attack Gabes Airdrome and the town's marshalling yard. The P-38s also strafe Gabes Airdrome. One B-26 is downed over the target and the crew of another that is forced to crash-land in the desert due to battle damage is rescued by a 15th Light Bombardment Squadron A-20 dispatched for the purpose from Tebessa Airdrome.

15th Light Bombardment Squadron A-20s, escorted by P-38s, attack a bridge and the railway station at Djedeida.

During the course of two of the day's three fighter actions, 14th Fighter Group P-38 pilots down two GAF fighters, and a 52d Fighter Group Spitfire pilot downs a GAF fighter. This mission marks the 52d Fighter Group's combat debut in North Africa, and the victory is its first of the war.

DECEMBER 1942

December 1, 1942

ENGLAND: Upon receiving orders from LtGen Dwight D. Eisenhower, LtGen Carl Spaatz leaves for Algeria to serve as Eisenhower's air adviser. MajGen Ira C. Eaker replaces Spaatz as commanding general of the Eighth Air Force.

TUNISIA: A regular pattern of air attacks is opened by the Twelfth Air Force against Tunis/El Aouina Airdrome. In the first of these, conducted before 0900 hours, the base is attacked by six A-20s and 13 B-17s, which are followed closely by nine A-20s and six RAF Bristol Bisley light bombers. An estimated 30 aircraft are destroyed on the ground, and a 14th Fighter Group P-38 pilot downs an Bf-109 in the air over the airdrome. During the afternoon, an attack by 12 B-26s destroys an estimated 15 GAF aircraft on the ground.

XII Fighter Command P-38s attack German Army tanks near Djedeida.

December 2, 1942

ENGLAND: BriGen Newton Longfellow replaces MajGen Ira C. Eaker as command-ing general of the VIII Bomber Command.

TUNISIA: Twelfth Air Force A-20s, followed by B-26s, attack Tunis/El Aouina Airdrome; Twelfth Air Force B-17s attack Bizerte/Sidi Ahmed Airdrome and Bizerte harbor; and Twelfth Air Force B-25s attack flak batteries near Gabes Airdrome.

A total of nine GAF fighters are downed during the day by pilots of the 1st, 14th, and 52d Fighter groups undertaking a number of escort missions and aggressive sweeps into enemy territory.

December 3, 1942

TUNISIA: 97th Heavy Bombardment Group B-17s attack shipping and port facilities at Bizerte at about 1030 hours. Forewarned by radar, GAF fighters attack the bombers, but they are attacked in turn by 1st Fighter Group P-38s. Three Bf-109s are downed against the loss of five P-38s.

15th Light Bombardment Squadron A-20s, escorted by P-38s, attack Tunis/El Aouina Airdrome, and P-38s and Spitfires attack a variety of ground targets while on far-ranging sweeps and reconnaissance missions. While on these missions, pilots of the 14th and 52d Fighter groups down three Bf-109s.

December 4, 1942

ITALY: In the first USAAF air attack directly upon the territory of a European Axis nation, Italian Navy warships and port facilities in Naples harbor are attacked by 20 IX Bomber Command B-24s. Hits are claimed on several of the warships, including a battleship. There are no USAAF losses.

TUNISIA: XII Bomber Command B-17s, followed a half hour later by B-26s, attack shipping and port facilities in Bizerte harbor. While escorting the bombers and conducting far-ranging sweeps and reconnaissance missions, pilots of the 1st, 14th, and 52d Fighter groups down five Bf-109s and a Bf-110.

December 5, 1942

ALGERIA: LtGen Carl Spaatz is named Acting Deputy Commander-in-Chief for Air of the Allied Force in Northwest Africa.

The 3d Reconnaissance Group, equipped with F-4 and F-5 aircraft (P-38 variants), arrives at Oran/La Senia Airdrome to support the Twelfth Air Force.

LIBYA: The Ninth Air Force's 12th Medium Bombardment Group, in B-25s, is recommitted to combat following a period of retraining. From its new base at Gambut, the group is to join the 57th Fighter Group and RAF light-bomber units in applying pressure to Axis air groups supporting the German Army battle line at El Agheila. During the early part of the month, USAAF and RAF pressure specifically against the Axis air establishment eventually drives all Axis aircraft from all the landing grounds within 90 miles of the front.

TUNISIA: Aircraft of the Twelfth Air Force's XII Bomber Command and XII Air Support Command open a concerted bombing campaign against German-held port facilities in Tunisia. The objective is to hamper the flow of German troops and supplies into Tunisia while Allied ground forces prepare for an all-out offensive to liberate the entire country. Kicking off the new venture, XII Bomber Command B-17s, escorted by 14th Fighter Group P-38s, attack shipping and port facilities at Tunis. 14th Fighter Group P-38 pilots down two Bf-109s near Bizerte Airdrome.

Twelfth Air Force B-25s attack Bizerte/Sidi Ahmed Airdrome, and A-20s attack German Army positions at Faid Pass.

December 6, 1942

ENGLAND: The 93d Heavy Bombardment Group, in B-24s, is reassigned to the VIII Bomber Command's 2d Heavy Bombardment Wing.

FRANCE: In the day's main effort, 37 of 66 VIII Bomber Command B-17s dispatched attack a locomotive factory at Lille. Losses are one B-17 downed and nine damaged, one crewman killed, two crewmen wounded, and ten crewmen missing.

Although 44th Heavy Bombardment Group B-24s are recalled from a mission against Abbeville/Drucat Airdrome, a squadron of six of the heavy bombers fails to receive the order and presses on. One B-24 is lost and another is damaged, at a cost of ten crewmen missing and three crewmen wounded.

TUNISIA: Fifteen XII Bomber Command B-17s attack the port of Tunis; 15th Light Bombardment Squadron A-20s attack the bridge over the Medjerda River at El Bathan; and 14th Fighter Group P-38 pilots down a Ju-88, two Bf-110s, and a Ju-52 in two separate actions.

The 33d Fighter Group's 58th Fighter Squadron, in P-40s, moves to the rather sparse forward fighter field at Thelepte and thus becomes the first USAAF unit to be based inside Tunisia. The unit will be primarily responsible for supporting ground troops and for undertaking low-level attacks on transportation targets such as rail lines, bridges, and road traffic.

December 7, 1942

ALGERIA: Three squadrons of the Eighth Air Force's 93d Heavy Bombardment Group, in B-24s, arrive in Algeria to bolster XII Bomber Command. (The group's fourth squadron remains in England to conduct night-operations experiments.)

TUNISIA: XII Bomber Command B-17s, escorted by P-38s, attack shipping and port facilities at Bizerte. Also, A-20s, escorted by P-38s, attack German Army tanks in the Teboura–El Bathan area, but other A-20s dispatched to attack La Hencha and Sousse are turned back by bad weather.

Two Ju-52 tri-motor transports are downed by a pair of 14th Fighter Group P-38 pilots near Sfax.

December 8, 1942

FRANCE: Findings of a recent bomb-damage assessment reveal that low-level bombing of submarine pens in western France has not been able to penetrate the roofs of the pens with the bombs available in the U.K. at this time.

ITALY: IX Bomber Command B-24s attack targets at Naples. One 376th Heavy Bombardment Group B-24 is downed by flak.

LIBYA: 57th Fighter Group P-40 pilots down seven Bf-109s in a morning battle over the Marble Arch Airdrome.

TUNISIA: Although bad weather halts bomber operations, numerous sweeps and reconnaissance missions are mounted by Twelfth Air Force fighter units.

December 9, 1942

ALGERIA: One Ju-88 medium bomber is downed by a 33d Fighter Group P-40 pilot in his unit's first combat encounter of the war.

December 10, 1942

EGYPT: On the first anniversary of Germany's and Italy's declarations of war on the United States, a 57th Fighter Group P-40 pilot downs an BF-109 in a battle over the Marble Arch Airdrome.

December 11, 1942

ALGERIA: Col Charles T. Phillips replaces Col Claude E. Duncan as commanding officer of the XII Bomber Command.

To better oversee flight operations and administration in the huge area for which it is responsible, Twelfth Air Force establishes five regional commands: the Moroccan Composite Wing, the West Algerian Composite Wing, the Central Algerian Composite Wing, XII Bomber Command; and XII Fighter Command.

ITALY: IX Bomber Command B-24s attack port facilities and the area surrounding the Naples port. One 98th Heavy Bombardment Group B-24 is downed by flak.

LIBYA: In anticipation of a British Eighth Army offensive against the Axis El Agheila Line—set to begin December 14—the 57th Fighter Group moves forward to a landing ground at Belandah.

TUNISIA: XII Bomber Command B-25s, with fighter escort, attack rail bridges at La Hencha.

December 12, 1942

ALGERIA: A pair of 1st Fighter Group P-38 pilots down an Italian Air Force flying boat over the Mediterranean north of Philippeville.

ENGLAND: The 315th Troop Carrier Group air echelon arrives from the United States following a forced one-month layover in Greenland caused by bad weather. The C-47 unit is assigned to the VIII Air Support Command as a general transportation organization.

FRANCE: Seventy-eight VIII Bomber Command B-17s are dispatched against Romilly-sur-Seine Airdrome, but they are prevented from bombing by heavy cloud cover. In the end, 17 of these B-17s do manage to locate the Rouen/Sotteville marshalling yard, upon which they drop 40 tons of bombs.

TUNISIA: XII Bomber Command B-17s attack the port facilities at Sfax for the first time; B-17s, escorted by P-38s, also attack port and rail facilities at Tunis; and B-26s dispatched to Sousse and La Hencha abort due to bad weather.

1stLt Virgil H. Smith, a P-38 pilot with the 14th Fighter Group's 48th Fighter

Squadron, achieves ace status when he downs an FW-190 over Gabes Airdrome during an afternoon mission.

December 13, 1942

LIBYA: Following a stalemate of several weeks—during which the British Eighth Army prepares for an all-out offensive to clear Libya—German Army forces holding the El Agheila Line suddenly withdraw at the last minute toward Tunisia. As British ground forces struggle to pursue the Germans, the WDAF, including the Ninth Air Force's 12th Medium Bombardment Group and 57th Fighter Group, maintain pressure and attempt to interdict routes of retreat.

57th Fighter Group P-40 pilots down two Bf-109s near El Agheila.

TUNISIA: Seventeen 97th Heavy Bombardment Group B-17s attack port facilities at Tunis; ten 301st Heavy Bombardment Group B-17s and 19 93d Heavy Bombardment Group B-24s attack port facilities at Bizerte; B-25s attack port facilities at Sousse; B-26s attack a bridge north of Sfax; P-38s escort the medium-bomber missions, fly patrols, and attack Axis road convoys and individual vehicles north of Gabes.

December 14, 1942

ENGLAND: A new report points out that efforts to build up and supply the Twelfth Air Force at the expense of the Eighth Air Force is producing a critical drain on the latter's ability to complete training cycles and mount combat operations.

LIBYA: 57th Fighter Group P-40 pilots down two Bf-109s at the cost of one P-40 and its pilot lost.

TUNISIA: XII Bomber Command B-24s attack shipping and port facilities at Bizerte, and B-17s attack shipping and port facilities at Tunis.

During the morning, nine 15th Light Bombardment Squadron A-20s, escorted by eight 14th Fighter Group P-38s and twelve 33d Fighter Group P-40s, attack the Sfax railroad station. During the afternoon, nine

15th Light Bombardment Squadron A-20s, escorted by P-38s, attack the same target.

P-38s attack several Axis vessels at sea off the Tunisian coast, strafe traffic on the coast highway between Tunis and Bizerte, and strafe trains near Kerker and La Hencha.

December 15, 1942

ALGERIA: Col Carlyle H. Ridenour replaces Col Charles T. Phillips as commanding officer of the XII Bomber Command.

LIBYA: Ninth Air Force B-25s and P-40s continue to attack tactical ground targets in support of the British Eighth Army. Eighteen 12th Medium Bombardment Group B-25s join with 36 RAF light bombers in a particularly effective attack against a motor-vehicle concentration west of the Marble Arch.

While flying with the 57th Fighter Group, a 79th Fighter Group P-40 pilot draws "first blood" for his unit when he downs a Bf-109.

TUNISIA: Three 15th Light Bombardment Squadron A-20s attack several bridges linking Gabes with Sfax; six A-20s attack Pont-du-Fahs; XII Bomber Command B-26s attack Tunis/El Aouina Airdrome; and XII Bomber Command B-17s attack port facilities at Bizerte.

In the IX Bomber Command's first mission to Tunisia—to help XII Bomber Command close Tunisian ports and lines of supply to German reinforcements and supplies—nine 376th Heavy Bombardment Group B-24s attack a railroad yard, roundhouse, and repair facilities at Sfax. The B-24s obliterate a locomotive repair shop.

December 16, 1942

LIBYA: Ninth Air Force B-25s and P-40s attack and harass German Army troops in the El Agheila area.

TUNISIA: In separate missions, A-20s of the 15th Light Bombardment Squadron and the 47th Light Bombardment Group's 86th Light Bombardment Squadron (the latter on their unit's first combat mission of the war) attack Axis vehicle columns on the road between Mateur and Massicault. These are the first of many such attacks that will destroy an estimated 100 vehicles along this road by the end of the month.

XII Fighter Command P-38s attacking Axis ships at sea off Tunisia's northern coast claim a direct bomb hit on one vessel, and a pair of 1st Fighter Group P-38 pilots down a lone Ju-88 at around noon.

December 17, 1942

TUNISIA: A total of 36 XII Bomber Command B-17s attack port facilities at Tunis and Bizerte; A-20s attack targets north and west of Gabes Airdrome and the Axis landing ground at Sidi Tabet; XII Bomber Command B-25s and B-26s dispatched to attack Axis ships in the Gulf of Tunis fail to locate their targets; XII Fighter Command P-38s escort all the bombing missions; and 1st Fighter Group P-38 pilots down a Ju-88 and two Bf-109s in separate midday actions.

December 18, 1942

LIBYA: The pursuit by the British Eighth Army of German forces retreating toward Tunisia bogs down.

XII Bomber Command B-17s attack shipping and port facilities at Sousse.

The Eighth Air Force's 93d Heavy Bombardment Group, in B-24s, is transferred from the operational control of the Twelfth Air Force to that of the Ninth Air Force. The group begins moving to the Gambut Main Airdrome.

TUNISIA: Thirty-six XII Bomber Command B-17s, escorted by 16 1st Fighter Group P-38s, attacking Bizerte through German fighters and flak claim a direct hit on one vessel. However, four P-38s and a B-17 are downed over the target by GAF fighters, and another B-17 is written off after it crash-lands at a friendly base.

Eleven XII Bomber Command B-26s, escorted by P-38s, attack a marshalling yard

and other rail facilities at Sousse. Flak downs two B-26s.

Twelfth Air Force A-20s, escorted by P-38s, attack a landing ground, dispersal areas, and the rail facilities at Mateur.

One Ju-88 and an FW-190 are downed during the day by 33d Fighter Group P-40 pilots.

December 19, 1942

TUNISIA: Twelfth Air Force A-20s, escorted by 33d Fighter Group P-40s, attack the marshalling yards at Sfax, and a 33d Fighter Group P-40 pilot downs a Ju-88 near Sfax.

December 20, 1942

FRANCE: In the first mission in which the Eighth Air Force's four operational B-17 groups operate under the supervision of the 1st Heavy Bombardment Wing and its one operational B-24 group operates under the supervision of the 2d Heavy Bombardment Wing, 60 B-17s and 12 B-24s drop more than 167 tons of bombs on Romilly-sur-Seine Airdrome. Fighter opposition is extremely heavy. Whereas bomber gunners claim an incredible 53 GAF fighters downed and 13 probably downed, enemy fighters and flak definitely down six B-17s, cause unrepairable damage to one B-17, and damage 29 B-17s and one B-24. Also, two B-17s crash-land in England. Crew losses amount to two killed, 58 missing, and 12 wounded. Overall, these are the worst losses for a single day sustained by the Eighth Air Force so far in the war.

TUNISIA: IX Bomber Command B-24s dispatched against Sousse harbor abort in the face of bad weather, but three of them claim the destruction of an Axis ship north of Sfax.

December 21, 1942

ALGERIA: 14th Fighter Group P-38s scrambled from their base at Youk-les-Bains down three Ju-88s during the afternoon.

TUNISIA: XII Bomber Command B-17s

are prevented by bad weather from attacking Sfax or Gabes, and 93d Heavy Bombardment Group B-24s, operating under IX Bomber Command control, are prevented by bad weather from attacking the port at Sousse. However, XII Fighter Command P-40s destroy a tank and several motor vehicles near Kairouan.

December 22, 1942

TUNISIA: Bad weather prevents XII Bomber Command B-17s from attacking Bizerte or secondary targets at Sfax and Sousse; and only two 93d Heavy Bombardment Group B-24s dispatched against Sousse penetrate bad weather to the target, but a number of those aborting manage to attack Monastir and railway facilities at Mahdia.

Two GAF medium bombers are downed during a midday mission by 33d Fighter Group P-40 pilots.

December 23, 1942

ALGERIA: The 17th Medium Bombardment Group, in B-26s, arrives following a direct move from the United States via the southern ferry route.
BAY OF BISCAY: Two Ju-88 medium bombers are downed by 82d Fighter Group P-38 pilots while the unit is transiting from England to Gibraltar for eventual deployment in North Africa as part of the XII Fighter Command. This unexpected encounter is the 82d Fighter Group's combat debut.
EGYPT: The 376th Heavy Bombardment Group, in B-24s, moves to a base in Egypt from Palestine, and the 8th Fighter Wing headquarters begins overseeing several Ninth Air Force fighter groups.
ITALY: During the night of December 23–24, IX Bomber Command B-24s attack Naples harbor and one B-24 attacks Taranto.
TUNISIA: The winter rainy season officially begins. Impenetrable cloud cover causes XII Bomber Command B-17s to abort their briefed attacks on airdromes at Tunis and Bizerte.

December 24, 1942

ENGLAND: The first consignment of USAAF P-47 fighters arrives aboard ship from the United States.
TUNISIA: LtGen Dwight D. Eisenhower decides to abandon the Allied ground attack on Tunis until the rainy season ends in early 1943. However, the British Eighth Army will continue a cautious advance in Libya.

IX Bomber Command B-24s dispatched to attack Tunis abort in the face of bad weather.

December 25, 1942

ALGERIA: 82d Fighter Group P-38s arrive at Oran/Tafaraoui Airdrome from England by way of Gibraltar. A number of them are immediately dispatched to fly a long anti-submarine patrol to protect two Allied convoys that are moving into the area.
ICELAND: The 25th Composite Wing is activated in Iceland to oversee USAAF units and personnel assigned to the defense of the strategically important island.
TUNISIA: XII Fighter Command P-40s bomb German Army troops near Sfax.

A pair of Italian Air Force Mc.202 fighters are downed by a pair of 52d Fighter Group Spitfire pilots.

December 26, 1942

TUNISIA: XII Bomber Command B-17s attack shipping and port facilities at Sfax. GAF fighters and heavy flak down two B-17s and two P-38s, but a flight of four P-38 pilots from the 1st Fighter Group's 94th Fighter Squadron down three of the GAF fighters.

XII Bomber Command B-17s, escorted by P-40s, claim three Axis ships damaged while mounting a second attack against shipping and port facilities at Sfax.

While conducting reconnaissance

patrols, XII Fighter Command P-38s strafe three locomotives and a number of motor vehicles.

During the night of December 26–27, three IX Bomber Command B-24s attack port facilities at Tunis, one B-24 attacks Sfax, and one B-24 attacks Sousse.

December 27, 1942

TUNISIA: XII Bomber Command B-17s, escorted by P-38s, attack shipping and port facilities at Sousse and claim direct hits on four vessels.

December 28, 1942

TUNISIA: IX Bomber Command, XII Bomber Command, and RAF heavy bombers (the latter controlled by IX Bomber Command) mount four separate attacks during the day and evening against shipping and port facilities at Sousse. Claims are made for heavy damage to shore facilities and direct hits on several vessels.

During the course of several air-to-air actions through the day, P-38 pilots of the 1st and 14th Fighter groups down a Ju-88 and four Bf-109s.

December 29, 1942

ALGERIA: A 52d Fighter Group Spitfire pilot downs a BF-109 near Bone.
TUNISIA: XII Bomber Command B-17s, escorted by P-38s, attack the harbor at Sousse; Twelfth Air Force A-20s attack bridges at La Hencha, and escorting P-40s strafe a locomotive and rail cars at Ste.-Juliette; and XII Fighter Command P-38s attack a German Army tank depot near Pont-du-Fahs, followed by an attack on the same target by A-20s.

IX Bomber Command B-24s dispatched to attack Tunis harbor during the night of December 29–30 are diverted to Sousse because of bad weather.

December 30, 1942

FRANCE: Forty of 77 VIII Bomber Command B-17s dispatched attack the U-boat base at Lorient with nearly 80 tons of bombs. Bomber gunners claim 29 GAF fighters downed and seven probably downed. Three B-17s are lost and 22 are damaged, with crew losses put at two killed, 30 missing, and 17 wounded.

TUNISIA: In their unit's combat debut, six 17th Medium Bombardment Group B-26s, escorted by 14th Fighter Group P-38s, attack Gabes Airdrome during the afternoon. Five of the B-26s sustain damage from flak and attacks by Bf-109s, and one B-26 is written off following a belly landing at Telergma Airdrome. A P-38 pilot downs one Bf-109 near the target.

XII Bomber Command B-17s, escorted by P-38s, attack the marshalling yards and port facilities at Sfax, and then XII Bomber Command B-25s attack the marshalling yards again; Twelfth Air Force A-20s attack German Army troop concentrations, Gabes Airdrome, and a fuel dump near El Aouinet; and P-40s escorting the A-20s strafe ground targets of opportunity near El Guettar.

1stLt Virgil H. Smith, a P-38 pilot with the 14th Fighter Group's 48th Fighter Squadron, who achieved ace status on December 11, is shot down and killed near Gabes.

December 31, 1942

TUNISIA: IX Bomber Command B-24s, accompanied by RAF Liberators, attack shipping and port facilities at Sfax; XII Bomber Command B-17s, with fighter escort, also attack Sfax harbor; Twelfth Air Force A-20s, with fighter escort, mount two attacks against the marshalling yards and port at Sousse; Twelfth Air Force B-26s, with fighter escort, attack Gabes Airdrome and shipping and rail bridges in the Bizerte and Tunis areas; and XII Fighter Command P-38s on reconnaissance missions claim the destruction of several motor vehicles.

JANUARY 1943

January 1, 1943

ALGERIA: BriGen John K. Cannon replaces Col Carlyle H. Ridenour as commander of the XII Bomber Command, and Col Peter S. Rask assumes command of the XII Air Support Command from BriGen Cannon.

SICILY: Several IX Bomber Command B-24s attack unspecified targets along the southeastern and southwestern coasts.

TUNISIA: XII Bomber Command B-17s and IX Bomber Command B-24s attack the harbor at Tunis in separate missions; XII Bomber Command B-26s attack the Tunis marshalling yards; and XII Bomber Command B-25s dispatched to attack Axis shipping near La Goulette abort in the face of bad weather.

Four 1st Fighter Group P-38 pilots down three Ju-52 transports near Cape El Fortress at 1515 hours.

January 2, 1943

ALGERIA: A status report issued by Headquarters, Twelfth Air Force, shows 520

operational aircraft of 755 assigned. It is estimated at this time that the GAF has 610 aircraft available for the defense of Tunisia, of which approximately 225 are Ju-88 bombers and 150 are FW-190 or Bf-109 fighters. The Italian Air Force in the region is thought to have 560 aircraft assigned, of which half are fighters, but of which only half are thought to be operational.

CRETE: To help stem Axis air attacks against Allied convoys bound for Malta, 12 376th Heavy Bombardment Group B-24s join 36 RAF light bombers for an attack against Kastelli/Pediada Airdrome, and 11 12th Medium Bombardment Group B-25s attack Heraklion Airdrome. This is the 12th Group's first combat mission outside of North Africa. During the return flight, two B-25s are lost over the sea for unknown reasons.

GERMANY: Four radar-equipped B-24s from the 93d Heavy Bombardment Group's 329th Heavy Bombardment Squadron conduct separate "moling" intruder-type sorties over the Ruhr region of northwestern Germany to test the efficacy of dispatching special bombers to harass and confuse the German air-defense system. The B-24s are equipped with British-made GEE navigational equipment, which can be used for precise location fixes at night or in cloudy weather (the better to conceal single aircraft over hostile territory). It is the goal of the moling experiment to trigger German air-raid warning defenses on days on which the VIII Bomber Command is grounded by bad weather. It is thought that doing so will inflict operational casualties upon GAF interceptors scrambled in inclement weather as well as disrupt work in German industrial areas when air-raid warnings are sounded. Perversely, the four initial moling sorties are foiled by *good* weather over the target area.

TUNISIA: XII Bomber Command B-17s attack shipping and port facilities at La Goulette. 1st Fighter Group P-38 pilots escorting the bombers down three Bf-109s, but two P-38s and their pilots are also lost.

XII Fighter Command A-20s, escorted by P-38s, attack Sousse harbor in two waves in the morning; A-20s return to attack Sousse in the afternoon; and XII Bomber Command B-26s, escorted by fighters, attack a bridge north of El Djem.

52d Fighter Group Spitfire pilots down two Ju-87s and an FW-190 between Bone and Cape Rosa between 0835 and 0915 hours.

January 3, 1943

FRANCE: Of 72 VIII Bomber Command B-17s and 13 B-24s dispatched, 60 B-17s and eight B-24s attack the St.-Nazaire U-boat base between 1130 and 1140 hours with 171 tons of bombs. GAF fighter opposition is heavy, and USAAF losses amount to seven B-17s downed and 44 B-17s and three B-24s damaged. Crew losses are two killed, six wounded, and 70 missing. On return to their bases, three B-24s crash-land owing to fuel depletion. All three B-24s are written off due to damage, and crew casualties amount to three killed and 17 injured.

On this mission, as an experiment aimed at promoting a more effective use of defensive machine guns, 305th Heavy Bombardment Group B-17s fly a so-called "stagger" formation. Also for the first time, precision bombing is undertaken by formations dropping on a designated lead bombardier rather than by individual aircraft bombardiers.

TUNISIA: All XII Fighter Command fighters and A-20s are assigned to attack German Army tanks involved in overrunning the Free French Army position at Fondouk el-Aouareb.

January 4, 1943

EGYPT: Col Robert Kauch relieves MajGen Elmer E. Adler as commander of the IX Air Support Command.

TUNISIA: XII Bomber Command B-25s attack the marshalling yard at Kairouan; XII Fighter Command A-20s attack Cherichera; and two formations of XII Bomber Command B-17s dispatched to attack Bizerte are thwarted by heavy cloud cover over the target.

Six GAF Ju-88s, escorted by Bf-109s, bomb the exposed forward fighter strip at Thelepte. A Ju-88 and a Bf-109 are downed when five 33d Fighter Group P-40 pilots based at Thelepte intercept the departing strike group.

January 5, 1943

FRENCH NORTHWEST AFRICA: LtGen Carl Spaatz is given command of the newly created Allied Air Force, which consists of the USAAF's Twelfth Air Force, the RAF's Eastern Air Command, and Free French Air Force units.

LIBYA: The 57th Fighter Group's "A" Party displaces forward to Hamraiet North Airdrome and is immediately bombed by 24 Axis fighter-bombers (the first of numerous similar raids mounted three or four times a day for three days).

TUNISIA: XII Bomber Command B-17s, escorted by P-38s, attack the power station at Sfax; XII Bomber Command B-26s, also escorted by P-38s, attack Kairouan; and

B-24s of IX Bomber Command's 93d Heavy Bombardment Group encountering heavy clouds over their primary target, Tunis, attack the harbor at Sousse instead.

The 82d Fighter Group, a new P-38 unit, arrives at Telergma Airdrome.

January 6, 1943

FRENCH MOROCCO: The 350th Fighter Group, in P-39s, arrives at Oujda Airdrome following a seven-hour, 1,200-mile direct flight from England. Of the 62 P-39s dispatched, two are lost without a trace, ten are interned in Portugal, and one is interned in Spain.
TUNISIA: Two formations of XII Fighter Command A-20s attack the military base at Kairouan, and XII Bomber Command B-25s attack the city's rail facilities.

A 52d Fighter Group Spitfire pilot downs an FW-190 near Cape Rosa at 1305 hours.
UNITED KINGDOM: The 56th Fighter Group, the first P-47 unit to be deployed overseas, arrives by ship from the United States and is assigned to the VIII Fighter Command.

January 7, 1943

GREECE: A single IX Bomber Command B-24 on a special mission attacks a quay in Piraeus harbor.
SICILY: Ten IX Bomber Command B-24s of 25 dispatched attack Axis shipping in Palermo harbor. This is the first USAAF attack against Palermo.
TUNISIA: XII Bomber Command B-26s attack the harbor and airdrome at Gabes. While escorting the B-26s to Gabes in his unit's North Africa combat debut, an 82d Fighter Group P-38 pilot downs a Bf-109.

January 8, 1943

TUNISIA: XII Bomber Command B-17s attack the naval base at Bizerte and the port facilities at Ferryville; XII Bomber Command B-26s attack Kairouan Airdrome; XII Bomber Command B-25s attack bridges and rail lines at Graiba and Kalaa Srira; XII

Fighter Command A-20s and P-40s attack German Army tanks near Gabes; and IX Bomber Command B-24s attack Tunis after being diverted by bad weather from the briefed primary, Bizerte.

While escorting and supporting the various bombing missions, fighter pilots of the 1st, 14th, 33d, 52d, and 82d Fighter groups down a total of eight GAF fighters.

January 9, 1943

LIBYA: XII Bomber Command B-26s attack Tripoli/Castel Benito Airdrome.
TUNISIA: XII Bomber Command B-25s attack Axis shipping at sea off Tunisia's northern coast.

January 10, 1943

ALGERIA: BriGen Howard A. Craig assumes command of the XII Air Support Command from Col Peter S. Rask.
TUNISIA: XII Bomber Command B-26s attack the marshalling yards and oil depot at Gabes; XII Bomber Command B-26s dispatched against Sousse abort in the face of bad weather; XII Fighter Command A-20s and P-40s attack the Axis military camp at Kebili; and IX Bomber Command B-24s attack La Goulette after being thwarted by bad weather over Bizerte.

During a fighter raid against Kairouan, Maj Philip G. Cochran, the commanding officer of the 33d Fighter Group's 58th Fighter Squadron, is credited with scoring a direct hit with a bomb on the building housing the regional German Army headquarters. In return, however, six Bf-109s strafe the 33d Fighter Group's advance fighter base at Thelepte.

January 11, 1943

ITALY: IX Bomber Command B-24s attack the port of Naples with 40 1,000-pound bombs, but results are obscured by the cloud cover over the target. Two B-24s are lost to enemy fire. (This is the only one of many missions against Naples to actually reach the assigned target in the month of January 1943. Because of poor weather conditions and low visibility over the throughout the month, twenty-two other missions against Naples are diverted to Palermo, Messina, and other secondary targets.)

LIBYA: In two separate afternoon actions, 57th Fighter Group P-40 pilots down three Bf-109s and an Italian Air Force Mc.202.

TUNISIA: XII Bomber Command B-17s attack fortifications in and around Gadames and the rail and highway bridge spanning the Oued el-Akarit River, near Gabes. In a 25-minute running battle, two escorting 1st Fighter Group P-38s and their pilots are lost against one Bf-109 confirmed destroyed.

XII Bomber Command B-25s attack Axis shipping at sea off the northern Tunisian coast. While escorting the B-25s, 14th Fighter Group P-38s pilots down two Ju-52s and a six-engine flying boat.

While attacking German Army tanks near Fondouk el-Aouareb, 33d Fighter Group P-40 pilots down two FW-190s.

GAF fighters strafe the advance fighter strip at Thelepte.

January 12, 1943

LIBYA: Twelve B-17s of XII Bomber Command's 97th Heavy Bombardment Group, escorted by 15 1st Fighter Group P-38s, attack Tripoli/Castel Benito Airdrome from medium altitude at about 1400 hours. At least 20 of the estimated 110 bombers, fighters, and other aircraft parked at the airdrome are claimed as destroyed. During the withdrawal, a large number of Italian fighters attack the bombers, but only one bomber is damaged. Two Italian fighters are claimed as probably downed by a pair of the P-38 pilots, and bomber gunners claim 14 enemy fighters destroyed and three probably destroyed.

MEDITERRANEAN: XII Bomber Command B-25s dispatched to attack Axis ships at sea in the Gulf of Gabes and the Straits of Sicily fail to locate any targets.

TUNISIA: XII Bomber Command B-26s attack bridges at Chaaba and La Hencha.

1st Fighter Group P-38s attack trucks and moored seaplanes during a sweep over

the Ben Gardane region. One Fi-156 observation plane is downed.

Seven GAF Ju-88s and five Bf-109s attack the advance fighter base at Thelepte, and two of the Ju-88s are downed by 33d Fighter Group P-40 pilots.

January 13, 1943

FRANCE: Sixty-four VIII Bomber Command B-17s, escorted by 4th Fighter Group Spitfires, strike industrial targets in the Lille area with 125 tons of bombs. After dropping their bombs, two 306th Heavy Bombardment Group B-17s collide. Both bombers are lost and all 20 crewmen are listed as missing. Other losses amount to one B-17 missing and 15 B-17s damaged with two crewmen killed, ten crewmen missing, and nine crewmen wounded in battles with GAF fighters.

LIBYA: IX Bomber Command B-24s and B-25s abort their respective missions in the face of bad weather, but 57th Fighter Group P-40 pilots down two Bf-109s in one of two separate fighter actions.

MEDITERRANEAN: XII Bomber Command B-25s attack a sinking Axis freighter midway between Sicily and Tunisia.

TUNISIA: Five GAF Ju-88s bomb the advance fighter base at Thelepte early in the evening, but two are downed and another is damaged by 33d Fighter Group P-40 pilots based there.

January 14, 1943

BELGIUM: While attacking ground targets, 4th Fighter Group Spitfire pilots down two FW-190s.

One squadron of the 4th Fighter Group becomes the first Eighth Air Force operational unit to completely re-equip with P-47 fighters.

FRENCH MOROCCO: Top Allied leaders, including President Franklin D. Roosevelt and Prime Minister Sir Winston S. Churchill, open a conference at Casablanca to formulate international war plans for 1943.

LIBYA: In two separate actions near

Gheddhia, 57th Fighter Group P-40 pilots down three Bf-109s and an Italian Air Force Mc.202.

MEDITERRANEAN: XII Bomber Command B-25s and P-38s are dispatched to attack Axis shipping at sea in the Straits of Sicily, but no ships are located. On the return flight, the P-38s strafe German Army vehicles and troop concentrations along the coast.

TUNISIA: During the afternoon, 26 XII Bomber Command B-17s, escorted by 17 1st Fighter Group P-38s, drop more than 63 tons of bombs on the port facilities and shipping at Sfax and Sousse. No bombers are lost, but one P-38 is downed by a Bf-109. Also, a Bf-109 is downed by a P-38 pilot.

XII Bomber Command B-26s attack the rail junction at Kalaa Srira and warehouses and rail facilities at Mahares.

A 52d Fighter Group Spitfire pilot downs a Bf-109 near Cape Rosa at 1215 hours.

January 15, 1943

LIBYA: In a move to thwart German efforts to seal the entrance to the Tripoli harbor, IX Bomber Command B-24s attack the remains of previously disabled and wrecked ships at Tripoli that can be used for that purpose. (These attacks will continue through January 21, when the Germans nonetheless sink four wrecks and actually do block the harbor.)

The British Eighth Army reopens its stalled final drive to clear Tripoli, and soon overruns forward German Army positions. 57th Fighter Group P-40s support the ground attack by strafing and bombing German Army positions.

MEDITERRANEAN: XII Bomber Command B-25s and B-26s leave an Axis vessel in flames while conducting anti-shipping searches. While escorting the bombers, 14th Fighter Group P-38 pilots down three Ju-52s near Marettimo Island and two Ju-52s and a six-engine transport

at an undisclosed location. On the return to base, the P-38 pilots also strafe German Army trucks along the coast.

TUNISIA: XII Bomber Command B-26s attack the rail and highway bridge across the Oued el-Akarit River, and an escorting 82d Fighter Group P-38 pilot downs a Bf-109.

When nine Ju-88s, escorted by GAF fighters, attack the advance fighter base at Thelepte without warning at about 1420 hours, 33d Fighter Group P-40s on patrol drive off the escorts while P-40s on strip-alert status scramble through falling bombs to take on the bombers. Flak accounts for one Ju-88, and four P-40 pilots from the 33d Fighter Group's 59th Fighter Squadron are credited with the remaining eight Ju-88s, of which four are downed by Capt Carmon B. Boone. However, a similar attack on the 33d Fighter Group's other base, at Youks-les-Bains, is not challenged, and heavy damage is inflicted upon facilities and aircraft. The 33d Fighter Group, which entered combat on December 6 with 71 operational P-40s, is now down to just 30 operational fighters.

The day's tally of 15 Axis aircraft downed over Tunisia and the Mediterranean is the USAAF's highest one-day total against Germany and her allies since the start of the war.

The 81st Fighter Group, a P-39 unit that has been staging into North Africa bases since late December, conducts its first ground-support missions from Thelepte as part of the XII Air Support Command.

January 16, 1943

LIBYA: IX Bomber Command B-24s attack port facilities and the town of Tripoli.

MEDITERRANEAN: XII Bomber Command B-26s dispatched to attack Axis ships at sea in the Straits of Sicily fail to locate any targets.

TUNISIA: XII Fighter Command A-20s dispatched on an armed reconnaissance fail to locate any targets.

January 17, 1943

LIBYA: IX Bomber Command B-24s attack the harbor at Tripoli, and Ninth Air Force P-40s undertake fighter-bomber missions in support of the British Eighth Army advance.

Allied reconnaissance aircraft discover that the Axis air forces have concentrated 200 combat aircraft at Tripoli/Castel Benito Airdrome. In the main, these aircraft have been forced to take refuge at Castel Benito after being driven out of forward bases by relentless pressure from RAF and Ninth Air Force units.

The 57th Fighter Group "B" Party moves forward to the landing ground at Darragh West.

MEDITERRANEAN: While escorting XII Bomber Command B-25s on an anti-shipping sweep to Sicily, P-38 pilots of the 82d Fighter Group's 97th Fighter Squadron down two Ju-52s and one Ju-88 encountered along the way. The B-25s are unable to locate any targets and return to base with their bombs.

TUNISIA: XII Bomber Command B-25s attack the rail junction at Graiba.

January 18, 1943

LIBYA: XII Bomber Command B-17s attack Tripoli/Castel Benito Airdrome, and IX Bomber Command B-24s attack Tripoli harbor. In an engagement with GAF fighters over both targets between 1410 and 1430 hours, 1st Fighter Group P-38 pilots down three Bf-109s and damage as many as nine others.

The 57th Fighter Group "A" Party joins the "B" Party at Darragh West and immediately resumes fighter-bomber missions in support of the British Eighth Army advance.

During the night of January 18–19, nine 12th Medium Bombardment Group B-25s join RAF light bombers in an attack against Axis aircraft concentrated at Castel Benito Airdrome.

MEDITERRANEAN: XII Bomber Command B-26s attack two Axis vessels in the Gulf of Hammamet.

January 19, 1943

ENGLAND: The 3d Bombardment Wing headquarters is remanned and reactivated following a long hiatus caused by the transfer of U.K.-based groups to North Africa.

LIBYA: IX Bomber Command B-24s attack the city of Tripoli, and IX Bomber Command B-25s attack Tripoli/Castel Benito Airdrome and motor vehicles.

TUNISIA: IX Bomber Command B-24s attack Sousse; XII Bomber Command B-17s attack industrial targets south of Tunis and the marshalling yard at Jabal al-Jallud; and XII Bomber Command B-25s attack the town of Medenine and a nearby motor park.

January 20, 1943

LIBYA: IX Bomber Command B-24s attack Tripoli harbor.

One Bf-109 is downed in a midday fighter battle involving 57th Fighter Group P-40s engaged in supporting the British Eighth Army.

MEDITERRANEAN: Six 310th Medium Bombardment Group B-25s, escorted by twelve 14th Fighter Group P-38s, sink an Axis tanker carrying fuel from Sicily to Tunisia.

TUNISIA: Thwarted from attacking Tripoli by bad weather, XII Bomber Command B-17s attack Cap Mangin, near Gabes.

January 21, 1943

ALGERIA: The 68th Observation Group's 154th Observation Squadron, in P-39s, moves from Oujda, French Morocco, to Youks-les-Bains Airdrome to prepare to enter combat.

FRENCH MOROCCO: The CCS "Casablanca Directive" reaffirms that the primary objective of the Allied air forces in Europe is the destruction of Germany's military, industrial, and economic base and the morale of the German people. Listed in order of importance are the following targets:

submarine-construction facilities, the aircraft industry as a whole, transportation, oil plants, and other war industries. Also, the new directive formally relieves VIII Bomber Command of the burden of supporting the North African Campaign.

MajGen Ira C. Eaker, Eighth Air Force commanding general, presents to Gen Henry H. Arnold a paper entitled "The Case for Day Bombing." Later, in a conversation with Prime Minister Sir Winston S. Churchill, Eaker successfully argues his case, and wins Churchill's approval. The paper and Churchill's support eventually lead to the formulation of the strategic Combined Bomber Offensive against Germany.

LIBYA: IX Bomber Command B-24s attack Tripoli harbor; IX Bomber Command B-25s attack targets of opportunity along an interior road; and Ninth Air Force P-40s support ground attacks by the British Eighth Army.

Under relentless pressure, especially from WDAF and IX Bomber Command bombers, the Axis air forces abandon Tripoli/Castel Benito Airdrome, their last base inside Libya.

MEDITERRANEAN: During a morning anti-shipping mission, six 319th Medium Bombardment Group B-26s, escorted by 82d Fighter Group P-38s, attack an Axis convoy bound from Sicily to Tunisia, sinking one freighter and damaging another near Cap Bon. Then, in a running battle between Bizerte and Cap Bon, 82d Fighter Group P-38 escort pilots down a total of seven German and Italian fighters and transports. Two P-38s and their pilots are lost in this action.

TUNISIA: XII Bomber Command B-25s attack the highway and rail bridge just north of Pont-du-Fahs; while strafing a long German Army road column along the Gabes–Ben Gardane road in southern Tunisia, 24 1st Fighter Group P-38 pilots destroy 65 vehicles and also down two Bf-109s at 1430 hours; and XII Fighter Command A-20s attack advancing German Army tanks and troops in the Ousseltia Valley in support of

a ground counterattack by the U.S. 1st Armored Division.

January 22, 1943

ALGERIA: The Allied Air Support Command is established as a component of LtGen Carl Spaatz's Allied Air Force. The new headquarters is to coordinate air support for and operations with the Allied ground forces active in North Africa. Command of the new echelon is given to BriGen Laurence S. Kuter.

FRANCE: While supporting RAF light bombers in a raid over the French coast, 4th Fighter Group Spitfire pilots down four Bf-109s around Dunkirk. One Spitfire and its pilot are lost in the fight, and a damaged Spitfire is further damaged beyond repair when it crash-lands at a base in England.

LIBYA: XII Bomber Command B-25s attack a road junction near Tripoli, and Ninth Air Force P-40s support the British Eighth Army.

MEDITERRANEAN: Six XII Bomber Command B-26s severely damage an Axis freighter while on an anti-shipping sweep between Sicily and Tunisia; and 14th Fighter Group P-38 pilots down two Ju-88s near the Egadi Islands at 1110 hours.

TUNISIA: Two formations of XII Bomber Command B-17s attack Tunis/El Aouina Airdrome in the morning; XII Bomber Command B-26s attack Tunis/El Aouina Airdrome shortly after noon; and XII Bomber Command B-25s attack Tunis/ El Aouina Airdrome again during the afternoon.

While helping Allied ground forces hold against a German Army counterattack in the Pont-du-Fahs area, the 81st Fighter Group makes its combat debut with an attack by ten 92d Fighter Squadron P-39s against vehicles and gun positions. Also participating in the day's numerous ground-support missions are 16 33d Fighter Group P-40s, and P-40s of the USAAF-equipped Lafayette Escadrille, a Free French Air Force unit operating as part of the Twelfth Air Force. In addition to the USAAF fighter attacks, 47th Light Bombardment Group A-20s attack a German Army tank depot near Ousseltia. Only one 33d Fighter Group P-40 is lost in the course of the group's many dangerous low-level attacks. Also, two 1st Fighter Group P-38s and their pilots are lost to GAF fighters while attacking German Army road columns in southern Tunisia.

January 23, 1943

FRANCE: Thirty-five of 73 VIII Bomber Command B-17s dispatched against the Lorient port area attack that target while 18 B-17s of the leading 305th Heavy Bombardment, plus one B-17 from another group, opt for the Brest U-boat base following a temporary bombsight malfunction in the lead bomber while over Lorient. Losses to flak and GAF fighters amount to five 303rd Heavy Bombardment Group B-17s missing with all 50 crewmen, two B-17s damaged beyond repair in crash-landings in the U.K., two crewmen killed, and 26 crewmen wounded or injured. It is noted that, for the first time, GAF fighters encountered over Lorient are attacking in groups of up to six at a time against a single bomber.
FRENCH MOROCCO: Results of the Casablanca Conference are determined. In the war against Germany, upon completion of the Tunisian Campaign, the Allies are to attack Sicily and shift the weight of the Anglo-American offensive from the south to northwestern Europe, from the U.K.
LIBYA: The British Eighth Army drives into Tripoli and secures the port facilities. The pursuit of retreating Axis forces toward Tunisia continues without pause. 57th Fighter Group P-40s support the British Eighth Army.
MEDITERRANEAN: XII Bomber Command B-26s attacking an Axis convoy between Sicily and Tunisia leave one ship listing and another exploding and capsizing. An escorting 82d Fighter Group P-38 pilot downs an Italian Air Force flying boat near Pantelleria Island, and other escorting fighters attack Axis trucks and tanks near Enfidaville, Tunisia during the return flight.

SICILY: During the night of January 23–24, IX Bomber Command B-24s attack Palermo harbor.
TUNISIA: Two formations of XII Bomber Command B-17s attack the Bizerte naval base and Axis shipping at sea in the area. One vessel is claimed as being sunk. As many as 100 GAF fighters attack the heavy bombers over and near the target, and bomber gunners claim 20 of them.

XII Fighter Command A-20s and P-40s attack German Army artillery, machine guns, and two infantry companies while supporting U.S. Army ground forces in the Ousseltia Valley. While attacking German Army road columns along the Gabes–Ben Gardane road, six 1st Fighter Group P-38s and their pilots are lost in a counterattack by GAF fighters, and a Bf-109 is downed in the area by a 14th Fighter Group P-38 pilot.

In two separate actions, pilots of the 52d and 82d Fighter groups down a Bf-109 and an Italian Air Force flying boat.

January 24, 1943

ALGERIA: Col Paul L. Williams replaces BriGen Howard A. Craig as commander of the XII Air Support Command.
LIBYA: 57th Fighter Group P-40s support the British Eighth Army.
TUNISIA: XII Bomber Command B-17s attack Sousse harbor; XII Bomber Command B-25s and B-26s, and IX Bomber Command B-25s attack Medenine Airdrome during three separate missions; and Twelfth Air Force fighters attack Axis vehicles and troop concentrations in support of Allied ground forces.

January 25, 1943

NORTH AFRICA: Nearly all theater air operations are shut down by bad weather, but several missions are mounted by Ninth Air Force P-40s in support of the British Eighth Army in Libya.

January 26, 1943

ALGERIA: The 68th Observation Group's

154th Observation Squadron, in P-39s, flies its first combat-reconnaissance missions of the war.

ITALY: During the night of January 26–27, IX Bomber Command B-24s attack Naples.

LIBYA: 57th Fighter Group P-40 fighter-bombers supporting the British Eighth Army become the first Allied aircraft to refuel at the newly captured Tripoli/Castel Benito Airdrome.

MEDITERRANEAN: XII Bomber Command B-26s dispatched on anti-shipping sweeps are recalled or abort because of bad weather.

SICILY: IX Bomber Command B-24s encounter such stiff headwinds while on a late-afternoon attack against Naples that they divert to Messina, where they attack the town and the train ferry terminal. Also, IX Bomber Command B-24s attack Messina again during the night of January 26–27.

January 27, 1943

FRENCH MOROCCO: The newly arrived 2d Air Defense Wing (which will be redesignated the 63d Fighter Wing in July 1943) replaces the Twelfth Air Force's provisional Moroccan Composite Wing in overseeing the operations of several Twelfth Air Force fighter groups.

GERMANY: In the first USAAF attack against a target on German soil, 55 VIII Bomber Command heavy bombers (of 91 B-17s and B-24s dispatched) attack the Wilhelmshaven U-boat base and port shortly after 1100 hours with more than 120 tons of bombs. The two B-24 groups involved are unable to locate the target due to poor visibility and poor navigation, and they return to base with their bombs. Two B-17s that cannot locate Wilhelmshaven drop their bombs on Emden. GAF fighters damage 32 B-17s and nine B-24s, force 30 crewmen to bail out (they are listed as missing), and kill two and wound three crewmen.

MEDITERRANEAN: XII Bomber Command B-25s attacking two Axis destroyers at sea off Algeria's northern coast leave one on fire. However, XII Bomber Command B-26s dispatched on a separate anti-shipping strike are unable to attack any of several targets sighted because of bad weather.

SICILY: IX Bomber Command B-24s attack Palermo after being diverted by bad weather from the briefed primary, Naples.

TUNISIA: XII Fighter Command A-20s attack Mezzouna.

January 28, 1943

FRENCH MOROCCO: Following a voyage from Norfolk, Virginia, the USS *Ranger* launches 72 325th Fighter Group P-40s, which land at Cazes Airdrome. Unbelievably, the base has received no advance warning from higher authority that the fresh group will be arriving.

LIBYA: In order to reach Axis supply sources and lines of supply with more efficiency, IX Bomber Command's 98th Heavy Bombardment Group displaces forward to the Gambut Airdrome complex from its former bases in the Nile Delta.

TUNISIA: XII Bomber Command B-17s, B-25s, and B-26s, respectively, attack the port, shipping, and marshalling yards at Sfax in three waves during the early afternoon. One B-26 and one P-38 are downed by GAF fighters, but bomber gunners claim five enemy fighters, and a Bf-109 is downed by a 14th Fighter Group P-38 pilot.

XII Air Support Command P-40s attack German Army artillery and infantry in direct support of U.S. Army and Free French ground forces attacking in the Ousseltia Valley.

The 14th Fighter Group (just two squadrons strong) is withdrawn from combat to give the overstressed pilots time to rest and recuperate. The unit's P-38s are turned over to the 82d Fighter Group, whose pilots are in better shape but which is experiencing equipment shortages. (The 14th Fighter Group, by then including a new third squadron, will not return to active combat until May 1943.)

January 29, 1943

MEDITERRANEAN: XII Bomber Command B-26s claim direct hits on an Axis passenger liner encountered during an anti-shipping sweep between Sicily and Tunisia.

TUNISIA: Three waves of XII Bomber Command B-17s attack port facilities and shipping at Bizerte.

While escorting XII Bomber Command B-26s in an attack against Tunis/El Aouina Airdrome, 82d Fighter Group P-38 pilots down two Bf-109s.

January 30, 1943

ALGERIA: The newly arrived 1st Air Defense Wing (which will be redesignated the 62d Fighter Wing in July 1943) assumes command-and-control responsibilities for units formerly overseen by the Twelfth Air Force's provisional West Algerian Composite Wing.

TUNISIA: Twelfth Air Force A-20s and fighters conduct numerous attacks on Axis troops, positions, and facilities between Faid and El Guettar; at least 50 XII Bomber Command B-17s attack the port facilities and shipping at Ferryville; XII Bomber Command B-26s attack the rail line south of Reyville; and XII Bomber Command B-25s attack rail installations and warehouses at El Aouinet. While escorting the latter attack, seven P-38 pilots of the 82d Fighter Group's 96th Fighter Squadron down eight Bf-109s at about 1040 hours.

January 31, 1943

EGYPT: In addition to his duties as Ninth Air Force commanding general, LtGen Lewis H. Brereton assumes command of U.S. Army Forces in the Middle East (USAFIME).

The headquarters of BriGen Auby C. Strickland's IX Fighter Command is formally established at El Kabrit Airdrome to oversee the operations of USAAF fighter groups flying in support of the British Eighth Army.

SICILY: IX Bomber Command B-24s attack the ferry terminal at Messina.

TUNISIA: XII Bomber Command B-17s attack port facilities and shipping at Bizerte; XII Bomber Command B-26s attack Gabes Airdrome, and escorting 1st Fighter Group P-38 pilots down two Bf-109s west of Gabes; and many Twelfth Air Force fighters attack ground targets and directly support Allied ground forces, mainly in the embattled area between Faid and Gafsa.

82d Fighter Group P-38 pilots down two Bf-110s north of the Gulf of Tunis at 1300 hours.

FEBRUARY 1943

February 1, 1943

EGYPT: The 9th Fighter Wing headquarters arrives in Egypt and is placed under the control of IX Fighter Command.

TUNISIA: XII Bomber Command B-17s attack the port and shipping at Tunis and shipping at La Goulette; Twelfth Air Force fighters provide direct support for Allied ground forces in the Sened-Maknassy area; and Twelfth Air Force A-20s and P-40s bomb tanks and vehicles near Sidi Khalif.

P-40s pilots of the 33d Fighter Group's 59th Fighter Squadron attack a force of fighter-escorted Ju-87 dive-bombers between Gafsa and Maknassy at about 0730 hours. During the brief running fight, four Ju-87s and an FW-190 are downed and others are damaged.

February 2, 1943

NORTH SEA: A VIII Bomber Command heavy-bomber force dispatched to Hamm, Germany, is recalled over the North Sea due to dangerous weather conditions at altitude.

TUNISIA: Separate formations of XII Bomber Command B-25s and B-26s mount a coordinated attack against Sfax\El Maou Airdrome; A-20s, escorted by P-39s and P-40s, attack an Axis munitions dump near the central battle area; and other Twelfth Air Force fighters mount many attacks in direct support of Allied ground forces.

In a morning action near Kairouan, 33d Fighter Group P-40 pilots down two FW-190s and a Ju-87. However, in several other fighter actions throughout the day, the 33d Fighter Group loses six fighters shot down or missing, and two others must be written off following crash-landings. The group is down to just 13 operational fighters, so it is hastily withdrawn to Telergma, Algeria, for rest, recuperation, and reequipping. (To accomplish the latter, most of the fresh 325th Fighter Group's brand-new P-40s soon will be shifted to the 33d Fighter Group.)

P-38 pilots of the 82d Fighter Group's 96th Fighter Squadron intercept a mixed flight of GAF single- and multi-engine aircraft off Cap Bon and down three Bf-109s and four multi-engine aircraft.

February 3, 1943

LIBYA: Two squadrons of the Ninth Air Force's 12th Medium Bombardment Group are detached for temporary service with the XII Air Support Command in Algeria.

MEDITERRANEAN: XII Bomber Command B-26s attack Axis ships at sea between Sicily and Tunisia.

SICILY: IX Bomber Command B-24s attack the harbors at Palermo and Messina.

TUNISIA: Fifteen XII Bomber Command B-26s attack Gabes Airdrome at about 1100 hours, and 82d Fighter Group P-38 pilots escorting the bombers down a Ju-88, two twin-engine fighters, and a Bf-109; XII Bomber Command B-25s attacking bridges north of Maknassy claim severe damage on one rail span; and XII Fighter Command A-20s attack tanks and motor vehicles in the northern ground-battle area and an artillery position and numerous trucks in the eastern Ousseltia Valley,

February 4, 1943

ENGLAND: LtGen Frank M. Andrews, USAAF, assumes command of ETOUSA, officially replacing Gen Dwight D. Eisenhower.

GERMANY: Sixty-seven VIII Bomber Command B-17s and 21 B-24s are dispatched to Hamm, Germany, but extreme cold forces the B-24s to abort over the North Sea, and cloudiness over the primary target causes 39 of the B-17s to opt for attacking industrial targets of opportunity around Emden. The 44th Heavy Bombardment Group, plus one B-17, attacks an Axis shipping convoy it encounters in the North Sea, but without known results. In attacks by GAF fighters against the B-17s, five B-17s are reported missing, including one that is seen to collide with an FW-190. Seventeen B-17 crewmen are wounded and 50 are counted as missing in action. This is the first time that Bf-110 twin-engine fighters are encountered by USAAF heavy bombers in northern Europe.

LIBYA: In order to reach Axis supply sources and lines of supply with more efficiency, IX Bomber Command's 376th Heavy Bombardment Group displaces forward to the El Adem Airdrome (near Gambut) from its former bases in the Nile Delta.

NORTH AFRICA: North African Theater of Operations, United States Army (NATOUSA) is created, and Gen Dwight D. Eisenhower is named as its commanding general.

TUNISIA: In the morning, 18 XII Bomber Command B-17s attack Gabes Airdrome and a landing ground west of town. In the afternoon, 24 B-17s attack Gabes Airdrome again, and P-38 escort pilots down a Bf-109 and an FW-190 during the second mission.

Advance elements of the British Eighth Army cross from Libya into southern Tunisia.

February 5, 1943

ENGLISH CHANNEL: Six 4th Fighter Group Spitfires strafe and damage two German Navy corvettes and a merchantman. One Spitfire is downed by flak, and the pilot is declared missing.

TUNISIA: XII Bomber Command bombing missions are canceled due to bad weather, but some fighter units are able to operate in direct support of Allied ground forces.

February 6, 1943

MEDITERRANEAN: Axis aircraft from Sardinia's Elmas Airdrome, outside Cagliari, inflict heavy damage upon several ships in an unescorted Allied convoy caught between Oran and Algiers.

TUNISIA: Bad weather in the region continues to force a halt in XII Bomber Command bombing operations, but several P-39 and P-40 units are able to mount reconnaissance and strafing missions, and some Spitfires are used to escort transport and evacuation flights.

February 7, 1943

ITALY: IX Bomber Command B-24s attacking Naples harbor score hits on several vessels.

SARDINIA: In retaliation for the February 6 attack by Axis aircraft on an Allied convoy, XII Bomber Command dispatches 32 B-17s and 19 B-26s against Elmas Airdrome, from which the Axis attack originated. The XII Bomber Command attack takes place at about 1500 hours. Bombs are also dropped on the seaplane base at Cagliari. Bomber crews claim 25 Axis aircraft destroyed on the ground and numerous fires started, bomber gunners claim five Bf-109s downed in the air, and 82d Fighter Group P-38 escort pilots down two Bf-109s. During the evening, RAF Beaufighters escorting the convoy, which is still within range of Sardinia, repulse a weak attack mounted from the crippled Axis airdrome.

TUNISIA: XII Fighter Command A-20s and fighters mount numerous reconnaissance missions over eastern Tunisia, and some fighters strafe artillery batteries in the Gafsa-Maknassy area.

The 31st Fighter Group, in Spitfires, moves from Algeria to Thelepte to replace the 33d Fighter Group, which departed the advance fighter strip on February 2.

February 8, 1943

ITALY: IX Bomber Command B-24s attack the ferry terminal at Messina.

TUNISIA: Forty-two XII Bomber Command B-17s attack the port facilities at Sousse. During the return flight, a 1st Fighter Group P-38 pilot downs an FW-190 at 1158 hours.

XII Bomber Command B-25s and B-26s attack the marshalling yard and airdrome at Gabes during the afternoon. 82d Fighter Group P-38 pilots escorting the B-26s down eight Bf-109s over the target and during the withdrawal, between 1235 and 1315 hours.

Two Twelfth Air Force A-20 formations

mount separate attacks on Axis vehicles and troop concentrations east of Faid, and escorting fighters strafe troop positions in the Sened-Maknassy area and the Axis landing ground at Kebili.

February 9, 1943

CRETE: IX Bomber Command B-25s attack several Axis airdromes.

LIBYA: IX Bomber Command's 98th Heavy Bombardment Group displaces forward from Gambut to several Benghazi-area bases.

TUNISIA: During the afternoon, XII Bomber Command bombers attack Kairouan Airdrome. While escorting the bombers, Capt Newell O. Roberts, a P-38 pilot with the 1st Fighter Group's 94th Fighter Squadron, achieves ace status when he downs a Bf-109.

Twelfth Air Force fighters strafe German Army machine-gun emplacements and trucks in and around Faid Pass, Axis-occupied buildings near Mezzouna, and trucks near Station de Sened.

February 10, 1943

MEDITERRANEAN: XII Bomber Command B-25s conducting anti-shipping sweeps between Sicily and Tunisia claim one ferry sunk and one badly damaged near Cap Bon.

SICILY: Bad weather forces IX Bomber Command B-24s to abort on the way to Palermo.

TUNISIA: Although bad weather forces the cancellation of bomber missions over the interior, XII Air Support Command P-39s and Spitfires strafe numerous German Army ground emplacements and motor vehicles in a large area centered on Station de Sened.

February 11, 1943

TUNISIA: All Twelfth Air Force heavy and medium bombers are grounded because of bad weather, but fighter-escorted A-20s attack ground targets around Station de Sened.

February 12, 1943

TUNISIA: All Twelfth Air Force heavy and medium bombers are grounded by bad weather, but fighter-escorted A-20s attack Axis gun emplacements west of Station de Sened.

February 13, 1943

ITALY: Despite storms in the area, IX Bomber Command B-24s attack Crotone Airdrome and various targets around the Naples area.

MEDITERRANEAN: 1st Fighter Group P-38 pilots down three Ju-52s 50 miles north of Bizerte at 1500 hours.

TUNISIA: XII Bomber Command B-26s attack Tunis/El Aiouna Airdrome and, during the return, escorting fighters strafe German Army tanks near Station de Sened and motor vehicles near Faid.

February 14, 1943

MEDITERRANEAN: XII Bomber Command B-25s on an anti-shipping sweep fail to locate any targets.

NORTH SEA: Seventy-four VIII Bomber Command B-17s bound for Hamm, Germany, abort in the face of bad weather.

TUNISIA: German Army forces mount a major counterattack against U.S. and Free French ground forces around Faid Pass. All Twelfth Air Force heavy and medium bombers are grounded by bad weather, but fighters strafe ground targets in a large area centered on Station de Sened and attack tanks and trucks near Sidi Saad. Also, Twelfth Air Force A-20s bomb tanks in Faid Pass, the town of Maknassy, and the rail yard at Station de Sened.

During the evening, as a result of lightning German and Italian advances on the ground, the Twelfth Air Force begins to evacuate forward air bases.

February 15, 1943

FRANCE: Twenty-one B-24s from the 44th Heavy Bombardment Group and one squadron of the 93d Heavy Bombardment Group attack the port of Dunkirk with 62 tons of bombs. GAF fighters and flak down two B-24s and damage eight, of which one that crash-lands has to be written off. Crew losses are one killed and 24 missing.

ITALY: IX Bomber Command B-24s attacking Naples harbor claim two direct hits on Axis ships.

LIBYA: In a new reorganization of Allied air commands in Libya and Egypt, BriGen Auby C. Strickland forms a new Desert Air Task Force (DATF) to undertake operational and administrative oversight of Ninth Air Force units west of the Marble Arch. Strickland will also serve as commanding general of all U.S. troops in the area.

IX Bomber Command headquarters displaces to Benghazi, and Col Hugo P. Rush relieves BriGen Patrick W. Timberlake as commander.

SICILY: Nineteen XII Bomber Command B-17s attack shipping and port facilities at Palermo.

TUNISIA: XII Bomber Command B-25s and B-26s attack Kairouan Airdrome at about 1450 hours, and 82d Fighter Group P-38 pilots down three GAF fighters. 2dLt William J. Sloan, a P-38 pilot with the 82d Fighter Group's 96th Fighter Squadron, achieves ace status when he downs a Bf-109.

The 350th Fighter Group's 346th Fighter Squadron, in P-39s, enters combat and scores its first aerial victories (two Bf-109s) over Thelepte Airdrome in the morning; and 31st Fighter Group Spitfire pilots down four GAF fighters in two separate engagements.

Despite extensive assistance by numerous close-support aircraft, Allied ground forces are pushed back in many places along a broad front, and the forward base at Sbeitla is abandoned.

February 16, 1943

FRANCE: Following the collision and loss of two B-24s and 20 crewmen over the English Channel, 59 VIII Bomber Command B-17s and six B-24s attack the St.-Nazaire port facilities with 160 tons of bombs shortly before 1100 hours. GAF fighter opposition, which is considered heavy, accounts for six B-17s downed and 28 B-17s and two B-24s damaged, against claims by bomber gunners amounting to 20 GAF fighters downed and 12 probably downed. Overall USAAF crew losses, counting the 20 men lost in the collision, are one killed, seven wounded, and 80 missing. Returning B-17 crews of the 91st Heavy Bombardment Group report seeing two GAF fighters dropping what are thought to be experimental time-delay fragmentation bombs on their unit's formation.

MEDITERRANEAN: XII Bomber Command B-25s dispatched on anti-shipping sweeps abort in the face of bad weather.

TUNISIA: XII Bomber Command cancels all pending medium and heavy bomber operations because of bad weather. However, Twelfth Air Force A-20s attack German Army gun positions near Sidi bou Zid in support of Allied ground forces, and many USAAF fighters attack German Army troop concentrations and vehicles around Gafsa.

February 17, 1943

ENGLAND: Col Frank A. Armstrong, Jr., forms the 101st Provisional Combat Bombardment Wing. The new provisional headquarters, formed under the authority of the Eighth Air Force, will more directly oversee the operations of several B-17 groups than can the burgeoning 1st Heavy Bombardment Wing, of which it will be a subunit. At the time of his transfer, Armstrong is promoted to the rank of brigadier general.

The 91st and 306th Heavy Bombardment groups are assigned to the 101st Provisional Combat Bombardment Wing.

NORTH AFRICA: The Mediterranean Air Command (MAC) is formed under RAF Air Chief Marshal Sir Arthur W. Tedder. It is a unified command with control over all the Allied air forces based in the region: the USAAF's Ninth and Twelfth air forces; the RAF's Eastern Air Command; the RAF's Middle East Air Command (later

redesignated RAF Middle East); and RAF units at Gibraltar and Malta. Also formed to handle the bulk of operational oversight directly beneath MAC is the new Northwest African Air Force (NAAF), which displaces the short-lived Allied Air Forces but which retains LtGen Carl Spaatz as its commanding general. NAAF initially consists of the Twelfth Air Force, the RAF's Eastern Air Command, and the RAF's Western Desert Air Force (supporting the British Eighth Army). In reality, when Spaatz commandeers the entire Twelfth Air Force headquarters organization, the Twelfth Air Force becomes a paper organization with Spaatz as its de facto commander.

SARDINIA: More than 40 XII Bomber Command B-17s attack Elmas Airdrome, and B-25s and B-26s attack Villacidro and Decimomannu airdromes. Two Italian Air Force aircraft are downed by 1st and 82d Fighter group P-38 pilots escorting the bombers.

TUNISIA: Twelfth Air Force A-20s and fighters mount numerous attacks in direct support of Allied ground forces in the Sbeitla-Kasserine-Feriana area.

The two forward fighter strips at Thelepte Airdrome are abandoned in the face of intense pressure on the ground by Axis forces. The precipitous withdrawal forces the destruction of 18 aircraft that are unable because of mechanical problems to fly out, and 60,000 gallons of fuel are pumped onto the ground from storage tanks.

Displaced by the abandonment of Thelepte Airdrome, two 47th Light Bombardment Group A-20 squadrons pull back to Youks-les-Bains, Algeria; 31st Fighter Group Spitfires move back to Tebessa, Algeria; two squadrons of 81st Fighter Group P-39s move back to Le Kouif, Algeria; two squadrons of 52d Fighter Group Spitfires move back to Youks-les-Bains and Telergma, Algeria.

February 18, 1943

ALGERIA: The independent 15th Light Bombardment Squadron, which was the first USAAF unit to see combat in Europe (on July 4, 1942) and which has participated in two air campaigns, is withdrawn from combat and reassigned to Nouvion Airdrome as part of the new Northwest African Training Command. (The squadron will be permanently disbanded on October 1, 1943.)

NORTH AFRICA: MAC and NAAF are formally activated, and NAAF is formally divided into fivecomponents: Northwest African Tactical Air Force (NATAF, to which XII Air Support Command and the Western Desert Air Force [incorporating the Ninth Air Force's medium-bomber and fighter groups] are assigned); Northwest African Strategic Air Force (NASAF, to which XII Bomber Command and the Middle East Air Command [incorporating IX Bomber Command] are assigned); Northwest African Coastal Air Force (NACAF, to which XII Fighter Command is assigned); Northwest African Troop Carrier Command (NATCC); and Northwest African Training Command (NATC). The Northwest African Photographic Reconnaissance Wing is also formed as a USAAF-RAF conglomerate.

SARDINIA: USAAF and RAF heavy and medium bombers attack Elmas Airdrome, the Cagliari seaplane base, and Villacidro Airdrome. However, the results of the bombings are obscured by poor visibility.

TUNISIA: XII Bomber Command medium and heavy bombers are grounded by bad weather, but Twelfth Air Force fighters are able to support the British First Army in the Sbeitla-Kasserine-Feriana region.

February 19, 1943

TUNISIA: As powerful German Army ground forces press massive attacks around Kasserine Pass, all Twelfth Air Force aircraft are grounded by bad weather.

IX Bomber Command B-25s attack Gabes through heavy clouds.

February 20, 1943

ITALY: IX Bomber Command B-24s attack Amantea, Crotone, Naples, Nicotera, Palmi, and Rosarno.

TUNISIA: Bad weather prevents all but a handful of Twelfth Air Force P-39s from getting airborne. The P-39s strafe German Army trucks and armored vehicles around Kasserine Pass as powerful German Army ground units break through the Allied front line and proceed toward Thala and Tebessa.

February 21, 1943

LIBYA: The 93d Heavy Bombardment Group, an Eighth Air Force B-24 unit on loan to the Ninth Air Force, is ordered to stand down pending its return to England. During its attachment to the XII and IX Bomber commands, the 93d Group mounted more than 200 effective sorties in North Africa.

MEDITERRANEAN: During the afternoon, 82d Fighter Group P-38 pilots down nine GAF multi-engine aircraft between Sicily and Bizerte.

NORTH AFRICA: NATAF assumes control of the RAF component of the WDAF, which will continue to support the British Eighth Army. However, the Ninth Air Force is not subordinated to the new NAAF command structure, and the USAAF component of the WDAF remains under Ninth Air Force control.

TUNISIA: Due as much to muddy conditions on the runway as to the pressure of being overrun by Axis ground forces, the 31st Fighter Group moves from Tebessa to Youks-les-Bains, Algeria.

Although NASAF B-25s are able to attack the rail yards at Gafsa, there is virtually no air action over Algeria or Tunisia because of overwhelming rain and fog. Throughout the day, only two P-39s are able to attack German Army ground forces.

February 22, 1943

ALGERIA: Pressured by Axis forces on the ground, two squadrons of 81st Fighter Group P-39s abandon Le Kouif Airdrome, on the Algeria-Tunisia frontier, and pull south to Youks-les-Bains. The advance runway at Kalaa Djerda Airdrome is also abandoned.

LIBYA: IX Bomber Command's 376th Heavy Bombardment Group displaces forward from Gambut to a Benghazi-area base.

TUNISIA: XII Bomber Command B-17s attack German Army units inside the Kasserine Pass, 12th Medium Bombardment Group B-25s attack a bridge near the pass, and escorting P-38s strafe troops. In an unrelated action, XII Bomber Command B-25s attack the Gafsa rail yards.

Although undermanned and undersupplied and despite horrid weather, 47th Light Bombardment Group A-20s mount eleven separate minimum-altitude missions through the day to help stem the advance of German armored columns from around Kasserine Pass toward Tebessa and Thala. Despite intense fire from the ground, only one A-20 is lost during the day, in a crash-landing after it is attacked by three Bf-109s.

154th Observation Squadron P-39s destroy three German tanks and ten trucks while conducting 14 armed reconnaissance missions during the day. One P-39 is downed by ground fire.

In all, XII Air Support Command aircraft mount 114 combat sorties against ground targets associated with the Axis advance toward Algeria. Thanks in part to these relentless attacks from the air, Allied ground forces are able to stop the Axis attack, and even to begin pushing it back at several points. At 1915 hours, the Axis ground forces begin withdrawing. The day's events, in fact, bring to an end the Battle of Kasserine Pass.

In the only air-to-air fighter engagements of the day, pilots of the 31st and 82d Fighter groups down two GAF bombers in separate afternoon confrontations.

February 23, 1943

ALGERIA: The 3d Air Defense Wing (which will be redesignated the 64th Fighter Wing in July 1943) assumes responsibility for overseeing operations formerly overseen by the Twelfth Air Force's provisional Central Algerian Composite Wing.

MEDITERRANEAN: NASAF B-25s attacking Axis shipping at sea north of Cap Bon claim one ship sunk.

SICILY: IX Bomber Command B-24s attack the ferry installation at Messina.

TUNISIA: NASAF B-17s attack Kairouan; NASAF B-17s, B-25s, B-26s, and NATAF A-20s and fighters attack German Army units retreating through Kasserine Pass; and IX Bomber Command B-25s attack Arram, a position along the German Army's new Mareth Line, in southern Tunisia.

NAAF fighter pilots down two Axis aircraft during the day.

February 24, 1943

ENGLAND: In an advisory message from the U.S. War Department, MajGen Ira C. Eaker is informed that, henceforth, VIII Fighter Command fighters will be employed *offensively* in the direct escort of VIII Bomber Command bombers.

ITALY: During the night of February 24-25, IX Bomber Command B-24s attack Naples harbor and Crotone.

TUNISIA: NASAF B-17s attack Kairouan Airdrome; NASAF B-25s attack and sink several Axis supply barges at sea near Cap Bon; NASAF B-17s and B-26s attack the town of Kasserine and German Army troop and motor columns in and around the Kasserine Pass; NASAF B-25s attack road traffic on the highway near Sbeitla; and NATAF A-20s and fighters attack German Army motor vehicles in a wide area around Sbeitla and the Kasserine Pass.

52d Fighter Group Spitfire pilots down three Bf-109s during a running noontime engagement near Tunis.

February 25, 1943

ENGLAND: The final element of the 2d Bombardment Wing's 93d Heavy Bombardment Group returns from nearly three months' service in North Africa.

EUROPE: RAF units based in the U.K. open around-the-clock offensive operations over northwestern Europe.

TUNISIA: NASAF B-17s attack Tunis/El Aouina Airdrome; NATAF A-20s and fighters attack German Army road traffic in the Thala-Kasserine-Sbeitla region and along the Gafsa-Feriana road; and IX Bomber Command B-25s attack German Army motor traffic along the roads around Arram.

Elements of the British First Army and the U.S. II Corps reoccupy Kasserine Pass.

February 26, 1943

ALGERIA: MajGen James H. Doolittle replaces BriGen John K. Cannon head of the XII Bomber Command, a sign that the Twelfth Air Force has been effectively supplanted by NAAF.

GERMANY: When the primary target, Bremen, is found to be obscured by cloud cover, 59 VIII Bomber Command B-17s and six B-24s (of 76 B-17s and 17 B-24s dispatched) attack the Wilhelmshaven submarine yard at about 1125 hours with 164 tons of bombs. Seven heavy bombers are lost, and a B-24 that crash-lands at a base in the U.K. is written off. Crew losses are 73 missing and 14 injured. In addition to USAAF crewmen, one of the missing is Robert B. Post, a correspondent for the *New York Times* who goes down in a 44th Heavy Bombardment Group B-24. Post is the first American war correspondent to be lost in the air over Europe. Bomber gunners claim 21 GAF fighters downed and nine probably downed.

SARDINIA: Nineteen XII Bomber Command B-17s attack the docks and rail lines at Cagliari.

TUNISIA: Thirty-two NASAF B-17s attack the port facilities and shipping at Bizerte, and escorting 1st Fighter Group P-38 pilots down four Bf-109s over Bizerte at 1215 hours.

IX Fighter Command P-40s attack German Army positions along the Mareth Line. One Bf-109 is downed in southern Tunisia by a 57th Fighter Group P-40 pilot at 1545 hours.

During the night of February 26–27, as a first step to supporting the British Eighth Army's plan to attack the Mareth Line on March 20, IX Bomber Command B-25s attempt to damage the road system around Arram.

February 27, 1943

ALGERIA: The 319th Medium Bombardment Group, a XII Bomber Command B-26 unit that has conducted almost daily attacks on targets in Tunisia and the Mediterranean, is withdrawn from combat to rest and refit. (The unit will not be returned to operational status until May 1943.)

FRANCE: Sixty VIII Bomber Command heavy bombers attack the Brest U-boat base with 155 tons of bombs. Opposition is negligible and only two B-24s are damaged, without crew loss. It is discovered after the mission that the 305th Heavy Bombardment Group, represented by 12 B-17s, aborted the mission within sight of Brest after receiving a bogus recall message, presumably from a German station on the ground.

SARDINIA: NASAF B-17s attack Cagliari and ships at sea north of Cape d'Orlando.

TUNISIA: NATAF fighters attack German Army forces mounting an unsuccessful ground attack near Medjez el-Bab, and IX Fighter Command P-40s strafe German Army positions along the Mareth Line.

February 28, 1943

TUNISIA: NATAF fighters and fighter-bombers attack German Army tanks, troops, and motor vehicles in the battle areas southwest of Mateur, at Sidi Nsir, near Bedja, and around Goubellat.

MARCH 1943

March 1, 1943

ALGERIA: LtGen Carl Spaatz formally replaces MajGen James H. Doolittle as commanding general of the Twelfth Air Force, a bureaucratic ploy that will allow Twelfth Air Force headquarters to administer all the USAAF components of Spaatz's NAAF, which has been assigned no administrative branch of its own. Doolittle, who would have been displaced, has already moved down to head the XII Bomber Command, on February 26. Also, Col Lawrence P. Hickey replaces BriGen Thomas W. Blackburn as commander of the XII Fighter Command, and BriGen John K. Cannon, formerly commanding general of the XII Bomber Command, assumes command of NATC.

ITALY: IX Bomber Command B-24s attack Naples harbor and several targets of opportunity in southwestern Italy.

MEDITERRANEAN: NASAF B-26s attack an Axis freighter at sea north of Bizerte.

SARDINIA: Forty-six NASAF B-17s at- tack the docks, town, and rail lines at Cagliari. 1st and 82d Fighter group P-38 escort pilots down five GAF and Italian fighters in several running battles over the island between 1400 and 1415 hours.

TUNISIA: Nine 17th Medium Bombard- ment Group B-26s, escorted by 82d Fighter Group P-38s, are dispatched to bomb the La Hencha bridge, on the road between Gabes and Sfax. When the P-38s are engaged by Bf-109s, the B-26s turn back for their base. In the fighter action, 2dLt Thomas A. White, a P-38 pilot with the 82d Fighter Group's 97th Fighter Squadron, achieves ace status when he downs a Bf-109 at 1430 hours.

NATAF B-25s attack German Army positions near Mateur, and NATAF fight- ers provide direct support for Allied ground forces around Bedja and Sidi Nsir.

March 2, 1943

SICILY: Thirty-eight NASAF B-17s attack the port facilities at Palermo during the af- ternoon, destroying drydocks and ship- building facilities and setting five ships on fire. A 1st Fighter Group P-38 escort pilot downs an Italian Air Force Mc.200 over Palermo.

TUNISIA: Having failed to attack the La Hencha bridge from medium altitude on March 1, nine 17th Medium Bombardment Group B-26s, escorted by 82d Fighter Group P-38s, conduct a bombing attack on the link at a mere 60 feet through heavy flak and despite determined opposition by GAF fighters. Although two B-26s are shot down and two are damaged beyond repair, the bridge is utterly demolished. In fending off GAF fighters, P-38 escort pilots of the 82d Fighter Group's 96th Fighter Squadron down five Bf-109s.

As German Army forces renew their ground attack along the Mateur-Taberka road near Jefna, NATAF fighters attack German Army tanks, troops, and motor vehicles northeast of Bedja and south of Mateur.

March 3, 1943

ITALY: IX Bomber Command B-24s attack bridges at Bianco and Siderno Marina.
SICILY: IX Bomber Command B-24s dispatched to attack Naples divert to Messina.
TUNISIA: Thirty-six NASAF B-17s attack port facilities at Tunis and La Goulette; NATAF medium bombers and fighters attack German Army ground forces around Bedja, Bou Arada, and Mateur, but enemy forces capture Sedjenane; and IX Fighter Command P-40s attack German Army units engaged in probing attacks along the Mareth Line.

1stLt Jack M. Ilfrey, a P-38 pilot with the 1st Fighter Group's 94th Fighter Squadron, achieves ace status when he downs one of two Bf-109s credited to his unit in an engagement over Tunis/El Aouina Airdrome at 1545 hours.

March 4, 1943

GERMANY: Despite adverse weather conditions and heavy attacks by GAF fighters, 28 of 71 VIII Bomber Command B-17s dispatched drop 90 tons of bombs on a marshalling yard at Hamm. Also, 16 91st Heavy Bombardment Group B-17s, after becoming separated from the main force, drop the USAAF's first bombs (20 tons) on targets of opportunity in the Ruhr region of Germany. Five of the attacking B-17s (including four from the errant 91st Group) are lost and 24 (including nine from the 91st) are damaged. Crew losses amount to one killed, seven wounded, and 42 missing. Seven crewmen are picked up by the Air-Sea Rescue Service after their damaged B-17 ditches.

Several B-24s taking part in a diversionary sweep of the English Channel are damaged by empty cartridges from bullets fired by aircraft ahead in the formation. This and the general dismay emerging over the defensive qualities of bomber formations of the day militate toward renewed efforts to develop better, safer, and more-defensible formations.

MEDITERRANEAN: NASAF B-25s dispatched on anti-shipping sweeps between Sicily and Tunisia fail to locate any targets, but NASAF B-17s that find and attack an Axis convoy at sea northwest of Bizerte claim four ships sunk.
TUNISIA: IX Fighter Command fighters provide cover for British Eighth Army forces concentrating to meet a renewed German Army attack in southern Tunisia. A 57th Fighter Group P-40 pilot downs a Bf-109 in an engagement over the Mareth Line at about 1500 hours.

March 5, 1943

LIBYA: Because of the recent replacement of many veteran crews with fresh crews, all IX Bomber Command aircraft and personnel are temporarily withdrawn from combat to begin a seven-day training program in night operations, rendezvous techniques, and precision bombing.

March 6, 1943

FRANCE: Sixty-five VIII Bomber Command B-17s attack the Lorient U-boat base with more than 162 tons of bombs. Losses are three B-17s missing and eight damaged, plus 30 crewmen missing. Also, 15 B-24s conduct a diversionary attack against the Brest U-boat base, in which three B-24s are damaged.

TUNISIA: German Army forces attacking the British Eighth Army along the Mareth Line, in southern Tunisia, are turned back. Thirty-five IX Fighter Command fighters take part in the defense by strafing and bombing German Army positions along the Mareth Line.

NAAF aircraft are grounded by bad weather.

March 7, 1943

ENGLAND: The first air echelon of the 322d Medium Bombardment Group, in B-26s, arrives from the United States via the southern ferry route for service with the VIII Bomber Command. Subsequent echelons will arrive as aircraft become available in the United States.

MEDITERRANEAN: Between 0930 and 0945 hours, at a position about 75 miles northeast of Tunisia's Cap Bon, P-38s of the 82d Fighter Group's 97th Fighter Squadron down two Ju-88s, an Italian fighter, and an Italian tri-motor floatplane.

NASAF B-25s attack Axis shipping at sea between Sicily and Tunisia, and NASAF B-17s attack a convoy in the Gulf of Tunis.

TUNISIA: NASAF B-17s attack the marshalling yard and shipping at Sousse.

March 8, 1943

FRANCE: Fifty-four VIII Bomber Command B-17s attack marshalling yards at Rennes with more than 135 tons of bombs, and 13 B-24s attack marshalling yards at Rouen with 39 tons of bombs. Two B-17s and two B-24s are downed, one each is damaged beyond repair in crash-landings in the U.K., and nine B-17s and three B-24s are damaged. Crew losses are five killed, 37 missing, and 11 wounded or injured. It is noted that GAF fighters attack in two waves, the first to engage the escort fighters and the second to directly attack the bombers.

MEDITERRANEAN: NASAF B-17s and B-25s attacking a variety of Axis ships between Sicily and Tunisia claim hits on and the possible sinking of several vessels.

TUNISIA: NASAF B-17s attack the marshalling yard and port at Sousse; and USAAF P-40s and RAF Spitfires attached to the WDAF attack the rear of German Army units moving through Medenine.

One FW-190 is downed in the morning by a 31st Fighter Group Spitfire pilot and, between 1200 and 1220 hours, 1st Fighter Group P-38 pilots down seven GAF fighters in a melee near Bizerte.

UNITED STATES: The Committee of Operations Analysts, a group of civilian and military experts, submits a report to Gen Henry H. Arnold setting forth the German aircraft industry as the top-most objective of the Allied strategic-bombing campaign and listing other German industries in order of priority. This document is the basis for the eventual Combined Bomber Offensive.

March 9, 1943

TUNISIA: All USAAF flight operations are suspended in the face of bad weather.

March 10, 1943

EGYPT: The flight echelon of the 340th Medium Bombardment Group, in B-25s, reaches El Kabrit Airdrome.

FRANCE: USAAF P-47 fighters make their combat debut in an unchallenged and uneventful fighter sweep over the French coast. Included in this mission are 14 P-47s of the newly committed 56th Fighter Group and 12 P-47s from the 4th Fighter Group, which is in the process of transitioning to the new fighter type from Spitfires. Also in the process of transitioning to the P-47 is the 78th Fighter Group, which has been headquartered in the U.K. but without airplanes since its original complement of P-38s and most of its junior pilots were transferred to other units in October 1942 to take part in Operation TORCH.

TUNISIA: NASAF B-17s attack Tunis/El Aouina Airdrome. Three Bf-109s are downed by 1st Fighter Group P-38 pilots in an action over the target between 1515 and 1530 hours.

GAF Ju-52 transports parked at the La Marsa Airdrome are attacked by NASAF B-17s, but results are not determined.

The rested and reequipped 33d Fighter Group, in brand-new P-40s, is shifted forward from Algeria to begin operations from several new rudimentary fighter strips around Sbeitla.

March 11, 1943

MEDITERRANEAN: NASAF B-26s attack an Axis convoy at sea between Sicily and Tunisia, but B-25s on anti-shipping sweeps in the area are not able to locate any targets.

Two Me-210s are downed by 82d Fighter Group P-38 pilots during a fighter sweep to Sicily.

TUNISIA: NAAF medium bombers and fighters attack German Army tanks and vehicles in the Bedja, Jefna, and Sedjenane areas.

March 12, 1943

FRANCE: Sixty-three VIII Bomber Command B-17s attack the Rouen/Sotteville marshalling yard against little or no opposition.

One of 41 4th Fighter Group Spitfires on a fighter sweep over France is downed by a GAF fighter over St.-Omer. The pilot, who is seen to bail out, is listed as missing. One FW-190 is downed by a 4th Fighter Group Spitfire pilot, the first and only claim of any sort in the theater since January 22 (and the last until April 15). Many people associated with USAAF operations in northwestern Europe are beginning to question in private the efficacy of the fighter-sweep philosophy of the VIII Fighter Command chief, MajGen Frank O'D. Hunter.

MEDITERRANEAN: NASAF B-25s attack Axis ships at sea between Sicily and Tunisia, and two Italian flying boats are

downed by 82d Fighter Group P-38 pilots near the Egadi Islands at 1345 hours.

TUNISIA: Thirty-eight NASAF B-17s attack the port facilities and marshalling yard at Sousse, and a 1st Fighter Group escort P-38 pilot downs a Bf-109 over Sousse at 1405 hours.

NASAF B-26s attack supply dumps and bridges at Enfidaville. Fighters escorting the B-26s attack various ground targets of opportunity around Pichon and Pont-du-Fahs. One Bf-109 is downed by the commanding officer of the newly recommitted 33d Fighter Group.

A 31st Fighter Groups Spitfire pilot downs a Bf-109 near Thelepte Airdrome during an early-afternoon sweep.

March 13, 1943

EGYPT: LtGen Lewis H. Brereton renames Headquarters, Desert Air Task Force, as Advanced Headquarters, Ninth Air Force, but he also designates all tactical units assigned to the advanced headquarters as the Desert Air Task Force.

FRANCE: Forty-four VIII Bomber Command B-17s attack the Amiens/Longeau marshalling yard, as assigned, but 31 B-17s fail to find the primary and therefore attack four targets of opportunity, including the rail line at Romescamps (21 B-17s) and the Abbeville/Drucat Airdrome (eight B-17s). Also, adding to the day's inept showing, 27 4th Fighter Group Spitfires that, for once, are assigned to bomber escort, fail to make the rendezvous. A total of 11 B-17s are damaged by enemy fire (including GAF fighter attacks), and six crewmen are wounded.

ITALY: IX Bomber Command B-24s attack Naples harbor through heavy cloud cover.

MEDITERRANEAN: NASAF B-25s dispatched on anti-shipping sweeps between Sicily and Tunisia fail to locate any targets.

TUNISIA: NATAF and IX Fighter Command fighters attack German Army positions along the Mareth Line.

In a long, running engagement centered on Gabes, 57th Fighter Group P-40 pilots down four Bf-109s and damage five or six others between 1405 and 1505 hours. And a Bf-109 downed over La Fauconnerie Airdrome at 1755 hours by an 81st Fighter Group P-39 fighter-bomber pilot is that unit's first victory of the war.

Following an exceptionally long break-in period (and de facto status as a manpower pool), IX Fighter Command's 79th Fighter Group is certified for combat duty, and it moves to a landing ground directly behind the British Eighth Army battle zone.

March 14, 1943

TUNISIA: In their unit's first official combat operation of the war, 12 79th Fighter Group P-40s escort 11 IX Bomber Command B-25s on an attack against gun emplacements on the Mareth Line. Otherwise, except for a few reconnaissance flights over eastern Tunisia and along shipping routes from Sicily, NAAF operations are canceled because of bad weather.

March 15, 1943

ALGERIA: BriGen Delmar H. Dunton is named to command the new Northwest African Air Service Command (NAASC), which will incorporate the XII Air Force Service Command and all USAAF and RAF organizations servicing NAAF's various operational commands.
MEDITERRANEAN: NASAF B-17s attack Axis shipping off northern Tunisia.
TUNISIA: NASAF B-26s attack the Italian Air Force airdrome Mezzouna. Later, in the afternoon, in their unit's combat debut, 25 321st Medium Bombardment Group B-25s, escorted by 33d Fighter Group P-40s, also attack Mezzouna. The B-25s complete their bomb run without encountering Axis fighters, but the escort is attacked by fighters, of which two Bf-109s and an Italian Air Force Mc.202 are downed. By downing the Mc.202, Maj Levi R. Chase, the commanding officer of the 33d Fighter Group's 60th Fighter Squadron, achieves ace status.

IX Bomber Command B-25s, escorted by 79th Fighter Group P-40s, attack Axis

troop positions at Zarat, and IX Fighter Command fighters strafe and bomb various ground targets.

In two separate fighter actions in southern Tunisia, an 82d Fighter Group P-38 pilot downs a Bf-109 near Maknassy at 1455 hours, and a 31st Fighter Group Spitfire pilot downs a Bf-109 over Sbeitla at about 1500 hours.
UNITED STATES: The 37th Fighter Squadron is formally transferred to the Twelfth Air Force's 14th Fighter Group from the 55th Fighter Group, a P-38 unit in training in Washington State. The 37th Squadron will replace the 50th Fighter Squadron, which was permanently detached from the 14th Fighter Group for service in Iceland.

March 16, 1943

EGYPT: Using personnel drawn from IX Fighter Command headquarters and the headquarters of the 8th and 9th Fighter wings, the 1st Provisional Training Group is established to oversee in-theater training of replacement fighter and medium-bomber pilots and crewmen.
MEDITERRANEAN: NASAF B-17s attacking an Axis convoy at sea between Sicily and Tunisia leave two small vessels burning from bomb hits.
TUNISIA: All NAAF bombers are grounded by bad weather.

IX Fighter Command fighter-bombers support British Eighth Army troops preparing to conduct limited assaults against the Mareth Line.

March 17, 1943

ENGLAND: All VIII Fighter Command fighters are grounded by extremely bad weather, and 78 VIII Bomber Command B-17s on their way to attack the Rouen/Sotteville marshalling yard are recalled before they leave English airspace. Also, of 44 2d Heavy Bombardment Wing B-24s dispatched on a diversionary mission over the North Sea, only 28 leave British airspace, and all of them are soon recalled.

TUNISIA: NAAF bombing operations are canceled because of bad weather, but A-20s and fighters conduct sweeps and armed-reconnaissance missions over a broad area and support U.S. II Corps infantry attacks leading to the capture of Gafsa.

IX Fighter Command fighters directly support the British Eighth Army along the Mareth Line.

March 18, 1943

ALGERIA: The Northwest African Provisional Troop Carrier Command (NATCC) is formally established as a component of the NAAF under the command of Col Ray A. Dunn. Initially, the new command consists solely of a headquarters element and the 51st Troop Carrier Wing and its subordinate units.

GERMANY: In VIII Bomber Command's forty-fifth mission of the war, 97 B-17s and B-24s attack the Vegesack U-boat yard with 268 tons of bombs. During the final moments of his unit's bomb run, 1stLt Jack W. Mathis, the 303d Heavy Bombardment Group lead bombardier, is thrown from his bombsight by the near detonation of an antiaircraft shell. Despite the traumatic amputation of an arm and many other dreadful shrapnel wounds that will prove to be mortal, Mathis struggles back to his post and releases the bombs, an act for which he is awarded a posthumous Medal of Honor. Air opposition is the heaviest encountered to date, as revealed in claims by bomber gunners of 52 GAF fighters downed and 20 probably downed. However, USAAF aircraft losses amount to one B-17 and one B-24 missing, one B-17 written off due to damage, and nine B-17s and 14 B-24s damaged. Crew losses are one killed, 16 wounded, and 20 missing, plus three crewmen injured in an emergency landing.

The Vegesack mission also marks the first successful use of experimental automatic flight control equipment (AFCE), a device that links the bombardier with the automatic pilot and thus allows the bombardier to fly the airplane during the final approach on the target. Modified AFCE devices eventually will be installed in all Eighth Air Force lead bombers.

ITALY: IX Bomber Command B-24s, escorted by IX Fighter Command P-40s, attack Naples harbor. This is IX Bomber Command's first heavy-bomber mission undertaken at maximum bombing altitude (28,000 to 30,000 feet), a move to defeat the effects of increasingly dense and accurate flak concentrations around the oft-targeted port area.

TUNISIA: All NAAF bombers are grounded by bad weather, but NATAF fighters fly numerous reconnaissance and sweep missions, and attack many ground targets of opportunity.

March 19, 1943

EGYPT: Col Uzal G. Ent replaces Col Hugo P. Rush as commander of the IX Bomber Command.

TUNISIA: All NAAF bombers are grounded by heavy rain.

March 20, 1943

ALGERIA: The Northwest African Tactical Bomber Force (NATBF) is established under NATAF control from the 47th Light Bombardment Group (A-20s), the RAF's 236 Wing, and the air echelons of two 12th Medium Bombardment Group B-25 squadrons.

ITALY: During the night of March 20–21, IX Bomber Command B-24s attack Naples harbor and city areas.

MEDITERRANEAN: 82d Fighter Group P-38s escorting NASAF B-25s on an anti-shipping sweep between Sicily and Tunisia are attacked by a reported 50 Axis aircraft from the direction of Tunis. In the ensuing battle, the P-38 pilots down two Ju-88s, eight Bf-109s, and an Italian fighter in an action 30 miles east-northeast of Pantelleria Island. In this action, which occurs at about 1230 hours, 2dLt Claude R. Kinsey, Jr., a P-38 pilot with the 82d Fighter Group's 96th Fighter Squadron, achieves ace status when he downs the Italian fighter.

In an unrelated action, a force of 17th Medium Bombardment Group B-25s on an anti-shipping sweep over the Straits of Sicily is jumped by a reported 30 GAF fighters. Taking advantage of experimental waist and tail gun positions that have been fitted out for test purposes only in 17th Group B-25s, gunners are able to hold the attacking fighters at bay. Claims for enemy fighters downed amount to seven, including four to improvised waist and tail guns. One B-25 is lost in the battle, and one is damaged beyond repair by more than 500 bulletholes.

TUNISIA: NASAF B-25s and B-26s in separate formations mount successive attacks on the Axis landing ground at Djebel Tebaga; IX Bomber Command B-25s attacking the Mareth Line through intense flak sustain many damaging hits; and, as the British Eighth Army opens what will turn out to be the final assault on the German Army's Mareth Line, IX Fighter Command fighters provide direct support against infantry and artillery emplacements.

March 21, 1943

TUNISIA: NASAF B-17s, escorted by P-38s, attack the Axis landing ground at Djebel Tebaga; NATBF A-20s and B-25s attack Djebel Tebaga and Mezzouna; and under escort by nearly 100 IX Fighter Command P-40s, IX Bomber Command B-25s attack the road through Gabes.

Between 1045 and 1055 hours, as elements of the U.S. 1st Armored Division drive to within artillery range of Maknassy, 31st Fighter Group Spitfire pilots down four Ju-87 dive-bombers and damage several Bf-109s. Also, a 1st Fighter Group P-38 pilot downs a Bf-109 over Gabes Airdrome at about 1445 hours.

March 22, 1943

EGYPT: Col John D. Corkille replaces BriGen Robert Kauch as commander of the IX Air Support Command.

GERMANY: Eighty-four of 102 VIII Bomber Command B-17s and B-24s dis-patched attack the Wilhelmshaven U-boat yards in the middle of the afternoon with 224 tons of bombs. Three bombers are lost, 22 bombers are damaged, one crewman is killed, 18 crewmen are wounded, and 32 crewmen are listed as missing in action.

MEDITERRANEAN: NASAF B-26s conducting an anti-shipping sweep between Sicily and Tunisia attack several Axis vessels at sea near Zembra Island.

SICILY: In the first bomber mission mounted against Sicily from Northwest Africa, 24 301st Heavy Bombardment Group B-17s attack port facilities at Palermo harbor with nearly 72 tons of bombs. Two 120-foot vessels are demolished, other ships are damaged, and major damage is caused to docking and warehouse facilities.

TUNISIA: IX Bomber Command B-25s attack road junctions, troop concentrations, and motor transport throughout the Gabes area; and NATBF A-20s attack Mezzouna Airdrome. 82d Fighter Group P-38 pilots down two Italian Air Force Mc.202s and nine Bf-109s north of Bizerte between 1345 and 1400 hours; 52d Fighter Group Spitfire escort pilots down two Ju-88s, two FW-190s, and six Bf-109s over Mezzouna Airdrome at about 1530 hours; and a 79th Fighter Group P-40 pilot downs one Bf-109 (the unit's first official score) near Mareth at 1610 hours. The final fighter tally—22 Axis aircraft downed—is the best one-day score run up by USAAF pilots so far in the war against Germany and her allies.

March 23, 1943

TUNISIA: While attacking numerous ground targets throughout eastern Tunisia, pilots of the 31st, 52d, and 82d Fighter groups are engaged in several aerial actions in which two Bf-109s are downed and six are damaged between 0950 and 1030 hours.

NASAF B-17s attack shipping in Bizerte harbor, and 1st Fighter Group P-38 escort pilots down three Bf-109s at 1235 hours. One of the Bf-109s is credited to

1stLt John L. Wolford, of the 27th Fighter Squadron, who thus achieves ace status.

March 24, 1943

SICILY: IX Bomber Command B-24s attack the ferry terminal, rail yard, and fuel storage tanks in and around the Messina port area.

TUNISIA: NASAF B-17s attack port facilities and shipping at Ferryville; NASAF B-26s attack the La Smala des Souassi landing ground; NASAF B-25s attack the Djebel Tebaga landing ground; and NATBF A-20s and B-25s attack Axis troop concentrations in direct support of the U.S. 1st Armored Division attack on El Guettar, as well as the Djebel Tebaga landing ground.

Two 81st Fighter Group P-39 dive-bomber pilots share in the downing of an Fi-156 observation plane at about 0700 hours; 33d Fighter Group P-40 pilots down seven Bf-109s in a sporadic engagement around Djebel Tebaga between 0905 and 1035 hours; and 52d Fighter Group Spitfire pilots down three Bf-109s and an FW-190 between Gafsa and Maknassy during the late afternoon.

IX Bomber Command B-25s directly supporting a British Eighth Army ground assault continuously attack German Army defensive positions around Zarat for three hours. Following the breakthrough, however, the ground forces are halted by German artillery, which is relentlessly attacked for more than two hours by RAF fighters and IX Fighter Command P-40s from the 57th, 79th, and 324th Fighter groups. (The 324th Fighter Group is represented by two squadrons that happen to be in the forward area as part of IX Fighter Command's combat-familiarization training syllabus. One of the 324th's squadrons is attached to the 57th Fighter Group, and the other is attached to the 79th Fighter Group.) As a result of the continuous air attacks, the ground forces are able to break through on the Mareth Line's inland flank. Five P-40s are downed, one pilot is lost, and two pilots are taken prisoner.

During the night of March 24–25, NATBF A-20s and B-25s attack German Army motor vehicles west of Sfax and Sousse.

March 25, 1943

ENGLAND: The Eighth Air Force establishes the 201st Provisional Combat Bombardment Wing to oversee combat operations of B-24 groups assigned to VIII Bomber Command's 2d Heavy Bombardment Wing. Col Edward J. Timberlake, the commanding officer of the 93d Heavy Bombardment Group, is reassigned as commander of the provisional wing.

The 44th and 93d Heavy Bombardment groups are assigned to the 201st Provisional Combat Bombardment Wing.

TUNISIA: NASAF B-17s attack port facilities and shipping at Sousse; through the day, the Djebel Tebaga landing ground is attacked, in succession, by NASAF B-25s, NATBF A-20s and B-25s, and XII Air Support Command B-25s and escorting fighters; and numerous NAAF fighters undertake attacks on various kinds of ground targets throughout eastern Tunisia.

Two Bf-109s and an FW-190 are downed by USAAF fighter pilots in at least three separate actions during the day.

March 26, 1943

TUNISIA: NASAF B-25s attack targets around Grombalia, but all other NASAF missions are aborted or canceled because of bad weather. However, 81st Fighter Group P-39s destroy several German Army trucks, and NATAF fighters, A-20s, and B-25s attack a fuel dump, roads, rail lines, and the Sfax dock area, and strafe the Djebel Tebaga landing ground and motor vehicles encountered between Faid and Gabes. Also, one Ju-88 is downed near the coast at 0940 hours by an 82d Fighter Group P-38 pilot.

IX Bomber Command B-25s mount two missions against targets along the Mareth Line, and P-40s damage an estimated 50 trucks, tanks, and other vehicles in strafing and bombing attacks. However, several USAAF fighters are lost to intense ground fire.

The British Eighth Army renews its ground attack on the Mareth Line.

March 27, 1943

TUNISIA: NATAF fighters attack numerous ground targets, but NAAF bombers are grounded by bad weather.

March 28, 1943

ENGLAND: The Eighth Air Force's "moling" experiment—attempts to trigger German air-defense systems on days on which the VIII Bomber Command is grounded by bad weather—is abandoned following seven failures since January 2 (see explanation), all caused by *good* weather over Germany. Despite the failure of the moling experiment, Eighth Air Force B-24 crews from the 93d Heavy Bombardment Group's 329th Heavy Bombardment Squadron have gained valuable blind-bombing experience that will prove to be crucial in coming months.

FRANCE: Seventy VIII Bomber Command B-17s attack the Rouen/Sotteville marshalling yard with 209 tons of bombs, but all 23 B-24s dispatched are recalled due to bad weather. Losses are one B-17 downed and nine damaged, two crewmen wounded, and 10 crewmen missing.

In the first sortie of its kind undertaken under Eighth Air Force command, a 13th Photographic Squadron F-5A (P-38 variant) photographs enemy positions north of Dieppe. Based on the findings, an RAF bomber mission will be mounted the next day against a marshalling yard at Le Treport.

ITALY: Three IX Bomber Command B-24s dispatched via Malta to mount an experimental low-level attack against the ferry terminal at Messina fail to rendezvous, but one B-24 attacks a chemical plant at Crotone, Italy, and another attacks the Vibo Valentia Airdrome, in Sicily.

TUNISIA: Although most NAAF bombers are grounded by bad weather, NASAF B-26s attacking Gabes Airdrome find that the base has been abandoned (presumably the day before) by its complement of GAF fighters, which have apparently been withdrawn to the Cap Bon area.

NATAF fighters conduct numerous offensive sweeps throughout eastern Tunisia, especially in support of heavy ground fighting near Mezzouna; and IX Fighter Command P-40 fighter-bombers attack ground targets at El Hamma, which German Army ground units are using as an escape route from the collapsing Mareth Line.

During the night of March 28–29, NAAF bombers attack roads, rail lines, and military transport in the Sfax and Sousse areas.

March 29, 1943

TUNISIA: All NAAF aircraft are grounded by bad weather, but some NATAF fighters are able to attack various motor transport and troop concentrations along the battlefront. In the course of these attacks, 33d Fighter Group P-40 pilots down seven Bf-109s in desultory morning engagements centered on Faid Pass; and 31st Fighter Group Spitfire pilots down three FW-190s over El Guettar between 1430 and 1450 hours.

IX Bomber Command B-25s attack the Sfax/El Maou Airdrome, and IX Fighter Command P-40s complete numerous fighter-bomber missions in support of British Eighth Army units pursuing fleeing German Army forces through Gabes. By the end of the day, Gabes falls to British ground forces, and the Eighth Army completes the occupation of the Mareth Line.

March 30, 1943

TUNISIA: All NAAF medium and heavy bombers are grounded by bad weather, but NATBF A-20s that are able to get airborne attack La Fauconnerie Airdrome as well as directly support an attack by U.S. Army ground forces on Djebel Berda; NAAF fighters attack numerous ground targets; IX

Bomber Command B-25s attack Sfax/El Maou Airdrome; and IX Fighter Command P-40s support British Eighth Army ground attacks.

Pilots of the 33d and 52d Fighter groups down ten Bf-109s and damage 11 others during a major engagement over and around La Fauconnerie Airdrome between 0807 and 0945 hours.

As German Army forces in southern Tunisia establish a new defensive line along the Oued el-Akarit River, the British Eighth Army halts its advance to reorganize and await reinforcements.

March 31, 1943

MEDITERRANEAN: NASAF B-25s dispatched on anti-shipping sweeps between Sicily and Tunisia attack several Axis ships at sea off northeastern Tunisia.

82d Fighter Group P-38 pilots down a Bf-109 and a Ju-88 off Cap Zambra during the late afternoon.

NETHERLANDS: Following the collision and loss of two 303d Heavy Bombardment Group B-17s during the assembly, an attack by 103 VIII Bomber Command heavy bombers fizzles when heavy cloud cover is encountered over the target. Thirty-three B-17s drop a total of 99 tons of bombs on several shipyards, but the others return to their bases fully loaded. Losses due to enemy action are three B-17s and a B-24 missing, one battle-damaged B-17 written off after its entire crew bails out over England, and four B-17s and one B-24 damaged. Crew losses are one killed by enemy fire, 15 killed in the collision, ten wounded, and ten missing.

SARDINIA: NASAF B-17s—including a number compiling the combat debut of the 99th Heavy Bombardment Group—simultaneously attack the Decimomannu, Monserrato, and Villacidro airdromes and Cagliari harbor.

TUNISIA: NATAF A-20s, B-25s, and fighters attack La Fauconnerie Airdrome and numerous tactical targets throughout the shrinking Axis holdings in eastern Tunisia; IX Bomber Command B-25s and elements of the WDAF attack the Sfax/El Maou Airdrome; and IX Fighter Command P-40s attack numerous ground targets of opportunity, particularly motor vehicles along the highway north of Gabes.

While supporting a late-afternoon ground-attack mission, 33d Fighter Group P-40 pilots down nine Bf-109s and four Ju-87s near El Guettar. All of the Ju-87s are credited to Col William W. Momyer, the commanding officer of the 33d Fighter Group, who thus achieves ace status and a final personal tally of eight confirmed victories.

The attack by IX Bomber Command B-25s on Sfax/El Maou Airdrome includes aircraft and crews from the 340th Medium Bombardment Group, which are undertaking a combat-familiarization course following the recent arrival of their unit in Egypt via the southern ferry route. In this combat debut, however, two of the 340th Group's aircraft are lost at sea, but both crews are recovered.

APRIL 1943

April 1, 1943

SICILY: Two IX Bomber Command B-24s staging through Malta mount an experimental low-level attack (from 100 feet) against the ferry terminal at Messina. Many direct hits are observed, and the B-24's low-level bombing capability is confirmed.

TUNISIA: NATBF A-20s attack La Fauconnerie Airdrome and the El Djem landing ground, and conduct numerous attacks against the German Army in the Sidi Mansour-Djebel Tebaga region; and IX Bomber Command medium and light bombers attack flak batteries and Axis aircraft parked at Sfax/El Maou Airdrome.

By helping to down a Ju-88 during the day, SSgt James E. Butler, a 52d Fighter Group Spitfire pilot, becomes the only USAAF enlisted fighter pilot to score an aerial victory in World War II. (Butler will score a total of four aerial victories while flying with enlisted rank.) In other fighter action, pilots of the 31st, 33d, and 52d Fighter groups are credited with five Bf-109s and four Ju-88s, bringing the day's tally to ten.

UNITED STATES: The advance air echelons of the 94th and 351st Heavy Bombardment groups, both in B-17s, depart for England for service with the 1st Heavy Bombardment Wing's 101st Provisional Combat Bombardment Wing.

April 2, 1943

ITALY: When 27 IX Bomber Command B-24s dispatched against Naples find the target area totally obscured by clouds, nine release their bombs through the clouds and three attack targets of opportunity their bombardiers can see.

SICILY: Two IX Bomber Command B-24s conduct a special mission in which one each attacks the ferry terminals at Messina and Villa San Giovanni, Italy. However, 24 IX Bomber Command B-24s dispatched to attack Palermo abort in the face of heavy clouds obscuring the target area.

TUNISIA: NATBF A-20s and B-25s attack La Fauconnerie Airdrome.

USAAF fighter pilots down four Bf-109s in at least three separate actions during the day. One of them, Capt Lyman Middleditch, Jr., a P-40 pilot with the 57th

Fighter Group's 64th Fighter Squadron, achieves ace status when he downs a Bf-109 at 1540 hours.

April 3, 1943

TUNISIA: All NASAF bombers are grounded by bad weather; NATAF aircraft attack Axis military vehicles in eastern Tunisia; NATBF B-25s attack Ste.-Marie du Zit Airdrome; IX Bomber Command B-25s attack Sfax/El Maou Airdrome; and WDAF A-20s attack Axis motor vehicles and gun emplacements.

In a lopsided attack near El Guettar at about 1730 hours, Spitfire pilots of the 52d Fighter Group's 2d Fighter Squadron down 13 Ju-87 dive-bombers in a matter of minutes. Four 2d Fighter Squadron pilots each down two of the Ju-87s, but high-scoring honors go to Capt Norman L. McDonald, who achieves ace status when he downs three Ju-87s. Also achieving ace status is Capt Arnold E. Vinson, who downs one Ju-87. Unfortunately, Vinson is shot down and killed.

The main body of the IX Bomber Command's 12th Medium Bombardment Group displaces forward to Medenine Airdrome.

April 4, 1943

FRANCE: Eighty-five VIII Bomber Command B-17s conduct a precision-bombing attack against the Paris Renault Billancourt works, the first USAAF mission within Paris city limits. Despite intense flak and concerted attacks by GAF fighters, 251 tons of bombs fall more or less within the target area. Four B-17s are listed as missing and 16 are damaged. Crew losses are 39 missing and six wounded.
ITALY: Ninety-nine IX Bomber Command B-17s and 64 XII Bomber Command B-24s attack the Capodichino Airdrome, port facilities, barracks, power plants, and gas works throughout Naples; and NASAF B-25s attack several small Axis ships at Carloforte, San Pietro Island.
TUNISIA: NASAF B-25s attack the El

Djem landing ground; NAAF P-38s dive-bomb a beached freighter at Cape Zebib; NATBF A-20s attack La Fauconnerie Airdrome; and NATBF B-25s attack the El Djem landing ground and Ste.-Marie du Zit Airdrome.

NAAF and IX Fighter Command fighters accompanying the various bomber missions attack numerous ground targets throughout the battle area. In the course of at least four separate afternoon aerial engagements, USAAF pilots down five Bf-109s and an Mc.202.
UNITED STATES: The first air echelon of the 96th Heavy Bombardment Group, in B-17s, departs for England via the northern ferry route for service with the Eighth Air Force.

April 5, 1943

BELGIUM: Sixty-four VIII Bomber Command B-17s and 18 B-24s attack industrial targets around Antwerp with more than 245 tons of bombs. Flak and GAF fighter opposition account for four B-17s missing, 12 B-17s and B-24 damaged, 40 crewmen missing, and three crewmen wounded, of whom one will die several weeks later. The Belgian ambassador to the U.S. protests the high casualty rate among civilians caused by misdropped bombs.
NORTH AFRICAN THEATER: Operation FLAX is launched by Allied air commands to cut off the flow of reinforcements and supplies being flown from Italy to Axis-held air bases in Tunisia. The general air offensive of which FLAX is a part is in support of Operation VULCAN, the upcoming final Allied ground offensive in Tunisia.

At 0800 hours, during a sweep over the Straits of Sicily aimed at interdicting the German aerial line of supply, 26 1st Fighter Group P-38s encounter a formation of 50 to 70 multi-engine aircraft (mostly transports) and 30 escort fighters, all about 25 miles northeast of Cap Bon. In relentless attacks in which just two P-38s are lost, the USAAF pilots down 11 Ju-52s, one FW-187, two Ju-87s, three Bf-109s, and two other unidentified aircraft. Capt Darrell G. Welch, a P-38 pilot with the 1st Fighter Group's 27th Fighter Squadron, achieves ace status when he downs three Ju-52s.

Within twenty minutes of the first attack, a force of 18 310th Medium Bombardment Group B-25s, escorted by 82d Fighter Group P-38s, arrives in the same area to attack an Axis surface resupply convoy from Sicily that is being covered by a force of GAF fighters from bases in Tunisia. As the B-25s attack and demolish a destroyer and damage two freighters, the P-38s engage the covering GAF fighters and another aerial resupply convoy that happens to fly into the fight. In this battle, the 82d Fighter Group P-38 pilots are credited with nine Ju-52s, three Ju-87s, three Bf-109s, one Bf-110, and one Me-210. USAAF losses are four P-38s and their pilots and one B-25 and its crew.

Next, late in the morning, 36 321st Medium Bombardment Group B-25s, escorted by 18 82d Fighter Group P-38s, attack Bo Rizzo Airdrome, Sicily, one of the originating points for the Axis aerial resupply effort. Light fragmentation bombs are thought to destroy or damage as many as 90 airplanes parked at Bo Rizzo. The P-38s engage GAF fighters on the way home over the Egadi Islands, downing two Bf-109s. Also downed on this mission are two B-25s.

Afternoon bombing missions associated with Operation FLAX are as follows: 18 B-17s escorted by USAAF Spitfires attack Bizerte/Sidi Ahmed Airdrome with unknown results; 22 B-17s escorted by USAAF Spitfires attack Tunis/El Aouina Airdrome, destroying an estimated 30 Axis aircraft, mostly transports; an attack by 22 B-17s on Bocca di Falco Airdrome, Sicily, is thought to destroy or damage as many as 150 Axis aircraft on the ground, and bomber gunners claim three fighters shot down; and 28 B-17s, escorted by 16 P-38s, attack Trapani/Milo Airdrome, Sicily, where an estimated 52 Axis transports and bombers are damaged or destroyed.

Two afternoon P-38 fighter sweeps over the Mediterranean fail to encounter any Axis aircraft but throughout the day, in addition to credits already cited, pilots of the 31st, 33d, and 52d Fighter groups down a total of 14 Axis fighters, bringing the day's tally to 47, the highest so far in the war against Germany and her allies. Also of special note this day is the accomplishment of Maj Levi R. Chase, Jr., the commanding officer of the 33d Fighter Group's 60th Fighter Squadron. By downing two Bf-109s in an afternoon action over La Fauconnerie Airdrome, Tunisia, Chase becomes the first USAAF double ace in the theater. (In 1945, by shooting down two Japanese fighters in the same action over Burma, Chase also will become one of only three USAAF pilots to score confirmed victories against German, Italian, and Japanese aircraft.) (It should be noted that German records show that, among GAF transports lost throughout April 5, 1943, only 14 Ju-52s were shot down, only 11 Ju-52s and Me-323s were destroyed on the ground, and only 67 other transports were damaged in the air and on the ground.)

TUNISIA: NATBF A-20s attack the El Djem landing ground and La Fauconnerie Airdrome; NAAF fighters attack German Navy E-boats encountered off Pont-du-Fahs and German Army motor vehicles near Bou Hamran; and WDAF aircraft attack various ground targets in support of Allied ground operations.

April 6, 1943

MEDITERRANEAN: Acting on short notice, 301st Heavy Bombardment Group B-17s launch against a convoy of Axis transports and freighters that is approaching Bizerte. Attacking through extremely intense flak sent up by both shipboard and shore-based batteries, the B-17s hold formation at 10,500 feet, hit the largest ship, which is filled with munitions, and blow it clean out of the water. The detonation is large enough to damage several of the bombers. Near misses are also scored against another freighter and an escort vessel. GAF fighters attack the withdrawing bombers. No bombers are lost, but the attacks by the GAF fighters account for nine crewmen wounded. Bomber gunners claim eight GAF fighters downed, plus three probably downed.

Shortly after the 301st Heavy Bombardment Group B-17s return to their base at St.-Donat Airdome, Algeria, an Allied reconnaissance airplane locates two of the Italian Navy's three remaining cruisers, the *Trieste* and the *Gorizia*. The two are anchored behind a wall of submarine nets in a cove near La Maddalena, in northern Sardinia. All available NAAF B-17s are immediately armed with 1,000-pound bombs and dispatched with a heavy long-range fighter escort. The attack force is divided into three groups: one mixed group of 24 B-17s is sent to bomb the harbor installations; one group of 36 97th Bombardment Group B-17s is sent after the *Gorizia;* and one group of 24 301st Heavy Bombardment Group B-17s is sent after the *Trieste*. The harbor facilities and the *Gorizia* are badly damaged by bombs, and the *Trieste* is sunk by several direct hits.

SICILY: NAAF B-17s attack port facilities and shipping at Trapani, and IX Bomber Command B-24s attack the ferry terminal at Messina.

TUNISIA: NATBF A-20s and B-25s attack Enfidaville Airdrome, La Fauconnerie Airdrome, and the El Djem landing ground.

The day's only confirmed aerial victory is scored by a 31st Fighter Group Spitfire pilot over La Fauconnerie Airdrome in the morning.

In direct support of a new British Eighth Army offensive that quickly breaches the German Army defenses along the Oued el-Akarit River, IX Bomber Command B-25s mount two separate missions against German Army troop concentrations.

April 7, 1943

SICILY: IX Bomber Command B-24s attack Palermo harbor.

TUNISIA: All NASAF bombers are grounded by bad weather, but IX Bomber Command, IX Fighter Command, XII Air Support Command, and the WDAF mount an all-out effort to harry German Army forces retreating before massive Allied ground attacks throughout Tunisia. USAAF fighter pilots, whose units are involved in numerous escort and ground-support missions, down three Bf-109s during at least three separate fighter actions.

By day's end, the British Eighth Army and U.S. II Corps are in direct physical contact on the ground for the first time. Further pointing up the ascendancy of the Allied war effort in the region, following weeks of unremitting attacks by USAAF and RAF tactical and strategic bombers, Axis air units are withdrawn from nearly all their airdromes and landing grounds in southern Tunisia.

April 8, 1943

FRANCE: The 56th and 78th Fighter groups are declared fully operational. An unchallenged fighter sweep (RODEO mission) between Dunkirk and Sangatte is the first all-P-47 operation of the war. Participating are 17 P-47s from the 4th Fighter Group (which has transitioned completely from Spitfires), with 12 78th Fighter Group P-47s and four 56th Fighter Group P-47s attached for purposes of giving their pilots operational experience.

TUNISIA: All NASAF bombers are grounded by bad weather, but NATAF and WDAF fighters manage to get airborne to attack retreating German Army units. Also, IX Bomber Command and IX Fighter Command aircraft mount an all-out effort to harass the retreating Axis forces.

One Bf-109 is downed by a 52d Fighter Group Spitfire pilot in an engagement near Kairouan at 1650 hours.

April 9, 1943

LIBYA: Following completion of its in-theater training cycle, the 340th Medium Bombardment Group, in B-25s, is declared operational and formally released to the IX Bomber Command for combat duty.

TUNISIA: All NASAF bombers are grounded by bad weather, but NAAF and IX Fighter Command fighters attack Axis troops and facilities throughout northern Tunisia.

52d Fighter Group Spitfire pilots down nine Ju-88s around Kairouan at about 1740 hours.

While on a photo-reconnaissance sortie from Sbeitla to Kairouan, a 154th Observation Squadron pilot engages in the first combat mission in the theater by a North American P-51A Mustang fighter, one of several on loan to his unit for combat testing.

April 10, 1943

ITALY: IX Bomber Command B-24s attack Naples.

LIBYA: The IX Fighter Command headquarters displaces from Egypt to Tripoli.

MEDITERRANEAN: As part of Operation FLAX, 1st Fighter Group P-38 pilots down eight Axis fighters and twenty GAF Ju-52 transports in an attack on the Axis air line of supply linking Sicily with German bases in Tunisia. The attack takes place between 0747 and 0757 hours over the sea about 20 miles east-northeast of Cap Bon. High-scoring honors go to 1stLt Meldrum W. Sears of the 71st Fighter Squadron, whose credits for four Ju-52 transports renders him an ace with seven confirmed victories overall. 2dLt Walter J. Rivers, also of the 71st Fighter Squadron, is also credited with four victories in this action, two Ju-52s and two Mc.200 fighters.

In an unrelated action that begins at 1240 hours, 82d Fighter Group P-38s attack another Axis air-supply convoy, this time just a mile north of Cap Bon. In this action, 13 GAF transports and fighters are downed. 2dLt Ray Crawford of the 95th Fighter Squadron achieves ace status when he downs two Ju-52s.

SARDINIA: NASAF B-17s attack La Maddalena.

TUNISIA: NASAF B-26s and NATAF fighter-bombers attack German Army troops and motor vehicles around Enfidaville, and 33d Fighter Group P-40 pilots down five Bf-109s in a midafternoon engagement north of Enfidaville.

Late in the day, Sfax falls to the British Eighth Army.

April 11, 1943

EGYPT: Col John D. Corkille is replaced as commander of IX Air Support Command by Col Wycliffe E. Steele.

ITALY: IX Bomber Command B-24s attacking Naples harbor are assailed by intense flak and fighter attacks from all quarters. One B-24 is downed.

MEDITERRANEAN: P-38 pilots of the 82d Fighter Group's 95th Fighter Squadron intercept an Axis air convoy over the Straits of Sicily and down 20 Ju-52s, two Ju-88s, and five GAF fighters between Marsala, Sicily, and Cap Bon, Tunisia, at about 0800 hours. 1stLt William J. Schildt achieves ace status when he downs three Ju-52s.

At 1030 hours, P-38 pilots of the 82d Fighter Group's 96th Fighter Squadron down five Ju-52s near Marettimo Island.

SICILY: NASAF B-17s attack Marsala and Trapani.

TUNISIA: NASAF B-17s attack Tunis; NAAF B-26s attack Oudna Airdrome; NAAF B-25s attack Ste.-Marie du Zit Airdrome; IX Bomber Command B-25s attack Axis motor vehicles and troop concentrations near Sfax; and NATBF A-20s and NATAF fighter-bombers attack German Army motor columns around Enfidaville.

Kairouan falls to British and American ground forces.

April 12, 1943

ENGLAND: In accordance with a directive issued during the Casablanca Conference, a plan for the proposed Combined Bomber Offensive is completed by a panel of RAF and USAAF officers.

ITALY: B-24s of the IX Bomber

Command's 376th Heavy Bombardment Group dispatched to attack Naples harbor turn back in the face of bad weather over the target. Approximately half the group returns to base with bombs aboard, but the remaining B-24s attack targets of opportunity at Cosenza and Crotone. A second mission is mounted later in the day, also by the 376th; Naples is attacked, as is the briefed secondary, Pizzo.

MEDITERRANEAN: NASAF B-17s attack Axis ships in the Straits of Sicily.

SICILY: NASAF B-17s attack the harbor at Trapani.

TUNISIA: NASAF B-17s attack Bizerte harbor; NATBF A-20s and B-25s attack Oudna and Ste.-Marie du Zit airdromes; and NAAF fighters mount numerous attacks on Axis ground forces and installations throughout northern Tunisia.

1st Fighter Group P-38 pilots down four GAF fighters in a morning action just to the west of Tunis at about 0800 hours. The 71st Fighter Squadron's Capt Lee V. Wiseman achieves ace status in this fight when he downs a Bf-109.

Sousse falls to the British Eighth Army.

April 13, 1943

ENGLISH CHANNEL: In the first of two separate fighter missions, 20 4th Fighter Group P-47s are joined while escorting RAF bombers (RAMROD mission) by four 56th Fighter Group P-47s and 12 78th Fighter Group P-47s. In what is considered to be the 78th Fighter Group's official combat debut, one of its P-47s suffers an engine failure over the English Channel, but the pilot is picked up by the Air-Sea Rescue Service after bailing out. The mission is unchallenged.

FRANCE: The 56th Fighter Group clocks its first official mission of the war when 12 of its P-47s join 12 from the 78th Fighter Group and 16 from the 4th Fighter Group for an unchallenged fighter sweep (RODEO mission) to St.-Omer.

SARDINIA: XII Fighter Command P-38s mount bombing attacks against an Italian

Navy cruiser at La Madallena and other Axis ships at Porto Torres.

SICILY: NASAF B-17s attack Castelvetrano and Trapani/Milo airdromes, but IX Bomber Command B-24s dispatched to attack the harbor at Catania are thwarted by heavy cloud cover over the target.

TUNISIA: NAAF B-25s attack Oudna Airdrome.

April 14, 1943

SARDINIA: NASAF B-17s attack Elmas and Monserrato airdromes.

TUNISIA: NASAF B-17s attack Tunis/El Aouina Airdrome, and escorting P-38s strafe an Axis ship beached near Cape Zebib; NATBF A-20s attack Bordj Toum; and NATAF fighter-bombers attack an Axis truck convoy and an artillery battery.

IX Fighter Command's 79th Fighter Group displaces forward to La Fauconnerie Airdrome, near Sfax.

April 15, 1943

BELGIUM: During a series of fighter sweeps between Furnes and St.-Omer, France, by 57 P-47s of the 4th, 56th, and 78th Fighter groups, three 4th Fighter Group P-47 pilots down three FW-190s between Knocke and Ostend. These are the first enemy airplanes ever downed by P-47s. However, three 4th Fighter Group P-47s are also downed. Two pilots are lost, but the third is rescued from the North Sea.

ENGLAND: The first air echelon of the 95th Heavy Bombardment Group, in B-17s, arrives from the United States via the southern ferry route.

MEDITERRANEAN: NACAF B-26s on an anti-shipping sweep in the Naples area attack an Axis ship at sea south of Ustica Island.

SICILY: IX Bomber Command B-24s attack the harbors and Catania and Palermo.

TUNISIA: NATAF fighters attack ground targets of opportunity throughout northern Tunisia, and IX Bomber Command B-25s attack the airdrome and a large fuel dump at Ste.-Marie du Zit.

The main body of IX Bomber Command's 12th Medium Bombardment Group displaces forward to Sfax\El Maou Airdrome. Also, the new 340th Medium Bombardment Group is ordered to displace to Sfax from its training base in Egypt.

UNITED STATES: The 379th Heavy Bombardment Group air echelon, in B-17s, begins moving to England via the southern ferry route for service with the 1st Heavy Bombardment Wing's 101st Provisional Combat Bombardment Wing.

April 16, 1943

FRANCE: Fifty-nine of 83 VIII Bomber Command B-17s dispatched attack the Lorient U-boat base against moderate opposition with 147 tons of bombs. Losses are one B-17 missing and eight damaged, ten crewmen missing, and seven crewmen wounded. An attempt by an F-5 photo-reconnaissance plane to assess the bomb damage—the first such mission by an Eighth Air Force unit—is hindered by cloud cover.

In a second attack, this by 2d Bombardment Wing B-24s, 52 tons of bombs are dropped through a heavy smokescreen on the Brest U-boat base. Losses in this action are three B-24s missing and nine damaged, 31 crewmen missing, and three crewmen wounded.

MEDITERRANEAN: NAAF P-38s mount bombing attacks against Axis ships at sea near Cape Zebib and Cape el-Ahmr. Also, while on fighter sweeps over the Mediterranean associated with Operation FLAX, 82d Fighter Group P-38 pilots down a flying boat south of Sicily at 0745 hours and a Bf-109 near Marettimo Island at 1550 hours.

SICILY: NASAF B-17s attack Palermo harbor, and IX Bomber Command B-24s attacking a tanker at Catania harbor claim several hits.

TUNISIA: NATAF bombers, fighter-bombers, and fighters mount an all-out effort against Axis ground forces, and NASAF B-26s attack the Oudna Airdrome.

The British Eighth Army links up with the U.S. II Corps.

April 17, 1943

GERMANY: Breasting what crew reports describe as the heaviest opposition to date, the largest force of VIII Bomber Command heavy bombers to reach a target so far in the war—107 B-17s—attack aircraft-industry targets at Bremen with more than 265 tons of bombs. Bomber gunners claim 63 GAF fighters downed and 15 probably downed against the heaviest losses sustained until now by the Eighth Air Force in a single mission—16 bombers missing and 39 damaged, two crewmen killed, 159 crewmen missing, and four crewmen wounded. Six of the lost crews are from the 91st Heavy Bombardment Group's 401st Heavy Bombardment Squadron. It is noted that FW-190 fighters unveil a new tactic, that of attacking the heavy bombers in waves so as to bring a maximum amount of firepower to bear at one time.

MEDITERRANEAN: NACAF bombers and fighters attack Axis ships at sea in the Straits of Sicily. In an action at 1540 hours, 82d Fighter Group P-38 pilots down one Ju-88 and four Italian Fiat Br.20 medium bombers near Zembra Island. Maj Harley C. Vaughn, the commanding officer of the 82d Fighter Group's 96th Fighter Squadron, achieves ace status when he downs the Ju-88.

SICILY: NASAF B-17s attack shipping and port facilities at Palermo, and escorting P-38 pilots of the 1st Fighter Group's 94th Fighter Squadron down three Ju-88s and damage at least ten other GAF aircraft in an engagement over the target at 1300 hours. Also, IX Bomber Command B-17s and a squadron of RAF Liberators attack Catania.

TUNISIA: NASAF B-17s attack shipping and port facilities at Ferryville, and NATBF A-20s attack a variety of targets in support of Allied ground units.

In their unit's combat debut, 36 P-40s of the 325th Fighter Group's 318th and

319th Fighter squadrons escort B-25s of NASAF's 319th Medium Bombardment Group on an afternoon mission against the GAF airdrome at Mateur. When GAF fighters attack the strike group, the P-40s keep them at bay, but one of the P-40s and its pilot are lost. On the other hand, a pilot from the 318th Fighter Squadron scores the group's first confirmed victory of the war. (The 325th Fighter Group arrived in North Africa in late February, but its aircraft were soon commandeered for use by the 33d Fighter Group. Only enough new aircraft have been received to date to reequip the two squadrons in action this day; there are not enough yet to reequip the group's 317th Fighter Squadron.)

IX Fighter Command's 79th Fighter Group displaces forward to the landing ground at Hani, and the 57th Fighter Group displaces forward to the El Djem landing ground. Both units are thus able to reach a considerable distance across the Axis Mediterranean aerial resupply routes.

April 18, 1943

MEDITERRANEAN: Beginning at about 1750 hours, at least 61 Ju-52s and 15 Bf-109s are downed over the Gulf of Tunis when they are engaged by 12 RAF Spitfires and 46 P-40s from the IX Fighter Command's 57th Fighter Group and an attached squadron of the 324th Fighter Group. In the course of the so-called Palm Sunday Massacre, three of the USAAF fighter pilots are credited with five aerial victories apiece: 2dLt Richard E. Duffy of the 324th Fighter Group (five Ju-52s); 2dLt MacArthur Powers of the 324th Fighter Group (four Ju-52s and a Bf-109 fighter—plus 2.5 victory credits that might have been awarded while he served earlier with the RAF); and 2dLt Arthur B. Cleaveland of the 57th Fighter Group (five Ju-52s). Also achieving ace status in this action is Capt Roy E. Whittaker of the 57th Fighter Group's 65th Fighter Squadron, whose downing of three Ju-52s and a Bf-109 brings his final personal tally to seven confirmed

victories. Six P-40s and a Spitfire are lost in the action.

SARDINIA: NASAF B-25s attack Alghero/Fertilla Airdrome and shipping at Porto Torres.

SICILY: Seventy-five NASAF B-17s attack a marshalling yard at Palermo and the Bocca di Falco Airdrome, and IX Bomber Command B-24s attack Catania.

TUNISIA: Ninth Air Force fighters attack a variety of tactical ground targets throughout Axis-held Tunisia, and IX Bomber Command B-25s attack several Axis landing grounds.

1stLt Sylvan Feld, a Spitfire pilot with the 52d Fighter Group's 2d Fighter Squadron, achieves ace status when he downs an FW-190 east of Tunis at 1530 hours.

April 19, 1943

TUNISIA: NASAF B-17s attack shipping at Tunis; NATBF A-20s attack La Sebala Airdrome; NATAF fighter-bombers attack German Army tanks along the active battlefront; and IX Bomber Command B-25s attack Axis landing grounds and German Army defensive positions.

In the course of three separate aerial engagements between 1040 and 1730 hours, pilots of the 31st and 52d Fighter groups down five GAF fighters.

April 20, 1943

MEDITERRANEAN: During a dawn sweep over the sea northwest of Cap Bon, 79th Fighter Group P-40 pilots down three Bf-109s and two Ju-88s.

TUNISIA: NASAF B-17s and B-25s attack the Axis landing grounds and airdromes at Creteville, La Marsa, La Sebala, Mabtouha, Protville, and Bizerte/Sidi Ahmed.

52d Fighter Group Spitfire pilots down five Bf-109s and two FW-190s north and west of Tunis between 0915 and 0920 hours.

The British Eighth Army captures Enfidaville.

April 21, 1942

MEDITERRANEAN: 79th Fighter Group

P-40 pilots down three Bf-109s near Cap Bon during a dawn sweep, and IX Fighter Command P-40s strafe and bomb barges along the coast.

NETHERLANDS: In VIII Fighter Command's deepest penetrations to date, a total of 82 P-47s conduct high-altitude fighter sweeps over three distinct areas of the Netherlands. For all that, GAF fighters fail to rise to the bait, and the sweeps are unchallenged.

TUNISIA: NASAF medium and heavy bombers are grounded by bad weather, but NATBF A-20s, fighters, and fighter-bombers mount a variety of missions in support of Allied ground forces.

31st Fighter Group Spitfire pilots down three Bf-109s, two FW-190s, and two FW-190s, respectively, in three separate missions.

April 22, 1943

ITALY: NASAF B-26s attack the harbor at Carloforte, San Pietro Island.

TUNISIA: NASAF B-25s attack two Axis landing grounds near Protville, and NATAF A-20s and fighters and IX Fighter Command P-40s attack numerous targets in support of Allied ground units.

In the course of three separate aerial engagements between 1135 and 1645 hours, 31st Fighter Group Spitfire pilots down three GAF fighters.

April 23, 1943

ITALY: NASAF B-25s and B-26s attack Arbatax harbor.

MEDITERRANEAN: NASAF B-17s attack Axis ships at sea north of Sicily. Also, in the course of four separate engagements while patrolling along the coast or out to sea, pilots of the 1st, 31st, and 52d Fighter groups down three Axis flying boats and damage a Bf-109.

TUNISIA: NASAF B-25s and B-26s attack motor vehicles and the rail line at Mateur, and various targets found along the Mateur-Bedja road; 320th Medium Bombardment Group B-26s undertake that unit's first

combat mission of the war against Pont-du-Fahs; NATAF A-20s, B-25s, fighter-bombers, and fighters, and IX Fighter Command P-40s mount an all-out effort against Axis ground forces throughout the battle area; and IX Bomber Command B-25s attack Axis troop concentrations, artillery positions, and a landing ground north of Enfidaville.

April 24, 1943

ICELAND: A Ju-88, presumably on a reconnaissance mission, is downed by two P-38 pilots of the Iceland Air Command's 50th Fighter Squadron.

TUNISIA: All NASAF bombers are grounded by bad weather, but NATAF fighters are able to mount attacks against ground targets in the Pont-du-Fahs area, and IX Fighter Command P-40s attack German Army troops north of Enfidaville.

April 25, 1943

TUNISIA: All NASAF bombers are grounded by bad weather, but NATAF fighters are able to mount direct-support missions in the battle area, and NATBF A-20s and B-25s and IX Bomber Command B-25s and P-40s attack a landing ground near Enfidaville and other targets in Axis-held territory.

USAAF fighter pilots down two Axis fighters in the course of at least three separate afternoon actions.

April 26, 1943

ITALY: NASAF B-17s attack Grosseto Airdrome; and, in IX Bomber Command's largest mission to date, 70 B-24s attack Bari Airdrome.

MEDITERRANEAN: NASAF B-26s and P-38 escorts attack Axis shipping at sea near Marettimo Island and Porto Ponte Romano, Sardinia; and NATBF B-25s attack Axis ships at sea off Cap Bon.

TUNISIA: NASAF B-25s attack the rail line at Mateur and the town of Teboura, and NATBF A-20s and B-25s attack numerous targets, including transportation targets, throughout the battle area in northeast Tunisia.

31st Fighter Group Spitfire pilots down five Bf-109s in the course of several aerial engagements over the battle area between 1105 and 1400 hours. Also, while escorting IX Bomber Command B-25s in an attack against the landing ground at Soliman South, 1stLt Robert J. Byrne and 1stLt Robert J. Overcash, of the 57th Fighter Group's 64th Fighter Squadron, both achieve ace status when they each down two Bf-109s at 1440 hours.

April 27, 1943

ALGERIA: BriGen Elwood R. Quesada officially replaces Col Lawrence P. Hickey as commander of the XII Fighter Command, a post Quesada has filled since mid March.
MEDITERRANEAN: NASAF B-25s attack Axis shipping at sea west of Zembra Island.
SARDINIA: NASAF B-17s attack Villacidro Airdrome.
TUNISIA: NATAF aircraft mount numerous ground-support attacks throughout the battle area, and IX Fighter Command P-40s bomb and strafe Axis positions north of Enfidaville.

April 28, 1943

ITALY: IX Bomber Command B-24s attack Naples harbor.
MEDITERRANEAN: NASAF B-25s and P-38 escorts attack two Axis vessels at sea off northeastern Sicily, and 82d Fighter Group P-38 pilots down six Axis fighters near the Egadi Islands at about 0830 hours.
SARDINIA: In their unit's combat debut of the war, B-17s of the 2d Heavy Bombardment Group (a linear descendent of a famous World War I bombardment unit) attack the port facilities at Terranova.
SICILY: IX Bomber Command B-24s attack the ferry terminal at Messina.
TUNISIA: NASAF B-25s attack shipping in Tunis harbor; NASAF B-26s attack the landing grounds at Mabouban and Mabtouha; NATAF aircraft attack Axis

shipping near Tunis and undertake numerous ground-support attacks throughout northeastern Tunisia; and IX Fighter Command P-40s attack embattled German Army troops near Enfidaville.

A 31st Fighter Group Spitfire pilot downs a Bf-109 during a morning engagement over the desert.

April 29, 1943

MEDITERRANEAN: NASAF P-38s attack Axis ships at sea near Marettimo Island; NAAF P-40s attack Axis ships at sea along Tunisia's northeastern coast; NATAF bombers and fighters attack Axis ships at sea in the Gulf of Tunis; and IX Fighter Command P-40s bomb and strafe Axis vessels encountered at sea between the Tunisian coast and Zembra Island.

In the course of at least four separate engagements through the day over or near Marettimo Island, Cap Bon, and the Gulf of Tunis, USAAF fighter pilots down 11 Bf-109s and three Mc.202s. Capt T H McArthur, a P-38 pilot with the 82d Fighter Group's 95th Fighter Squadron, achieves ace status when he downs a Bf-109 off Cap Bon at 1450 hours.
NORTHWESTERN EUROPE: In the largest VIII Fighter Command offensive operation to date, 112 P-47s from the 4th, 56th, and 78th Fighter groups conduct a series of high-altitude fighter sweeps from Pas-de-Calais to The Hague. In the only action of the day, however, a pair of 56th Fighter Group P-47s are downed by GAF fighters, and two others are damaged. No GAF fighters are officially credited, but three are claimed.

The VIII Fighter Command program of mounting fighter sweeps (rather than bomber-escort missions in support of the increasingly hard-pressed VIII Bomber Command) is drawing sharper criticism from many quarters, but the VIII Fighter Command chief, MajGen Frank O'D. Hunter, is steadfast in his conviction that sweeps are the best way to draw the GAF into battle—even though the GAF is rather pointedly ignoring VIII Fighter Command operations to the increasing peril of VIII Bomber Command heavy bombers and their crews. Hunter is aided in his fight to maintain sweeps by the philosophy of MajGen Ira C. Eaker, the Eighth Air Force commanding general, who is a champion of the view that heavy bombers are self-defending and thus not in need of fighter escort—only better formations and defensive tactics.

TUNISIA: During the afternoon, NASAF B-26s attack a landing ground near Protville, and NATAF and Ninth Air Force bombers and fighters mount numerous attacks on a variety of targets in the ground-battle area.

April 30, 1943

MEDITERRANEAN: NASAF B-26s and P-38s attack Axis ships at sea off Tunis; NASAF B-25s attack Axis ships at sea near Cap Bon; NATAF fighters and bombers attack Axis ships at sea in the Gulf of Tunis; and IX Fighter Command P-40s on anti-shipping sweeps claim one destroyer and three other ships sunk and two destroyers and two ships damaged. Although three IX Fighter Command P-40s are reported missing with two of their pilots following a midair collision, 57th and 79th Fighter group P-40 pilots down five Axis fighters over the Gulf of Tunis or near Cap Bon in three of the day's at least four separate actions between 1115 and 1655 hours.

SICILY: IX Bomber Command B-24s attack the ferry terminal at Messina, also hitting a nearby marshalling yard and sections of the city.

TUNISIA: NASAF B-25s attack Axis road convoys along the Tunis–Medjez el-Bab highway, and NATAF bombers and fighters attack Axis ground forces and installations throughout the shrinking battle area.

MAY 1943

May 1, 1943

FRANCE: Poor weather prevents all but 29 of 78 VIII Bomber Command B-17s dispatched from attacking the day's primary target, the St.-Nazaire U-boat base. Only 59 tons of bombs are released. Most of the day's losses are precipitated by a navigational error during the withdrawal. This error carries the main bomber formation over the heavily defended Brest Peninsula, where dense flak downs three B-17s and results in a dispersion of the bomber formations that work to the advantage of pursuing GAF fighters that until then are mostly heckling the formations. In all, seven B-17s are lost to enemy fire, two others are damaged beyond repair, and 20 are damaged. Crew losses amount to three killed, 73 missing, and 17 wounded.

Sgt Maynard H. Smith, a gunner aboard a 306th Heavy Bombardment Group B-17, is awarded a Medal of Honor for his heroic actions after enemy bullets ignite fires in the radio compartment and waist sections of his airplane. Sgt Smith, who is on his first combat mission, throws explod-ing ammunition overboard and then remans his machine gun to help fight off attacking GAF fighters. Despite severe battle damage, Smith's B-17 lands safely in the U.K. and is ultimately salvaged.

ITALY: IX Bomber Command B-24s attack the harbor at Reggio di Calabria, directly opposite the Sicilian port of Messina.

MEDITERRANEAN: NASAF B-26s and P-38s on anti-shipping sweeps between Sicily and Tunisia are unable to locate any Axis shipping in their zone, but NATAF A-20s and fighters attack Axis ships at sea in the Gulf of Tunis as well as harbor facilities at several small Tunisian ports.

In the day's only fighter engagement, two 33d Fighter Group P-40 pilots team up to down an FW-190 over the Gulf of Tunis, near Cape Carthage.

TUNISIA: NATAF A-20s and fighters attack Axis forces on the ground, and IX Fighter Command P-40s strafe port facilities and Axis shipping at sea along the northeastern coast.

May 2, 1943

MEDITERRANEAN: Bad weather re-

stricts NAAF flight operations over the sea to reconnaissance missions, but IX Fighter Command P-40s manage to attack Axis ships at sea off the northeastern coast of Tunisia.
TUNISIA: NATAF fighters attack Axis tanks and troops around Massicault and Teboura.

May 3, 1943

ICELAND: LtGen Frank M. Andrews, ETOUSA commanding general and an American military aviation pioneer, is killed in an air crash on the way to the United States.
TUNISIA: NASAF B-17s attack Axis shipping at Bizerte; NASAF B-25s attack the Axis landing ground at Protville; NATAF fighter-bombers attack ground targets around Massicault; and IX Fighter Command P-40 fighter-bombers attack targets in northeastern Tunisia.

Mateur falls to U.S. Army ground forces.

May 4, 1943

BELGIUM: Sixty-five of 79 VIII Bomber Command B-17s dispatched attack Antwerp industrial areas with 161 tons of bombs. No bombers are lost, but 16 are damaged and crew losses amount to three wounded. Of special note on this mission is the participation of Capt Clark Gable, who heads a film crew gathering material for a USAAF instructional film on combat gunnery. While flying with a cameraman as observers aboard the lead 305th Heavy Bombardment Group B-17 (also the mission lead airplane), Gable mans a radio-room machine gun and helps fend off attacking GAF fighters. The B-17 is slightly damaged in the attack, but no one, including America's leading male film star, is injured. This is the first of four combat missions that Gable will undertake with the Eighth Air Force.
ITALY: IX Bomber Command B-24s attack shipping at Reggio di Calabria and Taranto.
MEDITERRANEAN: NASAF bombers dispatched on anti-shipping sweeps are unable to locate any targets.

A 33d Fighter Group P-40 pilot downs a Bf-109 over the Gulf of Tunis during an afternoon engagement.
TUNISIA: NATBF A-20s and B-25s attack ground targets around Zaghoun in support of a ground attack by Free French ground units; NATAF fighters attack gun positions and motor vehicles near Massicault and Zaghoun; IX Air Support Command B-25s attack Zaghoun, the Zaghoun landing ground, and road traffic between Zaghoun and Bou Ficha; and IX Fighter Command P-40 fighter-bombers attack ground targets around Zaghoun.

May 5, 1943

MEDITERRANEAN: NASAF B-17s attack Axis ships at sea off Capo San Vito, Sicily; NASAF B-25s and B-26s attack Axis ships at sea east of Cape Zebib and off Marettimo Island; and NAAF fighters attack Axis ships at sea in the Gulf of Tunis.

In a single action at 0745 hours, seven P-38 pilots of the 82d Fighter Group's 95th Fighter Squadron down six Italian SM.82 transports, two Bf-109s, and one Mc.200 near Marettimo Island. During the early afternoon, a 79th Fighter Group P-40 pilot downs a Bf-109 over the Gulf of Tunis.
TUNISIA: NASAF B-17s attack port facilities and ships at Tunis and port facilities at La Goulette; NASAF B-25s, B-26s, and fighters attack two Axis landing grounds in northeastern Tunisia; NATAF bombers and fighters mount six separate missions against Axis defensive positions in support of a ground attack by a British Army infantry division; and IX Fighter Command P-40 fighter-bombers attack shipping, warehouses, and port facilities at Nabeul.

May 6, 1943

ITALY: IX Bomber Command B-24s attacking the harbor at Reggio di Calabria claim hits on several ships.
MEDITERRANEAN: NASAF B-25s and B-26s attacking numerous Axis ships at sea between Sicily and Tunisia claim the sinking of six ferries and five small boats laden

with Axis military evacuees. IX Fighter Command P-40s also attack Axis ships at sea in the Gulf of Tunis.

SICILY: NASAF B-17s attack the Marsala and Milo/Trapani airdromes.

TUNISIA: Following weeks of positioning and preparation, Operation VULCAN, the Allied final offensive in Tunisia, opens at dawn with massed artillery fire and the largest air offensive of the North Africa Campaign. Following attacks by NATAF aircraft during the night of May 5–6 against Tunis/El Aouina, and La Sebala airdromesand the landing ground at Ariana, NATAF and IX Fighter Command mount more than 1,400 fighter, bomber, and fighter-bomber sorties on May 6 against all types of targets throughout northeastern Tunisia.

In several separate morning aerial engagements over land and sea near the coast, pilots of the 1st, 31st, 52d, 82d, and 325th Fighter groups down ten GAF fighters and a Ju-52 transport. During the afternoon, 31st Fighter Group Spitfire pilots down seven Bf-109s, one FW-190, and one Mc.202 near Tunis. In all, 18 Axis aircraft are downed by USAAF pilots. During the afternoon action, LtCol Harrison R. Thyng and Maj Frank A. Hill, respectively the commanding officer and executive officer of the 31st Fighter Group's 309th Fighter Squadron, both achieve ace status, Hill by downing his third Bf-109 of the day and Thyng by downing his fifth enemy fighter in the war.

Except for reconnaissance aircraft, this is the last day in which Axis aircraft appear over Tunisia.

May 7, 1943

ENGLAND: LtGen Jacob L. Devers is appointed ETOUSA commanding general.

MEDITERRANEAN: IX Fighter Command P-40 fighter-bombers attacking Axis ships at sea in the Gulf of Tunis sink a destroyer loaded with evacuees and claim severe damage on three other destroyers.

TUNISIA: NAAF P-40s attack small ships and port facilities at Tunis; NATBF A-20s,

B-25s, and fighter-bombers attack Axis road traffic around Tunis and the Tunis/El Aouina Airdrome; and IX Bomber Command B-25s attack Keliba.

Tunis and Bizerte fall to Allied ground forces.

May 8, 1943

ENGLAND: The first YB-40 gunships (B-17s converted for use as heavily-armed bomber escorts) arrive from the United States. They are turned over to crews from the 92d Heavy Bombardment Group's 327th Heavy Bombardment Squadron, which will begin testing them in combat in June.

FRENCH MOROCCO: The 52d Troop Carrier Wing begins overseeing transport and cargo operations for the Twelfth Air Force's 61st, 313th, and 314th Troop Carrier groups.

MEDITERRANEAN: Although most planned NAAF anti-shipping sweeps are canceled because of bad weather, NASAF B-26s and P-40s attack small Axis ships at sea off the northeastern Tunisia coast; NATAF A-20s and fighters attack Axis shipping at sea between Sicily and Tunisia; and IX Fighter Command P-40 fighter-bombers attack Axis ships at sea in the Gulf of Tunis.

PANTELLERIA: P-38 fighter-bombers attack the Italian Army garrison on Pantelleria Island, and NATBF B-25s and NATAF A-20s and fighters attack the landing ground.

TUNISIA: NAAF B-25s attack the road junction and rail line at Korba and the highway north of Beni Khaled; NAAF P-40s attack port facilities near Thona; and NATAF aircraft attack numerous ground targets in support of Allied advances throughout northeastern Tunisia.

In what turn out to be the last fighter engagements of the North African Campaign, USAAF fighter pilots down a total of 11 Bf-109s and an Fi-156 observation plane over Tunisia or near the coast in at least two separate actions between 1140 and 1850 hours.

May 9, 1943

PANTELLERIA: Preparations begin for Operation CORKSCREW, the massive air and naval bombardment of the island of Pantelleria. The NAAF is ordered to turn its entire attention to the bombardment, which will last until the island is to be invaded on June 11.

NATAF A-20s and fighters and IX Bomber Command B-25s attack the landing ground.

SICILY: A total of 122 USAAF B-17s, 89 USAAF B-25s and B-26s, and 23 RAF Wellingtons attack various targets in Palermo with 485 tons of bombs. One B-17 is lost and approximately 50 others are damaged by flak. P-38 pilots of the 1st and 14th Fighter groups down four Axis aircraft in two separate actions over Palermo between 0915 and 1415 hours. Also, IX Bomber Command B-24s attack the Messina ferry terminal.

TUNISIA: Even though the Axis high command in Tunisia surrenders unconditionally, some German units continue to fight on. And, though the focus USAAF air operations in the North African Theater of Operations shifts immediately and sharply against targets in the Mediterranean, NATAF A-20s and fighters and IX Fighter Command fighters mount an all-out ground-support effort throughout the ground battle zone.

May 10, 1943

PANTELLERIA: NATAF A-20s, B-25s, and fighters attack the harbor, and IX Bomber Command B-25s attack the landing ground.

SICILY: Forty-five NAAF B-17s attack Trapani/Milo Airdrome, and 46 NAAF B-17s attack Bo Rizzo Airdrome, where one B-17 is lost.

Pilots of the 1st, 14th, and 82d Fighter groups down four GAF fighters in three separate engagements over Sicily between 1040 and 1705 hours. Maj Joel A. Owens, Jr., newly transferred from the 1st Fighter

Group to the position of 14th Fighter Group operations officer, achieves ace status when he downs two Bf-109s over Bo Rizzo Airdrome.

TUNISIA: NATAF A-20s, B-25s, and fighters and IX Fighter Command P-40s continue to attack Axis troops and vehicles on the Cap Bon Peninsula and in other areas in which Axis units are still putting up resistance.

May 11, 1943

ENGLAND: The VIII Bomber Command's 94th Heavy Bombardment Group is assigned to the new 4th Heavy Bombardment Wing's 401st Provisional Combat Bombardment Wing.

ITALY: XII Fighter Command P-40 fighter-bombers attack the harbor at San Michele.

SICILY: IX Bomber Command B-24s attacking port facilities and ships at Catania harbor sink a tanker and damage two freighters, and 180 NASAF B-17s, B-26s, and B-25s attack rail and port facilities at Marsala with 450 tons of bombs.

Three Axis fighters are downed over Marsala between 1130 and 1150 hours by 14th and 82d Fighter group P-38 pilots. Capt Ernest K. Osher, a P-38 pilot with the 82d Fighter Group's 95th Fighter Squadron, achieves ace status when he downs a Bf-109 on this mission, at 1150 hours.

TUNISIA: NATAF A-20s, B-25s, and fighters, IX Bomber Command B-25s, and IX Fighter Command P-40s continue to attack Axis forces that are still resisting in northeastern Tunisia.

May 12, 1943

ALGERIA: BriGen John K. Cannon replaces BriGen Paul L. Williams as commanding general of the XII Air Support Command.

ENGLAND: The VIII Bomber Command's 95th and 96th Heavy Bombardment groups, both in B-17s, are assigned to the new 4th Heavy Bombardment Wing's 401st Provisional Combat Bombardment Wing.

TUNISIA: NATAF A-20s, B-25s, and fighters and IX Bomber Command B-25s continue to attack Axis forces that are still resisting in northeastern Tunisia.

UNITED STATES: With President Franklin D. Roosevelt, Prime Minister Sir Winston S. Churchill, and the CCS in attendance, the TRIDENT Conference convenes in Washington, D.C. to reconsider strategy set at the Casablanca Conference.

May 13, 1943

FRANCE: Eighty-eight 1st Heavy Bombardment Wing B-17s attack Albert/Meaulte Airdrome with more than 218 tons of bombs. Three B-17s are lost and 11 are damaged, and crew losses amount to 31 missing and one wounded.

The 4th Heavy Bombardment Wing—comprising the virgin 94th, 95th, and 96th Heavy Bombardment groups, in 72 B-17s—makes an inauspicious combat debut with an independent attack against the St.-Omer/Longuenesse Airdrome. The mission does not go well: One 96th Heavy Bombardment Group B-17 crashes shortly after takeoff, after a stowed machine gun accidentally fires and disables the horizontal stabilizer and control cables; when the lead 96th Heavy Bombardment Group B-17 is forced to abort due to an oxygen leak, the entire group abandons the mission and follows it back to base; and when all 14 B-17s of the newly committed 351st Heavy Bombardment Group, which is attached to the 4th Wing, fail to join the main formation, they abandon the mission over the English Channel. Once over the target, only 31 of the 72 B-17s originally dispatched manage to drop their bombs. The B-17 that shot itself down is the only airplane lost outright, but one other is damaged beyond repair, and another is damaged and two crewmen are wounded by enemy fire. The only fatality is the pilot of the crashed 96th Group B-17, who is somehow killed after baling out. However, the rest of his crew is saved.

ITALY: IX Bomber Command B-24s attacking the harbor at Augusta damage oil storage tanks and a number of anchored motor vessels and seaplanes.

SARDINIA: Ninety-six USAAF B-25s, 107 USAAF B-17s, and 22 RAF Wellingtons, escorted by four fighter groups, attack port facilities, marshalling yards, an oil dump, and a chemical plant at Cagliari with 438 tons of bombs. Three Axis fighters are downed near Cagliari by 1st and 82d Fighter group P-38 pilots between 1240 and 1330 hours.

TUNISIA: The last organized German Army force holding out in Tunisia formally surrenders.

UNITED STATES: The TRIDENT conferees set July 10 as the date for the Anglo-American invasion of Sicily.

May 14, 1943

BELGIUM: Thirty-eight 94th and 95th Heavy Bombardment group (4th Heavy Bombardment Wing) B-17s attack industrial targets around Antwerp with nearly 87 tons of bombs. Losses are one heavy bomber missing and 15 damaged, ten crewmen missing and three wounded.

Escorting the Antwerp mission are 118 P-47s of the 4th, 56th, and 78th Fighter groups, which down five GAF fighters—including the first of the war for the 56th and 78th Fighter groups. Losses among the fighters are one 78th Fighter Group P-47 down at sea due to a mechanical failure, three 78th Fighter Group P-47s downed by GAF fighters, and one P-47 damaged. The pilots of all four downed fighters are listed as missing. Counting three GAF aircraft downed while serving with the Eagle squadrons and an FW-190 downed on April 15, Maj Donald J. M. Blakeslee, the commander of the 4th Fighter Group's 335th Fighter Squadron, achieves ace status with the confirmed destruction of an FW-190 over Knocke. (It is apparently lost on VIII Fighter Command—but not on bomber crewmen or fighter pilots—that the highest single-day score yet achieved by the Eighth Air Force fighters is directly linked to escorting the bombers, and not to fighter sweeps that pointedly remain unchallenged by GAF fighters.)

In a separate mission over Belgium, 21 B-17s of the 96th Heavy Bombardment Group (4th Heavy Bombardment Wing's 401st Provisional Combat Bombardment Wing) and 13 B-17s of the 351st Heavy Bombardment Group (1st Heavy Bombardment Wing's 101st Provisional Combat Bombardment Wing) attack Courtrai Airdrome with more than 75 tons of bombs. Losses are two B-17s missing, ten B-17s damaged, and 20 crewmen missing. This is the combat debut of both groups.

ENGLAND: To supervise medium bombardment groups arriving in the theater, Eighth Air Force headquarters activates the 3d Provisional Medium Bombardment Wing, which immediately begins operations.

GERMANY: One hundred nine 1st Heavy Bombardment Wing B-17s and 17 2d Heavy Bombardment Wing B-24s attack the Kiel shipyard at high noon with more than 291 tons of bombs. Flak and GAF fighters down three B-17s and eight B-24s and damage 27 B-17s and nine B-24s. Crew losses are three killed, 81 missing, and 17 wounded. Several GAF fighters are seen to drop parachute bombs into the bomber formation, but the effectiveness of the new weapon is unknown. Participating in this mission is the 92d Heavy Bombardment Group, which is being recommitted to combat after training replacement crews since October 9, 1942.

For its part in the Kiel mission, the 44th Heavy Bombardment Group, in B-24s, becomes the first Eighth Air Force unit to be awarded the Distinguished Unit Citation. Carrying incendiary bombs to be dropped in the wake of the B-17 groups, the 44th is exceptionally vulnerable to flak and GAF fighter attacks, and it suffers accordingly— all aircraft being damaged or lost. Nevertheless, the B-24s carry out an extremely accurate drop that blankets the target.

ITALY: NASAF B-17s attack Civitavecchia.

NETHERLANDS: In its first combat mission of the war and the Eighth Air Force's first medium-bomber mission, the specially trained 322d Medium Bombardment Group dispatches 12 B-26s to attack, at very low level, the power plant at Ijmuiden. Ten of the B-26s are damaged while dropping 43 500-pound bombs, and seven crewmen are wounded. After ordering his five crewmen to bail out over their base, the pilot of one of the battle-damaged B-26 is killed when his airplane crashes during a landing attempt.

PANTELLERIA: A full air and sea blockade of the island is officially ordered by the Mediterranean Air Command.

SARDINIA: NAAF P-38s escorting an attack on Cagliari by RAF Wellington bombers attack a tunnel, a barracks, an airdrome, a power station, and several factories. Three Axis aircraft are downed during these sweeps, at about 1300 hours, by 82d Fighter Group P-38 pilots. Also, NASAF B-26s attack Porto Ponte Romano, and NASAF B-25s and escorting P-38s attacking Olbia claim the destruction of three Axis vessels.

SICILY: One GAF medium bomber is downed over Gela at 1300 hours by a 14th Fighter Group P-38 pilot.

May 15, 1943

GERMANY: Of 80 1st and 4th Heavy Bombardment wing B-17s dispatched to Emden, 59 attack the target with 139 tons of bombs. GAF fighter opposition is heavy, but USAAF losses are only one B-17 missing with its crew of ten and nine B-17s damaged.

NETHERLANDS: Although briefed to bomb Wilhemlshaven, 76 of 113 1st Heavy Bombardment Wing B-17s dispatched attack targets of opportunity along the Dutch coast with 186 tons of bombs. Five B-17s are lost in the face of heavy fighter opposition, one B-17 is damaged beyond repair, and 27 are damaged. Crew losses are one killed, 51 missing, and seven wounded.

One hundred sixteen VIII Fighter

Command sorties are mounted over the Continent or the English Channel, and several GAF fighters are engaged by 56th Fighter Group pilots over Rotterdam, but only two GAF fighters are damaged.

UNITED STATES: The 381st Heavy Bombardment Group air echelon, in B-17s, begins moving to England via the northern ferry route for service with the 1st Heavy Bombardment Wing's 101st Provisional Combat Bombardment Wing.

May 16, 1943

NORTHWESTERN EUROPE: A total of 227 P-47 sorties are mounted over France, Belgium, and the Dutch coast by the 4th, 56th, and 78th Fighter groups. During afternoon sweeps, pilots of the 4th and 78th Fighter groups are engaged by several FW-190 squadrons. Three GAF fighters are downed, but a 78th Fighter Group P-47 and its pilot are also lost. Also, an F-5 of the 13th Photographic Squadron fails to return from a sortie to Paris.

May 17, 1943

FRANCE: Ninety 1st Heavy Bombardment Wing B-17s attack the Lorient U-boat base, and 38 4th Heavy Bombardment Wing B-17s attack power facilities at Lorient in the face of heavy GAF fighter opposition and flak. Five B-17s are downed and 29 are damaged, of which one is written off after crash-landing at a base in the U.K. and another makes a forced landing at sea during the withdrawal. Five of the ditched B-17's crew are rescued. In all, B-17 crew losses are one killed, 57 missing, and eight wounded.

Approaching their target at low level (2,500 feet) from the sea, 34 2d Heavy Bombardment Wing B-24s attack the Bordeaux U-boat base with more than 85 tons of bombs. Opposition is light and only one B-24 is damaged and two men are wounded. However, a B-24 that develops engine trouble is forced to crash-land in Spain, and its crew is interned.

NETHERLANDS: In its second such mis-

sion in three days, the 322d Medium Bombardment Group dispatches 11 B-26s to undertake a minimum-level attack on power stations at Ijmuiden and Haarlem. One airplane aborts and heads home early, and *all* of the remaining B-26s, with 60 crewmen aboard, are lost. Seven are downed by flak or GAF fighters, but two collide and the resulting detonation of their bombs brings down two other B-26s. Of all the crewmen lost, two are picked up from the North Sea by a Royal Navy destroyer following two days in the water. LtCol Robert M. Stillman, the group commander, is among the pilots and aircrewmen taken prisoner.

May 18, 1943

ALGERIA: BriGen Paul L. Williams assumes command of the NAAF Provisional Troop Carrier Command.

NORTHWESTERN EUROPE: One hundred VIII Fighter Command P-47s are dispatched on sweeps over France, Belgium, and the Netherlands. Two 4th Fighter Group P-47 pilots down two Bf-109s over Belgium. However, one 4th Fighter Group P-47 is shot down at sea, and its pilot is listed as missing.

PANTELLERIA: Allied warplanes open an unremitting offensive against Axis forces on the island, with special emphasis on the port and Marghana Airdrome. At least 80 B-25s and B-26s—and P-38 escorts—attack these targets.

SICILY: NAAF B-17s attack Trapani. 14th Fighter Group P-38 escort pilots down six Axis fighters during the return flight to their base in Tunisia.

UNITED STATES: The CCS approves plans for the Combined Bomber Offensive against Germany's war-making industries. At the top of the target list is German fighter production, followed by submarine yards and bases, the German aircraft industry as a whole, and oil production and distribution.

May 19, 1943

GERMANY: The Kiel U-boat yard is attacked at about 1330 hours by 103 1st Heavy Bombardment Wing B-17s, which drop 237 tons of bombs despite heavy fighter opposition that downs six and damages 28 of the heavy bombers. USAAF crew losses are one killed, 60 missing, and seven wounded. In a separate but coordinated attack, 55 4th Heavy Bombardment Wing B-17s attack the Flensburg U-boat yard with 134 tons of bombs. Nine B-17s are damaged, two crewmen are killed, and four crewmen are wounded.

A diversionary mission by 24 379th Heavy Bombardment Group B-17s (in its combat debut) and 117 VIII Fighter Command P-47s fails to attract any GAF fighter opposition.

SARDINIA: While escorting a force of NASAF B-26s against Cagliari, 325th Fighter Group P-40s, in their first major clash of the war, are engaged over land and sea by many Bf-109s. During a series of swirling, running dogfights, 325th Fighter Group pilots succeed in downing six Bf-109s.

In a second action at almost the same time, 82d Fighter Group P-38s are challenged by Axis fighters as they escort a force of NASAF B-25s against Villacidro Airdrome. In another running dogfight over land and sea, six Bf-109s and one Mc.200 are downed. 2dLt Louis E. Curdes, a pilot with the group's 95th Fighter Squadron, achieves ace status when he downs two of the Bf-109s.

NASAF medium bombers also attack Elmas, Milis, and Monserrato airdromes.

SICILY: 14th Fighter Group P-38s are engaged by Bf-109s while escorting NASAF B-17s on a midday attack against Trapani/Milo Airdrome, but no confirmed victories are credited.

May 20, 1943

ITALY: NASAF B-17s attack Grosseto Airdrome.

PANTELLERIA: NAAF P-38s and P-40s bomb and strafe targets of opportunity.

SARDINIA: 325th Fighter Group P-40

pilots down six Axis fighters, plus seven Me-323 six-engine heavy transports that are caught fleeing Decimomannu Airdrome ahead of an attack by NASAF B-25s; while escorting other NASAF B-25s against Villacidro Airdrome, 82d Fighter Group P-38 pilots down seven Axis fighters and one Ju-88; NASAF B-25s also attack Alghero Airdrome; and P-38s attack Milis Airdrome, various port facilities, and targets of opportunity around the island.

SICILY: A 1st Fighter Group P-38 pilot downs an Fi-156 observation plane near Trapani/Milo Airdrome.

May 21, 1943

BELGIUM: During a sweep between Ostend and Ghent by 105 VIII Fighter Command P-47s, three P-47s are downed and their pilots are listed as missing. In return, one GAF fighter is damaged.

GERMANY: Seventy-seven 1st Heavy Bombardment Wing B-17s attack the Wilhelmshaven U-boat yards at 1245 hours with 193 tons of bombs. GAF fighters and flak down seven B-17s and damage 24, from which crew losses amount to one killed, 60 missing, and nine wounded. The entire crew is saved from a B-17 that goes down at sea.

Also at 1245 hours, 46 4th Heavy Bombardment Wing B-17s attack the Emden U-boat yards with 110 tons of bombs, but all the bombs miss the target. GAF fighters and flak account for five B-17s lost, two damaged beyond repair, and nine damaged. Crew losses are two killed, 50 missing, and five wounded.

ITALY: IX Bomber Command B-24s attack Reggio di Calabria and Villa San Giovanni.

PANTELLERIA: NAAF P-40 fighter-bombers attack gun emplacements and various targets of opportunity.

SARDINIA: NASAF B-25s and B-26s attack Decimomannu and Villacidro airdromes and various targets of opportunity. 325th Fighter Group P-40 pilots down four Bf-109s over land and sea between 1610 and 1655 hours, and P-38 pilots of the 14th and 82d Fighter groups down seven Axis

fighters over Villacidro Airdrome at about
1700 hours. Two of the P-38 pilots achieve
ace status in this action, each by downing a
Bf-109: 2dLt Paul R. Cochran of the 14th
Fighter Group's 49th Fighter Squadron, and
1stLt Charles J. Zubarik of the 82d Fighter
Group's 96th Fighter Squadron.
SICILY: NASAF B-17s, escorted by 14th
Fighter Group P-38s, attack Castelvetrano
Airdrome at 0945 hours. The P-38s are en-
gaged by GAF fighters near the target, but
no confirmed victories are credited.
UNITED STATES: The 100th Heavy Bom-
bardment Group, in B-17s, departs for
England via the northern ferry route for
service with the Eighth Air Force.

May 22, 1943

MEDITERRANEAN: A 14th Fighter
Group P-38 pilot downs a Bf-109 near
Favignana Island, in the Egadi group.
TUNISIA: The entire 324th Fighter Group,
together for the first time since its arrival
in North Africa, moves into the Kairouan
Airdrome, from which it will fly coastal
patrols under NACAF control.

May 23, 1943

ALGERIA: Col John W. Monahan succeeds to the command of the NATC.
ITALY: NAAF P-38s attack the zinc works
at Iglesias and the port at Carloforte, San
Pietro Island.
PANTELLERIA: NASAF B-25s and
B-26s attack the port and Marghana Airdrome, and NAAF P-40s attack gun
emplacements throughout the island.

May 24, 1943

ALGERIA: Col Lawrence P. Hickey replaces BriGen John K. Cannon as head of
the XII Air Support Command.
ITALY: IX Bomber Command B-24s attack
the ferry terminal and a tanker at Reggio di
Calabria, and the ferry terminal and rail
yards at Villa San Giovanni.
PANTELLERIA: NASAF and NATAF
fighters attack Marghana Airdrome through
the day.

SARDINIA: NAAF medium bombers and
fighters attack numerous targets throughout the island. During a mission against
Alghero Airdrome and nearby satellite airfields, 82d Fighter Group P-38 pilots down
three SM.79 tri-motor medium bombers,
three Bf-109s, and two Mc.202s in running
fights between 1410 and 1435 hours.

May 25, 1943

ENGLAND: Col Stanley R. Wray turns
over command of the 91st Heavy Bombardment Group in order to form the headquarters of the 103d Provisional Heavy
Bombardment Wing, which, with similar
provisional headquarters, will serve as a
command-and-control subunit of the
burgeoning 1st Heavy Bombardment Wing.
Col Wray's job, for the time being, is to
oversee the final training cycle of several
B-17 groups as they arrive in the U.K. from
the United States.
    The 303d Heavy Bombardment Group
is reassigned to the 103d Provisional Combat Bombardment Wing (from the 101st).
    The first air echelon of the 384th Heavy
Bombardment Group arrives from the
United States via the northern ferry route
and is assigned to the 1st Heavy Bombardment Wing's 103d Provisional Combat
Bombardment Wing.
PANTELLERIA: NATAF B-25s and P-40s
attack Marghana Airdrome, shipping, and
troop concentrations.
SICILY: IX Bomber Command B-24s
attack the Messina ferry terminal and rail
yards; and NASAF B-17s, B-25s, B-26s,
and fighters attack numerous targets
throughout the island.
    1st Fighter Group P-38 pilots down 11
Bf-109s between 1110 and 1130 hours in
an action off Capo San Vito. During this
engagement, 2dLt John A. Mackay, a P-38
pilot with the 1st Fighter Group's 27th
Fighter Squadron, achieves ace status when
he downs two Bf-109s. Also, at 1545 hours,
a pair of 14th Fighter Group P-38 pilots
down a Do-217 medium bomber over Gela.
UNITED STATES: The TRIDENT Confer-

ence ends with a decision to launch a cross-Channel attack from England to France around May 1, 1944. In the meantime, the various air forces arrayed against northwestern and southern Europe are to open a long-term aerial offensive aimed at destroying the effectiveness of the Axis air forces and generally disrupt the ability of the Axis nations to withstand the cross-Channel invasion and subsequent drive into Germany. Until the invasion, the chief means of striking at the Axis in northwestern Europe will by a prolonged aerial offensive. Among the specific goals set forth for the air offensive are forcing Italy out of the war and destroying the Axis-held oil fields in Romania.

May 26, 1943

ITALY: 14th Fighter Group P-38s attack the harbor at Golfo Aranci. There, in the day's only fighter engagement, one of the P-38 pilots downs an Italian flying boat at 1215 hours. NAAF P-38s also attack the power dam at Tirso.
PANTELLERIA: NAAF and NATAF P-40 fighter-bombers attack gun emplacements, motor vehicles, and troop concentrations along the southeastern coast.
SARDINIA: NAAF P-38s attack Villacidro Airdrome and shipping at Porto Ponte Romano.
SICILY: NASAF B-17s, B-25, and B-26s attack Biscari, Comiso, and Gela/Ponte Olivo airdromes.

May 27, 1943

ENGLAND: The first air echelon of the 323d Medium Bombardment Group, in B-26s, arrives from the United States via the southern ferry route for service with VIII Bomber Command's 3d Medium Bombardment Wing.
PANTELLERIA: NAAF P-40s attack harbor defenses, and NATAF P-40s attack various targets along the south coast.
SARDINIA: NASAF B-25s and B-26s attack Decimomannu and Villacidro airdromes.

May 28, 1943

ITALY: NASAF B-17s attack the harbor, oil facilities, and a marshalling yard at Leghorn; IX Bomber Command B-24s attack Augusta; and two separate IX Bomber Command B-24s formations attack the important Axis air-base complex at Foggia for the first time.
MEDITERRANEAN: 14th Fighter Group P-38 pilots down two Bf-109s at about 1800 hours near Favignana Island, in the Egadi group.
SARDINIA: NAAF P-40s and NATAF A-20s attack various targets.
SICILY: NASAF medium bombers attack the Bo Rizzo, Castelvetrano, Trapani/Milo, and Sciacca airdromes; and three 325th Fighter Group P-40 pilots down three Bf-109s over Trapani/Milo Airdrome.

May 29, 1943

ENGLAND: Following the day's mission, the 44th and 93d Heavy Bombardment groups, in B-24s, stand down prior to a temporary move of unknown duration to the North African theater. Both units begin training to approach targets at and drop bombs from a mere 150 feet.
FRANCE: VIII Bomber Command schedules three missions as continuations of its ongoing campaign against the German Navy. At 1600 hours, against heavy opposition, 57 4th Heavy Bombardment Wing B-17s attack the Rennes Naval Storage Depot with more than 132 tons of bombs. Six B-17s are lost, one is damaged beyond repair, and 30 are damaged. Crew losses are one killed, 64 missing, and ten wounded. Next, just after 1700 hours, 147 1st Heavy Bombardment Wing B-17s attack the St.-Nazaire U-boat base with 277 2,000-pound bombs, and 34 2d Heavy Bombardment Wing B-24s attack the La Pallice U-boat base with 99 2,000-pound bombs. The B-24s are unopposed and unscathed, but seven B-17s are downed by enemy fire, one is lost in a crash-landing at sea (nine crewmen rescued), one is damaged beyond

repair in a crash-landing in England, and 58 are otherwise damaged. Crew losses are 71 missing and ten wounded. Of special note on this mission is the first use of experimental YB-40 gunships—B-17 variants fitted out with extra armor and machine guns and tasked with protecting the bomber formations against attacking fighters. Eight YB-40s are dispatched, of which one is lost.

VIII Fighter Command dispatches 131 P-47 escorts, but results are negligible owing to the short range of the USAAF fighters. One GAF fighter is listed as probably downed by a 56th Fighter Group P-47 pilot.

PANTELLERIA: NASAF B-26s, P-38s, and P-40s and NATAF P-40s attack gun emplacements, a radar installation, and the town.

SARDINIA: P-38 fighter-bombers attack Porto Ponte Romano.

May 30, 1943

ITALY: NASAF B-17s attack an aircraft-industry factory and landing ground at Pomigliano and the airdrome and marshalling yards at Capodichino; IX Bomber Command B-24s attack the air-base complex and facilities at Foggia; and NAAF P-38 fighter-bombers attack Chilivani and the port and railway station at Aranci.

A 1st Fighter Group P-38 pilot downs an Italian Re.2001 fighter over the Golfo Aranci at 1705 hours.

PANTELLERIA: IX Bomber Command B-25s attack troop concentrations, and NAAF fighters and medium bombers and NATAF fighters attack various targets around the island.

SARDINIA: NAAF P-38s attack the marshalling yard at Chilivani and strafe various targets of opportunity throughout the island.

May 31, 1943

ALGERIA: The 319th Medium Bombardment Group, a veteran B-26 unit that had to be withdrawn from combat on February 27 to rest and refit, arrives at Sedrata Airdrome, Algeria, from Oujda Airdrome, French Morocco, to resume combat operations.

ITALY: NASAF B-17s attack a marshalling yard and air-base complex at Foggia.

PANTELLERIA: NAAF medium bombers and fighters attack defensive positions, and NATAF P-40s attack numerous other ground targets.

SARDINIA: NAAF P-38 fighter-bombers attack Cagliari, a factory at Guspini, and the power station at Santa Caterina.

JUNE 1943

June 1, 1943

ITALY: NASAF P-40s strafe the seaplane base at Stagnone Island, and P-38 fighter-bombers attack the rail line near Balestrate.
PANTELLERIA: NASAF B-17s and P-38s attack targets throughout the island, and NATAF P-40s attack gun emplacements. The B-17s are the first heavy bombers to attack the island. Also, incessant aerial bombardment of the island is supplemented for the first time by what will be an ongoing naval bombardment.
SARDINIA: NASAF B-25s, B-26s, and P-38s attack Olbia, Porto Ponte Romano, and the harbor at Porto Torres.
TUNISIA: Two B-25s squadrons of the Ninth Air Force's 12th Medium Bombardment Group that have been on detached duty with XII Air Support Command since February are returned to the Ninth Air Force and reunited with the remainder of their group.

June 2, 1943

PANTELLERIA: NAAF fighters and medium bombers attack targets throughout the island all morning and into the afternoon.
SARDINIA: NAAF P-40s attack targets of opportunity throughout the island.
SICILY: NAAF P-38s attack Trapani/Milo Airdrome.
TUNISIA: The 79th Fighter Group moves to El Haouaria Airdrome to be in position to support the Allied air attacks against Pantelleria. Also, the 12th and 340th Medium Bombardment groups displace to Hergla Airdrome, also for better access to Pantelleria Island and other Mediterranean islands.

June 3, 1943

EGYPT: Col Charles D. McAllister replaces BriGen Auby C. Strickland as commander of the IX Fighter Command. McAllister also assumes command of the Desert Air Task Force.
PANTELLERIA: NAAF mounts an all-out effort against the island's defenses using medium bombers, light bombers, and fighters.
TUNISIA: One FW-190 is downed by a 52d

Fighter Group Spitfire pilot near Cap Bon.

June 4, 1943

ENGLAND: The 386th Medium Bombardment Group air echelon, in B-26s, arrives from the United States via the southern ferry route for service with VIII Bomber Command's 3d Medium Bombardment Wing.

ITALY: IX Bomber Command B-24s attack Grottaglie Airdrome.

PANTELLERIA: The NAAF mounts an all-out effort against the island's defenses using heavy bombers, medium bombers, light bombers, and fighters.

June 5, 1943

ITALY: NASAF B-17s attack the harbor at La Spezia.

MEDITERRANEAN: 1st Fighter Group P-38 pilots down two Bf-109s near Cape St. Elia.

PANTELLERIA: NASAF B-25s and P-38s attack gun emplacements and other positions.

SARDINIA: NASAF B-26s attack Porto Ponte Romano, and P-38s attack Capoterra and Monserrato airdromes.

SICILY: IX Bomber Command B-24s attack the harbor at Catania.

June 6, 1943

ENGLAND: The 95th and 100th Heavy Bombardment groups are assigned to the 4th Heavy Bombardment's Wing's 402d Provisional Combat Bombardment Wing.

ITALY: IX Bomber Command B-24s attack the harbors at Reggio di Calabria and Villa San Giovanni.

PANTELLERIA: At the official commencement of Operation CORKSCREW, air attacks by NAAF medium and light bombers and fighters are intensified, with special attention being paid to the destruction of shore batteries. Operating from its base at Korba, Tunisia, the 27th Fighter-Bomber Group makes its combat debut on a mission against Pantelleria. The 27th is the first USAAF unit to enter combat with

the new A-36 Apache dive-bomber. During two separate fighter actions, 52d and 325th Fighter group pilots down seven Bf-109s.

SICILY: IX Bomber Command B-24s attack the ferry terminal at Messina.

SCOTLAND: The 353d Fighter Group, in P-47s, arrives by ship from the United States for service with the VIII Fighter Command.

June 7, 1943

PANTELLERIA: NASAF and NATAF bombers and fighters and IX Bomber Command B-25s attack the entire island through the afternoon. P-40 pilots of the 57th and 79th Fighter groups down two Bf-109s and two Mc.202s in two separate afternoon fighter actions.

TUNISIA: Two 52d Fighter Group Spitfire pilots down a Bf-109 near Cap Bon.

June 8, 1943

PANTELLERIA: A total of eight Axis fighters are downed by USAAF fighter pilots during the course of three separate aerial engagements over or near the island.

SARDINIA: NAAF P-38s attack the Italian Army barracks at Segariu, and the Villacidro Airdrome.

June 9, 1943

PANTELLERIA: NASAF, NATAF, and IX Bomber Command bombers and fighters, and Allied naval forces bombard the entire island throughout the day. USAAF fighter pilots down 13 Axis fighters over or near the island in three separate aerial engagements. 1stLt Daniel Kennedy, a P-38 pilot with the 1st Fighter Group's 27th Fighter Squadron, achieves ace status when he downs three Bf-109s over the island at about 1415 hours.

During the night of June 9–10, NAAF fighter-bombers attack the island.

SICILY: IX Bomber Command B-24s attack Catania and Gerbini airdromes.

June 10, 1943

NORTHWESTERN EUROPE: The CCS

direct the initiation of the Combined Bomber Offensive. This coordinated strategic-bombing campaign against Germany will involve USAAF precision bombing during the day and RAF area bombing during the night. A Combined Operational Planning Committee is to be established under CCS auspices to coordinate the multinational effort.

Under Combined Bomber Offensive directives, first priority will be given to German Navy submarine bases and yards, the German aircraft industry, oil production, and ball-bearing production. Secondary priority is given to production facilities for military vehicles and synthetic rubber. However, in light of heavy and growing strategic-bomber losses, the directive contains an enigmatic conclusion that states, "German fighter production must be considered an Intermediate Objective second to none in priority."

MEDITERRANEAN: In the course of at least two large running afternoon fighter battles, 31st Fighter Group Spitfire pilots and 79th and 325th Fighter group P-40 pilots down a total of 34 Axis fighters from over Pantelleria to within 5 miles of Sicily.

PANTELLERIA: More than 1,000 combat sorties are mounted throughout the day by NAAF bombers and fighters. Also, IX Bomber Command B-25s and fighter-bombers mount additional attacks.

June 11, 1943

GERMANY: In VIII Bomber Command's largest heavy-bomber attack to date, 248 B-17s on their way to attack U-boat yards at Wilhelmshaven are forced to disperse by heavy clouds. Moreover, Germans on the ground blanket the immediate target area with smoke. As a result, only 218 B-17s manage to drop more than 426 tons of bombs over a wide area of Wilhelmshaven and several scattered targets of opportunity. Losses among the B-17s against GAF fighter opposition rated as heavy are eight missing (including one lost in a midair collision with an FW-190) and 62 damaged,

with crew losses of three killed, 80 missing, and 20 wounded. These losses and the inaccurate bombing, caused in part by flak and GAF fighter attacks, bring a number of high-ranking proponents of the USAAF daylight-bombing strategy to reassess the need for long-range escort fighters.

LAMPEDUSA: IX Bomber Command B-25s and fighters and Royal Navy warships open an intense bombardment that continues through the night of June 11–12.

PANTELLERIA: During a brief lull following a final crescendo of around-the-clock aerial and naval bombardment—as soldiers of the 1st British Infantry Division prepare to land on the island—a large formation of bomb-equipped GAF FW-190s and Bf-109s attempts to attack Royal Navy ships and landing craft. However, the attack is turned back by 57th Fighter Group P-40 pilots.

Shortly, at 0735 hours—just as the first British troops are stepping ashore against nominal opposition—the island's Italian commander issues a proclamation calling for unconditional surrender by the entire garrison. For the first time in history, an aerial bombardment campaign is given full credit for a victory over a land objective. In all, between May 5 and the landings, Pantelleria Island has been subjected to 5,285 combat sorties dispensing 6,200 tons of bombs.

Despite the surrender of the island's garrison in the morning, Axis fighters continue to attack Allied aircraft and ships in the area. In the course of two morning attacks, pilots of the 52d and 57th Fighter groups down eight GAF fighters. Next at about 1300 hours, 81st Fighter Group P-39 dive-bomber pilots down three FW-190s. And, finally, while defending against an attack at about 1540 hours, three 31st Fighter Group Spitfire pilots down six GAF fighters. In this final action, all three Spitfire pilots of the 31st Fighter Group's 307th Fighter Squadron achieve ace status: 1stLt J D Collinsworth, who downs a Bf-109; 1stLt Charles R. Fischette, who downs two

Bf-109s; and 1stLt John H. White, who downs an FW-190.

June 12, 1943

BELGIUM: While on fighter sweeps involving 140 4th, 56th, and 78th Fighter group P-47s, a 56th Fighter Group pilot downs an FW-190 over Ypres.
ENGLAND: The 322d Medium Bombardment Group is transferred to the administrative control of the VIII Air Support Command, which is not yet an operational component of the Eighth Air Force.
LAMPEDUSA: Following the start of scheduled day-long attacks by NAAF and Ninth Air Force fighters and bombers, the Italian garrison surrenders to avoid further bombardment, and a British Army infantry company is landed to take possession of the island. (On June 13 and 14, the two remaining islands of the Pelagie group, Lampione and Linosa, will be surrendered by their garrisons without a fight. Thus, the right flank of the proposed Allied invasion route to Sicily has been secured.)
PANTELLERIA: 52d Fighter Group Spitfire pilots down three FW-190s during a morning engagement over the island.
SICILY: NASAF B-26s attack Bocca di Falco, Castelvetrano, and Trapani/Milo airdromes.

June 13, 1943

ALGERIA: MajGen Edwin J. House replaces Col Lawrence P. Hickey as head of the XII Air Support Command.
FRANCE: 140 VIII Fighter Command short-range P-47s are dispatched on sweeps over France, Belgium, and the Netherlands. For once, GAF fighters engage the 56th Fighter Group formation over northern France, with the result that three FW-190s are downed, including two by Col Hubert Zemke, the 56th Fighter Group commanding officer.
GERMANY: Although the main daylight-bombing attack against Bremen by 122 1st Heavy Bombardment Wing B-17s is lightly opposed by GAF fighters (four

B-17s missing and 31 damaged), 22 of the 72 4th Heavy Bombardment Wing B-17s dispatched on a diversionary strike against Kiel are downed and 24 are damaged, one beyond repair. 1st Heavy Bombardment Wing crew losses are 32 missing and eight wounded, but the 4th Heavy Bombardment Wing's crew losses are an unprecedented and utterly shocking three killed, 20 wounded, and 213 missing. Among the missing is BriGen Nathan B. Forrest, the commander of the new 401st Provisional Combat Bombardment Wing, and the first general officer downed on an Eighth Air Force combat mission. Forrest is in fact killed when the lead 95th Heavy Bombardment Group B-17 in which he is a passenger is downed by a GAF fighter. As a result of the mission's high losses, ranking proponents of the daylight bombing strategy are given more than ample justification for reassessing the need for changing strategies to favor long-range fighter escorts.
MEDITERRANEAN: 350th Fighter Group P-39 dive-bomber pilots down two FW-190s over Pantelleria during the afternoon.
SICILY: Twenty-four 376th Heavy Bombardment Group B-24s attack Gerbini Airdrome, and 22 98th Heavy Bombardment Group B-24s join RAF bombers for an attack against Catania Airdrome.
UNITED STATES: The first air echelon of the 389th Heavy Bombardment Group, in B-24s, departs for England for service with the 2d Bombardment Wing's 201st Provisional Bombardment Wing.

June 15, 1943

ALGERIA: Col Harold A. Barton assumes command of the XII Air Force Service Command.
ENGLAND: The 6th Air Defense Wing (which will be redesignated as the 67th Fighter Wing in July 1943) is activated to oversee the operations of several VIII Fighter Command fighter groups, a task it will begin in December 1943.

The 323d and 386th Medium Bombardment groups, in B-26s, are transferred to the administrative control of the VIII Air Support Command.

ENGLISH CHANNEL: All 155 VIII Bomber Command B-17s dispatched on a mission to France are recalled because of the weather before any reach the French coast. Fighter operations are also canceled.

SICILY: During the morning, NAAF B-17s, B-25s, B-26s, and P-38s attack Bocca di Falco, Bo Rizzo, Castelvetrano, Sciacca, and Trapani/Milo airdromes, as well as several radio stations near Marsala. 1st and 82d Fighter group P-38 pilots and 325th Fighter Group P-40 pilots down three Italian and two GAF fighters over the airdromes or near the coast between 0610 and 1020 hours.

June 17, 1943

SICILY: IX Bomber Command B-24s attack the airdromes at Biscari and Comiso, putting the latter out of commission.

June 18, 1943

MEDITERRANEAN: NASAF B-25s, B-26s, and P-38s attack Axis ships at sea in the Golfo Aranci. P-38 pilots of the 82d Fighter Group's 96th Fighter Squadron down 16 Italian Air Force fighters and an FW-190 over the Golfo Aranci at about 1000 hours. One of the P-38 pilots, 2dLt Lawrence P. Liebers, achieves ace status when he downs two Mc.202s and an Mc.205.

SARDINIA: NASAF B-25s, B-26s, and P-38s attack port facilities and shipping at Olbia. Two Bf-109s and an Fi-156 observation plane are downed by 1st and 325th Fighter group pilots during the morning.

SICILY: Allied fighters and bombers based in North Africa open a systematic air campaign supporting in advance the upcoming invasion of the first Allied land objective in western Europe. Initial focus is placed on targets around the narrow Straits of Messina, over which the island's large garrison is most likely to be reinforced.

NAAF B-17s attack the ferry terminal and rail yards at Messina, and P-38 fighter-bombers attack Trapani/Milo Airdrome.

June 19, 1943

ITALY: IX Bomber Command B-24s attack ferries in the Straits of Messina, the harbor at Reggio di Calabria, and the rail yards and ferry terminal at Villa San Giovanni.

PANTELLERIA: The 33d Fighter Group, in P-40s, displaces forward to the island's newly rehabilitated Marghana Airdrome.

TUNISIA: A P-39 pilot from NACAF's 350th Fighter Group downs a Ju-88 (presumably on a reconnaissance mission) just off the coast at 0745 hours.

June 20, 1942

LAMPEDUSA: The recently captured airfield becomes operational, thus shortening the range to targets on and around Sicily.

SICILY: NASAF B-26s attack Bo Rizzo, Castelvetrano, and Trapani/Milo airdromes, and P-38 escort pilots of the 1st and 14th Fighter groups down 15 Bf-109s during an engagement over Sicily between 0830 and 0855 hours.

June 21, 1943

ITALY: NASAF B-17s attack a marshalling yard at Battipaglia, an air depot at Cancello Arnone, rail yards at Naples, and marshalling yards and a railway trestle at Salerno. Also, IX Bomber Command B-24s attack port facilities and rail yards at Reggio di Calabria, and the ferry terminal at Villa San Giovanni.

June 22, 1943

BELGIUM: Thirty-nine B-17s of the 381st and 384th Heavy Bombardment groups, in their combat debuts as part of the 1st Heavy Bombardment Wing, attack industrial targets around Antwerp with more than 95 tons of bombs. Losses sustained by the newcomers are four B-17s missing and 18 damaged. Crew losses are one killed, 40 missing, and three wounded. 4th Fighter Group P-47s escort the B-17s part of the way home from the target, but no known contacts with GAF fighters result from the effort.

GERMANY: In the Eighth Air Force's main event of the day, 183 of the 224 1st and 4th Heavy Bombardment wing B-17s dispatched and 11 YB-40s attack a synthetic-rubber plant at Huls with 422 tons of bombs. Results of this first large-scale strategic mission against an industrial target in the Ruhr region of Germany are considered particularly good, but losses from heavy flak and determined GAF fighter attacks are high: 15 B-17s and one YB-40 are lost and 75 B-17s damaged, with crew losses of two killed, 151 missing, and 16 wounded. A diversionary mission by the 100th Heavy Bombardment Group, making its combat debut, fails to confuse the German defenses on account of a late start.

NETHERLANDS: Between 0915 and 0925 hours, P-47 pilots of the 4th and 78th Fighter groups down seven GAF fighters over Walcheren Island without sustaining any losses.

SARDINIA: NACAF Beaufighters claim a small vessel sunk off the coast.

June 23, 1943

ENGLAND: While being prepared for the day's mission, a 381st Heavy Bombardment Group B-17 blows up, killing 22 USAAF personnel and one British civilian and damaging another B-17. Then, after 180 VIII Bomber Command B-17s are dispatched on two separate missions against targets in France, all are recalled due to bad weather.

The 4th Heavy Bombardment Wing's 96th Heavy Bombardment Group is reassigned to the 4th Heavy Bombardment Wing's new 403d Provisional Combat Bombardment Wing.

The final air echelon of the 388th Heavy Bombardment Group, in B-17s, arrives from the United States via the northern ferry route and is assigned to the 4th Heavy Bombardment Wing's 403d Provisional Combat Bombardment Wing.

June 24, 1943

BELGIUM: Of 128 P-47 sorties launched over northern Europe, one 78th Fighter Group P-47 pilot downs an FW-190 near Ostend at 0910.

FRANCE: Joining the veteran 13th Photographic Squadron, the 22d Photographic Squadron mounts its first combat reconnaissance sorties of the war.

GREECE: Forty-nine IX Bomber Command B-24s attack Salonika/Sedhes Airdrome.

MEDITERRANEAN: An Me-210 is downed at sea at 1910 hours by an 81st Fighter Group P-39 on convoy-escort duty.

SARDINIA: NASAF B-25s and B-26s attack the Alghero/Fertila and Venafiorita airdromes, the rail junction at Chilivani, Axis ships at sea off the coast, and various targets of opportunity. Also, while conducting aggressive sweeps over southern Sardinia, NAAF P-40s attack motor vehicles near La Maddalena, sink two small vessels off the coast, and strafe Axis aircraft on the ground at Capoterra Airdrome.

While escorting the morning bombing attacks or conducting sweeps, 14th Fighter Group P-38 pilots down seven Bf-109s over Alghero Airdrome, 325th Fighter Group P-40 pilots down five Bf-109s over the Gulf of Palmas, and 1st Fighter Group P-38 pilots down eight Bf-109s over Chilivani.

June 25, 1943

ENGLAND: The final air echelon of the 387th Medium Bombardment Group, in B-26s, arrives from the United States via the northern ferry route and is attached administratively to the Eighth Air Force's VIII Air Support Command.

NETHERLANDS: Due to extremely poor visibility over much of northwestern Europe, 149 1st Heavy Bombardment Wing B-17s—of 190 B-17s and seven YB-40s dispatched—attack targets of opportunity and targets of last resort, including a convoy underway at sea. GAF fighters and flak account for 15 B-17s missing and 39 damaged, and crew losses of three killed, 142 missing, and 11 wounded. All crewmen are rescued from a B-17 that is abandoned near the English coast and one that ditches at sea.

Also hampered by poor visibility, 18 of the 78 4th Heavy Bombardment Wing B-17s dispatched attack a convoy off Juist Island. Three B-17s are downed and 22 are damaged, and crew casualties are 20 missing and three wounded. This is the first actual combat mission undertaken by the 100th Heavy Bombardment Group, but only two of the 18 B-17s dispatched by the unit drop their bombs.

SICILY: In their heaviest single raid of the month, NAAF B-17s attack Messina with 300 tons of bombs.

June 26, 1943

ALGERIA: A 350th Fighter Group P-39 pilot downs a Ju-88 near Algiers at 1530 hours.

ENGLAND: Thirty-nine 93d Heavy Bombardment Group B-24s are dispatched to Benghazi, Libya, for temporary duty with the Ninth Air Force. The 93d, which has previously served on detached duty with the Ninth Air Force in North Africa, is the first to go of three 2d Bombardment Wing's 201st Provisional Combat Bombardment Wing B-24 groups that are to be dispatched to Libya for a special IX Bomber Command operation code-named TIDALWAVE.

The 385th Heavy Bombardment Group air echelon, in B-17s, arrives from the United States via the northern ferry route for service with the 4th Heavy Bombardment Wing's 401st Provisional Combat Bombardment Wing.

FRANCE: Of 123 1st Heavy Bombardment Wing B-17s and five YB-40s dispatched on a late-afternoon mission against Villacoublay Airdrome, a total of only 17 B-17s attack an aircraft-industry plant at Villacoublay or Poissy Airdrome (secondary targets); 39 of 42 B-17s dispatched by the 305th and 306th Heavy Bombardment groups attack their primary, Tricqueville

Airdrome; and all 81 4th Heavy Bombardment Wing B-17s dispatched against Le Mans Airdrome abort before reaching the target. Moderate GAF opposition over the targets and during the withdrawal accounts for five B-17s lost and 14 damaged, and crew losses of one killed, 51 missing, and three wounded.

Between 1850 and 1915 hours, while escorting withdrawing heavy bombers, 4th and 56th Fighter group P-47s are engaged over Dieppe by FW-190s and Bf-109s. The P-47 pilots receive credit for four confirmed victories, but four 56th Fighter Group P-47s are downed, four pilots are missing, and the wounded pilot of another 56th Group P-47 crash-lands his battle-damaged P-47 at a base in England. Also, the pilot of a damaged 56th Fighter Group P-47 is rescued from the English Channel after abandoning his airplane following an abortive landing attempt in which only one wheel comes down.

MEDITERRANEAN: A Spitfire pilot with the 52d Fighter Group downs one FW-190 and damages another north of Pantelleria at 1700 hours.

June 27, 1943

ENGLAND: Thirty-eight 44th Heavy Bombardment Group B-24s are dispatched to Benghazi, Libya, for temporary duty with the Ninth Air Force. The 44th is the second 201st Provisional Combat Bombardment Wing B-24 groups to be dispatched to take part in a special IX Bomber Command operation code-named TIDALWAVE.

June 28, 1943

ALGERIA: A 350th Fighter Group P-39 pilots downs a Ju-88 near Algiers at 1930 hours. This is the second downing of a GAF airplane in this area in three days.

ENGLAND: Although the final air echelon has been in England for only three days, a large detachment of 389th Heavy Bombardment Group B-24s is dispatched to Libya to join the rest of the 2d Bombardment Wing's 201st Combat Bombardment Wing in IX Bomber Command's upcoming Operation TIDALWAVE.

FRANCE: Of 185 1st and 4th Heavy Bombardment wing B-17s and six YB-40s dispatched, 158 B-17s attack port facilities at St.-Nazaire between 1655 and 1713 hours with 300 tons of bombs. Losses to flak and GAF fighters are eight B-17s missing and 57 damaged, three crewmen killed, 50 crewmen missing, and 14 crewmen wounded. The crews of three 95th Heavy Bombardment Group B-17s—30 men in all—are saved by the Air-Sea Rescue Service. Of special note is the first appearance in combat of longer-ranged B-17s. The new airplanes, first used by the 4th Heavy Bombardment Wing, incorporate extra wing tanks ("Tokyo tanks") that raise the fuel capacity of B-17Fs from 1,730 gallons to 2,810 gallons.

Forty-three 1st Heavy Bombardment Wing B-17s attack the Beaumont-le-Roger Airdrome with 103 tons of bombs at 1736 hours.

One hundred thirty 4th, 56th, and 78th Fighter group P-47s escort the 1st Heavy Bombardment Wing B-17s partway to St.-Nazaire, but they are not challenged.

GREECE: Twenty-four 98th Heavy Bombardment Group B-24s attack Athens/Eleusis Airdrome, and 22 376th Heavy Bombardment Group B-24s attack Athens/Kalamaki Airdrome.

ITALY: NASAF B-17s attack Leghorn.

SARDINIA: NASAF B-25s attack Alghero and Olbia airdromes, B-26s attack Milis Airdrome, and NASAF fighters attack Decimomannu Airdrome.

A total of 11 Axis fighters are downed by NAAF fighter pilots during the afternoon. 1stLt Edward T. Waters, a P-38 pilot with the 82d Fighter Group's 96th Fighter Squadron, achieves ace status when he downs an Mc.202 over Alghero Airdrome at 1230 hours.

June 29, 1943

FRANCE: All 146 1st Heavy Bombardment Wing B-17s and two YB-40s dispatched against Villacoublay and Tricqueville airdromes return to England with their bombs aboard after finding solid cloud cover over both targets. Fourteen of these B-17s are damaged by GAF fighters, but none are lost and no casualties are sustained. Likewise, no losses, damage, or crew casualties are sustained by a force of 86 4th Heavy Bombardment Wing B-17s that attacks marshalling yards and an aircraft-industry factory at Le Mans with 181 tons of bombs at about 2000 hours. During the bomber withdrawal, a 78th Fighter Group P-47 pilot downs two Bf-109s near Gournay.

June 30, 1943

ENGLAND: The RAF formally relinquishes operational control of all VIII Fighter Command units, and the 4th Air Defense Wing assumes operational control.

The 56th and 78th Fighter groups are assigned to the 4th Air Defense Wing.

MEDITERRANEAN: NACAF aircraft sink two schooners off the Sardinian coast and damage an Axis vessel at sea off the west coast of Italy.

SICILY: NASAF B-17s attack Bocca di Falco Airdrome and the city of Palermo; NASAF B-25s attack Sciacca Airdrome; and NASAF B-26s attack Bo Rizzo Airdrome. 82d Fighter Group P-38 pilots down three GAF fighters over Sciacca Airdrome at 1130 hours.

Since the air offensive opened on June 18, NAAF and IX Bomber Command medium and heavy bombers have completed 990 combat sorties against targets in Sicily and Italy, most of them against railroad marshalling yards, ports, and supply points—i.e., against the Axis supply system.

JULY 1943

July 1, 1943

ENGLAND: MajGen Frederick L. Anderson replaces MajGen Newton Longfellow as commanding general of the VIII Bomber Command.

NETHERLANDS: In the day's only combat air engagement in the theater, 78th Fighter Group P-47 pilots down two FW-190s over the Dutch coast. One P-47 and its pilot are lost—Col Arman Peterson, the 78th Fighter Group commander, who is killed.

TUNISIA: In the day's only combat air engagement in the theater, patrolling Spitfires of the 52d Fighter Group's 5th Fighter Squadron down four GAF fighters northeast of Cap Bon.

UNITED STATES: Gen Henry H. Arnold is informed that the present ratio of one fighter group for every four bomber groups operating from the U.K. must be changed to no fewer than one fighter group for every one or two bomber groups.

July 2, 1943

ENGLAND: Forty B-24s from the 2d Heavy Bombardment Wing's brand-new 389th Heavy Bombardment Group are dispatched to a base near Benghazi, Libya, to take part in a special IX Bomber Command operation code-named TIDALWAVE. It is the last of three VIII Bomber Command B-24 groups to be so dispatched. Operation TIDALWAVE is considered to be so important that the 389th Group is dispatched to take part even though it has *no* combat experience and is incompletely trained; its lead flight echelon reached England from the United States only on June 11, and the final flight echelon arrived on June 25.

ITALY: In the largest mission of its kind so far in the Mediterranean, 91 IX Bomber Command B-24s mount a preemptive attack against Axis airdromes in the "heel" of Italy—at Grottaglie, Lecce, and San Pancrazio Salentino. Four B-24s are lost, including at least two downed by aerial rockets—the first such use in the theater.

Among the B-24 groups participating in the airfield strikes are the 44th and 93d, which are on loan from VIII Bomber Command's 2d Heavy Bombardment Wing for Operation TIDALWAVE. However, due to the urgent need for every available warplane to take part in softening up targets for the impending invasion of Sicily (Operation HUSKY), Operation TIDALWAVE is put on hold, and VIII Bomber Command's entire 201st Provisional Combat Bombardment Wing (three B-24 groups) is committed to preinvasion strikes.

MEDITERRANEAN: NACAF aircraft attack two Axis ships at sea off Italy's west coast.

SICILY: The intensified final phase of Operation HUSKY, the pre-invasion bombardment of military targets in Sicily, formally begins. NATAF B-25s attack Castelvetrano Airdrome; IX Bomber Command B-25s attack Sciacca Airdrome; and NATAF's 86th Fighter-Bomber Group, in A-36s, makes its combat debut in attacks on Sicily mounted from its base at Korba, Tunisia.

1stLt Charles B. Hall, a "Tuskegee airman" flying a P-40 with the independent 99th Fighter Squadron, scores that unit's first aerial victory of the war, an FW-190 downed over southwestern Sicily on a morning mission. Hall is the first African-American airman ever to down an enemy airplane in combat. Three other FW-190s are damaged in the action by other 99th Squadron pilots, but two P-40s and their pilots are lost.

July 3, 1944

ENGLAND: A report from LtGen Jacob L. Devers, ETOUSA commanding general, to Gen Henry H. Arnold praises VIII Bomber Command bombardiers but stresses the dire need to better train gunners for high-altitude combat.

LIBYA: The 389th Heavy Bombardment Group, a B-24 unit of the Eighth Air Force's 201st Provisional Combat Bombardment Wing, arrives at Benghazi from England for special duty in IX Bomber Command's Operation TIDALWAVE. The 389th is a virgin unit that has only just been declared combat-operational.

SARDINIA: NASAF B-17s and B-25s attack Alghero, Chilivani, and Monserrato airdromes; and NASAF B-26s attack Capoterra and Milis airdromes. A 14th Fighter Group P-38 pilot downs a Bf-109 near Cagliari while covering one of the afternoon bombing missions.

SICILY: IX Bomber Command B-25s attack Comiso Airdrome. 33d and 325th Fighter group P-40 pilots down two GAF fighters in separate actions over Sciacca and Trapani/Milo airdromes, respectively.

July 4, 1943

FRANCE: On the first anniversary of the first USAAF bombing mission against targets in Occupied Europe—while on VIII Bomber Command's seventy-first mission of the war—166 1st Heavy Bombardment Wing B-17s attack aircraft-industry targets in Le Mans and Nantes at about 1245 hours with more than 404 tons of bombs. Seven B-17s are lost and 54 are damaged, of which one is written off after crash-landing in the U.K. Crew losses are one killed, 70 missing, and nine wounded. Ninety-three 4th and 78th Fighter group P-47s dispatched to provide withdrawal cover are recalled due to bad weather.

On a separate mission, 71 4th Heavy Bombardment Wing B-17s attack La Pallice at about noon with more than 137 tons of bombs. One B-17 is lost and one is damaged, and crew losses are ten missing.

SICILY: NASAF B-17s and B-26s attack Catania and Gerbini airdromes; NASAF B-25s attack two of Gerbini Airdrome's satellite fields; NATAF A-20s and B-25s attack Castelvetrano, Comiso, Sciacca, and Trapani/Milo airdromes; and IX Bomber Command B-25s attack Comiso Airdrome.

324th Fighter Group P-40 pilots down five Axis fighters while covering the NATAF morning mission against Sciacca Airdrome; and 82d Fighter Group P-38 pilots down three Italian Air Force fighters while covering NASAF's two afternoon attacks against the Gerbini Airdrome complex, at about 1315 hours and between 1500 and 1530 hours, respectively.

July 5, 1943

SICILY: NASAF B-17s, B-25s, and B-26s attack various parts of the Gerbini Airdrome complex and the radar stations at Licata and Marsala; NATAF aircraft attack the Biscari, Comiso, Sciacca, and Trapani/Milo; 86 IX Bomber Command B-24s attack port facilities, oil storage, and rail yards at Messina; and IX Bomber Command B-25s attack Biscari and Sciacca airdromes.

In the most strongly opposed bombing mission of the preinvasion bombardment cycle, 27 B-17s of NASAF's 99th Heavy Bombardment Group bound for the Gerbini Airdrome complex are attacked by an estimated 100 Axis fighters as they near the target. Three B-17s are lost, but the formation succeeds in dropping 3,240 fragmentation bombs on the airdrome, resulting in damage or loss to an estimated 28 Axis fighters on the ground. Bomber gunners claim 38 Axis fighters downed and 11 probably downed, but these are certainly liberal estimates. P-38 pilots of the 82d Fighter Group's 95th Fighter Squadron down five Italian and German fighters.

July 6, 1943

SCOTLAND: The 352d Fighter Group, in P-47s, arrives by ship from the United States for service with VIII Fighter Command.

SICILY: Beginning before dawn, NATAF aircraft mount day-long attacks against the Biscari, Comiso, Sciacca, and Trapani/Milo airdromes; NASAF B-17s and IX Bomber Command B-24s attack the Gerbini Airdrome complex; and NASAF B-25s attack Biscari Airdrome. In an engagement over Gerbini at about 1520 hours, 1st Fighter Group P-38 pilots claim seven Bf-109s as damaged or probably downed, but no victory credits are awarded.

During the night of July 6-7, NATAF light bombers attack Sciacca Airdrome.

July 7, 1943

ENGLAND: The headquarters echelon of the 7th Photographic Reconnaissance and Mapping Group arrives from the United States and is assigned to the Eighth Air Force.

ITALY: IX Fighter Command P-40 fighter-bombers attack Lucca Airdrome.

SICILY: NASAF B-17s, B-25s, and B-26s attack the Gerbini Airdrome complex and Bo Rizzo Airdrome; NATAF A-20s attack Biscari, Bo Rizzo, Comiso, Mazara del Vallo, and Trapani/Milo airdromes, as well as the Marsala radar station and several other targets; IX Bomber Command B-24s attack the Gerbini Airdrome complex and the rail line north of Brucoli; IX Bomber Command B-25s attack Biscari and Comiso airdromes.

In one of at least three fighter engagements during the day, P-40 pilots of the 325th Fighter Group's 317th Fighter Squadron down five Bf-109s and an Mc.202 during an attack on Trapani/Milo Airdrome at about 1030 hours.

July 8, 1943

ENGLAND: The 7th Photographic Reconnaissance and Mapping Group assumes operational control over the 13th, 14th, and 22d Photographic Reconnaissance squadrons, which have been operating as independent elements of the Eighth Air Force.

MEDITERRANEAN: Two Ju-88 reconnaissance aircraft are downed, one near Bizerte and the other over the Algerian coast, by pilots of NACAF's 350th and 52d Fighter groups, respectively.

SICILY: NASAF B-25s and B-26s mount several attacks against the Gerbini Airdrome complex; NASAF P-38s strafe radar installation in the eastern part of the island; NATAF B-25s attack Biscari and Comiso airdromes; NATAF A-20s attack Sciacca Airdrome; NATAF A-36s attack a sulfur plant, a rail yard, and numerous rail and road targets throughout the island; IX Bomber Command B-24s attack the railroad station, a marshalling yard, and telephone and telegraph links at Catania; IX Bomber Command B-25s attack Biscari and Comiso airdromes; and IX Fighter Command P-40s attack Biscari Airdrome. Also, three Bf-109s are downed in a large afternoon fighter battle involving 324th Fighter Group and 99th Fighter Squadron P-40s over Sciacca Airdrome.

During the night of July 8–9, NATAF aircraft attack Sciacca and Trapani/Milo airdromes.

July 9, 1943

CRETE: IX Bomber Command B-24s attack Maleme Airdrome.

The Maleme mission is the combat debut for the 389th Heavy Bombardment Group, one of three VIII Bomber Command B-24 groups on loan to the IX Bomber Command.

MEDITERRANEAN: The theater's first USAAF night-fighter unit, the Twelfth Air Force's independent 415th Night-Fighter Squadron in British-built Beaufighters, becomes operational.

SICILY: Throughout the day, NAAF and Ninth Air Force bombers and fighters attack numerous targets, especially airdromes, throughout Sicily. In a special last-minute reaction to late-breaking intelligence, 18 IX Bomber Command B-24s successfully mount a low-level attack against a hotel at Taormina that is thought to house the main headquarters overseeing all German forces in Sicily.

P-40 pilots of the 324th Fighter Group's 316th Fighter Squadron engaged by Bf-109s over the Castelvetrano Airdrome during a morning mission receive credit for five confirmed victories and five probables. In other morning action, a 14th Fighter Group P-38 pilot downs a Bf-109 near Sciacca Airdrome, and 324th Fighter Group P-40 pilots down four Bf-109s over Trapani/Milo Airdrome.

As the Allied invasion fleet approaches the landing beaches, Allied air commanders declare that their air forces have attained air supremacy over Sicily. By the time the Allied amphibious and airborne assaults begin, only two airfields on Sicily are fully operational—Sciacca and Trapani/Milo

airdromes; all the others have been abandoned or cannot be used because of damage.

July 10, 1943

FRANCE: Thirty-six of 64 1st Heavy Bombardment Wing B-17s attack Abbeville/Drucat Airdrome at about 0730 hours with just over 62 tons of bombs, and 34 of 116 1st Heavy Bombardment Wing B-17s and five YB-40s dispatched attack Caen Airdrome at about 0830 hours with more than 74 tons of bombs. Losses against light GAF flak and fighter opposition are one B-17 lost and 33 damaged, and ten crewmen missing and one wounded.

One hundred one 4th Heavy Bombardment Wing B-17s dispatched against Paris/Le Bourget Airport abort over France because of thick cloud cover.

In all, 128 4th, 56th, and 78th Fighter group P-47s are dispatched to escort the bombers during the penetration and withdrawal phases, but no GAF fighters are spotted within range of the USAAF fighters.

SICILY: In history's first mass airborne assault, which begins at 0245 hours, 133 tow planes, including 105 51st Troop Carrier Wing C-47s, release glider-borne British Army airborne troops near Syracuse (Operation LADBROKE). The landing itself is a shambles due to bad weather and inexact techniques, but the British troops manage to secure their objectives. Of the 133 gliders released, only 12 come down in the landing zone and 47 are lost at sea, most with all the troops aboard. The remaining 74 gliders come to rest pretty much all over the island.

A concurrent parachute drop by American paratroopers against Gela (Operation HUSKY No. 1) meets pretty much the same difficulties. A total of 226 52d Troop Carrier Wing C-47s drop 2,781 paratroopers and 891 parachute equipment packs, but barely enough of both to secure the vital Gela crossroads actually hit the drop zone.

During the day, elements of the U.S. 82d Airborne Division and U.S. Army ground forces landing from the sea near Gela link up on the high ground overlooking the Gela/Ponte Olivo Airdrome. Also, British Army ground forces capture the airfield at Pachino.

Throughout the day, NAAF and Ninth Air Force bombers, fighters, and fighter-bombers undertake a dizzying variety of missions in support of the Allied invasion forces.

Although NAAF fighters mount a maximum effort over the invasion fleet and the entire island, the day's momentous events are not strongly opposed by Axis air forces. Throughout the day, in fact, only 24 Axis aircraft are downed by NAAF fighters. In the day's biggest air action, which takes place over southwestern Sicily between 1800 and 1820 hours, P-38 pilots of the 82d Fighter Group's 96th Fighter Squadron down nine Axis fighters and a Ju-88. Two new aces emerge from this action: FO Frank D. Hurlbut, who downs three FW-190s, and 2dLt Ward A. Kuentzel, who downs the Ju-88 and an FW-190.

During the night of July 10–11, NASAF aircraft attack Sciacca and Trapani/Milo airdromes. All planned follow-up airborne operations scheduled for the night of July 10–11 are canceled.

July 11, 1942

ITALY: IX Bomber Command B-24s attack the port area at Reggio di Calabria, directly opposite Messina.

SICILY: NASAF B-17s attack the marshalling yards at Catania; NASAF B-26s attack the Gerbini Airdrome complex and Trapani/Milo airdrome; NASAF B-25s and P-38s attack Sciacca Airdrome and a town; IX Bomber Command B-24s attack a town; and IX Bomber Command B-25s attack the Bo Rizzo and Trapani/Milo airdromes as well as several area targets.

If anything, Axis air forces are even less aggressive in the defense of Sicily than they were on D day. Despite an all-out effort by USAAF fighters to stop penetrations by Axis warplanes, only 16 confirmed

victories are declared, of which half are against GAF medium bombers. Capt Carl W. Payne, a Spitfire pilot with the 31st Fighter Group's 309th Fighter Squadron, achieves ace status when he downs a GAF fighter near Pazzollo at 1615 hours.

Overall, the invasion is going well. U.S. ground forces capture Comiso Airdrome, but it is unusable due to bomb damage.

During the day, Axis ground forces mount a major counterattack toward Gela, which is being held in part by elements of the U.S. 82d Airborne Division. It is decided by the high command to conduct a reinforcement of the threatened area by a follow-on airborne landing during the night. Some 2,000 U.S. Army paratroopers are assigned to the night drop (Operation HUSKY No. 2), which will be carried out from bases in North Africa to the vicinity of Gela by 144 C-47s from four troop-carrier groups operating under the control of the 52d Troop Carrier Wing. The drop zone is to be the Gela/Farello Airdrome. Using Malta as a turning point in their flight from the rendezvous off Tunisia, the C-47s reach Sicily on time and in the right place despite strong headwinds, a low haze, and a lack of navigational aids. Unknown to the flight commanders, however, the drop zone has only recently fallen back into the hands of Axis ground troops. Also, no one has bothered to tell the ships of the invasion force, nor the troops manning newly erected coast-defense positions, that the air armada is to be expected. As the C-47s reach the fleet, they are taken under intense antiaircraft fire, and even more fire is added as the airplanes fly over the coast. Aircraft losses—which in many cases include crewmen and passengers—are put at 23, and many crewmen and passengers in aircraft that make it through the maelstrom are nonetheless killed or wounded by penetrating bullets and shrapnel. Half the C-47s returning to Tunisia report heavy damage. A number of pilots who are faced with the need to overfly the landing zone several times in the end refuse to drop vulnerable troops into the maelstrom, and so the reinforcement is further weakened. Perhaps as a result of the diluted and scattered reinforcement effort, the paratroop force already on the ground is unable to fight its way out of an isolated position produced by the enemy counterattack, and so the situation on the ground is at least as bad as it was before the reinforcement effort began.

July 12, 1943

ITALY: IX Bomber Command B-24s attack the port facilities, ferry terminal, and marshalling yards at Reggio di Calabria, and the ferry terminal and rail yards at Villa San Giovanni.

SICILY: NASAF B-17s attack rail bridges around Messina; NASAF and NATAF B-25s, B-26s, and A-20s attack the Gerbini satellite fields, and Agrigento, Canicatti, and Trapani/Milo airdromes; NATAF A-20s and fighters attack Trapani/Milo airdrome and numerous rail and communications targets throughout the island; and IX Bomber Command B-25s attack Bo Rizzo Airdrome.

Efforts by Axis aircraft to penetrate the Allied air cover over the fleet and the invasion beaches are virtually nil; throughout the day, only ten Axis fighters are downed in the area. Maj John L. Bradley, the commanding officer of the 33d Fighter Group's 58th Fighter Squadron, achieves ace status when he downs a Bf-109 during a morning mission near Licata.

Gela/Ponte Olivo Airdrome is captured intact by U.S. Army ground units.

July 13, 1943

BAY OF BISCAY: The 479th Antisubmarine Group, formed in England on July 8 and equipped with B-24s, begins mounting anti-submarine patrols out of the English coastal base at St. Eval in search of surfaced German Navy submarines. By July 18, the group will have virtually swept the Bay of Biscay clean of surfaced German submarines. Despite continued vigorous patrolling, there are to be no sightings of surfaced enemy submarines after August 2, and the group will cease operations in October.

ENGLAND: The first air echelon of the 390th Heavy Bombardment Group, in B-17s, arrives from the United States via the northern ferry route. The unit is assigned to the 4th Heavy Bombardment Wing's 402d Provisional Combat Bombardment Wing.

ITALY: IX Bomber Command B-24s attack Crotone Airdrome.

SICILY: NASAF B-17s, B-25s, and B-26s attack the Carcitela, Enna, and Trapani/Milo airdromes; the town of Randazzo; and numerous targets of opportunity around the island. Also, NATAF bombers and fighters attack tactical and communications targets, including Axis troop concentrations; IX Bomber Command B-24s attack a town; and IX Bomber Command B-25s attack road targets and several towns in the British Eighth Army zone.

Pachino Airdrome is open to RAF fighters, which arrive from bases in North Africa to begin ground-support operations. It is noted that Axis aircraft are no longer offering resistance over the island; only three Bf-109s and an Mc.202 are downed over Sicily by USAAF fighters.

The 31st Fighter Group moves from Gozo Island (next to Malta) to Gela/Ponte Olivo Airdrome and immediately begins flight operations.

In the Sicilian Campaign's fourth and final airborne mission, 51st Troop Carrier Wing C-47s are charged with dropping a force of British Army paratroopers at night against a bridge near Catania. Of the 124 C-47s dispatched from North Africa, 11 are shot down, 50 are damaged by friendly fire, and 27 return to their bases with paratroopers aboard. Despite the rough handling, the British force does succeed in securing its objective.

During the night of July 13–14, NATAF bombers, fighters, and fighter-bombers attack numerous tactical and communications targets throughout the island.

July 14, 1943

FRANCE: The day's heavy-bomber activity is undertaken in three phases. In the first, after a 381st Heavy Bombardment Group B-17 explodes in midair and crashed during assembly, 53 of 64 1st Heavy Bombardment Wing B-17s dispatched attack Amiens/Glisy Airdrome at about 0745 hours with 83 tons of bombs. GAF flak and fighters down one B-17 and damage 36, including one in a collision with an FW-190. This and one other damaged B-17 crash-land in the U.K. Of the ten men in the B-17 that explodes and crashes during assembly, six are killed and four are rescued. Overall crew casualties in this phase of the day's operations are six killed, ten missing, and three wounded.

In the second phase of the day's operations, 52 of 84 4th Heavy Bombardment Wing B-17s attack Paris/Le Bourget Airport with nearly 123 tons of bombs. Heavy GAF fighter opposition and flak down four B-17s and damage 51, of which one is abandoned by its entire crew over the U.K. Crew losses are 41 missing and 16 wounded.

In the third phase, 101 of 111 1st Heavy Bombardment Group B-17s and five YB-40s attack Villacoublay Airdrome with more than 232 tons of bombs at about 0810 hours. Two B-17s are lost and 68 are damaged. One of the damaged B-17s ditches off the English coast and the entire crew is rescued. Crew losses for this phase are one killed, 21 missing, and three wounded.

As is now becoming commonplace, VIII Fighter Command P-47s provide escort to the extremity of their range during both the penetration and withdrawal phases of VIII Bomber Command heavy-bomber missions. On this day, however, only the Amiens/Glisy bomber force is escorted by all 128 operational P-47s of the 4th, 56th, and 78th Fighter groups. In several running engagements during the penetration, two FW-190s are downed by 4th and 78th Fighter group pilots, but three P-47s are lost, including a battle-damaged P-47 that is abandoned by its pilot off Newhaven. This pilot is rescued, but the other two are carried as missing.

ITALY: Allied air commanders order a major intensification of the air effort to interdict the flow of Axis reinforcements and supplies to Sicily from the Italian mainland, and Naples is designated as the primary target of the effort. The first attack under this edict is undertaken during the night of July 14–15 by RAF Wellingtons under NASAF control.

SICILY: NASAF B-17s, B-25s, and B-26s attack Enna, Marsala, Messina, Randazzo, and numerous targets of opportunity all across the island; IX Bomber Command B-24s and RAF heavy bombers under IX Bomber Command control attack the rail line, marshalling yards, port facilities, and oil storage at Messina; and IX Bomber Command B-25s attack targets around Enna.

Only one GAF airplane is credited in the entire theater, an HS-129 ground-attack plane that is downed near Agrigento at 0905 hours by a P-51 pilot of the 68th Reconnaissance Group's 111th Reconnaissance Squadron.

Biscari Airdrome is captured by U.S. Army infantrymen.

During the night of July 14–15, IX Bomber Command B-25s attack Palermo.

July 15, 1943

ITALY: NASAF B-17s attack Villa San Giovanni, and IX Bomber Command B-24s attack the main airdrome and two satellite fields at Foggia.

SICILY: NASAF medium bombers attack Vibo Valentia; NATAF A-20s and fighters attack Palermo and targets of opportunity around the island; NAAF fighters mount numerous ad hoc strafing missions wherever tactical and communications targets can be located; and IX Bomber Command B-25s attack Randazzo.

During the night of July 15–16, NATAF A-20s and B-25s attack Randazzo and nearby roads.

July 16, 1943

FRANCE: In the VIII Air Support

Command's inaugural operational combat mission, 14 323d Medium Bombardment Group B-26s conduct a medium-altitude attack with about 17 tons of bombs against a marshalling yard at Abbeville. Ten of the B-26s are damaged by flak, and two crewmen are wounded. This is the 323d Medium Bombardment Group's combat debut.

ITALY: IX Bomber Command B-24s attacking Bari Airdrome are attacked by Axis fighters. Three B-24s are downed against gunners' claims for 11 Axis fighters.

MEDITERRANEAN: Axis air units, which have all but disappeared from the skies within range of North Africa–based Allied day fighters, intensify their efforts to bomb Allied shipping and ground targets around Sicily at night. The only Axis airplane downed in the theater is an Fi-156 observation plane that falls prey over Sicily to a 27th Fighter-Bomber Group A-36 during an afternoon ground-support mission.

At 1950 hours, 17 325th Fighter Group P-40s attack and knock out the Axis radar station on Ustica Island, northwest of Sicily. This allows an RAF bomber formation attacking targets around Capodichino at about midnight to do so without advance warning.

SICILY: NATAF aircraft attack a town and numerous targets of opportunity, and IX Bomber Command aircraft attack two towns.

During the night of July 16–17, IX Bomber Command B-25s attack Catania in support of the British Eighth Army.

July 17, 1943

ENGLAND: The 322d Medium Bombardment Group, which lost ten B-26s and 60 crewmen in a minimum-level raid over Holland on May 17, is returned to combat status following retraining as a medium-altitude bombing unit. The group comes under the operational control of the VIII Air Support Command.

FRANCE: Weather causes severe disruptions after several hundred VIII Bomber Command heavy bombers are already over the Continent. Briefed for a mission against rail-industry targets in Hannover, 205 1st Heavy Bombardment Wing B-17s and two YB-40s are recalled at 0955 hours, but 33 B-17s attack various targets of opportunity along the return route. GAF fighters dog the bombers all the way, damaging 52, of which one is written off in a forced landing in the U.K. after seven crewmen bail out. Also, one returning 351st Heavy Bombardment Group B-17 that is attacked by GAF fighters over the North Sea ditches, but its crew is rescued. Crew casualties are one killed, three missing, nine wounded.

B-26s of the VIII Air Support Command's 3d Medium Bombardment Wing conduct an unchallenged diversionary mission to the Cayeaux area, and the 13th Photographic Reconnaissance Squadron dispatches five F-5s to France, of which one is lost.

ITALY: At approximately 1430 hours, 77 IX Bomber Command B-24s attack marshalling yards and rail installations around Naples. This attack is followed at 1530 hours by 49 NASAF B-17s going after the same targets. Next, at about 1600 hours, 107 NASAF B-26s, escorted by 98 P-38s, also attack Naples. During this attack, in the theater's only fighter action of the day, P-38s from the 1st, 14th, and 82d Fighter groups take on a feeble effort by a handful of Axis fighters to get at the bombers. Only one Axis fighter is downed in this action, and several other Axis fighters are damaged. Finally, within the hour, 48 NASAF B-17s and 72 NASAF B-25s attack targets around Naples under escort by 67 NASAF P-38s. In all (including an unspecified mission by 59 bombers), 868 tons of bombs dropped in 408 NASAF bomber sorties exact a heavy toll in damage in and immediately around Naples. The day's effort costs NASAF eight bombers, seven downed by flak and one downed by an enemy fighter. Also, 80 IX Bomber Command B-24s attack Naples through fighter opposition described as "fierce." Two B-24s are lost.

NETHERLANDS: The 4th Heavy Bombardment Wing is recalled at 0955 hours because of bad weather encountered on the way to its briefed target, an aircraft factory in Hamburg. On the way home, 22 B-17s of the 385th and 388th Heavy Bombardment groups, making their combat debuts with the 401st and 403d Provisional Combat Bombardment wings, respectively, drop 49 tons of bombs through holes in the clouds on what they believe to be the Fokker aircraft factory in Amsterdam. Unfortunately, no bombs hit the Fokker plant, but 150 Dutch civilians are killed. One 4th Heavy Bombardment Wing B-17 from one of the veteran groups drops ten 500-pound bombs on an Axis convoy seen through a hole in the clouds, but results are unobserved. In all, one 4th Heavy Bombardment Wing B-17 is lost to enemy fire, one is damaged beyond repair, and 41 are otherwise damaged. Crew losses are one killed, 14 missing, and three wounded.

One hundred twenty-six 4th, 56th, and 78th Fighter group P-47s escort the bombers, but two-thirds of the fighters are recalled due to bad weather.

SICILY: Following through on night-long attacks against tactical targets, NATAF aircraft attack Catania and Paterno, the Riposto railroad station, and tanks, guns, trains, and trucks throughout the island. Also, IX Bomber Command B-25s attack Catania and rail lines and roads around Paterno.

July 18, 1943

SICILY: NATAF A-20s attack Catania; NATAF A-36s attack several towns in the battle area; and IX Bomber Command B-25s attack Catania and Randazzo. Between 1918 and 1923 hours, 14th Fighter Group P-38 pilots down 15 Ju-52s between Ischia and Ustica Island.

The 33d Fighter Group moves from Marghana Airdrome, Pantelleria, to Licata Airdrome, Sicily, and the 27th Fighter-Bomber Group moves from Korba Airdrome, Tunisia, to Gela/Ponte Olivo, Sicily. Both units immediately begin flight operations from their new Sicilian bases.

During the night of July 18–19, NATAF A-20s attack Catania.

July 19, 1943

ITALY: As part of an ongoing effort to force Italy out of the war by psychological means, more than 500 Allied bombers attack military targets in and around Rome with more than 1,000 tons of bombs. IX Bomber Command contributes all five of its B-24 groups to the undertaking, and the NASAF dispatches four groups amounting to 150 B-17s. Taking special care to avoid priceless ruins and other important historical and cultural sites—a feat sometimes accomplished by flying difficult and disadvantageous courses to various targets—the heavy bombers are credited with putting the Lorenzo and Littoria marshalling yards out of action. Also taking part in the attacks are two NASAF B-25 groups and three NASAF B-26 groups, escorted by 169 P-38s. The medium bombers attack and cause severe damage to the Littoria Airdrome and the two airfields of the Ciampino Airdrome complex. The only mishap with respect to historical and art treasures is the inadvertent bombing of the Basilica of San Lorenzo by NASAF B-17s. Despite the fact that warning leaflets had been dropped for two days prior to the attack, and even though the precise hour of the attack had been given, opposition is nil. The only serious flak concentration is encountered over Ciampino, and the only aircraft losses of the day are a B-25 and a B-26 downed by flak. Only one Italian fighter is downed over Rome, by an 82d Fighter Group P-38 pilot. In fact, this is the only victory credit awarded in the entire theater.

The result of the Rome attacks, coupled with earlier heavy attacks on Naples, is a 200-mile gap in the Italian rail system at a time when Axis forces need to move reinforcements and supplies to Sicily and southern Italy.

In other action over the mainland, NASAF B-25s and B-26s attack Ciampino.

Following the Rome mission, all IX Bomber Command B-24s based in the Benghazi, Libya, area are ordered to stand down from combat operations in order to train for Operation TIDALWAVE, which is set for August 1.

SICILY: NAAF P-40s attack rail facilities around Alcamo; NATAF A-36s attack railroads and road traffic throughout western Sicily; and IX Bomber Command B-25s attack Catania and Randazzo.

The 57th Fighter Group's "A" Party moves from Tunisia to Pachino Airdrome.

During the night of July 19–20, NATAF A-20s and B-25s attack roads and towns near the battle area.

July 20, 1943

ITALY: In all of Italy, including Sicily, only one Axis airplane is credited, an Italian SM.82 encountered and brought down between Naples and Palermo in a shared effort by three 1st Fighter Group P-38 pilots.

SARDINIA: Forty-eight P-40 dive-bombers from the 325th Fighter Group attack Monserrato Airdrome. Seven of about 40 Italian and German fighters that rise to meet the attack are downed in a running dogfight between 0700 and 0720 hours with 317th Fighter Squadron P-40s. In this fight, Capt Ralph G. Taylor, Jr., achieves ace status when he downs two Mc.202s and a Bf-109. One P-40 and its pilot are lost.

SICILY: NAAF fighter-bombers attack numerous targets of opportunity in western Sicily; IX Bomber Command B-25s attack two towns; and NASAF B-25s attack Montecorvino Airdrome.

NATAF's 86th Fighter-Bomber Group moves from Korba, Tunisia, to join the 27th Fighter-Bomber Group at Gela.

During the night of July 20–21, NATAF A-20s attack an Axis motor column near Randazzo.

July 21, 1943

ITALY: NASAF B-17s attack Grosseto Airdrome.

SICILY: About 20 IX Bomber Command B-25s attack Randazzo.

U.S. Army ground forces capture the Castelvetrano Airdrome.

July 22, 1943

ENGLAND: An Allied intelligence report given in connection with an assessment of the efficacy of the Combined Bomber Offensive to date indicates that half the GAF's fighter strength is deployed in the defense of the bomber routes from the U.K. to targets in Germany and Occupied Europe. It is noted that these deployments are being made at the expense of other fronts and theaters where active ground fighting is under way.

ITALY: NASAF B-17s attack the Foggia Airdrome complex and a marshalling yard at Battipaglia, and NASAF B-26s attack a bridge and a marshalling yard at Salerno.

SARDINIA: The 325th Fighter Group returns to Sardinia in an ongoing effort to break the will of the Axis air units defending the island. In the course of several simultaneous sweeps over the island's airdromes, the P-40 pilots down 12 Mc.202s, two Me-209s, two Ju-52s, and two Fi-156s between 0940 and 0950 hours. Two P-40s and their pilots are lost on this mission.

SICILY: NATAF A-20s attack Randazzo and roads, rail lines, and other ground targets near the battlefront. The 27th and 31st Fighter groups begin flying missions from Agrigento Airdrome, the former to support U.S. Army ground forces and the latter to stave off Axis air attacks from close range.

1stLt William J. Sloan, a P-38 ace with the 82d Fighter Group's 96th Fighter Squadron, downs a Bf-109 over Battipaglia, bringing his final personal tally to 12 confirmed victories. One other Bf-109 is downed in this action, by a member of Sloan's squadron.

The city of Palermo is surrendered without opposition to U.S. Army ground forces.

July 23, 1943

ITALY: NASAF B-17s attack Leverano Airdrome, NASAF B-25s attack Crotone Airdrome, and NASAF B-26s attack Aquino Airdrome.

SICILY: NATAF B-25s and fighters attack vehicles and bridges near Randazzo and Axis landing craft off the coast.

July 24, 1943

ENGLAND: MajGen Frederick L. Anderson, VIII Bomber Command commanding general, declares Blitz Week, an effort to mount seven major bombing missions on seven consecutive days in order to stress the GAF fighter defenses.

ITALY: NASAF B-17s and B-25s attack the rail yards at Bologna, and NASAF B-26s attack the rail yards at Paola.

MEDITERRANEAN: NACAF's independent 414th Night-Fighter Squadron, in Beaufighters, mounts its first operational sorties of the war. Coincidentally, the 415th Night-Fighter Squadron's Capt Nathaniel H. Lindsay and his radar operator, FO Austin G. Petry, succeed in scoring their unit's first and the day's only confirmed victory in the entire theater, an He-115 reconnaissance floatplane downed over the Tyrrhenian Sea at an undisclosed time.

NORWAY: In the Eighth Air Force's first-ever attack on targets in Norway—and its longest mission undertaken to date (a 1,900-mile round trip)—167 1st Heavy Bombardment Wing B-17s accompanied by one YB-40 and 41 4th Heavy Bombardment Wing long-range B-17s attack a nitrate plant near Heroya and the naval base at Trondheim, respectively, with more than 495 tons of bombs. Both forces are virtually unopposed, but 64 B-17s in all are damaged, of which one is written off after crash-landing in England and another after crash-landing in Sweden, where the crew is interned. In all, three crewmen are wounded and ten are interned. Due to solid cloud cover, a third force composed of 84 4th Heavy Bombardment Wing long-range

B-17s is prevented from attacking its briefed target, the Bergen port area, and it returns to the U.K. with its bombs.

This mission also marks the first use of splasher beacons to facilitate assembly in bad weather. After taking off individually, the heavy bombers fly out to sea to the location of a designated radio beacon. There, individual groups formate and then fly on to acquire a course to the target by overflying three additional designated splasher beacons. This experiment is deemed a complete success and will be used in the future to thwart the effects of bad flying conditions.

SICILY: NATAF fighter-bombers attack an Axis transport at sea near Mt. Etna and port facilities, barges, and several Italian Navy warships in and around Messina harbor. 33d Fighter Group P-40s fly combat and armed-reconnaissance missions in support of ground troops and attack motor vehicles.

July 25, 1943

BELGIUM: Thirteen 323d Medium Bombardment Group B-26s, of 18 dispatched, attack coke ovens near Ghent from medium altitude with 16 tons of bombs. Six of the B-26s are damaged, but there are no crew casualties.

GERMANY: A force of 123 1st Heavy Bombardment Wing B-17s briefed for a mission against a diesel-engine factory in Hamburg is diverted by cloud cover against the city's shipyards and various targets of opportunity. In all, 100 of the B-17s drop nearly 196 tons of bombs between 1317 and 1414 hours, but losses are excessive—15 B-17s missing and 67 damaged by heavy flak and GAF fighter opposition. From this force alone, crew losses are one killed, 150 missing, and five wounded.

A second mission by three 1st Heavy Bombardment Wing B-17 groups bound for the Kiel shipyards is abandoned altogether when the aircraft are unable to assemble in bad weather over England.

The day's third heavy-bomber mission is conducted by 118 of 141 4th Heavy

Bombardment Wing B-17s dispatched against aircraft factories in Warnemunde. Unable to locate this target because of bad weather, 118 B-17s attack the Kiel shipyards and other targets of opportunity with total of just over 522 tons of bombs between 1630 and 1700 hours. Faced with flak and modest GAF fighter opposition, this force sustains four B-17s lost and 51 damaged, of which one ditches at sea and another crash-lands in the U.K. and from which both crews are rescued. Crew casualties are one killed, 40 missing, and three wounded.

ITALY: Benito Mussolini's rule is declared at an end by King Victor Emmanuel III, who appoints himself to head the Italian Army and Marshal Pietro Badoglio to head the government.

SICILY: NATAF A-20s and B-25s mount around-the-clock attacks on docking facilities, shipping, road traffic, and Axis tanks; IX Bomber Command B-25s attack docking facilities and shipping at Milazzo; and nearly 100 IX Fighter Command P-40 fighter-bombers attack the harbors at Catania, Milazzo, and Taormina.

During the night of July 25–26, NATAF B-25s attack Adrano, Milazzo, and Paterno.

July 26, 1943

FRANCE: Although briefed to attack the St.-Omer/Ft. Rouge Airdrome, 15 of 18 323d Medium Bombardment Group B-26s dispatched are only able to find the St.-Omer/Longuenesse Airdrome, on which they drop nearly 15 tons of bombs at about 1115 hours. Four of the B-26s are damaged by flak.

GERMANY: Attacking through heavy flak and GAF fighter opposition, 50 1st Heavy Bombardment Wing B-17s and two YB-40s and 44 4th Heavy Bombardment Group B-17s bomb two separate rubber factories in Hannover between noon and 1245 hours with a total of nearly 134 tons of bombs. Fourteen B-17s are lost over enemy territory, one is written off after reaching a base in the U.K., and two ditch near England during the return flight, but both crews are

rescued. Crew losses are four killed, 126 missing, and 22 wounded.

When the pilot of a 92d Heavy Bombardment Group YB-40 becomes crazed from a bullet wound to the head during a fighter attack over the target, FO John C. Morgan, the co-pilot, flies the airplane in formation with one hand for two hours while restraining the struggling pilot with the other hand, until a fellow crewman can relieve the situation. Morgan is awarded a Medal of Honor for this feat.

Unable to attack the briefed target in Hannover, B-17s from three groups of the 4th Heavy Bombardment Wing attack targets of opportunity, including Wilhelmshaven, Wesermunde, and a convoy at sea. These groups suffer aggregate losses of five B-17s missing, one B-17 ditched (from which the crew is saved), and one B-17 damaged, with crew losses of one killed, 51 missing, and three wounded.

A separate mission by 121 1st Heavy Bombardment Wing B-17s is dispatched against the Hamburg U-boat yards, but, thanks to bad weather, only 54 of the heavy bombers drop just over 126 tons of bombs at noon. Lost against light opposition are two B-17s, and crew losses are one killed, 20 missing, and three wounded.

A total of 86 heavy bombers are damaged by flak or fighters in all three phases of the day's mission.

ITALY: NASAF B-26s attack a marshalling yard at Paola.

MEDITERRANEAN: Events in Sicily and Italy are going so well that the CCS direct Gen Dwight D. Eisenhower to begin immediate planning for Operation AVALANCHE, the invasion of Italy. The main objectives outlined are the port of Naples and nearby airfields.

SARDINIA: Maj Robert L. Baseler, 325th Fighter Group operations officer, achieves ace status when he downs an Mc.202 over the island at about 0930 hours. Altogether on this mission, 325th Fighter Group P-40 pilots down four Mc.202s and a Bf-109.

SICILY: NATAF A-20s repeatedly attack

Regalbuto through the day; NATAF fighters attack Axis troop and supply movements via road, rail, and shipping; IX Bomber Command B-25s attack Milazzo; and IX Fighter Command P-40 fighter-bombers attack Catania and shipping at Riposto.

The 79th Fighter Group "A" Party moves to Cassible Airdrome.

July 27, 1943

FRANCE: Seventeen 323d Medium Bombardment Group B-26s, escorted by 119 P-47s, attack the Tricqueville Airdrome with 18 tons of bombs at 1825 hours. After the bombers are safely on their way home, the fighters conduct an unchallenged sweep around Rouen.

ITALY: NASAF B-17s attack Capua Airdrome and the rail line at Lioni.

MEDITERRANEAN: Gen Dwight D. Eisenhower directs subordinate commanders to plan for a dual invasion of Italy. U.S. forces will land near Naples while British forces will land in Calabria, on the "toe" of Italy. D-Day is to be on or around September 7.

In the day's only air action in the theater, a 414th Night-Fighter Squadron Beaufighter crew downs an SM.82 transport over the sea west of Sicily.

SICILY: NASAF B-25s and B-26s attack the landing ground at Scalea; NATAF aircraft attack a wide range of transportation targets and docking areas throughout the island; and IX Fighter Command P-40s attack shipping at Catania and numerous tactical targets throughout northeastern Sicily.

July 28, 1943

BELGIUM: Seventeen 323d Medium Bombardment Group B-26s attack coke ovens at Zeebrugge with 33 1,000-pound bombs at 1105 hours.

FRANCE: Eighteen 323d Medium Bombardment Group B-26s dispatched against Tricqueville Airdrome are recalled after failing to rendezvous with P-47 escorts on the way to the target.

GERMANY: Of 182 1st Bombardment Heavy Wing B-17s dispatched to Kassel in bad weather, 58 attack the Fieseler Aircraft factory, and 37 of 120 4th Bombardment Wing B-17s dispatched to Oschersleben attack the assigned target or targets of opportunity in Germany and the Netherlands with a total of 177 tons of bombs. Losses from heavy flak and determined GAF fighter attacks are heavy: A total of 22 B-17s are lost, three battle-damaged B-17s are written off after crash-landing in the U.K., and 118 B-17s are damaged, including one in a crash-landing in the U.K. Crew losses are 205 missing and 15 wounded

This day marks a turning point in fighter operations over northwestern Europe. In the first use of jettisonable belly tanks (albeit bulky, unpressurized Fiberglas models normally used for ferry flights) by VIII Fighter Command aircraft, 4th Fighter Group P-47s assigned to withdrawal support for the B-17s become the first USAAF fighters to penetrate into German airspace. During the withdrawal, for the loss of one P-47 and its pilot, 4th Fighter Group pilots down nine FW-190s and Bf-109s in a running fight between Utrecht and Rotterdam from 1155 to 1220 hours. 1stLt Duane W. Beeson, a P-47 pilot with the 4th Fighter Group's 334th Fighter Squadron, achieves ace status when he downs a Bf-109 near Rotterdam at about 1215 hours. (Two of Beeson's earlier victories were scored while he was flying with 71 RAF Eagle Squadron.)

Also of special note is the first known use by GAF fighters of aerial rockets, whose firing is observed and even photographed with a gun camera by a 78th Fighter Group P-47 pilot. Although highly inaccurate, the Germany Army 21cm rocket adapted for use by twin-engine fighters is capable of destroying any heavy bomber it strikes. This fact is driven home at this very first encounter when one of the rockets blows apart a 385th Heavy Bombardment Group B-17 that then crashes into two other B-17s in the same formation. All three B-17s are lost. It is also noted that the GAF rocket can be fired from outside the effective range of machine guns aboard the B-17s. It is viewed as something of a miracle that USAAF fighters equipped with long-distance tanks appear on the very day this dreaded stand-off weapon makes its combat debut.

SARDINIA: In the day's only air action in the theater, P-40 pilots of the 325th Fighter Group's 318th Fighter Squadron down two Mc.202s near Monserrato Airdrome during a morning sweep.

SICILY: NATAF A-20s attack Centuripe, Milazzo, and Regalbuto; NAAF A-36s and P-40s attack traffic, bridges, and roads near the battlefront; and IX Fighter Command P-40s attack shipping at Catania and Santa Teresa.

The 79th Fighter Group "B" Party arrives from Tunisia to join the "A" Party at Cassible Airdrome.

July 29, 1943

ENGLAND: Eighteen 323d Medium Bombardment Group B-26s briefed for an attack on Amsterdam/Schipol Airport land back at their base with all bombs aboard.

FRANCE: Nineteen 323d Medium Bombardment Group B-26s attack the St.-Omer/Ft. Rouge Airdrome at about 1830 hours with more than 18 tons of bombs. Eight B-26s are damaged by flak, but there are no crew casualties.

Twenty 386th Medium Bombardment Group B-26s, in their unit's combat debut, mount a diversion for the St.-Omer mission. The bombers are covered by 128 P-47s, but only one FW-190 is damaged in the only fighter action of the day.

GERMANY: Ninety-one of 167 1st Heavy Bombardment Wing B-17s and one YB-40 dispatched attack the day's primary target, the shipyards at Kiel, at 0900 hours, but all the other B-17s either abort or attack targets of opportunity or targets of last resort because of the heavy cloud cover encountered over Kiel. In all, 139 B-17s attack targets in and around Kiel with just over 315

tons of bombs. Also, 767,000 leaflets are released over the city. GAF flak and fighter opposition account for six B-17s lost and 63 damaged, of which one is written off following a safe landing in the U.K.

In the second phase of the mission, 54 of 81 4th Heavy Bombardment Wing B-17s dispatched attack the Heinkel aircraft factory at Warnemunde at about 0920 hours with 129 tons of bombs. This formation loses two B-17s in a collision near the U.K. coast, plus two B-17s downed and seven damaged by enemy fire. Crew losses are 40 missing from four downed B-17s.

ITALY: NASAF B-17s attack Viterbo Airdrome, and NASAF B-26s attack Aquino Airdrome;.

MEDITERRANEAN: The day's only confirmed victory in the theater is awarded to a 414th Night-Fighter Squadron Beaufighter crew for bringing down an Italian Air Force transport 50 miles off the coast of Sardinia at an undisclosed time.

SICILY: NATAF A-20s and fighters attack Milazzo and Regalbuto, shipping off Messina, and gun emplacements and motor vehicles in northeastern Sicily; and at least 200 IX Fighter Command P-40 sorties are mounted against Axis shipping at several Axis-held coastal towns and in the Straits of Messina.

July 30, 1943

BELGIUM: A strike by 24 B-26s of the 323d Medium Bombardment Group against the Courtrai/Wevelghem Airdrome is recalled because of fog over the target.

GERMANY: Of 119 1st Heavy Bombardment Wing B-17s dispatched, 94 attack Kassel's Bettenhausen Fieseler aircraft factory, and 40 of 67 4th Heavy Bombardment Wing B-17s attack the Waldau Fieseler Aircraft factory, also in Kassel, all between 0900 and 0930 hours. Losses are six B-17s from each wing, plus 82 B-17s damaged, and five lost in crashes, crash-landings, and ditchings. Overall crew losses are 11 killed (including ten in the crash of their B-17 in England), 97 missing (including five who bail out of a damaged B-17 that ultimately returns to the U.K.), 11 wounded, and six injured when their B-17 crash-lands in the U.K.

When 107 P-47s of the 4th, 56th, and 78th Fighter groups undertake the Eighth Air Force's second long-range escort mission of the war with dropable Fiberglas ferry tanks, they down a total of 24 GAF fighters over Germany and the Netherlands. Claims for four GAF fighters probably destroyed and eight damaged are also made. With the downing of his fourth and fifth confirmed victims—an FW-190 and Bf-109 over Haltern, Germany, at 1020 hours—Capt Charles P. London, a P-47 pilot with the 78th Fighter Group's 83d Fighter Squadron, becomes the Eighth Air Force's first fighter ace. Also, Maj Eugene P. Roberts, the commanding officer of the 78th Fighter Group's 84th Fighter Squadron, is credited with VIII Fighter Command's first triple victory of the war, over the Netherlands. And, on the way back to its base, in the first strafing attack undertaken by a P-47, the 78th Fighter Group's 2dLt Quince L. Brown damages a train. USAAF losses sustained at this epic turning point in the air war over northwestern Europe are seven P-47s lost and six pilots missing. Among the missing is LtCol Melvin F. McNickle, the brand-new 78th Fighter Group commander, who is shot down and taken prisoner on his maiden combat mission.

ITALY: NASAF B-17s attack Grottaglie Airdrome, and NASAF B-25s attack Pratica di Mare Airdrome. Three Axis fighters are damaged and one Bf-109 is downed in a melee with 82d Fighter Group P-38s over Pratica di Mare at about 1050 hours.

NETHERLANDS: On their unit's first combat mission of the war, 11 of 24 B-26s dispatched by the 386th Medium Bombardment Group attack Woensdrecht Airdrome at about 0700 hours with just over 13 tons of bombs. During a running battle with GAF fighters—the first in the theater against B-26s flying at medium altitude—the new group loses one B-26, but gunners claim six

GAF fighters downed and five probably downed. Five B-26s land safely in England with battle damage, but another is written off following a crash-landing. Crew losses are six missing and seven wounded.

Two crews from the Eighth Air Force's moribund 67th Reconnaissance Group fly with an RAF strike against Amsterdam/Schipol Airport in order to gain combat experience, but one crew is reported missing over the North Sea.

SARDINIA: While undertaking a fighter sweep over the island, 20 P-40s of the 325th Fighter Group's 317th Fighter Squadron and 16 from the 319th Fighter Squadron are attacked by 40 Bf-109s at about 0950 hours. During the course of a 35-minute melee over the Sassari area, 21 Bf-109s are downed against the loss of one P-40 and its pilot. 1stLt Walter B. Walker, Jr., of the 317th Fighter Squadron, achieves ace status in this action when he downs three of the Bf-109s. For once, GAF records show USAAF claims to be on the slim side; apparently 30 Bf-109s fail to return to their bases.

SICILY: At 0745 hours, as the 52d Fighter Group undertakes a permanent move from La Sebala Airdrome, Tunisia to Sicily's Bocca di Falco Airdrome, two 5th Fighter Squadron Spitfire pilots each down an FW-190 from a pair encountered 30 miles northeast of Bizerte. The veteran group begins flight operations as soon as it arrives at Bocca di Falco.

NATAF A-20s attack gun emplacements near the battle area, and more than 100 IX Fighter Command P-40s attack shipping at Messina, Milazzo, and Riposto, and targets of opportunity throughout the battle area.

July 31, 1943

ALGERIA: The 42d Medium Bombardment Wing is assigned, without personnel or equipment, to the Twelfth Air Force to oversee combat operations of groups to be assigned at a later date.

FRANCE: VIII Air Support Command

mounts four separate B-26 attacks, the largest number thus far undertaken by the command on a single day. Two of the attacks are undertaken by the 323d Medium Bombardment Group at about 1120 hours when 20 and 19 aircraft, respectively, bomb the Merville and Poix/Nord airdromes with an aggregate of more than 44 tons of bombs. One B-26 from the Poix/Nord force is lost and seven B-26s from both forces are damaged. Crew losses are seven missing.

In the afternoon, at about 1620 hours, 21 386th Medium Bombardment Group B-26s and 18 322d Medium Bombardment Group B-26s attack the Abbeville/Drucat and Tricqueville airdromes, respectively, with an aggregate of about 30 tons of bombs. Five B-26s are damaged during this mission, but there are no crew casualties. This is the first mission for the 322d Medium Bombardment Group since its disastrous May 17 mission.

In its operational debut, the 387th Medium Bombardment Group, in B-26s, dispatches a diversionary mission with a heavy P-47 escort during the afternoon to an area north of Dunkirk, but no opposition is encountered.

SICILY: NASAF B-26s attack Adrano; NATAF aircraft attack numerous Axis-held towns and various targets of opportunity; NATAF aircraft attack shipping in the Milazzo-Orlando area; and IX Fighter Command P-40s attack shipping near Milazzo.

The 79th Fighter Group moves from Cassible Airdrome to Palagonia Airdrome.

AUGUST 1943

August 1, 1943

MEDITERRANEAN: NACAF Beaufighters claim hits on Axis shipping at sea between Sardinia and Italy.

Two Do-217s are downed over the sea by 52d Fighter Group Spitfire pilots at about 0605 hours, and an Mc.202 is downed over the sea by a 14th Fighter Group P-38 pilot at 1115.

ITALY: NASAF B-17s attack Capodichino Airdrome.

ROMANIA: On a special mission designated Operation TIDALWAVE, 177 IX Bomber Command B-24s based around Benghazi, Libya (including three VIII Bomber Command groups on loan), conduct a low-level attack on the strategic oil-refining facilities at Ploesti and Campina. The damage inflicted is severe, but 41 B-24s are downed, 13 are lost in operational accidents, and seven are interned with their crews after being forced to land in Turkey. Crew losses are 532 from all causes.

Col Leon Johnson, the commanding officer of the 44th Heavy Bombardment Group (Eighth Air Force B-24s) earns a Medal of Honor for his daring leadership over Ploesti, as does Col John R. Kane, the commanding officer of the 98th Heavy Bombardment Group (Ninth Air Force B-24s). Also receiving Medals of Honor are LtCol Addison E. Baker, the commanding officer of the 93d Heavy Bombardment Group (Eighth Air Force B-24s), and Maj John L. Jerstad, Baker's volunteer co-pilot. Although their lead B-24 is severely damaged by enemy fire during the final approach to the target, and should be landed immediately, Baker and Jerstad nonetheless continue to lead their formation, and both are killed when the bomber crashes shortly after its bombs have been dropped. 2dLt Lloyd H. Hughes, the pilot of a 389th Heavy Bombardment Group (Eighth Air Force) B-24, is awarded a Medal of Honor for refusing to turn for home after flak damage causes fuel to stream from his airplane. Despite the fuel leak, Hughes bombs his by-then-blazing target. However, the airplane crashes after its bombs are released, and all aboard are killed.

SICILY: NASAF B-25s attack Milazzo; NATAF A-20s and B-25s attack Bronte, Paterno, Randazzo, and Santa Maria di Licondia, and motor vehicles near Orlando; IX Bomber Command B-25s attack Adrano; and IX Fighter Command P-40s conduct a record 230 sorties against a variety of Sicilian towns and Axis ships at sea in the Straits of Messina.

August 2, 1943

ENGLAND: A scheduled attack against the Woensdrecht Airdrome in the Nerherlands by the 322d Medium Bombardment Group is canceled.
FRANCE: Forty-nine 323d and 386th Medium Bombardment Group B-26s attack the Merville and St.-Omer/Ft. Rouge airdromes, respectively. Twenty-eight B-26s are damaged by flak, and one B-26 is written off after it makes a forced landing in the U.K. In all, six crewmen are wounded by enemy fire.

During the morning, the 387th Medium Bombardment Group, in its combat debut, mounts a diversionary mission with a large fighter escort, but no action results.
ITALY: NATAF aircraft attack port facilities and shipping at Reggio di Calabria.
SARDINIA: The only confirmed aerial victories in the theater are awarded for four GAF fighters downed during an afternoon mission by 14th Fighter Group P-38s.
SICILY: NATAF aircraft attack ammunition and supply dumps, motor vehicles, and road junctions throughout southeastern Sicily; docking facilities and shipping at Messina and Milazzo; and various targets of opportunity in the battle area. Also, IX Bomber Command B-25s attack Adrano, and IX Fighter Command P-40s attack shipping off Milazzo and in the Straits of Messina.

The 340th Medium Bombardment Group advance echelon, in B-25s, moves to Comiso Airdrome from Tunisia, and the 12th Medium Bombardment Group advance echelon, also in B-25s, moves to Gela/Ponte Olivo Airdrome.

August 3, 1943

SICILY: NATAF A-20s attack tactical targets in the battle area; NAAF A-20s, medium bombers, and fighters attack Adrano and Biancaville, shipping at Milazzo and in the Straits of Messina, and gun emplacements in the battle area; IX Bomber Command B-25s attack Adrano three times during the day and interdict roads into the town; and IX Fighter Command P-40s mount a record 320 sorties against docking facilities and shipping at Milazzo and Messina, and provide direct air support for British Army ground forces around Bronte and Catania. Four 79th Fighter Group P-40s and their pilots are lost while attacking ground targets.

August 4, 1943

FRANCE: Thirty-three 322d Medium Bombardment Group B-26s attack the shipyards at Le Trait at about 1930 hours. There are no losses or casualties.
ITALY: NASAF B-17s attack the Naples submarine base; NASAF medium bombers attack the rail bridges at Catanzaro and Paola; and NATAF aircraft attack rail sidings throughout the Calabria region.

14th Fighter Group P-38 pilots down seven Bf-109s and an Mc.202 between Cape Vaticano and Pizzo, in Calabria, at about 1715 hours.
SICILY: NATAF aircraft attack a wide variety of tactical and communications targets in and around the battle area as well as shipping in the Straits of Messina. And IX Fighter Command P-40s attack shipping at Messina and provide direct support for Allied ground forces fighting near Mt. Etna.

August 5, 1943

ICELAND: Two P-38 pilots of the Iceland Air Command's 50th Fighter Squadron down an FW-200 flying boat over the island. This is the last of five GAF aircraft downed over or near Iceland during the war.
SARDINIA: NASAF B-25s attack the switching station at Guspini, and P-40

escorts claim a U-boat sunk off of south-western Sardinia.

Although air opposition over the island has virtually dried up, NAAF aircraft continue to pound the Sardinian airdromes and other facilities. A new weapon is added to the Allied arsenal when four 321st Medium Bombardment Group special B-25s, each equipped with a nose-mounted 75mm cannon, attack the Guspini rail switching station. Thirty-six 75mm rounds are fired during several 300-foot firing passes by each B-25, and several of the rounds score direct hits that set the target afire. As a result of this test, the 321st Group is ordered to establish a separate "gun" squadron.

SICILY: Two forces of NASAF B-17s mount separate attacks on the port facilities and rail yards at Messina; NATAF aircraft attack a variety of tactical targets, including troop positions and gun emplacements, in direct support of Allied ground forces; NATAF aircraft also attack motor vehicles behind the lines and all manner of ships and craft encountered in the Straits of Messina or along the coasts on either side of the straits; IX Bomber Command B-25s attack roads and road junctions around Francavilla three times and troop concentrations around Adrano twice in support of British Eighth Army ground attacks; and IX Fighter Command P-40s attack Messina harbor and shipping in the Straits of Messina.

The rear flight echelon of the Ninth Air Force's 12th Medium Bombardment Group, in B-25s, arrives at Gela/Ponte Olivo Airdrome from Tunisia and immediately resumes flight operations.

British Eighth Army ground forces take Catania and Paterno.

August 6, 1943

MEDITERRANEAN: A P-39 pilot with the 350th Fighter Group's 346th Fighter Squadron downs a Ju-88 reconnaissance bomber at sea 100 miles off the coast from Cherchell, Algeria, at 1355 hours; and a 52d Fighter Group Spitfire pilot downs a Bf-109 40 miles northeast of Palermo at 1740 hours.

SICILY: NASAF B-17s attack the coastal roads leading to Messina; NASAF B-25s attack rail bridges and road junctions; NATAF aircraft attack a dizzying array of frontline targets, including Axis-occupied towns; NAAF and IX Fighter Command fighter-bombers mount aggressive anti-shipping sweeps and attacks from Vito Valentia to the Straits of Messina; and, in direct support of attacks by British Eighth Army ground forces, IX Bomber Command bombers attack Axis-held towns north of the Biancaville-Adrano road.

During the night of August 6–7, British Eighth Army ground forces capture Adrano and Biancaville.

August 7, 1943

ENGLAND: The VIII Fighter Command's 4th Air Defense Wing is formally redesignated as the 65th Fighter Wing.

MEDITERRANEAN: 82d Fighter Group P-38 pilots down two FW-190s off Pizzo at about 1620 hours.

ITALY: Two separate formations of NASAF B-25s attack Crotone Airdrome, and NASAF B-26s attack highway and rail bridges at Marina di Catanzaro.

SARDINIA: 325th Fighter Group P-40 pilots down two Bf-109s and damage five others during a morning sweep over southern Sardinia.

SICILY: Randazzo, the final escape route of many Axis units, is attacked through the day by NATAF A-20s and B-25s, and 150 IX Bomber Command B-25s. NATAF bombers also attack Maletto; NATAF A-36s and P-40s attack motor vehicles near Randazzo; and NATAF A-36s and P-40s, and IX Fighter Command P-40s attack numerous small vessels at sea between Sicily and the Italian mainland, and a variety of communications targets near the battle area and supply points in northeastern Sicily.

August 8, 1943

FRANCE: Thirty-six B-26s from the 323d

Medium Bombardment Group abort in the face of bad weather while on their way to attack Poix/Nord Airdrome.

ITALY: NASAF B-26s attack the highway and rail bridges at Angitola, and escorting P-38s strafe trains and other targets of opportunity.

MEDITERRANEAN: Eight GAF aircraft are downed in the theater during the day: A Ju-88 reconnaissance bomber off Algiers, and seven GAF fighters over Italy at various times and places between 0940 and 1830 hours.

NACAF's independent 417th Night-Fighter Squadron, in Beaufighters, clocks its first operational sorties.

SICILY: NATAF A-20s and NATAF and IX Bomber Command B-25s attack Randazzo; and NAAF fighters attack motor vehicles north of Mt. Etna and Axis ships at sea in the Straits of Messina, and support Allied ground forces. More than 130 P-40 sorties are mounted against ships, boats, and barges in the Straits of Messina and in support of Allied ground forces.

UNITED STATES: Headquarters, U.S. Army Air Forces, decides to transfer the Ninth Air Force to England to serve as a tactical air force in northern Europe once the invasion of France begins in mid-1944. Headquarters, Ninth Air Force, and several subordinate headquarters will make the move, but all remaining operational units will be transferred to the Twelfth Air Force. Once the Ninth Air Force is established in England, the Eighth Air Force's VIII Air Support Command will be redesignated and transferred to it. LtGen Lewis H. Brereton will retain command of the Ninth Air Force.

August 9, 1943

ENGLAND: The 301st Heavy Bombardment Group, in B-17s, is assigned to the VIII Bomber Command.

FRANCE: Seventy-two 322d and 386th Medium Bombardment group B-26s arrive over the St.-Omer/Ft. Rouge Airdrome at 1904 hours, but all but one are prevented from dropping their bombs because of heavy

cloud cover. Eleven of the B-26s are damaged by flak, and six crewmen are wounded.

Elements of the newly committed 353d Fighter Group, in 16 P-47s, join the 4th, 56th, and 78th Fighter groups for a sweep through the Abbeville-Poix area, but the 139 fighters dispatched encounter no opposition.

ITALY: NASAF B-25s attack bridges at Catanzaro and Soverato, and P-38s attack targets of opportunity in southern Italy.

SARDINIA: NAAF P-40s mount sweeps across southern Sardinia.

SICILY: NASAF B-17s attack a vital crossroads north of Messina; NATAF bombers attack the road junction at Gesso; NAAF fighters mount numerous attacks against road targets, rail sidings, gun emplacements, and various military targets of opportunity; IX Bomber Command B-25s attack Divieto, a tunnel west of Spadafora San Martino, and selected targets near the front lines; and IX Fighter Command P-40s attack shipping at Messina, Milazzo, and Palmi, Italy.

August 10, 1944

ALGERIA: BriGen Ray A. Dunn assumes command of the NAAF Provisional Troop Carrier Command.

ITALY: NASAF P-38 fighter-bombers attack communications targets throughout the toe of Italy, and bridges at Angitola and near Locri.

SICILY: NATAF aircraft and IX Bomber Command P-40s attack Randazzo; NATAF aircraft and IX Fighter Command mount anti-shipping sweeps over the Straits of Messina and northeastern Sicily; and NATAF aircraft conduct numerous attacks in direct support of Allied ground forces.

August 11, 1943

CANADA: The QUADRANT Conference, attended by President Franklin D. Roosevelt and Prime Minister Sir Winston S. Churchill, is convened in Quebec to discuss and adjust the Allied war strategies.

ITALY: NASAF B-17s attack a marshalling yard at Terni; NASAF B-25s attack bridges spanning the Angitola River; and NASAF B-26s and P-38s attack the bridge at Catanzaro.

SICILY: NATAF fighter-bombers provide close tactical support for landings by U.S. Army forces at Orlando; NAAF and IX Bomber Command medium bombers and IX Fighter Command P-40s support British Eighth Army ground forces attacking in the Randazzo area; and IX Fighter Command P-40s attack shipping at Messina and Milazzo, Axis troop concentrations awaiting evacuation to the Italian mainland, and a train near Messina.

Only three Axis aircraft are encountered and downed in the theater, all during afternoon missions.

August 12, 1943

BELGIUM: In their unit's first individual mission, 27 353d Fighter Group P-47s conduct an unchallenged and uneventful sweep across the Belgian coast.

FRANCE: Thirty-four 322d Medium Bombardment Group B-26s attack the Poix/Nord Airdrome at 1052 hours. Thirteen of the B-26s are damaged by defensive fire, but none is lost and no crew casualties are sustained. The 323d Medium Bombardment Group, briefed for the same mission, is recalled while still over the English Channel.

GERMANY: One hundred thirty-three 1st Heavy Bombardment Wing B-17s attack Bochum, Gelsenkirchen, Recklinghausen, and several targets of opportunity. Flak and GAF fighter opposition down an unprecedented 23 of these heavy bombers, a staggering 103 are damaged, and two that crash-land in the U.K. are written off. Crew casualties are five killed, 232 missing, and 49 wounded. These are by far the worst losses inflicted on any U.S. bomber force so far in the war.

In a separate phase of the day's mission, 110 4th Heavy Bombardment Wing B-17s (including the 390th Heavy Bombardment Group, in its combat debut) attack the city of Bonn and several targets

of opportunity between 0850 and 0900 hours. Losses against light opposition are two B-17s downed and 70 damaged, of which one is written off. Crew losses are one killed, 21 missing, and seven wounded.

Using pressurized steel belly tanks (good at high altitude) for the first time, 131 P-47s of the 4th, 56th, and 78th Fighter groups undertake penetration and withdrawal escort sorties, during which four GAF fighters are downed by pilots of the 4th Fighter Group. There are no USAAF fighter losses.

ITALY: NASAF B-25s attack Crotone Airdrome, and NASAF B-26s attack Grazzanise Airdrome. In a rather large engagement over Grazzanise Airdrome at about 1300 hours, 1st Fighter Group P-38 pilots down two and damage or possibly down eight Axis fighters. Also, B-26 gunners claim nine Axis fighters during the Grazzanise action.

SICILY: NATAF A-20s and NATAF and IX Bomber Command B-25s attack several Axis-held towns near the battlefront. NATAF A-36s and P-40s provide direct support for Allied ground forces and, with IX Fighter Command P-40s, attack Axis shipping in the Straits of Messina and along the northeastern coast. In their unit's first aerial engagement of the Sicily Campaign, while on an afternoon mission aimed at interdicting Axis shipping traffic in the Straits of Messina, 79th Fighter Group P-40 pilots down an FW-190 and damage or possibly down five other Axis fighters.

TUNISIA: 52d Fighter Group Spitfire pilots down an FW-190 and damage another in an engagement 10 miles off Bizerte at 1850 hours.

August 13, 1943

AUSTRIA: In the first Allied bombing mission against a target inside Austria (Operation JUGGLER), 61 of 114 IX Bomber Command B-24s dispatched attack an aircraft factory and ball-bearing factory at Wiener-Neustadt. The flight to the target and back from bases around Benghazi,

Tunisia, is 1,200 miles. Flak and fighter opposition over the target is extremely light, but two B-24s are lost. The aircraft factory's output of Bf-109 airframes is reduced by one-third in the wake of the attack, and the ball-bearing plant is severely damaged. **ITALY:** Fighter-escorted NASAF bombers totaling 106 B-17s, 66 B-25s, and 102 B-26s attack several marshalling yards in and around Rome with more than 500 tons of bombs. Although fighter opposition is reported as being "strong," only two B-26s are lost, and 1st and 14th Fighter group P-38 escort pilots account for only one Bf-109 and an Mc.202.

NASAF B-25s attack an Axis ship off Pizzo; NATAF bombers and IX Bomber Command B-25s attack Piedimonte; and IX Fighter Command P-40s attack bridges and shipping along the southwestern coast.
SARDINIA: While conducting a sweep over southern Sardinia, NAAF P-40s strafe a rail junction, small boats, and a power station.
SICILY: NATAF bombers and IX Bomber Command B-25s attack Falcone; NATAF bombers attack bridges near Scaletta; NATAF A-36s, IX Bomber Command B-25s, and IX Fighter Command P-40s attack shipping in the Straits of Messina; and NATAF A-36s and IX Fighter Command P-40s attack various targets of opportunity in northeastern Sicily and along the battlefront.

1stLt Paul G. McArthur, a P-40 pilot with the 79th Fighter Group's 87th Fighter Squadron, achieves ace status when he downs a Bf-109 near the Straits of Messina during a morning mission. Three other members of McArthur's squadron also down a Bf-109 apiece.

Randazzo falls to elements of the U.S. Seventh Army.

August 14, 1943

AUSTRIA: Sixty-one IX Bomber Command B-24s attack the Bf-109 factory at Wiener-Neustadt.
ITALY: The Italian government declares

Rome an open city, thus obviating the threat of further bombing attacks.

NATAF aircraft and IX Bomber Command B-25s attack a road junction near Palmi, but NASAF P-38 conducting sweeps over the toe of Italy find little movement along the area's roads.
SICILY: NATAF aircraft attack a refueling point near Gesso, shipping in the Straits of Messina, and numerous targets of opportunity in northeastern Sicily and southern Sicily. IX Fighter Command P-40s attack shipping around Milazzo and Messina.

August 15, 1943

BELGIUM: On a mission confused by bad weather, 91 of 180 1st Heavy Bombardment Wing B-17s dispatched attack their secondary target, Flushing/Vlissingen Airdrome, at about 1930 hours. At about same time, 56 other B-17s from the original formation attack the Poix and Amiens/Glisy airdromes in France. No aircraft are lost in the attacks, but 48 are damaged and three crewmen are wounded.
FRANCE: Of 147 4th Heavy Bombardment Wing B-17s dispatched, 82 of the airplanes drop half their bombs on Merville Airdrome and half on Lille/Vendeville Airdrome. Sixty-one other B-17s attack Vitry-en-Artois Airdrome. Two B-17s are lost in these attacks—including one in a midair collision—11 B-17s are damaged, one crewman is killed, 20 crewmen are missing, and three crewmen are wounded.

In the VIII Air Support Command's first mission of the day, 31 387th Medium Bombardment Group B-26s—in their unit's combat debut—attack the St.-Omer/Ft. Rouge Airdrome at about 1000 hours. Eighteen B-26s are damaged, but there are no crew casualties.

Nineteen 323d Medium Bombardment Group B-26s attack the Abbeville marshalling yard with 54 1,000-pound bombs at about 1930 hours. Nine B-26s are damaged and one crewman is wounded.
ITALY: NASAF B-25s and B-26s attack the rail junction and marshalling yard at Sibari,

and NASAF P-38s attack the tracks and tunnel at Sibari as well as trains, troops, and radar installations throughout the Sibari area.

MEDITERRANEAN: Two Bf-109s are downed over the Isle of Capri by a 1st Fighter Group P-38 pilot.

The U.S. Fifth Army issues its plan for Operation AVALANCHE, the invasion of Italy at Salerno.

NETHERLANDS: The 386th Medium Bombardment Group turns back at the Dutch coast late in the day while on its way to attack Woensdrecht Airdrome.

NORTHWESTERN EUROPE: The Eighth Air Force opens Operation STARKEY, an effort to make the German Army and GAF believe that an invasion at the Pas-de-Calais is imminent and thus halt the movement of fresh units to Italy and Russia. (STARKEY is also seen as a means to test a preliminary air plan leading to the *actual* invasion of France, now set for mid-1944.) The focus of the STARKEY attacks will be GAF airfields in France, Belgium, and the Netherlands. As well as being a ruse and a test, the operation, which will continue until September 9, will cause great collateral damage to the GAF forward bases.

SARDINIA: NAAF P-40s attack a troop bivouac near Monserrato.

SICILY: The Allied air forces formally begin an around-the-clock campaign to interdict Axis forces attempting to conduct an orderly withdrawal from Sicily across the Straits of Messina. IX Bomber Command B-25s attack ships picking up troops along the beaches, and IX Fighter Command P-40s mount more than 180 sorties against ships and craft in the Straits of Messina.

SPAIN: A representative of the Italian Supreme Command opens armistice negotiations in Madrid with representatives of the Allied powers

August 16, 1943

ENGLAND: The 2906th Provisional Observation Training Group is established at Atcham Airdrome from various fighter-training organizations already in residence. The new unit is to process and provide advanced theater training to replacement fighter pilots for the Eighth Air Force and, eventually, the Ninth Air Force.

FRANCE: One hundred seventy-one 1st Heavy Bombardment Wing B-17s attack Paris/Le Bourget Airport with more than 397 tons of bombs at about 0930 hours. Flak and moderate GAF fighter opposition account for four bombers lost (including one down in the North Sea from which the crew is rescued) and 46 damaged. Crew losses are one killed, 31 missing, and four wounded.

In a separate attack between 0911 and 0923 hours, 66 4th Heavy Bombardment Group B-17s each drop half their bombs on Poix Airdrome and half on Abbeville/Drucat Airdrome, for a total of nearly 79 tons of bombs. Losses are 38 B-17s damaged, and there are no crew casualties.

VIII Air Support Command B-26s mount two missions: 31 387th Medium Bombardment Group B-26s attack Bernay St.-Martin Airdrome at about 1115 hours; and, at 1700 hours, 29 322d Medium Bombardment Group B-26s attack Beaumont-le-Roger Airdrome and three B-26s attack Conches Airdrome (target of opportunity).

4th Fighter Group P-47 pilots down 18 GAF aircraft while escorting 1st Heavy Bombardment Group B-17s over and around Paris. Of 180 P-47 escorts dispatched, the 4th, 56th, and 353d Fighter groups each lose one plane and one pilot missing, plus two P-47s written off after crash-landing in the U.K. Among the missing is LtCol Joseph A. Morris, the 353d Fighter Group commander, who is killed.

ITALY: NASAF B-25s and B-26s attack Staletti and a temporary bridge across the Angitola River at Angitola; NATAF A-36s and P-40s attack various communication targets throughout the toe of Italy; and 86 IX Bomber Command B-24s attack the airdrome complex and city of Foggia.

SICILY: NATAF A-20s, NATAF and IX Bomber Command B-25s, and IX Fighter

Command aircraft attack shipping and landing craft in and around the Straits of
Messina.

Organized resistance all but ceases as
the last of the Axis forces withdraw across
the Straits of Messina behind collapsing
rearguards. Before midnight, U.S. Army
ground patrols enter the outskirts of
Messina, which is under fire from Axis
gun emplacements on the nearby Italian
mainland.

TUNISIA: A 415th Night-Fighter Squadron Beaufighter downs an Italian Air Force
float-reconnaissance plane between Tunis
and Bizerte at about 0435 hours.

August 17, 1943

FRANCE: Twenty-nine 386th Medium
Bombardment Group B-26s attack Bryas
Sud Airdrome at 1051 hours with nearly
35 tons of bombs. Two B-26s are damaged,
but there are no crew casualties. In the
afternoon, the entire 387th Medium Bombardment Group is recalled, 35 323d
Medium Bombardment Group B-26s attack
Poix/Nord Airdrome. Twenty B-26s are
damaged and one crewman is wounded.

Based on reconnaissance findings
indicating that 140 GAF twin-engine fighters are based in the Marseille area, 180
Tunisian-based NASAF B-17s attack the
Istres-le-Tube and Salon-de-Provence airdromes, dropping 25,619 20-pound fragmentation bombs and claiming 94 enemy
aircraft destroyed on the ground. One GAF
airplane, probably a Ju-88, is downed by an
escort fighter, and bomber crews claim 23
GAF airplanes downed, undoubtedly an
inflated figure.

GERMANY: The VIII Bomber Command
mounts its notorious attack against ball-
bearing–industry targets in and around
Schweinfurt—The Schweinfurt Raid:

First, between 1148 and 1207 hours,
127 4th Heavy Bombardment Wing B-17s
attack aircraft factories at Regensburg with
nearly 299 tons of bombs. This attack is met
with resolute opposition from GAF fighters and flak, which down 24 B-17s and

damage 50 others. The 4th Heavy Bombardment Wing long-range B-17s then fly on to
friendly bases in North Africa. Along the
way, two battle-damaged bombers crash-
land in Switzerland, where their crews are
interned, and eight ditch in the Mediterranean, mostly because of fuel depletion. Crew
losses are four killed, 200 missing, and nine
wounded.

In the second phase of the mission, 183
1st Heavy Bombardment Wing B-17s attack
the Schweinfurt ball-bearing plants with
more than 424 tons of bombs between 1459
and 1511 hours. Flak and GAF fighter
opposition is extremely heavy and resolute.
B-17 gunners alone claim 148 GAF fighters downed and 18 GAF fighters probably
downed, but actual losses are lower by several orders of magnitude. Losses sustained
by the 1st Heavy Bombardment Wing, however, are nothing less than harrowing: 36
B-17s downed outright, from which the
crews of two that crash into the North Sea
are rescued; and 121 B-17s damaged, of
which three crash-land at bases in the U.K.
Overall crew casualties are put at three
killed, 352 missing, and 12 wounded.

Aggregate B-17 losses for the day are
60 B-17s missing, four damaged beyond repair, and 168 damaged. Aggregate crew
losses are a staggering seven killed, 552
missing, and 21 wounded. Overall, this is
the equivalent of airplanes and crewmen
needed for nearly two operational heavy-
bomber groups. Although heavy damage is
claimed at both targets, it is known that only
one bomb in nine dropped by heavy bombers during World War II actually hit the
intended target.

P-47s from the 56th, 78th, and 353d
Fighter groups are also pressed to find new
limits of endurance. After flying early-pen-
etration escort for the 4th Heavy Bombardment Wing B-17s, the 56th and 353d
Fighter groups return to the extremity of
their range to fly late-withdrawal escort for
the returning 1st Heavy Bombardment Wing
B-17s. In all, faced with an all-out effort by
scores of GAF fighters, the P-47 pilots of

the 4th, 56th, 78th, and 353d Fighter groups down a total of 19 GAF fighters in a series of sharp fighter battles over Germany, Belgium, and the Netherlands between 1028 and 1630 hours. Sixteen of these victories are credited to the 56th Fighter Group alone.

ITALY: Approximately 100 NASAF medium bombers attack Battipaglia and Castrovillari, in the toe of Italy, and escorting P-38s strafe numerous targets of opportunity in the region; NATAF aircraft and IX Fighter Command P-40s attack shipping in the Straits of Messina and neighboring bodies of water; and NATAF aircraft attack the rail junction at Lamezia and strafe and bomb Axis troops moving through the area.

MEDITERRANEAN: The air-support plan for Operation AVALANCHE is issued.

SICILY: Messina is liberated and the campaign for Sicily is officially concluded.

August 18, 1943

BELGIUM: Although briefed to attack the Lille/Vendeville Airdrome in France, 22 of 36 322d Medium Bombardment Group B-26s dispatched are forced by bad weather to settle for a target of opportunity, the Ypres/Vlamertinghe Airdrome in Belgium, on which they drop 31 tons of bombs at 1016 hours. Twenty-three of the group's airplanes are damaged by enemy fire, but no crew casualties result.

ENGLAND: The 353d Fighter Group, in P-47s, is assigned to the VIII Fighter Command's 66th Fighter Wing.

FRANCE: Two 67th Photographic Reconnaissance Group A-20s, escorted by RAF Spitfires, undertake that unit's first official operational mission of the war, a photographic reconnaissance of the Brest Peninsula. Also, one of four 7th Photographic Reconnaissance Group F-5s dispatched on missions to France is so badly damaged by hail that it breaks up in flight. The pilot bails out and is carried by the wind to the English coast.

ITALY: NASAF medium bombers and fighters attack bridges and a road junction

at Angitola, barracks and a rail line at Gonessa, rail facilities and a bridge at Soverato, and a road junction and highway at Staletti; NATAF aircraft attack road and rail targets and gun emplacements throughout southern Italy; and IX Fighter Command P-40s attack road targets and shipping around Scilla.

MEDITERRANEAN: A 414th Night-Fighter Squadron Beaufighter downs a reconnaissance Ju-88 off Cap Bon at 1530 hours.

NETHERLANDS: Thirty-six 386th Medium Bombardment Group B-26s attack Woensdrecht Airdrome with 45 tons of bombs at 1032 hours.

August 19, 1943

FRANCE: Thirty-six 323d Medium Bombardment Group B-26s attack the Amiens/Glisy Airdrome at 1130 hours; 35 387th Medium Bombardment Group B-26s attack the Poix/Nord Airdrome at about 1215 hours; and the 322d Medium Bombardment Group aborts due to thick cloud cover over it target, Bryas Sud Airdrome.

ITALY: NAAF P-40s sweeping across southern Italy attack a train and strafe several trucks; IX Fighter Command P-40s sweeping across southern Italy bomb roads and buildings; more than 150 NASAF B-17s and 70 IX Bomber Command B-24s, in separate formations, attack marshalling yards at Foggia; and approximately 100 NASAF medium bombers attack marshalling yards at Salerno and Sapri. 14th Fighter Group P-38 escort pilots down seven Axis fighters in a running fight southwest of Foggia and Salerno between noon and 1220 hours

A 27th Fighter-Bomber Group A-36 pilot downs a Bf-109 while attack a marshalling yard at Catanzaro.

NETHERLANDS: A total of 93 1st Heavy Bombardment Wing B-17s, of 125 dispatched, attack Gilze-Rijen and Flushing/Vlissingen airdromes at about 1800 hours, but the entire 4th Heavy Bombardment Wing aborts its attack on the Woensdrecht

Airdrome following two complete circuits over the target area in search of holes in the clouds through which bombs can be dropped. Losses from both wings are five B-17s downed and 50 damaged, plus one 4th Wing B-17 that is written off after crash-landing off the English coast after catching fire during the assembly. Crew casualties are nine wounded and 51 missing.

4th and 78th Fighter group P-47s undertake the penetration escort, and the 56th and 353d Fighter groups undertake withdrawal escort. A 78th Fighter Group pilot downs one GAF airplane, and 56th Fighter Group pilots down nine GAF fighters.

August 20, 1943

ENGLAND: The Eighth Air Force activates the 482d Heavy Bombardment Group as a special testing and training unit for experimental radar blind-bombing devices. Personnel are drawn from the 92d Heavy Bombardment Group's 329th Heavy Bombardment Squadron, which has already conducted experiments with British-made GEE blind-bombing radar, and from the moribund 479th Antisubmarine Group. Equipped with B-17s and B-24s, the new unit, which is operationally attached to the 1st Heavy Bombardment Wing and administratively overseen by the 92d Heavy Bombardment Group headquarters, is to take part in combat operations to test new equipment and techniques, test various radar devices, and train pathfinder lead-bomber crews from operational groups.

ITALY: NASAF B-25s attack a marshalling yard at Benevento; B-26s attack marshalling yards at Aversa and Capua; and NATAF and IX Fighter Command P-40s attack road and rail targets while conducting several sweeps across the toe of Italy.

In a large fighter battle near the Naples coast at about 1230 hours, 1st and 82d Fighter group P-38 pilots down 13 Axis fighters and damage many others.

SARDINIA: NAAF P-40s attack a marshalling yard at Monserrato.

August 21, 1943

ITALY: NASAF B-17s and B-26s attack marshalling yards at Aversa and Villa Literno, 1st and 82d Fighter group P-38 escort pilots down five Axis fighters near Villa Literno at 1300 hours; IX Bomber Command B-24s attack an air depot and rail facilities at Cancello Arnone; and NATAF fighter-bombers attack road traffic in the toe of Italy.

TUNISIA: The 42d Medium Bombardment Wing headquarters begins overseeing operations of the Twelfth Air Force's 17th, 319th, and 320th groups (all in B-26s), and the 325th Fighter Group, in P-40s.

August 22, 1943

FRANCE: Thirty-five 386th Medium Bombardment Group B-26s attack Beaumont-le-Roger Airdrome at 2110 hours, but the 322d Medium Bombardment Group aborts its attack on Poix/Nord Airdrome after its RAF escort fails to rendezvous.

ITALY: NASAF B-26s and escorting NATAF A-36s attack marshalling yards at Salerno, and NATAF P-40s conducting an armed reconnaissance attack motor vehicles in southern Italy. 86th Fighter-Bomber Group A-36 pilots down three Axis fighters and damage or possibly down four others in a running fight 25 miles west-southwest of Naples.

MEDITERRANEAN: As Headquarters, Ninth Air Force, prepares for its move to England, where it will serve as the USAAF's tactical air force in northwestern Europe, it begins to divest itself of operational control of various headquarters and operational units: the 57th, 79th, and 324th Fighter groups (all in P-40s) are transferred to the XII Air Support Command; and the 12th and 340th Medium Bombardment groups (both in B-25s) are transferred to the XII Bomber Command.

August 23, 1943

FRANCE: Cloud cover forces the 322d and 386th Medium Bombardment groups to forgo planned attacks against the Gosnay power station and Poix/Nord Airdrome, respectively.

ITALY: NASAF B-26s attack a marshalling yard at Battipaglia, and IX Bomber Command B-24s attack a marshalling yard at Bari.

MEDITERRANEAN: A 14th Fighter Group P-38 pilot downs one Bf-109 over the sea.

The 316th Troop Carrier Group is transferred from the Ninth Air Force to the XII Troop Carrier Command.

NETHERLANDS: In the hope of drawing GAF interceptors into a trap to be sprung by 158 P-47s from all four VIII Fighter Command groups, the 353d Fighter Group attempts to simulate a heavy-bomber formation on its way to a target. However, no GAF interceptors rise to the bait, and the ruse is never repeated.

SARDINIA: NAAF fighter-bombers attack barracks and a factory near Cagliari.

August 24, 1943

CANADA: At the conclusion of the QUADRANT Conference in Quebec, Allied leaders agree that the target date for Operation OVERLORD, the invasion of France, will be May 1, 1944. Leading up to the invasion, the Combined Bomber Offensive—now known as Operation POINTBLANK—will seek the annihilation of the German Air Force in the West by means of a bombing campaign aimed at destroying the German aircraft industry and an attritional fighter campaign aimed at destroying the German Air Force in the air. Operational plans for the simultaneous British and American invasions of Italy (Operations AVALANCHE and BAYTOWN, respectively) are also approved.

FRANCE: Of 85 4th Heavy Bombardment Wing B-17s on their way back to the U.K. from bases in North Africa [see August 17, 1943], 58 attack the Bordeaux/Merignac Airdrome at about noon. Nine of the B-17s dispatched return to North Africa due to various mechanical problems, and one of these is written off. Combat losses are

three B-17s downed, one written off after crash-landing in the U.K., and 40 damaged. Crew losses are the 30 men in the three missing bombers plus two missing after their bomber ditches off Land's End due to fuel starvation.

The 4th Heavy Bombardment Wing gets off a late-afternoon strike against airfields in France, but only 22 of the 42 B-17s dispatched are able to find targets in the bad weather, and only about 30 tons of bombs are dropped on the Conches and Evreux/Fauville airdromes between 1844 and 1900 hours. Losses are one B-17 ditched (one crewman killed and nine rescued), 15 B-17s damaged, and nine crewmen wounded.

While 36 1st Heavy Bombardment Wing B-17s conduct a diversionary flight, 86 1st Heavy Bombardment Wing B-17s attack the Villacoublay Airdrome with 257 tons of bombs at 1800 hours. Sixty-four B-17s are damaged and ten crewmen are wounded.

While escorting the afternoon bombing mission, P-47 pilots down six GAF fighters over France. Of these, one is the first confirmed victory awarded to a pilot of the 353d Fighter Group, and another is the first confirmed victory awarded to Capt Francis S. Gabreski, a 56th Fighter Group P-47 pilot who will one day become the top-scoring USAAF fighter ace in the war against Germany (28 victories). Also, Maj Eugene P. Roberts, the commanding officer of the 78th Fighter Group's 84th Fighter Squadron, in P-47s, achieves ace status when he downs an FW-190 and a Bf-109, his fifth and sixth confirmed victories, near Evreux at 1800 hours.

ITALY: NATAF fighter-bombers attack an Italian Navy cruiser off Sapri as well as various communications targets throughout southwestern Italy.

LIBYA: Following two months' temporary duty with the IX Bomber Command (for Operation TIDALWAVE), the Eighth Air Force's 93d Heavy Bombardment Group departs for England.

August 25, 1943

FRANCE: Twenty-one 387th Medium Bombardment Group B-26s attack the Rouen power station with 63 1,000-pound bombs at 1832 hours, and 31 322d Medium Bombardment Group B-26s attack the Tricqueville Airdrome at 1834 hours with 44 tons of bombs. Two B-26s from each group are damaged, but there are no crew casualties.

ITALY: Seventy-five 82d Fighter Group P-38s and 65 1st Fighter Group P-38s mount a devastating low-level strafing raid against the Foggia Airdrome complex. The P-38s claim 137 Axis airplanes destroyed or damaged and also strafe numerous anti-aircraft emplacements, airfield buildings, and such equipment as can be seen from the air. All told, two 1st Fighter Group P-38s and their pilots are lost. The raid is so effective that not one Axis airplane is encountered in the air over the multiple targets. Then, as soon as the P-38s depart the Foggia area, 136 NASAF B-17s, escorted by the 14th Fighter Group, drop 240 tons of bombs on four of the Foggia satellite fields. An estimated 60 Axis aircraft are damaged or destroyed on the ground in this phase of the attack. Also, IX Bomber Command B-24s attack the Foggia marshalling yards.

LIBYA: Following two months' temporary duty with IX Bomber Command (for Operation TIDALWAVE), the Eighth Air Force's 44th and 389th Heavy Bombardment groups depart for England.

UNITED KINGDOM: The 20th Fighter Group, in P-38s, arrives in Scotland by ship and is formally assigned to the VIII Fighter Command. Owing to a shortage of P-38 aircraft in the Mediterranean, the 20th Fighter Group will take an inordinately long time becoming fully operational.

August 26, 1943

ALGERIA: A 350th Fighter Group P-38 pilot downs two Bf-109s 15 miles off Taher at 1725 hours.

ENGLAND: The 356th Fighter Group, in P-47s, is assigned to the VIII Fighter Command's 65th Fighter Wing. (The new unit's ground echelon is in England and the pilots and aircraft are on the way.)

FRANCE: Thirty-six 323d Medium Bombardment Group B-26s attack the Caen/Carpiquet Airdrome at 1846 hours with more than 47 tons of bombs. There are no losses to enemy action, but a B-26 is damaged beyond repair when it overshoots the runway while landing.

ITALY: At least 80 NASAF B-17s attack Capua Airdrome. Two P-38 pilots with the 14th Fighter Group's 48th Fighter Squadron, Capt Herbert E. Ross and Capt Sidney W. Weatherford, achieve ace status at about noon when they each down a Bf-109 over Capua Airdrome. Two other Bf-109s are also downed in this action by 48th Fighter Squadron pilots.

More than 100 NASAF medium bombers attack Grazzanise Airdrome and a satellite runway, and a 1st Fighter Group P-38 escort pilot downs one Bf-109 over the target at 1245 hours.

NATAF P-40 fighter-bombers attack Carloforte, San Pietro Island, and NATAF A-20s and B-25s attack a variety of communications targets and gun emplacements throughout southern Italy. 33d Fighter Group P-40 pilots down three Bf-109s over southern Italy during the afternoon.

MEDITERRANEAN: RAF aircraft of the WDAF and former IX Fighter Command units are assigned operationally to NATAF.

SARDINIA: NAAF P-40s strafe targets of opportunity during a sweep across southern Sardinia.

August 27, 1943

FRANCE: Thirty-five 386th Medium Bombardment Group B-26s attack Poix/Nord Airdrome with more than 542 tons of bombs at 0826 hours. This attack is unopposed, but the 322d Medium Bombardment Group sustains one B-26 missing and six damaged in an attack by GAF fighters after aborting its attack on a power station at Rouen because of heavy cloud cover. Crew losses are six missing and two wounded.

In support of Operation CROSSBOW, the RAF bombing campaign against German V-weapons facilities and factories, 187 1st and 4th Heavy Bombardment wing B-17s, of 224 dispatched, attack V-1 launching sites around Watten with 368 2,000-pound bombs between 1846 and 1941 hours. Four B-17s are lost, one ditches (crew saved), and 98 are damaged, of which one is written off after crash-landing at its base. Crew losses are one killed, 32 missing, and 18 wounded.

A 56th Fighter Group P-47 escorting the B-17s is attacked and damaged by an RAF Spitfire, and a 353d Fighter Group P-47 is downed in an engagement with GAF fighters.

ITALY: Thirty-six unescorted 310th Medium Bombardment Group B-25s dispatched against a marshalling yard at Benevento, northeast of Naples, are met over the shoreline by an estimated 50 Axis fighters, which make repeated attacks on the bomber formation all the way through the flight to the target and early in the withdrawal phase. Also, flak over the target is extremely heavy. Nevertheless, all the B-25s attack the target, including one B-25 that completes the bomb run with both engines on fire. For the loss of three B-25s, the target area is left in flames and a subsequent bomb-damage assessment indicates that the attack has severed three main rail lines running through Benevento.

NASAF B-17s attack a marshalling yard at Sulmona; NASAF medium bombers attack a marshalling yard at Caserta; and NATAF aircraft attack a large number of transportation targets and gun emplacements throughout southern Italy.

1stLt Carroll S. Knott, a P-38 pilot with the 14th Fighter Group's 49th Fighter Squadron, achieves ace status when he downs an FW-190 over Sulmona at 1145 hours. This is one of six Axis aircraft downed over southern Italy within the hour by P-38 pilots of the 1st, 14th, and 82d Fighter groups.

August 28, 1943

ITALY: NASAF B-17s attack a marshalling yard at Terni; NASAF B-25s attack a marshalling yard at Cancello Arnone; NASAF B-26s attack Sparanise and a marshalling yard at Aversa; and NATAF A-20s, B-25s, and P-40 fighter-bombers attack numerous rail targets and road junctions throughout southern Italy.

NAAF fighters down 13 Axis fighters over Italy throughout the day. 1stLt Richard A. Campbell, a P-38 pilot with the 14th Fighter Group's 37th Fighter Squadron, achieves ace status when he downs two Bf-109s over Lake Belsena at 1220 hours. Campbell's credits are among six Bf-109s downed by 14th Fighter Group pilots at about 1220 hours. Also, 1stLt Herman "W" Visscher, a P-38 pilot with the 82d Fighter Group's 97th Fighter Squadron, achieves ace status when he downs a Bf-109 over Caviano at 1500 hours. Visscher's is one of four Axis fighters downed in the Naples area by the 82d Fighter Group between 1500 and 1545 hours.

SARDINIA: NAAF P-40s bomb and strafe targets of opportunity all across southern Sardinia. Capt Frank J. Collins, a P-40 pilot with the 325th Fighter Group's 319th Fighter Squadron, achieves ace status when he downs a Bf-109 during a group fighter sweep over southern Sardinia. In all, seven Bf-109s are downed over Sardinia by 325th Fighter Group pilots between 0930 and 1030 hours.

August 29, 1943

ENGLAND: MajGen William E. Kepner succeeds MajGen Frank O'D. Hunter as commanding general of the VIII Fighter Command. Although Hunter's failed fighter-sweep strategy has been rendered moot for several weeks already by an aggressive new fighter-escort strategy, it is Hunter's replacement by the sanguinary Kepner that marks the actual rise of the USAAF fighter force to the status of a strategic weapon in northwestern Europe.

ITALY: NASAF B-17s attack a marshalling yard at Orte; NASAF B-26s attack Torre Annunziata; and NATAF fighters escorting the NASAF bombers attack rail targets and gun emplacements along the bomber routes.

A 52d Fighter Group Spitfire pilot downs an Me-210 over Ustica Island at 0950 hours, and 14th Fighter Group P-38 pilots down three Mc.202s and damage or possibly down a dozen Bf-109s over Orte between 1020 and 1030 hours.

August 30, 1943

FRANCE: Thirty-three 323d Medium Bombardment Group B-26s attack an ammunition dump at Eperlecques with nearly 49 tons of bombs about 1900 hours. Fourteen B-26s are damaged and three crewmen are wounded.

ITALY: NASAF B-26s, escorted by 44 1st Fighter Group P-38s, attack marshalling yards at Aversa at about noon. As the formation crosses the Italian coast on the way to the target, it is attacked by an estimated 75 Axis fighters, which are immediately engaged by the outnumbered P-38s. Despite the loss of 13 P-38s and their pilots, no GAF fighter gets through to the bombers. Eight GAF fighters and an Mc.202 are downed by the P-38s in this determined defensive battle, and the B-26s cause extreme damage to the target during an unmolested bombing run that results in no bomber losses.

NASAF B-26s attack Viterbo Airdrome; NASAF B-25s attack marshalling yards at Civitavecchia; NATAF A-20s and B-25s attack marshalling yards at Marina di Catanzaro and Paola, and gun emplacements and troop bivouacs near Reggio di Calabria; and NATAF A-36s attack Pellaro and marshalling yards at Lamezia and Sapri.

SARDINIA: NAAF P-40s strafe the radar station at Pula.

August 31, 1943

FRANCE: Thirty-three 322d Medium Bombardment Group B-26s attack the Mazingarbe power plant at 0718 hours with 48 tons of bombs. One B-26 is damaged. At 0721 hours, 36 387th Medium Bombardment Group B-26s attack Lille/Vendeville Airdrome with nearly 54 tons of bombs. One B-26 is downed, 11 are damaged, and crew losses are six missing and two wounded. Solid cloud cover over the area prevents 72 322d and 386th Medium Bombardment group B-26s from attacking their target.

One hundred seventy 1st Heavy Bombardment Wing B-17s are unable to locate their briefed target, Romilly Airdrome, through thick clouds, so between 1807 and 1824 hours, 105 of these heavy bombers drop 1,240 500-pound bombs (310 tons) on Amiens/Glisy Airdrome. Losses are one B-17 missing and two lost in a collision over the English Channel on the way to the target, one lost in a crash-landing in the U.K., and 35 damaged by flak and GAF fighters. Crew losses are five killed, 33 missing, and eight wounded. It is worth noting that the switch in targets by a large proportion of the bombers is effected by orders directly transmitted via VHF radio by the mission commander, the 101st Provisional Combat Bombardment Wing's Col William Gross. This is the first instance in which an Eighth Air Force mission commander is permitted to break radio silence to redirect a bombing force once it has left English airspace. Such on-the-spot direction will soon become the norm and will profoundly influence the efficiency of the Eighth Air Force heavy-bomber forces.

In contrast, however, 149 4th Heavy Bombardment Wing B-17s briefed for an attack on the Meulan aircraft factory are unable to locate any target through the cloud cover and thus return to their bases with bombs aboard after sustaining 19 bombers damaged and one crewman wounded.

While providing escort for the B-17s, two 353d Fighter Group P-47s and their pilots are lost following a collision near St.-Omer. In all, 160 P-47 escort sorties are provided for the B-17s by the VIII Fighter

Command, but only two GAF fighters are damaged.

ITALY: IX Bomber Command B-24s attack a marshalling yard at Pescara; approximately 150 NASAF B-17s attack a marshalling yard at Pisa; NATAF A-20s and B-25s mount a morning attack against a road and rail junction at Catanzaro, and afternoon attacks on Cosenza; and NAAF fighter-bombers attack the seaplane base and rail line at Sapri.

During the night of August 31–September 1, NATAF A-20s attack troop bivouacs near Reggio di Calabria.

SEPTEMBER 1943

September 1, 1943

ALGERIA: NAAF formally relinquishes administrative control of all subordinate units to appropriate subordinate headquarters: NAAF headquarters to Twelfth Air Force headquarters; NASAF aircraft to XII Bomber Command; NACAF aircraft to XII Fighter Command; and so forth. However, the Twelfth Air Force still remains operationally subordinate to NAAF, and LtGen Carl Spaatz remains commanding general of both organizations. Also, NATAF continues to function as an operational command overseeing the XII Air Support Command (31st and 33d Fighter groups, in Spitfires and P-40s respectively; 27th and 86th Fighter-Bomber groups, in A-36s; and 111th Tactical Reconnaissance Squadron), NATBF (47th Light Bombardment Group, in A-20s), and the RAF's Western Desert Air Force.

ITALY: A-20s and B-25s under NATAF control attack several towns, a bridge, a lighthouse, and a radar station in southern Italy; and Twelfth Air Force P-40s attack a zinc plant and strafe a factory.

September 2, 1943

ENGLAND: The 44th and 392d Heavy Bombardment groups are assigned to the 2d Heavy Bombardment Wing's 202d Provisional Combat Bombardment Wing.

FRANCE: Three hundred nineteen 1st and 4th Heavy Bombardment wing B-17s dispatched against GAF airdromes in France are recalled as they approach the French coast due to heavy cloud cover. Only 34 4th Wing B-17s attack targets of opportunity—Mardyck and Denain/Prouvy airdromes—with a total of 101 tons of bombs at about 1905 hours. Three of 182 escort P-47s are lost while conducting ad hoc fighter sweeps.

Of 216 3d Medium Bombardment Wing B-26s dispatched, 104 are able to find holes in the cloud cover and drop nearly 150 tons of bombs on several GAF airfields and fuel dumps.

ITALY: Intelligence estimates indicate that all Axis airfields in the BAYTOWN invasion area except Foggia have been neutralized by intense Allied preinvasion bombing efforts, which numbers approximately 3,000 air-combat sorties since August 18. Now the great weight of the air attacks shifts to preinvasion targets in the AVALANCHE area, around Salerno.

Seventy-five XII Bomber Command B-26s, escorted by 82d Fighter Group P-38s, attack a marshalling yard at Cancello Arnone, near Naples, at about 1330 hours through relentless Axis fighter attacks that begin during the approach to the target and continue until the withdrawing bombers are 100 miles out to sea. Twenty-three Axis fighters are downed by 82d Fighter Group P-38 pilots against no USAAF losses.

In an effort to at least temporarily interdict military traffic from Germany, a small number of XII Bomber Command B-17s attack rail lines in Brenner Pass, the shortest route from Germany (via Austria) to Italy. Other XII Bomber Command B-17s and B-25s attack marshalling yards at Bologna, Bolzano, and Trento.

In the south, closer to the invasion area, tactical aircraft, including RAF units flying under Twelfth Air Force control, attack gun emplacements, road and rail targets, an ammunition dump, and barge traffic.

September 3, 1943

FRANCE: Of 233 1st and 4th Heavy Bombardment Wing B-17s dispatched, 216 drop a total of 587 tons of bombs on five GAF airfields in northwestern France between 0843 and 0955 hours. Also, 37 of 65 4th Heavy Bombardment Wing B-17s dispatched attack the Caudron-Renault aircraft factory and an airdrome, both in Paris, with a total of 111 tons of bombs between 0845 and 0925 hours.

While escorting the heavy bombers, and at a cost of one P-47 and its pilot lost, 56th Fighter Group P-47 pilots down four FW-190s near Paris between 0840 and 0900 hours.

Ninety-eight of 141 3d Medium Bombardment Wing B-26s dispatched attack three GAF airfields in northwestern France with a total of 146 tons of bombs between 0828 and 1007 hours.

ITALY: The British Eighth Army opens

Operation BAYTOWN—and the Allied liberation of the European continent—with landings on the Italian mainland, in Calabria, just across the 3-mile-wide Straits of Messina.

NATAF A-20s, A-36s, and fighters, with RAF light bombers, attack gun emplacements throughout the toe of Italy, Camigliatello and Crotone airdromes, rail yards, troop concentrations, bridges, and road junctions. Six IX Bomber Command B-24s are downed by Axis fighters while attacking a marshalling yard at Sulmona.

A 57th Fighter Group P-40 pilot downs a Bf-109 over Catanzaro at 0800 hours.

SARDINIA: Twelfth Air Force P-40s attack radar installations at Capo Carbonara and Pula.

SICILY: Representatives of the Italian government of Marshal Pietro Badoglio sign an armistice with the Allies, which will become effective and made public on September 8.

TUNISIA: 81st Fighter Group P-38 pilots down an FW-190 and probably down another about 50 miles off Bizerte at 0750 hours.

September 4, 1943

BELGIUM: Thirty-three 387th Medium Bombardment Group B-26s attack a marshalling yard at Courtrai at 1756 hours.

FRANCE: Ninety 3d Medium Bombardment Wing B-26s attack marshalling yards at Hazebrouck, Lille, and St- Pol-sur-Mer between 1756 and 1833 hours.

ITALY: XII Bomber Command B-17s dispatched to attack airdromes in southern Italy are forced to abort in the face of bad weather; Twelfth Air Force P-38s dispatched to attack Grazzanise Airdrome are unable to find their target, but they attack targets of opportunity on the return flight to their bases; and USAAF fighter-bombers and RAF light bombers attached to NATAF attack motor vehicles, roads, and rail junctions all across the toe of Italy, and gun emplacements around Reggio di Calabria.

A 1st Fighter Group P-38 pilot downs

an Fi-156 observation plane near Cancello Arnone at 1800 hours.

SICILY: The 57th Medium Bombardment Wing (formerly the 8th Fighter Wing) is reassigned from the Ninth Air Force to the Twelfth Air Force, and it begins overseeing operations of the 12th, 321st, and 340th Medium Bombardment groups, all in B-25s.

The Twelfth Air Force's 416th Night-Fighter Squadron, in Beaufighters, mounts its first operational sorties of the war.

September 5, 1943

BELGIUM: Sixty-three 3d Medium Bombardment Wing B-26s attack a marshalling yard at Ghent at about 0830 hours.

ITALY: Approximately 130 XII Bomber Command B-17s attack Civitavecchia and Viterbo Airdrome, and more than 200 XII Bomber Command B-25s and B-26s attack landing grounds around Grazzanise.

14th and 82d Fighter group P-38 pilots down three Axis fighters over the Grazzanise area at about 1300 hours.

NATAF operations are impeded by bad weather, and only a few sorties are successfully mounted against tactical targets in and around the BAYTOWN battle area.

LIBYA: Col John C. Kilborn assumes command of the IX Bomber Command from MajGen Uzal G. Ent.

MEDITERRANEAN: As the British Eighth Army expands its holdings on the Italian mainland, the American AVALANCHE assault forces leave North African ports on their way to the Gulf of Salerno.

SARDINIA: Twelfth Air Force medium bombers and fighters attack Pabillonis and the radar station at Pula.

September 6, 1943

BELGIUM: Thirty-two B-26s of the 3d Medium Bombardment Wing's 386th Medium Bombardment Group attack a marshalling yard at Ghent at 0739 hours.

FRANCE: 3d Medium Bombardment Wing B-26s attack marshalling yards at Rouen at 0738 hours, and at Amiens and Serqueux at about 1800 hours.

GERMANY: Provisionally reorganized into the new 1st, 2d, and 3d Bombardment divisions (B-17s, B-24s, and B-17s, respectively), VIII Bomber Command heavy bombers mount their largest bombing mission to date—338 1st and 3d Bombardment division B-17s dispatched against aircraft-industry targets in Stuttgart. However, only a very few of the B-17s are able to locate the assigned target due to foul weather conditions. In the end, after the bomber formations become hopelessly disorganized and separated, 262 B-17s release their bombs—a few over Stuttgart and the rest over a broad array of "targets of opportunity" between 0940 and 1230 hours. Losses amount to 45 B-17s, but less through enemy action than fuel depletion in many 1st Bombardment Division short-range B-17s. One B-17 crashes in a Swiss lake and four make forced landings on Swiss runways. Crew losses amount to two killed and 333 missing, but 118 crewmen from 12 fuel-starved B-17s that ditch in the North Sea are recovered by Air-Sea Rescue Service boats.

A 353d Fighter Group P-47 is lost while escorting the B-17s, but a 4th Fighter Group P-47 pilot downs an FW-190 near Chateau Thierry, France, at 1125 hours.

In their first U.K.-based mission since returning from North Africa, 60 2d Bombardment Division B-24s stage a diversion over the North Sea that attracts no attention.

ITALY: XII Bomber Command B-17s attack Capodichino Airdrome, the harbor at Gaeta, rail facilities at Minturno, and a marshalling yard at Villa Literno; bad weather turns back a force of XII Bomber Command B-17s dispatched against Pomigliano Airdrome; despite bad weather, a small number of NATAF aircraft are able to attack a few rail targets and targets of opportunity; and XII Bomber Command B-25s and B-26s attack Capua and Grazzanise airdromes.

1st, 14th, and 81st Fighter group escort pilots down 11 Axis fighter during noon-hour actions over Capua and Grazzanise airdromes.

SARDINIA: Twelfth Air Force P-40s attack the landing ground at Pabillonis.

September 7, 1943

ALGERIA: A 350th Fighter Group P-38 pilot downs two Bf-109s at sea 10 miles northwest of Bougie at 1306 hours.

BELGIUM: 105 1st Bombardment Division B-17s attack Brussels/Evere Airdrome with 315 tons of bombs at about 0850 hours.

ENGLAND: The 422d Heavy Bombardment Squadron is formally detached from the 305th Heavy Bombardment Group to train in night-bombing techniques.

FRANCE: Thanks to a botched rendezvous, only 81 of 144 3d Medium Bombardment Wing B-26s dispatched attack marshalling yards at Lille and St.-Pol-sur-Mer between 0854 and 0858 hours.

Fifty-eight of 147 3d Bombardment Division B-17s dispatched overcome bad weather to attack V-weapons sites at Watten with 116 tons of bombs between 0820 and 0854 hours.

ITALY: XII Bomber Command B-17s attack two of the satellite fields in the Foggia Airdrome complex; XII Bomber Command B-25s and B-26s attack roads and bridges behind the BAYTOWN battle area; and NATAF A-20s and B-25s attack a gun battery and a roadblock near Catanzaro and Crotone Airdrome.

During the night of September 7–8, NATAF A-20s support a British Eighth Army landing at Pizzo.

NETHERLANDS: Only three of the 29 2d Bombardment Division B-24s dispatched are able to attack Bergen/Alkmaar Airdrome through bad weather, but 19 other B-24s attack an Axis convoy at sea off Texel Island. This is the first mission from England undertaken by the veteran 389th Heavy Bombardment Group.

While providing escort for 3d Bombardment Division B-17s, 56th Fighter Group P-47 pilots down two Bf-109s near Texel Island at 0900 hours.

SARDINIA: Twelfth Air Force P-40s attack the landing ground at Pabillonis and barges off Portoscuso.

September 8, 1943

ENGLAND: The 44th, 93d, and 389th Heavy Bombardment groups, all in B-24s, are returned to operational status with the 2d Bombardment Division following several months' temporary service with IX Bomber Command (Operation TIDALWAVE).

The Eighth Air Force activates the 652d Heavy Bombardment Squadron as a provisional weather-reconnaissance unit charged with conducting meteorological missions over the North Atlantic. The unit is equipped with B-17s.

FRANCE: A total of 135 3d Medium Bombardment Wing B-26s attack the Lille/Nord and Lille/Vendeville airdromes between 0922 and 1013 hours; and 68 3d Medium Bombardment Wing B-26s attack German Army coastal defenses around Boulogne between 1756 and 1818 hours.

During the night of September 8–9, five B-17s from the Eighth Air Force's independent 422d Heavy Bombardment Squadron join RAF bombers in a raid against targets in the Boulogne area. The B-17s drop 43 500-pound general-purpose bombs and five special Photoflash bombs. This is the first Eighth Air Force night-bombing mission of the war.

ITALY: At 1830 hours, on the eve of the AVALANCHE landings, Gen Dwight D. Eisenhower announces the armistice with Italy. This is followed at 1945 hours by a similar announcement from Marshal Pietro Badoglio. Upon Badoglio's announcement, the Italian Fleet and many Italian warplanes head for predetermined points to surrender to the Allies.

Strikes by Allied aircraft on targets near Salerno continue right up until the landings begin: IX Bomber Command B-24s attack the Foggia satellite fields; about 130 XII Bomber Command B-17s attack Frascati; XII Bomber Command medium bombers attack highways and bridges; and

Twelfth Air Force fighters support the British Eighth Army around Pizzo.

During the night of September 8–9, Twelfth Air Force fighters bomb and strafe roads behind the invasion area, and medium bombers attack roads and junctions in the Naples area.

SARDINIA: Twelfth Air Force P-40s attack the landing ground at Pabillonis.

TUNISIA: The 5th Photographic Reconnaissance Group reaches its new base at La Marsa Airdrome and is assigned to the Twelfth Air Force. The new unit is equipped with F-5 photo-reconnaissance aircraft, a P-38 variant.

September 9, 1943

ALGERIA: BriGen Paul L. Williams assumes command of the XII Provisional Troop Carrier Command.

FRANCE: The Eighth Air Force concludes Operation STARKEY, a dress rehearsal for the air plan drawn up for the invasion of France in mid-1944: Between 0830 and 0840 hours, 1st Bombardment Division B-17s seed Lille/Nord, Lille/Vendeville, and Vitry-en-Artois airdromes with thousands of 20-pound fragmentation bombs designed to damage airplanes, buildings, and equipment; four 2d Bombardment Division B-24 groups (including the 392d Heavy Bombardment Group, in its combat debut) attack the Abbeville/Drucat, St.-Omer/Ft. Rouge, and St.-Omer/Longuenesse airdromes with general-purpose and fragmentation bombs; 20 of 87 3d Bombardment Division B-17s briefed to attack an aircraft plant in Paris do so at 0903 hours while 48 B-17s divert to a secondary target, the Beaumont-sur-Oise Airdrome, between 0855 and 0916 hours; also, at about 0815 hours, 59 3d Bombardment Division B-17s attack their briefed target, the Beauvais/Tille Airdrome.

Two hundred fifteen P-47 escort are launched in support of the heavy-bomber attacks, including a patrol over the English coast by the 352d Fighter Group, in its combat debut with VIII Fighter Command. Just one GAF airplane is claimed, an FW-109 downed near Beauvais at 0817 by a 56th Fighter Group P-47 pilot.

Two hundred two 3d Medium Bombardment Wing B-26s drop more than 334 tons of bombs on coast-defense positions around Boulogne between 0745 and 0915 hours at a cost of three B-26s lost to enemy fire, 18 B-26s damaged, and two B-26s lost in operational accidents. Crew losses amount to 11 killed, 19 missing, and eight wounded.

ITALY: When the U.S. Fifth Army, including some attached British Army units, invades southern Italy at Salerno and Paestum, powerful German Army ground forces are immediately dispatched from other areas to counterattack the beachhead. The entire Twelfth Air Force is ordered aloft to stem the flow of German troops and vehicles.

IX Bomber Command B-24s attack the Foggia satellite fields; XII Bomber Command B-17s attack bridges at Cancello Arnone and Capua; more than 240 B-25 and B-26 sorties are mounted against rail bridges at Potenza and the landing ground at Scanzano; and NATAF aircraft patrol over the landing beaches, provide on-call air support against all manner of tactical targets, and mount sweeps against motor vehicles and other targets of opportunity.

During the course of hundreds of fighter sorties, only three GAF aircraft are engaged: a Do-217 bomber that is damaged by a 325th Fighter Group P-40 pilot during a morning mission; and an FW-190 and an Fi-156 that are downed by 86th Fighter-Bomber Group A-36 pilots, also during the morning.

September 10, 1943

ITALY: The German Army occupies the city of Rome.

XII Bomber Command B-17s, B-25s, and B-26s attack the communications network leading to the Salerno area from throughout central Italy; IX Bomber Command B-24s attack a Foggia satellite field;

and NATAF aircraft provide direct and general support for Allied forces within the beachhead area.

At 0740 hours, while conducting an armed reconnaissance over southern Italy, 12 27th Fighter-Bomber Group A-36s come upon a German Army road column amounting to more than 500 trucks and armored vehicles moving north through Lagonegro, 70 road miles from Salerno. In the attack that follows, and numerous others mounted on this column during the day by the 27th Fighter-Bomber Group, an estimated 177 German vehicles are destroyed and an estimated 246 are damaged. The road column, which equals the strength of three armored divisions, is completely stalled. The decisive nature of this single interdiction—one among many performed by Twelfth Air Force aircraft—can be seen when it is taken into account that concerted German Army counterattacks at Salerno nearly drive their way through the beachhead to the sea.

Throughout the 27th Fighter-Bomber Group attacks on the German Army road column, only one GAF fighter is engaged, a Bf-109 that is downed by a 524th Fighter-Bomber Squadron A-36 pilot. In other, extremely light fighter action, three GAF fighters are downed over or near the invasion beaches by 1st and 31st Fighter group pilots.

Within only one day of the landings, the former Axis airdrome at Paestum, in the British zone, is made operational in anticipation of an early occupation by the 33d Fighter Group, which has made something of a specialty of being the first Allied air unit into a forward location.

During the night of September 10–11, the 12th Medium Bombardment Group, in B-25s, attacks several communications centers.

September 11, 1943

FRANCE: Thirty-two 323d Medium Bombardment Group B-26s attack Beaumont-le-Roger Airdrome at 1756 hours; and 14 of 19 322d Medium Bombardment Group B-26s are damaged by enemy fire during an attack at 1704 hours on the day's briefed secondary target, the Le Trait shipyard.

ITALY: XII Bomber Command B-17s attack a marshalling yard, a bridge, and a highway junction in and around Benevento; XII Bomber Command B-25s and B-26s attack highways and road junctions serving German Army forces moving on the beachhead area; and NATAF aircraft provide support throughout the day for Allied forces in the beachhead, and attack a broad band of routes leading into the area.

In all, nine GAF fighters and a Ju-52 are downed by USAAF fighter pilots during several afternoon engagements, all more or less over the Salerno beachhead. 1stLt Gerald L. Rounds, a P-38 pilot with the 82d Fighter Group's 97th Fighter Squadron, achieves ace status when he downs a Bf-109 while patrolling over the Salerno beachhead area at 1440 hours. Rounds's fighter is damaged in this action and he is forced to crash-land at his base in Sicily. And 1stLt Rodney W. Fisher, a P-38 pilot with the 1st Fighter Group's 71st Fighter Squadron, achieves ace status when he downs an FW-190 and two Bf-109s at 1745 hours while defending the Salerno beachhead.

SARDINIA: Axis forces begin a peaceful evacuation of the island via Corsica, where Free French Army troops are aiding citizens in an uprising against the German garrison.

UNITED KINGDOM: In anticipation of the transfer of the Ninth Air Force to England, MajGen Ira C. Eaker, the commanding general of the Eighth Air Force, is named commander of all USAAF units and personnel in the United Kingdom.

September 12, 1943

GREECE: IX Bomber Command B-24s attack Kalathos and Maritsa airdromes.

ITALY: As German Army pressure mounts on the Salerno beachhead, XII Bomber Command B-17s attack road defiles

at Mignano, a road bridge at Benevento, and
the Frosinone Airdrome; and NATAF aircraft provide support for Allied forces in
the beachhead throughout the day, and
attack numerous communications targets in
the area.

In the day's only fighter action, 82d
Fighter Group P-38 pilots probably down
two GAF fighters over the sea near Salerno
during the afternoon.

Engineers complete a new runway near
Paestum.

The Isle of Capri, in the Gulf of Naples,
is occupied.

During the night of September 12–13,
NATAF aircraft fly numerous intruder
missions over six Axis airdromes between
Rome and Pizzo.

September 13, 1943

ENGLAND: In a major reorganizational
move based on assessments of combat
command-and-control experience over the
preceding year, the Eighth Air Force
officially activates the three heavy bombardment divisions that have overseen combat
missions on a provisional basis on September 6, 7, and 9. The 1st Bombardment
Division, commanded by MajGen Robert
B. Williams, assumes responsibility for
overseeing the combat operations of the 1st
Heavy Bombardment Wing (B-17s); the 2d
Bombardment Division, commanded by
BriGen James P. Hodges, assumes responsibility for overseeing all Eighth Air Force
B-24 units; and the 3d Bombardment Division, commanded by MajGen Curtis E.
LeMay, assumes responsibility for overseeing the 4th Heavy Bombardment Wing
(B-17s). Each bombardment division will
also eventually have particular fighter and
other operational units assigned.

The 1st and 40th Combat Bombardment wings begin overseeing several 1st
Bombardment Division B-17 groups; the
2d, 14th, 20th, and 41st Combat Bombardment wings begin overseeing several 2d
Bombardment Division B-24 groups; and
the 4th, 13th, and 45th Combat Bombard-

ment wings each begin overseeing several
3d Bombardment Division B-17 groups.
Also, the various provisional combat
bombardment wings and the 6th Fighter
Group (responsible for training the Eighth
Air Force's replacement fighter pilots) are
disbanded.

The 91st, 351st, and 381st Heavy Bombardment groups are assigned to the 1st
Bombardment Division's 1st Combat Bombardment Wing.

The 92d and 305th Heavy Bombard-
ment groups are assigned to the 1st Heavy
Bombardment Division's 40th Combat
Bombardment Wing.

The 303d, 379th, and 384th Heavy
Bombardment groups are assigned to the
1st Heavy Bombardment Division's 41st
Combat Bombardment Wing.

The 389th Heavy Bombardment Group
is assigned to the 2d Bombardment
Division's 2d Combat Bombardment Wing.

The 44th and 392d Heavy Bombard-
ment groups are assigned to the 2d
Bombardment Division's 14th Combat
Bombardment Wing.

The 92d Heavy Bombardment Group
is assigned to the 2d Bombardment
Division's 20th Combat Bombardment
Wing.

The 94th and 385th Heavy Bombardment groups are assigned to the 3d Bombardment Division's 4th Combat Bombardment Wing.

The 95th, 100th, and 390th Heavy
Bombardment groups are assigned to the
3d Bombardment Division's 13th Combat
Bombardment Wing.

The 96th and 388th Heavy Bombardment groups are assigned to the 3d Bombardment Division's 45th Combat Bombardment Wing.

ITALY: XII Bomber Command B-17s and
B-25s, and NATAF light and medium
bombers attack roads and highways leading to the Salerno area; and NATAF A-36s
destroy as many as 30 German Army
vehicles near Potenza. (While doing so,
27th and 86th Fighter-Bomber group A-36

pilots down six GAF fighters in two separate morning engagements.)

The 33d Fighter Group moves forward from Sicily to Paestum Airdrome, in the Salerno beachhead.

During the night of September 13–14, in a rush operation, 600 U.S. Army paratroopers are dropped at Agropoli, south of Salerno, by 82 52d Troop Carrier Wing C-47s and C-53s. The drop is flawless; the paratroopers are dropped exactly on the drop zone, and no airplanes are lost.

LIBYA: Col Frederick M. Byerly replaces Col Charles D. McAllister as commanding officer of the IX Fighter Command.

September 14, 1943

ENGLAND: The 55th Fighter Group, a P-38 unit, arrives from the United States aboard ship for duty with the VIII Fighter Command.

EUROPEAN THEATER OF OPERATIONS (ETO): Scheduled attacks by more than 100 3d Medium Bombardment Wing B-26s against GAF airdromes are aborted due to bad weather.

The 355th Fighter Group, in P-47s, makes its combat debut in an uneventful fighter sweep over the North Sea coast.

ITALY: As part of an all-out air, naval, and ground effort to stem German Army counterattacks against the Salerno beachhead, XII Bomber Command B-17s, B-25s, and B-26s, IX Bomber Command B-24s, and RAF heavy bombers attack highways, bridges, defiles, road centers, rail lines, marshalling yards, a barracks, gun emplacements, and numerous other targets in a wide band around the battle area. Also, NATAF aircraft mount more than 500 combat sorties in direct support of the Allied ground forces. By day's end, the German Army counterattack against the Salerno beachhead is stemmed, thanks in large part to relentless air-interdiction operations conducted by USAAF and RAF air units.

Two FW-190s and an Fi-56 are downed during several morning engagements over the Salerno beachhead by 27th and 86th

Fighter-Bomber group A-36 pilots and 82d Fighter Group P-38 pilots.

British Eighth Army troops enter Bari.

During the night of September 14–15, XII Troop Carrier Command C-47s drop U.S. Army paratroopers near the Sele River.

September 15, 1943

FRANCE: Eighty-seven 1st Bombardment Division B-17s attack Romilly-sur-Seine Airdrome with nearly 268 tons of bombs at 1850 hours; and 47 2d Bombardment Division B-24s attack Chartres Airdrome with 141 tons of bombs at about 0905 hours; 78 3d Bombardment Division B-17s attack the Hispano-Suiza aircraft-engine factory in Paris with 229 tons of bombs at about 1855 hours; 21 3d Bombardment Division B-17s attack the Billancourt-Renault works in Paris with 63 tons of bombs at 1854 hours; and 40 3d Bombardment Division B-17s attack the Caudron-Renault aircraft factory in Paris with 119 tons of bombs at 1855 hours. Five B-17s and one B-24 are lost.

Sixty-eight 3d Medium Bombardment Wing B-26s attack the Merville Airdrome with 100 tons of bombs at about 1745 hours, but 72 B-26s dispatched to attack Lille/Nord Airdrome return to their bases without completing the mission.

During the night of September 15–16, at about 2340 hours, five B-17s from the Eighth Air Force's independent 422d Heavy Bombardment Squadron join RAF bombers on a mission against an aircraft-industry target in France.

ITALY: XII Bomber Command B-17s, B-25s, and B-26s attack numerous highways and road junctions surrounding the Salerno beachhead area; IX Bomber Command B-24s attack a marshalling yard at Potenza, various rail lines, and several warehouses; and NATAF aircraft attack rail lines, highways, motor vehicles, and German-occupied buildings.

GAF attempts to penetrate to the beachhead area throughout the day result in the confirmed downing, between 0730 and 1900 hours, of 11 FW-190s by pilots of the 31st and 33d Fighter groups and the 86th Fighter-Bomber Group.

The 57th and 79th Fighter groups move from Sicily to Rocco Bernardo and Crotone airdromes, respectively.

German Army counterattacks against the Salerno beachhead subside.

September 16, 1943

FRANCE: Seventy-nine 1st Bombardment Division B-17s attack the Nantes port area, and 51 1st Bombardment Division B-17s attack Nantes/Chateau Bougon Airdrome between 1502 and 1512 hours. Two of the seven B-17s that are lost are brought down by aerial bombs dropped by GAF aircraft.

While escorting the 1st Bombardment Division B-17s on target penetration, 56th Fighter Group P-47 pilots down two GAF fighters over northwestern France at 1430 hours.

Ninety-three of 148 3d Bombardment Division B-17s dispatched attack the La Pallice port area, and the La Rochelle/Laleau and Cognac/Chateaubernard airdromes between 1731 and 1758 hours. Four B-17s are brought down by enemy action and five are lost in accidents during night landings, with the result that 44 crewmen are killed and 30 are missing in action.

Sixty-seven 3d Medium Bombardment Wing B-26s attack Beaumont-le-Roger and Tricqueville airdromes with 92 tons of bombs at 1735 hours.

ITALY: XII Bomber Command B-17s attack rail and road targets in and around Benevento and Caserta; XII Bomber Command B-25s and B-26s attack road and rail targets at Capua, Formia, and Mignano; IX Bomber Command B-24s attack a supply dump and road junctions in and around Potenza; NATAF aircraft attack motor vehicles, troop concentrations, communications targets, and Axis aircraft on the ground in and around Contursi and Eboli; and XII Air Support Command fighter-bombers provide constant on-call support for Allied ground forces in the Salerno beachhead area.

Three GAF fighters and a Ju-88 are downed by USAAF fighters pilots over southern Italy in a series of minor engagements between 0720 and 1440 hours.

The 68th Reconnaissance Group's 111th Reconnaissance Squadron, in P-51As, moves from Algeria to Sele Airdrome.

September 17, 1943

FRANCE: Five B-17s from the Eighth Air Force's independent 422d Heavy Bombardment Squadron join an RAF attack on the marshalling yards at Mondane between 0029 and 0044 hours.

ITALY: XII Bomber Command B-17s and B-26s attack Ciampino and Pratica di Mare airdromes; XII Bomber Command B-25s attack barges and small craft around the mouth of the Tiber River; IX Bomber Command B-24s attack road and rail junctions at Pescara, in eastern Italy; Twelfth Air Force P-38 fighter-bombers mount 27 separate dive-bombing attacks against rail and road targets and targets of opportunity in the Salerno beachhead area; and NATAF aircraft mount day-long sweeps over the beachhead area and attack numerous rail and road targets servicing German Army forces in southern Italy.

Four GAF fighters are downed by pilots of the 33d Fighter and 27th Fighter-Bomber groups during two separate afternoon actions over the Salerno beachhead area.

Thanks in large measure to the unremitting pressure exerted by the Allied air forces, German Army forces withdraw from the Salerno area to a new defensive battle line north of the beachhead.

TUNISIA: A detachment of the 2d Bombardment Division's 93d Heavy Bombardment Group arrives from England for temporary duty with IX Bomber Command.

September 18, 1943

FRANCE: Although 162 3d Medium Bombardment Wing B-26s are briefed for attacks on three targets in France, only 25 from the 387th Medium Bombardment Group overcome bad weather to drop 37 tons of bombs on the Beauvais/Tille Airdrome.

ITALY: XII Bomber Command B-17s attack Viterbo Airdrome and the road between Salerno and Avellino; XII Bomber Command B-25s and B-26s attack Ciampino and Pratica di Mare airdromes; IX Bomber Command B-24s attack a marshalling yard at Pescara; 321st Medium Bombardment Group B-25 gunships attack a lighthouse and small vessels near Capraia and at sea between Italy and Corsica; and P-38s under temporary NATAF control strafe four satellite fields in the Foggia Airdrome complex and attack numerous roads, rail lines, and bridges with bombs and machine guns.

A 14th Fighter Group P-38 pilot downs a Ju-52 during the morning strafing attack at Foggia.

The 27th Fighter-Bomber Group, in A-36s, moves forward from Sicily to Capaccio Airdrome.

SARDINIA: Preparations are begun to take over Sardinia's airfields as soon as the island surrenders to a small Allied landing force without a shot being fired.

September 19, 1943

FRANCE: Of 144 3d Medium Bombardment Wing B-26s dispatched against Lille/Nord and Merville airdromes, only 18 from the 386th Medium Bombardment Group attack Lille/Nord with 26 tons of bombs at 1139 hours.

ITALY: NATAF aircraft mount numerous attacks on rail and road targets around the expanding Salerno beachhead.

Allied ground forces secure Auletta and Potenza.

TUNISIA: Detachments of the 2d Bombardment Division's 44th and 389th Heavy Bombardment groups arrive from England for temporary duty with the IX Bomber Command.

September 20, 1943

ITALY: XII Bomber Command B-17s and B-26s attack road and rail targets around

the expanding beachhead area; XII Air Support Command A-36s and NATAF aircraft attack German Army forces concentrating in the Nocera area.

In its last operational mission against targets in Italy, the IX Bomber Command dispatches 98th and 376th Heavy Bombardment group B-24s against a marshalling yard at Castelfranco Veneto. Clouds obscure the target, but the 98th Group bombers release their bombs on the basis of a time-to-target estimate, and the 376th Group B-24s attack the airdrome and marshalling yards on the return leg.

The 31st Fighter Group, in Spitfires, moves forward from Sicily to Montecorvino Airdrome.

LIBYA: Upon their return from the day's mission to Italy, the 98th and 376th Heavy Bombardment groups—and the 43d Service Group and all Ninth Air Force military police and engineering units—are ordered to move to Tunis, where, upon arrival, they will be formally transferred to the Twelfth Air Force.

September 21, 1943

FRANCE: Forty-four of 73 3d Medium Bombardment Wing B-26s dispatched attack Beauvais/Tille Airdrome with 65 tons of bombs at 0937 hours.

ITALY: XII Bomber Command B-17s attack the bridge and town at Benevento; VIII Bomber Command B-24s on detached service with the XII Bomber Command attack Bastia and Leghorn; XII Bomber Command B-25s and B-26s attack landing craft and a ferry near Elba and bridges at Cancello Arnone and Capua; and NATAF aircraft attack troop concentrations, tanks, motor vehicles, and German-occupied towns beyond the expanding Salerno beachhead area.

LIBYA: Headquarters, Ninth Air Force, ceases operations at Tripoli to prepare for its move to the U.K.

September 22, 1943

FRANCE: Seventy B-26s from the 3d

Medium Bombardment Wing attack Evreux/Fauville Airdrome with 105 tons of bombs at 1613 hours, but 72 other B-26s are prevented by bad weather from attacking Beauvais/Tille Airdrome.

GERMANY: Five B-17s from the Eighth Air Force's independent 422d Heavy Bombardment Squadron join and RAF attack against Hannover between 2143 and 2209 hours.

GREECE: In its final mission in the theater, IX Bomber Command dispatches the last of its B-24 groups against Athens/Eleusis and Maritsa airdromes.

ITALY: XII Bomber Command B-25s and B-26s attack bridges and rail and road targets around the Salerno beachhead area; 321st Medium Bombardment Group B-25 gunships operating under NATAF control attack small ships and craft near Elba; NATAF aircraft attack German Army troop concentrations, gun emplacements, tanks, and motor vehicles in and around the battle area, the landing ground at Capua, and docking facilities and ships at Manfredonia.

LIBYA: Upon their return from the day's mission to Greece, the last Ninth Air Force B-24 groups are formally transferred to the Twelfth Air Force, leaving the Ninth with no operational units.

NETHERLANDS: While conducting a fighter sweep along the North Sea coast, 353d Fighter Group P-47 pilots down two GAF fighters near Utrecht between 1215 and 1220.

September 23, 1943

FRANCE: Forty-six of 117 1st Bombardment Division B-17s dispatched attack the Nantes port area with 134 tons of bombs at about 0815 hours. While escorting the 1st Bombardment Division B-17s over the target and during the withdrawal, 353d Fighter Group P-47 pilots down five GAF fighters near Nantes and Chateaubriant between 0815 and 0845 hours.

Fifty-three 3d Bombardment Division B-17s attack the Kerlin/Bastard Airdrome with 155 tons of bombs at about 0815 hours,

and 55 3d Bombardment Division B-17s attack Vannes/Meucon Airdrome with 165 tons of bombs at 0825 hours.

Seventy 3d Medium Bombardment Wing B-26s attack Conches Airdrome at 0907 hours, and 69 B-26s attack Beauvais/Tille Airdrome at 1545 hours.

Sixty-one 1st Bombardment Division B-17s attack the Nantes port area with 174 tons of bombs at about 1810 hours; and 19 1st Bombardment Division B-17s attack Rennes/St.-Jacques Airdrome (secondary) with 57 tons of bombs at 1834 hours. This is the first time in which two entirely separate heavy-bomber missions have been mounted from the U.K. in one day.

GERMANY: Four B-17s from the Eighth Air Force's independent 422d Heavy Bomber Squadron join an RAF attack against Mannheim between 2211 and 2222 hours.

ITALY: XII Bomber Command B-26s attack bridges at Cancello Arnone and near Capua; and NATAF aircraft attack numerous towns, roads, railroads, and motor vehicles in and around the battle area.

September 24, 1943

CORFU: The island is seized by a German Army landing force.

FRANCE: Seventy-one 3d Medium Bombardment Wing B-26s attack Evreux/Fauville Airdrome at 1149 hours, and 66 B-26s attack Beauvais/Tille Airdrome at 1602 hours.

ITALY: XII Bomber Command B-25s and B-26s attack numerous roads, road junctions, bridges, and rail lines in and around the battle area; VIII Bomber Command B-24s on detached service with the XII Bomber Command attack marshalling yards at Pisa; and NATAF aircraft attack numerous tactical and communications targets throughout southern Italy.

The XII Air Support Command's 47th Light Bombardment Group, in A-20s, moves forward from Sicily to Grottaglie Airdrome.

MEDITERRANEAN: XII Bomber Command medium bombers attack an Italian Navy destroyer between Elba and Corsica.

September 25, 1943

FRANCE: Sixty-eight 3d Medium Bombardment Wing B-26s attack St.-Omer/Longuenesse Airdrome with 100 tons of bombs at 1718 hours.

ITALY: XII Bomber Command B-17s attack marshalling yards at Bologna and a rail bridge at Bolzano; XII Bomber Command B-25s and B-26s attack the Bastia/Borgo, Lucca, and Pisa airdromes, a road junction, and several rail and road bridges; and NATAF aircraft attack numerous tactical targets.

In the first air-to-air engagements over Italy in a week, a 31st Fighter Group Spitfire pilot downs an FW-190 during the morning near Montecorvino Airdrome, and 27th Fighter-Bomber Group A-36 pilots down three Bf-109s around Aquino Airdrome at 1220 hours.

September 26, 1943

FRANCE: Although the day's primary mission against various targets around Paris has to be abandoned in the face of bad weather, 40 3d Bombardment Division B-17s manage to attack Reims/Champagne Airdrome with 118 tons of bombs at 1751 hours. Also, 72 3d Medium Bombardment Wing B-26s on their way to attack Conches Airdrome are recalled due to bad weather.

ITALY: NATAF aircraft attack numerous communications and tactical targets, including German Army troop concentrations and gun emplacements in and around the battle area.

The 86th Fighter-Bomber Group, in A-36s, moves forward from Sicily to join the 27th Fighter-Bomber Group at Sele Airdrome.

September 27, 1943

GERMANY: On a mission to bomb the Emden port facilities and industrial areas, 246 1st and 3d Bombardment division B-17s make the first combat use of the British-built H2S airborne radar system, which will allow radar-equipped pathfinder bombers to "see" targets through thick cloud cover. The radars are aboard four B-17s of the 482d Heavy Pathfinder Bombardment Group, which makes its combat debut leading various groupings of the heavy-bomber force. Unfortunately, three of the H2S sets fail before they arrive over the target, so the bulk of the bombing effort is scattered throughout the city. A total of 505 tons of bombs are dropped on what are hoped to be industrial targets in Emden between 0957 and 1008 hours, and 181 tons of bombs are dropped on various targets of opportunity. Eight B-17s are lost and 78 are damaged, and crew losses are one killed, 71 missing, and 18 wounded.

For the first time, also, rotations of VIII Fighter Command P-47s with new 108-gallon long-range drop tanks are able to provide escort all the way to the target and back, an event that results in the confirmed downing of 18 GAF fighters over the target area between 1005 and 1025 hours by P-47 pilots of the 4th, 78th, and 353d Fighter groups as well as four over the Netherlands coast between 1030 and 1045 hours by 56th Fighter Group P-47 pilots. Of 262 P-47 escort sorties, one P-47 and its pilot are lost in action, and one is lost in an operational accident.

Sixty-five 3d Medium Bombardment Wing B-26s attack Beauvais/Tille Airdrome at 1045 hours, and 68 B-26s attack Conches Airdrome at 1729 hours.

Four B-17s from the Eighth Air Force's independent 422d Heavy Bombardment Squadron join the RAF attack on Hannover between 2208 and 2217 hours. One of the night bombers is lost.

ITALY: Although bad weather forces the cancellation of most scheduled Twelfth Air Force missions, XII Air Support Command fighters are able to strafe Viterbo Airdrome and the Bracciano seaplane base, and attack a number of rail and road targets in southern Italy. Also, NATAF aircraft attack motor vehicles near Benevento, and 86th

Fighter-Bomber Group A-36 pilots down a Ju-52 and an He-111 while conducting a morning mission near Rome.

The complete terms of surrender are presented by Allied representatives to Marshal Pietro Badoglio.

Axis forces abandon the Foggia Airdrome complex in the British Eighth Army zone, an event of major importance.

September 28, 1943

ITALY: Most of the Twelfth Air Force is grounded by bad weather, but NATAF fighter-bombers are able to attack several targets.

September 29, 1943

ITALY: XII Bomber Command B-25s and B-26s attack bridges at or near Amorosi, Cancello Arnone, Castelvenere, and Piana; Twelfth Air Force P-38 fighter-bombers attack a bridge near San Apollinare and the defile at Ausonia; and NATAF aircraft attack tactical targets in and around the battle area.

MALTA: During a meeting aboard the battleship HMS *Nelson* off Malta, Gen Dwight D. Eisenhower and Marshal Pietro Badoglio sign Italy's complete instrument of surrender.

September 30, 1943

ITALY: XII Bomber Command B-25s, B-26s, and P-38s, and NATAF aircraft mount numerous attacks on a variety of tactical targets throughout southern and south-central Italy.

The final air-to-air victory of a slow month that has seen the GAF all but concede the air over Italy to Allied aircraft comes at 1620 hours when Col Charles M. McCorkle, the commanding officer of the 31st Fighter Group, downs an Me-210.

Despite the invasion of an Axis partner and the European mainland itself—and in sharp contrast to bitter battles on the ground—the Axis air forces (of which one stops flying altogether midway through the month) launch such desultory resistance that the Allied air forces are able to achieve and maintain virtual air supremacy over southern Italy. Only 94 Axis aircraft of all types are downed throughout the theater in September 1943, a total indicative of a lukewarm effort on the part of the GAF.

OCTOBER 1943

October 1, 1943

AUSTRIA: XII Bomber Command B-24s attack the Bf-109 factory at Wiener-Neustadt with 187 tons of bombs.

ENGLAND: Intelligence reports made available to the Eighth Air Force indicate that German aircraft production is on the rise and that there are more GAF fighters than ever before defending the bomber routes from England to Germany.

GERMANY: XII Bomber Command B-17s prevented by bad weather from bombing their primary target at Augsburg, Germany, attack targets of opportunity during the return flight over Austria, Italy, Corsica, and Elba.

ITALY: XII Bomber Command B-26s attack communications targets at Arce, Capua, Grazzanise, and Mignano; and NATAF aircraft attack Benevento, a marshalling yard and bridge at Capua, and transportation targets from Isernia north to Avezzano.

A-36 pilots from the 27th Fighter-Bomber Group A-36 down two Ju-52s over Italy, one at 0830 hours and the other at 1330 hours.

Naples falls without a fight to the U.S. Fifth Army.

October 2, 1943

FRANCE: Due to poor visibility, just six of 72 3d Medium Bombardment Wing B-26s attack St.-Omer/Longuenesse Airdrome at 1715 hours.

GERMANY: With two H2S-equipped 482d Heavy Pathfinder Bombardment Group B-17s guiding them, 339 1st and 3d Bombardment division B-17s attack aircraft-industry targets at Emden through cloud cover with 953 tons of bombs between 1557 and 1603 hours. Losses are two B-17s downed and 34 B-17s damaged.

In all, VIII Fighter Command fighters mount 227 escort sorties. Six GAF fighters are downed over the Netherlands and northern Germany between 1600 and 1635 hours by P-47 pilots of the 4th, 56th, and 353d Fighter groups. While flying withdrawal escort for the heavy bombers on their way home from Germany, Col Hubert Zemke, the commanding officer of the 56th Fighter Group, in P-47s, achieves ace status when he downs an FW-190 near Groningen, Holland, at 1635 hours.

ITALY: Air operations are severely limited due to bad weather, but some XII Air Support Command aircraft are able to attack roads, bridges, and motor vehicles while conducting armed-reconnaissance missions.

NETHERLANDS: A scheduled attack by 392d Heavy Bombardment Group B-24s against Woensdrecht Airdrome is completely thwarted by heavy clouds.

TUNISIA: BriGen Gordon P. Saville replaces MajGen Elwood R. Quesada as commanding general of the XII Fighter Command.

Following several weeks' service with IX Bomber Command, a detachment of the Eighth Air Force's 93d Heavy Bombardment Group departs for England.

October 3, 1943

CORSICA: 14th Fighter Group P-38 pilots engaged by Bf-109s over Bastia down one and damage two others.

FRANCE: Sixty-three 3d Medium Bombardment Group B-26s attack Beauvais/Tille Airdrome at about 1725 hours.

ITALY: XII Bomber Command B-25s, B-26s, and P-38s attack numerous bridges (including pontoon bridges) throughout south-central Italy; and XII Bomber Command fighter-bombers attack German Army vehicles in the battle area.

The 321st Medium Bombardment Group, in B-25s, and the 82d Fighter Group, in P-38s, move from Tunisia to bases in Italy.

U.S. Fifth Army troops capture Benevento.

MEDITERRANEAN: XII Bomber Command P-38s attack Axis ships at sea between Italy and Corsica.

NETHERLANDS: One hundred thirty-one 3d Medium Bombardment Wing B-26s attack Amsterdam/Schipol, Haamstede, and Woensdrecht airdromes.

TUNISIA: Following several weeks' service with IX Bomber Command, a detachment of the Eighth Air Force's 389th Heavy Bombardment Group departs Libya for England.

October 4, 1943

CORSICA: Allied ground forces, including local partisans, take complete control of the island and its former Axis air bases.

FRANCE: 3d Bombardment Division B-17s attack St.-Dizier/Robinson Airdrome and a marshalling yard at Sarreguemines, both at about 1140 hours.

Twenty-five 3d Medium Bombardment Wing B-26s dispatched against several GAF airdromes in France are recalled due to bad weather.

GERMANY: When mission leaders fly 100 miles off the projected course, only 15 1st Bombardment Division B-17s attack the day's primary target, an aircraft-industry factory at Wiesbaden, with 45 tons of bombs. Meanwhile, the 77 B-17s that are off course reach Frankfurt am Main, where they join a planned attack by 37 1st Bombardment Division B-17s against aircraft-industry targets and the city itself. Altogether, Frankfurt am Main is struck by about 304 tons of bombs between about 1100 and 1111 hours.

3d Bombardment Division B-17s attack marshalling yards at Saarbrucken and an aircraft-industry factory at Saarlautern between about 1133 and 1139 hours.

The VIII Fighter Command mounts 223 P-47 escort sorties in support of the various VIII Bomber Command missions. In all, 18 GAF fighters are downed along the bomber routes between 1030 and 1203 hours. Capt Walker M. Mahurin, a P-47 pilot with the 56th Fighter Group's 63d Fighter Squadron, achieves ace status when he downs three Bf-110s near Duren between 1132 and 1140 hours.

ITALY: XII Bomber Command B-17s attack bridges at Bolzano and marshalling yards at Pisa; XII Bomber Command B-25s and B-26s attack the Argos Airdrome, shipping at Bastia, a highway overpass at

Mignano, and road defiles at Isernia and Terracina; and NATAF aircraft attack numerous road, rail, and vehicles targets in and around the battle area.

LIBYA: LtCol Ray J. Stecker replaces Col Frederick M. Byerly as commanding officer of the IX Fighter Command, which is in the process of transferring its headquarters operation to England.

MEDITERRANEAN: Combined with bombardments undertaken by ships of the Royal Navy (part of an attempt by the British to draw Turkey into the war on the Allied side), Twelfth Air Force B-17s, B-24s, B-25s, and P-38s begin a week-long offensive against German air bases in Greece, Crete, and the Dodecanese Islands.

NORWAY: Twenty U.S. Navy SBD dive-bombers and ten TBF torpedo bombers (rigged out as light vertical bombers) from the USS *Ranger* attack merchant ships tied up in the harbor at Bodø in two waves beginning at 0830. Altogether, the Navy bombers—which drop a total of 50 500- and 1,000-pound bombs—claim the sinking of five merchant ships, totaling 23,000 tons, and damage to at least seven other ships. Two SBDs and one TBF are lost with a total of three pilots and five aircrewmen. Operation LEADER, as it is called, is the first and only U.S. Navy carrier raid in the European Theater.

TUNISIA: Following several weeks' service with IX Bomber Command, a detachment of the Eighth Air Force's 44th Heavy Bombardment Group departs Libya for England.

October 5, 1943

ENGLAND: The 55th Fighter Group, in P-38s, is assigned to the VIII Fighter Command's 66th Fighter Wing.

ITALY: XII Bomber Command B-17s attack marshalling yards at Bologna; XII Bomber Command B-25s and B-26s attack several roads; and NATAF aircraft attack tactical targets in the battle area and several fuel dumps and railroad trains.

27th Fighter-Bomber Group A-36

pilots down two Ju-52s over Italy, one at 0850 hours and the other at 1115 hours.

October 6, 1943

ENGLAND: The 20th Fighter Group, which is training in P-38s, is formally assigned to the 67th Fighter Wing; and the 352d Fighter Group, in P-47s, is assigned to the 67th Fighter Wing.

GREECE: XII Bomber Command P-38s strafe the Araxos Airdrome.

ITALY: XII Bomber Command B-17s attack a marshalling yard at Mestre; XII Bomber Command B-26s attack roads and highways; and NATAF aircraft attack numerous tactical targets in and around the battle area.

October 7, 1943

FRANCE: Four B-17s from the independent 422d Heavy Bombardment Squadron undertake the first Eighth Air Force night leaflet drop of the war when they disperse more than 240,000 leaflets over Paris between 2257 and 2307 hours.

ITALY: Most Twelfth Air Force flight operations are canceled because of bad weather, but NATAF aircraft, including A-20s and B-25s, are able to attack towns and rail and road targets around Capua, Guglionesi, and Termoli.

MEDITERRANEAN: A 1st Fighter Group P-38 pilot based at Gambut Airdrome, Libya, downs a Ju-88 near Leros, in the Dodecanese Islands, at 1600 hours.

October 8, 1943

ENGLAND: Attacks by 144 3d Medium Bombardment Wing B-26s against several GAF airdromes in France are abandoned due to unfavorable weather conditions. At the conclusion of the day's activities, the 322d and 386th Medium Bombardment groups stand down pending their transfer to the Ninth Air Force.

GERMANY: 158 1st Bombardment Division B-17s and 156 3d Bombardment Division B-17s attack the city of Bremen, the Bremen shipyards, Bremen aircraft-industry targets, and various targets of opportunity at Vegesack, Meppen, Oldenburg, and Emden with a total of 459 tons of bombs between 1505 and 1527 hours. The Allied radio countermeasure known as Carpet (employed to jam ground-based gun-laying radars) is used for the first time, but losses due to attacks by GAF fighters are considered heavy. Overall losses in these attacks are 27 B-17s downed, two damaged beyond repair, and 205 damaged. Crew losses are three killed and 271 missing.

Providing escort for the B-17s are 274 P-47s from six VIII Fighter Command groups, which account for 12 GAF fighters over the Netherlands and Germany between 1445 and 1545 hours. Maj Roy W. Evans, the commanding officer of the 4th Fighter Group's 335th Fighter Squadron, achieves ace status when he downs a Bf-109 near Oldenburg at 1455 hours.

Forty-three unescorted 2d Heavy Bombardment Division B-24s attack the Vegesack U-boat base with more than 85 tons of bombs at about 1620 hours.

GREECE: XII Bomber Command B-24s based in Libya attack Athens/Eleusis, Athens/Tatoi, Heraklion (Crete), Kastelli/Pediada (Crete), and Rhodes/Maritsa airdromes. Also, 48 321st Medium Bombardment Group B-25s based in Italy attack Athens/Eleusis Airdrome in the morning. Although two B-25s are downed and 26 are damaged by flak and GAF fighters, the group claims many GAF bombers destroyed on the ground and numerous buildings set on fire. 82d Fighter Group P-38s escorting the B-25s down two Bf-109s over the Gulf of Corinth.

ITALY: NATAF aircraft attack a bridge at Minturno and a German Army troop concentration and road junction at Termoli.

October 9, 1943

FRANCE: Two B-17s from the Eighth Air Force's 422d Heavy Bombardment Squadron drop more than 266,000 leaflets over Rennes between 0005 and 0111 hours. This is the last of eight essentially experimental night missions undertaken by the 422d Squadron.

GERMANY: One hundred six 1st Bombardment Division B-17s attack an aircraft-industry factory at Anklam with more than 185 tons of bombs at about 1145 hours; 23 2d Bombardment Division B-24s attack the Danzig U-boat yards with 50 tons of bombs at 1305 hours; 18 2d Bombardment Division B-24s attack the Gdynia (Poland) port area (secondary) with 36 tons of bombs; a total of 109 1st and 3d Bombardment division B-17s attack the Gdynia port area with 272 tons of bombs between 1304 and 1324 hours; and 96 3d Bombardment Division B-17s attack aircraft-industry targets at Marienburg with 218 tons of bombs between 1253 and 1302 hours. Eighteen B-17s from the Anklam force and six B-17s from the Gdynia force are lost. In the longest Eighth Air Force mission to date, many of the heavy bombers are in the air for more than ten hours and fly as many as 1,500 miles.

The Marienburg force makes use for the first time in combat of a 100-pound jellied-gasoline incendiary bomb.

GREECE: XII Bomber Command B-17s attack airdromes at Athens, Larissa, and Salonika; and B-24s attack Kastelli/Pediada Airdrome in Crete.

ITALY: NATAF aircraft attack a German Army headquarters at Palata, roads and railroads north of Naples, gun emplacements near Capua, and road traffic around Montenero and Termoli; and XII Bomber Command B-17s attack Argos Airdrome.

MEDITERRANEAN: While guarding a flotilla of Royal Navy warships that have just bombarded German bases in the Dodecanese Islands, Maj William L. Leverette, the commanding officer of the 14th Fighter Group's 37th Fighter Squadron, downs *seven* Ju-87 dive-bombers in a single pass at about 1215 hours. This is the highest single-mission score in either the ETO and Mediterranean Theater of Operations (MTO) throughout World War II. 2dLt Harry T. Hanna, also of the 37th Fighter Squadron, downs five Ju-87s in the same action and also achieves "instant-ace" status. In all, 17 Ju-87s and one Ju-88 are downed by Leverette and the handful of P-38 pilots under his command during this mission. There are no USAAF losses.

NETHERLANDS: Sixty-six B-26s of the 3d Medium Bombardment Wing's 323d and 387th Medium Bombardment groups conduct their final mission under the operational control of the Eighth Air Force—an attack on Woensdrecht Airdrome with 98 tons of bombs between 1516 and 1526 hours. At the conclusion of the day's activities, the 323d and 387th Medium Bombardment groups stand down pending their transfer to the Ninth Air Force.

UNITED STATES: Gen Henry H. Arnold recommends that the Twelfth Air Force be divided into two parts, a tactical air force to support Allied ground forces in Italy and a new independent strategic air force to undertake heavy-bomber missions against strategic targets in southern and central Europe as part of the Anglo-American Combined Bomber Offensive.

October 10, 1944

GERMANY: Two hundred six 1st and 3d Bomber division B-17s attack rail targets and canals in and around Munster with more than 700 tons of bombs between 1503 and 1518 hours. GAF fighter opposition is fierce, particularly against the lead 3d Bombardment Division. In the 100th Heavy Bombardment Group formation alone, 12 of 14 B-17s are downed, and one of the two survivors eventually crash-lands in the U.K. due to battle damage. Overall losses are 30 B-17s downed—25 from the 13th Combat Bombardment Wing alone—three damaged beyond repair, and 102 damaged. Crew losses are two killed and 306 missing. One of the missing airmen is 1stLt John Winant, the son of the United States ambassador to Great Britain, who is taken prisoner after the 390th Heavy Bombardment Group B-17 he is piloting goes down.

A total of 216 P-47s from five VIII Fighter Command groups provide escort and support for the Munster mission, including an early fighter sweep designed to disrupt GAF defensive operations along the Dutch coast. In all, P-47 pilots of the 4th, 56th, 78th, and 353d Fighter groups down 20 GAF fighters over the Netherlands and Germany between 1204 and 1550 hours. Maj David C. Schilling, 56th Fighter Group operations officer, in a P-47, achieves ace status when he downs an FW-190 near Altenberg at 1515 hours. Two P-47 pilots with the 56th Fighter Group's 61st Fighter Squadron also achieve ace status: 1stLt Robert S. Johnson, when he downs a Bf-110 and an FW-190 near Munster at 1530 hours, and Capt Gerald W. Johnson, when he downs a Bf-109 and a Bf-110 near Münster at 1535 hours. Also, Capt Walter C. Beckham, a P-47 pilot with the 353d Fighter Group's 351st Fighter Squadron, achieves ace status when he downs an Me-210 and two Bf-110s near Munster between 1530 and 1550 hours.

GREECE: XII Bomber Command B-17s attack two airdromes at Athens, and B-24s attack the airdromes at Calato, Heraklion (Crete), and Maritsa.

ITALY: NATAF aircraft attack numerous gun emplacements, a variety of road and rail targets, vehicles, and tactical targets throughout the U.S. Fifth Army battle area.

MEDITERRANEAN: XII Bomber Command P-38s escorting heavy bombers to Greece attack Antimachia Airdrome, in the Dodecanese Islands, and Axis ships at sea and in several Aegean harbors.

NETHERLANDS: Although briefed for the main Eighth Air Force attack against Munster, 30 1st Bombardment Division B-17s of the 305th and 379th Heavy Bombardment groups go off course and finally attempt to bomb Twente/Enschede Airdrome. However, most of the bombs land in the adjacent town and kill 155 civilians.

October 11, 1943

GREECE: XII Bomber Command B-25s attack Rhodes/Maritsa Airdrome.

ITALY: Most NATAF operations are

canceled because of bad weather; only a few RAF components are able to attack various tactical targets.
MEDITERRANEAN: XII Bomber Command P-38s attack ships in the harbor at Corfu.

October 12, 1943

ITALY: Although planned operations are severely hampered by bad weather, NATAF aircraft attack Aquino Airdrome, several road junctions, road and rail traffic, rail facilities, and gun emplacements in and around the battle area.
SICILY: The 81st Fighter Group, which has been conducting coastal operations while based in Tunisia, is transferred to Castelvetrano Airdrome.
TUNISIA: XII Bomber Command bombers are grounded by bad weather.

October 13, 1943

ALBANIA: XII Bomber Command medium bombers attack Tirana Airport.
ITALY: XII Bomber Command medium bombers attack the town of Alife and a road junction; and NATAF aircraft directly support the U.S. Fifth Army's assault crossing of the Volturno River.

The Badoglio government formally declares war on Germany.

October 14, 1943

ENGLAND: LtGen Lewis H. Brereton activates the U.S. Army Air Forces in the United Kingdom (USAAFUK) to oversee the U.S. Eighth and Ninth Air forces.
GERMANY: Of 291 1st and 3d Bombardment division B-17s and 29 2d Bombardment Division B-24s dispatched against Schweinfurt, only 229 B-17s reach the objective, where they drop 483 tons of bombs on various aircraft-industry targets. Sixty B-17s—nearly one in four—are lost to flak or fighter opposition, seven are damaged beyond repair, and 138 are damaged. Crew losses are a staggering five killed and 594 missing, plus 40 wounded.

One hundred ninety-six VIII Fighter Command P-47s from four groups are dispatched for bomber-escort duty, but the entire 4th Fighter Group is recalled after going astray in heavy clouds, and the 352d Fighter Group accompanies the 2d Bombardment Division B-24s, which eventually abandon the mission. The remaining 56th and 353d Fighter groups give a good accounting of themselves—13 GAF fighters downed over Belgium and northwestern Germany between 1300 and 1345 hours—but they are able to provide only penetration support owing to limited range. As a result of the unacceptably heavy bomber and crew losses beyond the range of friendly fighters, the Eighth Air Force curtails missions deep inside Germany until enough fighters with sufficient range can be amassed for escort duty all the way to the target and back.

Capt Frank E. McCauley, a P-47 pilot with the 56th Fighter Group's 61st Fighter Squadron, achieves ace status when he downs a Bf-110 near Aachen at 1345 hours.
ITALY: XII Bomber Command B-17s and B-24s attack bridges and towns in east-central Italy, and XII Bomber Command B-25s attack Argos Airdrome. However, bad weather severely limits the support that NATAF aircraft are able to provide to the U.S. Fifth Army along the Volturno River.

October 15, 1943

ENGLAND: LtGen Lewis H. Brereton resumes command of the Ninth Air Force, following its moved to England from North Africa. Although the Ninth Air Force is slated to provide tactical coverage for U.S. Army ground forces following the projected invasion of France, its fighters will be on loan to the Combined Bomber Offensive until shortly before the mid-1944 invasion.

LtGen Ira C. Eaker assumes command of the newly formed USAAFUK, in addition to his ongoing duties as Eighth Air Force commanding general.
GREECE: XII Bomber Command B-25s attack Megalo Mikra and Salonika/Sedhes airdromes.

ITALY: NATAF aircraft attack a vast array of communications and transportation targets servicing the battle area, as well as tactical targets within the battle area, especially around the Volturno River.

The 340th Medium Bombardment Group, in B-25s, moves from Sicily to San Pancrazio Salentino Airdrome.

NETHERLANDS: The 356th and 55th Fighter groups, in P-47s and P-38s, respectively, make their combat debuts in a pair of fighter sweeps over the Frisian Islands. The 55th is the first P-38–equipped fighter group to operate from the U.K. since the commitment of all U.K.-based P-38s to Operation TORCH a full year earlier. It is also the first VIII Fighter Command unit to actually enter combat in P-38s.

UNITED STATES: The U.S. Joint Chiefs of Staff accept Gen Henry H. Arnold's proposal to split the Twelfth Air Force and propose to Gen Dwight D. Eisenhower that he reconstitute the XII Bomber Command as a new Fifteenth Air Force, which will take part, with the U.S. Eighth Air Force and RAF Bomber Command, in the strategic Combined Bomber Offensive.

October 16, 1943

ENGLAND: Headquarters, Ninth Air Force, is formally reactivated at Sunninghill Park, England, following its transfer from Egypt. LtGen Lewis H. Brereton resumes his duties as commanding general, and BriGen Victor H. Strahm as chief of staff. The IX Bomber Command is reactivated under the command of MajGen Samuel E. Anderson; the IX Fighter Command is reactivated under the temporary command of LtCol Ray J. Stecker; the IX Air Support Command is reactivated under the command of MajGen Henry J. Miller; and a new IX Troop Carrier Command is activated under the command of BriGen Benjamin F. Giles. Simultaneously, VIII Air Support Command is effectively disbanded when the 3d Medium Bombardment Wing headquarters and all four of its B-26 groups are transferred to the Ninth Air Force. Numerous

service and support units, many transferred from the Eighth Air Force, are organized into a newly activated IX Air Force Service Command, which is commanded by MajGen Henry J. Miller.

The new IX Troop Carrier Command assumes control of all Eighth Air Force troop-carrier units—the 315th Troop Carrier Group (consisting of just six C-47 aircraft, two squadron headquarters, and the group headquarters), and the 434th Troop Carrier Group. These units are assigned to the control of the 50th Troop Carrier Wing.

GREECE: Twelfth Air Force P-38 fighter-bombers attack ships at sea off the west coast.

ITALY: XII Bomber Command B-25s attack rail lines, a rail tunnel, marshalling yards, a highway underpass, a gas works, and industrial buildings in and around Bologna; and NATAF aircraft attack a large number of communications and transportation targets, troop concentrations, road traffic, and a landing ground from the battle area north to around the city of Rome.

October 17, 1943

ENGLAND: The 50th Troop Carrier Wing headquarters is assigned to the IX Troop Carrier Command.

GERMANY: A VIII Bomber Command heavy-bomber force dispatched against Duren is recalled over the North Sea due to bad weather.

ITALY: XII Bomber Command aircraft are grounded because of bad weather, and NATAF is forced to cancel many missions. However, NATAF aircraft, especially A-20s and B-25s, attack numerous rail, road, and tactical targets.

October 18, 1943

ENGLAND: LtCol Ray J. Stecker is replaced by BriGen Elwood R. Quesada as commander of the IX Fighter Command, which is in transit to England from Libya.

FRANCE: Throughout the day, in its first missions since being reconstituted in England, the IX Air Support Command dispatches 228 B-26s against airdromes in France. However, bad weather forces the bombers to abort all the missions before reaching their targets.

ITALY: XII Air Support Command A-36s attack the rail yards at Venafro; Twelfth Air Force fighter-bombers attack troops, gun emplacements, and the railroad stations at Boiano, Petacciato, and Vairano; Twelfth Air Force fighters and fighter-bombers strafe the seaplane base at Bracciano and airdromes at Grosseto, Rome, and Viterbo, and attack trains on several lines through Rome; and 47th Light Bombardment Group A-20s attack road and rail targets in central Italy.

86th Fighter-Bomber Group A-36 pilots down two Bf-109s and an Fi-156 in two separate actions.

YUGOSLAVIA: XII Bomber Command B-25s attack marshalling yards at Skoplje, and escorting P-38s attack locomotives and motor vehicles.

October 19, 1943

ITALY: NAAF opens an air offensive against railroad bridges throughout Italy in the hope of forcing the German Army in Italy to make greater reliance upon vulnerable coastal shipping and motor transport to keep its combat divisions at the front supplied.

XII Bomber Command B-24s flying at low level attack a number of rail bridges; and NATAF aircraft attack rail lines, trains, tunnels, gun emplacements, two landing grounds, an ammunition dump, motor vehicles, and German troops.

A 33d Fighter Group P-40 pilot downs an FW-190 at 1040 hours.

SOVIET UNION: The TRIPARTATE Conference between the American, British, and Soviet foreign ministers opens in Moscow to discuss ways to shorten the war and bring about postwar cooperation.

UNITED KINGDOM: The 359th Fighter Group, in P-47s, arrives by ship from the United States for service with VIII Fighter Command's 66th Fighter Wing.

October 20, 1943

ENGLAND: The 358th Fighter Group, in P-47s, arrives by ship from the United States for service with the VIII Fighter Command.

GERMANY: Two hundred twelve VIII Bomber Command B-17s are dispatched to attack aircraft-industry targets at Duren, but only 86 from the 3d Bombardment Division are able to complete the attack, releasing 209 tons of bombs over the city at about 1415 hours. Due to the failure of the new Oboe pathfinding equipment aboard the lead 1st Bombardment Division B-17, the entire formation aborts, except for the 379th Heavy Bombardment Group's 17 B-17s, which attack Woensdrecht Airdrome in the Netherlands, with nearly 42 tons of bombs at 1430 hours. Also, 11 B-17s of the 3d Bombardment Division's 385th Heavy Bombardment Group attack Aachen when they are unable to locate Duren. Losses are nine B-17s missing, ten damaged, and one written off following a crash-landing. Crew losses are one killed and 85 missing, plus three gunners asphyxiated due to an oxygen-system failure in their airplane.

Three hundred twenty-one VIII Fighter Command P-47s and 39 P-38s are launched to escort and support the heavy bombers. In sporadic action, four GAF fighters are downed over the Netherlands and Belgium between 1400 and 1435 hours.

ITALY: XII Bomber Command B-17s, B-25s, B-26s, and P-38s attack the Cervetri and Marcigliana airdromes, the Rome/Casale Airdrome, and rail bridges in and near Grosseto, Montalto di Castro, and Orvieto; and NATAF aircraft attack numerous gun emplacements, motor vehicles, and rail and road targets.

YUGOSLAVIA: XII Bomber Command bombers attack a marshalling yard at Nis, and NATAF fighter-bombers sink two ships off the Dalmatian.

October 21, 1943

ALBANIA: XII Bomber Command B-17s attack rail and road bridges.

FRANCE: Seventy-two 3d Medium Bombardment Wing B-26s dispatched against the Evreux/Fauville Airdrome abort in the face of bad weather.

ITALY: XII Bomber Command B-17s attack a rail viaduct at Terni; XII Bomber Command B-24s attack a rail bridge at Orvieto; XII Bomber Command B-25s and B-26s attack bridges at Acquapendente and Montalto di Castro, and the rail line at Orbetello; XII Bomber Command P-38s attack a radar station at Pellegrino; NATAF A-20s and B-25s attack the town area, a rail line, and troop concentrations at Cassino; and XII Air Support Command fighter-bombers attack numerous tactical, rail, and road targets in and around the battle area.

P-40 pilots of the 33d Fighter Group's 66th Fighter Squadron down six Ju-87s in an engagement at 0755 hours, and P-38 pilots of the 1st and 82d Fighter groups down eight GAF fighters over Orvieto between 1145 hours and noon. Finally, between 1800 and 1830 hours, P-39 pilots from the 350th Fighter Group's 345th Fighter Squadron score their squadron's first confirmed victory of the war (of seven altogether) when they intercept GAF night raiders over a convoy off Cape Tenos and down one He-111 and damage another.

Col Arthur Thomas assumes command of the XII Air Support Command.

YUGOSLAVIA: XII Bomber Command P-38 fighter-bombers attack a marshalling yard at Skoplje, and NATAF aircraft attack Axis ships at sea off the Dalmatian coast.

October 22, 1943

FRANCE: Although approximately 160 of nearly 200 3d Medium Bombardment Wing B-26s dispatched on morning and afternoon missions against, respectively, Evreux/Fauville and Cambrai/Epinoy airdromes abort in the face of bad weather, the remainder are able to complete their attacks.

GREECE: XII Bomber Command B-25s attack Athens/Eleusis Airdrome, and 82d Fighter Group P-38 escort pilots down two

Bf-109s near the target at about 1230 hours.

ITALY: XII Bomber Command B-26s attack rail bridges near Orvieto; XII Bomber Command B-25s attack rail bridges near Grosseto; and NATAF aircraft attack Aquino Airdrome and numerous rail, road, and tactical targets in and around the battle area.

A 27th Fighter-Bomber Group A-36 pilot downs two Bf-109s near Viterbo Airdrome at 0845 hours.

TUNISIA: The XII Air Force Provisional Engineer Command is activated.

UNITED STATES: The CCS agree to the establishment of the Fifteenth Air Force to oversee the conduct of strategic Combined Bomber Offensive operations out of bases in the Mediterranean and Italy.

October 23, 1943

ALBANIA: XII Bomber Command B-25s attack a bridge. Also, during an attack by XII Bomber Command P-38s on Tirana Airport, an 82d Fighter Group P-38 pilot downs a Ju-52 over the target at 0830 hours.

ITALY: XII Bomber Command B-26s attack road and rail bridges at Marsciano and Montalto di Castro; and NATAF aircraft attack a German Army troop concentration near Spinete and numerous road, rail, and tactical targets in or near the battle area.

1st Fighter Group P-38 pilots down two Bf-109s and damage or probably down several others over Marsciano at 1340 hours.

October 24, 1943

ALBANIA: XII Bomber Command medium bombers attack Tirana Airport.

AUSTRIA: Eighty-nine XII Bomber Command B-17s and 25 B-24s, escorted by 36 P-38s, attack the Bf-109 factory at Wiener-Neustadt. Total cloud cover prevents all but the 98th Heavy Bombardment Group, in B-24s, from dropping bombs on the target. 301st Heavy Bombardment Group B-17s are able to attack a marshalling yard north of Wiener-Neustadt.

FRANCE: Two hundred 3d Medium

Bombardment Wing B-26s, escorted by 205 VIII Fighter Command P-47s and 48 P-38s, attack Beauvais/Nivillers, Montdidier, and St.-Andre-de-L'Eure airdromes.

ITALY: XII Bomber Command medium bombers attack a rail bridge near Orvieto and the viaduct at Terni; and NATAF aircraft attack numerous road, rail, and tactical targets in and around the battle area.

P-38 pilots of the 1st Fighter Group's 27th Fighter Squadron down an Mc.202 and two Bf-109s in an engagement over Lake Bracciano, near Rome, at 1135 hours. Also, during the course of several afternoon actions, A-36 pilots of the 27th Fighter-Bomber Group's 522d Fighter-Bomber Squadron down three Bf-109s and an Fi-167 biplane.

YUGOSLAVIA: NATAF aircraft attack road and rail targets along the Dalmatian coast.

October 25, 1943

ITALY: NATAF aircraft attack Tarquinia Airdrome and numerous roads and bridges servicing German Army forces in and around the battle area

YUGOSLAVIA: Twelfth Air Force P-39 fighter-bombers attack the landing ground at Podgorica, and NATAF aircraft attack road and rail targets along the Dalmatian coast.

October 26, 1943

ENGLAND: The 2906th Provisional Observation Training Group is redesignated the 495th Fighter Training Group. The unit processes and provides advanced theater training to replacement fighter pilots for both the Eighth and Ninth air forces.

GREECE: XII Bomber Command B-25s and P-38s attack Megalo Mikra and Salonika/Sedhes airdromes.

ITALY: NATAF B-25s attack Terracina and an ammunition dump; and other NATAF aircraft attack parked Axis aircraft near Ancona, and road, rail, and tactical targets from central Italy south to the battle area.

October 27, 1943

AUSTRIA: More than 150 XII Bomber Command B-17s and B-24s attack aircraft-industry targets at Wiener-Neustadt and bridges and rail lines at two other locations.

ITALY: Although most NATAF missions are canceled in the face of bad weather, XII Air Support Command aircraft are able to provide some support for Allied ground forces in the battle area, and fighter-bombers attack Gaeta.

YUGOSLAVIA: NATAF fighter-bombers attack small ships and craft at Opuzen.

October 28, 1943

ITALY: Most of the Twelfth Air Force is grounded by bad weather, but XII Air Support Command A-36s are able to attack gun emplacements and several highways and bridges between Rome and the battle area.

During a mission to the Rome area, A-36 pilots of the 27th Fighter-Bomber Group's 522d Fighter-Bomber Squadron down six Bf-109s between 1100 and 1130 hours. Later, during an afternoon engagement over Civita Castellana, a pair of A-36 pilots from the 86th Fighter-Bomber Group's 526th Fighter-Bomber Squadron down three Bf-109s.

October 29, 1943

ITALY: XII Bomber Command B-17s attack marshalling yards at Genoa and Sampierdarena, several industrial plants at San Giorgio, and bridges around Genoa-Ansaldo. Although bad weather prevents extensive coverage of the battle area, NATAF aircraft attack two gun emplacements, several bridges, and ships and port facilities at Giulianova.

October 30, 1943

FRANCE: Five IX Air Support Command A-20s—the first of their kind to operate from bases in the U.K. since October 1942—attack Cherbourg/Maupertus Airdrome.

ITALY: XII Bomber Command B-24s attack steel works at Genoa-Ansaldo and Sampierdarena and marshalling yards at Genoa; XII Bomber Command B-17s attack marshalling yards at Imperia, Porto Maurizio, Savona, and Varazze; NATAF B-25s attack Frosinone; and NATAF fighter-bombers attack various road, rail, and tactical targets in and around the battle area.

Following a hiatus from combat since July—in order to retrain to conduct infantry-support operations—the 324th Fighter Group, a former Ninth Air Force P-40 unit, is transferred from Tunisia to Cercola Airdrome, where it joins the XII Air Support Command.

SOVIET UNION: The TRIPARTATE Conference of foreign ministers is concluded in Moscow with an agreement to force an "unconditional surrender" from Germany and to establish a world peace organization.

October 31, 1943

ALBANIA: 82d Fighter Group P-38 pilots down an Fi-156 and three Bf-109s between 1500 and 1520 hours during a bombing and strafing attack on Tirana Airport.

FRANCE: XII Bomber Command B-17s attack a viaduct at Antheor.

ITALY: Although most NATAF aircraft are grounded by bad weather, XII Bomber Command B-25s attack Anzio, and XII Bomber Command B-26s attack port facilities and shipping at Civitavecchia.

NOVEMBER 1943

November 1, 1943

ENGLAND: The Ninth Air Force is placed under the operational control of the Allied Expeditionary Air Force (AEAF), which is activated to oversee operations of the British and American tactical air forces for Operation OVERLORD.

The 92d Combat Bombardment Wing is activated to oversee several 1st Bombardment Division B-17 groups, and the 93d Combat Bombardment Wing is activated to oversee several 2d Bombardment Division B-24 groups.

The veteran 351st Heavy Bombardment Group is reassigned to the 92d Combat Bombardment Wing, as is the newly arrived 401st Heavy Bombardment Group.

ITALY: On the day it becomes operational, the new Fifteenth Air Force dispatches the B-17s of all four groups of its 5th Heavy Bombardment Wing from their bases in Tunisia against the former Italian naval base at La Spezia, in northern Italy, and against a nearby rail bridge at Vezzano. Also, 47th Medium Bombardment Wing B-25s—now also part of the Fifteenth Air Force—attack marshalling yards at Ancona and Rimini.

NATAF aircraft attack port facilities and shipping at Ancona, and transportation and tactical targets in or near the battle area.

MEDITERRANEAN: A 57th Fighter Group P-40 pilot downs a Do-24 rescue-and-reconnaissance flying boat at sea during the afternoon.

TUNISIA: The Fifteenth Air Force is activated at Tunis under the command of MajGen James H. Doolittle. To implement the new command, Headquarters, XII Bomber Command, is redesignated Headquarters, Fifteenth Air Force, a move that effectively disbands the XII Bomber Command. Initially, the new air force consists of the 5th Heavy Bombardment Wing, composed of four B-17 groups (2d, 97th, 99th, and 301st) and two B-24 groups (98th and 376th); the 42d Medium Bombardment Wing, composed of three B-26 groups (17th, 319th, and 320th); the 47th Medium Bombardment Wing, composed of two B-25 groups (310th and 321st); the new 306th Fighter Wing, composed of three P-38 groups (1st, 14th, and 82d) and one P-40 group (325th); and the veteran but newly redesignated 68th Tactical Reconnaissance Group.

UNITED STATES: A U.S. military mission to the Soviet Union is organized under MajGen John R. Deane with the purpose of establishing facilities in Russia to support shuttle-bombing operations against Germany by Eighth and Fifteenth air force heavy bombers.

YUGOSLAVIA: NATAF aircraft attack shipping and port facilities at Split.

November 2, 1943

AUSTRIA: In its first Combined Bomber Offensive mission of the war, the Fifteenth Air Force dispatches 139 B-17s and B-24s, escorted by 72 P-38s, against the Bf-109 factory at Wiener-Neustadt. Opposition from flak and fighters is heavy, but the attack is considered punishing when 74 B-17s and 38 B-24s drop 327 tons of bombs with results that are reported as being "excellent." Accurate, heavy flak and attacks by an estimated 160 GAF fighters result in the loss of six B-17s and five B-24s.

ITALY: Fifteenth Air Force B-25s attack a marshalling yard at Ancona; Fifteenth Air Force B-26s attack a rail bridge at Amelia and the harbor at Civitavecchia; and NATAF A-20s and B-25s attack an ammunition dump and gun emplacements in the zone of the British Eighth Army, the coastal road at Terracina, the town of Fondi, rail facilities at Aquila, and several bridges and road junctions near the battle area.

A 31st Fighter Group Spitfire pilot downs a Bf-109 near Rome at 1135 hours.

The Twelfth Air Force's 12th Medium Bombardment Group, in B-25s, moves from Sicily to the Foggia Airdrome complex.

November 3, 1943

ENGLAND: The 435th Troop Carrier Group arrives in England and is assigned to the IX Troop Carrier Command's 50th Troop Carrier Wing.

FRANCE: Seventy-one IX Bomber Command B-26s attack Tricqueville Airdrome, and 71 B-26s attack St.-Andre-de-L'Eure Airdrome. One B-26 is lost over the latter target.

GERMANY: In its largest daylight mission to date, VIII Bomber Command dispatches a total 566 B-17s and B-24s against the Wilhelmshaven port area. Led by 11 482d Heavy Pathfinder Bombardment Group B-17s equipped for the first time with new H2X guidance radar, a total of 434 B-17s and 105 B-24s drop a record 1,448 tons of bombs on the briefed target area between 1307 and 1335 hours. Opposition is meager, but seven B-17s are downed with their 70 crewmen. This mission also marks the first time that a heavy-bomber group—the 96th—goes out at double strength, in this case 50 B-17s.

Three hundred thirty-three VIII Fighter Command P-47 and 45 P-38 escorts down 14 GAF fighters over the Netherlands and the Wilhelmshaven area between 1226 and 1350 hours. Fighter losses are two P-47s missing with their pilots, five P-47s damaged, and one P-47 written off following a rough landing.

The newly committed 20th Fighter Group's 79th Fighter Squadron, in P-38s, makes its combat debut when it accompanies the 55th Fighter Group on the bomber-escort mission to Wilhelmshaven. The 20th Fighter Group has a full complement of pilots in the U.K., but there is a shortage of up-to-date P-38s that will persist for several months and prevent the new group from becoming fully operational.

GREECE: Twelfth Air Force B-25s, escorted by Fifteenth Air Force P-38s, attack Axis aircraft on the ground at Araxos Airdrome.

ITALY: NATAF aircraft attack Cisterna di Latina Airdrome and the landing grounds at Ancona and Pescara, plus numerous road, rail, and tactical targets in and around the battle area, especially in support of the British Eighth Army.

NETHERLANDS: Sixty-five IX Bomber

Command B-26s attack Amsterdam/Schipol Airport.

TUNISIA: The 310th and 321st Medium Bombardment groups, in B-25s, are transferred from the Fifteenth Air Force back to the Twelfth Air Force.

November 4, 1943

ENGLAND: The Eighth Air Force officially promulgates Operation ARGUMENT, the air campaign specifically aimed at destroying the GAF interceptor force over Germany.

Headquarters, Ninth Air Force, creates the IX Engineer Command under Col Karl B. Schilling. The command will be responsible for building, rehabilitating, and maintaining airstrips in northern Europe following the invasion of France. Meantime, the command's aviation engineer battalions will build fighter strips and emergency bomber strips in southern England.

354th Fighter Group personnel arrive in England by ship without any airplanes. Although trained in P-39s, the 354th is assigned to become the first fighter group in Europe or the Mediterranean to be equipped with the new P-51B Mustang long-range fighter.

The newly arrived 445th Heavy Bombardment Group, in B-24s, is assigned to the 2d Bombardment Division's 2d Combat Bombardment Wing; and the newly arrived 446th Heavy Bombardment Group, also in B-24s, is assigned to the 2d Bombardment Division's 20th Combat Bombardment Wing.

ITALY: B-17s of the Fifteenth Air Force's 5th Heavy Bombardment Wing attack the highway between Leghorn and Rome and three separate rail lines; Fifteenth Air Force P-38 fighter-bombers attack a tunnel near Terni and strafe ground targets around Montalto di Castro; and NATAF aircraft attack Furbara and Tarquinia airdromes, small ships off Pescara and Solta, and trains and motor vehicles between Avezzano and Sora.

27th Fighter-Bomber Group A-36

pilots down an Me-210 and a pair of Bf-109s near Guidonia Airdrome at about 1100 hours.

TUNISIA: BriGen Donald A. Davison assumes command of the new XII Air Force Provisional Engineer Command.

November 5, 1943

ALBANIA: XII Air Support Command B-25s attack Berat/Kocove Airdrome.

FRANCE: Despite numerous aborts caused by bad weather, more than 150 IX Bomber Command B-26s attack a secret military construction site* at Mimoyecques. One B-26 is lost.

GERMANY: Three hundred twenty-three 1st and 3d Bombardment division B-17s and five B-17 pathfinders attack the oil refinery and marshalling yard at Gelsenkirchen with 739 tons of bombs between 1313 and 1350 hours. Flak and GAF fighters account for eight B-17s lost, three damaged beyond repair, and 216 damaged. Crew casualties are four killed, 84 missing, and 31 wounded.

One hundred four 2d Bombardment Division B-24s plus four B-17 pathfinders attack a marshalling yard at Munster with 284 tons of bombs between 1349 and 1358 hours. Three B-24s are lost, one is written off, and 43 are damaged. Crew losses are seven killed, 31 missing, and 22 wounded.

Escort and support for the heavy bombers is provided by 336 P-47s and 47 P-38s, whose pilots down 19 GAF fighters, mostly over the Netherlands, between 1300 and 1430 hours at a cost of four P-47s and their pilots missing.

ITALY: NATAF aircraft attack roads and bridges in or near Atina, Cassino, Castrocielo, Isernia, Lucana, Rome, Pescara, and Vasto.

SARDINIA: The 350th Fighter Group, which has been involved in coastal-protection operations from Algerian bases, is transferred to Sardinia, from which it will conduct ground-support missions over Italy.

YUGOSLAVIA: NATAF aircraft attack ships off Split.

November 6, 1943

ENGLAND: IX Fighter Command head-quarters personnel arrive in England by ship from the Middle East.

ITALY: Seven Fifteenth Air Force B-17s attack rail bridges at Orbetello; Fifteenth Air Force P-38 fighter-bombers attack bridges near Orvieto and Monte Molino, and strafe Tarquinia Airdrome, motor vehicles, and a train; and NATAF aircraft attack road, rail, and tactical targets.

YUGOSLAVIA: NATAF aircraft attack road and rail targets.

November 7, 1943

FRANCE: More than 200 IX Bomber Command B-26s dispatched against Meulan/Les Mureaux and Montdidier airdromes abort in the face of bad weather. However, 49 P-47s and 54 P-38s dispatched by the VIII Fighter Command to escort the IX Bomber Command B-26s sweep the English Channel coast from Ostend, Belgium, to Calais. Results of the sweep are nil, but two P-38s are lost.

GERMANY: Restricted and dispersed by bad weather, 112 B-17s of the 122 that are actually dispatched attack a variety of targets in Germany: 37 3d Bombardment Division B-17s attack their briefed primary, an aircraft-industry plant at Duren, with 84 tons of bombs at 1114 hours; 53 1st Bombardment Division B-17s attack their briefed primary, an aircraft-industry plant at Wesel, with 125 tons of bombs at 1125 hours; and 20 3d Bombardment Division B-17s attack their briefed secondary, at Randerath, with 48 tons of bombs between 1114 and 1125 hours.

283 VIII Fighter Command P-47s escort and support the heavy bombers, but only one GAF fighter is downed. The 56th Fighter Group posts one P-47 missing, and the 355th Fighter Group posts five P-47s missing. The 78th Fighter Group flies the VIII Fighter Command's first group double escort mission with "A" and "B" fighter formations.

November 8, 1943

ENGLAND: The new 354th Fighter Group, which is transitioning from P-39s into P-51s, becomes the first tactical fighter unit formally assigned to the IX Fighter Command.

ITALY: The Twelfth Air Force is grounded by bad weather, but NATAF aircraft are able to mount six small missions against gun emplacements and motor vehicles along the battle line and a few trains near the battle area. During an afternoon mission, a 57th Fighter Group P-40 pilot downs a Ju-88 off Pescara.

Eighty-one Fifteenth Air Force B-17s attack the Fiat ball-bearing plant, marshalling yards, and an aircraft-engine factory at Turin.

November 9, 1943

ALBANIA: NATAF fighters strafe gun emplacement, ships, and radio stations along the Albanian coast.

ITALY: NATAF aircraft attack Formia and Itri as a diversion for a bombardment of Formia and Gaeta by Allied naval forces; NATAF aircraft also attack road, rail, and tactical targets; Fifteenth Air Force B-17s attack the Genoa-Ansaldo steel works; and 20 Fifteenth Air Force B-24s miss the target entirely when they attack Turin's Villaperosa ball-bearing plant at 1230 hours.

One FW-190 is downed over Turin at 1220 hours by an 82d Fighter Group P-38 escort pilot.

YUGOSLAVIA: NATAF fighter-bombers attack shipping in Split harbor.

November 10, 1943

ALBANIA: NATAF bombers attack Durazzo.

BELGIUM: Approximately 60 IX Bomber Command B-26s attack Chievres Airdrome.

FRANCE: All the IX Bomber Command B-26s dispatched to attack Lille/Vendeville Airdrome abort in the face of bad weather, as do most of the 72 B-26s dispatched against Montdidier Airdrome. Six B-26s attack Amiens/Glisy Airdrome.

Two hundred eight VIII Fighter Command P-47s and 58 P-38s escort and support the B-26s over France and Belgium.
ITALY: For the second day in a row, 20 Fifteenth Air Force B-24s attempt to attack the Villaperosa ball-bearing plant in Turin; Fifteenth Air Force B-17s attack a marshalling yard at Bolzano; NATAF fighter-bombers attack gun emplacements around Rocca and troop concentrations and troop trains south of Rome; and NATAF fighters strafe trucks and trains between Rome and La Spezia and between Piombino and Leghorn.
YUGOSLAVIA: NATAF bombers attack Split.

November 11, 1943

ALGERIA: 417th Night-Fighter Squadron Beaufighters down one Ju-88 and damage another off Arzieu between 1720 and 1950 hours.
ENGLAND: The Eighth Air Force's 479th Antisubmarine Group is officially disbanded. Groundcrews from the 22d Antisubmarine Squadron are assigned to the 482d Heavy Pathfinder Bombardment Group. Also, flying personnel from the 22d Antisubmarine Squadron and groundcrews from the 4th Antisubmarine Squadron are assigned to a nascent and as-yet-unofficial Eighth Air Force special operations group, which is being prepared to drop agents and supplies by parachute to assist partisan organizations in France and the Low Countries.
FRANCE: Thirty-one Fifteenth Air Force B-24s cause no damage when they drop 90 tons of bombs on a ball-bearing factory and viaduct at Annecy. One B-24 is lost to flak.

One hundred sixty-two IX Bomber Command B-26s attack a secret military construction site* and targets of opportunity in an area of the Cherbourg Peninsula centered on Martinvast.
GERMANY: The 1st Bombardment Division abandons its mission to Wesel due to bad weather, but 59 3d Bombardment Division B-17s (from three of seven groups dispatched) and one B-17 pathfinder attack their briefed primary, a marshalling yard at Munster, with 122 tons of bombs at 1408 hours. The other four 3d Division groups turn back over the Dutch coast because of a navigational error and the failure of the pathfinder equipment.

Three hundred forty-two VIII Fighter Command P-47s and 59 P-38s—a one-day record—escorting and supporting the heavy bombers account for nine GAF fighters downed along the bomber routes between 1345 and 1500 hours.
ITALY: NATAF and RAF light bombers and fighter-bombers attack numerous tactical targets in the Palena and Rocca areas in support of the British Eighth Army; NATAF fighters attack motor vehicles along the coast between the Pescara and Sangro rivers; and NATAF aircraft attack Rocca, an explosives factory, the port of Civitavecchia, and German Army strongpoints at two locations.

During a series of midmorning engagements over central Italy, 31st Fighter Group Spitfire pilots down two FW-109s and damage several other GAF fighters. Also, an FW-190 is downed during the afternoon by a 27th Fighter-Bomber Group A-36 pilot.

The 47th Bombardment Wing headquarters is transferred without its B-26 groups or aircraft from Tunisia to Manduria, Italy, near Taranto. The wing headquarters will eventually oversee operations of Fifteenth Air Force B-24 groups (initially the 98th and 376th).

November 12, 1943

ALBANIA: After failing to locate their assigned targets near Athens, Twelfth Air Force B-25s returning from Greece attack Berat/Kocove Airdrome and an Albanian oil refinery.
ENGLAND: The 97th Combat Bombardment Wing headquarters is activated to oversee operations of several Ninth Air Force light bombardment (A-20) groups; the 3d Medium Bombardment Wing head-

quarters (B-26s) is redesignated the 98th Medium Combat Bombardment Wing; and the headquarters of the Eighth Air Force's 44th Bombardment Wing is transferred to the Ninth Air Force and redesignated the 99th Medium Combat Bombardment Wing. All three wings are attached to IX Bomber Command. Also, the 323d and 387th Medium Bombardment groups are placed under the control of the 98th Wing, and the 322d and 386th Medium Bombardment groups are placed under the control of the 99th Wing. For the time being, the three wing headquarters are restricted to overseeing training of their subordinate units, and not combat operations.

ITALY: Fifteenth Air Force B-26s dispatched to attack rail lines and bridges around Montalto di Castro and Orbetello are dispersed by heavy cloud cover, and the attacks are largely ineffectual. NATAF aircraft attack road, rail, and tactical targets in support of the U.S. Fifth and British Eighth armies.

27th Fighter-Bomber Group A-36 pilots down two Ju-88s north of Rome during an afternoon mission.

During the night of November 12–13, NATAF A-20s attack a marshalling yard at Arezzo and Perugia Airdrome.

November 13, 1943

ENGLAND: The 67th Reconnaissance Group is transferred from the VIII Air Support Command to the Ninth Air Force and reequipped with P-51A aircraft.

GERMANY: Bad weather over England creates havoc with the day's mission against Bremen. The 1st Bombardment Division abandons the mission owing to immense problems during assembly; the only two 1st Bombardment Division B-17s that get over the Continent attack targets of opportunity through holes in the clouds; and 73 3d Bombardment Division B-17s, 53 2d Bombardment Division B-24s, and three pathfinder B-17s manage to attack the primary target, the Bremen port area, but many bombs are expended on unidentified "targets of oppor-

tunity" that happen to lay beneath holes in the cloud cover. Three B-17s and 13 B-24s are downed by flak and fighters, but a high proportion of heavy bombers are lost or severely damaged in a rash of operational accidents: two B-17s crash separately during assembly, killing a total of 17 crewmen; a B-17 is abandoned by its crew over England when it catches fire; when two B-17s collide en route to the target, one ditches and the other crashes into the sea, fortunately without loss of life; two B-17s collide during the bomb run over Bremen; a B-24 crashes while landing; and another B-24 crash-lands on return to England. Also on this mission, B-24 groups fly 12-plane section formations for the first time.

Three hundred forty-five VIII Fighter Command P-47s and 45 P-38s escort and support the heavy bombers, but their range is severely limited by strong headwinds. The fighters take part in several running battles across the Netherlands and over Bremen, and they are credited with downing seven GAF fighters and two Ju-88s, but seven P-38s and three P-47s are also lost with nine pilots, and two other P-38s crash-land at U.K. bases and must be written off.

ITALY: The Fifteenth Air Force is grounded by bad weather, but NATAF A-20s attack Atina, Palena, and the harbor at Civitavecchia; and other NATAF aircraft attack tactical targets in the battle area, three Axis landing grounds, and the harbor at Giulianove.

31st Fighter Group Spitfire pilots down four Bf-109s over the port of Gaeta at about 1630 hours.

November 14, 1943

BULGARIA: Twelfth Air Force B-25s, escorted by P-38s of the Fifteenth Air Force's 82d Fighter Group, attack marshalling yards at Sofia. Eighteen Axis fighters attack the bombers over the target, but they are driven off by 82d Fighter Group P-38s, whose pilots down three Bf-109s and two FW-190s against the loss of one P-38.

ITALY: NATAF operations over Italy are

virtually shut down by bad weather, but fighters are able to strafe Furbara and Tarquinia airdromes and attack trains near Avezzano.

November 15, 1943

ENGLAND: On an undisclosed date in mid-November, the 447th Heavy Bombardment Group, in B-17s, arrives in England and is assigned to the 3d Bombardment Division's 4th Combat Bombardment Wing.
GREECE: XII Air Support Command B-25s attack Athens/Kalamaki Airdrome. Also, while Fifteenth Air Force B-24s attack the Athens/Eleusis Airdrome at about 1300 hours, P-38 escorts from the 82d Fighter Group stave off attacks by GAF fighters, damaging six and downing an FW-190 and a Ju-87.
ITALY: NATAF fighters attack road traffic south of Ancona.

November 16, 1943

ENGLAND: Air Marshal Sir Trafford Leigh-Mallory, RAF, is named Air Commander-in-Chief of the Allied Expeditionary Air Force (AEAF), and BriGen William O. Butler, USAAF, is named as his deputy.
FRANCE: Fifteenth Air Force B-17s attack the Istres-le-Tube and Istres/Les Pates airdromes, and Fifteenth Air Force B-26s attack Salon-de-Provence Airdrome.
GREECE: Twelfth Air Force B-25s attack Athens/Eleusis Airdrome.
NORWAY: One hundred thirty 1st Bombardment Division B-17s attack aircraft-industry targets at Knaben with 313 tons of bombs between 1138 and 1238 hours; 147 3d Bombardment Division B-17s attack aircraft-industry targets at Rjukan with more than 355 tons of bombs at 1145 hours; and 29 2d Bombardment Division B-24s attack Rjukan with 74 tons of bombs between 1204 and 1212 hours.
YUGOSLAVIA: Twelfth Air Force B-25s attack Sibenik Airdrome.

November 17, 1943

GREECE: Fifteenth Air Force B-17s

attack the Athens/Eleusis Airdrome, and Twelfth Air Force B-25s attack the Kalamaki Airdrome. One Bf-109 is downed over Athens by an 82d Fighter Group P-38 escort pilot.
ITALY: Twelfth Air Force fighters attack motor vehicles north of Ancona.
　　The Fifteenth Air Force's 376th Heavy Bombardment Group, a B-24 unit, is transferred from Tunisia to San Pancrazio.

November 18, 1943

ENGLAND: Aircraft from the IX Troop Carrier Command's 50th Troop Carrier Wing and the 101st Airborne Division conduct the first of several preliminary rehearsals for the projected airborne-assault phase of Operation OVERLORD.
GREECE: Fifteenth Air Force B-17s attack the Athens/Eleusis Airdrome; and NATAF A-20s, B-25s, and RAF aircraft attack Larissa Airdrome.
ITALY: NATAF aircraft attack several roads and towns, German Army troop billets, and tactical targets along the front lines.
　　The Fifteenth Air Force's 98th Heavy Bombardment Group, in B-24s, is transferred from Tunisia to Brindisi.
NORWAY: Eighty-two 2d Bombardment Division B-24s attack the Oslo/Kjeller Airdrome with more than 209 tons of bombs. Nine B-24s are lost and three land in Sweden, where they and their crews are interned.
YUGOSLAVIA: NATAF fighter-bombers attack a marshalling yard at Knin, boat traffic on the Krka River, several trains, the landing ground at Sinj, and port facilities at ships at Sibenik.

November 19, 1943

FRANCE: All of the more than 100 IX Bomber Command B-26s dispatched against several airdromes in France abort in the face of bad weather.
GERMANY: Although briefed to attack Gelsenkirchen, bad weather and the failure of the Oboe equipment aboard six pathfinder B-17s oblige 130 of 167 3d Bombardment

Division B-17s to scatter 281 tons of bombs on many targets of opportunity on both sides of the German-Netherlands frontier. The failure of the Oboe equipment on this mission puts its use to an end as primary guidance on high-altitude bombing missions. The Oboe equipment, which relies upon radio signals from ground stations in England, is transferred to the Ninth Air Force, whose medium-altitude work does not interfere with the Oboe guidance technique. Meanwhile, the Eighth Air Force falls back upon H2S and H2X airborne ground-radar equipment, which provides much better results for high-altitude work.

Two hundred eighty-eight VIII Fighter Command P-47s provide escort and support for the B-17s.

ITALY: NATAF A-36s and P-40s attack bridges near Cassino and Pontecorvo, trucks and trains near Rieti, and German Army strongpoints around Barrea.

YUGOSLAVIA: NATAF aircraft attack trains and trucks around Metkovic.

November 20, 1943

ITALY: Bad weather grounds most Twelfth and Fifteenth air force aircraft, but some NATAF aircraft are able to attack a rail junction and several towns in the German Army zone.

November 21, 1943

ITALY: NATAF B-25s attack gun emplacements around Gaeta; NATAF fighter-bombers attack several German Army strongpoints along the battle lines; and Fifteenth Air Force B-26s attack a marshalling yard at Chiusi, the harbor at Civitavecchia, and a bridge at Fano.

November 22, 1943

EGYPT: The SEXTANT Conference opens in Cairo between President Franklin D. Roosevelt, Prime Minister Sir Winston S. Churchill, and Generalissimo Chiang Kai-shek, of China.

ITALY: Fifteenth Air Force B-26s attack a rail center at Foligno and a bridge at Cicerna; more than 100 NATAF fighters and bombers attack gun emplacements and strongpoints in the Fossacesia region of the battle area; A-36s attack the harbor, a chemical plant, and rail yards at Civitavecchia; and A-36s and P-40s attack roads, rail lines, and villages in and around the battle area.

TUNISIA: The 90th Photographic Reconnaissance Wing is activated at La Marsa Airdrome to oversee the Twelfth Air Force's 3d and 5th Photographic Reconnaissance groups.

November 23, 1943

FRANCE: Eighty-three IX Bomber Command B-26s attack the Berck-sur-Mer and St.-Omer/Longuenesse airdromes.

ITALY: The Twelfth Air Force is grounded by bad weather.

November 24, 1943

BULGARIA: Fifteenth Air Force B-24s, escorted by P-38s, attack a marshalling yard at Sofia. However, due to poor weather and visibility, only 17 B-24s are able to drop their bombs. An estimated dozen Axis fighters attack the bombers and, although 82d Fighter Group P-38 pilots are able to down two Bf-109s, two B-24s and a P-38 are also lost.

ENGLAND: The 100th Fighter Wing is activated to oversee fighter groups yet to be assigned to the Ninth Air Force.

FRANCE: Following two consecutive cancellations on account of weather, 103 Fifteenth Air Force B-17s attack the Vichy French fleet and the Toulon submarine pens and drydocks with 315 tons of bombs. Several vessels including a cruiser are claimed as sunk. Fifteen B-17s that are unable to locate Toulon attack the viaduct at Antheor. GAF fighters mount sustained attacks on the bombers for about 30 minutes, but no B-17s are lost or seriously damaged, and one GAF fighter is claimed.

IX Bomber Command B-26s attack Berck-sur-Mer and St.-Omer/Longuenesse airdromes.

ITALY: Flight operations are severely limited due to bad weather.

The 47th Heavy Bombardment Wing begins overseeing the two B-24 groups thus far assigned to the Fifteenth Air Force.

November 25, 1943

AUSTRIA: Fifteenth Air Force B-24s attack Klagenfurt Airdrome.

ENGLAND: Air Chief Marshal Sir Trafford Leigh-Mallory, commander of the Allied Expeditionary Air Force (AEAF) activates the headquarters of the RAF's Second Tactical Air Force, which he will command. In time, LtGen Lewis H. Brereton's U.S. Ninth Air Force will also come under Leigh-Mallory's supervision.

FRANCE: The 56th and 353d Fighter groups conduct the first dive-bombing attack by P-47s in the theater against St.-Omer/Longuenesse Airdrome. One 353d Fighter Group P-47 and its pilot are lost in the attack, but results are deemed acceptable. The missing pilot is LtCol Loren G. McCollum, the 353d Fighter Group commander, who is taken prisoner.

The 20th Fighter Group's 77th Fighter Squadron makes its combat debut as an attachment to the 55th Fighter Group.

ITALY: NATAF aircraft attack German Army gun emplacements and defensive points around Ancona and in several contested sectors of the battle area.

YUGOSLAVIA: Twelfth Air Force B-25s attack Sarajevo and Travnik.

November 26, 1943

ALGERIA: P-39 pilots of the 350th Fighter Group's 347th Fighter Squadron, and Beaufighter pilots of the 414th Night Fighter Squadron team up with British and French airmen to beat off an attack by 30 GAF night bombers against Allied shipping in Bougie harbor. At least five FW-200s, four He-177s, and two Do-217s are downed by the Allied fighters, and several others are damaged or possibly downed, but not before a glider bomb released by one of the GAF bombers sinks a troop transport.

EGYPT: Although Operation OVERLORD has been discussed at length, no conclusive decisions are reached by the time the SEXTANT Conference ends.

FRANCE: Three hundred fifty VIII Bomber Command B-17s, 77 B-24s, and 13 pathfinder B-17s attack the city of Bremen with 1,205 tons of bombs between 1145 and 1228 hours. Losses are 22 B-17s and three B-24s downed (including one B-17 by friendly incendiary bombs) and 165 heavy bombers damaged, plus crew losses of ten killed and 215 missing.

The 1st Bombardment Division's 401st Heavy Bombardment Group, in B-17s, makes its combat debut.

VIII Fighter Command dispatches 353 P-47s and 28 P-38s to escort and support the bombers. The fighter pilots down a one-day theater record of 34 GAF aircraft over Germany, the Netherlands, and France between 1030 and 1400 hours.

Maj Jack C. Price, the commanding officer of the 78th Fighter Group's 84th Fighter Squadron, achieves ace status when he downs an FW-190 and a Bf-109 near Paris at 1100 hours. (Price's and several other victories over Paris are associated with an aborted morning attack against a ball-bearing plant by 3d Bombardment Division B-17s.) Capt Walker M. Mahurin, a P-47 pilot with the 56th Fighter Group's 63d Fighter Squadron, becomes VIII Fighter Command's first double ace when he downs two Bf-110 fighters near Oldenburg between 1207 and 1229 hours; Capt Walter V. Cook, a P-47 pilot with the 56th Fighter Group's 62d Fighter Squadron achieves ace status when he downs two Bf-110s near Papenburg at 1215 hours; and Maj Francis S. Gabreski, a P-47 pilot with the 56th Fighter Group's 61st Fighter Squadron, achieves ace status when he downs two Bf-110s near Oldenburg at 1215 hours.

During the morning, IX Bomber Command's 323d Medium Bombardment Group attacks Cambrai/Epinoy Airdrome, and the 322d and 386th Medium Bombardment groups mistakenly attack Roye/Amy Airdrome (instead of the Rosieres-en-Santerre landing ground).

During the afternoon, secret military construction sites* at Audinghen are attacked by B-26s from the 323d, 386th, and 387th Medium Bombardment groups.

ITALY: 376th Heavy Bombardment Group B-24s attack rail bridges at four locations; 2d and 99th Heavy Bombardment group B-17s attack a viaduct; 301st Heavy Bombardment Group B-17s attack a marshalling yard and a bridge at Rimini; 17th Medium Bombardment Group B-26s attack Cassino; and NATAF aircraft attack a marshalling yard and the harbor at Ancona, troop concentrations at two locations, and several strongpoints in the battle area.

November 27, 1943

ITALY: Fifteenth Air Force B-17s attack a marshalling yard at Rimini, a marshalling yard and rail bridges at Grizzano, and a rail bridge at Vergato; XII Bomber Command B-25s attack Porto Civitanova; and NATAF aircraft mount day and night attacks against road, rail, and tactical targets.

YUGOSLAVIA: XII Air Support Command B-25s attack Sibenik.

November 28, 1943

FRANCE: P-38 pilots of the 1st Fighter Group's 71st Fighter Squadron down three FW-190s over the French coast at 1210 hours while on the way to attack the Salon-de-Provence Airdrome, but they and the Fifteenth Air Force B-26s they are escorting against targets in southern France are recalled because of bad weather.

IRAN: President Franklin D. Roosevelt and Prime Minister Sir Winston S. Churchill meet with Marshal Josef Stalin at the Eureka Conference in Tehran.

ITALY: Fifteenth Air Force B-24s, Fifteenth Air Force P-38 fighter-bombers, and XII Air Support Command B-25s attack a rail tunnel at Dogna, north of Trieste; Fifteenth Air Force B-17s attack the Rome/Ciampino Airdrome; and NATAF fighter-bombers attack motor vehicles, troops, trucks, trains, and buildings in the battle area.

YUGOSLAVIA: XII Air Support Command B-25s attack barracks, port facilities, ships, and warehouses at Dubrovnik, Sibenik, and Zara.

November 29, 1943

BELGIUM: Fifty-three IX Bomber Command B-26s attack Chievres Airdrome.

FRANCE: Seventy-one IX Bomber Command B-26s attack Cambrai/Epinoy Airdrome.

GERMANY: Although the cloud cover reaches as high as 29,000 feet in places, 137 VIII Bomber Command B-17s, of 360 dispatched, are able to attack the city of Bremen with 410 tons of bombs between 1430 and 1550 hours, and 17 B-17s attack various targets of opportunity.

Three hundred fourteen VIII Fighter Command P-47s and 38 P-38s escort and support the bombers, but heavy winds result in high fuel consumption that prevents deep penetrations. VIII Fighter Command pilots down 14 GAF fighters over Germany and the Netherlands between 1210 and 1504 hours, but seven P-38s and nine P-47s are lost with their pilots.

ITALY: Fifteenth Air Force B-17s attack Grossetto Airdrome; Fifteenth Air Force B-24s attack Rome/Casale Airdrome; XII Air Support Command B-25s attack road and rail bridges at Giulianova; and NATAF aircraft attack German Army strongpoints in and near the battle area.

SCOTLAND: 357th Fighter Group personnel arrive by ship from the United States for training as a P-51 unit and service with the IX Fighter Command; and the 361st Fighter Squadron, in P-47s, arrives for service with VIII Fighter Command.

YUGOSLAVIA: XII Air Support Command B-25s attack Sarajevo.

November 30, 1943

AUSTRIA: Fifteenth Air Force B-24s attack Klagenfurt Airdrome.

ENGLAND: The IX Fighter Command formally reestablishes its headquarters in the U.K. following its move from Libya.

The 357th and 362d Fighter groups arrive in England aboard ship and are assigned to the IX Fighter Command's 70th Fighter Wing. The 357th will transition from P-39s to P-51s, and the 362d will transition from P-39s to P-47s.

The newly arrived 448th Heavy Bombardment Group, in B-24s, is assigned to the 2d Bombardment Division's 20th Combat Bombardment Wing.

FRANCE: Fifteenth Air Force B-17s attack the submarine pens at Marseille.

GERMANY: Although 352 B-17s and 29 B-24s are dispatched to Solingen to attack aircraft-industry targets, all the B-24s and all the 1st Bombardment Division B-17s but one turn back because of extremely high cloudiness. In the end, 78 3d Bombardment Division B-17s, the one 1st Bombardment Division B-17, and one pathfinder B-17 attack the briefed primary with 224 tons of bombs between 1155 and noon. Losses are three B-17s downed, three B-17s lost in operational accidents, nine B-17s damaged, 11 crewmen killed (in one of the accidents), 23 crewmen missing, and 20 crewmen wounded.

The VIII Fighter Command dispatches 327 P-47s and 20 P-38s to escort and support the bomber force, but only one victory credit is awarded to a 78th Fighter Group P-47 pilot who downs an FW-190 near Eupen, Belgium, at 1235 hours. Also, one P-38 and five P-47s and their pilots are lost in action.

IRAN: Under pressure from Premier Josef Stalin, and in return for an agreement that the Soviet Union will declare war on Japan, President Franklin D. Roosevelt and Prime Minister Sir Winston S. Churchill agree to make Operation OVERLORD their nations' main effort in mid-1944 and to undertake an invasion of southern France (Operation ANVIL) as well. As a result of this agreement, American and British representatives return to Cairo to renew the previously inconclusive portion of the SEXTANT Conference on the OVERLORD and ANVIL operations.

ITALY: Although severely hampered by overcast conditions, Fifteenth Air Force B-24s attack Fiume; Fifteenth Air Force B-26s attack Montalto di Castro, a rail bridge at Monte Molino, and targets around Bastia and Torgiano; and NATAF aircraft mounting numerous sorties against tactical targets in the German Army battle line provide a U.S. Army division with decisive assistance in turning back a German Army counterattack.

---

*   The "secret military construction sites" are later identified as V-1 rocket launching sites.

DECEMBER 1943

December 1, 1943

ALBANIA: An 82d Fighter Group P-38 pilots downs a Ju-52 near Alessio at 1530 hours.

FRANCE: One hundred seventy-six IX Bomber Command B-26s attack Cambrai/Epinoy, Cambrai/Niergnies, Chievres (Belgium), and Lille/Vendeville airdromes.

Twenty-eight 354th Fighter Group P-51s conduct their unit's maiden combat mission, an uneventful sweep over the Pas-de-Calais and Belgium. This is also the first combat mission to be made over northwestern Europe under IX Fighter Command control.

GERMANY: Two hundred six 1st Bombardment Division B-17s and 69 2d Bombardment Division B-24s, guided by six pathfinder B-17s, attack aircraft-industry targets at Solingen and Leverkusen with a total of 702 tons of bombs. Several targets of opportunity are also attacked. 3d Bombardment Division B-17s slated for the mission abort due to bad weather. Losses are 19 B-17s and five B-24s downed, 13 crewmen killed (including nine in an operational accident), and 227 crewmen missing.

Of 374 P-47s from seven groups and 42 55th Fighter Group P-38s escorting the heavy-bomber mission, five P-47s and two P-38s are declared missing. Fifteen GAF fighters are downed by VIII Fighter Command pilots over Belgium and Germany between 1130 and 1240 hours.

ITALY: B-24s of the Fifteenth Air Force's 47th Heavy Bombardment Wing dispatched against a marshalling yard at Bolzano in the early afternoon are recalled because of bad weather. 1st Fighter Group P-38 escort pilots down two Bf-109s between 1245 and 1305 hours.

One hundred eighteen B-17s of the Fifteenth Air Force's 5th Heavy Bombardment Wing, escorted by 14th Fighter Group P-38s, drop 354 tons of bombs in a damaging attack on industrial targets in Turin, including the Fiat ball-bearing plant. A 14th Fighter Group P-38 pilot downs a Bf-109 over the target shortly after 1400.

Fifteenth Air Force B-26s attack bridges and rail facilities at three locations;

XII Air Support Command B-25s attack gun emplacements; and NATAF fighter-bombers attack gun emplacements, motor vehicles, and other military targets in direct support of Allied ground forces.

Headquarters, Fifteenth Air Force, displaces from Tunis, Tunisia, to Bari, Italy, and the headquarters of the Fifteenth Air Force's 5th Heavy Bombardment Wing displaces from Tunisia to Foggia, Italy.

December 2, 1943

ENGLAND: The CCS authorizes the AEAF to attack construction sites in the Cherbourg and Pas-de-Calais areas of northern France that appear to be missile-launching facilities.

FRANCE: One hundred eighteen Fifteenth Air Force B-17s, escorted by 14th Fighter Group P-38s, attack the submarine pens being constructed at Marseille. Damage is counted as heavy despite flak and attacks by GAF fighters, of which two FW-190s are downed by P-38 pilots and several others are claimed by bomber gunners.

ITALY: Thirty-five Fifteenth Air Force B-24s, escorted by 82d Fighter Group P-38s, attack a marshalling yard at Bolzano with 106 tons of bombs. Rolling stock and tracks are severely damaged. P-38 pilots down four of the 33 GAF fighters that attack the formation, but three P-38s are also downed.

Fifteenth Air Force B-26s attack a marshalling yard at Arezzo, the town area at Orvieto, and a rail bridge; NATAF aircraft provide direct support to Allied ground forces; XII Air Support Command B-25s attack bridges and bridge approaches; and NATAF fighters and fighter-bombers attack gun emplacements, trains, and motor vehicles in and around the battle area.

In a spectacularly successful night raid on Allied shipping in Bari harbor, approximately 30 GAF tactical bombers succeed in blowing up two ammunition ships, which in turn results in the sinking of another 17 ships and the closing of the port for three weeks.

YUGOSLAVIA: Twelfth Air Force fighters attack harbors and shipping at several points along the coast.

December 3, 1943

EGYPT: The SEXTANT Conference is reopened in Cairo by Allied representatives seeking to reach firm decisions regarding the OVERLORD and ANVIL landings in France.

ENGLAND: Air Chief Marshal Sir Charles F. Portal, RAF, notes in a letter to the CCS that Operation POINTBLANK (the Combined Bomber Offensive) is three months behind schedule in achieving specific goals prior to May 1, 1944, the earliest possible date for the launching of the cross-Channel attack, Operation OVERLORD.

ETO: Operation CROSSBOW, the campaign against German V-weapons sites (at first code-named SKI, but later and more popularly known as NOBALL), is given top priority for the Allied tactical air forces.

ITALY: Despite bad weather, Fifteenth Air Force B-24s are able to attack the Rome/Casale Airdrome, but Fifteenth Air Force B-26s are recalled on their way to the day's targets.

NATAF fighter-bombers attack Anzio and Nettuno, and tanks and motor vehicles in the battle area and north of Rome.

A 27th Fighter-Bomber Group A-36 pilot downs an He-111 north of Rome at 1415 hours.

The entire II Air Service Area Command is transferred from the Twelfth to the Fifteenth Air Force, where it will be redesignated the XV Air Force Service Command.

YUGOSLAVIA: XII Air Support Command B-25s attack the marshalling yard and port facilities at Sibenik, and XII Air Support Command fighter-bombers attack ships in the harbor at Sibenik.

December 4, 1943

ENGLAND: The Ninth Air Force's IX Air Support Command is activated in England under the command of Col Clarence E. Crumrine. It will begin training units for tactical operations in support of the projected invasion of France by the U.S. First Army.

Using personnel and equipment from the disbanded 479th Antisubmarine Group [see November 11, 1943], the Eighth Air Force activates the 36th and 406th Heavy Bombardment squadrons for service with its nascent and as-yet-unofficial special operations group, which is being prepared to drop agents and supplies by parachute to assist partisan organizations in France and the Low Countries. The new squadrons are placed under the temporary administrative control of the 482d Heavy Pathfinder Bombardment Group.

ETO: The reconnaissance phase of Operation CROSSBOW begins with an intense schedule of missions.

FRANCE: Two hundred three IX Bomber Command B-26s are dispatched against the Chievres (Belgium) and Lille/Vendeville airdromes, but all are recalled because of bad weather.

ITALY: The entire Twelfth and Fifteenth air forces are grounded by bad weather.

NETHERLANDS: Sixteen 353d Fighter Group P-47s dive-bomb the Gilze-Rijen Airdrome under escort from the remainder of the 343d Fighter Group and the 56th Fighter Group. Also, 352d Fighter Group P-47 pilots conducting a sweep down three GAF fighters near Rotterdam between 1500 and 1510 hours. There are no USAAF losses.

December 5, 1943

EGYPT: At the SEXTANT Conference, Gen Dwight D. Eisenhower is confirmed as the OVERLORD supreme commander.

FRANCE: The VIII Bomber Command mounts its inaugural Operation CROSSBOW mission against NOBALL V-weapons sites in France, but uniformly bad weather prevails, and only three of 548 VIII Bomber Command heavy bombers dispatched actually release their bombs. Nine heavy bombers are lost through various mishaps.

The day is also marked by the bomber-

escort debut of the Ninth Air Force's 354th Fighter Group, the first operational P-51B Mustang fighter unit to enter combat in Europe. The 354th Fighter Group is officially assigned to the IX Fighter Command, but it will be on loan to the VIII Fighter Command, as will be other units that will be assigned to the IX Fighter Command over the winter months.

The 20th Fighter Group's 55th Fighter Squadron, in P-38s, makes its combat debut as an attachment to the VIII Fighter Command's 55th Fighter Group.

More than 200 IX Bomber Command B-26s taking part in the Ninth Air Force's inaugural CROSSBOW mission are forced to turn for home in the face of bad weather, but a total of 52 B-26s are able to attack NOBALL V-weapons sites at three locations.

ITALY: Despite bad weather, a number of XII Air Support Command B-25s attack a bridge at Pescara; and NATAF fighters and fighter-bombers attack Aviano and Piombino airdromes, gun emplacements, trains, motor vehicles, and several bridges in and around the battle area.

Headquarters, Twelfth Air Force, moves to Italy from Tunisia.

MEDITERRANEAN: The CCS authorize the creation of a new headquarters to be known as the Mediterranean Allied Air Forces (MAAF), which will consolidate the operations of MAC and NAAF.

YUGOSLAVIA: XII Air Support Command B-25s attack a marshalling yard and shipyards at Split, and NATAF fighters attack a ship in the harbor at Poljud.

December 6, 1943

ENGLAND: The 70th Fighter Wing headquarters is assigned to the IX Fighter Command to oversee fighter units assigned to the Ninth Air Force.

The 354th Fighter Group is assigned to the 70th Fighter Wing.

FRANCE: P-39 pilots of the 350th Fighter Group's 345th Fighter Squadron down two Ar-196 float reconnaissance airplanes near Cannes at about 1500 hours.

GREECE: Many Fifteenth Air Force heavy bombers are unable to locate targets due to poor weather conditions, but 45 47th Heavy Bombardment Wing B-24s attack Athens/ Eleusis Airdrome, and 56 5th Heavy Bombardment Wing B-17s attack Athens/ Kalamaki Airdrome. One B-24 is downed by flak, but 82d Fighter Group P-38 escort pilots down four GAF fighters over Athens between 1150 and 1230 hours.

ITALY: Although most flight operations over Italy are canceled in the face of bad weather, Fifteenth Air Force B-17s are able to attack a marshalling yard and rail bridges at Grizzano, and Twelfth Air Force A-36s and P-40s are able to attack bridges at two locations.

December 7, 1943

CORSICA: A 52d Fighter Group Spitfire pilot downs an Me-210 off Corsica.

EGYPT: The SEXTANT Conference concludes with, among other things, firm decisions regarding the invasion of France in mid-1944.

ITALY: The Fifteenth Air Force is grounded because of bad weather, but XII Air Support Command B-25s and A-36s attack the town and harbor at Civitavecchia; XII Air Support Command B-25s attack the rail line, a road, and the town area at Pescara; and NATAF fighter-bombers attack gun emplacements, a bridge, and several defended towns in and around the battle area. Spitfire pilots of the 31st Fighter Group's 309th Fighter Squadron down six GAF fighters over central Italy at about 1500 hours.

The 5th Heavy Bombardment Wing's 301st Heavy Bombardment Group, in B-17s, moves from Tunisia to a base in Italy.

December 8, 1943

ETO: Gen Carl Spaatz is informed by Gen Henry H. Arnold that he will command the new U.S. Strategic Air Forces in Europe (USSAFE). The new command, which will be headquartered in England, will oversee the efforts of the Eighth and Fifteenth air forces in the conduct of the Combined Bomber Offensive.

GREECE: Fifteenth Air Force B-24s, escorted by 82d Fighter Group P-38s, attack the Athens/Tatoi Airdrome; and Fifteenth Air Force B-17s attack the Athens/Eleusis Airdrome.

ITALY: Fifteenth Air Force B-17s attack the port area and shipping at San Stefano al Mare, and rail bridges at Orbetello; XII Air Support Command B-25s attack industrial targets, bridges, marshalling yards, and town areas at Ancona, Aquila, and Pescara; XII Air Support Command A-20s attack a troop bivouac and gun emplacements; and NATAF A-20s, fighters, and fighter-bombers attack gun emplacements, troop concentrations, roads, railroads, and bridges in and around the battle area.

A 27th Fighter-Bomber Group A-36 pilot downs a Ju-52 at 0930 hours over Avezzano Airdrome.

The 1st Fighter Group, in P-38s, moves from Sardinia to a new base in Italy.

December 9, 1943

ITALY: Fifteenth Air Force B-17s attack the rail bridges at Levanto; XII Air Support Command B-25s attack an ironworks and a marshalling yard at Terni, and rail and road bridges and tracks at three locations; XII Air Support Command A-20s attack a bivouac area and gun emplacements; and NATAF fighters and fighter-bombers attack a variety of transportation and tactical targets in and around the battle area.

Fifteenth Air Force B-24s and B-26s are grounded by bad weather, and the 5th Heavy Bombardment Wing's 2d and 99th Heavy Bombardment groups, in B-17s, are recalled due to bad weather while on the way to their targets.

The 5th Heavy Bombardment Wing's 2d Heavy Bombardment Group, in B-17s, is transferred from Tunisia to a base in Italy.

BriGen George H. Beverley assumes command of the XII Provisional Troop Carrier Command.

December 10, 1943

BULGARIA: Thirty-one Fifteenth Air Force B-24s attack the marshalling yard at Sofia, and 82d Fighter Group P-38 escort pilots down nine of the estimated 30 GAF fighters that attack the formation over Sofia at about 1220 hours. Two P-38s are also downed.

ENGLAND: Between 1920 and 2000 hours, 20 GAF attack aircraft raid Ninth Air Force bases at Andrews Field and Earls Colne, Gosfield, and Great Dunmow airdromes. Eight USAAF personnel are killed, and 20 are wounded at Great Dunmow.

ITALY: XII Air Support Command A-36s and P-40s attack warehouses, oil tanks, rail facilities, and a ship at Civitavecchia; a defended town; tactical targets in the British Eighth Army battle area; and road traffic at or near the front. Also, Fifteenth Air Force B-26s attack bridge approaches around Ventimiglia.

MEDITERRANEAN: The Mediterranean Theater of Operations (MTO) is formally activated, but the new Mediterranean Allied Air Forces (MAAF) is not yet made operational.

YUGOSLAVIA: XII Air Support Command fighter-bombers attack a ship in the harbor at Split.

December 11, 1943

GERMANY: Four hundred thirty-seven VIII Bomber Command B-17s and 86 B-24s attack aircraft-industry targets at Emden with 1,407 tons of bombs. Losses are 15 B-17s and two B-24s. Also, in a GAF experiment, one B-24 is damaged when an FW-190 tows a cable through a bomber formation.

The 3d Bombardment Division's 92d Combat Bombardment Wing makes its combat debut.

Bomber escort and support is provided by 313 P-47s, 31 P-38s, and 44 P-51s, which down two Ju-88 attack aircraft and 19 GAF fighters over the Netherlands and northern

Germany between 1203 and 1305 hours. 1stLt Glenn D. Schiltz, Jr., a P-47 pilot with the 56th Fighter Group's 63d Fighter Squadron, achieves ace status when he downs an Me-210 near Emden at 1230 hours.

ITALY: The entire Fifteenth Air Force and XII Air Support Command B-25s are grounded by bad weather, but numerous fighter and fighter-bomber missions are mounted in support of Allied ground forces. 31st Fighter Group Spitfire pilots down one and damage two Bf-109s over central Italy at 0935 hours.

The 5th Heavy Bombardment Wing's 99th Heavy Bombardment Group, in B-17s, is transferred from Tunisia to a base in Italy. Also, after being reequipped with P-47s and transferred from the Twelfth Air Force to the Fifteenth Air Force, the veteran 325th Fighter Group arrives at Foggia Airdrome to begin escorting heavy bombers over southern Europe.

December 12, 1943

ENGLAND: The 94th Heavy Combat Bombardment Wing is activated to oversee several B-17 groups of the VIII Bomber Command's 1st Bombardment Division.

The 361st Fighter Group, in P-47s, is assigned to the VIII Fighter Command's 66th Fighter Wing.

ITALY: All Fifteenth Air Force flight operations and many scheduled Twelfth Air Force missions are canceled in the face of bad weather, but XII Air Support Command B-25s are able to attack the landing ground, road, and rail line at Terracina; and A-36s and P-40s bomb Itri and attack motor vehicles.

The Fifteenth Air Force's 14th Fighter Group, in P-38s, moves from Tunisia to a new base in Italy.

December 13, 1943

FRANCE: The 67th Fighter Wing's 359th Fighter Group, in P-47s, completes its first combat mission, an unchallenged fighter sweep over the Pas de Calais area.

GERMANY: One hundred sixty-nine 1st Bombardment Division B-17s and four pathfinder B-17s attack the Bremen port area with 457 tons of bombs at about noon. There are no losses in this attack.

Four hundred sixty-seven VIII Bomber Command B-17s, 99 B-24s, and eight pathfinder B-17s attack the Kiel port area with 1,147 tons of bombs between 1245 and 1305 hours. (The totals include a small number of B-17s that attack Hamburg and other targets of opportunity when poor visibility due to frosting prevents them from bombing the primary.) Five heavy bombers are lost.

The 2d Bombardment Division's 445th Heavy Bombardment Group, in B-24s, makes its combat debut.

Bomber escort is provided by 322 P-47s, 31 P-38s, and 41 P-51s, which down one Ju-88. One P-47 and one P-51 are lost.

Of special note on the Kiel mission, the new P-51s set a record for depth of penetration by escort fighters over Europe. And, in the first combat in World War II to involve a P-51B Mustang fighter, the 354th Fighter Group's 1stLt Glenn T. Eagleston is given credit for the probable destruction of a Bf-110 over Frederickstadt at 1325 hours.

ITALY: The entire Fifteenth Air Force is grounded in the face of bad weather, but XII Air Support Command A-36s and P-40s conduct a wide variety of attacks against targets in and around the battle area.

NETHERLANDS: Two hundred eight IX Bomber Command B-26s attack Amsterdam/Schipol Airport with 787 1,000-pound bombs. Two B-26s are lost to heavy flak concentrations.

YUGOSLAVIA: XII Air Support Command B-25s attack warehouses, an oil depot, port facilities, and a railway yard at Sibenik and Split.

December 14, 1943

GREECE: Thirty-three Fifteenth Air Force B-24s attack Athens/Tatoi Airdrome; 76

Fifteenth Air Force B-17s attack Athens/Kalamaki and Athens/Eleusis airdromes; and 27 Fifteenth Air Force B-17s that are unable to find Athens/Eleusis attack the port area and shipping at Piraeus. One B-17 is lost.

14th Fighter Group P-38 escort pilots down two Bf-109s.

On its first mission with the Fifteenth Air Force, the 325th Fighter Group, in P-47s, provides target withdrawal escort.

ITALY: XII Air Support Command B-25s attack the town area and marshalling yard at Orte; A-20s attack a road bridge; and A-36s and P-40s attack the town and port areas at Civitavecchia, and several bridges in and around the battle area.

December 15, 1943

AUSTRIA: Fifteenth Air Force B-17s attack marshalling yards at Innsbruck.

ENGLAND: The Ninth Air Force is formally placed under AEAF operational control. Under a new directive issued by AEAF, the first priority of U.K.-based tactical bombers (RAF and USAAF) is the GAF fighter force. Also, a Ninth Air Force planning staff is established in London.

The 1st Bombardment Division's 351st and 401st Heavy Bombardment groups are reassigned to the new 94th Combat Bombardment Wing.

ITALY: Fifteenth Air Force B-24s attack the viaduct at Avisio; Fifteenth Air Force B-17s attack a marshalling yard at Bolzano; XII Air Support Command A-20s and B-25s attack roads around Frosinone and Pontecorvo; and XII Air Support Command fighter-bombers attack gun emplacements all along the U.S. Fifth Army front. 324th Fighter Group P-40 pilots and 31st Fighter Group Spitfire pilots down four GAF fighters in several actions over central Italy.

YUGOSLAVIA: XII Air Support Command B-25s attack Mostar Airdrome; and XII Air Support Command A-36s and P-40s attack ships, motor vehicles, and parked airplanes in and around the Peljesac Peninsula.

December 16, 1943

GERMANY: Three hundred ninety-two VIII Bomber Command B-17s, 133 B-24s, and two pathfinder B-17s attack the Bremen port area. Eight B-17s are lost.

The 2d Bombardment Division's 446th Heavy Bombardment Group, in B-17s, makes its combat debut.

Bomber escort is provided by 131 P-47s, 31 P-38s, and 39 P-51s, but the 55th Fighter Group cannot complete its part of the escort plan owing to the late arrival of the bomber formations. 1stLt Charles F. Gumm, Jr., of the 354th Fighter Group, becomes the first USAAF P-51B pilot to be given credit for a confirmed victory over a GAF airplane and the first IX Fight Command pilot to down an enemy airplane over northwestern Europe. While providing target escort for the heavy bombers over the port of Bremen, Gumm damages a Ju-88 medium bomber and downs a Bf-109 at 1330 hours. The only other victory credit awarded is for a Ju-88 downed by several 4th Fighter Group P-47 pilots near the Zuider Zee at 1310 hours.

ITALY: Fifteenth Air Force B-24s attack the rail bridge and rail tunnel at Dogna, and the rail line between Dogna and Chiusaforte; P-38s escorting the B-24s strafe oil tanks and trains; Fifteenth Air Force B-17s attack the rail junction and marshalling yard at Padua; XII Air Support Command A-20s attack gun emplacements; XII Air Support Command A-36s and P-40s attack gun batteries, gun emplacements, troop concentrations, and strongpoints in direct support of the U.S. Fifth and British Eighth armies; and XII Air Support Command A-36s and P-40s bomb the port area at Civitavecchia and a town.

YUGOSLAVIA: XII Air Support Command B-25s attack a marshalling yard and the port area at Sibenik, and ships at Zara; and Twelfth Air Force P-40s and P-47s strafe targets of opportunity in the Peljesac Peninsula.

1stLt Alfred C. Froning, of the 57th Fighter Group's 65th Fighter Squadron, achieves ace status when he downs two Bf-109s near Trpanj during the morning. Froning's victories are among six credited to 57th Fighter Group pilots, who have just transitioned from P-40s to P-47s.

December 17, 1943

ENGLAND: Representatives from the AEAF, the Ninth Air Force, the RAF's Second Tactical Air Force, and 21st Army Group begin formulating the preliminary joint plan for support of the Allied ground forces in northern Europe by the components of AEAF.

ITALY: All XII Air Support Command B-25s abort in the face of bad weather, but XII Air Support Command A-20s are able to attack a German Army artillery concentration; and XII Air Support Command A-36s and P-40s attack barracks, warehouses, port facilities, and marshalling yards at Anzio and Nettuno, and troop positions at three locations.

YUGOSLAVIA: Twelfth Air Force P-40s and P-51s, escorted by South African Air Force fighters, attack a ship near Trpanj; and 57th Fighter Group P-47 pilots down three Bf-109s near Metkovic during an afternoon mission.

December 18, 1943

FRANCE: Fifteenth Air Force B-26s attack the Antheor viaduct and several road and rail bridges along the Var River.

ITALY: Weather severely limits the bulk of flight operations by Twelfth and Fifteenth air force units, but XII Air Support Command A-36s and P-40s are able to attack a variety of tactical and communications targets in central Italy.

December 19, 1943

AUSTRIA: Fifteenth Air Force B-17s attack a marshalling yard at Innsbruck.

GERMANY: In the Fifteenth Air Force's first attack on a target on German soil, 50 unescorted B-24s attack the Messerschmitt research and experimental facility and Bf-110 assembly plant in Augsburg with 86 tons of bombs through a near-total undercast. Fifty GAF fighters attack the formation and down four B-24s while bombers gunners claim 21 GAF fighters destroyed or probably destroyed.

ITALY: Fifteenth Air Force B-26s attack rail facilities and marshalling yards at three locations; XII Air Support Command B-25s attack the marshalling yards and airdrome at Orte and the marshalling yards at Terni; XII Air Support Command A-20s attack Orte and Cassino; XII Air Support Command A-36s attack the rail line and port at Civitavecchia; XII Air Support Command P-40s attack a dump near Arce and two towns; and, after missing its rendezvous with heavy bombers, the Fifteenth Air Force's 325th Fighter Group, in P-47s, strafes Ancona Airdrome, a ship, a train, and several truck convoys.

YUGOSLAVIA: XII Air Support Command P-40s attack ships at Solin, Split, and Trogir.

December 20, 1943

BULGARIA: Approximately 30 Fifteenth Air Force B-24s attack marshalling yards at Sofia, and 82d Fighter Group P-38 escort pilots down four GAF fighters over the target at about 1250 hours.

FRANCE: Thirty-five of more than 150 IX Bomber Command B-26s dispatched against several V-weapons construction sites attack a V-weapons site in northern France, but the rest are thwarted by heavy cloud cover.

The 358th Fighter Group, in P-47s, completes its first combat mission, an unchallenged fighter sweep over the Pas-de-Calais area. (The tempo of the buildup of strategic fighter forces based in the U.K. is noticeably increasing.)

GERMANY: Three hundred fifty seven VIII Bomber Command B-17s, 103 B-24s, and 12 pathfinder B-17s attack the Bremen port area. Twenty-seven heavy bombers are lost.

Following the attack by his bomber box, TSgt Forrest L. Vosler, the radioman-gunner of a 303d Heavy Bombardment Group B-17, is wounded in the legs and thighs by a burst of antiaircraft fire that also knocks out two of the bomber's engines, disables the radio equipment, and seriously injures the tail gunner. Moments later, Vosler is blinded by a 20mm shell. Despite his wounds, Vosler continues to fire his machine gun in defense of the airplane. Later, when the pilot announces that the plane must ditch in the English Channel, Vosler repairs the radio by touch alone and successfully transmits distress signals. Finally, after the B-17 successfully ditches, Vosler rescues the wounded tail gunner and drags him to a wing to await rescue. For his actions this day, TSgt Vosler is awarded a Medal of Honor.

Bomber escort is provided by 26 P-38s, 47 P-51s, and a record 418 P-47s, which down 19 GAF aircraft over the Netherlands and northern Germany between 1125 and 1245 hours. LtCol Glenn E. Duncan, the commanding officer of the 353d Fighter Group, in P-47s, achieves ace status when he downs an FW-190 over Falkenburg at 1210 hours; and 1stLt Joe H. Powers, a P-47 pilot with the 56th Fighter Group's 61st Fighter Squadron, achieves ace status when he downs a Bf-109 near Bremen at 1215 hours. VIII Fighter Command losses are four P-51s and three P-47s, including a P-47 that crashes after it collides with a B-24 (which also crashes).

The first "freelance" fighter mission of the air war over northwestern Europe occurs when the bomber stream arrives 30 minutes late for its rendezvous with 55th Fighter Group P-38s. Rather than waste time and fuel waiting, the group leader puts into action a plan much-discussed by fighter pilots—ranging far ahead of the bombers to try to break up GAF fighter formations as they converge along the bomber path. The 55th Fighter Group scores no victories this day, but its use of the new tactic gets the attention of VIII Fighter Command, and there ensues a healthy debate that, in the end, will free the fighters from the outmoded close-escort doctrine of the day.

Another important first is the use of "window"—strips of metal foil cut in such a way as to thwart German early-warning radar when dropped from bombers in the bomber stream.

GREECE: Fifteenth Air Force B-17s attack the Athens/Eleusis Airdrome, and 14th Fighter Group P-38 escort pilots down eight Bf-109s and an FW-190 over the target at about 1240 hours.

ITALY: XII Air Support Command A-36s and P-40s attack numerous tactical and transportation targets in central Italy.

The 5th Heavy Bombardment Wing's 97th Heavy Bombardment Group, in B-17s, is transferred from Tunisia to a base in Italy.

The 450th Heavy Bombardment Group, in B-24s, arrives in Italy and is attached to the Fifteenth Air Force 47th Heavy Bombardment Wing. Although nine new heavy-bomber groups have been promised to the new strategic air force by the end of the year, the 450th, with its 62 B-24s, is the first and only new heavy-bomber group to reach the Fifteenth Air Force in 1943.

MEDITERRANEAN THEATER OF OPERATIONS (MTO): The Mediterranean Allied Air Forces (MAAF) is formally activated to oversee all the Allied air forces and commands in the new MTO, including USAAF, RAF, French, and Italian units. Air Chief Marshal Sir Arthur W. Tedder is named the theater air commander-in-chief, and Gen Carl Spaatz, the theater USAAF commander, is to be his deputy until Spaatz's scheduled departure for England to head the new U.S. Strategic Air Forces in Europe (USSAFE). MAC and NAAF are disbanded.

MAAF is now composed of three subordinate commands: the Mediterranean Allied Strategic Air Force (MASAF, of which the Fifteenth Air Force is to be a part); the Mediterranean Allied Tactical Air Force (MATAF, of which the Twelfth Air Force is to be a part); and the Mediterranean Allied Coastal Air Force (MACAF).

Also formed—under Gen Carl Spaatz's command—is USAAF in the North African Theater of Operations (USAAFNATO), a non-operational body that will coordinate operations undertaken by the Twelfth and Fifteenth air forces.

UNITED KINGDOM: In the IX Troop Carrier Command's first operational mission of the war, two C-47s evacuate hospitalized American personnel to England from Ireland.

December 21, 1943

FRANCE: Eighty-four IX Bomber Command B-26s from two groups, escorted by 208 VIII Fighter Command P-47s, are dispatched against two V-weapons sites, but one B-26 group completely misses its target (by miles!). Targets of opportunity are also attacked.

ITALY: XII Air Support Command B-25s and P-40s attack Terracina; and XII Air Support Command A-36s and P-40s attack numerous transportation and tactical targets, including a fuel dump and a munitions plant at Cervaro and a radar station and other targets between Civitavecchia and Rome.

LtGen John K. Cannon replaces Gen Carl Spaatz as commanding general of the Twelfth Air Force.

December 22, 1943

ENGLAND: The 365th Fighter Group arrives aboard ship from the United States and is assigned to the IX Fighter Command's 70th Fighter Wing to train in P-47s.

The independent 810th Medical Evacuation Squadron is assigned to the IX Troop Carrier Command's 50th Troop Carrier Wing.

ETO: Gen Carl Spaatz is ordered to England at once to assume command of the new U.S. Strategic Air Forces in Europe (USSAFE).

FRANCE: Two humdred ten IX Bomber Command B-26s dispatched against

V-weapons sites in France are recalled because of bad weather.

GERMANY: Although more than 100 heavy bombers are thwarted by heavy cloud cover, 145 1st Bombardment Division B-17s, 87 2d Bombardment Division B-24s, and two B-17 pathfinders are able to attack a marshalling yard at Osnabruck. Also, 161 3d Bombardment Division B-17s, 30 2d Bombardment Division B-24s, and three pathfinder B-17s attack a marshalling yard at Munster. Five B-17s and 12 B-24s are lost from the Osnabruck force.

The 2d Bombardment Division's 448th Heavy Bombardment Group, in B-24s, makes its combat debut.

Bomber escort is provided by 40 P-38s, 448 P-47s, and 28 P-51s. Although two P-38s and two P-47s are downed by GAF fighters, USAAF fighter pilots are credited with downing 15 GAF fighters over the Netherlands and northern Germany between 1345 and 1500 hours.

ITALY: The Fifteenth Air Force is grounded by bad weather, but Twelfth Air Force P-40s and Spitfires attack German Army strongpoints, and P-40s attack bridges, road and rail targets, and motor vehicles.

MajGen Paul L. Williams replaces BriGen George H. Beverley as commanding general of the XII Provisional Troop Carrier Command.

MTO: LtGen Ira C. Eaker is ordered to the Mediterranean as MAAF commander-in-chief-designate; he will replace Air Chief Marshal Sir Arthur W. Tedder as soon as Tedder is ordered to England to become deputy commander-in-chief of Operation OVERLORD. However, Eaker's departure is to be delayed until after the arrival in England of Gen Carl Spaatz and Eaker's own replacement as Eighth Air Force commanding general, MajGen James H. Doolittle.

YUGOSLAVIA: 57th Fighter Group P-47s attack targets of opportunity around Zara.

December 23, 1943

ENGLAND: The 363d Fighter Group ar-

rives aboard ship from the United States and is assigned to the IX Fighter Command's 70th Fighter Wing to train in P-47s.

FRANCE: Fifteenth Air Force B-26s attack the Antheor viaduct.

ITALY: Fifteenth Air Force B-26s attack a marshalling yard and rail bridge at Imperia, and various targets around Ventimiglia.

NETHERLANDS: 353d Fighter Group P-47s dive-bomb the Gilze-Rijen Airdrome.

YUGOSLAVIA: Bad weather prevents Twelfth Air Force P-40s and P-47s from directly supporting Yugoslav partisans resisting a German Army invasion of Korcula Island, off the Peljesac Peninsula.

December 24, 1943

FRANCE: In connection with Operation CROSSBOW, the Eighth Air Force mounts its largest mission to date—722 heavy bombers and 541 fighters.

Of the heavy bombers dispatched, a total of 670 (478 B-17s and 192 B-24s) attack V-weapons sites around Pas-de-Calais with 1,745 tons of bombs. Thanks in large part to the GAF's having been run out of the forward areas over the preceding months, not one heavy bomber or fighter is lost to enemy action.

The 3d Bombardment Division's 447th Heavy Bombardment Group, in B-17s, makes its combat debut.

Approximately 60 IX Bomber Command B-26s attack V-weapons sites around Pas-de-Calais, but 30 other B-26s abort in the face of bad weather.

ITALY: The Twelfth and Fifteenth air forces are virtually grounded by bad weather. Of more than 100 Fifteenth Air Force B-26s dispatched to attack a marshalling yard at Pisa, all fail to locate the target, but 24 attack a marshalling yard at Cecina.

YUGOSLAVIA: Twelfth Air Force fighters dispatched in the morning to attack a ship off Ugljan Island fail to locate the target, but a pair of 57th Fighter Group P-47 pilots down a Ju-88 over the sea near Sibenik.

December 25, 1943

ITALY: Fifteenth Air Force B-24s attack a marshalling yard at Udine and Vicenza Airdrome; Fifteenth Air Force B-17s attack marshalling yards at Udine and Bolzano; and Fifteenth Air Force B-26s attack several marshalling yards in the Pisa-Porta Nuova area. An 82d Fighter Group P-38 escort pilot downs a Bf-109 over Udine at about 1100 hours.

December 26, 1943

ITALY: The entire Twelfth Air Force and Fifteenth Air Force heavy bombers are grounded by bad weather, but Fifteenth Air Force B-26s are able to attack marshalling yards at three locations.

December 27, 1943

ENGLAND: The 27th Photographic Squadron, newly arrived from the United States, is assigned to the Eighth Air Force's 7th Photographic Reconnaissance Group.

Operational fighter training organizations long established at Goxhill Airdrome are formally reorganized into the 496th Fighter Training Group, which will oversee advanced P-51 theater training for replacement fighter pilots bound for both the Eighth and Ninth air forces. At the same time, at Atcham Airdrome, the previously established 495th Fighter Training Group begins specializing in advanced P-47 theater training for the two air forces.

ITALY: Fifteenth Air Force B-26s attack two viaducts, but they are prevented by bad weather from attacking the marshalling yards at Poggibonsi; XII Air Support Command A-36s attack port and rail facilities at Civitavecchia, several gun emplacements and troop positions along the battle lines, a factory, a rail line, and a bridge.

YUGOSLAVIA: XII Air Support Command B-25s attack a ship near Zara.

December 28, 1943

ITALY: A total of about 100 Fifteenth Air Force B-17s and B-24s attack a marshal-ling yard at Rimini, and 17 unescorted Fifteenth Air Force B-24s attack a marshalling yard at Vincenza. During the Vincenza attack, ten 376th Heavy Bombardment Group B-24s are downed over the target in an attack by an estimated 50 GAF fighters, the largest single loss sustained thus far on a Fifteenth Air Force mission. As a result of this heavy loss, the 47th Heavy Bombardment Wing is immediately withdrawn from combat for five weeks to undergo thorough retraining of the many green crews that, because of end-of-tour rotations, have recently filled the ranks of the wing's veteran 98th and 376th Heavy Bombardment groups.

Approximately 100 Fifteenth Air Force B-26s attack Centocelle and Guidonia airdromes and rail bridges around Orvieto; XII Air Support Command A-20s, B-25s, and A-36s support an attack by RAF medium and heavy bombers against a variety of targets in the Rome area; and Twelfth Air Force tactical aircraft attack Ciampino Airdrome, road and rail targets around Roccasecca, rail sidings at Frosinone, port facilities and ships at Civitavecchia, the harbor at Anzio, and communications targets around Atina and Pontecorvo.

The 15th Combat Mapping Squadron (a Mediterranean Allied Photographic Reconnaissance Wing unit) is attached to the Fifteenth Air Force to begin reconnoitering targets and potential targets throughout southern Europe.

MEDITERRANEAN: A 52d Fighter Group Spitfire pilot downs a GAF twin-engine fighter at sea east of Elba.

NETHERLANDS: The 20th Fighter Group, in P-38s, which has been staging into combat one squadron at a time for over a month, undertakes its first combat mission as a complete unit—an uneventful sweep over the Dutch coast.

December 29, 1943

ITALY: Fifteenth Air Force B-17s attack industrial targets at Reggio Emilia and marshalling yards at Rimini and Ferrara;

Fifteenth Air Force B-26s attack a viaduct, bridges at two locations, and marshalling yards at two locations; XII Fighter Command A-36s attack a rail yard and port facilities at Civitavecchia, a truck park, and a railroad station; and XII Air Support Command P-40s attack the railroad station at Anagni.

The 304th Heavy Bombardment Wing establishes its headquarters at Cerignola Airdrome to oversee several new B-24 groups that are expected to arrive in Italy in January 1944 for duty with the Fifteenth Air Force.

YUGOSLAVIA: Twelfth Air Force P-40s attack a ship near the Peljesac Peninsula.

December 30, 1943

FRANCE: Approximately 100 IX Bomber Command B-26s attack an airdrome at St.-Omer and a V-weapons sites near the English Channel coast, but 100 other B-26s abort in the face of bad weather.

GERMANY: Five hundred thirteen VIII Bomber Command B-17s and 145 B-24s attack the port area and an oil refinery at Ludwigshafen with 1,394 tons of bombs. Twenty-three heavy bombers are lost, five are written off, and 117 are damaged. Crew losses are 11 killed and 200 missing.

The VIII Fighter Command dispatches 79 P-38s (including the fully operational 20th Fighter Group), 463 P-47s, and 41 P-51s to escort the bombers and undertake several fighter sweeps over France. P-47 pilots down seven GAF fighters over France between 1115 and 1420 hours, but a total of 11 P-47s, two P-51s, and 12 fighter pilots are lost during the day. Two of the P-47s and two of the P-51s, and all their pilots, are lost in midair collisions.

ITALY: Fifteenth Air Force B-17s attack marshalling yards at Verona, Rimini, and Padua, and rail bridges around Padua; Fifteenth Air Force B-26s attack marshalling yards at two locations, a road junction, and a viaduct; XII Air Support Command A-20s attack Atina; and XII Air Support

Command A-36s and P-40s attack troops and a variety of tactical targets in and around the battle area.

14th Fighter Group P-38 escort pilots down three GAF fighters over or near Padua at about 1250 hours; and 325th Fighter Group P-47 pilots down three Bf-109s over central Italy at about 1400 hours.

1stLt Michael T. Russo, of the 27th Fighter-Bomber Group's 524th Fighter-Bomber Squadron, becomes history's first and only A-36 Apache fighter-bomber ace when he downs two Bf-109s over central Italy at 1015 hours.

MEDITERRANEAN: The theater's last aerial victory credited in 1943 is a Ju-88 downed at sea at 1530 hours by a 52d Fighter Group Spitfire pilot.

YUGOSLAVIA: XII Air Support Command B-25s attack a variety of targets at Zara, and XII Air Support Command fighters attack a ship at Crkvice.

December 31, 1943

ENGLAND: The 71st Fighter Wing headquarters is assigned to the IX Fighter Command to oversee fighter units yet to be assigned to the Ninth Air Force.

FRANCE: Two hundred VIII Bomber Command B-17s and 144 B-24s attack the Bordeaux/Merignac, Cognac/Chateaubernard, and St.-Jean-d'Angely airdromes, and 120 VIII Bomber Command B-17s attack aircraft-industry targets around Paris. A total of 25 heavy bombers are lost to enemy fire and 15 are lost to a combination of bad landings and ditchings caused by battle damage, fuel shortages, and operational accidents. Among airmen lost is Col William A. Hatcher, Jr., the 351st Heavy Bombardment Group commander, who is killed.

Escort and support for the heavy bombers is provided by 74 P-38s, 441 P-47s, and 33 P-51s, which down nine GAF fighters over France between 1030 and 1400 hours. Four USAAF fighters and two of their pilots are lost.

Approximately 200 IX Bomber Command B-26s attack V-weapons sites along the Channel coast.

ITALY: MAAF fighters and fighter-bombers support the British Eighth Army with attacks against German Army artillery and troop displacements all along the battle line, and XII Air Support Command A-36s attack gun emplacements and the town area at Formia.

JANUARY 1944

January 1, 1944*

ENGLAND: USSAFE is formally established under the command of Gen Carl Spaatz to provide operational control over the Eighth and Fifteenth air forces for the conduct of the USAAF portion of the Combined Bomber Offensive (Operation POINTBLANK).

The 452d Heavy Bombardment Group, in B-17s, arrives from the United States via the southern ferry route for service with the 3d Bombardment Division's 45th Combat Bombardment Wing.

MTO: In a complete reorganization of USAAF theater commands, U.S. Army Air Forces, North African Theater of Operations (USAAFNATO), is redesignated U.S. Army Air Forces, Mediterranean Theater of Operations (USAAFMTO); the II Air Service Area Command is redesignated XV Air Force Service Command; the III Air

* Due to the vastly increasing tempo of the air war, only significant fighter and bomber actions will be described from this date onward to the end of the war in Europe.

Service Area Command is redesignated XII Air Force Service Command; the old XII Air Force Service Command is redesignated Army Air Forces Service Command, MTO; the XII Provisional Air Force Engineer Command is redesignated Army Air Forces Provisional Engineer Command, MTO; the XII Air Force Training Command is redesignated XII Air Force Training and Replacement Command; and the XII Bomber Command is reinstated under the command of BriGen Robert D. Knapp to oversee the three B-26 groups of the 42d Medium Bombardment Wing (formerly assigned to the Fifteenth Air Force) and the three B-25 groups formerly attached to the XII Air Support Command.

For the moment, the combat arms of the Fifteenth Air Force comprise: the 5th Heavy Bombardment Wing (2d, 93d, 97th, and 301st Heavy Bombardment groups, in B-17s); the 47th Heavy Bombardment Wing (99th and 376th Heavy Bombardment groups, in B-24s); and the 1st, 14th, and 82d Fighter groups, in P-38s, and the 325th Fighter Group, in P-47s.

The combat arms of the Twelfth Air Force comprise: the XII Bomber Command, consisting of three B-25 groups (12th, 321st, and 340th Medium Bombardment groups) and the 42d Medium Bombardment Wing (17th, 319th, and 320th Medium Bombardment groups, in B-26s); the XII Air Support Command, consisting of the 47th Light Bombardment Group (A-20s), the 27th and 86th Fighter-Bomber groups (A-36s), the 57th Fighter Group (P-47s), the 31st Fighter Group (Spitfires), the 33d, 79th, and 324th Fighter groups (P-40s), the 415th Night-Fighter Squadron (Beaufighters), and the 111th Tactical Reconnaissance Squadron (mixed aircraft types); the XII Fighter Command, consisting of the 81st and 350th Fighter groups (P-39s), the 52d Fighter Group (Spitfires), the 414th, 416th, and 417th Night-Fighter squadrons (Beaufighters), and the 310th Medium Bombardment Group (B-25s and B-25 gunships); the XII Troop Carrier Command, consisting of the 51st and 52d Troop Carrier wings (seven groups in C-47s and some C-54s); and the 90th Photographic Reconnaissance Wing, consisting of the 3d and 5th Photographic Reconnaissance groups (mixed aircraft types).

January 2, 1944

ITALY: XII Bomber Command B-26s attack a marshalling yard and two bridges; XII Bomber Command B-25s attack a barracks, an iron works, and a marshalling yard; XII Air Support Command A-36s attack the marshalling yards and harbor at Civitavecchia, a marshalling yard, gun emplacements, and targets of opportunity; XII Air Support Command P-40s attack various tactical targets, including a German Army road column mired in the snow in the Avezzano-Popili area; and P-47s of the Fifteenth Air Force's 325th Fighter Group conduct an uneventful sweep over Rome.

January 3, 1944

ITALY: Fifty-three B-17s of the 5th Heavy Bombardment Wing's 2d and 99th Heavy Bombardment groups attack the ball-bearing plant at Villarperosa, scoring 12 direct hits; 50 B-17s of the 5th Heavy Bombardment Wing's 97th and 301st Heavy Bombardment groups attack a marshalling yard at Turin; XII Air Support Command A-36s and P-40s attack a rail station, gun emplacements around Cassino, the harbor at Civitavecchia, assorted rail and tactical targets, and motor vehicles.

MajGen Nathan F. Twining replaces MajGen James H. Doolittle as commanding general of the Fifteenth Air Force, and BriGen Edward M. Morris replaces BriGen Gordon P. Saville as commanding general of the XII Fighter Command.

YUGOSLAVIA: XII Bomber Command B-25s attack Sibenik, Spilt, and German Army troop concentrations at Projedor.

January 4, 1944

BULGARIA: A force of 108 Fifteenth Air Force B-17s briefed for an attack against marshalling yards at Sofia is forced to abort by cloud cover over the target. However, 40 of the B-17s drop about 81 tons of bombs on the rail lines around Dupnica.

ENGLAND: The headquarters of the Ninth Air Force's new XIX Air Support Command is activated under the temporary command of MajGen Elwood R. Quesada, who is also serving as commanding general of the IX Fighter Command.

FRANCE: Despite poor weather and visibility, 253 IX Bomber Command B-17s attack V-weapons sites in France.

During the night of January 4–5, Operation CARPETBAGGER, the parachuting of agents and supplies by air to anti-Axis partisan forces in western Europe, begins with a drop by Eighth Air Force special-operations B-24s over northern France. In this and numerous other clandestine missions, the supply drop takes place under the cover of a leaflet drop.

GERMANY: Of 569 VIII Bomber Command heavy bombers dispatched, 313 B-17s and 132 B-24s attack the Kiel port area with more than 1,000 tons of bombs. Also, seven

B-17s and 34 B-24s attack various targets of opportunity. Seventeen heavy bombers and their crews are lost.

Fighter support for the Kiel mission consists of 70 P-38s of the 20th and 55th Fighter groups and 42 P-51s of the 354th Fighter Group. Several GAF fighters are damaged over the target by USAAF fighters, and a 354th Fighter Group P-51 pilot downs a Ju-88 over Kiel at 1225 hours, but one of each type of airplane is lost.

On a separate mission, 68 3d Bombardment Division B-17s attack the city of Munster. The only losses are two B-17s that collide over Germany.

Fighter support for the Munster mission consists of 430 VIII Fighter Command P-47s from nine fighter groups. Seven GAF fighters are downed by P-47 pilots of the 56th, 78th, and 353d Fighter groups over northern Germany and Belgium between 1030 and 1100 hours. 1stLt Peter E. Pompetti, a P-47 pilot with the 78th Fighter Group's 84th Fighter Squadron, achieves ace status when he downs a Bf-109 near Coesfeld at 1045 hours.

Employed in a combat mission for the first time, on a 56th Fighter Group P-47 is a new paddle-bladed propeller that significantly increases the performance of the P-47 fighter.

YUGOSLAVIA: XII Bomber Command B-25s attack Brodac and the marshalling yard and town area at Travnik.

January 5, 1944

ENGLAND: USSAFE formally begins coordinating the strategic-bombing offensives by the Eighth and Fifteenth air forces.

FRANCE: One hundred twelve 3d Bombardment Division B-17s, escorted by 76 78th Fighter Group P-47s (split into "A" and "B" groups), attack the Bordeaux/ Merignac Airdrome. Eleven B-17s and five P-47s are lost with all hands. An escort pilot downs two Bf-109s over La Rochelle at 1017 hours.

Seventy-eight 1st Bombardment Division B-17s, escorted by 149 4th and 352d

Fighter group P-47s, attack Tours Airdrome. One B-17 is lost with its crew. Escort pilots down an He-177 and two FW-190s between 1145 hours and noon.

The 1st Bombardment Division's 91st Heavy Bombardment Group becomes the first Eighth Air Force bomber unit to complete 100 combat missions.

GERMANY: Escorted by 70 P-38s and 41 P-51s, 119 1st Bombardment Division B-17s and 96 2d Bombardment Division B-24s attack the shipyards and aircraft-industry targets at Kiel. Five B-17s, five B-24s, and seven P-38s are lost.

Of 78 3d Bombardment Division B-17s briefed for an attack on ball-bearing factories at Elberfield, 73 attack various targets of opportunity after running into bad weather. Escort for this attack is provided by 243 P-47s from four VIII Fighter Command groups.

In all, USAAF fighter pilots taking part in escort missions over Germany are credited with 27 GAF aircraft downed between 1120 and 1230 hours.

ITALY: The bulk of the Twelfth Air Force is grounded by bad weather, but some XII Air Support Command A-36s are able to attack gun emplacements and other tactical targets.

January 6, 1944

ETO: Gen Carl Spaatz assumes command of USSAFE, and LtGen James H. Doolittle formally succeeds LtGen Ira C. Eaker as Eighth Air Force commanding general. To implement his new command, Spaatz redesignates Headquarters, Eighth Air Force, as Headquarters, USSAFE, and names as his deputies for administration and operations, respectively, BriGen Hugh J. Knerr and MajGen Frederick L. Anderson. On the same day, Headquarters, VIII Bomber Command, is redesignated Headquarters, Eighth Air Force, and the VIII Bomber Command ceases to exist as such.

ITALY: XII Bomber Command B-26s attack an aircraft factory at Piaggio and marshalling yards at two locations; and XII

Air Support Command A-36s and P-40s attack gun emplacements, rail lines, and railroads in and around the battle area.

January 7, 1944

AUSTRIA: P-38 pilots of the 1st and 14th Fighter groups down five GAF fighters and damage or possibly down several others in a running fight from Wiener-Neustadt southward between 1100 and 1140 hours.
FRANCE: Thirty-five IX Bomber Command B-26s attack the Cherbourg/Maupertus Airdrome, but all other IX Bomber Command missions are canceled due to bad weather.
GERMANY: Of 502 Eighth Air Force B-17s and B-24s dispatched, 417 attack the I.G. Farben plant at Ludwigshafen with nearly 1,000 tons of bombs. Twelve bombers are lost with their crews, and 14 crewmen are killed in their airplanes by enemy fire.

Escort and support for the bomber mission is provided by 71 P-38s, 463 P-47s, and 37 P-51s, of which a P-38 and five P-47s are lost with their pilots. Seven GAF fighters are downed over France and Germany between 1145 and 1340 hours. Capt James A. Goodson, a P-47 pilot with the 4th Fighter Group's 336th Fighter Squadron, achieves ace status when he downs two FW-190s near Bethune, France, at about 1335 hours.

For the first time, fighters employ the phased-escort tactic, in which specific groups relieve specific groups at specific times and places along the bomber route after flying by way of the most direct route from the U.K. The technique is designed to conserve fuel and thus allow each group to stay with the bombers longer than they had been able to do previously. The phased-escort technique proves so efficacious that it will endure until the end of the war.
ITALY: Fifteenth Air Force B-17s attack a torpedo factory at Fiume; XII Bomber Command B-25s attack Perugia Airdrome; XII Bomber Command B-26s attack marshalling yards at two locations and a bridge;

and XII Air Support Command A-20s, A-36s, and P-40s attack road, rail, and tactical targets in or near the battle area.
YUGOSLAVIA: Forty-eight Fifteenth Air Force B-17s attack an aircraft factory at Maribor.

January 8, 1944

ENGLAND: The 303d Heavy Bombardment Group is reassigned to the 1st Bombardment Division's 40th Combat Bombardment Wing.

The new 453d Heavy Bombardment Group, in B-24s, is assigned to the 2d Bombardment Division's 2d Combat Bombardment Wing.
ITALY: One hundred nine Fifteenth Air Force B-17s destroy two-thirds of the aircraft factory at Reggio Emilia, thereby reducing production of Regianne Re.2005 and Savoia-Marchetti SM.79 fighters; XII Bomber Command B-26s attack marshalling yards at two locations; XII Air Support Command A-20s and A-36s attack rail targets in or near the battle area; and XII Air Support Command P-40s provide direct support for U.S. Army ground forces.
YUGOSLAVIA: The B-24 equipped 449th and 450th Heavy Bombardment groups, of the Fifteenth Air Force's 47th Heavy Bombardment Wing, make their combat debuts with an attack on the Mostar Airdrome. There is virtually no opposition, and no losses.

XII Bomber Command B-25s attack the port area, warehouses, and the rail line at Metkovic.

January 9, 1944

ITALY: Fifteenth Air Force B-17s attack the aircraft factory and a marshalling yard at Reggio Emilia; XII Bomber Command B-25s attack a marshalling yard and docking facilities at Ancona; and XII Air Support Command A-36s and P-40s attack tanks, trucks, and troop positions in and around the battle area.
YUGOSLAVIA: Fifteenth Air Force B-24s attack Mostar Airdrome.

January 10, 1944

BULGARIA: Fifteenth Air Force B-17s attacking a marshalling yard at Sofia are attacked by an estimated 60 Axis fighters. Two B-17s are downed, but 14th Fighter Group P-38 escort pilots down nine GAF fighters over Sofia at about 1230 hours.

ITALY: XII Bomber Command B-25s attack a town, and XII Air Support Command aircraft attack numerous rail, road, tactical, and communications targets throughout central Italy.

During the night of January 10–11, XII Bomber Command B-26s attack iron and steel works at Piombino.

YUGOSLAVIA: Fifteenth Air Force B-24s attack a marshalling yard at Skoplje.

January 11, 1944

ENGLAND: The 96th Heavy Combat Bombardment Wing headquarters is activated to oversee several Eighth Air Force B-24 groups.

GERMANY: The Allied strategic air offensive against Germany (Operation POINTBLANK) is officially inaugurated with the dispatch of 663 Eighth Air Force heavy bombers against several industrial targets in Germany.

One hundred fifty-nine 1st Bombardment Division B-17s attack aircraft-industry targets at Oschersleben. Thirty-four B-17s are downed and 83 are damaged by intense flak and fighter attacks. Crew losses are 349 missing and nine killed.

One hundred seven 1st Bombardment Division B-17s attack aircraft-industry targets at Halberstadt. Eight B-17s and their crews are lost, and 42 B-17s are damaged.

Escort for the 1st Bombardment Division is provided by 177 P-47s and 44 P-51s, whose pilots down 27 GAF fighters against the loss of two P-47s and their pilots missing.

In the first *officially sanctioned* test of the "freelance" fighter tactic [see December 20, 1943], the 56th Fighter Group mounts two small fighter groups, 56A (36 P-47s) and 56B (48 P-47s), both to range ahead and far to the flanks of two separate bomber streams in the hope of disrupting GAF fighter formations as they gather for mass attacks on the heavy bombers. The 56A Group is credited with 11 confirmed victories in the vicinity of Osnabruck between 1105 and 1115 hours.

Maj James H. Howard, the commanding officer of the 354th Fighter Group's 356th Fighter Squadron, in P-51s, becomes the only U.K.-based fighter pilot to earn a Medal of Honor in the war when he single-handedly defends a small formation of B-17s that is under attack by a large force of GAF fighters over Halberstadt. Howard, a former U.S. Navy pilot who has already downed 2.333 Japanese airplanes over China and Burma while serving with the American Volunteer Group (Flying Tigers) and a GAF fighter over Germany, also achieves ace status in this heroic action when, without any backup whatsoever from other fighters, he downs two Bf-110s and an FW-190 (and probably downs another FW-190) between 1150 and 1215 hours.

Two hundred thirty-four 3d Bombardment Division B-17s and 138 2d Bombardment Division B-24s briefed to attack aircraft-industry targets at Brunswick are recalled because of bad weather. By then the bomber formations are over Germany, so a total of 285 heavy bombers attack various targets of opportunity through holes in the clouds. Sixteen B-17s and two B-24s are lost. Taking part in this mission is the first H2S-equipped B-24 to be dispatched on a combat mission.

Escort for the Brunswick mission is provided by 49 P-38s and 322 P-47s. One P-38 and one P-47 are lost, and a pair of P-47 pilots down two GAF fighters.

GREECE: Fifteenth Air Force B-17s attack the port and shipping in the harbor at Piraeus, and 1st Fighter Group P-38 pilots down two Bf-109s over the harbor area at about 1310 hours. Six B-17s are lost in a series of midair collisions in dense overcast.

ITALY: XII Bomber Command B-25s attack a rail yard and a rail junction, and XII Air Support Command A-36s and P-40s attack numerous gun emplacements and rail and road targets in the battle area and central Italy.

January 12, 1944

ITALY: XII Bomber Command B-25s and B-26s attack a dam and several bridges in central Italy; XII Air Support Command A-20s attack a town; XII Air Support Command A-36s and P-40s attack numerous German Army defensive positions along the battle line and many rail targets in or near the battle area; and the Fifteenth Air Force's 325th Fighter Group, in P-47s, strafes a marshalling yard and numerous buildings across central Italy during a fighter sweep to Rome.

Col Archibald Y. Smith assumes command of the XII Air Force Training and Replacement Command.

YUGOSLAVIA: 57th Fighter Group P-47 pilots down three Bf-109s off the coast at Korcula during a morning mission, and XII Air Support Command P-40s attack a ship in the Krka River.

January 13, 1944

FRANCE: One hundred ninety-three IX Bomber Command B-26s attack V-weapons sites in France.

ITALY: As part of the preparation for the upcoming amphibious landings at Anzio, 100 Fifteenth Air Force B-17s and B-24s and 241 XII Bomber Command B-25s and B-26s, escorted by fighters from both air forces, attack the Rome-area airdromes at Centocelle, Ciampino, Guidonia, and Perugia. The bombers are credited with destroying or disabling most of the GAF aircraft based in central Italy.

In the course of the bomber attacks, which take place at about noon, eight Bf-109s are downed and 11 others are damaged or possibly downed by pilots of the 14th and 325th Fighter groups. 2dLt Paul H. Wilkins, a P-38 pilot with the 14th

Fighter Group's 37th Fighter Squadron, achieves ace status when he downs one of the Bf-109s.

XII Air Support Command A-36s and P-40s mount numerous tactical missions and attack road and rail targets in and around the battle area.

YUGOSLAVIA: MATAF fighter-bombers attack shipping at Sibenik and along the Krka River.

January 14, 1944

FRANCE: Due to bad weather over Germany, 552 Eighth Air Force heavy bombers are dispatched to attack 21 V-weapons sites around Pas-de-Calais. In the end, 522 B-17s and B-24s attack 20 of the briefed targets with more than 1,500 tons of bombs, and 19 B-24s attack various targets of opportunity. Two B-17s and one B-24 are lost with their crews.

Escort and support for the heavy bombers is provided by 645 USAAF fighters whose pilots are credited with downing 13 GAF fighters over France and Belgium between 1448 and 1530 hours. Three USAAF fighters are lost with their pilots. Capt Don S. Gentile, a P-47 pilot with the 4th Fighter Group's 336th Fighter Squadron, achieves ace status when he downs two FW-190s over the Bois de Compiegne between 1500 and 1520 hours. (Two of Gentile's earlier victories were scored while he was flying a Spitfire with the RAF's 133 Eagle Squadron.)

ITALY: XII Bomber Command B-25s attack a bridge; XII Air Support Command A-20s provide direct support for U.S. Fifth Army ground forces around Monte Trocchio; and XII Air Support Command A-36s and P-40s attack numerous tactical, transportation, and communications targets, including an A-36 strike against the harbor at Anzio.

YUGOSLAVIA: Approximately 200 Fifteenth Air Force B-17s and B-24s attack the Mostar Airdrome, and 82d Fighter Group P-38 pilots down three GAF fighters and damage several others over the target.

January 15, 1944

ITALY: Fifteenth Air Force B-24s attack a marshalling yard at Prato, nearby roads, and the town area at Pistoia; Fifteenth Air Force B-17s attack marshalling yards at eight locations and two rail bridges; XII Bomber Command B-25s attack a rail junction; XII Bomber Command B-26s attack bridges at Orvieto; the XII Air Support Command's 79th Fighter Group, in P-40s, and an RAF fighter wing attack a railroad station; XII Air Support Command A-36s and P-40s attack gun emplacements and troop positions in direct support of the U.S. Fifth Army; and Twelfth Air Force P-40s on an armed reconnaissance attack several rail targets.

52d Fighter Group Spitfire pilots down three He-115 reconnaissance float planes over Savona harbor at 1545 hours.

The 306th Heavy Bombardment Wing headquarters is activated in anticipation of its becoming a heavy-bomber component of the Fifteenth Air Force. However, in May 1944, it will be redesignated the 306th Fighter Wing and will oversee the operations of all fighter groups assigned to the Fifteenth Air Force.

MTO: LtGen Ira C. Eaker formally assumes command of MAAF and AAFMTO.

January 16, 1944

AUSTRIA: Sixty-one Fifteenth Air Force B-17s damage the Bf-109 components factory at Klagenfurt. Two Bf-109s are downed and two are probably downed by 14th Fighter Group P-38 pilots south of the target at 1150 hours. Three P-38s are lost.
ETO: Gen Dwight D. Eisenhower formally assumes his duties in England as Supreme Commander, Allied Expeditionary Force.
ITALY: Fifteenth Air Force B-24s attack the landing ground at Osoppo; Fifteenth Air Force B-17s attack Villaorba Airdrome; XII Bomber Command B-25s attack a marshalling yard and rail lines at Terni; XII Bomber Command B-26s attack a marshalling

yard and a bridge at Orte; XII Air Support Command A-20s attack Atina; XII Air Support Command A-36s attack rail lines, rail junctions, and several towns in and around the battle area; and XII Air Support Command P-40s attack gun emplacements in and around Cassino and several other frontline towns.

33d Fighter Group P-40 pilots down an FW-190 in a morning clash over Anzio, and 31st Fighter Group Spitfire pilots down three Bf-109s and damage several others near Cassino at 1030 hours.
YUGOSLAVIA: Fifteenth Air Force B-24s attack the town area at Zara.

January 17, 1944

ITALY: Fifteenth Air Force B-24s attack a marshalling yard at Arezzo; Fifteenth Air Force B-17s attack marshalling yards at two locations; XII Bomber Command B-25s attack marshalling yards at three locations; XII Bomber Command B-26s attack a rail bridge and a marshalling yard; XII Air Support Command A-36s attack Anzio, Avezzano, and Tarquinia; and XII Air Support Command P-40s attack the docks at Anzio and gun emplacements at two locations.
YUGOSLAVIA: XII Air Support Command P-40s attack the harbor at Sibenik.

January 18, 1944

ENGLAND: Gen Dwight D. Eisenhower directs that USSAFE assume administrative responsibility for all USAAF commands and units in the United Kingdom.
ITALY: Fifteenth Air Force B-24s attack the marshalling yards at Pisa; Fifteenth Air Force B-17s attack marshalling yards at three locations and rail bridges at two locations; XII Bomber Command B-26s attack the harbor at Piombino, factories, a bridge, and a rail line; XII Air Support Command A-20s attack gun emplacements; and XII Air Support Command A-36s and P-40s attack troops, motor vehicles, and gun emplacements in and around the battle area, and rail targets throughout central Italy.

YUGOSLAVIA: XII Air Support Command P-40s attack ships, port facilities, and railroads around Metkovic and Ploca.

January 19, 1944

ENGLAND: The Eighth Air Force establishes a radio countermeasures detachment based on technology available from the RAF. Designated the 803d Provisional Bombardment Squadron, the detachment is equipped with several B-17s and assigned for training by RAF personnel.

ITALY: Fifteenth Air Force B-17s and B-24s attack three airdromes around Rome; XII Bomber Command B-25s attack Rieti Airdrome; XII Bomber Command B-26s attack Viterbo Airdrome; XII Air Support Command A-36s attack troop positions and rail and communications targets along the U.S. Fifth Army battlefront at the Garigliano River; and XII Air Support Command P-40s attack German Army troop positions and defended villages in the battle area.

YUGOSLAVIA: XII Air Support Command P-40s attack two schooners at Makarska.

January 20, 1944

ENGLAND: In accordance with Gen Dwight D. Eisenhower's January 18 directive, Gen Carl Spaatz's USSAFE formally assumes administrative responsibility for all USAAF commands and units in the United Kingdom.

ITALY: Fifteenth Air Force B-17s and B-24s attack the Centocelle, Ciampino, and Guidonia airdromes, around Rome; XII Bomber Command B-25s attack rail lines around Carsoli; XII Bomber Command B-26s attack a bridge and a marshalling yard; XII Air Support Command A-20s provide close support for U.S. Fifth Army ground forces around Minturno; and XII Air Support Command A-36s and P-40s attack rail targets and mount more than 200 close-support sorties in conjunction with the U.S. 36th Infantry Division's crossing of the Rapido River.

31st Fighter Group Spitfires down three GAF fighters and damage or possibly down four others during afternoon missions over central Italy.

January 21, 1944

ENGLAND: The first air echelon of the 457th Heavy Bombardment Group, in B-17s, arrives from the United States for service with the 1st Bombardment Division's 94th Combat Bombardment Wing.

FRANCE: After being grounded for a full week by bad weather over the Continent, 795 Eighth Air Force B-17s and B-24s are dispatched against 36 V-weapons sites in the Cherbourg and Pas-de-Calais areas. Results are decidedly mixed due to heavy cloud cover. Four hundred one of the heavy bombers never drop their bombs, but 26 V-weapons sites and several targets of opportunity, including three airdromes, are eventually attacked by 394 heavy bombers releasing 1,141 tons of bombs. Six bombers are lost.

Escort and support for the mission is provided by a record 628 USAAF fighters (including a new P-47 unit, the 361st Fighter Group, in its combat debut). USAAF P-47 pilots down seven GAF fighters against the loss of one P-47 and its pilot. 56th Fighter Group P-47s turn in the first claims in the theater for GAF fighters destroyed during a strafing attack on an enemy airdrome.

One hundred nineteen IX Bomber Command medium bombers also attack V-weapons sites.

In an effort to stop at the source GAF bomber attacks on shipping and bases in Corsica and Sardinia, a total of 72 Fifteenth Air Force B-17s attack the GAF airdromes at Salon-de-Provence and Istres-le-Tube at about noon with an aggregate of 228 tons of bombs. Damage is heavy and both bases are put out of commission temporarily just as a major Allied amphibious landing is about to take place in central Italy. Six GAF fighters are downed over southern France by 1st and 82d Fighter group P-38 escort pilots.

ITALY: Fifteenth Air Force B-24s attack marshalling yards at Pisa, Pontedera, and Prato; Fifteenth Air Force B-17s attack marshalling yards and a bridge at Rimini, and a marshalling yard at Porto Civitanova; XII Bomber Command B-26s attack rail bridges around Orvieto; XII Bomber Command B-25s attack a bridge at Pontecorvo and rail lines around Rome; XII Air Support Command A-20s attack Atina; and XII Air Support Command A-36s and P-40s attack numerous tactical targets, troop concentrations, and a radar station in the U.S. Fifth Army zone.

325th Fighter Group P-47 pilots down four FW-190s near Florence at about 1230 hours.

January 22, 1944

ITALY: Beginning at 0200 hours, the Anzio beachhead is established by an Anglo-American invasion force supported by air and naval bombardment. Thanks to Fifteenth Air Force attacks on GAF bomber bases in southern France on January 21, only two of the 58 GAF aircraft that attack the beachhead and fleet on January 22 are bombers. Nearly the entire Twelfth Air Force is dedicated to supporting the invasion.

Fifteenth Air Force B-24s attack the marshalling yard at Arezzo and a road defile at Terracina; and Fifteenth Air Force B-17s attack a marshalling yard and the airdrome at Pontedera, a marshalling yard and rail bridges at Terni, and highway and rail bridges around Pontecorvo and Stazione di Campoleone.

In several afternoon clashes, Twelfth and Fifteenth air force fighter pilots down 12 GAF fighters over central Italy, especially between Anzio and Rome.

January 23, 1944

FRANCE: Approximately 200 IX Bomber Command B-26s attack V-weapons sites along the Channel coast.

ITALY: Fifteenth Air Force B-24s attack marshalling yards at three locations, Rieti Airdrome, a landing ground near Iesi, a bridge, and several targets of opportunity; Fifteenth Air Force B-17s attack marshalling yards at two locations, a rail line, a rail bridge, and two highway bridges; XII Bomber Command B-25s and B-26s attack targets in and around Avezzano, and B-25s also attack a road junction; XII Air Support Command A-20s attack Vallecorsa; XII Air Support A-36s attack numerous tactical targets; and XII Air Support Command fighters cover the Anzio beachhead throughout the day.

Spitfire pilots of the 52d Fighter Group's 2d Fighter Squadron down two Ju-88s and three He-111s near the port of Viareggio at about 1650 hours.

The 414th Night-Fighter Squadron moves nine of its twelve Beaufighters, with air and maintenance crews, into the Anzio beachhead area. At 1940 hours, following 30 minutes of stalking and chasing, a 414th Squadron aircrew downs a Do-217 that had been picked up on the Beaufighter's airborne radar as it crossed the northern tip of Sardinia. Twenty minutes later, a second 414th Squadron Beaufighter crew downs a Ju-88 from the same GAF night-raiding formation.

Col William S. Gravely is named to head the XII Air Force Training and Replacement Command.

YUGOSLAVIA: 57th Fighter Group P-47 fighter-bombers attack a bridge at Skradin.

January 24, 1944

BULGARIA: Fifteenth Air Force B-17s attack marshalling yards at two locations.

1stLt David D. Kienholz, a P-38 pilot with the 1st Fighter Group's 94th Fighter Squadron, achieves ace status when he downs an FW-190 over the airdrome at Sofia. Altogether, three GAF fighters are downed and four others are damaged or possibly downed over Sofia by 1st and 82d Fighter group P-38 pilots between 1215 and 1230 hours.

FRANCE: Approximately 175 IX Bomber Command B-26s attack V-weapons sites along the Channel coast.

GERMANY: The Eighth Air Force's briefed mission against aircraft-industry targets and marshalling yards at Frankfurt am Main turns into a complete shambles when the 857 B-17s and B-24s encounter immense problems forming up over England. Only 563 bombers are actually dispatched, none from the 2d Bombardment Division, which is recalled while still over England. Finally, as the lead 3d Bombardment Division combat wing is approaching the German frontier at 1020 hours, the mission is canceled and all bombers are recalled. Nevertheless, the 56 3d Bombardment Division B-17s in the lead wing, plus two stray 1st Bombardment Division B-17s, elect to carry out an attack on a target of opportunity, and they drop 143 tons of bombs on a power station at Eschweiler. Two 95th Heavy Bombardment Group B-17s are downed by enemy fire and two other B-17s are lost in operational accidents during takeoffs.

The VIII Fighter Command dispatches a record 678 fighters to escort and support the heavy bombers. An attempt is made to test a new area-patrol technique—tying specific groups to specific areas along the bomber route—but the effort is abandoned due to the weather-related problems encountered by the bombers. Twenty-one GAF fighters are downed over France, Belgium, and western Germany between 1115 and 1310 hours. Losses among USAAF fighters, however, amount to four P-38s, three P-47s, and two P-51s, and all their pilots.

ITALY: All Twelfth Air Force bombers are grounded by bad weather, but XII Air Support Command A-36s and P-40 fighter-bombers are able to attack various communications targets in central Italy. Also, Twelfth Air Force fighters provide continuous cover over the Anzio beachhead.

52d Fighter Group Spitfire pilots down two Do-217s and damage another near Pisa at 1635 hours.

YUGOSLAVIA: Fifteenth Air Force B-24s attack the town airdrome at Skoplje.

January 25, 1944

ENGLAND: The 391st Medium Bombardment Group, in B-26s, arrives from the United States for duty with the IX Bomber Command's 98th Combat Bombardment Wing.

FRANCE: All of approximately 150 IX Bomber Command B-26s dispatched to attack V-weapons sites abort in the face of bad weather.

ITALY: Although many Fifteenth Air Force B-17s dispatched to attack the marshalling yards at Arezzo and Perugia are thwarted by bad weather and poor visibility, a number attack targets of opportunity, including several road and rail bridges; XII Bomber Command B-26s attack Amelia, marshalling yards at two locations, and a road; XII Bomber Command B-25s attack Valmontone; XII Air Support Command A-20s attack Terelle; and XII Air Support Command A-36s and P-40s cover the Anzio beachhead and attack motor vehicles, railroads, and rolling stock throughout central Italy, and a bridge on the British Eighth Army front.

79th Fighter Group P-40 pilots down three Bf-109s and damage five other GAF fighters over the Anzio beachhead area during two separate engagements, one in the morning and one at 1215 hours.

NETHERLANDS: Escorted and supported by 174 P-47s from four other groups, 44 353d Fighter Group P-47s conduct a dive-bombing attack with 500-pound bombs against Leeuwarden Airdrome.

YUGOSLAVIA: XII Air Support Command P-40s and P-47s attack ships off Dubrovnik and road and rail traffic around the city.

January 26, 1944

CORSICA: 414th Night-Fighter Squadron Beaufighters damage and possibly down a Ju-88 and an He-111 while patrolling off Calvi between 1945 and 2015 hours.

FRANCE: One hundred forty-four IX Bomber Command B-26s dispatched to attack V-weapons sites are recalled because of bad weather.

ITALY: All Fifteenth Air Force heavy bombers and Twelfth Air Force medium bombers are grounded by bad weather, but XII Air Support Command A-20s are able to attack German Army troops defending Cisterna di Latina against a ground attack by the U.S. Fifth Army, and XII Air Support Command fighters and fighter-bombers attack numerous rail, road, and tactical targets in and around the battle area.

Spitfire pilots of the 31st Fighter Group's 307th Fighter Squadron down three GAF fighters in an engagement over Nettuno, in the Anzio beachhead area, at 1525 hours. One of the victors is Capt Virgil C. Fields, Jr., who achieves ace status when he downs an FW-190.

January 27, 1944

FRANCE: In an effort to prevent GAF bombers from attacking shipping and harassing the Anzio beachhead and invasion fleet, the Fifteenth Air Force goes after three GAF bomber bases in southern France.

After running a gauntlet of about 30 GAF fighters and while facing moderate to intense flak over the target, 64 Fifteenth Air Force B-17s, escorted by 27 14th Fighter Group P-38s, attack the Salon-de-Provence Airdrome at about 1215 hours. One B-17 and a P-38 are lost, and 20 B-17s are damaged in a running 30-minute fight in which the P-38s down 32 GAF fighters and damage six others.

Sixty-eight Fifteenth Air Force B-17s, escorted by 19 1st Fighter Group P-38s, attack Montpellier/Frejorgues Airdrome at about 1225 hours. Approximately 20 GAF fighters attack the P-38 escorts, but they leave the bombers alone. Three Bf-109s are downed and several others are damaged or possibly downed against the loss of one P-38. Only one B-17 is damaged over the target by flak.

In the third phase of the mission 27 450th Heavy Bombardment Group B-24s, escorted by 28 P-38s, crater the runways and damage the facilities at Istres-le-Tube Airdrome with 80 tons of bombs dropped at about 1235 hours. This force encounters no enemy fighters, but flak downs one B-24, severely damages another, moderately damages 11, and lightly damages all the rest.

Overall, the attack is successful in that Montpellier/Frejorgues and Salon-de-Provence airdromes are closed down and Istre-le-Tube can operate only at a diminished capacity.

ITALY: XII Bomber Command B-26s attack bridges and a marshalling yard; XII Bomber Command B-26s attack a rail line, a marshalling yard, and roads; XII Air Support Command A-20s provide close support for U.S. Fifth Army troops attacking Terelle; XII Air Support Command A-36s and P-40s attack defended towns and road and rail targets in and around the battle area; XII Air Support Command P-40s attack gun emplacements and provide on-call close air support for U.S. Fifth Army troops battling in the Atina and Cisterna di Latina areas; Fifteenth Air Force P-38s sweep the area around Rome; and Fifteenth Air Force P-47s sweep the area around Florence.

Throughout the day, P-40 pilots of the Twelfth Air Force's 57th and 79th Fighter groups and the independent 99th Fighter Squadron down 16 GAF fighters over Anzio, half between 0840 and 0850 hours and half between 1130 and 1500 hours.

January 28, 1944

FRANCE: Led by pathfinder B-24s equipped with new GH radar, B-24s of the 2d Bombardment Division's 93d and 446th Heavy Bombardment groups (escorted by 122 P-47s) are dispatched to attack two V-weapons sites near Bonnieres. Both groups are subsequently ordered to bomb the same target, but an early accidental release of bombs results in a widely dispersed and largely ineffectual bombing pattern.

ITALY: Fifteenth Air Force B-24s attack a marshalling yard at Ferrara; Fifteenth Air Force B-17s attack a marshalling yard at Verona; and 64 Fifteenth Air Force B-17s drop more than 9,000 20-pound fragmentation bombs on Aviano Airdrome to prevent the GAF from staging aircraft through it for attacks on the Anzio beachhead. At the time of the attack, 56 GAF aircraft are counted in dispersal areas on the ground, but only one is definitely destroyed in the attack.

XII Bomber Command B-26s attack bridges at two locations; XII Bomber Command B-25s attack a marshalling yard at Orte; XII Air Support Command A-20s attack Cisterna di Latina; XII Air Support Command A-36s attack Atina, tactical targets in the U.S. Fifth Army battle area, and a marshalling yard and other rail targets; XII Air Support Command P-40 and P-47 fighter-bombers attack a road junction; and XII Air Support Command P-40s attack several defended towns.

Throughout the morning, from about 0720 to 1150 hours, fighter pilots of the Twelfth Air Force's 31st, 33d, 79th, and 324th Fighter groups and the independent 99th Fighter Squadron down 23 GAF fighters and damage or possibly down 11 others.

NETHERLANDS: 359th Fighter Group P-47s are dispatched to dive-bomb the Leeuwarden Airdrome, but the mission is canceled when they fail to rendezvous with their escort, the 352d Fighter Group.

January 29, 1944

FRANCE: Approximately 80 IX Bomber Command B-26s attack V-weapons sites along the Channel coast.

GERMANY: In the largest USAAF strategic mission to date, 863 Eighth Air Force B-17s and B-24s are dispatched against industrial targets in and around Frankfurt am Main. In the end, a record 806 heavy bombers release more than 1,895 tons of bombs against the primary or, in the case of one 3d Bombardment Division formation,

against targets of opportunity at Ludwigshafen. Losses to enemy flak and fighter attacks are 24 B-17s and five B-24s missing and crew losses of 299 missing and 22 killed. (The 3d Bombardment Division formation bombing Ludwigshafen is savaged by GAF fighters due to a lack of escorting fighters, and it loses 11 B-17s shot down.) Operational accidents and writeoffs claim five additional bombers.

Escort and support for the Frankfurt am Main mission is provided by 632 USAAF fighters, whose pilots down 44 GAF fighters along the bomber route over France, Belgium, and Germany between 1100 and 1305 hours.

ITALY: Fifteenth Air Force B-24s attack a marshalling yard at Siena; Fifteenth Air Force B-17s attack marshalling yards at Ancona, Fabriano, Prato, and Rimini; XII Bomber Command B-26s attack bridges north of Rome; XII Bomber Command B-25s attack a marshalling yard; XII Air Support Command P-47 fighter-bombers attack a munitions plant; and XII Air Support Command A-36s and P-40s attack tactical targets in and around the Anzio beachhead and U.S. Fifth Army battle area.

Twelfth Air Force fighters and fighter-bombers down three Bf-109s and an Fi-156 in several early-afternoon engagements over central Italy.

January 30, 1944

GERMANY: Unable to visually pinpoint their briefed aircraft-industry targets in and around Brunswick, 599 Eighth Air Force B-17s and 104 B-24s attack the various industrial sites throughout the area that they can locate. Also, 39 B-24s divert to Hannover due to heavy smoke and contrails encountered over Brunswick. In all, the Eighth Air Force heavy bombers drop 1,747 tons of bombs, mostly on Brunswick. Losses are 18 B-17s (including two involved in a midair collision) and two B-24s.

A total of 635 USAAF fighters providing escort and support for the heavy bombers account for 47 GAF aircraft over

Germany and the Netherlands between 1130 and 1345 hours. 1stLt Michael J. Quirk, a P-47 pilot with the 56th Fighter Group's 62d Fighter Squadron, achieves ace status when he downs a Bf-109 near Almelo (Netherlands) at 1315 hours; and 1stLt Virgil K. Meroney, a P-47 pilot with the 352d Fighter Group's 487th Fighter Squadron, achieves ace   status when he down a Bf-109 near Zwolle at 1330 hours.

ITALY: Fifteenth Air Force B-24s attack strike targets in the Po River valley.

When the four GAF airfields and landing grounds in the Udine Airdrome complex, in northeastern Italy, are targeted, it is decided to send the 325th Fighter Group, in 60 P-47s, early and below the effective level of German radar in order to take advantage of the GAF practice of flying all their serviceable aircraft to safety as soon as incoming bombers are pinpointed. After flying more than 300 miles at wavetop height, the 325th's P-47s suddenly gain altitude and fly directly into the GAF formations just as they are being scrambled. The resulting ambush nets 37 confirmed victories for 325th Fighter Group P-47 pilots alone. Indeed, Capt Herschel H. Green, the 317th Fighter Squadron operations officer, is credited with downing four Ju-52s, a Do-217, and a Mc.202, a record that brings his personal score from three to nine victories and renders him the MTO's top-scoring ace. 2dLt George P. Novotny, also a member of the 317th Fighter Squadron, also achieves ace status when he downs two Ju-52 transports and an Hs-126 reconnaissance biplane between 1145 and 1155 hours.

Five minutes after the 325th Fighter Group opens its attack, 152 Fifteenth Air Force B-17s and 63 B-24s, escorted by 14th and 82d Fighter group P-38s, attack all four airfields in the Udine complex, causing heavy destruction.

In all, 45 GAF aircraft are downed by the fighters, numerous others are claimed by bomber gunners, and as many as two dozen are destroyed or severely damaged

on the ground. Fifteenth Air Force losses are one B-17 and two B-24s. Thanks to this attack, and that on the Aviano Airdrome on January 28, the GAF is forced to shift the weight of its regional air effort to the Klagenfurt Airdrome, just north of the Austro-Italian frontier.

All XII Bomber Command B-26s and many B-25s are grounded by bad weather, but some XII Bomber Command B-25s are able to attack towns and two road junctions; XII Air Support Command A-20s attack a town and a road junction; and XII Air Support Command fighter-bombers attack a town.

The 451st Heavy Bombardment Group, in B-24s, makes its combat debut with the Fifteenth Air Force, and the veteran 12th Medium Bombardment Group, in B-25s, stands down from combat operations with the XII Bomber Command in anticipation of its transfer to the Tenth Air Force in India.

YUGOSLAVIA: XII Air Support Command fighter-bombers attack barges and fishing boats off Zara.

January 31, 1944

AUSTRIA: Seventy-four Fifteenth Air Force B-17s attack the Klagenfurt Airdrome, just north of the Austro-Italian border. Of 67 aircraft counted on the ground at the time of the attack, 11 are claimed as destroyed and seven are claimed as damaged.

ENGLAND: The Ninth Air Force's 357th Fighter Group, in P-51s, is traded to the Eighth Air Force in return for the 358th Fighter Group, in P-47s. The 357th is assigned to the 66th Fighter Wing.

FRANCE: Seventy-four Eighth Air Force B-24s, escorted by 114 P-47s, make an unopposed attack on V-weapons sites at St.-Pol/Siracourt.

ITALY: Forty-one Fifteenth Air Force B-24s attack Aviano Airdrome; 70 Fifteenth Air Force B-17s attack the Udine Airdrome; XII Air Support Command A-20s attack a town and a road junction; XII Air Support

Command A-36s and P-40s attack several towns and a road junction east of the Anzio beachhead; and XII Air Support Command P-47 fighter-bombers attack a town.

325th Fighter Group P-47 escort pilots down two Bf-109s and three SM.82s near Udine between 1255 and 1315 hours.

NETHERLANDS: Seventy-five 4th, 78th, and 355th Fighter group P-47 dive-bombers are dispatched, along with an escort composed of 47 P-38s and 87 P-47s, to attack the Gilze-Rijen Airdrome. In all, 70 of the P-47 dive-bombers attack the briefed primary with one 500-pound bomb apiece. Also, 4th Fighter Group P-47 escort pilots down five Bf-109s near the Gilze-Rijen Airdrome between 1445 and 1500 hours, and 55th Fighter Group P-38 pilots down six Bf-109s and two FW-190s between 1520 and 1630 hours, while conducting a sweep over the Eindhoven-Venlo-Arnhem area.

FEBRUARY 1944

February 1, 1944

ENGLAND: MajGen Elwood R. Quesada replaces Col Clarence E. Crumrine as head of the IX Air Support Command, and Crumrine replaces Quesada as head of the XIX Air Support Command. Following the change of command, the IX Fighter Command effectively becomes a paper organization without personnel, and the IX Air Support Command assumes control of the Ninth Air Force fighter wings, which in turn control the Ninth Air Force operational fighter groups. In sum, IX Air Support Command is the Ninth Air Force's top fighter command.

ETO: Joint invasion planners issue a document known as the Initial Joint Plan, the air-ground-naval plan (Operation NEPTUNE) for the cross-Channel movement phase of Operation OVERLORD.

ITALY: Except for a sweep by 325th Fighter Group P-47s over the Orvieto-Viterbo area, the Fifteenth Air Force is grounded by bad weather. However, XII Bomber Command B-25s are able to attack a road junction, and XII Air Support Command A-36s, P-40s, and P-47s attack three towns, respectively.

February 2, 1944

FRANCE: Ninety-five 2d Bombardment Division B-24s, escorted by 183 P-47s, attack V-weapons sites around Pas-de-Calais.

Thirty-six IX Bomber Command B-26s, escorted by 20th Fighter Group P-38s, attack Tricqueville Airdrome.

HUNGARY: Fifteenth Air Force B-17s attack industrial targets in Budapest.

ITALY: Fifteenth Air Force B-24s attack a radar station; XII Bomber Command B-25s attack a road junction; XII Air Support Command A-20s attack a town; and XII Air Support Command A-36s and P-40s attack villages, a supply dump, and road and rail targets.

The 33d Fighter Group, an original Twelfth Air Force combat element, stands down in anticipation of its transfer to the Tenth Air Force, in India.

BriGen Gordon P. Saville replaces

MajGen Edwin J. House as commanding general of the XII Air Support Command.

February 3, 1944

GERMANY: Five hundred fifty-three 1st and 3d Bombardment division B-17s attack the Wilhelmshaven port area (primary), and 56 1st Bombardment Division B-17s attack targets of opportunity in and around Emden. However, of 193 2d Bombardment Division B-24s that get airborne for an attack on the Emden port area, only 53 are actually dispatched to the target, and even these abandon the mission after encountering heavy cloud cover over the Zuider Zee. Four B-17s are lost.

Escort and support for the heavy bombers is provided by 632 USAAF fighters, of which eight are lost with their pilots to both enemy action and various operational accidents, including fuel starvation due to severe headwinds encountered on the way to the target. USAAF fighter pilots down six GAF fighters over Germany between 1043 and 1130 hours.

ITALY: Diverted from their briefed targets because of bad weather, Fifteenth Air Force B-24s attack the railroad stations at Stimigliano and Sulmona; Fifteenth Air Force P-47s sweep over the Prato and Pontassieve areas; various XII Bomber Command medium-bomber missions are aborted in the face of bad weather; XII Air Support Command A-36s attack roads and targets of opportunity south of Rome, and bomb two towns in support of U.S. Army ground forces driving on Cassino; and XII Air Support Command P-47s attack a town and rail facilities.

February 4, 1944

ENGLAND: The United States Strategic Air Forces in Europe acronym is changed to from USSAFE to USSTAF.

MajGen Otto P. Weyland replaces Col Clarence E. Crumrine as commander of the XIX Air Support Command, and the IX Air Support Command formally assumes control of the 84th Fighter Wing headquarters (which for the moment controls no fighter groups).

The 436th Troop Carrier Group arrives in England and is assigned to IX Troop Carrier Command's 50th Troop Carrier Wing.

FRANCE: Fifteenth Air Force B-17s attack the Vichy French naval base at Toulon, but all the B-24s dispatched on the same mission abort in the face of bad weather. Also, a number of B-17s that become separated from the main force attack the rail viaduct at Antheor.

GERMANY: Three hundred forty-six 1st and 3d Bombardment Division B-17s and 27 2d Bombardment Division B-24s attack marshalling yards at Frankfurt am Main, and 197 B-17s and 63 B-24s attack numerous targets of opportunity throughout northwestern Germany. Two B-24s and 18 B-17s are lost with 203 crewmen, and three bombers are written off.

Escort and support for the bombers is provided by 56 P-38s, 537 P-47s, and 44 P-51s, of which one P-38 and its pilot are lost. 56th and 352d Fighter group P-47 pilots down eight GAF aircraft along the bomber track over Belgium between 1300 and 1330 hours.

ITALY: Almost the entire Twelfth Air Force is grounded due to bad weather, but P-40s and Spitfires are able to patrol the Anzio beachhead area, where a powerful German Army ground offensive is launched.

February 5, 1944

FRANCE: Three hundred fifty-four Eighth Air Force B-17s and 98 B-24s attack six GAF airdromes with an aggregate of 1,313 tons of bombs. Two B-24s are lost and three bombers are written off.

The 452d Heavy Bombardment Group, in B-17s, and the 453d Heavy Bombardment Group, in B-24s, make their combat debuts.

Escort and support for the heavy bombers is provided by 634 USAAF fighters, whose pilots down four GAF fighters, an He-111, and an FW-200 between 1045 and 1215 hours.

Approximately 226 IX Bomber Command B-26s attack six V-weapons sites around St.-Omer. Six B-26s are lost to typically heavy flak concentrations around the sites.

ITALY: XII Bomber Command B-25s attack a marshalling yard at Terni; XII Air Support Command A-20s attack various targets around Lanuvio and Piedimonte; and XII Air Support Command A-36s and P-40s attack numerous motor vehicles and road junctions in central Italy.

The 332d Fighter Group, the USAAF's only African-American combat unit, begins combat operations in P-39s with the Twelfth Air Force from its base at Montecorvino Airdrome, at which the group has arrived only two days earlier. The veteran, independent 99th Fighter Squadron is operationally attached to the new group.

February 6, 1944

FRANCE: Although deterred by bad weather from attacking their primary targets (several GAF airdromes in France) 160 Eighth Air Force B-17s (of 492 dispatched) and 37 B-24s (of 150 dispatched) attack three other airdromes, and nine B-24s attack a V-weapons site.

Escort and support for the bombers is provided by 638 USAAF fighters, whose pilots down 12 GAF fighters between 1045 and 1310 hours. Capt Robert A. Lamb, a P-47 pilot with the 56th Fighter Group's 61st Fighter Squadron, achieves ace status when he downs a Bf-109 near Beauvais at 1045 hours.

IX Bomber Command B-26s attack the Amiens/Glisy Airdrome, a factory, and several V-weapons sites in northern France.
ITALY: The Fifteenth Air Force is grounded by bad weather; XII Bomber Command B-25s attack a road junction at Frascati, XII Bomber Command B-26s attack a marshalling yard at Orte, and XII Air Support Command A-36s and P-40s attack numerous towns, motor vehicles, and railroad cars.

Col Charles M. McCorkle, the commanding officer of the Twelfth Air Force's 31st Fighter Group, achieves ace status when he downs a Bf-109 while flying a Spitfire over Anzio during a late-morning mission. This is one of eight GAF aircraft downed over Italy during the day by Twelfth Air Force fighter pilots.

Capt Virgil C. Fields, Jr., a six-victory Spitfire ace with the 31st Fighter Group's 307th Fighter Squadron, is shot down and killed in a dogfight over the Anzio beachhead.

February 7, 1944

ITALY: The Fifteenth Air Force is grounded by bad weather; XII Bomber Command B-25s attack a marshalling yard at Viterbo and support a withdrawal by U.S. Army troops in the face of a massive German Army counteroffensive around Anzio; XII Bomber Command B-26s attack bridge approaches; XII Air Support Command A-20s attack Piedimonte and the railroad station and road junction at Campoleone; XII Air Support Command A-36s provide direct support for U.S. Army ground forces and attack several rail targets; and XII Air Support Command P-40s attack numerous tactical targets in the Anzio and Cassino battle areas.

Twelfth Air Force fighter pilots down 20 GAF airplanes over central and northern Italy in at least seven separate engagements between 0810 and 2245 hours.

February 8, 1944

ENGLAND: With D day fast approaching (the target date is in early May), Ninth Air Force planners begin considering targets other than V-weapons sites and airfields.
FRANCE: One hundred ten 2d Bombardment Division B-24s attack V-weapons sites around the Pas de Calais with 364 tons of bombs. Escort is provided by 89 Ninth Air Force P-47s operating under VIII Fighter Command control, including the newly committed 362d Fighter Group.

In the IX Bomber Command's first two-mission day, more than 200 B-26s attack V-weapons sites and targets of opportunity in northwestern France during the morning, and more than 100 B-26s return to northwestern France to attack V-weapons sites and military installations.

GERMANY: Eighty-six Eighth Air Force B-17s attack the briefed primary, a marshalling yard at Frankfurt am Main, but 107 B-17s divert to various targets of opportunity. Thirteen B-17s are lost. Among the airmen lost is LtCol Herbert O. Wangeman, the 452d Heavy Bombardment Group commander, who is killed.

Escort and support for the heavy bombers is provided by 553 USAAF fighters, whose pilots down 14 GAF fighters over Belgium, France, Luxembourg, and western Germany between 1030 and 1215 hours. Also, seven locomotives are destroyed by 20th and 354th Fighter group pilots during the return legs of their escort missions. Three 354th Fighter Group P-51s and their pilots are lost during the strafing attacks.

ITALY: The Fifteenth Air Force's 304th Heavy Bombardment Wing takes part in its first combat operation of the war when 454th Heavy Bombardment Group B-24s, in their unit's combat debut, attack Orvieto Airdrome. Also, 47th Heavy Bombardment Wing B-24s attack the Tarquinia and Viterbo airdromes and a marshalling yard at Prato; and 5th Heavy Bombardment Wing B-17s attack marshalling yards at Verona.

XII Bomber Command B-25s attack Cisterna di Latina; XII Bomber Command B-26s attack a rail bridge, warehouses, and a marshalling yard; XII Air Support Command A-20s attack Piedimonte; XII Air Support Command A-36s and P-40s attack numerous tactical and transportation targets; and XII Air Support Command P-47s attack Atina.

February 9, 1944

CORSICA: The Twelfth Air Force's 350th Fighter Group, which is still flying P-39s bolstered by a few P-38s, is transferred from Sardinia to undertake coastal defense flights closer to the European mainland.

ENGLAND: The 344th Medium Bombardment Group, in B-26s, arrives in England for service with the IX Bomber Command.

FRANCE: In the first mission of its kind undertaken by IX Bomber Command bombers, 54 B-26s from the 322d and 386th Medium Bombardment groups attack the marshalling yard at Tergnier with excellent results. Also, 79 IX Bomber Command B-26s attack various V-weapons sites and several targets of opportunity.

ITALY: The Fifteenth Air Force is grounded by bad weather; XII Bomber Command B-25s and B-26s provide close support for U.S. Army ground forces; XII Air Support Command A-20s attack troop concentrations; and XII Air Support Command A-36s and P-40s attack troop positions, assembly points, and gun emplacements in and around the battle areas.

February 10, 1944

ENGLAND: The newly arrived 364th Fighter Group, in P-38s, is assigned to the VIII Fighter Command's 67th Fighter Wing.

FRANCE: One hundred fourteen IX Air Force B-26s attack the Poix and Beauvais/Tille airdromes, a bridge, a coastal battery, and several V-weapons sites along the Channel coast.

GERMANY: One hundred forty-one 1st Bombardment Division B-17s, escorted by 446 fighters, attack aircraft-industry targets at Brunswick. Losses are an unsustainable 29 bombers missing (20 percent of the force) with 295 crewmen.

In one of the hardest fought air battles to date over northwestern Europe, USAAF fighter pilots down a record 60 GAF fighters along the bomber routes between 1045 and 1330 hours. However, five P-38s and four P-47s are lost with their pilots. 1stLt Vermont L. Garrison, a P-47 pilot with the 4th Fighter Group's 336th Fighter Squadron, achieves ace status when he downs a Bf-109 near Dummer Lake at 1110 hours.

ITALY: All Twelfth Air Force bombers are grounded by bad weather, but XII Air Support Command A-36s, P-40s, and P-47s, and Fifteenth Air Force B-17s and B-24s conduct missions in support of Allied ground forces in the Anzio beachhead.

The 304th Heavy Bombardment Wing's 456th Heavy Bombardment Group, in B-24s, makes its combat debut.

NETHERLANDS: Due to frost and poor visibility caused by contrails, only 27 of 81 2d Bombardment Division B-24s dispatched are able to attack the Gilze-Rijen Airdrome. No aircraft are lost to enemy fire, but four B-24s are lost in operational accidents.

February 11, 1944

FRANCE: Ninety-four of 201 2d Bombardment Division B-24s dispatched attack the St.-Pol/Siracourt V-weapons site, near Pas-de-Calais. Escort is provided by 85 P-47s.

One hundred thirty-nine IX Bomber Command B-26s are dispatched to attack V-weapons sites in northern France. Most of them are recalled in the face of bad weather, but 35 are able to attack a marshalling yard at Amiens.

The 357th Fighter Group, the theater's second and the VIII Fighter Command's first P-51 unit, makes its combat debut with an unchallenged fighter sweep to Rouen.

GERMANY: One hundred fifty-seven 1st Bombardment Division B-17s attack a marshalling yard at Frankfurt am Main, and 55 B-17s attack various targets of opportunity, including Ludwigshafen.

Escort and support is provided by 82 P-38s, 486 P-47s, and 38 P-51s whose pilots down 30 GAF fighters over France, Belgium, Germany, and Luxembourg between 1055 and 1400 hours. USAAF fighter losses are eight P-38s, four P-47s, and two P-51s with all their pilots. 1stLt Stanley B. Morrill, a P-47 pilot with the 56th Fighter Group's 62d Fighter Squadron, achieves ace status when he downs a Bf-109 near Dison, Belgium, at 1100 hours; 1stLt Frederick J. Christensen, Jr., a P-47 pilot with the 56th Fighter Group's 62d Fighter Squadron, achieves ace status when he downs a Bf-109 over Bierset at 1130

hours; 1stLt James M. Morris, a P-38 pilot with the 20th Fighter Group's 77th Fighter Squadron, achieves ace status when he downs a Bf-109 near Giessen at 1156 hours; Capt Richard E. Turner, a P-51 pilot with the 354th Fighter Group's 356th Fighter Squadron, achieves ace status when he downs a Bf-109 near Luxembourg City at 1300 hours; and Col Kenneth R. Martin, the commanding officer of the 354th Fighter Group, in P-51s, achieves ace status when he downs an Me-410 over Frankfurt am Main at 1222 hours. However, Col Martin is taken prisoner after colliding with another P-51.

ITALY: The Twelfth and Fifteenth air forces are both grounded by bad weather.

February 12, 1944

ENGLAND: All the personnel of the IX Bomber Command's first A-20 unit, the 416th Light Bombardment Group, arrive in England, but the airplanes have been shipped in crates and must be painstakingly reassembled, thus delaying the group's training cycle and commitment to combat. The new group is temporarily assigned to the 99th Combat Bombardment Wing for administrative and training purposes.

The Ninth Air Force's 370th Fighter Group, in P-38s, arrives in England.

FRANCE: Ninety-seven 2d Bombardment Division B-24s, including four GH-equipped pathfinders, attack the V-weapons site at St.-Pol/Siracourt. No bombers are lost, but 29 are damaged by intense flak. Close escort is provided by 84 P-47s, and 41 354th Fighter Group P-51s conduct a sweep of the area.

ITALY: All Fifteenth Air Force B-17 and B-24 sorties that can be launched in the face of bad weather are made in support of Allied ground forces in the Anzio beachhead. Making its combat debut is the 304th Heavy Bombardment Wing's 455th Heavy Bombardment Group, in B-24s, which attacks a German Army headquarters at Grottaferrata.

XII Bomber Command B-25s attack

gun emplacements in and around Campoleone, B-26s attack Cecina, and XII Air Support Command A-36s and P-40s attack Fabrica di Roma Airdrome as well as numerous tactical targets and towns in and around the battle areas.

UNITED STATES: The entire 467th Heavy Bombardment Group flight echelon, in B-24s, departs for England via the southern ferry route.

February 13, 1944

ENGLAND: The IX Bomber Command activates the 1st Provisional Pathfinder Squadron, employing British-made GEE navigational equipment mounted in B-26s.

ETO: The CCS reaffirm that the Allied air forces in Europe will conduct a combined offensive aimed at destroying Axis "military, industrial, and economic systems," reducing Axis air power, and disrupting Axis lines of communication. However, the target list assigned in the current directive is shorter than previous lists so as to allow the Allied strategic air forces to decisively demolish each target rather than spreading themselves too thin to attack too many targets. Top priority is given to industrial targets, especially those associated with the German aircraft industry.

FRANCE: Two hundred sixty-six 3d Bombardment Division B-17s attack 12 V-weapons sites, and 138 2d Bombardment Division B-24s attack five V-weapons sites, all in the Pas-de-Calais area. Four B-24s are lost, but 16 of 40 crewmen aboard are rescued when two of them ditch off the English coast.

Escort is provided by 189 P-47s and 43 P-51s. In the day's only fighter action, 356th Fighter Group P-47 pilots down six FW-190s in running dogfights between Paris and the Channel coast between 1500 and 1520 hours.

One hundred eighty-two IX Bomber Command B-26s attack V-weapons sites along the Channel coast, and 25 B-26s confounded by bad weather attack secondary targets in the same area.

ITALY: XII Bomber Command B-26s attack a viaduct; and XII Bomber Command B-25s and XII Air Support Command A-20s, A-36s, and P-40s attack tactical targets around the Anzio beachhead.

The 81st Fighter Group stands down from combat operations preparatory to its transfer to the Fourteenth Air Force in China.

February 14, 1944

ENGLAND: A shortage of aerial bombs threatens to halt IX Bomber Command missions, and does in fact curtail a number of planned attacks while emergency stocks are scoured from the Middle East and Iceland.

The 482d Heavy Pathfinder Bombardment Group (radar and pathfinding) is transferred from the administrative control of the 1st Bombardment Division to that of the new VIII Air Force Composite Command. The unit, which has been providing pathfinder crews and airplanes on operational missions, is now tasked almost exclusively with training blind-bombing radar operators for the Eighth Air Force bomber groups, as well as with continuing experimentation with new equipment and improved techniques.

The 422d Heavy Bombardment Squadron (night leaflets) is transferred from the administrative control of the 1st Bombardment Division to that of the VIII Air Force Composite Command.

ETO: Gen Dwight D. Eisenhower establishes Supreme Headquarters, Allied Expeditionary Force (SHAEF) to oversee and direct the invasion of France and the subsequent air, sea, and land campaign in northern Europe.

ITALY: Fifteenth Air Force B-24s attack marshalling yards at eight locations and several targets of opportunity; and Fifteenth Air Force B-17s attack the marshalling yards at three locations and targets of opportunity that include the aircraft factory and airdrome at Pontedera.

Maj Lewis W. Chick, Jr., the commanding officer of the 325th Fighter Group's

317th Fighter Squadron, a P-47 unit, achieves ace status when he downs a Bf-109 while escorting B-24s near Ferrara at 1310 hours. Chick's victim is one of four GAF fighters downed by 317th Fighter Squadron pilots at this time. Overall, in various fighter actions supporting several heavy-bomber missions, Fifteenth Air Force P-38 and P-47 pilots down ten GAF fighters during the afternoon.

XII Bomber Command B-25s attack a marshalling yard; XII Air Support Command A-20s attack Grottaferrata; XII Air Support Command A-36s attack gun emplacements, motor vehicles, and rail yards in and around the battle areas; XII Air Support Command P-40s attack German Army troops and equipment around the Anzio beachhead; and XII Air Support Command P-47s attack a defended town and a dump.

NETHERLANDS: Forty-eight 353d Fighter Group P-47s, of which 23 are equipped with one 500-pound bomb apiece, are deterred by cloud cover from attacking the Eindhoven Airdrome, so they dive-bomb the Gilze/Rijen Airdrome instead.

YUGOSLAVIA: Twelfth Air Force P-40s attack a ship and a fuel dump.

February 15, 1944

BELGIUM: Forty-two VIII Fighter Command P-47 dive-bombers unable to locate their primary target in France bomb an airdrome thought to be in Belgium, either at Nieuport or Coxyde.

ENGLAND: The Eighth Air Force's independent 803d Provisional Bombardment Squadron (Radio Counter Measures) is transferred from the administrative control of the 1st Bombardment Division to that of the VIII Air Force Composite Command.

FRANCE: Fifty-two 2d Bombardment Division B-24s of the 93d, 389th, 445th, and 453d Heavy Bombardment groups attack V-weapons sites in the Pas-de-Calais area with 150 tons of bombs. Escort is provided by 95 P-47s of the 4th and 356th Fighter groups.

During the morning, 247 IX Bomber Command B-26s attack Cherbourg/ Maupertus Airdrome, several V-weapons sites, and several targets of opportunity. During the afternoon, 141 IX Bomber Command B-26s attack V-weapons construction sites along the Channel coast.

The IX Bomber Command's 391st Medium Bombardment Group, in B-26s, makes its combat debut.

ITALY: Fifteenth Air Force B-17s mount the first heavy-bomber attack on German Army fortifications on Monte Cassino, where the entire Allied ground effort has come to a halt in the face of unprecedented German resistance enhanced by a seemingly unbreachable defensive position. The 142 B-17s assigned to the mission drop 353 tons of bombs on the monastery, which, along with XII Bomber Command B-25s and B-26s, reduce the irreplaceable historical treasure to rubble. For all that, German Army resistance to follow-on ground attacks appears unfazed.

More than 60 Fifteenth Air Force B-24s attack marshalling yards at two locations; XII Bomber Command B-26s attack a rail line and a marshalling yard; XII Air Support Command A-20s attack road targets; and XII Air Support Command fighters and fighter-bombers attack numerous tactical and transportation targets in and around Rome and the battle areas.

52d Fighter Group Spitfire pilots down four GAF fighters and damage several other aircraft near Viterbo Airdrome, in central Italy, at about 1635 hours.

February 16, 1944

ITALY: Sixteen German Army divisions open an offensive against the Anzio beachhead, and so all available aircraft in the theater are ordered to conduct an all-out aerial counteroffensive against the German forces. During the first day, more than 250 fighter and fighter-bomber sorties are mounted by the XII Air Support Command and the Fifteenth Air Force. To help stem the flow of German Army troops and materiel toward

Anzio, unescorted Fifteenth Air Force B-24s attack rail lines, road and rail bridges, and marshalling yards at six locations.

XII Bomber Command B-25s attack the targets in the Campoleone area and the marshalling yard at Orte; XII Bomber Command B-26s attack a rail station, a factory, bridges at two locations, and a town; XII Air Support Command A-20s join RAF light and medium bombers in attacks on German Army troop concentrations all around the Anzio beachhead; and XII Air Support Command fighters and fighter-bombers also attack tactical targets along the U.S. Fifth Army front.

February 17, 1944

ENGLAND: The Ninth Air Force establishes an advance headquarters at Uxbridge, from which it will oversee tactical operations in France immediately following the OVERLORD invasion. The new advance headquarters will also liase with the RAF's Second Tactical Air Force.

The 52d Troop Carrier Wing headquarters begins operating with the IX Troop Carrier Command following its transfer, along with its four troop carrier groups from the Twelfth Air Force.

ITALY: Allied naval bombardment and air attacks, including more than 800 medium- and heavy-bomber sorties, help prevent the German Army counterattack from breaking into the Anzio beachhead area. The Twelfth Air Force is engaged to the hilt in turning back the German Army counterattack against the beachhead, and all types of aircraft, including Fifteenth Air Force fighters and fighter-bombers, are employed in direct- and close-support tactical missions as well as attacks on German Army lines of supply and communication. Also, unescorted Fifteenth Air Force heavy bombers attack motor-vehicle parks, troop concentrations, and storage dumps.

In the day's only air action in support of the U.S. Fifth Army, XII Air Support Command A-36s attack Monte Cassino Monestary.

The Fifteenth Air Force's 455th and 456th Heavy Bombardment groups, in B-24s, are declared operational.

February 18, 1943

ENGLAND: Headquarters, Eighth Air Force, establishes the 8th Provisional Photographic Reconnaissance Wing and appoints Col Elliott Roosevelt (the Ninth Air Force Director of Reconnaissance) as its commanding officer.

The final air echelon of the 458th Heavy Bombardment Group, in B-24s, arrives for service with the 2d Bombardment Division's 96th Combat Bombardment Wing.

ITALY: The Fifteenth Air Force and the XII Bomber Command are grounded by bad weather; XII Air Support Command A-20s attack troop concentrations at Piedimonte; and A-36s and P-40s mount numerous direct-support missions and sorties against German Army forces trying to break into the Anzio beachhead.

Several attempted GAF attacks against the Anzio beachhead are turned back by patrolling USAAF fighters, and one Bf-109 is downed over the beachhead by a 31st Fighter Group Spitfire pilot.

February 19, 1944

ITALY: XII Bomber Command B-25s attack German Army troop concentrations north of the Anzio beachhead area, and XII Air Support Command A-36s and P-40s mount more than 200 sorties against tactical targets along the Anzio battle lines.

52d Fighter Group Spitfire pilots down 12 Bf-109s in a running fight over central Italy between 1310 and 1355 hours, and other Twelfth Air Force fighter pilots down six other GAF fighters throughout the day.

Col Peter S. Rask becomes commanding officer of the XII Troop Carrier Command, which is slated to be disbanded within several weeks.

February 20, 1944

GERMANY: The Eighth Air Force kicks

off the "Big Week" bomber offensive (Operation ARGUMENT) against German industrial targets. The objective is to mount at least one large bomber strike every day for a full week, and the goal, aside from damaging industrial targets, is to draw large parts of the GAF interceptor force into attritional battles. The February 20 mission against aircraft-industry targets in and around Leipzig (1st Bombardment Division) and Brunswick (2d Bombardment Division), and the Tutow Airdrome (3d Bombardment Division) is the first 1,000-bomber mission ever attempted, but aborts for various reasons pare the actual number of heavy bombers completing the mission from 1,003 dispatched to 823 effective.

Two hundred seventy-six 1st Bombardment Division B-17s attack the Leipzig/Mockau Airdrome and several briefed aircraft-industry plants, and 64 1st Bombardment Division B-17s attack Oschersleben and other targets of opportunity. Seven B-17s are lost.

During the 1st Bombardment Division Leipzig attack, 1stLt William R. Lawley, Jr., the pilot of a 305th Heavy Bombardment Group B-17, is awarded a Medal of Honor after being severely wounded, as are most of his crewmembers. After pulling out of a steep dive, Lawley realizes that most of his crewmen would be unable to bail out, so he stays at the control sand nurses the damaged airplane back to England, where he makes a successful crash-landing. Also, in a 351st Heavy Bombardment Group B-17, in which the co-pilot is killed and the pilot is too severely wounded to fly the damaged airplane, 2dLt Walter E. Truemper, the navigator, and Sgt Archibald Mathies, the flight engineer, bring the plane back to England. After the rest of the crew—except for the wounded pilot—has bailed out over their home base at Polebrook, Truemper and Mathies attempt to land. However, the airplane crashes on the fourth attempt, and all three men aboard are killed. Truemper and Mathies are awarded posthumous Medals of Honor.

One hundred sixty-three 2d Bombardment Division B-24s attack several aircraft-industry factories around Brunswick and Gotha, as briefed, but 81 other B-24s are obliged for various reasons to attack several wide-ranging targets of opportunity. Eight B-24s are lost.

Severe cloud cover renders the planned 3d Bombardment Division attacks something of a shambles, but 296 B-17s nevertheless attack Tutow Airdrome and several wide-ranging targets of opportunity. Six B-17s are lost and one B-17 lands in Sweden.

Of the record 835 USAAF fighters dispatched, four are lost with their pilots. USAAF fighter pilots down 59 GAF fighters and two Ju-88 attack aircraft over Germany and Belgium between 1230 and 1520 hours. Two P-51 pilots of the 354th Fighter Group's 353d Fighter Squadron achieve ace status: Capt Don M. Beerbower, when he downs a Bf-109 near Oschersleben at 1310 hours and a Bf-110 near Muhlhausen at 1345 hours; and Capt Jack T. Bradley, when he downs a Bf-109 near Dessau at 1320 hours. Also, Capt Lindol F. Graham, a P-38 pilot with the 20th Fighter Group's 79th Fighter Squadron, achieves ace status when he downs two Bf-110s near Brunswick at 1330 hours; Capt Leroy A. Schreiber, a P-51 pilot with the 56th Fighter Group's 62d Fighter Squadron, achieves ace status with 7.5 victories, when he downs three Bf-109s near Steinhuder Lake at 1345 hours; Capt Norman E. Olson, a P-47 pilot with the 355th Fighter Group's 357th Fighter Squadron, achieves ace status when he downs a Bf-109 over Siegen at 1422 hours; and 2dLt Grant M. Turley, a P-47 pilot with the 78th Fighter Group's 82d Fighter Squadron, achieves ace status when he downs a Bf-109 near Koblenz at 1450 hours.

This day's action is marked by two other special events: the first use in combat of the 150-gallon jettisonable belly tank by USAAF fighters supporting the 1st Bombardment Division over Leipzig, and the first double missions flown by the 55th, 356th, 361st, and 362d Fighter groups.

The day's planned mission by the Fifteenth Air Force B-17s against aircraft-industry targets at Regensburg is aborted due to icing conditions at altitude over the Alps. **ITALY:** One hundred five Fifteenth Air Force B-24s support Allied ground forces in the Anzio beachhead; XII Bomber Command B-25s attack assembly areas and dumps north of the Anzio beachhead; XII Bomber Command B-26s attack troop concentrations along roads around Vallalta; XII Air Support Command A-20s attack troop concentrations and numerous motor vehicles; and XII Air Support Command A-36s and P-40s attack two towns, troops, trucks, tanks, and a factory.

Thanks in large part to the response of the theater air forces, the German Army offensive against the Anzio beachhead is decisively defeated. **NETHERLANDS:** Thirty-five IX Bomber Command B-26s attack Haamstede Airdrome (target of opportunity), but approximately 100 other B-26s dispatched against several airdromes are forced to abort in the face of bad weather.

February 21, 1944

BELGIUM: Of more than 200 IX Bomber Command B-26s dispatched in the morning against Coxyde/Furnes Airdrome, only 18 locate and attack the target, and all the rest abort in the face of bad weather. It is well worth noting that the B-26 leading the successful attack is a pathfinder model from IX Bomber Command's 1st Provisional Pathfinder Squadron—making that unit's combat debut. The B-26 pathfinder crew is able to locate the target through the weather because of the GEE navigational radar it has aboard. This is the Ninth Air Force's first use of blind-bombing equipment. **ENGLAND:** One hundred eighty-five IX Bomber Command B-26s dispatched against airdromes in France and the Netherlands are recalled because of bad weather.

MajGen Elwood R. Quesada is reap-

pointed to head the moribund IX Fighter Command, temporarily an unmanned paper organization subordinate to Headquarters, Ninth Air Force. The reconstituted IX Fighter Command will oversee operations and training of all Ninth Air Force fighter units. Until operational units are assigned, however, the small XIX Air Support Command headquarters establishment will handle administrative duties for the IX Fighter Command.

The veteran 52d Troop Carrier Wing arrives in England from the Mediterranean area and is assigned to the IX Troop Carrier Command. It consists of the 61st, 313th, 315th, and 316th Troop Carrier groups. (The last named was the old Ninth Air Force's first and only troop carrier unit in North Africa and Sicily.)

The 466th Heavy Bombardment Group, in B-24s, arrives from the United States via the southern ferry route for service with the 2d Bombardment Division.

The 440th Troop Carrier Group arrives from the United States for service with the IX Troop Carrier Command.

The Ninth Air Force's 10th Photographic Reconnaissance Group headquarters and the group's 30th Photographic Reconnaissance Squadron arrive from the United States. (The group's 31st, 33d, and 34th Photographic Reconnaissance squadrons are slated to arrive over the next two months.) The entire group is equipped with F-5 aircraft. **GERMANY:** Although briefed for attacks against airdromes at Gutersloh, Lippstadt, and Werl, 285 of 336 1st Bombardment Division B-17s are obliged by bad weather to attack targets of opportunity—seven airdromes and a marshalling yard at Lingen.

The 457th Heavy Bombardment Group, in B-17s, makes its combat debut as part of the 1st Bombardment Division's 94th Combat Bombardment Wing.

The 2d Bombardment Division is briefed to attack the Achmer and Handorf airdromes, but bad weather disperses the B-24 formations. Achmer Airdrome is attacked by only 11 aircraft while 203 others attack targets of opportunity—three other airdromes and Lingen.

One hundred seventy-five of the 281 3d Bombardment Division B-17s dispatched attacked their briefed primaries, Diepholz Airdrome and the city of Brunswick, but bad weather obliges 88 other B-17s to divert to targets of opportunity—two GAF airdromes and the city of Hannover.

Overall, 13 B-17s and three B-24s are lost with 163 crewmen, and six B-17s and one B-24 written off.

Escort and support is provided by 69 P-38s, 542 P-47s, and 68 P-51s, of which two P-47s and three P-51s are lost with their pilots. USAAF fighter pilots down 27 GAF fighters over Germany and the Netherlands between 1320 and 1545 hours. 1stLt Charles F. Gumm, Jr., a P-51 pilot with the 354th Fighter Group's 355th Fighter Squadron, achieves ace status when he downs a Bf-110 over Brunswick at about 1430 hours; and Capt Robert W. Stephens, a P-51 pilot with the 354th Fighter Group's 355th Fighter Squadron, achieves ace status when he downs a Bf-110 over Brunswick at 1430 hours. Gumm and Stephens are the Ninth Air Force's first aces since the move to England.

ITALY: Fifteenth Air Force heavy bombers are grounded by bad weather; XII Bomber Command B-25s attack the marshalling yards at Orte; XII Bomber Command B-26s and XII Air Support Command A-36s and P-40s attack troop concentrations, a fuel dump, and tanks and motor vehicles around Campoleone; and XII Air Support Command fighter-bombers also block the Itri-Gaeta road.

USAAF fighter pilots down three Bf-109s over Italy.

February 22, 1944

ENGLAND: Headquarters, Eighth Air Force, is officially reconstituted as Headquarters, U.S. Strategic Air Forces in Europe (USSTAF), and the VIII Bomber Command headquarters is officially renamed Headquarters, Eighth Air Force. Unofficially, this arrangement has been in effect since January 6.

The 53d Troop Carrier Wing headquarters arrives in England and is assigned to the IX Troop Carrier Command. Its subordinate units are the 437th, 438th, and 439th Troop Carrier groups, which all arrived in England earlier in the month.

GERMANY: As part of the Big Week operation, in the first successful coordinated attack of its kind, Eighth and Fifteenth air force heavy bombers strike targets in Germany from two directions at the same time. However, in the case of the U.K.-based heavy bombers, severe weather conditions over northwestern Europe oblige 544 of 799 B-17s and B-24s to be recalled or abort on their own. Just 81 of 289 1st Bombardment Division B-17s attack the briefed primaries—aircraft-industry factories at Aschersleben and Bernburg—while 100 others attack various targets of opportunity. The entire 3d Bombardment Division (333 B-17s) is recalled. And only 74 of 177 2d Bombardment Division B-24s dispatched drop their bombs—and blanket four Dutch towns in the mistaken notion that they are over Germany. To top off this incredibly bad day, 38 B-17s, three B-24s, and 397 crewmen are lost, four B-17s are written off, and 35 crewmen are killed.

Escort and support for the Eighth Air Force heavy bombers is provided by 659 USAAF fighters, of which eight P-47s and three P-51s are lost with their pilots. One of the missing pilots is Maj Walter C. Beckham, an 18-victory P-47 ace with the 353d Fighter Group's 351st Fighter Squadron, who is shot down and taken prisoner while strafing parked FW-190s at the Ostheim Airdrome. At the time he is downed, Beckham is the Eighth Air Force's top-scoring ace.

While escorting the bombers and looking for targets to attack, USAAF fighter pilots down 57 GAF fighters, a Ju-88, and an Italian-made flying boat over Germany,

Belgium, and the Netherlands between 1215 and 1555 hours. 1stLt George F. Hall, a P-47 pilot with the 56th Fighter Group's 63d Fighter Squadron, achieves ace status when he downs two Bf-110s near Paderborn at 1245 hours; Capt John W. Vogt, Jr., a P-47 pilot with the 56th Fighter Group's 63d Fighter Squadron, achieves ace status when he downs a Bf-110 near Paderborn at 1245 hours; 1stLt Donovan F. Smith, a P-47 pilot with the 56th Fighter Group's 61st Fighter Squadron, achieves ace status when he downs an FW-190 near Lippstadt at 1350 hours; Capt James N. Poindexter, a P-47 pilot with the 353d Fighter Group's 352d Fighter Squadron, achieves ace status when he downs two Bf-109s near Cologne at 1510 hours; and Maj Jack J. Oberhansly, the commanding officer of the 78th Fighter Group's 82d Fighter Squadron, in P-47s, achieves ace status when he shares in the downing of two FW-190s over Walcheren Island (Netherlands) at 1510 hours.

The 365th Fighter Group, a IX Fighter Command P-47 unit, makes its combat debut while on loan to the Eighth Air Force.

In the main Fifteenth Air Force attack of the day—against aircraft factories in the city of Regensburg, in southern Germany—118 B-24s demolish a good part of the Obertraubling Messerschmitt fighter assembly plant, but an attack by an estimated 120 GAF fighters downs 14 B-24s. At the same time, 65 B-17s attack the nearby Prufening Messerschmitt components factory with 153 tons of bombs, losing five aircraft to GAF fighters. Also hit by 42 tons of bombs is the marshalling yard at Peterhausen, a secondary target that is struck after 21 Fifteenth Air Force B-17s go astray of the main body of heavy bombers bound for Regensburg.

Penetration and target escort is provided by 122 Fifteenth Air Force P-38s, and withdrawal escort is provided by 63 P-47s. One P-38 and one P-47 are lost. Despite the ample opportunities to score, no GAF fighters are downed on this mission by Fifteenth Air Force fighters.

ITALY: XII Bomber Command B-25s attack a marshalling yard and a rail bridge; XII Bomber Command B-26s attack a rail bridge; XII Air Support Command A-20s, P-40s, and P-47s attack targets near Campoleone; XII Air Support Command A-36s attack gun emplacements and troops near Carroceto; and XII Air Support Command P-47s attack the road net around Roccasecca.

Fighter pilots of the Twelfth Air Force's 31st and 324th Fighter groups down nine Bf-109s and damage or possibly down eight other GAF fighters in two separate engagements over central Italy between 0750 and 0910 hours.

NETHERLANDS: Sixty-six IX Bomber Command B-26s attack Gilze-Rijen Airdrome, but more than 100 others abort in the face of bad weather.

YUGOSLAVIA: 304th Heavy Bombardment Wing B-24s attack port facilities at Sibenik, and 28 5th Heavy Bombardment Wing B-17s attack the airdrome at Zagreb.

February 23, 1944

AUSTRIA: Eighty-one Fifteenth Air Force B-24s attack an aircraft assembly plant at Steyr, and 21 B-24s demolish much of the Steyr factory responsible for 10 percent of Germany's anti-friction ball-bearing production. Although the bombing results are excellent, the bomber force is attacked over the Alps during the withdrawal by an estimated 120 GAF fighters, and it sustains the Fifteenth Air Force's worst one-day loss ratio to date: 17 B-24s downed against just one Me-210 downed and two Bf-110s damaged by 14th Fighter Group P-38 escort pilots.

GERMANY: 1stLt John B. Carder, a P-51 pilot with the 357th Fighter Group's 364th Fighter Squadron, shoots down over Germany a P-47 with GAF markings. Although the markings and the downing show up clearly on Carder's gun-camera film, the victory is not officially awarded.

ITALY: Almost the entire Twelfth Air Force is grounded by bad weather, but a small number of XII Air Support Command

P-40s are able to patrol the Anzio beach-head area and attack gun emplacements near Campoleone.

February 24, 1944

AUSTRIA: In another mission coordinated with the Eighth Air Force, Fifteenth Air Force B-17s attack aircraft-components targets at Steyr. Beginning 100 miles short of the target, at least 130 GAF fighters arriving in waves mount unrelenting attacks, including aerial-rocket attacks, that down ten 2d Heavy Bombardment Group B-17s before a single bomb is dropped. Despite intense flak coverage, a total of 87 B-17s drop 261 tons of bombs that completely level the primary target and also destroy a large supply of ball bearings stored in another facility. Once beyond the flak belt, the bombers are again attacked by waves of GAF fighters, some firing rockets. Although a withdrawal-escort force of 87 P-38s and 59 P-47s arrives, four more 2d Heavy Bombardment Group B-17s and two B-17s from other groups are lost. Three P-38s are also lost, but 82d Fighter Group P-38 pilots down two Bf-109s and eight Bf-110s and Me-210s after 1300 hours, and a 325th Fighter Group P-47 pilot is credited with downing two Bf-109s, bringing the total score to 12 GAF fighters downed by USAAF fighters plus 11 GAF fighters claimed as destroyed by bomber gunners.
ENGLAND: The IX Air Support Command advance headquarters at Uxbridge assumes operational control for fighter groups that have been on loan to the VIII Fighter Command. Also, the 70th Fighter Wing headquarters begins overseeing operations of several Ninth Air Force fighter groups.
FRANCE: One hundred forty-five IX Bomber Command B-26s mount afternoon attacks against V-weapons sites between St.-Omer and Abbeville.
GERMANY: Continuing the Big Week operation, the Eighth Air Force dispatches 505 heavy bombers against aviation-industry targets at Gotha, Kreising, Posen (Poznan,

Poland), Schweinfurt, and Tutow. In the end, due to mishaps and bad weather, 295 3d Bombardment Division B-17s attack Rostock and other targets of opportunity; 238 1st Bombardment Division B-17s attack Schweinfurt, as briefed; 169 2d Bombardment Division B-24s attack Gotha, as briefed; and 44 B-24s accidentally release their bombs over Eisenach. Losses for the day are 16 B-17s and 33 B-24s with 484 crewmen missing and five crewmen killed, plus two writeoffs and a B-17 interned in Sweden.

Escort and support for the Eighth Air Force bombers sent against Gotha and Schweinfurt is provided by 70 P-38s, 609 P-47s, and 88 P-51s, including double missions flown by the 359th and 365th Fighter groups. Against credits for downing 36 GAF fighters and a Ju-88 over Germany (and one FW-190 over Linz, Austria) between 1215 and 1430 hours, USAAF fighter losses are four P-38s, four P-47s, and two P-51s and their pilots.

1stLt John H. Truluck, Jr., a P-47 pilot with the 56th Fighter Group's 63d Fighter Squadron, achieves ace status when he downs an FW-190 over Herford at 1255 hours; and Maj James C. Stewart, the commanding officer of the 56th Fighter Group's 61st Fighter Squadron, in P-47s, achieves ace status when he downs an FW-190 over Kassel at 1300 hours.

The 363d Fighter Group, a IX Fighter Command P-51 unit, makes its combat debut while on loan to the Eighth Air Force; and the 458th Heavy Bombardment Group, in B-24s, makes its combat debut.

Demonstrating the awesome potential of the Combined Bomber Offensive, RAF heavy bombers follow up on the Eighth Air Force's daylight attack on Schweinfurt with an attack on the city during the night of February 24–25.
ITALY: XII Bomber Command B-26s attack Fabrica di Roma Airdrome; and XII Air Support Command A-36s, P-40s, and P-47s attack gun emplacements, tanks, troops, trucks, motor vehicles, and a bridge.

Twenty-seven Fifteenth Air Force B-17s that become separated from the force bound for Steyr, Austria, attack the oil refinery at Fiume. One B-17 is lost.

NETHERLANDS: During the morning, 226 IX Bomber Command B-26s attack the Deelen, Leeuwarden, and Gilze-Rijen airdromes.

February 25, 1944

AUSTRIA: A small force of Fifteenth Air Force B-17s attacks the Klagenfurt Airdrome, and 16 Fifteenth Air Force B-24s that become separated from the day's main effort against Regensburg, Germany, attack a marshalling yard at Zell-am-See. A 14th Fighter Group P-38 escort pilot downs a Bf-110 south of Salzburg at 1340 hours.

BELGIUM: IX Bomber Command B-26s mount a morning attack against St.-Trond Airdrome.

ENGLAND: MajGen Paul L. Williams succeeds MajGen Benjamin F. Giles as head of the IX Troop Carrier Command.

FRANCE: IX Bomber Command B-26s mount a morning attack against Cambrai/Epinoy Airdrome, but 164 B-26s dispatched in the afternoon against various military targets in northern France are recalled because of bad weather.

Aircraft from the Ninth Air Force's 10th Photographic Reconnaissance Group complete their unit's first operational mission, over the Cherbourg Peninsula.

GERMANY: The Eighth and Fifteenth air forces conclude Big Week with coordinated attacks on aircraft-industry targets, including a one-two punch against Regensburg.

One hundred ninety-six 1st Bombardment Division B-17s attack aircraft-industry factories at Augsburg; 50 1st Bombardment Division B-17s attack aircraft-industry factories at Stuttgart; 172 2d Bombardment Division B-24s attack aircraft-industry factories at Furth; and 267 3d Bombardment Division B-17s attack aircraft-industry factories at Regensburg. Twenty-five B-17s and six B-24s are lost with 305 crewmen killed or missing; three B-17s are written off, and one B-17 lands in Switzerland.

Escort and support for the bombers is provided by 899 Eighth and Ninth air force fighter sorties, including double missions flown by the 361st, 363d, and 365th Fighter groups. One P-47 and two P-51s are lost with their pilots.

USAAF fighter pilots down 25 GAF fighters and two Ju-88s over Germany, France, Luxembourg, and Belgium between 1206 and 1515 hours. 1stLt Frank Q. O'Connor, a P-51 pilot with the 354th Fighter Group's 356th Fighter Squadron, achieves ace status when he downs a Bf-109 near Mannheim at 1440 hours.

German opposition against the main Fifteenth Air Force strike against Regensburg is concentrated on the 36 B-17s that are leading the main body of 103 47th Heavy Bombardment Wing B-24s by a considerable margin. Owing to a lack of sufficient long-range fighters in the theater, the heavy bombers are not escorted during the target-penetration phase of the mission; 85 P-38s and 40 P-47s will be on hand, however, during target withdrawal. More than 100 GAF fighters attack the in-bound B-17s over Fiume and manage to down 11 301st Heavy Bombardment Group B-17s long before the target is reached. The bombing run by the 25 remaining lead B-17s hits the primary target with many bombs, but the GAF fighters return once the B-17s clear the flak belt, and they continue to make firing passes for another 30 minutes, albeit without downing any more B-17s. Claims by bomber gunners amount to an improbably high 31 GAF fighters downed, but many claims are undoubtedly correct.

During the second phase of the attack, by 103 304th Heavy Bombardment Wing B-24s, GAF fighters begin attacking the heavy bombers some 300 miles from the target, and continue to do so in several waves all the way to Regensburg and on the way out, beyond the flak belt. The Prufening Messerschmitt aircraft components factory is severely damaged by bombs.

In sum, of the 149 Fifteenth Air Force heavy bombers dispatched to attack the Prufening Messerschmitt factory, ten abort and 33 are downed. The onus for the exceptionally high 24 percent loss rate among the bombers is put on the inadequate number of long-range fighter escorts with sufficient range to reach Germany from bases in southern Italy.

Six Fifteenth Air Force heavy bombers are lost attacking other targets, as well as three P-38s and a P-47 engaged in the Regensburg withdrawal.

Shortly after the Fifteenth Air Force heavy bombers depart the Regensburg area, 267 Eighth Air Force B-17s arrive to find that most of the GAF fighters are on the ground being refueled and rearmed. Troubled by fewer than 50 GAF fighters (which nonetheless down 12 B-17s) the Eighth Air Force bombers complete the destruction of the Prufening factory and also severely damage the Obertraubling aircraft-industry plant.

Other Eighth Air Force bombers attack Furth and Stuttgart, and RAF Bomber Command bombers return to Stuttgart during the night of February 25–26.

ITALY: Sixteen 304th Heavy Bombardment Wing B-24s attack a marshalling yard at Fiume; and XII Air Support Command A-36s and P-40s attack numerous targets in or near the battle areas.

YUGOSLAVIA: Twenty-one Fifteenth Air Force B-17s attack warehouses in the dock area at Pola, and Fifteenth Air Force B-24s attack the port area at Zara.

February 26, 1944

YUGOSLAVIA: In the day's only air action in all of Europe, XII Air Support Command P-47s attack ships near Velaluka.

February 27, 1944

ENGLAND: The VIII Air Force Composite Command assumes control of the 36th and 406th Heavy Bombardment squadrons, special-operations units that have been under the temporary administrative control of

the 482d Heavy Pathfinding Bombardment Group since December 4, 1943.

FRANCE: Of 258 Eighth Air Force B-17s dispatched against a number of V-weapons sites around Pas-de-Calais, 109 attack assigned targets and 23 attack various targets of opportunity. Escort for the B-17s is provided by 197 fighters, including 21 P-51s of a newly reequipped squadron of the 4th Fighter Group. One GAF fighter is downed against no USAAF losses.

Three 2d Bombardment Division B-24 groups are dispatched against V-weapons sites but, of 81 B-24s dispatched, only 49 attack their assigned targets. Escort for the B-24s is provided by 61 56th Fighter Group P-47s.

ITALY: Most of the Twelfth Air Force is grounded by bad weather, but XII Air Support Command A-36s attack Guidonia and Littoria airdromes, the port area at Ladispoli, and rail cars north of Rome; and P-40s attack Littoria and nearby road targets.

February 28, 1944

FRANCE: One hundred eighty IX Bomber Command B-26s attack Rosieres-en-Santerre Airdrome and V-weapons sites, but bad weather hampers the bombing, and 34 other B-26s are unable to locate targets.

ITALY: XII Bomber Command B-26s attack the landing ground at Canino, but heavy cloud cover causes most bombs to miss the target. Also, XII Air Support Command A-36s attack Guidonia, Littoria, and Marcigliana airdromes.

YUGOSLAVIA: XII Air Support Command P-47s attack vessels off Dubrovnik as well as targets of opportunity on land.

February 29, 1944

FRANCE: Thirty-eight 2d Bombardment Division B-24s, escorted by 79 P-47s, attack a V-weapons site with more than 112 tons of bombs. One P-47 is lost over France due to engine failure, and its pilot is captured.

Nineteen IX Bomber Command B-26s

attack Breck-sur-Mer and nearby coastal fortifications, but 218 other B-26s dispatched to attack V-weapons sites abort in the face of bad weather.

GERMANY: Two hundred fifteen 3d Bombardment Division B-17s attack aircraft-industry targets in and around Brunswick with about 425 tons of bombs. One B-17 ditches off the Dutch coast and its crew is taken prisoner. Escort and support for the Brunswick mission is provided by 554 fighters, of which four are lost with their pilots.

One Ju-52 is downed over the Netherlands at 1025 hours. It is strikingly obvious to many of the men involved in this day's mission that the GAF has been exhausted by the Big Week offensive.

ITALY: The Fifteenth Air Force is grounded by bad weather over its scheduled targets; XII Bomber Command B-25s attack troop positions and gun emplacements; XII Bomber Command B-26s attack Viterbo Airdrome and satellite fields, as well as targets of opportunity in central Italy; XII Air Support Command A-20s, A-36s, and P-40s attack troop concentrations around the Anzio beachhead; XII Air Support Command P-40s attack German Army tanks near Littoria and a barracks and rail yard at Cisterna; and XII Air Support Command P-47s attack the railroad station at Giulianova.

Three FW-190s are downed over central Italy by 31st Fighter Group Spitfire pilots.

YUGOSLAVIA: IX Air Support Command P-47s attack ships off Dubrovnik.

MARCH 1944

March 1, 1944

ENGLAND: The VIII Air Force Service Command is redesignated Air Service Command, USSTAF; the VIII Strategic Air Depot Area is redesignated VIII Air Force Service Command; the IX Troop Carrier Command establishes a pathfinder school to train special crews for invasion duties; and the 71st Fighter Wing headquarters begins overseeing the operations of several Ninth Air Force fighter groups.

ITALY: Twelfth and Fifteenth air force bombers are grounded by bad weather; XII Air Support Command P-40s attack motor vehicles and gun emplacements in support of the U.S. Fifth Army; and XII Air Support Command P-47s attack a vessel in the Adriatic Sea.

The XII Provisional Troop Carrier Command is disbanded, and the 51st Troop Carrier Wing is placed directly under Head-quarters, Twelfth Air Force; Headquarters, XII Bomber Command, is effectively disbanded, and the 42d Medium Bombard-ment Wing (three B-26 groups) and the 57th Medium Bombardment Wing (three B-25 groups) are placed directly under Headquar-ters, Twelfth Air Force. The XII Air Sup-port Command and XII Fighter Command remain in operation as they are.

March 2, 1944

FRANCE: Eighty-four 3d Bombardment Division B-17s, escorted by 281 USAAF fighters, attack the Chartres Airdrome with 158 tons of bombs. One B-17 is lost.

In two separate missions, the IX Bomber Command mounts a total of 353 B-26 sorties against V-weapons sites and the Amiens/Glisy, Rosieres-en-Santerre, and Tergnier airdromes. Also, in IX Bomber Command's first directed mission against the Axis rail system, 126 B-26s attack a marshalling yard at Amiens.

GERMANY: Of 327 1st Bombardment Division B-17s and 154 2d Bombardment Division B-24s dispatched to attack mar-shalling yards at Frankfurt am Main, only 101 B-17s and 36 B-24s are able to locate the assigned target area through thick cloud cover. One hundred ninety-two

B-17s and 46 B-24s attack various targets of opportunity.

The 458th Heavy Bombardment Group, a B-24 unit assigned to the 2d Bombardment Division's 96th Combat Bombardment Wing, makes it combat debut.

Of 589 USAAF fighters assigned to escort and support the Frankfurt am Main mission, four are lost with three of the pilots.

VIII Fighter Command escort pilots down 16 GAF fighters along the heavy-bomber route, primarily over Belgium, between 1145 and 1420 hours. 1stLt Vasseure F. Wynn, a P-51 pilot with the 4th Fighter Group's 334th Fighter Squadron, achieves ace status when he downs a Bf-109 near Koblenz at 1155 hours. (Wynn's score includes 2.5 victories earned while he was flying with the RAF.)

ITALY: Fifteenth Air Force B-17s, B-24s, P-38s, and P-47s mount 351 bomber sorties and more than 150 fighter sorties against targets around the Anzio beachhead; Twelfth Air Force B-26s attack an assembly area near Carroceto, and B-25s and B-26s attack an assembly area and gun emplacements near Cisterna di Roma; and XII Air Support Command A-36s and P-40s attack troop positions and gun emplacements in the Anzio battle area and around Cisterna and Littoria.

The 304th Heavy Bombardment Wing's 459th Heavy Bombardment Group, in B-24s, makes its combat debut.

YUGOSLAVIA: XII Air Support Command P-47s attack a ship off Sibenik.

March 3, 1944

FRANCE: Two hundred eighteen IX Bomber Command B-26s attack German Army installations at two locations, and the Beauvais/Tille, Laon/Couvron, Montdidier, Rosieres-en-Santerre, and Roye/Amy airdromes.

GERMANY: Seven hundred forty-eight Eighth Air Force heavy bombers are dispatched against industrial and aviation-industry targets in Berlin, Oranienburg, and Erkner, but bad weather results in 669 aborts. Only 75 B-17s and four B-24s attack targets of opportunity. Eight heavy bombers are lost to enemy fire, and three are downed following a midair collision. Col Harold J. Rau, the commanding officer of the 20th Fighter Group, in P-38s, becomes the first USAAF fighter pilot to catch a distant glimpse of the city of Berlin.

A record 730 USAAF fighters are dispatched to escort the heavy bombers, including VIII Fighter Command's new 364th Fighter Group, in P-38s, in its combat debut. Of these, six P-51s and one P-38 are lost with six pilots, and one P-47 crash-lands at its base.

VIII Fighter Command escort pilots down eight GAF fighters over Germany between 1130 and 1230 hours. 1stLt Vermont Garrison, a P-47 ace with the 4th Fighter Group's 336th Fighter Squadron, downs a Bf-109 near Berlin at about 1215, bringing his personal tally to 7.333 confirmed victories, but he is downed by flak and taken prisoner.

HUNGARY: 1stLt Max J. Wright, a P-38 pilot with the 14th Fighter Group's 48th Fighter Squadron, achieves ace status when he downs an Me-210 over Budapest at 1103 hours.

ITALY: The Twelfth Air Force opens an offensive against rail lines running through Rome. All three B-25 groups of the 57th Medium Bombardment Wing are grounded by bad weather, but an attack by all three B-26 groups of the 42d Medium Bombardment Wing against a marshalling yard at Ostiense is among the most accurate of the war, with all bombs falling within 200 yards of the target. Damage to tracks, facilities, and rolling stock is extensive. B-26s also attack Benedetto de Marsi.

Fifteenth Air Force B-24s attack the landing ground at Canino, and the Fabrica di Roma and Viterbo airdromes, but results are poor due to cloudy weather over the targets; at least 80 B-24s and more than 100 P-38s abort in the face of bad weather; and Fifteenth Air Force B-17s attack Rome's

Littorio and Tiburtina marshalling yards with results rated as "good." While supporting the Viterbo attack, 325th Fighter Group P-47 pilots down seven GAF fighters between 1135 hours and noon.

XII Air Support Command A-36s attack a tent camp and a train between Rome and Magliano Romano, and P-40s attack gun emplacements north of the Anzio beachhead area.

March 4, 1944

ENGLAND: The 84th Fighter Wing headquarters begins overseeing the operations of several Ninth Air Force fighter groups.
FRANCE: Two hundred fifty-one IX Bomber Command B-26s and 21 A-20s dispatched against several airfields in France abort in the face of heavy cloud cover over the targets. This was to have been the combat debut of the 416th Light Bombardment Group, the Ninth Air Force's first operational A-20 unit.
GERMANY: Although 502 1st and 3d Bombardment division B-17s are dispatched to attack industrial suburbs of Berlin, unfavorable weather conditions over most of Germany prevent all but one 30-plane 3d Division combat wing from reaching its primary target. Of these 30 B-17s, five are lost to enemy action. A total of 219 1st and 3d Bomber division B-17s attack targets of opportunity in the Ruhr, and ten of these B-17s are lost to enemy action. All the remaining B-17s return to base with their bombs. Due to weather reports from Germany, the 2d Bombardment Division abandons this mission before leaving English airspace.

Of 770 USAAF fighters dispatched, a record 24 fail to return to their bases. Of these, it appears that 11 of 33 P-51s dispatched by the 363d Fighter Group are lost in weather-related accidents over the Dutch coast.

VIII Fighter Command escort pilots down seven GAF fighters over Germany between 1215 and 1340 hours.

A scheduled attack by Fifteenth Air Force B-17s against Breslau is aborted in the face of bad weather.
ITALY: Most of the Twelfth Air Force is grounded by bad weather, but a few XII Air Support Command P-40s attack gun emplacements in the battle area.

March 5, 1944

ENGLAND: The 405th Fighter Group, in P-47s, arrives in England for service with the Ninth Air Force.
FRANCE: Two hundred seven IX Bomber Command B-26s attack V-weapons sites around St.-Omer and Abbeville.

Two hundred nineteen 2d Bombardment Division B-24s are dispatched against three GAF airdromes in France, but cloud cover over the targets forces 164 to attack four *other* airdromes, and the rest abort.

Escort for the B-24s is provided by 307 USAAF fighters, of which five are lost in action with four pilots and three are lost in operational accidents with one pilot. One of the missing pilots is Col Henry R. Spicer, the 357th Fighter Group commander, who is shot down and taken prisoner.

VIII Fighter Command escort pilots down 16 GAF aircraft over France between 1130 and 1305 hours. 1stLt Spiros N. Pissanos, a P-51 pilot with the 4th Fighter Group's 334th Fighter Squadron, achieves ace status when he downs two Bf-109s near Bordeaux at noon. Engine trouble then forces Pissanos to make an emergency landing south of Le Havre, but he is able to evade capture and will return safely to Allied lines on September 9, 1944.
ITALY: Most of the Twelfth Air Force is grounded by bad weather, but XII Air Support Command A-36s attack Formia, and P-40s attack Pontecorvo.

The XII Provisional Troop Carrier Command is formally disbanded.

March 6, 1944

FRANCE: Two hundred sixty IX Bomber Command B-26s attack V-weapons sites, Beauvais/Tille Airdrome, and a marshalling yard at Hirson, but 50 other B-26s and

A-20s dispatched against a marshalling yard at Creil abort in the face of bad weather.

The 344th Medium Bombardment Group, in B-26s, makes its combat debut.

GERMANY: In the war's first attack on Berlin by USAAF day bombers, 504 Eighth Air Force B-17s and 226 B-24s are dispatched against industrial targets in and around the city. However, a total of 474 B-17s and 198 B-24s attack a wide variety of secondary targets and targets of opportunity in the Berlin area through breaks in the heavy cloud cover. GAF fighter opposition is concentrated and fierce (the GAF has had days to prepare a massive reception owing to earlier failures by the bombing forces to reach the target), and 53 B-17s and 16 B-24s are downed, 293 B-17s and 54 B-24s are damaged, and five B-17s and one B-24 are written off. Crew losses are 17 killed, 686 missing, and 31 wounded. Fifteen of the B-17s lost are from the 3d Bombardment Division's 100th Heavy Bombardment Group, the highest one-day toll to date sustained by a single bomber group.

Escort and support for the heavy bombers is provided by a record 801 USAAF fighters (86 P-38s, 615 P-47s, and 100 P-51s), of which five P-51s, five P-47s, and one P-38 are lost with their pilots. Maj Henry L. Mills, the commanding officer of the 4th Fighter Group's 334th Fighter Squadron, brings his personal tally to six confirmed victories when he downs an FW-190 near Brandenburg at 1330 hours, but Mills is forced down in this engagement and captured. And 2dLt Grant M. Turley, a six-victory P-47 ace with the 78th Fighter Group's 82d Fighter Squadron, is shot down and killed in air-to-air combat over Barenburg.

VIII Fighter Command fighters down a record 81 GAF fighters and attack aircraft along the bomber routes and over Berlin between 1130 and 1500 hours. 2dLt Joseph W. Icard, a P-47 pilot with the 56th Fighter Group's 62d Fighter Squadron, achieves ace status when he downs an FW-190 over Dummer Lake at noon (Icard will be lost two days later in the same area); 1stLt Glenn T. Eagleston, a P-51 pilot with the 354th Fighter Group's 353d Fighter Squadron, achieves ace status when he downs a Bf-109 near Burg; and 1stLt Pierce W. McKennon, a P-51 pilot with the 4th Fighter Group's 335th Fighter Squadron, achieves ace status when he downs a Bf-109 near Berlin at 1245 hours. (McKennon's first victory was scored while he was flying with the RAF.)

ITALY: XII Air Support Command A-36s attack motor vehicles and rail cars, and P-40s attack a town and gun emplacements near the Anzio beachhead.

March 7, 1944

ENGLAND: The 409th Light Bombardment Group, in A-20s, arrives in England for service with the IX Bomber Command. The 409th has been trained as a night-bomber unit, but it arrives in England with a shortage of night-qualified bombardier-navigators that must be made good by way of personnel transfers from operational B-26 units that are already experiencing severe personnel shortages.

The 458th Heavy Bombardment Group is assigned to the 2d Bombardment Division's 96th Combat Bombardment Wing.

FRANCE: Fifteenth Air Force B-17s attack the Toulon naval base.

A total of 112 IX Bomber Command B-26s and 18 A-20s attack military installations near Creil-sur-Mer and Greny, V-weapons sites along the Channel coast, and various targets of opportunity. One hundred fifty other B-26s dispatched against a marshalling yard at Creil are recalled in the face of bad weather.

ITALY: Fifteenth Air Force B-24s attack a defended town, marshalling yards at four locations, and the Fabrica di Roma, Orvieto, and Viterbo airdromes; Twelfth Air Force B-25s attack Rome's Ostiense marshalling yards; Twelfth Air Force B-26s attack a marshalling yard at Littoria; XII Air Support

Command A-20s attack a railroad station; and XII Air Support Command A-36s attack a railroad station near Civitavecchia, gun emplacements around Littoria Airdrome, communications targets, and a train.

March 8, 1944

ENGLAND: The 303d Fighter Wing headquarters arrives in England for eventual duty with the Ninth Air Force.

GERMANY: Three hundred twenty Eighth Air Force B-17s and 150 B-24s attack the Berlin/Erkner aircraft-industry complex with nearly 1,000 tons of bombs, and 36 B-17s and 33 B-24s attack targets of opportunity in the Berlin area. Twenty-eight B-17s and nine B-24s are lost, of which most of the former result from a massed GAF fighter assault on the leading B-17 formation, the 3d Bombardment Division's 45th Combat Bombardment Wing.

Escort and support for the heavy bombers is provided by a record 891 USAAF fighters, of which 18 are lost with their pilots and 16 are written off. The 352d and 355th Fighter groups, which are transitioning from P-47s to P-51s, each mount mixed formations of both types.

VIII Fighter Command escort pilots down 77 GAF fighters and attack aircraft over Germany between 1230 and 1620 hours. Capt Joseph H. Bennett, a P-47 pilot with the 56th Fighter Group's 61st Fighter Squadron, achieves ace status when he downs an FW-190 and two Bf-109s over Steinhuder Lake between 1245 and 1300 hours; and three 4th Fighter Group P-51 pilots achieve ace status near Berlin at 1350 hours: Maj James A. Clark, Jr., the commanding officer of the 334th Fighter Squadron, when he downs a Bf-109; 1stLt John T. Godfrey, of the 336th Fighter Squadron, when he downs two Bf-109s and shares in the downing of a third; and 1stLt Nicholas Megura, of the 334th Fighter Squadron, when he downs a Bf-109 and an FW-190.

ITALY: Twelfth Air Force B-25s attack the marshalling yard at Orte and the rail line between Orte and Fabrica di Roma; Twelfth Air Force B-26s attack Rome's Tiburtina marshalling yard and port facilities at Porto Santo Stefano; XII Air Support Command A-36s attack a castle, a bridge, gun emplacements, and a road junction; XII Air Support Command P-40s attack gun emplacements and a road junction near Rome and strafe motor vehicles on the Appian Way; and XII Air Support Command P-47s attack gun emplacements in the battle area.

NETHERLANDS: IX Bomber Command B-26s attack Volkel and Soesterberg airdromes in separate morning and afternoon missions, respectively.

March 9, 1944

ENGLAND: Because of ongoing combat-crew shortages resulting from physical exhaustion and war neurosis, Headquarters, Ninth Air Force, directs that IX Bomber Command B-26 and A-20 groups are to dispatch no more than 36 bombers apiece on normal operational missions, and 54 apiece on all-out missions.

GERMANY: Briefed for specific targets in the Berlin area, 339 Eighth Air Force B-17s are forced by weather conditions to execute an area attack with 795 tons of bombs. 2d Bombardment Division B-24 formations, which are also briefed for Berlin, attack various antiaircraft concentrations at Brunswick, Hannover, and Nienburg after the lead pathfinder experiences an equipment failure. Eight heavy bombers are downed.

Escort and support for the heavy bombers is provided by 808 USAAF fighters, which account for no enemy aircraft downed.

ITALY: Twelfth Air Force B-25s attack the port facilities at Porto Santo Stefano and a bridge; XII Air Support Command A-36s attack a railroad station; and XII Air Support Command P-40s attack several gun emplacements near the battle area.

March 10, 1944

ENGLAND: The Ninth Air Force, which has been supporting the Combined Bomber

Offensive through the loan of many of its assets to the Eighth Air Force, is formally authorized by Headquarters, AEAF, to shift the bulk of its efforts against preinvasion tactical targets within range of its bases in England.

ITALY: Twelfth Air Force B-25s attack a marshalling yard at Littoria; Twelfth Air Force B-26s attack Rome's Tiburtina marshalling yard and a rail bridge at Orvieto; and XII Air Support Command A-36s attack troop positions, tanks, gun emplacements, and railroad targets.

March 11, 1944

ENGLAND: The 53d Troop Carrier Wing begins operations with the IX Troop Carrier Command; the 441st Troop Carrier Group arrives in England for service with the IX Troop Carrier Command; and the 394th Medium Bombardment Group, in B-26s, arrives in England for service with the Ninth Air Force.

The VIII Fighter Command's 361st Fighter Group is reassigned to the 67th Fighter Wing.

The newly arrived 467th Heavy Bombardment Group, in B-24s, is assigned to the 2d Bombardment Division's 96th Combat Bombardment Wing.

FRANCE: Thirty-four B-24s of the 2d Bombardment Division's 44th and 93d Heavy Bombardment groups attack a V-weapons site at Wizernes with 127 tons of bombs. Escort was to have been provided by 213 P-47s of the 352d and 353d Fighter groups, but the fighters, which abort in the face of bad weather, undertake low-level sweeps resulting in the loss of three P-47s and two of the pilots.

Of 114 IX Bomber Command B-26s dispatched against V-weapons sites in northern France, 61 are able to attack the assigned targets and 53 abort in the face of bad weather.

Thirty-six 352d Fighter Group P-47s equipped with a single 500-pound bomb apiece attack the submarine pens at St.-Nazaire en masse at wave-top height from

the direction of the Bay of Biscay, then make their withdrawal across the Brittany Peninsula to the English Channel. The German defenses are caught by surprise by the wave-top skip-bombing attack, but results are unknown. During the withdrawal, P-47 pilots strafe targets of opportunity all across Brittany. Losses are one P-47 and its pilot missing, one battle-damaged P-47 that crashes in the English Channel after the pilot bails out (pilot not recovered), two P-47s damaged by enemy fire, and one P-47 written off   after crash-landing at a base in the U.K.

Fifteenth Air Force B-24s attack the harbor and naval base at Toulon. While escorting this mission, 1stLt Richard J. Lee, a P-38 pilot with the 1st Fighter Group's 94th Fighter Squadron, achieves ace status when he downs two Bf-109s near Toulon between 1150 and 1220 hours. In all, seven GAF fighters are downed on the Toulon mission by 1st Fighter Group P-38 pilots.

GERMANY: All 124 Eighth Air Force B-17s dispatched attack marshalling yards at Munster and nearby targets of opportunity. One B-17 is lost.

Escort is provided by 90 P-47s and 50 P-51s from three fighter groups. Two 355th Fighter Group P-51s and their pilots are lost, but no enemy aircraft are downed.

ITALY: Fifteenth Air Force B-24s attack the Iesi Airdrome and marshalling yards at two locations, and Fifteenth Air Force B-17s attack a marshalling yard at Padua. While on the Padua mission, Capt William A. Rynne, a P-47 pilot with the 325th Fighter Group's 317th Fighter Squadron, achieves ace status when he downs two Bf-109s near the target at about 1230 hours. In all, 325th Fighter Group P-47s pilots down 11 GAF fighters around Padua between 1120 and 1230 hours, but three P-47s are lost.

Twelfth Air Force B-25s and B-26s attack marshalling yards at three locations, and XII Air Support Command A-36s, P-40s, and P-47s attack rail and tactical targets in and around the battle areas.

March 12, 1944

ENGLAND: The 474th Fighter Group, in P-38s, arrives in England for service with the Ninth Air Force. It is the Ninth Air Force's first P-38 unit.

FRANCE: Despite bad weather, 52 2d Bombardment Division B-24s attack the St.-Pol/Siracourt Airdrome or nearby targets of opportunity.

March 13, 1944

FRANCE: A total of 271 Eighth Air Force B-17s and B-24s, escorted by 213 VIII Fighter Command P-47s, are dispatched against V-weapons sites around Pas-de-Calais, but bad weather is encountered and only seven B-17s attack a target of opportunity near Poix with a total of 21 tons of bombs. Two B-17s are downed by enemy fire, 74 are damaged, and one is written off. Crew losses are six killed, 20 missing, and one wounded.

Of 77 IX Bomber Command B-26s dispatched, 40 attack V-weapons sites and 37 abort in the face of bad weather.

ITALY: Twelfth Air Force B-25s attack marshalling yards at Perugia and Spoleto, and chokepoints around Terni; Twelfth Air Force B-26s attack rail lines and bridges between Florence and Rome, and a defended town; XII Air Support Command A-36s attack rail targets; and P-40s attack gun emplacements near the Anzio beachhead and a supply dump.

March 14, 1944

ENGLAND: The IX Fighter Command's new 366th and 368th Fighter groups (both in P-47s) are declared operational and placed on full combat status.

ITALY: Twelfth Air Force B-25s attack marshalling yards at Orte and Terni; Twelfth Air Force B-26s attack a marshalling yard and a chemical plant; XII Air Support Command A-20s attack a German Army tank repair shop; XII Air Support Command A-36s and P-47s attack Ostia and nearby railroad stations; and XII Air Sup-

port Command P-40s attack gun emplacements around the Anzio beachhead.

March 15, 1944

BELGIUM: One hundred eighteen IX Bomber Command B-26s attack Chievres Airdrome and the marshalling yards at two locations.

In an afternoon test of Oboe guidance equipment turned over by the Eighth Air Force, ten IX Bomber Command B-26s attack Coxyde Airdrome with poor results.

ENGLAND: As part of the preinvasion training syllabus, 50 IX Troop Carrier Command transports conduct Operation THRUST, a combined training mission with the British 6th Airborne Division. In general, in training exercises carried out through the entire month, USAAF troop carrier units are found to be deficient in virtually all requirements for airborne operations, including the dropping of troops and supplies and the release of gliders. A more rigorous training syllabus will be introduced in April.

FRANCE: During the afternoon, seven 366th Fighter Group P-47s conduct the Ninth Air Force's first dive-bombing mission when they attack St.-Valery-en-Caux Airdrome with one 250-pound bomb apiece.

GERMANY: One hundred eighty-five 3d Bombardment Division B-17s and 145 2d Bombardment Division B-24s attack aircraft-industry targets in Brunswick.

Escort and support for the heavy bombers is provided by 588 USAAF P-38s and P-47s, including 86 from the Ninth Air Force. Five fighters are lost with their pilots.

VIII Fighter Command escort pilots down 35 GAF fighters over Germany between 1015 and 1230 hours. 1stLt Joseph L. Egan, Jr., a P-47 pilot with the 56th Fighter Group's 63d Fighter Squadron, achieves ace status when he downs an FW-190 over Nienburg at 1105 hours; and 2dLt Frank W. Klibbe, a P-47 pilot with the 56th Fighter Group's 51st Fighter Squadron, achieves ace status when he downs an FW-190 near Bernburg at 1320 hours.

ITALY: In the largest air operation in the theater to date, more than 1,000 Allied warplanes level Monte Cassino monastery and nearby German Army defensive positions with 1,200 tons of bombs. The Twelfth and Fifteenth air forces provide 275 heavy bombers and nearly 200 medium bombers, which drop more than 2,000 thousand-pound bombs. Although the Benedictine monastery is utterly demolished, the ground attack fails.

Although no official start date is ever set, Allied warplanes in Italy effectively commence Operation STRANGLE, the aerial interdiction of the supply network in use by German Army forces in Italy. The wide-ranging operation will continue into late May and will eventually result in an 80 percent reduction in the German Army's ability to supply its combat divisions in Italy.

NETHERLANDS: As part of a test to increase the effectiveness of the P-47 as a fighter-bomber, two 353d Fighter Group P-47s equipped with two 1,000-pound bombs apiece attack a barge in the Zuider Zee.

March 16, 1944

GERMANY: Four hundred one Eighth Air Force B-17s attack Augsburg; 64 Eighth Air Force B-17s attack targets of opportunity at Ulm and Gessertshausen; 197 2d Bombardment Division B-24s attack Friedrichshafen; and 13 B-24s attack targets of opportunity. Eighteen B-17s and five B-24s are lost with a total of 217 crewmen, 179 heavy bombers damaged, and seven crewmen killed.

Escort and support for the heavy bombers is provided by a record 868 USAAF fighters, including 237 from the Ninth Air Force. Ten escorts are lost with nine pilots.

VIII Fighter Command escort pilots down 75 GAF fighters along the bomber routes between 1030 and 1335 hours. Capt Glendon V. Davis, a P-51 pilot with the 357th Fighter Group's 364th Fighter Squadron, achieves ace status when he downs a Bf-109 and shares in the downing of a

Bf-110 over Ulm between 1130 and 1145 hours; and Capt Jack R. Warren, a P-51 pilot with the 357th Fighter Group's 364th Fighter Squadron, achieves ace status when he downs an FW-190 and two Bf-110s near Augsberg between 1205 and 1215 hours. (Warren will be shot down and killed on March 18.)

ITALY: Fifteenth Air Force B-17s attack German Army troop concentrations; Twelfth Air Force medium bombers and XII Air Support Command aircraft attack gun emplacements in the Cassino battle area; and XII Air Support Command fighter-bombers attack gun emplacements around the Anzio beachhead area.

March 17, 1944

AUSTRIA: Fifteenth Air Force B-24s are dispatched to attack several Bf-109 component factories near Vienna, at Fischamend Markt and Schwechat. Weather forces 125 B-24s bound for Fischamend Markt to abort, and the 192 B-24s bound for Schwechat drop 379 tons of bombs through solid clouds simply by estimating their time of arrival over the target. Miraculously, many of the bombs strike an industrial area.

FRANCE: Seventy IX Bomber Command B-26s attack a marshalling yard at Creil.

The VIII Fighter Command dispatches 135 P-47s from the 78th, 353d, 359th, and 361st Fighter groups to deliver low-level strafing attacks against GAF airdromes in France. Weather disrupts several of the planned attacks, but all four groups do end up delivering attacks of one sort or another, at a loss of two 78th Fighter Group P-47s and their pilots. One of those lost is 1stLt Peter E. Pompetti, a five-victory P-47 ace with the 78th Fighter Group's 84th Fighter Squadron, who is shot down by flak and captured while strafing a GAF airdrome near Paris.

March 18, 1944

GERMANY: Two hundred eighty-four 1st Bombardment Division B-17s attack aircraft-industry targets at Oberpfaffenhofen and the Landsberg, Lechfeld, and Memmingen airdromes; 198 2d Bombardment Division B-24s attack aircraft-industry targets around Friedrichshafen; and 196 3d Bombardment Division B-17s attack Munich and other targets of opportunity in the Munich area. Fifteen B-17s and 28 B-24s are downed, four heavy bombers are written off, and crew losses are 438 missing, 10 killed, and 22 wounded. Among the lost airmen is Col Joseph A. Miller, the 453d Heavy Bombardment Group commander, who is killed.

Escort and support is provided by a record 925 USAAF fighters, including 261 from the Ninth Air Force. Thirteen escorts are lost with 12 pilots, and three are written off. The 78th Fighter Group flies the first triple mission of the campaign, employing "A", "B", and "C" formations totaling 96 aircraft.

USAAF escort pilots down 38 GAF aircraft over Germany and eastern France between 1230 and 1630 hours. FO Ralph K. Hofer, a P-51 pilot with the 4th Fighter Group's 334th Fighter Squadron, achieves ace status when he downs two Bf-109s near Mannheim at 1335 hours; and LtCol Mark E. Hubbard, who scored four victories during a first tour in the MTO, achieves ace status at the controls of a 20th Fighter Group P-38 when he downs two Bf-109s, shares in the downing of another, and probably downs yet another, in the vicinity of Memmingen at about 1400 hours. However, Hubbard is himself shot down by a GAF fighter pilot near Augsburg and taken prisoner. Less fortunate is Capt Lindol F. Graham, a P-38 ace with the 20th Fighter Group's 79th Fighter Squadron. Shortly after sharing in the downing of a Bf-110 near Ulm, Graham is killed when his P-38 hits the ground during a strafing run.

ITALY: Responding to reports that as many as 235 GAF fighters have returned to the Udine Airdrome complex in northeastern Italy, Fifteenth Air Force planners conceive a brilliant plan to eradicate them. First, 95 P-38s strafe lines of supply and communication in northeastern Italy and conduct a sweep over the Udine-Villaorba area, an operation that holds most GAF fighters in the area on the ground. Next, 113 B-17s make a feint toward southern Germany by way of the Yugoslav coast, a move that draws up GAF fighters based at Klagenfurt and Graz airdromes, in southern Austria. These B-17s next turn sharply west, which in turn draws the GAF interceptor force toward northeastern Italy. The B-17s drop 20-pound fragmentation bombs on Udine and Villaorba airdromes at 1013 hours, and the USAAF fighters in the area attack the GAF fighters out of Graz and Klagenfurt. As the B-17s and all the USAAF fighters leave the area, the GAF fighters must land at the Udine area's three undamaged airfields to rearm and refuel. As the GAF fighters are being serviced at the Gorizia, Lavariano, and Maniago satellite fields, those bases are bombed between 1059 and 1111 hours by, respectively, 72, 67, and 121 B-24s, which sow 32,370 20-pound fragmentation bombs that destroy or damage 56 GAF aircraft on the ground. Also, in the air between 0925 and 1005, Fifteenth Air Force P-38 and P-47 pilots down 17 GAF aircraft. The cost to the Fifteenth Air Force, in the course of 406 heavy-bomber and 168 fighter sorties, is seven bombers and four fighters lost.

In addition to attacks on the airdromes, Fifteenth Air Force P-38s and P-47s attack a tanker in Mariano Lagoon, destroy six seaplanes at Belvedere, and attack two trains and two railroad stations.

Twelfth Air Force B-25s and B-26s, and XII Air Support Command A-20s attack the rail line at Colleferro, the marshalling yard at Foligno, a rail bridge and marshalling yards at Orvieto, the port area at Piombino, a rail bridge at Poggibonsi, and an assembly area north of the Anzio beachhead. XII Air Support Command A-36s, P-40s, and P-47s attack tactical targets in and around the Anzio battle area, troop concentrations near Cassino, and various rail and road targets.

March 19, 1944

AUSTRIA: Although unable to reach their briefed target at Steyr because of bad weather, a total of 234 Fifteenth Air Force B-17s and B-24s attack Klagenfurt Airdrome with 589 tons of bombs. Also, 76 B-24s attack Graz Airdrome with 183 tons of bombs. Twelve B-24s are downed at Graz and six B-24s are lost at Klagenfurt, including two lost in a collision.

The new 55th Heavy Bombardment Wing's 460th Heavy Bombardment Group, in B-24s, makes its combat debut on this mission. This is also the 55th Wing's first mission.

FRANCE: During the morning, 16 Ninth Air Force P-47 dive-bombers attack a GAF airfield near Boulogne-sur-Mer; 173 1st and 3d Bombardment division B-17s, escorted by P-47s, attack V-weapons sites; and 152 IX Bomber Command B-26s attack V-weapons sites around St.-Omer.

During the afternoon, 65 IX Bomber Command A-20s attack the St.-Omer V-weapons sites again.

ITALY: Components of the Mediterranean Allied Tactical Air Force (MATAF), including the Twelfth Air Force, are directed to expand their ongoing attacks against Axis lines of communication throughout Italy by targeting ports, rail lines, and marshalling yards. The new operation is codenamed STRANGLE.

Twelfth Air Force B-25s attack the marshalling yard at Avezzano, a bridge and the marshalling yard at Orte, and a bridge near Orvieto; Twelfth Air Force B-26s attack a road bridge near Arezzo and port facilities at San Stefano al Mare; XII Air Support Command A-20s attack tank repair shops near Tivoli; and XII Air Support Command P-40s and P-47s attack gun emplacements and troop concentrations near the Anzio beachhead battle area.

NETHERLANDS: Twenty 78th Fighter Group P-47s, escorted by ten other P-47s, dive-bomb Gilze-Rijen Airdrome.

YUGOSLAVIA: Fifteenth Air Force B-24s attack marshalling yards at Knin and Metkovic.

March 20, 1944

FRANCE: IX Bomber Command B-26s and A-20s attack a marshalling yard, locomotive works, and rail bridge at Creil, and four V-weapons sites. Also, 85 IX Fighter Command P-47 dive-bombers and escorts attack Abbeville/Drucat, Conches, and Poix airdromes.

Maj James C. Stewart, the commanding officer of the 56th Fighter Group's 61st Fighter Squadron, in P-47s, brings his final personal tally to 11.5 confirmed victories when he downs two Bf-109s and probably downs another near Charleville at 1130 hours.

GERMANY: Of 353 Eighth Air Force B-17s dispatched, high cloud cover forces all but 146 to abort. The day's secondary target, Frankfurt am Main, and several targets of opportunity are attacked. Only one of 92 B-24s dispatched drops its bombs on a target of opportunity. Losses are five B-17s and two B-24s missing, and 165 heavy bombers damaged.

Escort for the heavy bombers is provided by 594 fighters, including 79 from the Ninth Air Force. Eight escorts are lost with their pilots.

ITALY: Twelfth Air Force B-25s attack marshalling yards at two locations and the port area at San Stefano al Mare; Twelfth Air Force B-26s attack Port Ercole, rail bridges at two locations, and ships and port facilities at Piombino; XII Air Support Command A-20s attack a factory; XII Air Support Command A-36s attack a rail line and drop food parcels to Allied ground troops around Cassino; XII Air Support Command P-40s attack fuel dumps, gun emplacements, and troop concentrations in the Cassino area; and XII Air Support Command P-47s attack fuel dumps.

March 21, 1944

FRANCE: Fifty-six 2d Bombardment Division B-24s dispatched attack V-weapons sites around Watten, but all of the IX Bomber Command B-26s dispatched against V-weapons sites are recalled due to bad weather.

VIII Fighter Command fighter pilots down ten GAF aircraft over France between 1345 and 1530 hours. During a sweep around Bordeaux by 48 4th Fighter Group P-51s, Capt Kenneth G. Smith, of the 335th Fighter Squadron, achieves ace status when he shares in the downing of an Fi-156 near Bordeaux at 1345 hours. However, Smith is himself shot down and taken prisoner. Maj George Carpenter, the 335th Fighter Squadron commanding officer, achieves ace status when he downs an FW-190 and shares in the downing of a second FW-190 near Bordeaux between 1415 and 1500 hours.

ITALY: The Fifteenth Air Force is grounded by bad weather, and several planned missions by Twelfth Air Force B-25s and A-20s are canceled because of the weather, but one group of Twelfth Air Force B-25s attacks a bridge at Poggibonsi. Also, Twelfth Air Force B-26s attack the viaducts at Arezzo and Bucine, and the rail bridges at Cecina and Poggibonsi; XII Air Support Command A-36s drop food parcels to ground troops around Cassino; P-40 fighter-bombers attack tactical targets around the Anzio beachhead; and XII Air Support Command P-47s attack rail bridges north of Rome.

1stLt Richard F. Hurd, a Spitfire pilot with the 31st Fighter Group's 308th Fighter Squadron, achieves ace status with his fifth and sixth confirmed victories when he downs two Bf-109s near Pignataro at about 1400 hours. In all during the day, 31st Fighter Group Spitfire pilots down five Bf-109s over central Italy.

March 22, 1944

GERMANY: Six hundred fifty-seven Eighth Air Force heavy bombers diverted by bad weather from attacking several aircraft factories at Oranienburg and Basdorf attack Berlin and a small number

of targets of opportunity with a total of 1,471 tons of bombs. Twelve heavy bombers are lost and one is interned in Sweden, and 347 bombers are damaged. Escort is provided by 817 fighters, including 221 from the Ninth Air Force, but only two GAF aircraft are downed.

The 466th Heavy Bombardment Group, in B-24s, makes its combat debut.

At the conclusion of this mission, the 482d Heavy Pathfinder Bombardment Group is formally withdrawn from combat and reassigned solely as a pathfinder training unit.

ITALY: Approximately 100 Fifteenth Air Force B-24s attack marshalling yards at Bologna and Rimini; more than 100 Fifteenth Air Force B-17s attack a marshalling yard at Verona; Twelfth Air Force B-25s attack the road bridge near Poggibonsi; Twelfth Air Force B-26s attack a viaduct near Arezzo and a rail bridge at Poggibonsi; and XII Air Support Command P-40s attack gun emplacements.

When Mt. Vesuvius erupts, the 340th Medium Bombardment Group, based at Pompeii Airdrome, is forced to evacuate on short notice. Few human casualties result from the rain of hot rocks, but every one of the group's 88 B-25s is destroyed.

March 23, 1944

AUSTRIA: Fifteenth Air Force B-17s on their way to attack aircraft-industry targets at Steyr are recalled because of bad weather.
FRANCE: During the morning, 220 IX Bomber Command B-26s mount an attack against the Beaumont-le-Roger and Beauvais/Tille airdromes and a marshalling yard at Creil.

During the afternoon, 146 IX Bomber Command B-26s attack a marshalling yard at Haine-St.-Pierre.

The 394th Medium Bombardment Group, in B-26s, makes its combat debut in the morning attack against Beaumont-le-Roger Airdrome.

GERMANY: Bad weather obliges 707 of 765 Eighth Air Force heavy bombers dispatched to attack secondaries and targets of opportunity with an aggregate of 1,755 tons of bombs. Twenty-two B-17s and six B-24s and lost, and 322 heavy bombers are damaged.

Escort and support for the heavy bombers is provided by 841 fighters, including 226 from the Ninth Air Force. Four escorts are lost with their pilots.

Escort pilots down 20 GAF fighters over Belgium and Germany between 0957 hours and noon. 1stLt William J. Simmons, a P-51 pilot with the 354th Fighter Group's 355th Fighter Squadron, achieves ace status when he downs a Bf-109 near Hannover at 1115 hours.

ITALY: Twelfth Air Force B-25s attack a rail bridge; Twelfth Air Force B-26s attack a marshalling yard at Florence; XII Air Support Command A-36s attack tactical targets in the Cassino battle area; and XII Air Support Command P-40s attack gun emplacements in the Cassino-Esperia battle area.

UNITED STATES: The 487th Heavy Bombardment Group, in B-24s, departs for England via the southern ferry route.

March 24, 1944

FRANCE: One hundred forty-eight 2d Bombardment Division B-24s attack St.-Dizier/Robinson Airdrome, and 33 B-24s diverting from Metz/Frescati Airdrome because of cloud cover attack Nancy/Essay Airdrome. Escort is provided by two P-47 groups.

GERMANY: Sixty 1st Bombardment Division B-17s attack the primary target, Schweinfurt, with 130 tons of bombs, and 162 B-17s attack the secondary, Frankfurt am Main, with 382 tons of bombs. There are no losses to enemy action, but 11 crewmen and eight servicemen and two children on the ground are killed when a pathfinder B-17 crashes during a premission flight. Also, two B-17s crash after colliding near Schweinfurt.

Although seven fighter groups are unable to take off because of bad weather,

escort is provided by nearly 450 fighters from nine groups. Four fighters and three of their pilots are lost in two separate midair collisions.

ITALY: Under relentless attack as part of Operation STRANGLE, the rail lines to Rome from northern Italy are completely severed following week-long attacks by the Twelfth and Fifteenth air forces. Hereafter, until the city is liberated in June, no rail car is able to get through Rome in any direction.

Although more than 200 Fifteenth Air Force B-17s and B-24s abort in the face of bad weather, approximately 100 B-24s attack a marshalling yard at Rimini, and 32 B-24s attack Ancona, Senigallia, and several rail and road bridges spanning the Vomano River.

Twelfth Air Force B-26s attack the rail line and a bridge at Orvieto; Twelfth Air Force B-26s attack port facilities at Leghorn, and bivouac areas and supply dumps; XII Air Support Command A-20s attack gun emplacements near Cassino; XII Air Support Command A-36s and P-40s attack gun emplacements, troop concentrations, and road targets in the Cassino battle area; and XII Air Support Command P-47s attack a train and a rail bridge near Rome.

March 25, 1944

ENGLAND: In a clarification of its March 10 directive, AEAF directs that all Ninth Air Force P-51s continue to provide fighter support for Operation POINTBLANK (i.e., to continue to escort bombers) whenever called upon to do so by the Eighth Air Force. Otherwise, Ninth Air Force fighters are to begin shifting increasingly to tactical missions in support of the upcoming invasion of France, Operation OVERLORD. Target priorities set out by AEAF for the entire Ninth Air Force are, in order of importance: rail centers, V-weapons sites (Operation CARPETBAGGER), specified industrial targets, and operational GAF airfields.

FRANCE: More than 140 IX Bomber Command B-26s attack a marshalling yard at Hirson.

ITALY: The entire Fifteenth Air Force and most of the Twelfth Air Force are grounded by bad weather, but Twelfth Air Force B-26s are able to attack a town and port facilities at Leghorn, and XII Air Support Command P-40s attack gun emplacements near the Anzio beachhead.

March 26, 1944

ETO: Gen Dwight D. Eisenhower approves a plan to isolate the OVERLORD invasion area by means of concentrated air attacks on the transportation system in western Europe, particularly the rail system.

FRANCE: A total of 500 Eighth Air Force heavy bombers attack 16 V-weapons sites around Pas-de-Calais and Cherbourg with 1,271 tons of bombs. Four B-17s and one B-24 are lost, and 236 bombers are damaged. Escort and support for the heavy bombers is provided by 266 VIII Fighter Command P-47s, of which just one is lost with its pilot.

Nearly 140 IX Air Support Command P-47s and P-51s from five groups attack a marshalling yard, V-weapons sites, and German Army installations throughout France.

ITALY: Forced to turn back by bad weather while bound for Steyr, Austria, Fifteenth Air Force B-24s attack the Udine Airdrome complex and marshalling yards at Rimini, and Fifteenth Air Force B-17s attack port facilities and shipping at Fiume. However, approximately 150 B-17s and B-24s return to their bases with bombs aboard. Also, faithful to its schedule, the 82d Fighter Group turns up over Steyr at about 1055 hours and is engaged by GAF fighters, of which five are downed and four are damaged or possibly downed by the P-38 pilots.

The 340th Medium Bombardment Group, which suffered the loss of all of its 88 B-25s when it was run out of Pompeii Airdrome on March 22, sets up new quarters at Paestum Airdrome and immediately mounts a strike against the rail bridge at Perugia with all six of the new B-25s it has received so far.

Twelfth Air Force B-26s attack viaducts at Arezzo; XII Air Support Command A-20s attack troop concentrations; XII Air Support Command P-40s attack gun emplacements around the Anzio beachhead area and near Fontana Liri; and XII Air Support Command P-47s attack two rail bridges.

NETHERLANDS: Three hundred thirty-eight IX Bomber Command B-26s and 35 A-20s attack the German Navy E-boat and R-boat (torpedo boats and gunboats) pens at Ijmuiden, but a misdrop by the lead bomber results in very little damage. One B-26 is lost.

March 27, 1944

FRANCE: Seven hundred one Eighth Air Force B-17s and B-24s attack 11 GAF airfields in France with 1,853 tons of bombs. Losses are three B-17s and three B-24s to enemy action and two B-24s destroyed in a collision during assembly over England.

Escort and support is provided by a record 960 USAAF fighters, of which ten are lost with their pilots and five are damaged.

USAAF escort pilots down 12 GAF aircraft over France between 1330 and 1615 hours. Maj Walker M. Mahurin, a P-47 ace with the 56th Fighter Group's 63d Fighter Squadron, brings his final tally in the ETO to 18.75 confirmed victories when he shares with three other pilots in the downing of a Do-217 near Chartres at 1500 hours. Shortly, Mahurin's P-47 is downed by flak, but he is able to evade capture, and he will be returned to the U.K. on May 7, 1944. (Mahurin subsequently downs a Japanese airplane in Southeast Asia in 1945, and he will down 3.5 jet interceptors in the Korean War.) Less fortunate than Walker Mahurin is Maj Gerald W. Johnson, a 16.5-victory P-47 ace with the 56th Fighter Group's 63d Fighter Squadron, who is taken prisoner after his P-47 is downed by flak during a strafing pass at a railroad train.

Of 53 IX Bomber Command B-26s dispatched against V-weapons sites in northern France, only 18 attack their assigned targets while the others abort in the face of bad weather.

ITALY: Twelfth Air Force B-25s attack road and rail bridges at three locations; Twelfth Air Force B-26s attack a rail bridge and other rail targets at Poggibonsi; XII Air Support Command A-20s and A-36s attack a railroad station; XII Air Support Command P-40s attack supply dumps and a German Army command post near Rome; and XII Air Support Command P-47s attack transportation targets along the rail line between Rome and Orvieto.

March 28, 1944

BALKANS: The Twelfth Air Force's 60th Troop Carrier Group is assigned to keep Yugoslav, Greek, and Albanian partisans supplied with weapons, munitions, and other military equipment and stocks, and to drop agents as needed. Hereafter (except for commitment to the invasion of southern France in August 1944) the group will more or less specialize in partisan-support operations.

ENGLAND: The Eighth Air Force's 652d Bombardment Squadron, a provisional weather-reconnaissance unit, is formally reconstituted as the 8th Provisional Heavy Weather Reconnaissance Squadron. At the same time, the Eighth Air Force forms the Provisional Light Weather Reconnaissance Squadron, a Mosquito unit that will conduct meteorological flights over northern Europe, and the Provisional Special Weather Reconnaissance Squadron, a Mosquito unit that will conduct day and night reconnaissance sorties. The latter two units are formed from a nucleus of P-38 pilots from the 50th Fighter Squadron, a former 14th Fighter Group component that has been serving in Iceland since mid-1942.

The 801st Provisional Heavy Bombardment Group is created under the auspices of the VIII Air Force Composite Command. Equipped with specially remodeled B-24s, the new unit will drop agents and supplies by parachute to assist partisan organizations in France and the Low Countries. The 801st is initially composed of former aircrews and groundcrews from the disbanded 479th Antisubmarine Group [see November 11, 1943].

The Eighth Air Force's 803d Provisional Bombardment Squadron (Radio Counter Measures) is redesignated as the 36th Provisional Bombardment Squadron and assigned to the 801st Provisional Heavy Bombardment Group.

FRANCE: Three hundred sixty-four 1st and 3d Bombardment division B-17s attack Dijon/Longvic, Chartres, Chateaudun, and Reims/Champagne airdromes with a total of 937 tons of bombs. Two B-17s are lost.

Escort and support for the bombers is provided by 453 USAAF fighters, of which three P-51s and their pilots are lost. Also, 355th Fighter Group P-51 pilots strafe the Dijon/Longvic Airdrome after it has been bombed.

ITALY: Fifteenth Air Force B-17s and B-24s attack marshalling yards at Verona; and B-24s attack bridges at Cessano and Fano, and a marshalling yard and industrial targets (including the Breda shipyard) at Mestre. The aggregate of bombs expended is 1,061 tons, making this the Fifteenth Air Force's first thousand-ton day.

Twelfth Air Force B-25s attack rail bridges and viaducts at two locations; Twelfth Air Force B-26s attack a marshalling yard and rail junction at Montepescali, and a bridge approach at Perugia; XII Air Support Command A-20s attack a tank factory; XII Air Support Command A-36s attack rail bridges at two locations; and XII Air Support Command P-40s attack numerous tactical targets around Cassino as well as motor-vehicle parks and supply dumps.

A total of 12 GAF fighters are downed over Italy during the day, by both Twelfth and Fifteenth air force fighter pilots engaged in either escort or ground-support missions.

NETHERLANDS: 2d Bombardment Division B-24s are recalled due to bad weather while en route to attack the German Navy base at Ijmuiden.

March 29, 1944

ENGLAND: The 442d Troop Carrier Group arrives in England for service with the IX Troop Carrier Command, and the 48th Fighter Group, in P-47s, arrives in England for service with the IX Fighter Command.

The IX Troop Carrier Command is reorganized as follows: 50th Troop Carrier Wing—439th, 440th, 441st, and 442d Troop Carrier groups; 52d Troop Carrier Wing—61st, 313th, 314th, 315th, and 316th Troop Carrier groups; and 53d Troop Carrier Wing—434th, 435th, 436th, 437th, and 438th Troop Carrier groups. This will be the IX Troop Carrier Command organization for Operation OVERLORD.

FRANCE: Thirty of 77 2d Bombardment Division B-24s dispatched attack the V-weapons sites around Watten. The only losses are two B-24s that collide during assembly, killing 18 crewmen. Also, 19 would-be rescuers and four civilians on the ground are killed and 38 servicemen are wounded when the bombs in one of the crashed airplanes detonate. Escort for this otherwise uneventful mission is provided by 37 361st Fighter Group P-47s.

GERMANY: Two hundred thirty-three 1st Bombardment Division B-17s attack the city of Brunswick and several targets of opportunity.

Escort and support for the bombers is provided by 428 USAAF fighters. Ten pilots are lost when 12 fighters are downed in action and six crash or ditch for various reasons.

USAAF escort pilots down 46 GAF fighters over Germany between 1315 and 1520 hours. LtCol Everett W. Stewart, the executive officer of the 355th Fighter Group, in P-51s, achieves ace status when he downs two fixed-gear trainers near Brunswick at 1350 hours; and 1stLt Charles F. Anderson, Jr., a P-51 pilot with the 4th Fighter Group's 335th Fighter Squadron, achieves ace status when he downs two FW-190s and shares in the downing of a

third FW-190 near Gifhorn between 1410 and 1425 hours.

ITALY: In the Fifteenth Air Force's largest mission so far in the war, nearly 300 Fifteenth Air Force B-24s attack marshalling yards at Bolzano and Milan; and 105 Fifteenth Air Force B-17s attack marshalling yards, a ball-bearing factory, and the Fiat airplane-engine factory at Turin.

A total of 13 GAF fighters are downed over Italy during the day by Twelfth and Fifteenth air force fighter pilots. Capt James E. Fenex, Jr., a P-40 pilot with the 324th Fighter Group's 316th Fighter Squadron, achieves ace status when he downs two FW-190s near Rome at 1530 hours.

Twelfth Air Force B-25s attack Viterbo Airdrome; Twelfth Air Force B-26s attack Leghorn; XII Air Support Command A-36s attack the harbors and port facilities at Civitavecchia and San Stefano al Mare; XII Air Support Command P-40s attack repair shops, supply dumps, and a bivouac area near Rome and a supply dump and gun emplacements near Velletri; and XII Air Support Command P-47s attack a rail overpass north of Rome.

March 30, 1944

BULGARIA: One hundred fourteen Fifteenth Air Force B-17s and 253 B-24s attack marshalling yards at Sofia, an industrial area at Imotski, and Imotski Airdrome.

The 463d Heavy Bombardment Group, in B-17s, makes its combat debut on this mission as part of the 5th Heavy Bombardment Wing.

Thirteen Axis fighters, many of which appear to be Bulgarian Air Force aircraft, are downed during the mission by P-38 pilots of the 1st and 82d Fighter groups. Also, while escorting the bombers en route over Yugoslavia, 14th Fighter Group P-38 pilots down an Axis fighter and damage or possibly down seven others.

ENGLAND: The IX Engineer Command is formally activated under the command of BriGen James B. Newman.

GERMANY: The Combined Bomber

Offensive suffers a major setback when nearly 100 RAF bombers are downed while taking part in a mission against Nurnberg, on the night of March 30–31. As a result of these losses, the RAF's night-bombing program is sharply curtailed.

ITALY: Twelfth Air Force B-25s attack port facilities at Leghorn and a rail bridge near Orte; and XII Air Support Command A-36s and P-40s attack a variety of scattered targets, including ammunition and supply dumps, rail bridges, and motor vehicles.

The 57th Fighter Group, the first Twelfth Air Force unit to be equipped with P-47s, moves temporarily from Italy to Corsica in order to be in a better position from which to conduct low-level sweeps against German Army lines of supply and communication. The uniquely equipped group is ordered to provide a minimum of 48 fighter-bomber sorties per day as well as its own top cover. This is the first effective test of the P-47 in a fighter-bomber roll, which includes low-level strafing and dive-bombing attacks. (Between April 1 and 14, the group exceeds all expectations by providing at least 80 fighter-bomber sorties per day.)

NETHERLANDS: Twelve P-47s each from the 359th and 361st Fighter groups dive-bomb Soesterberg and Eindhoven airdromes, respectively. Also, 22 78th Fighter Group P-47s strafe a marshalling yard, shipping on the Rhine River, a flak tower and gun emplacements, and the Deelen, Twente/Enschede, and Venlo airdromes.

March 31, 1944

ITALY: The Twelfth and Fifteenth air forces are grounded by bad weather—except for fighter sweeps carried out by the Corsica-based P-47s of the 57th Fighter Group.

APRIL 1944

April 1, 1944

GERMANY: Two hundred forty-five 3d Bombardment Division B-17s and 195 2d Bombardment Division B-24s are dispatched to attack chemical plants at Ludwigshafen. All the B-17s abort due to heavy cloud cover over France. Due to the weather and a pathfinding error, the 2d Bombardment Division B-24s end up more than 100 miles off course. Although completely lost, 101 B-24s attack Pforzheim, Germany; nine attack Grafenhausen, Germany; 17 B-24s attack Strasbourg, France; and 36 B-24s attack Schaffhausen, Switzerland. The U.S. government eventually pays Switzerland $1 million in reparations. Twelve B-24s are lost in action. Among the lost airmen is Col James M. Thompson, the 448th Heavy Bombardment Group commander, who is killed.

Of 17 VIII and IX Fighter command fighter groups scheduled to escort the heavy bombers, four are grounded by bad weather, including one group that is scheduled to report on weather conditions over Germany.

In all, 475 fighters participate in the mission, and 4th and 354th Fighter group P-51 pilots down five Bf-109s during the morning over France and Germany.

The 352d Fighter Group, which is transitioning from P-47s to P-51s flies a mixed-group formation in both types, even though the pilots flying the P-51s (480th Fighter Squadron) have accumulated no more than five hours experience in the new type.

ITALY: Twelfth Air Force B-25s attack the harbor at Leghorn, bridges, and a rail line; Twelfth Air Force B-26s attack several bridges across the Arno River; XII Air Support Command A-20s attack German Army ammunition dumps; XII Air Support Command P-40s attack a tunnel, bridges, fuel dumps, gun emplacements, and tactical targets in the battle areas; and XII Air Support Command P-47 fighter-bombers attack a bridge and a train.

The 31st and 52d Fighter groups are transferred from the Twelfth Air Force to the Fifteenth Air Force. Both veteran Spitfire units are temporarily dispatched to

Tunisia to transition to new P-51B long-range fighters and to train to undertake bomber-escort missions.

April 2, 1944

AUSTRIA: Following four aborts due to weather during the preceding two weeks, Fifteenth Air Force heavy bombers are finally able to get through heavy clouds to Steyr. A phased escort—the first of its kind in the theater—is provided by the Fifteenth Air Force's three P-38 groups and one P-47 group. Between 1213 and 1231 hours, 125 Fifteenth Air Force B-17s and 30 B-24s attack the ball-bearing plant; 168 Fifteenth Air Force B-24s attack the Steyr Airdrome; and 125 B-24s bomb the Daimler-Puch aircraft components factory. Of 280 heavy bombers taking part in this mission, 20 are lost to enemy fire.

In punishing series of fighter battles en route to and over the target area, Fifteenth Air Force escort pilots down 33 GAF aircraft against one P-38 written off after it makes a wheels-up landing at its home base.
ITALY: Twelfth Air Force B-25s and B-26s attack numerous rail bridges; and XII Air Support Command fighter-bombers attack numerous transportation targets, dumps, tactical targets, and targets of opportunity.
YUGOSLAVIA: Thirty-five Fifteenth Air Force B-24s attack marshalling yards at Bihac; 28 B-24s of the 55th Heavy Bombardment Wing's 461st Heavy Bombardment Group make their unit's combat debut in an attack on the Mostar Airdrome; and 29 B-17s of 5th Heavy Bombardment Wing's 463d Heavy Bombardment Group attack a marshalling yard at Brod. Three Bf-109s are downed near Zagreb at 1045 hours by P-47 pilots of the 325th Fighter Group's 317th Fighter Squadron.

April 3, 1944

HUNGARY: Fifteenth Air Force B-24s attack marshalling yards at Budapest, and Fifteenth Air Force B-17s attack Budapest's Csepel Island aircraft plant. P-38 pilots of the 1st, 14th, and 82d Fighter groups down seven GAF fighters and two He-111s in the Budapest area between 1020 and 1105 hours.
ITALY: Despite bad weather that causes many mission cancellations and aborts, Twelfth Air Force medium bombers cut the approaches to a bridge north of Orvieto; XII Air Support Command A-20s attack an ammunition dump; XII Air Support Command A-36s attack a rail line and underpass; XII Air Support Command P-40s attack the town area at Itri, a German Army bivouac, a railroad station, and a supply dump; and XII Air Support Command P-47s attack a road junction and town area.
UNITED STATES: The 489th Heavy Bombardment Group, in B-24s, departs for England via the southern ferry route.
YUGOSLAVIA: Fifteenth Air Force B-24s attack a marshalling yard at Brod.

April 4, 1944

ENGLAND: The 410th Light Bombardment Group, in A-20s, arrives in England for service with the Ninth Air Force. The 410th is the last of the Ninth Air Force's three A-20 groups to arrive in the war zone.

The 339th Fighter Group arrives by ship from the United States for service with the VIII Fighter Command. Trained as a P-39 fighter-bomber group, the 339th will be equipped with P-51s. The new unit is assigned to the 66th Fighter Wing.

The Ninth Air Force's 404th Fighter Group and the advance echelon of the 373d Fighter Group, both in P-47s, arrive in England by ship.
ITALY: Twelfth Air Force medium bombers abort in the face of bad weather; XII Air Support Command A-20s attack ammunition dumps; and XII Air Support Command fighter-bombers attack gun emplacements, a bivouac, and numerous transportation targets in the Rome area and along and around the battlefronts.
ROMANIA: In the first of many strategic missions made under a commitment by the Fifteenth Air Force to aid the advance of

the Red Army across the Balkans by disrupting Balkans transportation centers in use to supply the German Army in the East, 350 B-17s and B-24s, escorted by 119 P-38s, are dispatched to attack rail facilities in Bucharest. GAF fighter opposition is fierce, especially against the 449th Heavy Bombardment Group, a 47th Heavy Bombardment Wing B-24 unit that becomes separated from the rest of the wing in bad weather. Seven of the group's 28 B-24s are downed by the Axis fighters, but the survivors attack the target and make it home. Altogether, 93 B-17s and 220 B-24s drop 863 tons of bombs, mostly on marshalling yards at Bucharest. Also, 30 B-24s from two groups attack the Bucharest/Otopeni Airdrome. Bomber gunners are awarded credit for 50 GAF fighters, but the only victories credited to Fifteenth Air Force fighters taking part in the Bucharest mission (or at all in the theater) are a Bf-110 and two Ju-88s downed over Caracal, Romania, at 1428 hours by 82d Fighter Group P-38 pilots.

April 5, 1944

ENGLAND: The 397th Medium Bombardment Group, in B-26s, arrives in England for service with the IX Bomber Command. The 397th is the fourth and last B-26 unit assigned to the 98th Combat Bombardment Wing. Also, the Ninth Air Force's 50th Fighter Group, in P-47s, arrives in England by ship.

The newly arrived 486th and 487th Heavy Bombardment groups, both in B-24s, are assigned to the 3d Bombardment Division's 92d Combat Bombardment Wing.

FRANCE: Due to heavy cloud cover over the target area, only 21 of 50 2d Bombardment Division B-24s dispatched attack V-weapons sites at St.-Pol/Siracourt.

GERMANY: Despite heavy clouds and a snow storm that turns back numerous other groups, the 4th and 355th Fighter groups, in P-51s, strafe eleven airfields in the vicinity of Munich and claim 96 German aircraft destroyed on the ground. Also

damaged is a captured B-17 parked on one of the GAF airfields.

In addition to GAF aircraft destroyed on the ground, pilots of the 4th, 20th, and 355th Fighter groups down a total of 12 GAF aircraft over Germany between 1450 and 1515 hours. In all, ten USAAF fighters and eight pilots are lost in the day's action. Capt Duane W. Beeson, a 19-victory ace with the 4th Fighter Group's 334th Fighter Squadron, shares with two other pilots in the downing of a Ju-88 near Brandenburg at 1500 hours, but he is also shot down by flak near Brandenburg and taken prisoner.

ITALY: Twelfth Air Force bombers are grounded by bad weather; XII Air Support Command A-36s attack Formia and several railroad stations; and XII Air Support Command P-40s attack fuel dumps, a railroad station, and gun emplacements in the U.S. Fifth Army battle area.

POLAND: Heavy bombers of the Eighth Air Force's 45th Combat Bombardment Wing strike an aircraft components factory.

ROMANIA: Although SHAEF has officially proscribed attacks specifically aimed at gutting Axis oil facilities, the commanders of the Fifteenth Air Force heavy-bomber force claim that the 558 tons of bombs dropped by 95 B-17s and 135 B-24s on the Ploesti oil fields and refining facilities this day are aimed only at rail facilities. However, bombs that miss the rail facilities cause grave harm to adjacent oil facilities. Thus, this mission effectively begins a tacitly approved bombing campaign against oil targets, especially Ploesti. Five B-24s are lost, all from the 451st Heavy Bombardment Group, which is attacked fiercely by as many as 85 Axis fighters.

YUGOSLAVIA: Fifteenth Air Force B-24s attack a marshalling yard at Leskovac, and Fifteenth Air Force B-17s attack a marshalling yard at Nis.

April 6, 1944

FRANCE: Five 2d Bombardment Division B-24 groups are dispatched against the V-weapons site at Watten, but heavy clouds over the target prevent all but 12 B-24s from mounting the attack.

ITALY: Although some medium-bomber missions are canceled because of bad weather, Twelfth Air Force B-25s attack Perugia Airdrome, and B-26s attack a bridge near Orvieto. Also, XII Air Support Command fighter-bombers attack small ships in the Aegean Sea, and gun emplacements, railroad stations, and road and rail bridges throughout central Italy.

The 350th Fighter Group, in modified ground-attack P-39s, mounts an all-out effort against German Army lines of supply and communication. Operating from Corsica, the group mounts 75 sorties in ten missions through intense flak and severs a highway and knocks out two rail bridges, a barracks, and two air-warning systems. When a flight of six of the group's P-39s is attacked in the afternoon by ten FW-190s and Bf-109s in the Grosseto area, ten P-39s flying top cover down five of the GAF fighters and drive away the rest without loss.

The Fifteenth Air Force's new 49th Heavy Bombardment Wing becomes operational when the veteran 451st Heavy Bombardment Group, in B-24s, is transferred to its control from the 47th Heavy Bombardment Wing, and the 461st Heavy Bombardment Group is transferred from the 55th Heavy Bombardment Wing.

YUGOSLAVIA: Fifteenth Air Force B-17s attack an airdrome at Zagreb.

While escorting the B-17s, 325th Fighter Group P-47 pilots and 82d Fighter Group P-38 pilots down 13 GAF fighters over Yugoslavia and northern Italy. 1stLt Eugene H. Emmons, a P-47 pilot with the 325th Fighter Group's 317th Fighter Squadron, achieves ace status when he downs a Bf-109 over Trieste at 1540 hours.

April 7, 1944

ITALY: Fifteenth Air Force B-17s attack a marshalling yard at Treviso, and Fifteenth Air Force B-24s attack marshalling yards at Bologna and Mestre.

1stLt Robert K. Seidman, a P-38 pilot

with the 14th Fighter Group's 49th Fighter Squadron, achieves ace status when he downs a Bf-109 over Mestre at 1305 hours. Seidman's victory is one of ten Bf-109s downed by 14th Fighter Group P-38 pilots between 1245 and 1305 hours.

Twelfth Air Force B-25s and B-26s attack a marshalling yard at Prato, a viaduct, and several rail lines and bridges; XII Air Support Command A-20s attack an ammunition dump; XII Air Support Command A-36s attack gun emplacements, a train, and the rail line at Orvieto; XII Air Support Command P-40s attack several towns, dumps, and gun emplacements; and XII Air Support Command P-47s attack bridges near Rome and a marshalling yard.

April 8, 1944

AUSTRIA: Fifteenth Air Force B-17s attack aircraft-industry targets at Fischamend Markt.

BELGIUM: One hundred ninety-six IX Bomber Command B-26s attack Coxyde Airdrome and a marshalling yard at Hasselt, and 32 P-47 fighter-bombers attack targets around Hasselt.

ENGLAND: IX Bomber Command's 97th, 98th, and 99th Combat Bombardment wings are ordered to assume operational control of the B-26 and A-20 groups heretofore assigned to them administratively.

GERMANY: Although nearly the entire 1st Bombardment Division is grounded by fog at its bases, all 59 91st and 381st Heavy Bombardment group B-17s that are able to get airborne attack the assigned target, Oldenburg Airdrome.

Of 350 2d Bombardment Division B-24s dispatched, 190 attack the assigned target, an aircraft plant at Brunswick, and 113 attack several targets of opportunity, including Langenhagen Airdrome. Thirty B-24s are downed.

One hundred eighty-four of the 255 3d Bombardment Division B-17s dispatched attack their primary targets, the Achmer, Quakenbruck, and Rheine/Hopstein airdromes. In addition, 65 3d

Bombardment Division B-17s attack various targets of opportunity. Four B-17s are downed.

Escort for the heavy bombers is provided by 780 fighters, whose pilots down an unprecedented 88 GAF aircraft (mostly fighters) along the bomber routes between 1300 and 1630 hours. Forty-nine other GAF aircraft are claimed as destroyed on the ground in strafing attacks. 1stLt James B. Dalglish, a 354th Fighter Group P-51 pilot flying with the 363d Fighter Group's 381st Fighter Squadron, achieves ace status when he downs a Bf-109 over Gifhorn at 1124 hours; Capt Raymond C. Care, a P-51 pilot with the 4th Fighter Group's 334th Fighter Squadron, achieves ace status when he downs a Bf-109 over Ulzen at 1350 hours; 1stLt Willard W. Millikan, a P-51 pilot with the 4th Fighter Group's 336th Fighter Squadron, achieves ace status when he downs three Bf-109s near Ulzen at 1350 hours; and Capt Don S. Gentile, a P-51 ace with the 4th Fighter Group's 336th Fighter Squadron, brings his final personal tally to 21.833 confirmed victories when he downs three FW-190s near Ruhrburg at about 1350 hours.

Twenty-three USAAF fighters are lost with their pilots, either in air-to-air combat or while strafing ground targets of opportunity of Germany. Capt Virgil K. Meroney, a nine-victory ace with the 352d Fighter Group's 487th Fighter Squadron, is shot down by ground fire and captured while strafing an airdrome in northwestern Germany; and Capt Norman E. Olson, a six-victory P-47 ace with the 355th Fighter Group's 357th Fighter Squadron, is shot down by flak and killed near Celle Hofer.

The VIII Fighter Command's 352d Fighter Group flies its first group mission since transitioning to P-51s.
ITALY: Twelfth Air Force medium bombers attack a bridge near Orte; XII Air Support Command A-20s attack several supply dumps; and XII Air Support Command fighter-bombers attack bridges, motor vehicles, rail lines, and supply dumps.

YUGOSLAVIA: For the first time, Fifteenth Air Force heavy bombers take part in mining the Danube River. During this night mission, three B-24s accompanying RAF Wellingtons seed the river below Belgrade with 1,000-pound and 1,600-pound mines.

April 9, 1944

GERMANY: One hundred forty 1st Bombardment Division B-17s attack aircraft-industry targets at Marienburg and Rahmel; 126 2d Bombardment Division B-24s attack Parchim, an aircraft plant at Tutow, and several targets of opportunity; and 136 3d Bombardment Division B-17s attack aircraft-industry targets at Posen (Poznan, Poland) and Warnemunde, and the Rostock/Marienehe Airdrome. Thirty-two heavy bombers are lost.

Escort for the heavy bombers is provided by 719 fighters, whose pilots down 21 GAF fighters along the bomber routes between 1120 and 1545 hours. USAAF fighter losses are ten airplanes and nine pilots. Two P-51 pilots with the 354th Fighter Group's 356th Fighter Squadron achieve ace status near Kiel at 1445 hours: 1stLt Robert E. Goodnight, when he downs an FW-190, and 2dLt Thomas F. Miller, when he downs an FW-190 and shares in the downing of another FW-190.
ITALY: XII Air Support Command A-36s and P-40s attack two towns, the rail line between Rome and Bracciano, railroad repair shops, and gun emplacements.

April 10, 1944

BELGIUM: Two hundred fourteen 1st Bombardment Division B-17s attack aircraft-industry targets at Brussels and Evere, and Brussels/Melsbroek and Brussels/Evere airdromes; and 143 3d Bombardment Division B-17s that are unable to locate their assigned target in France, attack the airdromes at Beaumont-sur-Oise (France), Diest/Schaffen, and Maldagem.

During the afternoon, in their second mission of the day, 267 IX Bomber

Command B-26s and A-20s attack coastal defenses, V-weapons sites, marshalling yards, and airdromes at Charleroi/Montignies, Coxyde, Namur, and Nieuport.

ENGLAND: In response to reports of degraded bombing performance among IX Bomber Command units, LtGen Lewis H. Brereton orders that all bomber units be withdrawn from combat, in rotation, for training designed primarily to bring replacement-filled combat crews to top operational standards.

FRANCE: One hundred sixty-six 2d Bombardment Division B-24s attack their primary targets, the Marquise/Mimoyecques V-weapons site, an aircraft factory at Bourges, and Bourges Airdrome; and 49 B-24s attack assigned secondary targets, Orleans/Bricy and Romorantin/Prunieres airdromes.

The 467th Heavy Bombardment Group makes its combat debut in the attack on Bourges Airdrome.

Only 21 of 248 3d Bombardment Division B-17s dispatched attack their primary, the Courcelles-sur-Seine Airdrome, but 42 B-17s are able to attack the Florennes/Juzaine Airdrome in Belgium.

During the morning, 258 IX Bomber Command B-26s and 41 A-20s attack coastal batteries and military installations around Le Havre.

In the first mission of its kind, 29 20th Fighter Group P-38s are dispatched to bomb Florennes/Juzaine Airdrome while being led by a special "droopsnoot" airplane, a P-38 with a nose modified to carry a bombardier and his bombsight. However, all bombs are dropped in the English Channel after heavy clouds are encountered over the target.

In the second such mission in the theater, 16 of 34 55th Fighter Group P-38s led by a droopsnoot model divert from their cloud-obscured primary target, St.-Dizier/Robinson Airdrome, and drop 17 tons of bombs on Coulommiers Airdrome. Also, escorting 355th Fighter Group P-47s strafe Villaroche Airdrome. Two P-38s and their pilots are lost in the attack. One of the miss-

ing pilots is Col Jack S. Jenkins, the 55th Fighter Group commander, who is taken prisoner.

USAAF pilots escorting the various Eighth Air Force heavy-bomber formations down 15 GAF aircraft over Belgium, France, and the Netherlands. 1stLt Paul S. Riley, a P-51 pilot with the 4th Fighter Group's 335th Fighter Squadron, achieves ace status when he downs a Bu-131 trainer over Romorantin/Prunieres Airdrome at 1000 hours.

Ninth Air Force P-47s dive-bomb Evreux Airdrome.

GERMANY: Twenty-seven 20th Fighter Group P-38s, guided by a droopsnoot P-38 and escorted by 46 359th Fighter Group P-47s, attack Gutersloh Airdrome with 13 tons of bombs. One P-38 and its pilot are lost.

ITALY: Twelfth Air Force B-25s attack a marshalling yard at Orvieto and two bridges; Twelfth Air Force B-26s attack Poggibonsi, viaducts near Arezzo and at Bucine, and the rail line and rail bridges at Cecina; XII Air Support Command A-20s attack an ammunition dump; and XII Air Support Command fighter-bombers attack barracks and troop concentrations, rail bridges, rolling stock, and motor vehicles throughout central Italy.

When 30 GAF bombers attack the Anzio beachhead during the night of April 10–11, two 416th Night-Fighter Squadron Beaufighters are vectored to intercept them. The German aircraft are driven off by persistent attacks in which one bomber is probably destroyed and another is severely damaged. Unfortunately, one Beaufighter crashes in flames with its crew aboard, and the other is damaged.

NETHERLANDS: Unable to locate their primary target in Belgium, 20 1st Bombardment Division B-17s attack Bergen Op Zoom.

April 11, 1944

BELGIUM: Two hundred twenty-nine IX Bomber Command B-26s and A-20s attack

Charleroi/Montignies and Chievres airdromes and coastal military installations. **FRANCE:** More than 90 Ninth Air Force P-47s dive-bomb Gael Airdrome and nearby military installations.

GERMANY: A total of 311 1st Bombardment Division B-17s attack Cottbus and Sorau airdromes and several targets of opportunity. Nineteen 1st Division B-17s are lost.

1stLt Edward S. Michael, a B-17 pilot with the 1st Bombardment Division's 305th Heavy Bombardment Group, is critically injured by fire from a GAF fighter, but he remains at his post and recovers from a steep dive. Realizing that a crewman is too badly injured to bail out of the severely damaged bomber, Michael elects to fly to England, where he successfully crash-lands. Lieutenant Michael is awarded a Medal of Honor.

Two hundred forty-three 2d Bombardment Division B-24s attack aircraft-industry targets at Bernburg, Halberstadt, and Oschersleben, plus several targets of opportunity. Twelve B-24s are lost.

Two hundred seventy-four 3d Bombardment Division B-17s attack Politz, Rostock, an aircraft factory at Arnimswalde, and several targets of opportunity through heavy fighter opposition. Thirty-three B-17s are lost, including 11 that eventually turn up following landings in Sweden due to battle damage.

Escort for the various bombing missions is provided by a total of 819 USAAF fighters, of which 16 are lost with their pilots.

A total of 52 GAF aircraft, mostly fighters, are downed by USAAF fighter pilots over Germany between 1045 and 1530 hours. The USAAF fighter pilots also claim 65 GAF aircraft destroyed on the ground. 1stLt John B. Carder, a P-51 pilot with the 357th Fighter Group's 364th Fighter Squadron, achieves ace status when he downs a Bf-109 near Leipzig at 1130 hours; 1stLt Don McDowell, a P-51 pilot with the 354th Fighter Group's 353d Fighter Squadron, achieves ace status when he downs a

Bf-109 near Leipzig at 1140 hours; 1stLt Hipolitus T. Biel, a P-51 pilot with the 4th Fighter Group's 334th Fighter Squadron, achieves ace status when he downs an Me-410 and a Bf-110 near Stettin at 1225 hours; and 1stLt Robert L. Shoup, a P-51 pilot with the 354th Fighter Group's 356th Fighter Squadron, achieves ace status when he downs a Bf-109 near Munich at 1320 hours.

ITALY: Twelfth Air Force B-25s attack a rail bridge; Twelfth Air Force B-26s attack marshalling yards at Ancona and Siena; and XII Air Support Command fighter-bombers attack numerous rail targets northeast of Rome, the town of Gaeta, and several supply dumps.

April 12, 1944

AUSTRIA: In an all-out effort against aircraft-industry targets in the Vienna area, 172 Fifteenth Air Force B-17s attack the aircraft components factory at Fischamend Markt; 140 Fifteenth Air Force B-24s attack the Messerschmitt assembly plant at Bad Voslau; and 134 Fifteenth Air Force B-24s attack the Bf-109 components and assembly factory at Wiener-Neustadt. One B-17 and six B-24s are lost.

The 483d Heavy Bombardment Group, in B-17s, makes its combat debut as part of the 5th Heavy Bombardment Wing. It is the last of six B-17 groups to join the Fifteenth Air Force's only B-17 wing.

Escort for the heavy bombers is provided by more than 200 Fifteenth Air Force P-38s and P-47s, whose pilots down 17 GAF fighters between 1135 hours and 1220 hours. LtCol William L. Leverette, the commanding officer of the 14th Fighter Group's 37th Fighter Squadron, downs a Bf-110 near Fischamend Markt, bringing his final personal tally to 11 confirmed victories; and 2dLt Edsel Paulk, a P-47 pilot with the 325th Fighter Group's 317th Fighter Squadron, achieves ace status when he downs a Bf-109 near Wiener-Neustadt at 1215 hours.

BELGIUM: Two hundred thirty-one IX Bomber Command B-26s and 20 A-20s attack Coxyde/Furnes and Courtrai/ Wevelghem airdromes, and military bases, V-weapons sites, and rail targets in De Pannes-Bains, Dunkirk (France) and Ostend, and St. Ghislain.

FRANCE: More than 70 Ninth Air Force P-47s dive-bomb various German military installations in northern France.

The IX Fighter Command's 371st Fighter Group, in P-47s, makes its combat debut.

Twelfth Air Force medium bombers attack rail bridges spanning the Var River.

GERMANY: All 455 Eighth Air Force heavy bombers dispatched against various targets in Germany abort or are recalled in the face of heavy clouds and dense contrails. One pathfinder airplane is downed in the dark over England by a German intruder during assembly, and five 2d Bombardment Division B-24s are lost to GAF fighters near the German frontier.

Seven hundred eighty-eight USAAF fighters are dispatched to escort the abortive bomber missions. Four Ju-87s and 13 GAF fighters are downed over Belgium, northern France, and northwestern Germany. Capt John J. Hockery, a P-47 pilot with the 78th Fighter Group's 82d Fighter Squadron, achieves ace status when he downs a Ju-87 near Sedan at 1340 hours; and 1stLt Charles F. Anderson, Jr., a P-51 ace with the 4th Fighter Group's 335th Fighter Squadron, achieves double-ace status when he downs two Bf-109s near Brunswick at 1410 hours.

ITALY: Twelfth Air Force B-25s and B-26s attack rail targets and bridges at six locations; XII Air Support Command A-20s attack a supply dump; and XII Air Support Command fighter-bombers attack rail bridges, transportation targets, dumps, and motor vehicles throughout central Italy and on Elba Island.

UNITED STATES: The 490th Heavy Bombardment Group, in B-24s, departs for England via the southern ferry route for service with the 3d Bombardment Division's 93d Combat Bombardment Wing.

YUGOSLAVIA: Fifteenth Air Force B-17s attack the port at Split, and Fifteenth Air Force B-24s attack Zagreb Airdrome and several marshalling yards. One B-24 is downed over Zagreb.

April 13, 1944

BELGIUM: One hundred seventy-five IX Bomber Command A-20s and B-26s abort in the face of bad weather, but 121 B-26s and 37 A-20s attack airdromes, marshalling yards, coastal batteries, V-weapons sites, and other military targets along the Channel and North Sea coasts at Chievres, Le Havre (France), Namur, and Nieuport. Also, Ninth Air Force P-47s dive-bomb coastal V-weapons sites.

The 409th Light Bombardment Group, in A-20s, makes its combat debut.

CORSICA: At 0335 hours, GAF night bombers attack Alesan Airdrome, the new home of the 340th Medium Bombardment Group, whose entire complement of B-25s was destroyed in late March during an eruption of Mt. Vesuvius. The fragmentation bombs dropped by the GAF aircraft kill 20 members of the group, totally destroy 30 of the group's 90 B-25s, and severely damage 45 others. Later in the day, however, the battered 340th Medium Bombardment Group puts up a 12-plane mission.

ENGLAND: At the stroke of midnight, in formal recognition of what he has been doing since mid-March, Gen Dwight D. Eisenhower officially assumes supreme control of all Allied air operations mounted out of the U.K.

FRANCE: The U.S. Ninth and British Second Tactical air forces formally open a coordinated offensive against German Army shore defenses and batteries along the Normandy coast. However, to prevent the Germans from pinpointing the area as the OVERLORD invasion objective, attacks on targets in Normandy are to be mixed in with the general offensive, already under way, against numerous other targets in other areas of coastal France and Belgium.

GERMANY: One hundred fifty-four 1st

Bombardment Division B-17s attack aircraft-industry targets at Schweinfurt; 182 2d Bombardment Division B-24s attack Lauffern, Lechfeld Airdrome, and aircraft-industry targets at Oberpfaffenhofen; and 227 3d Bombardment Division B-17s attack the Messerschmitt factory and the town area at Augsburg. In the heaviest GAF fighter attack mounted since November 1943, 32 B-17s and six B-24s are lost and a total of 350 heavy bombers are damaged.

Escort for the various heavy-bomber missions is provided by 871 USAAF fighters, of which nine are lost with eight pilots.

Forty-two GAF fighters and a trainer are downed over Belgium, Germany, and Luxembourg between 1310 and 1645 hours. 1stLt Alwin M. Jucheim, Jr., a P-47 pilot with the 78th Fighter Group's 83d Fighter Squadron, achieves ace status when he downs an FW-190 over Beuchenbeuren; 1stLt Louis H. Norley, a P-51 pilot with the 4th Fighter Group's 336th Fighter Squadron, achieves ace status when he downs an FW-190 near Schweinfurt at 1400 hours; and 1stLt Carl M. Frantz, a P-51 pilot with the 354th Fighter Group's 353d Fighter Squadron, achieves ace status when he downs a Bf-109 near Darmstadt at 1410 hours.

This is the first anniversary of the combat debuts of the 56th and 78th Fighter groups.

HUNGARY: In the Fifteenth Air Force's largest mission to date (535 B-17s and B-24s dispatched, overall), 324 B-24s attack the aircraft components plant on Csepel Island, at Budapest, and the Tokol and Vesces airdromes; and 163 B-17s attack the Bf-109 components factory and airdrome at Gyor. Eighteen heavy bombers and three escort fighters are lost to enemy action. Pilots of the 1st, 82d, and 325th Fighter groups down 14 Axis fighters and five Ju-88s during various phases of the mission.

ITALY: Twelfth Air Force B-25s attack Terni and a bridge; Twelfth Air Force B-26s attack a rail bridge and a marshal-

ling yard; and XII Air Support Command fighter-bombers attack numerous rail and road targets throughout central Italy.

YUGOSLAVIA: Approximately 50 Fifteenth Air Force heavy bombers attack a marshalling yard at Brod.

April 14, 1944

ETO: The CCS shift direct operational control of the U.S. and British strategic air forces in Europe to Gen Dwight D. Eisenhower.

ITALY: Twelfth Air Force B-25s attack Viterbo Airdrome and a marshalling yard at Leghorn; Twelfth Air Force B-26s attack rail targets at six locations; and XII Air Support Command fighter-bombers attack rail targets, gun emplacements, supply dumps, and several factories in central Italy.

April 15, 1944

ETO: The Allied Expeditionary Air Force (Europe) issues its overall operational plan for Operation NEPTUNE, the cross-Channel phase of Operation OVERLORD.

GERMANY: Six hundred sixteen Eighth and Ninth air force fighters mount strafing missions against GAF bases in western and central Germany, but three fighter groups abort in the face of bad weather. Fifteen GAF fighters, an He-111, and an Fi-156 are downed in air-to-air combat, and 40 GAF aircraft are claimed as destroyed on the ground. In large part because of bad weather, USAAF losses are 33 fighters downed and 30 pilots lost. Capt Raymond C. Care, a six-victory ace with the 4th Fighter Group's 334th Fighter Squadron, is shot down by flak and captured near Celle; and Maj Leroy A. Schreiber, the commanding officer of the 56th Fighter Group's 62d Fighter Squadron and a 12-victory P-47 ace, is shot down by flak and killed over Flensburg Airdrome.

ITALY: The XII Air Support Command is redesignated XII Tactical Air Command (XII TAC).

Twelfth Air Force B-25s and B-26s attack a marshalling yard, a tunnel, and several rail bridges in central Italy; and XII TAC fighter-bombers attack ammunition dumps, rail lines, and bridges in central Italy, as well as numerous tactical targets, including gun emplacements and tanks, in the U.S. Fifth Army battle area.

The 332d Fighter Group is reassigned from the Twelfth Air Force to the Fifteenth Air Force's 306th Fighter Group, and it begins transitioning to P-47s and retraining for escort duty.

ROMANIA: Fifteenth Air Force B-24s attack marshalling yards at Bucharest, and Fifteenth Air Force B-17s attack a marshalling yard at Ploesti.

YUGOSLAVIA: Fifteenth Air Force B-17s attack a marshalling yard at Nis.

April 16, 1944

ITALY: Twelfth Air Force B-25s attack rail-bridge approaches at two locations; XII TAC A-20s attack fuel dumps; and XII TAC fighter-bombers attack a tunnel, a marshalling yard, a rail line, a town, and numerous targets of opportunity throughout central Italy.

ROMANIA: Fifteenth Air Force B-17s and B-24s attack marshalling yards at Brasov, and B-24s attack a marshalling yard at Turnu Severin.

In the first theater mission in P-51s, the 31st Fighter Group escorts heavy bombers to Turnu Severin. Fifty escort fighters that fail to rendezvous with the heavy bombers attack the rail lines around Craiova.

YUGOSLAVIA: Fifteenth Air Force B-17s attack an aircraft factory and airdrome at Belgrade.

April 17, 1944

BULGARIA: Fifteenth Air Force B-24s attack marshalling yards at Sofia, and seven GAF fighters are downed around Sofia between 1215 and 1300 hours by 31st Fighter Group P-51 pilots and 325th Fighter Group P-47 pilots.

ETO: Gen Dwight D. Eisenhower directs the Allied strategic air forces in Europe to focus the bulk of their power against the GAF and supporting industries. The objective is to prevent German tactical air units from mounting a counterattack against the invasion fleet and beaches during the landing or consolidation phases of Operation OVERLORD. In addition, Eisenhower explicitly adds strategic oil targets to the overall target list, with the specific intention of both diminishing the flow of oil products to the Axis armed forces and forcing GAF fighters into the air against what is perceived as being the overwhelming strength of the Allied fighter forces accompanying each strategic bomber mission.

FRANCE: Fourteen 2d Bombardment Division B-24s, including five pathfinder aircraft, conduct an experimental attack against the V-weapons site at Wizernes.

ITALY: Twelfth Air Force B-25s attack bridges at two locations; XII TAC A-20s attack fuel dumps near Rome; and XII TAC fighter-bombers attack various transportation targets, gun emplacements around Orte, and gun emplacements, motor vehicles, and dumps in the Anzio battle area.

YUGOSLAVIA: Fifteenth Air Force B-17s attack a marshalling yard at Sava, an aircraft factory in Belgrade, and the Belgrade/Rogozarski Airdrome. 82d Fighter Group P-38 pilots down an He-111 and two Ju-52 over Belgrade.

April 18, 1944

ENGLAND: The nascent XIX Air Support Command is redesignated XIX Tactical Air Command (TAC), and the IX Air Support Command is redesignated IX TAC.

The air echelon of the 34th Heavy Bombardment Group, in B-24s, arrives from the United States via the southern ferry route and is assigned to the 3d Bombardment Division's 93d Combat Bombardment Wing; and the air echelon of the 492d Heavy Bombardment Group, in B-24s, arrives from the United States via the southern ferry route and is assigned to the 3d Bombardment Divisions 14th Combat Bombardment Wing.

FRANCE: Two hundred seventy-seven IX Bomber Command B-26s and 37 A-20s attack marshalling yards and gun emplacements at Calais, Charleroi/St.-Martin, and Dunkirk.

Twelve 2d Bombardment Division B-24s conduct an experimental attack against V-weapons sites at Watten.

GERMANY: Two hundred seventy-five 1st Bombardment Division B-17s attack aircraft-industry targets at Oranienburg and several targets of opportunity, including Perleberg Airdrome; 159 2d Bombardment Division B-24s attack aircraft-industry targets at Brandenburg and Rathenow; 89 2d Bombardment Division B-24s attack various targets of opportunity; and 210 3d Bombardment Division B-17s attack Luneberg Airdrome, an aircraft-industry plant at Oranienburg, and several targets of opportunity. Nineteen heavy bombers are lost, including a B-17 interned in Switzerland.

Escort for the heavy bombers is provided by 634 USAAF fighters. 4th Fighter Group P-51 pilots down four GAF fighters over Germany between 1425 and 1500. While leading the 4th Fighter Group on a bomber-escort mission, Maj George Carpenter, the commanding officer of the group's 335th Fighter Squadron, brings his final personal tally to 13.833 confirmed victories when he downs a Bf-109 near Nauen at 1425 hours and an FW-190 near the Rhine Canal at 1435 hours. Unfortunately, Carpenter's P-51 is shot down over Stendal and he is taken prisoner. In all, five USAAF fighters and their pilots are lost.
ITALY: XII TAC P-40s and P-47s attack fuel dumps and rail and communications targets, and Fifteenth Air Force P-38s and P-47s down seven GAF fighters and damage or possibly destroy six others during a midafternoon fighter sweep to the Udine area.

April 19, 1944

FRANCE: Twenty-seven 93d and 448th Heavy Bombardment group B-24s attack V-weapons sites at Watten in a test of pathfinding equipment. Escort is provided by 47 P-47s of the IX Fighter Command's 405th Fighter Group, in their unit's combat debut.
GERMANY: Two hundred thirteen 1st Bombardment Division B-17s attack aircraft-industry targets at Kassel; 53 1st Bombardment Division B-17s attack Eschwege Airdrome; 62 2d Bombardment Division B-24s attack Gutersloh Airdrome; 117 2d Bombardment Division B-24s attack Paderborn Airdrome; 51 2d Bombardment Division B-24s attack various secondary targets and targets of opportunity; and 245 3d Bombardment Division B-17s attack Lippstadt and Werl airdromes. Five 1st Bombardment Division B-17s are lost.

Escort for the heavy bombers is provided by 697 USAAF fighters, and more than 500 other USAAF fighters undertake sweeps throughout northwestern Europe. Two USAAF fighters are lost with their pilots. One of the lost fighter pilots is 1stLt Charles F. Anderson, Jr., a 4th Fighter Group P-51 ace, who is killed in action over Brussels.

Sixteen of approximately 100 GAF fighters encountered along the bomber routes are downed between 1015 and 1045. 1stLt John F. Thornell, Jr., a 352d Fighter Group P-51 pilot achieves ace status when he downs two FW-190s near Kassel at 1030 hours; 1stLt Bernard J. McGratten, a P-51 pilot with the 4th Fighter Group's 335th Fighter Squadron, achieves ace status when he downs a Bf-109 and shares in the downing of an FW-190 over Eschwege between 1350 and 1400 hours; and Maj Thomas L. Hayes, Jr., the executive officer of the 357th Fighter Group, in P-51s, achieves ace status when he downs a Bf-109 near Kassel at 1035 hours.

More than 350 IX Bomber Command B-26s and A-20s attack city areas and marshalling yards at Donauworth, Gunzburg, Neu-Ulm, Schelklingen, and Ulm.
ITALY: Despite numerous mission cancellations and aborts because of bad weather,

Twelfth Air Force B-25s attack a marshalling yard at Piombino; Twelfth Air Force B-26s attack a marshalling yard at Ancona and a rail bridge at Cecina; and XII TAC P-47s attack numerous rail targets.

April 20, 1944

BELGIUM: Thirty-six 78th Fighter Group P-47s, escorted by 56 55th Fighter Group P-38s, dispatched to attack St.-Trond Airdrome jettison their bombs into the English Channel and abort in the face of bad weather.

FRANCE: Of 560 Eighth Air Force B-17s and 282 B-24s dispatched against 33 V-weapons sites in the Pas-de-Calais and Cherbourg areas, 375 B-17s and 174 B-24s attack 24 of the briefed targets, and 12 B-17s and seven B-24s attack various targets of opportunity. Nine heavy bombers are lost.

Escort for the heavy bombers is provided by 388 VIII Fighter Command fighters, whose pilots down four Bf-109s and a Ju-88 over central France between 1800 and 1945 hours. Two P-51s and their pilots are lost.

Nearly 400 IX Bomber Command B-26s and A-20s attack gun emplacements at five locations, V-weapons sites, Poix Airdrome, and targets of opportunity around Pas-de-Calais; and nearly 140 Ninth Air Force P-47s bomb the marshalling yards at Creil and Mantes-la-Jolie.

The IX Fighter Command's 48th Fighter Group, in P-47s, makes its combat debut, as does the IX Bomber Command's 397th Medium Bombardment Group, in B-26s.

In the first true fighter-bomber mission undertaken by VIII Fighter Command P-51s, 33 357th Fighter Group P-51s, escorted by 31 78th Fighter Group P-47s, attack Cambrai/Epinoy Airdrome with two 500-pound bombs apiece, and one P-51 attacks Vitry-en-Artois Airdrome.

ITALY: Although some Fifteenth Air Force heavy bombers dispatched against communications targets in northern Italy are forced to abort in the face of bad weather, B-24s are able to attack the naval base at Trieste, the harbor at Venice, the shipyard at Monfalcone, and marshalling yards at three locations; and B-17s attack the port facilities at Venice and marshalling yards at Ancona, Castelfranco, and Padua.

1stLt John W. McGuyrt, Jr., a P-38 pilot with the 14th Fighter Group's 48th Fighter Squadron, achieves ace status when he downs a Bf-109 over Trieste at 1300 hours.

Twelfth Air Force B-25s and B-26s, and XII TAC A-20s attack the Arezzo viaduct, bridges at two locations, and a marshalling yard and three fuel dumps at Leghorn; and XII TAC fighter-bombers attack fuel dumps and rail and road targets in central Italy, and numerous tactical targets in the Cassino area.

April 21, 1944

BELGIUM: More than 175 Ninth Air Force P-47 dive-bombers attack the marshalling yards and targets of opportunity at Haine-St.-Pierre (France), Hasselt, Montignies-sur-Sambre, and Namur.

ETO: Bad weather forces the indefinite cancellation of the start of the Eighth Air Force strategic heavy-bomber offensive against Axis oil targets.

FRANCE: Two hundred thirty-six IX Bomber Command B-26s and 34 A-20s attack V-weapons sites and coastal defenses at Abbeville, Amiens, Berck-sur-Mer, Etaples, and St.-Omer. Four B-26s are lost.

ITALY: XII TAC A-20s attack an ammunition dump; and XII TAC fighter-bombers attack road, rail, and tactical targets around Rome and throughout the battle area.

ROMANIA: Fifteenth Air Force B-17s attack the oil-producing and refining facilities at Ploesti.

While escorting the B-17s, in the first significant fighter action in the theater involving P-51s, 31st Fighter Group P-51 pilots down 13 Axis fighters and damage or possibly down 17 others between noon and 1215 hours. 1stLt Leland P. Molland, a P-51 pilot with the 308th Fighter Squadron, achieves ace status with 5.5 victories when he downs a Bf-109 and an Mc.202 over Ploesti. Two 31st Fighter Group P-51s are lost with their pilots.

More than 100 304th Heavy Bombardment Wing B-24s attack Turnu Severin and marshalling yards at Bucharest, and 14th Fighter Group P-38 pilots down ten Axis fighters between 1435 and 1445 hours.

UNITED STATES: The 491st Heavy Bombardment Group, in B-24s, departs for England via the southern ferry route.

April 22, 1944

BELGIUM: Approximately 275 Ninth Air Force P-47s and P-51s attack several marshalling yards in Belgium.

ENGLAND: Eighth Air Force headquarters activates the 802d Provisional Reconnaissance Group to oversee three independent reconnaissance units: the 8th Provisional Heavy Weather Reconnaissance Squadron (B-17s), the Provisional Light Weather Reconnaissance Squadron (Mosquitoes), and the Provisional Special Weather Reconnaissance Squadron.

The 398th Heavy Bombardment Group, in B-17s, arrives from the United States and is assigned to the 1st Bombardment Division's 1st Combat Bombardment Wing.

FRANCE: A total of more than 400 IX Bomber Command B-26 sorties and nearly 90 A-20 sorties are mounted throughout the day against V-weapons sites around St.-Omer and Hesdin.

GERMANY: Of 803 Eighth Air Force heavy bombers dispatched against marshalling yards at Hamm, 398 B-17s and 240 B-24s attack the primaries, 15 B-24s attack the city of Hamm, 20 B-24s attack Bonn, 50 B-17s attack Koblenz, 19 B-17s attack Soest, and 37 B-17s attack various targets of opportunity. Only one heavy bomber is lost over the Continent, but 14 other are downed when GAF fighters infiltrate the returning bomber streams over England after dark.

Escort for the heavy bombers is provided by 859 USAAF fighters, including 314 on loan from the IX Fighter Command. After leaving the bombers at the conclusion of their escort duties, 356th Fighter Group P-47s conduct dive-bombing attacks with 100-pound bombs (two per airplane) on targets of opportunity encountered during the return flight. Thirteen USAAF fighters are lost with 12 pilots.

Eighth and Ninth air force escort pilots down 36 GAF fighters over Germany between 1240 and 1530 hours. Capt Albert L. Schlegel, a P-51 pilot with the 4th Fighter Group's 335th Fighter Squadron, achieves ace status when he downs two Bf-109s near Kassel at 1750 hours; 1stLt Kendall E. Carlson, a P-47 pilot with the 4th Fighter Group's 336th Fighter Squadron, achieves ace status when he downs a Bf-109 and shares in the downing of a second Bf-109 near Kassel at 1800 hours; and Capt Robert L. Buttke, a P-38 pilot with the 55th Fighter Group's 343d Fighter Squadron, achieves ace status when he downs a Bf-109 near Hamm at 1935 hours.

ITALY: Twelfth Air Force B-25s and B-26s attack bridges and rail lines in central Italy, the town area at Orvieto, and the harbor at San Stefano al Mare; XII TAC A-20s attack a town and ammunition dumps; and XII TAC fighter-bombers attack gun emplacements around the Anzio beachhead, a marshalling yard at Siena, various rail targets in the Florence area; and four towns.

April 23, 1944

AUSTRIA: In the theater's largest heavy-bomber mission to date, 171 Fifteenth Air Force B-17s attack the Bf-109 assembly plant at Wiener-Neustadt; 33 B-24s attack the Wiener-Neustadt/Nord airdrome; 107 B-24s attack the Bf-109 assembly plant and GAF base at Bad Voslau; and 143 B-24s attack aircraft-industry factories at Schwechat. Two B-17s and 11 B-24s are lost, and many others are damaged by flak and unremitting GAF fighter attacks.

Escort pilots of the 1st, 31st, and 82d

Fighter groups down 26 GAF fighters along the bomber route over Hungary and Austria between 1320 and 1545 hours. 1stLt Frederick O. Trafton, Jr., a P-51 pilot with the 31st Fighter Group's 308th Fighter Squadron, achieves ace status when he downs two Bf-109s and an Mc.202 at about 1345 hours, while waiting for the bomber formation over Lake Balaton, Hungary. Trafton is subsequently wounded and shot down during a chase over Hungary and Yugoslavia, and he falls into the hands of Yugoslav partisans, with whom he stays for three months before returning to Italy. Also, while acting as an adviser to the 31st Fighter Group, which has recently transitioned to P-51 fighters, the 4th Fighter Group's Maj James A. Goodson downs two Bf-109s during the Wiener-Neustadt mission, between 1320 and 1440 hours. These victories bring former–RAF pilot Goodson's final tally to 14 enemy aircraft downed since June 1943.

BELGIUM: Seventeen 359th Fighter Group P-47s, escorted by 17 other P-47s from their group, mount a dive-bombing attack against Le Culot Airdrome; and 361st Fighter Group P-47s dive-bomb Chievres Airdrome.

FRANCE: Three hundred seven IX Bomber Command B-26s and 57 A-20s attack V-weapons sites, gun emplacements, and marshalling yards in the Pas-de-Calais area and on both sides of the Franco-Belgian frontier. Also, more than 1,000 Ninth Air Force P-47 and P-51 sorties are mounted against tactical targets in France, Belgium, and the Netherlands.

Forty-eight 55th Fighter Group P-38s, led by a droopsnoot model and escorted by 78th Fighter Group P-47s, attack an airdrome at Laon; 20th Fighter Group P-38s, led by droopsnoot models and escorted by 352d Fighter Group P-51s, attack Tours and Chateaudun airdromes (two P-38s are lost with their pilots); and 361st Fighter Group P-47s dive-bomb Denain/Prouvy Airdrome;

GERMANY: 353d Fighter Group P-47s strafe targets of opportunity in northwestern Germany (two P-47s are lost with their

pilots); 356th Fighter Group P-47s glide-bomb and strafe Haguenau Airdrome (three P-47s are lost with their pilots); and 357th Fighter Group P-51s conduct a dive-bombing attack against an unidentified airdrome, possibly Leningen.

ITALY: Twelfth Air Force B-25s attack bridges and bridge approaches around Attigliano; Twelfth Air Force B-26s attack a marshalling yard and several viaducts; and XII TAC fighter-bombers attack bridges and rail lines throughout central Italy.

April 24, 1944

FRANCE: IX Bomber Command B-26s dispatched against targets in France are recalled because of bad weather, but 32 Ninth Air Force P-47s dive-bomb a marshalling yard at Louvain.

GERMANY: One hundred nine 1st Bombardment Division B-17s attack Erding Airdrome; 57 1st Bombardment Division B-17s attack Landsberg Airdrome; 84 1st Bombardment Division B-17s attack aircraft-industry targets and the airdrome at Oberpfaffenhofen; 120 2d Bombardment Division B-24s attack Gablingen Airdrome; 98 2d Bombardment Division B-24s attack Leipheim Airdrome; 211 3d Bombardment Division B-17s attack aircraft-industry targets in and around Friedrichshafen; and 15 3d Bombardment Division B-17s attack an aircraft-industry target at Neckarslaum because of dense smoke cover at Friedrichshafen. Losses are 27 1st Bombardment Division B-17s, nine 2d Bombardment Division B-24s, and four 3d Bombardment Division B-17s.

Escort for the heavy bombers is provided by 867 USAAF fighters, of which 17 are lost with their pilots. One of the missing pilots is 1stLt Hipolitus T. Biel, a P-51 ace with the 4th Fighter Group's 334th Fighter Squadron, who is shot down and killed near Worms.

USAAF fighter pilots down 66 GAF aircraft over western Germany between 1240 and 1530 hours. After downing an FW-190 and probably downing another

FW-190 near Mannheim at about 1250 hours, 1stLt Paul S. Riley, a six-victory P-51 ace with the 4th Fighter Group's 355th Fighter Squadron, is himself shot down near Worms and taken prisoner; 1stLt Edward E. Hunt, a P-51 pilot with the 354th Fighter Group's 353d Fighter Squadron, achieves ace status when he downs a Bf-109 near Ingolstadt at 1325 hours; Capt Robert E. Woody, a P-51 pilot with the 355th Fighter Group's 354th Fighter Squadron, achieves ace status with seven victories when he downs four Bf-109s and shares in the downing of a fifth near Regoersdorf at about 1345 hours; 1stLt Fletcher E. Adams and 1stLt John B. England, fellow P-51 pilots with the 357th Fighter Group's 362d Fighter Squadron, both achieve ace status when they each down three Bf-110s over Munich at 1405 hours; and 2dLt Henry W. Brown, a P-51 pilot with the 355th Fighter Group's 354th Fighter Squadron, achieves ace status when he downs two Bf-109s near Munich at 1430 hours.

ITALY: Making the first use in the theater of radio-guided azimuth (Azon) bombs, five Fifteenth Air Force B-17s attack the Ancona-Rimini rail line; Twelfth Air Force B-25s and B-26s attack rail targets in central Italy; XII TAC A-20s attack a dump; and XII TAC fighter-bombers attack a railroad station, the landing ground at Canino, Axis shipping at sea off Leghorn, marshalling yards at Orvieto and Terni, and numerous other transportation targets in central Italy.

ROMANIA: Fifteenth Air Force B-24s attack marshalling yards at Bucharest, and B-17s and B-24s attack marshalling yards at Ploesti.

YUGOSLAVIA: Fifteenth Air Force B-17s attack aircraft-industry targets at Belgrade.

April 25, 1944

FRANCE: Ninety-eight 1st Bombardment Division B-17s attack Metz/Frescati Airdrome; 42 1st Bombardment Division B-17s attack Nancy/Essay Airdrome; and 121 3d Bombardment Division B-17s attack

Dijon/Longvic Airdrome. Two 1st Bombardment Division B-17s are lost.

In a special test of new GH pathfinding equipment, 27 2d Bombardment Division B-24s attack V-weapons sites at Wizernes.

55th Fighter Group P-38s, led by a droopsnoot model, bomb Amiens/Glisy Airdrome and then rendezvous with heavy bombers to provide withdrawal escort.

Seven hundred nineteen USAAF fighters provide escort for heavy bombers attacking targets in France and Germany. Two P-51s and their pilots are lost, and three GAF fighters and a Do-217 are downed during the morning.

The IX Fighter Command's 474th Fighter Group, in P-38s, makes its combat debut.

Two hundred forty IX Bomber Command B-26s and 69 A-20s attack V-weapons sites along the Channel coast and gun emplacements at seven locations; and nearly 150 Ninth Air Force P-47s dive-bomb airdromes in France and Belgium.

GERMANY: Of 199 2d Bombardment Division B-24s dispatched against marshalling yards at Mannheim, just seven attack the primary, 16 attack a marshalling yard at Landau, and eight attack other targets of opportunity. Losses are five B-24s, plus three B-24s interned in Switzerland.

ITALY: Although more than 300 Fifteenth Air Force heavy bombers abort in the face of bad weather, nearly 150 B-24s attack Varese and an aircraft factory at Turin, and Fifteenth Air Force B-17s attack the marshalling yards at Vicenza; Twelfth Air Force B-25s and B-26s attack dumps, a marshalling yard, and several bridges and bridge approaches; XII TAC A-20s attack dumps; XII TAC P-40s and P-47s attack gun emplacements, an ammunition dump, and roads and road traffic north of Rome; and XII TAC P-47s attack several Axis destroyers at sea off Elba Island.

April 26, 1944

ENGLAND: The Ninth Air Force issues

its "Ninth Air Force Tactical Air Plan for Operation NEPTUNE."

FRANCE: Thirty-three 55th Fighter Group P-38s, guided by a droopsnoot model, attack Le Mans Airdrome in the morning, and 24 352d Fighter Group P-51s dive-bomb Cormeilles-en-Vexin Airdrome in the afternoon. Also, 43 P-47s and 47 P-51s that were to have escorted B-17s to Cologne conduct sweeps over France.

GERMANY: After being diverted from their primary targets by heavy overcast, 165 1st Bombardment Division B-17s and 127 3d Bombardment Division B-17s attack aircraft-industry targets at Brunswick, and 47 3d Bombardment Division B-17s drop their bombs in the area between Hildesheim and Hannover. Unable to reach Paderborn, 238 2d Bombardment Division B-24s return to England with their bombs, and 62 1st Bombardment Division B-17s dispatched to Cologne are recalled while still over the English Channel because of an adverse weather report.

Escort for the heavy bombers is provided by 554 USAAF fighters, of which five are lost with their pilots over the Continent and two are lost, with one of the pilots killed, in a midair collision over their base. No GAF aircraft are downed.

Approximately 125 IX Bomber Command B-26s attack Plattling Airdrome.

ITALY: Most USAAF missions in the theater are canceled in the face of bad weather, but some XII TAC P-47s are able to attack road and rail targets of opportunity, the landing ground at Canino, a marshalling yard at Leghorn, and a fuel dump.

April 27, 1944

BELGIUM: On their second mission of the day, 118 3d Bombardment Division B-17s divert from their primary target in France because of cloud cover. Ninety-eight attack Le Culot Airdrome, and 20 attack Ostend/Middelkerke Airdrome. Two B-17s are lost. Also, one squadron of 353d Fighter Group P-47s dive-bombs Florennes/Juzaine Airdrome with 100-pound bombs before

rendezvousing with the heavy bombers to provide withdrawal support.

FRANCE: Nearly 450 IX Bomber Command B-26s and A-20s, along with 275 Ninth Air Force P-47 and P-51 dive-bombers, attack coastal batteries, gun emplacements, military encampments, airdromes, and marshalling yards in France and Belgium.

Due to ongoing poor weather conditions over Germany, Eighth Air Force heavy bombers are used to bolster the Ninth Air Force's offensive against transportation targets and V-weapons sites in France. In all, 307 1st and 3d Bombardment division B-17s and 169 2d Bombardment Division B-24s attack 21 of 25 briefed and five unbriefed V-weapons sites in the Cherbourg and Pas-de-Calais areas. Four heavy bombers are lost.

Escort for the heavy bombers is provided by 357 VIII Fighter Command fighters, of which one is downed in action and another is lost to engine failure. Both pilots are listed as missing. No GAF aircraft are claimed.

Finding their primary target obscured by clouds, 36 20th Fighter Group P-38s, led by a droopsnoot model, attack Albert/Meaulte Airdrome with 1,000-pound bombs. However, one P-38 squadron mistakenly attacked by P-47s is forced to jettison its bombs. Also, 53 55th Fighter Group P-38s, led by a droopsnoot model, attack Roye/Amy Airdrome with 1,000-pound bombs; and 23 356th Fighter Group P-51s dive-bomb Cormeilles-en-Vexin Airdrome.

Finally, in the Eighth Air Force's second round of heavy-bomber missions for the day, 103 1st Bombardment Division B-17s attack Nancy/Essay Airdrome; 60 1st Bombardment Division B-17s attack the Toul/Croix de Metz Airdrome; and 118 and 72 2d Bombardment Division B-24s, respectively, attack the marshalling yards at Blainville-sur-L'Eau and Chalons-sur-Marne. Two B-17s are lost.

In all, escort and support for the

afternoon heavy-bomber missions are provided by 543 VIII Fighter Command fighters, of which four are lost with three pilots. Four GAF FW-190s are downed by five 356th Fighter Group P-47 pilots at 1730 hours.
ITALY: Bad weather grounds the Twelfth and Fifteenth air forces, except for a small number of XII TAC P-40s that are able to attack a supply dump near Rome.

April 28, 1944

FRANCE: Unable to locate their primary target, 16 IX Bomber Command B-26s attack Cormeilles-en-Vexin Airdrome, and 250 IX Bomber Command B-26s dispatched to attack marshalling yards in France are recalled because of heavy cloud cover over the targets.

One hundred sixteen 1st Bombardment Division B-17s, escorted by 205 VIII Fighter Command fighters, attack Avord Airdrome. Losses are two B-17s with their crews and two P-51s with their pilots.

Of 106 3d Bombardment Division B-17s dispatched against V-weapons sites at Sottevast, just 18 attack the primary and targets of opportunity. Two B-17s are lost, and Col Robert H. Kelley, the 100th Heavy Bombardment Group commander, is killed.

Thirty-four 20th Fighter Group P-38s, led by a droopsnoot model, bomb Tours Airdrome. Forty-nine 55th Fighter Group P-38s, led by a droopsnoot model, bomb Chateaudun Airdrome, which is also dive-bombed by 32 353d Fighter Group P-47s.

During the afternoon, 47 2d Bombardment Division B-24s, escorted by 50 361st Fighter Group P-47s, attack the V-weapons sites at Marquise/Mimoyecques. One B-24 is lost.

Diverted from their primary target by cloud cover, 16 56th Fighter Group P-47s dive-bomb an unidentified Paris-area airdrome with 500-pound fragmentation bombs.
ITALY: One hundred sixty-eight Fifteenth Air Force B-24s attack the port area at San Stefano al Mare; 108 Fifteenth Air Force

B-24s attack the port area at Orbetello; 188 Fifteenth Air Force B-24s and B-17s attack a steel works and the port area at Piombino; Twelfth Air Force B-25s and B-26s attack rail bridges and viaducts; XII TAC A-20s attack a fuel dump; and XII TAC P-40s and P-47s attack a fuel dump, gun emplacements, and numerous rail targets throughout Italy.

April 29, 1944

FRANCE: Two hundred seventeen IX Bomber Command B-26s dispatched against marshalling yards in northern France abort in the face of heavy cloud cover over the targets.

Five hundred thirty-two Fifteenth Air Force heavy bombers attack the harbor area at Toulon with 1,312 tons of bombs.

A total of 11 GAF fighters are downed over southern France and the Mediterranean between 1130 and 1210 hours by escort pilots of the 1st, 31st, and 82d Fighter groups.

The 484th Heavy Bombardment Group, in B-24s, makes its combat debut with the Fifteenth Air Force's 49th Heavy Bombardment Wing.
GERMANY: Three hundred sixty-eight Eighth Air Force B-17s and 210 B-24s attack the city of Berlin, and 38 B-17s attack various targets of opportunity in the Berlin and Magdeburg areas. Thirty-eight B-17s and 25 B-24s are lost with a total of 18 crewmen killed and 606 missing.

Escort for the heavy bombers is provided by 814 USAAF fighters, of which 13 are lost with 12 pilots.

Despite the appearance of large numbers of GAF fighters over Berlin, only 11 of them are downed along the bomber routes between 1035 and 1305 hours. 1stLt Lowell K. Brueland, a P-51 pilot with the 354th Fighter Group's 355th Fighter Squadron, achieves ace status when he downs a Bf-109 near Stendal.
ITALY: Five Fifteenth Air Force B-17s attack the Ancona-Rimini rail line with radio-guided Azon bombs; Twelfth Air Force

B-25s attack a rail bridge and a viaduct; Twelfth Air Force B-26s attack bridges and bridge approaches at two locations; XII TAC A-20s attack a dump near Rome; and XII TAC P-40s and P-47s attack a town, gun emplacements near Anzio, the dock area at San Vincenzo, a marshalling yard, and road and rail targets.

April 30, 1944

FRANCE: More than 300 IX Bomber Command B-26s and A-20s attack V-weapons sites, construction sites, and marshalling yards.

One hundred fourteen 1st Bombardment Division B-17s attack Lyon/Bron Airdrome; 52 2d Bombardment Division B-24s attack V-weapons sites at St- Pol/Siracourt; and 118 3d Bombardment Division B-17s attack Clermont-Ferrand/Aulnat Airdrome. One B-17 is lost.

Escort for the Eighth Air Force heavy bombers is provided by 644 USAAF fighters, of which five are lost with four pilots.

Forty-four 20th Fighter Group P-38s, led by a droopsnoot model and escorted by 55th Fighter Group P-38s, bomb Tours Airdrome from high altitude with four 500-pound bombs apiece and then sweep ahead of the heavy bombers; the VIII Fighter Command's 339th Fighter Group, in P-51s, makes its combat debut by mounting a fighter sweep ahead of the heavy bombers; and a squadron of 353d Fighter Group P-47s dive-bombs Romorantin/Prunieres Airdrome before rendezvousing with the heavy bombers.

Eighteen GAF fighters are downed by USAAF fighters over France between 0920 hours and noon. 1stLt Richard A. Peterson, a P-51 pilot with the 357th Fighter Group's 364th Fighter Squadron, achieves ace status when he downs two FW-190s near Auxerre at 1140 hours; Capt Joseph E. Broadhead, a P-51 pilot with the 357th Fighter Group's 362d Fighter Squadron, achieves ace status when he downs a Bf-109 over Paris at 1145 hours; and 1stLt Joseph F. Pierce, a P-51 pilot with the 357th Fighter Group's 363d Fighter Squadron, achieves ace status when he downs two FW-190s near Orleans at 1150 hours.

In separate afternoon attacks, 22 20th Fighter Group P-38s, led by a droopsnoot model and escorted by 364th Fighter Group P-38s, attack Orleans/Bricy Airdrome from high altitude with nearly seven tons of fragmentation bombs; 21 353d Fighter Group P-47s dive-bomb Orleans/Bricy Airdrome; and five 353d Fighter Group P-47s dive-bomb a V-weapons site after becoming separated from the main force.

ITALY: Fifteenth Air Force B-24s attack marshalling yards at Alessandria and Milan; and Fifteenth Air Force B-17s attack the airdrome at Reggio Emilia and aircraft-industry targets at Milan and Varese.

The 464th Heavy Bombardment Group, in B-24s, makes its combat debut as part of the 55th Heavy Bombardment Wing.

MAY 1944

May 1, 1944

BELGIUM: During the afternoon, 13 3d Bombardment Division B-17s and 59 2d Bombardment Division B-24s attack a marshalling yard at Brussels, and 40 2d Bombardment Division B-24s attack a marshalling yard at Liege.

IX Bomber Command B-26s and A-20s attack a variety of industrial targets and marshalling yards.

The IX Bomber Command's 410th Light Bombardment Group, in A-20s, makes its combat debut. It is the last of eleven IX Bomber Command combat groups to enter combat.

ENGLAND: The Ninth Air Force's 50th, 370th, and 404th Fighter groups (in P-47s, P-47s, and P-38s, respectively) are declared operational.

FRANCE: Of 531 Eighth Air Force heavy bombers dispatched in the morning against 23 V-weapons sites in France, more than 400 abort in the face of bad weather. Only 22 3d Bombardment Division B-17s and 57 2d Bombardment Division B-24s attack assigned targets in the Pas-de-Calais area, and a total of 51 1st Bombardment Division B-17s attack Montdidier, Poix, and Roye/Amy airdromes as targets of opportunity.

IX Bomber Command B-26s and A-20s attack a variety of industrial targets and marshalling yards.

In the afternoon, 57 and 52 1st Bombardment Division B-17s, respectively, attack the marshalling yards at Reims and Troyes, and 42 and 64 3d Bombardment Division B-17s, respectively, attack the marshalling yards at Metz and Saarguemines.

GERMANY: 4th Fighter Group P-51 pilots down five Bf-109s, and a 355th Fighter Group P-51 pilot downs a sixth Bf-109 over northwestern Germany between 1810 and 1830 hours.

ITALY: Fifteenth Air Force B-24s attack Castel Maggiore and a rail bridge; Fifteenth Air Force B-17s attack a marshalling yard at Bolzano; Twelfth Air Force B-25s and B-26s attack several bridges in central and northern Italy and several marshalling yards in and around Florence; XII TAC A-20s attack an ammunition dump; and XII TAC fighter-bombers attack dumps, rail targets, a factory, several Axis ships at sea, and several tunnels.

UNITED STATES: The 493d Heavy Bombardment Group, in B-24s, begins its departure for England via the northern ferry route for service with the 3d Bombardment Division's 93d Combat Bombardment Wing. This group will be the last heavy-bomber unit to be assigned to the Eighth Air Force.

May 2, 1944

ETO: More than 250 IX Bomber Command B-26s and A-20s attack marshalling yards at three locations, and more than 400 Ninth Air Force P-47s and P-51s attack airdromes and marshalling yards throughout France, Belgium, and the Netherlands.

FRANCE: Fifty 2d Bombardment Division B-24s, escorted by 108 VIII Fighter Command fighters, attack V-weapons sites in the Pas-de-Calais area using GH blind-bombing equipment.

ITALY: Although more than 300 Fifteenth Air Force B-17s and B-24s abort in the face of bad weather, nearly 250 Fifteenth Air Force B-24s attack marshalling yards at Castel Maggiore and Parma, port facilities at La Spezia, and rail bridges at Faenza and Orbetello; Twelfth Air Force B-25s and B-26s attack bridges and marshalling yards; XII TAC A-20s attack an ammunition dump near Rome; and XII TAC fighter-bombers attack rail and road targets, bridges, landing grounds, and dumps in central and northern Italy.

May 3, 1944

FRANCE: Forty-seven 2d Bombardment Division B-24s, escorted by 101 VIII Fighter Command fighters, attack V-weapons sites around Wizernes using GH blind-bombing equipment.

ITALY: Twelfth Air Force B-25s and B-26s attack a marshalling yard and several bridges and bridge approaches; XII

TAC A-20s attack several ammunition dumps; and XII TAC fighter-bombers attack gun emplacements, bridges, rail lines, and buildings in the U.S. Fifth Army battle areas, plus rail lines, road bridges, dumps, and port facilities at Civitavecchia and Montalto di Castro, Axis vessels at sea, and numerous other targets of opportunity throughout northern and central Italy.

May 4, 1944

ENGLAND: The newly arrived 491st Heavy Bombardment Group, in B-24s, is assigned to the 2d Bombardment Division's 95th Combat Bombardment Wing.

FRANCE: Approximately 170 IX Bomber Command B-26s and 36 A-20s attack German Army gun and troop emplacements at six locations.

GERMANY: Three hundred sixty 1st Bombardment Division B-17s and 231 2d Bombardment Division B-24s are thwarted by heavy clouds from reaching assigned targets at Berlin and central Germany, but 40 of the B-17s are able to attack the Bergen/Alkmaar Airdrome (Netherlands) through holes in the clouds during their return flight to England.

Of 516 USAAF fighters dispatched to escort Eighth Air Force heavy bombers to Germany and back, three are lost in action and five are written off following various mishaps.

USAAF escort pilots down 11 GAF fighters in aerial engagements along the bomber routes. Capt Frank Q. O'Connor, a P-51 ace with the 354th Fighter Group's 356th Fighter Squadron, brings his final personal tally to 10.75 confirmed victories when he downs a Bf-109 near Hannover at 1045 hours.

ITALY: Twelfth Air Force B-25s and B-26s attack rail lines, marshalling yards, and rail bridges; and XII TAC fighter-bombers attack gun emplacements and a radar station near Anzio, marshalling yards at two locations, shipping at Leghorn, dumps, rail lines, a bridge, troop emplacements, and numerous other targets.

May 5, 1944

ENGLAND: BriGen Myron R. Wood assumes command of the IX Air Force Service Command.

The newly arrived 489th Heavy Bombardment Group, in B-24s, is assigned to the 2d Bombardment Division's 95th Combat Bombardment Wing.

FRANCE: Thirty-three 2d Bombardment Division B-24s led by a GH-equipped pathfinder attack the V-weapons site at Sottevast, but they are forced to bomb visually when the GH equipment malfunctions. Four crewmen are killed when a battle-damaged B-24 crashes while landing.

GERMANY: Capt Frank J. Koraleski, Jr., a P-51 pilot with the 355th Fighter Group's 354th Fighter Squadron, achieves ace status when he shares in the downing of a Do-217 (with four other pilots), a Bf-109 (with one other pilot), and an FW-44 biplane trainer (also with one other pilot) near Landsberg Airdrome between 1510 and 1530 hours.

ITALY: XII TAC A-20s attack a supply dump; and XII TAC fighter-bombers attack rail lines north and east of Rome, gun emplacements around Anzio, dumps, barges, the Canino landing ground, and numerous rail lines.

ROMANIA: Four hundred eighty-five Fifteenth Air Force heavy bombers attack marshalling yards and a pumping station at Ploesti; and 39 B-17s attack a marshalling yard at Turnu Severin. Nineteen bombers are lost over Ploesti to Axis fighters.

The 465th Heavy Bombardment Group, in B-24s, makes its combat debut over Ploesti as part of the 55th Heavy Bombardment Wing.

31st Fighter Group P-51 pilots down nine Axis fighters around Ploesti between 1355 and 1440 hours. 1stLt Raymond F. Harmeyer, a P-51 pilot with the 31st Fighter Group's 309th Fighter Squadron, achieves ace status when he downs a Bf-109 over Ploesti.

YUGOSLAVIA: One hundred sixteen

Fifteenth Air Force B-24s attack Axis troops around Podgorica;

May 6, 1944

FRANCE: Seventy 2d Bombardment Division B-24s attack the V-weapons sites at Siracourt, but 90 1st Bombardment Division B-17s dispatched against V-weapons sites in the Pas-de-Calais area abort in the face of heavy cloud cover over the target. Escort for the heavy bombers is provided by 185 USAAF fighters, including the veteran 359th Fighter Group, on its first P-51 mission.

The 398th Heavy Bombardment Group, in B-17s, makes its combat debut.

IX Bomber Command B-26s and A-20s dispatched to attack coastal-defense targets in France abort in the face of bad weather.

The Ninth Air Force's 10th Photographic Reconnaissance Group, in F-5s, begins an intense two-week effort to fully photo-map the OVERLORD invasion beaches and adjacent areas using the low-level oblique technique. (One F-5 and its pilot will be lost in the course of eleven single-plane sorties.)

ITALY: XII TAC A-20s attack storage dumps, and XII TAC fighter-bombers attack numerous rail and road targets, and several gun emplacements.

ROMANIA: Fifteenth Air Force B-17s and B-24s attack aircraft-industry targets around Brasov; B-17s attack a marshalling yard at Turnu Severin; and Fifteenth Air Force B-24s attack a marshalling yards at Campina, near the Ploesti oil complex.

1st, 14th, and 82d Fighter group P-38 pilots are credited with downing seven GAF fighters while escorting the heavy bombers on these various missions.

May 7, 1944

BELGIUM: An effort by 2d Bombardment Division B-24s to attack marshalling yards at Liege fails when the bombers are unable to assemble for the morning mission. A second attempt in the afternoon is somewhat more successful when 29 of 67 3d

Bombardment Division B-24s dispatched locate the target through heavy cloud cover. Unfortunately, all bombs miss the target.

The 486th and 487th Heavy Bombardment groups, in B-24s, make their combat debuts during the 3d Bombardment Division afternoon mission.

FRANCE: The Ninth Air Force opens a bombing campaign by bombers and fighter-bombers against rail bridges serving the OVERLORD invasion area, especially those spanning the Meuse and Seine rivers. Throughout the day, Ninth Air Force fighter-bombers attack airfields and bridges within 130 miles of the invasion beaches in Normandy. Among other damage, eight P-47s armed with two 1,000-pound bombs apiece completely destroy a bridge at Vernon following a low-level bombing run.

GERMANY: Two hundred eighty-three 1st Bombardment Division B-17s and 231 3d Bombardment B-17s attack the city of Berlin with more than 1,250 tons of bombs; 39 B-17s attack various targets of opportunity; 147 2d Bombardment Division B-24s attack Munster; and 165 2d Bombardment Division B-24s attack Osnabruck. Eight B-17s are lost and 265 B-17s are damaged. One B-24 ditches and all but two crewmen are lost.

Seven hundred fifty-four USAAF fighters escort and support the heavy-bomber missions to Germany at a cost of four fighters and three pilots lost.

ITALY: Twelfth Air Force medium bombers are grounded by bad weather; XII TAC A-20s attack a dump; and XII TAC fighter-bombers attack targets on Elba Island, and road and rail targets, several harbors, and other targets throughout central Italy.

ROMANIA: Fifteenth Air Force B-17s and B-24s attack marshalling yards at Bucharest.

14th and 31st Fighter group escort pilots down nine Axis fighters over and around Bucharest between 1100 and 1210 hours. Capt Samuel J. Brown and 1stLt Richard D. Faxon, P-51 pilots with the 31st Fighter Group, achieve ace status when each

downs a Romanian Air Force IAR.80 fighter over Bucharest at about noon.

YUGOSLAVIA: Fifteenth Air Force B-17s attack a rail bridge in Belgrade.

May 8, 1944

BELGIUM: During the afternoon, 57 3d Bombardment Division B-17s attack a marshalling yard at Brussels.

ENGLAND: The Ninth Air Force's 36th and 373d Fighter groups, both in P-47s, are declared operational.

ETO: Gen Dwight D. Eisenhower sets the Operation OVERLORD D day for June 5.

Approximately 450 IX Bomber Command B-26s and A-20s attack airdromes, V-weapons sites, and coastal-defense positions in northern France and Belgium.

FRANCE: During the afternoon, 92 1st and 3d Bombardment division B-17s attack V-weapons sites at Glacerie and Sottevast. Five B-17s are lost.

Throughout the day, approximately 450 IX Bomber Command B-26 and A-20 sorties, and numerous fighter-bomber missions are mounted against airfields and bridges spanning the Meuse River. In the first IX Bomber Command missions against specific rail bridges, B-26s attack a bridge spanning the Seine River at Oissel. (To help mask the intended OVERLORD invasion area, the Seine and Meuse bridges are to be attacked with equal intensity. Overall, despite the buildup of intense flak concentrations, the bombing campaign against such bridges prior to the invasion will be extremely successful. By D day, all rail bridges from Rouen to about 10 miles west of Paris will have been made impassable. And a similar effort against road bridges in the same region will be nearly as successful.)

GERMANY: Of 500 1st and 3d Bombardment division B-17s dispatched against Berlin, 386 attack the city, 17 attack the Brandenburg suburb, and 50 attack targets of last resort at Brunswick and Magdeburg. Also, 288 2d Bombardment Division B-24s attack the city of Brunswick, as planned.

Twenty-five B-17s and 11 B-24s are lost, and seven B-24s are written off.

Escort for the Eighth Air Force heavy bombers is provided by 729 USAAF fighters, of which 13 are lost with their pilots in fierce air-to-air combat over Germany, Belgium, and the Netherlands.

USAAF escort pilots down 56 GAF fighters along the bomber routes between 0930 and 1235 hours, and some USAAF fighter groups strafe targets of opportunity during their return legs. Capt Clayton E. Davis, a P-51 pilot with the 352d Fighter Group's 487th Fighter Squadron, achieves ace status when he downs three Bf-109s and shares in the downing of an FW-190 near Brunswick between 0930 and 1010 hours; 1stLt Carl J. Luksic, a P-51 pilot with the 352d Fighter Group's 487th Fighter Squadron, achieves ace status with a total of eight confirmed victories when he downs three FW-190s and two Bf-109s near Brunswick between 0935 and 1030 hours; LtCol John C. Meyer, the commanding officer of the 352d Fighter Group's 487th Fighter Squadron, achieves ace status when he downs three Bf-109s near Bremen between 0935 and 1030 hours; Capt Robert S. Johnson, a P-47 pilot with the 56th Fighter Group's 62d Fighter Squadron, brings his final personal tally to 27 confirmed victories when he downs an Bf-109 and an FW-190 near Hannover at 1000 hours; 1stLt Robert J. Booth, a P-51 pilot with the 359th Fighter Group's 369th Fighter Squadron, achieves ace status when he downs an FW-190 and two Bf-109s near Drakenburg between 1000 and 1010 hours; Maj Stephen W. Andrew, the commanding officer of the 352d Fighter Group's 486th Fighter Squadron, achieves ace status when he downs an FW-190 near Hannover at 1015 hours; and Capt Frank A. Cutler, a P-51 pilot with the 352d Fighter Group's 486th Fighter Squadron, achieves ace status when he downs two Bf-109s near Gifhorn at 1030 hours.

ITALY: XII TAC fighter-bombers attack a supply dump near Anzio as well as numerous road and rail targets in central Italy.

May 9, 1944

BELGIUM: Ninety-six 2d Bombardment Division B-24s attack Florennes/Juzaine Airdrome; 101 2d Bombardment Division B-24s attack St.-Trond Airdrome; and 63 2d Bombardment Division B-24s attack a marshalling yard at Liege.

ENGLAND: The Ninth Air Force's 367th and 406th Fighter groups, in P-38s and P-47s, respectively, are declared operational. These additions bring the IX Fighter Command to a final wartime strength of 18 combat groups.

ETO: The Allied Expeditionary Air Force, Eighth Air Force, and RAF Bomber Command open a full-scale bomber and fighter-bomber offensive against GAF bases in France and Belgium. The aim of the ongoing effort will be to drive the GAF from the OVERLORD invasion area by D day.

Escort for the USAAF heavy bombers attacking targets in France, Belgium, and Luxembourg is provided by 668 VIII Fighter Command and 202 IX Fighter Command fighters, of which seven are lost with their pilots. Five GAF fighters are downed over northern Europe during the morning.

FRANCE: Thirty-seven 1st Bombardment Division B-17s attack Thionville Airdrome; 37 1st Bombardment Division B-17s attack a marshalling yard at Thionville; 75 1st Bombardment Division B-17s attack St.-Dizier/Robinson Airdrome; a total of 16 2d Bombardment Division B-24s unable to attack their primary targets attack Hody and Nivelles airdromes; 71 3d Bombardment Division B-17s attack Juvincourt Airdrome; 113 3d Bombardment Division B-17s attack Laon/Athies Airdrome; 43 3d Bombardment Division B-17s attack Lille/Vendeville Airdrome; a total of 11 3d Bombardment Division B-17s unable to attack their primary targets attack Chievres (Belgium) and Lille/Vendeville airdromes; and 68 3d Bombardment Division B-24s attack Laon/Couvron Airdrome.

Forty IX Bomber Command B-26s attack bridges, V-weapons sites, and coastal-defense positions in northern France, and Ninth Air Force P-47s attack V-weapons sites.

The first successful B-24 mission overseen by groups of the 3d Bombardment Division is flown against Laon/Couvron Airdrome. In all, five B-24 groups will be added to the 3d Bombardment Division, but the logistics and maintenance problems inherent in mixing types of such complicated equipment as heavy bombers results in an early decision to reequip the five 3d Bombardment Division B-24 groups with B-17s. This program will not be completed until late in the year.

ITALY: Twelfth Air Force B-26s attack a rail bridge and viaduct; XII TAC A-20s attack several fuel dumps; and XII TAC fighter-bombers attack numerous road and rail targets in the region north of Rome.

LUXEMBOURG: Fifty-three 1st Bombardment Division B-17s attack a marshalling yard at Luxembourg City.

May 10, 1944

AUSTRIA: Despite bad weather along the bomber route that results in many aborts, 126 Fifteenth Air Force B-24s and 174 B-17s attack the Wiener-Neustadt Bf-109 plant with 795 tons of bombs, and 102 B-24s attack the Wiener-Neustadt/Nord Airdrome with 212 tons of bombs. Twenty-eight heavy bombers and three escort fighters are lost.

The 485th Heavy Bombardment Group, in B-24s, makes its combat debut as part of the 55th Heavy Bombardment Wing. It is the twenty-first and last heavy-bomber group to join the Fifteenth Air Force.

More than 200 Fifteenth Air Force fighters provide escort for the heavy bombers. P-38 pilots of the 1st, 14th, and 82d Fighter groups account for 13 GAF fighters on the way to or over the target. 2dLt Franklin C. Lathrope, a P-38 pilot with the 1st Fighter Group's 94th Fighter Squadron, achieves ace status when he downs a pair of Bf-109s south of Wiener-Neustadt.

The 52d Fighter Group undertakes its first escort mission with the Fifteenth Air Force since transitioning to P-51s.

BELGIUM: Ninth Air Force B-26s, P-47s, and P-51s attack airdromes, marshalling yards, and V-weapons sites.

ENGLAND: The day's planned Eighth Air Force mission to Germany is abandoned due to bad weather encountered over England during the early stages of the assembly. Many Ninth Air Force bomber and fighter-bomber missions are also canceled due to the bad weather.

FRANCE: Ninth Air Force B-26s, P-47s, and P-51s attack airdromes, marshalling yards, and V-weapons sites.

ITALY: Twelfth Air Force B-25s attack bridges at five locations; Twelfth Air Force B-26s attack bridges near Arezzo; and XII TAC fighter-bombers attack numerous road and rail targets.

NORTH SEA: The Eighth Air Force air-sea rescue squadron (officially designated the 65th Fighter Group Detachment "B") mounts its first sorties of the war in support of the RAF Air-Sea Rescue Service. The new USAAF unit initially employs war-weary P-47s in a spotter role only, but modifications to the airplanes will soon allow the unit to drop inflatable dinghies to aviators whose planes have gone down in the sea. The unit is composed of pilots and aircraft drawn from 16 VIII Fighter Command P-47 groups and stations. (Several modified B-17s and six Consolidated OA-10 Catalina flying boats will reach the unit in early 1945.)

YUGOSLAVIA: Nineteen Fifteenth Air Force heavy bombers unable to join the main attack on Wiener-Neustadt drop their bombs on Knin.

May 11, 1944

BELGIUM: During the morning, IX Bomber Command B-26s attack a marshalling yard at Aerschot. During the afternoon, 104 Eighth Air Force B-17s attack two marshalling yards in Brussels, 119 B-17s attack the marshalling yards at Liege, and 20 B-17s unable to attack their briefed targets attack the rail junction at Malines. Two B-17s are lost.

ENGLAND: Personnel and B-24 aircraft of the 467th Heavy Bombardment Group's 788th Heavy Bombardment Squadron and the 490th Heavy Bombardment Group's 850th Heavy Bombardment Squadron are transferred to the secret 801st Provisional Heavy Bombardment Group for eventual service parachuting agents and supplies to Occupied Europe.

ETO: More than 100 Ninth Air Force fighters abort or are recalled from planned fighter-bomber missions.

Escort for various Eighth Air Force afternoon B-17 missions against targets in France, Belgium, Germany, and Luxembourg is provided by a total of 471 VIII and IX Fighter command fighters, of which four are lost with their pilots.

FRANCE: Despite cloudy conditions, a total of 195 2d Bombardment Division B-24s attack the marshalling yards at Belfort, Epinal, and Mulhouse, as planned; 99 2d Bombardment Division B-24s attack various targets of opportunity; and 70 3d Bombardment Division B-17s dispatched against the marshalling yard at Chaumont fail to reach the target. Six B-24s are downed by flak, and two B-24s are interned in Switzerland.

The 492d Heavy Bombardment Group, in B-24s, makes its combat debut with the 2d Bombardment Division.

Escort and support for the 2d Bombardment Division are provided by 536 VIII Fighter Command fighters, of which five are lost with their pilots.

The Ninth Air Force turns the bulk of its attention against GAF bases within range of Caen by attacking airdromes at Beaumont-le-Roger and Cormeilles-en-Vexin, and IX Bomber Command B-26s also attack a marshalling yard at Mezieres.

During the afternoon, 12 Eighth Air Force B-17s unable to reach their briefed primary attack the marshalling yard at Thionville.

78th Fighter Group P-47 pilots down three GAF fighters over France between 1410 and 1445 hours.

GERMANY: During afternoon missions by Eighth Air Force B-17s, 19 attack a marshalling yard at Bettembourg, 60 attack a marshalling yard at Ehrgang, 55 attack a marshalling yard at Kons Karthaus, 58 attack a marshalling yard at Saarbrucken, and 16 attack a marshalling yard at Volkingen. Six B-17s are lost.

354th Fighter Group P-51 pilots down ten GAF fighters over Germany and Luxembourg between 1810 and 1900 hours. 1stLt Robert D. Welden, a P-51 pilot with the 354th Fighter Group's 356th Fighter Squadron, achieves ace status when he downs an FW-190 near Saarbrucken at 1845 hours, and Capt Charles W. Lasko, a P-51 pilot with the 354th Fighter Group's 355th Fighter Squadron, achieves ace status when he shares in the downing of a Bf-109 over Luxembourg at 1900 hours.

ITALY: Although many missions are canceled or redirected because of bad weather, Twelfth Air Force B-25s and B-26s attack a rail line, and bridges and viaducts at five locations; and XII TAC fighter-bombers attack Littoria Airdrome, rail targets throughout central Italy, and many German Army fighting positions along the front lines facing the U.S. Fifth and British Eighth armies.

LUXEMBOURG: During the afternoon, 53 Eighth Air Force B-17s attack a marshalling yard at Luxembourg City.

MTO: Operation STRANGLE, the aerial interdiction of the Germany Army's supply distribution system in Italy is concluded for lack of viable targets. Since March 15, MAAF units have mounted 65,000 effective bomber, fighter-bomber, and fighter sorties that have sown 33,100 tons of bombs against transportation targets and supply dumps throughout central and northern Italy.

Upon the cancellation of Operation STRANGLE, Operation DIADEM is launched in support of Allied ground attacks aimed at breaching the German Army's Gustav

Line and driving through to Rome. Operation DIADEM is billed as an all-out aerial offensive against the German Army in Italy.

May 12, 1944

BELGIUM: Despite thick haze that results in many aborts, Ninth Air Force B-26s attack V-weapons sites, bridges, rail targets, railroad guns, coastal defenses, and airdromes.

ENGLAND: IX Troop Carrier Command transport aircraft and U.S. Army paratroopers conduct Operation EAGLE, a full-dress rehearsal for the D-day airborne component.

FRANCE: Despite thick haze that results in many aborts, Ninth Air Force B-26s attack V-weapons sites, bridges, rail targets, railroad guns, coastal defenses, and airdromes.

GERMANY: In the Eighth Air Force's first mission of the war against oil-industry targets, 814 B-17s and B-24s escorted by an all-out USAAF and RAF fighter effort, drop nearly 1,700 tons of bombs on the German oil plants at Bohlen, Brux (Czechoslovakia), Lutzkendorf, Merseburg, Zeitz, and Zwickau, as well as several targets of opportunity. Many of the oil plants are severely damaged by the bombs, but of equal importance are the heavy losses sustained by the GAF interceptor force sent aloft to challenge the bombers. Nearly 200 German fighters are claimed as destroyed by escort fighter pilots and bomber gunners. However, GAF fighter opposition is especially violent against the leading 3d Bombardment Division formations, which lose 41 of 43 B-17s (and three B-24s).

Escort is provided by a record 735 VIII Fighter Command fighters and 245 IX Fighter Command fighters, of which ten are lost with their pilots. 1stLt John B. Carder, a seven-victory P-51 ace with the 357th Fighter Group's 364th Fighter Squadron, is shot down and captured.

Sixty-seven GAF fighters are downed along the bomber routes between 1140 and 1500 hours. Capt James W. Wilkinson, a P-47 pilot with the 78th Fighter Group's 82d Fighter Squadron, achieves ace status when he downs an FW-190 near Koblenz at 1220 hours; Capt Clarence E. Anderson, Jr., a P-51 pilot with the 357th Fighter Group's 363d Fighter Squadron, achieves ace status when he downs a Bf-109 near Frankfurt am Main at 1230 hours; Capt Joe H. Powers, a P-47 ace with the 56th Fighter Group's 61st Fighter Squadron, brings his final personal tally to 14.5 confirmed victories when he shares in the downing of a Bf-109 near Frankfurt am Main at 1230 hours; 1stLt Robert J. Rankin, a P-47 pilot with the 56th Fighter Group's 61st Fighter Squadron, achieves ace status with a total of nine confirmed victories when he downs five Bf-109s between Marburg and Koblenz between 1230 and 1300 hours; and 1stLt William C. Reese, a P-51 pilot with the 357th Fighter Group's 362d Fighter Squadron, achieves ace status when he downs a Bf-109 near Schweinfurt at 1250 hours.

The VIII Fighter Command's 361st Fighter Group completes its first combat mission since transitioning to P-51s from P-47s.

ITALY: During the course of the day, the Fifteenth Air Force mounts 1,143 heavy-bomber sorties loaded with 1,912 tons of bombs against numerous targets in Italy as part of Operation DIADEM, the general Allied air offensive aimed at breaking the will of German Army forces facing Allied ground troops. Among the many targets attacked are the German Army headquarters at Massa d'Albe and Monte Soratte. Harbors and rail targets are also attacked. Escort is provided by more than 250 Fifteenth Air Force fighter sorties, and 25 Fifteenth Air Force P-38s strafe Piacenza Airdrome.

Twelfth Air Force B-26s and XII TAC A-20s attack German Army troop concentrations around Fondi in support of the U.S. Fifth Army's advance toward Rome. Attacks by Twelfth Air Force medium bombers are also mounted against Pastena and Vallecorsa, as well as numerous tactical positions along the battle lines. XII TAC fighter-bombers attack numerous tactical targets and troop positions along the battle lines as well as rear-area troop concentrations and transportation targets.

324th Fighter Group P-40s are specially equipped with phosphorous and fragmentation cluster bombs and dispatched to attack Monte Cassino's Monastery Hill at low level. Diving through an undercast and heavy flak, 24 P-40s release more than five tons of bombs precisely on the target, thus eliminating resistance and allowing pinned-down Allied ground units to move freely through the area. Immediately after the successful attack, 12 additional 324th Fighter Group P-40s attack German Army troops as they mass for a counterattack near Monastery Hill. This attack is broken up before it begins by the accurate delivery of 12 500-pound bombs and three separate strafing passes by each fighter. Allied troops hunkered down within 75 yards of the target area are not molested.

During the day, Twelfth and Fifteenth Air Force fighter pilots are credited with downing eight GAF fighters over Italy and an He-177 near Elba Island.

May 13, 1944

BELGIUM: IX Bomber Command B-26s and A-20s attack coastal defenses and V-weapons sites, and P-47 dive-bombers attack tactical targets.
FRANCE: IX Bomber Command B-26s and A-20s attack coastal defenses and V-weapons sites, and P-47 dive-bombers attack tactical targets.
GERMANY: Two hundred seventy-two 1st Bombardment Division B-17s dispatched against oil-industry targets in western Poland are diverted because of bad weather against the Baltic coastal cities of Stettin and Straslund, where they drop a total of 763 tons of bombs. Ten B-17s are lost.

Two hundred twenty-eight 2d Bombardment Division B-24s attack an aircraft factory at Tutow, as briefed, and 12 B-24s attack targets of opportunity. One B-24 is lost.

One hundred seventy-eight 3d Bombardment Division B-17s attack a marshalling yard at Osnabruck. One B-17 is lost.

Escort for the heavy bombers is provided by a record 737 VIII Fighter Command fighters and 370 IX Fighter Command fighters, of which nine are lost with their pilots. Capt Frank A. Cutler, a 352d Fighter Group P-51 pilot who achieved ace status on May 8, is shot down and killed shortly after downing a Bf-109 near Neubrandenburg at 1420 hours.

USAAF escort fighters down 54 GAF aircraft. Capt Wallace N. Emmer, a P-51 pilot with the 354th Fighter Group's 353d Fighter Squadron, achieves ace status when he downs two Bf-109s over Germany during an afternoon mission; 1stLt Francis H. Horne, a P-51 pilot with the 352d Fighter Group's 328th Fighter Squadron, achieves ace status when he downs two FW-190s near Demmin at 1315 hours; Col Joe L. Mason, the commanding officer of the 352d Fighter Group, in P-51s, achieves ace status when he downs two Bf-109s and an FW-190 near Demmin at 1420 hours; and Maj George E. Preddy, the commanding officer of the 352d Fighter Group's 487th Fighter Squadron, achieves ace status when he downs two Bf-109s near Neubrandenburg at 1425 hours.

355th Fighter Group P-51s complete the deepest target penetration to date in the ETO, a 1,470-mile round trip to Posen (Poznan, Poland).
ITALY: The Fifteenth Air Force dispatches more than 670 heavy bombers on missions in support of the Allied ground offensive: B-24s attack marshalling yards at Bolgna, Piacenza, and Vicenza; and B-17s attack a rail bridge and the marshalling yard at Bolzano, and marshalling yards at Bronzola and Trento.

On a separate mission by the 301st Heavy Bombardment Group, four Azon-equipped B-17s lead a bombing run on a viaduct north of Trento. The guided bombs, and many others, blast a 70-foot gap in the viaduct and thus close down rail traffic from Brenner Pass.

The entire Twelfth Air Force devotes its energies to supporting the Allied ground attacks against the Gustav Line: Twelfth Air Force B-25s attack German-held towns directly behind the battle area; Twelfth Air Force B-26s attack several rail bridges; XII TAC A-20s attack a German Army command post; and XII TAC fighter-bombers attack an array of tactical targets in and around the battle area.

May 14, 1944

ITALY: Fifteenth Air Force B-24s attack the Piacenza and Reggio Emilia airdromes, and a marshalling yard at Vicenza; Fifteenth Air Force B-17s attack marshalling yards at Ferrara and Mantua and the Piacenza Airdrome; 48 Fifteenth Air Force P-38s strafe the Aviano and Villaorba airdromes; Twelfth Air Force B-25s and B-26s attack bridges, bridge approaches, and viaducts north and northwest of Rome; XII TAC A-20s attack German Army command posts in the battle area; and XII TAC fighter-bombers attack road and rail targets, gun emplacements, bridges, and an array of tactical targets throughout the battle area.

P-40 pilots of the XII TAC's 324th Fighter Group attack German Army ground forces in the enemy stronghold at Castellonorato, dropping fragmentation, demolition, and phosphorous bombs so accurately and with such force that the German garrison immediately surrenders to nearby Allied ground units.

SCOTLAND: The 479th Fighter Group, in P-38s, arrives from the United States aboard ship for service with the VIII Fighter Command's 65th Fighter Wing.

May 15, 1944

FRANCE: Thirty-eight 1st Bombardment Division B-17s attack V-weapons sites at Marquise/Mimoyecques, and 90 2d Bombardment Division B-24s attack V-weapons sites at Siracourt.

More than 300 IX Bomber Command B-26s and A-20s abort in the face of heavy clouds, but small groups amounting to 45 medium and light bombers attack a marshalling yard at Somain and the Creil and Evreux/Fauville airdromes.

The Ninth Air Force's 10th Photographic Reconnaissance Group, in F-5s, opens an intensive final preinvasion effort to photographically monitor all GAF airfields within range of the OVERLORD invasion beaches; produce photo mosaics of all the airborne-invasion landing areas and drop zones; cover all the main roads in the invasion area; cover all the Seine River bridges between Paris and the sea, and all Loire River bridges between Orleans and Nantes; and produce photo mosaics for a study by the IX Bomber Command of the flak defenses around Liege, Belgium.

ITALY: The Fifteenth Air Force is grounded by bad weather; Twelfth Air Force B-25s and B-26s, and XII TAC A-20s, attack road and rail targets north and northwest of the battle area, and port facilities and vessels along both coasts; and XII TAC fighter-bombers provide close and direct support for Allied ground forces battling through the Gustav Line.

May 16, 1944

ITALY: Twelfth Air Force B-25s and B-26s attack rail bridges and a tunnel in central Italy; XII TAC A-20s attack gun emplacements; and XII TAC fighter-bombers sweep vehicles and roads to the immediate rear of the Allied battle lines, thus isolating the German Army ground forces from reinforcement and resupply.

May 17, 1944

ITALY: Fifteenth Air Force heavy bombers attack the port facilities at Piombino and San Stefano al Mare, a marshalling yard at Ancona, a causeway at Orbetello, and a steel factory; Fifteenth Air Force P-38s attack the Forli, Ghedi, Modena, Reggio Emilia, and Villafranca di Verona airdromes; Twelfth Air Force B-25s attack Viterbo Airdrome; Twelfth Air Force B-26s attack road bridges directly behind the battle area; XII TAC A-20s attack a German Army command post at Valmontone and drop supplies to Free French Army troops; and XII TAC fighter-bombers attack gun emplacements at Cassino and elsewhere, and numerous bridges and road and rail targets throughout the battle area.

YUGOSLAVIA: Fifteenth Air Force heavy bombers attack Bihac.

May 18, 1944

FRANCE: An attempt by the Ninth Air Force's 404th Fighter Group to dive-bomb Beaumont-sur-Oise Airdrome is thwarted by bad weather.

ITALY: Twelfth Air Force B-25s and B-26s attack rail bridges throughout central and northern Italy; XII TAC A-20s attack supply dumps; and XII TAC fighter-bombers attack railroads, several defended towns, and scores of tactical positions in direct and close support of Allied ground forces.

ROMANIA: Approximately 700 Fifteenth Air Force heavy bombers are dispatched on the first *authorized* direct attack against the Ploesti oil-refining facilities, but most groups turn back because of extremely heavy cloud cover. Only 206 heavy bombers loaded with 493 tons of bombs complete their attacks, and 14 of these are downed by flak and fighters. While escorting the bombers, P-38 and P-51 pilots of the 1st, 14th, 31st, and 325th Fighter groups down 14 Axis fighters over Romania between 1025 hours and noon.

YUGOSLAVIA: A number of Fifteenth Air Force heavy bombers deterred from the day's main attack against Ploesti attack marshalling yards at Belgrade and Nis. Also, Fifteenth Air Force escort fighters strafe the airdromes at Scutari (Abania) and Nis.

May 19, 1944

FRANCE: Despite a thick haze over many targets that results in well over a hundred aborts, nearly 300 IX Bomber Command B-26s and A-20s, along with nearly 300 P-47 dive-bombers, attack coastal-defense positions, railroad guns, port facilities, and V-weapons sites. A P-47 pilot with the IX TAC's 404th Fighter Group downs a Bf-109 (that unit's first victory) near Rouen at 2040 hours.

GERMANY: Four hundred ninety-five 1st and 3d Bombardment division B-17s using H2X radar guidance attack the city of Berlin through very heavy cloud cover; 49 1st Division B-17s unable to locate the primary attack the port facilities at Kiel; and 272 2d Bombardment Division B-24s attack aircraft-industry targets at Brunswick. Sixteen B-17s and 12 B-24s are lost.

Escort for the heavy-bomber formation is provided by a total of 700 VIII Fighter Command fighters and 264 IX Fighter Command fighters, of which 19 aircraft and 17 pilots are lost.

USAAF escort pilots down a total of 71 GAF aircraft over Germany and the Baltic Sea between 1220 and 1615 hours. 1stLt Ray S. Wetmore, a P-51 pilot with the 359th Fighter Group's 370th Fighter Squadron, achieves ace status when he downs two Bf-109s near Stendal at 1245 hours; Maj Leslie C. Smith, the commanding officer of the 56th Fighter Group's 61st Fighter Squadron, in P-47s, achieves ace status when he downs two FW-190s near Oschersleben, between 1335 and 1350 hours; and two P-51 pilots with the 4th Fighter Group's 334th Fighter Squadron achieve ace status: Capt Howard D. Hively, when he downs three Bf-109s near Schwerin between 1515 and 1530 hours; and 1stLt David W. Howe, when he downs a Bf-109 over Neustadt Bay at 1530 hours.

ITALY: Fifteenth Air Force B-24s attack port facilities at Leghorn and La Spezia; Fifteenth Air Force B-17s attack oil-industry targets at Porto Marghera and rail bridges at three locations; Twelfth Air Force B-25s and B-26s attack rail bridges in north-central Italy; XII TAC A-20s attack an ammunition dump; and XII TAC fighter-bombers provide direct and close support for Allied ground forces advancing in many areas of central Italy.

May 20, 1944

FRANCE: Ninety and 73 1st Bombardment Division B-17s, respectively, attack Paris/ Orly Airport and Villacoublay Airdrome; 125 2d Bombardment Division B-24s attack Reims/Champagne Airdrome and marshalling yard; and 271 3d Bombardment Division B-17s abort in the face of heavy cloud cover. Losses to enemy action are two B-24s, but eight B-17s and three B-24s are lost in accidents during takeoffs and assembly in thick fog.

Escort for the heavy bombers is provided by 657 VIII Fighter Command fighters and 296 IX Fighter Command fighters, of which four aircraft and pilots are lost. Two GAF fighters are downed by 55th Fighter Group P-38 pilots near Sens at 1100 hours.

Although as many as 250 IX Bomber Command B-26s abort in the face of heavy clouds over many targets, approximately 200 B-26s attack airfields, V-weapons sites, and coastal defenses. Many Ninth Air Force P-47 fighter-bombers also attack the same types of targets.

ITALY: Twelfth Air Force bombers are grounded because of bad weather, but XII TAC fighter-bombers are extremely active against communications, transportation, and tactical targets.

May 21, 1944

ETO: Fighter units operating under the aegis of the AEAF open Operation CHATTA-NOOGA CHOO-CHOO against rail movements by German military forces throughout France, Belgium, and western Germany.

FRANCE: Twenty-five 1st Bombardment Division B-17s and 99 2d Bombardment Division B-24s, respectively, attack V-weapons sites at Marquise/Mimoyecques and Siracourt with the aid of GH blind-bombing equipment.

Fifty IX Bomber Command B-26s attack Abbeville/Drucat Airdrome.

An estimated 500 Ninth Air Force P-47s and P-51s attack locomotives and rail cars throughout France. For the loss of nine fighters, the Ninth Air Force fighters and fighter-bombers account for 46 locomotives destroyed and 11 probably destroyed, plus assorted other damage to locomotives, rolling stock, and rail facilities.

GERMANY: During their first missions posted under Operation CHATTANOOGA CHOO-CHOO, VIII Fighter Command fighters ranging over Germany destroy 91 locomotives of 225 attacked. Targets of opportunity, including many airdromes and rail bridges, are also attacked by the fighters.

Losses are the highest to date posted by the fighter units based in the U.K.: 27 fighters downed by enemy action and 26 pilots listed as missing. 1stLt Joseph F. Pierce, a seven-victory P-51 ace with the 357th Fighter Group's 363d Fighter Squadron, is shot down by flak and killed near Anklam; and 1stLt William C. Reese, a five-victory P-51 ace with the 357th Fighter Group's 362d Fighter Squadron, is shot down and killed by flak over Straslund.

Eighth and Ninth air force fighter pilots down 21 GAF aircraft, including as many as eight trainers and four or five other noncombatants, between 1220 and 1335 hours.

ITALY: Although flight operations are severely restricted because of bad weather, Twelfth Air Force B-25s and B-26s attack several roads and bridges in north-central Italy; XII TAC A-20s attack a German Army bivouac; and XII TAC fighter-bombers maintain pressure on German Army forces in the battle areas and also range throughout central Italy to attack rail and other communications targets.

May 22, 1944

BELGIUM: A total of 130 VIII Fighter Command P-47 fighter-bombers attack rail bridges at Hasselt (primary) and Liege (targets of opportunity). One P-47 and its pilot are lost.

ENGLAND: North Pickenham Airdrome becomes the last of 77 British airfields to be turned over to the USAAF.

FRANCE: Ninety-four 2d Bombardment Division B-24s attack the V-weapons sites at Siracourt.

1stLt Morris A. Stanley, a P-51 pilot with the 357th Fighter Group's 364th Fighter Squadron, achieves ace status when he downs two FW-190s near Strasbourg at 1220 hours.

Approximately 330 IX Bomber Command B-26s and A-20s attack airfields around Calais, Cherbourg, and Paris; and more than 300 Ninth Air Force P-47s and P-51s dive-bomb numerous marshalling yards in the same regions. 474th Fighter Group P-38s mount the Ninth Air Force's first attacks within the city of Paris when they bomb and strafe Paris/Orly Airport.

During the night of May 22–23, 16 322d Medium Bombardment Group B-26s attack Beaumont-le-Roger Airdrome (which the 322d had also attacked earlier in the day). This is the first USAAF group-strength B-26 night-bombing mission of the war against Germany.

GERMANY: Two hundred eighty-nine of 342 1st and 3d Bombardment division B-17s dispatched attack port facilities at Kiel. Five B-17s are lost.

Escort and support for the B-17s are provided by 568 VIII Fighter Command fighters, of which seven airplanes and six pilots are lost.

VIII Fighter Command escort pilots down 23 GAF fighters over Germany between 1150 and 1320 hours. FO Evan D. McMinn, a P-47 pilot with the 56th Fighter Group's 61st Fighter Squadron, achieves ace status when he downs two FW-190s near Rothenburg between noon and 1215 hours; and Capt Nicholas Megura, a P-51 ace with the 4th Fighter Group's 334th Fighter Squadron, brings his final personal tally to 11.833 victories when he shares in the downing of a Bf-109 near Kiel at 1315 hours. Unfortunately, the P-38 pilot with whom Megura shares the victory also damages Megura's P-51 to the point where Megura is forced to land in nearby Sweden, where he is interned.

ITALY: As a result of the Allied breakthrough at the Gustav Line, Operation DIADEM, the air-support phase of the Allied offensive, in canceled. Since May 12, as part of DIADEM, MAAF aircraft have flown nearly 73,000 effective sorties and have dropped 51,500 tons of bombs. Twelfth Air Force aircraft alone are credited with the destruction of 6,577 motor vehicles.

More than 550 Fifteenth Air Force B-17s and B-24s attack the Ancona-Pescara rail line, troop concentrations at Avezzano, an oil depot at La Spezia, ammunition and supply dumps Carrara, road and rail bridges at Pineto, port facilities at Piombino, and town areas at Palestrina, Pescina, and Valmontone.

Most Twelfth Air Force bombers are grounded or abort, but XII TAC fighter-bombers attack defended towns, roads, bridges, troop concentrations, and numerous other targets while supporting Allied advances on the ground.

The formal assignment of the 332d Fighter Group to the Fifteenth Air Force leaves only the 350th Fighter Group and several night-fighter squadrons remaining under the control of the XII Fighter Command.

May 23, 1944

BELGIUM: During the afternoon, 75 359th and 361st Fighter group P-51 fighter-bombers attack and demolish a rail bridge at Hasselt. One P-51 is lost with its pilot.

FRANCE: Fifteen IX Bomber Command B-26s mount a predawn attack against Beaumont-le-Roger Airdrome.

The Eighth Air Force dispatches 1,045 B-17s and B-24s—a record number launched for a single mission—against marshalling yards at Chaumont, Epinal, and Metz, and the Avord, Bourges, Chateaudun, Etampes/Mondesir, and Orleans/Bricy airdromes. In all, 814 heavy bombers actually attack these primary targets as well as four briefed secondaries—marshalling yards at Bayon, Neunkirchen and Saarbrucken (Germany), Caen/Carpiquet Airdrome, and several targets of opportunity. Two B-17s and one B-24 are downed by enemy fire, and two B-17s and one B-24 are lost in operational mishaps.

The 34th Heavy Bombardment Group undertakes its combat debut as part of the 3d Bombardment Division's 93d Combat Bombardment Wing.

Escort for the heavy bombers is provided by a record 1,206 USAAF fighters—562 from the VIII Fighter Command and 644 from the IX Fighter Command. Losses are four IX Fighter Command fighters.

During the afternoon, 58 IX Bomber Command B-26s attack the coastal batteries at three locations; and more than 120 Ninth Air Force P-38s attack locomotives and rail cars throughout central France.

ITALY: Fifteenth Air Force B-24s attack the marina and a marshalling yard at Frascati; Fifteenth Air Force B-17s attack marshalling yards at Avezzano and Ferentino; Fifteenth Air Force P-38s strafe Ferrara Airdrome; Twelfth Air Force B-25s and B-26s are grounded by bad weather; XII TAC A-20s attack communications targets; and XII TAC fighter-bombers attack numerous transportation targets, and provide direct and close support for Allied ground forces at Anzio as well as those advancing in the Liri River valley.

May 24, 1944

AUSTRIA: Fifteenth Air Force B-24s attack the GAF airdromes at Bad Voslau, Graz, Munchendorf, and Wollersdorf, and Fifteenth Air Force B-17s attack aircraft-industry targets near Wiener-Neustadt. In heavy fighter action during the penetration, target, and withdrawal phases of the various attacks, Fifteenth Air Force escort fighters are credited with downing 34 and probably downing nine GAF fighters between 0950 hours and noon.

FRANCE: During the afternoon, 400 2d and 3d Bombardment division B-24s attack the Creil, Melun, and Poix airdromes and Paris/Orly Airport. Thirty-three B-24s are damaged, but none is lost.

More than 450 IX Bomber Command B-26s attack V-weapons sites, coastal defenses, and airdromes, and Ninth Air Force P-38s and P-47s bomb four landing fields.

USAAF fighters down five GAF fighters between 1920 and 2010 hours.

GERMANY: Five hundred seventeen 1st and 3d Bombardment division B-17s attack the city of Berlin and targets of opportunity. Thirty-three B-17s are lost and 256 are damaged.

USAAF fighter pilots down 32 GAF aircraft between 1010 and 1155 hours, and 16 USAAF fighters are lost with their pilots, including a number that are downed during strafing attacks on rail targets during return flights to England.

ITALY: Fifteenth Air Force B-17s attack a rail viaduct at Avisio, and most Twelfth Air Force aircraft spend the day attacking scores of tactical, communications, and transportation targets at or behind the fluid battlelines. The destruction of five bridges by Twelfth Air Force medium bombers in the German Army rear virtually seals the battle area from resupply and reinforcement. Hundreds of motor vehicles are destroyed or disabled.

YUGOSLAVIA: Fifteenth Air Force heavy bombers attack marshalling yards at Varazdin and Zagreb.

May 25, 1944

BELGIUM: IX Bomber Command B-26s attack bridges around Liege, and Ninth Air Force P-47 fighter-bombers attack numerous other targets.

FRANCE: As part of an experiment to test heavy bombers against tactical targets, a total of 325 Eighth Air Force heavy bombers operating in small, independent formations attack German coastal batteries at Fecamp and St.-Valery as well as numerous marshalling yards and airdromes in France and Belgium. Two B-17s and two B-24s are lost.

Escort for the various heavy-bomber formations is provided by 604 VIII Fighter

Command fighters and 207 IX Fighter Command fighters, of which 12 are lost with their pilots. Twelve GAF fighters are downed, and a number of fighter groups attack ground targets on their way home following escort duty.

After downing two Bf-109s and probably downing two FW-190s near Strasbourg at about 1000 hours, Capt Joseph H. Bennett, a P-51 ace with the 4th Fighter Group's 336th Fighter Squadron, is forced down for unknown reasons and taken prisoner. At the time of his capture, Bennett's personal tally is 8.5 victory credits.

IX Bomber Command B-26s attack Lille/Nord and Monchy-Breton airdromes, and Ninth Air Force P-47 fighter-bombers attack numerous other targets.

Fifteenth Air Force B-24s attack marshalling yards at Toulon and two other locations, and Fifteenth Air Force B-17s attack a marshalling yard at Lyon.

ITALY: Following the Allied breakthrough near Cassino and the long-awaited continuation of the drive on Rome, the German Army attempts to establish a new defensive line between Frascati and Tivoli. Called upon to disrupt German efforts to rush troops and equipment to the new line, the 86th Fighter Group, in A-36s and P-40s, mounts an all-out low-level interdiction effort between 0650 and 2020 hours. During the course of 86 combat sorties in twelve separate missions, the group is credited with 217 vehicles destroyed and 245 damaged, which in turn effectively seals many roads into the proposed defensive zone. The 86th's fighter-bomber pilots also destroy several German artillery positions. The day's action costs the group two aircraft lost and five aircraft damaged beyond repair. As a result of this and similar efforts by the Twelfth Air Force—on its most active day of the war, so far—the German Army abandons its plans for the new defensive line and continues its fighting withdrawal in the face of relentless Allied pressure on the ground and from the air. (Before the Allied ground offensive runs out of steam in late

June, the German Army in Italy will have been pushed approximately 80 miles north of Rome.)

In a morning fighter engagement south of Orbetello, P-47 pilots of the 57th Fighter Group's 66th Fighter Squadron down five FW-190s.

Fifteenth Air Force B-24s attack the port area at Monfalcone, Piacenza Airdrome, and oil-industry targets at Porto Marghera. During the attack on Piacenza Airdrome, 2dLt Warren L. Jones, a P-38 pilot with the 14th Fighter Group's 49th Fighter Squadron, achieves ace status when he downs a Bf-109 at 1300 hours. In all, 14th Fighter Group P-38 pilots down eight Bf-109s in this action.

YUGOSLAVIA: Fifteenth Air Force B-17s attack German Army troop concentrations around Bihac.

May 26, 1944

FRANCE: The 479th Fighter Group, in P-38s, makes its combat debut by mounting two uncontested "familiarization" fighter sweeps along the Dutch coast. The 479th is the very last of fifteen fighter groups to be assigned to the VIII Fighter Command.

As many as 400 IX Bomber Command B-26s and A-20s attack Beaumont-le-Roger and Chartres airdromes, and bridges at Poissy and Vernon; 108 P-47 and P-51 fighter-bombers attack Cormeilles-en-Vexin, Creil, and Evreux/Fauville airdromes; and P-38s and P-47s sweep across France and nearby countries in search of targets of opportunity, of which many are bombed and strafed.

In the south, Fifteenth Air Force B-17s attack a marshalling yard at St.-Etienne, and B-24s attack a bridge spanning the Var River and marshalling yards at Chambery, Grenoble, Lyon, and Nice.

ITALY: Twelfth Air Force B-25s and B-26s attack various rail targets and roads around Florence, and XII TAC fighter-bombers sweep occupied Italy in their ongoing campaign against motor traffic.

YUGOSLAVIA: Fifteenth Air Force B-24s attack German Army troop concentrations around Bihac, and escort fighters dive-bomb and strafe an airdrome.

May 27, 1944

ENGLAND: 1,155 USAAF fighters are dispatched by VIII and IX Fighter commands (720 and 425, respectively) to escort and support Eighth Air Force heavy-bomber formations dispatched to France and Germany.

FRANCE: Thirty-six 3d Bombardment Division B-17s and 18 2d Bombardment Division B-24s, respectively, attack gun emplacements at Fecamp and the town of St.-Valery with the aid of H2X equipment; 102 3d Bombardment Division B-17s attack aircraft-industry targets and a marshalling yard at Strasbourg; and 69 3d Bombardment Division B-24s attack Woippy Airdrome.

USAAF escort pilots down 34 GAF fighters over France between 1045 and 1430 hours, but mostly in a major aerial engagement around Strasbourg at about 1230 hours. Maj George L. Merritt, Jr., the commanding officer of the 361st Fighter Group's 375th Fighter Squadron, in P-51s, achieves ace status when he downs an FW-190 near Lille at 1430 hours.

Nearly 590 IX Bomber Command B-26 and A-20 sorties, and several hundred P-47 sorties, are mounted against marshalling yards, rail lines, and bridges.

In southern France, nearly 700 Fifteenth Air Force B-17s and B-24s attack Montpellier and Salon-de-Provence airdromes, and marshalling yards at Avignon, Marseille, Montpellier, and Nimes. Also, Fifteenth Air Force B-17s attack a marshalling yard at Avignon.

The veteran 325th Fighter Group undertakes its first combat escort since transitioning from P-47s to P-51s.

Col Oliver B. Taylor, the commanding officer of the 14th Fighter Group, achieves ace status when he downs an FW-190 over Rimen during a morning mission.

GERMANY: Eighth Air Force heavy bombers attack briefed targets and several targets of opportunity as follows: 150 1st Bombardment Division B-17s attack a chemical plant at Ludwigshafen; 125 1st Bombardment Division B-17s attack a marshalling yard at Mannheim; 43 1st Bombardment Division B-17s attack targets of opportunity; 98 3d Bombardment Division B-17s attack a marshalling yard at Karlsruhe; 145 2d Bombardment Division B-24s attack a marshalling yard at Saarbrucken; 66 2d Bombardment Division B-24s attack a marshalling yard at Neunkirchen; and 72 2d Bombardment Division B-24s attack a marshalling yard at Kons Karthaus. Nineteen B-17s and five B-24s are lost.

Four GAF aircraft are downed over Germany by USAAF fighter pilots. Capt Thomas L. Harris, a P-51 pilot with the 357th Fighter Group's 364th Fighter Squadron, achieves ace status when he downs two Bf-109s over Colmar at 1300 hours.

ITALY: Twelfth Air Force B-25s and B-26s attack lines of communication running through and around Orvieto; XII TAC A-20s attack dumps; and XII TAC fighter-bombers continue to hunt for motor vehicles, attack bridges, strafe and bomb gun emplacements, and provide direct and close support for the Allied ground forces.

NETHERLANDS: Twenty-four 56th Fighter Group P-47 fighter-bombers attack a barge convoy.

YUGOSLAVIA: Fifteenth Air Force heavy bombers attack port facilities at Razanac.

May 28, 1944

BELGIUM: IX Bomber Command B-26s and A-20s attack rail bridges and marshalling yards.

FRANCE: IX Bomber Command B-26s and A-20s attack rail bridges, marshalling yards, naval facilities, and V-weapons sites.

GERMANY: A record 1,341 Eighth Air Force heavy bombers are dispatched against six oil and rail targets in Germany, but heavy clouds force nearly 500 bombers to abort, and several hundred of the remainder salvo their bombs on a dizzying array of targets of opportunity all along and around the bomber routes. The assigned targets attacked are as follows: 38 B-17s against an oil target at Ruhland; 12 B-17s against an aircraft-industry target at Dessau; 15 B-17s against a secondary aircraft-industry target at Zwickau; 28 B-17s against a secondary aircraft-industry target at Leipzig; 105 B-17s against an oil dump at Konigsburg; 55 B-17s against oil-industry target at Magdeburg; 17 B-17s against the city of Dessau; 66 B-24s against Lutzkendorf; 63 B-24s against an oil-industry target at Merseburg; 187 B-24s against an oil-industry target at Zeitz-Troglitz; and 58 B-17s against a marshalling yard at Cologne. Twenty-six B-17s and six B-24s are lost. Twelve of the B-17s are downed from the 94th Combat Bombardment Wing formation, which weathers the heaviest GAF fighter attacks of the afternoon.

In the attack on the marshalling yard at Cologne, B-17s of the 41st Combat Bombardment Wing test a special glide bomb, but the device is rated a failure.

Escort for the heavy bombers is provided by 697 VIII Fighter Command fighters and 527 IX Fighter Command fighters, adding up to a record 1,224 escort sorties. Fourteen escort fighters are lost with their pilots. Capt Alwin M. Jucheim, Jr., a seven-victory P-47 ace with the 78th Fighter Group's 83d Fighter Squadron, is taken prisoner following a midair collision with another P-47; and 1stLt Don McDowell, an 8.5-victory P-51 ace with the 354th Fighter Group's 353d Fighter Squadron, is lost without a trace during this mission.

GAF losses are 56 fighters and attack aircraft downed along the bomber routes between 1345 and 1530 hours. 1stLt Carl M. Frantz, a P-51 ace with the 354th Fighter Group's 353d Fighter Squadron, brings his final personal tally to 11 confirmed victories when he downs a Bf-109 over Neuhaldenleben at about 1400 hours; and 1stLt Leroy A. Ruder, a P-51 pilot with the 357th Fighter Group's 363d Fighter Squad-

ron, achieves ace status when he downs a Bf-109 over Germany at 1400 hours.

ITALY: Approximately 100 Fifteenth Air Force B-24s attack port facilities at Genoa and a marshalling yard; Twelfth Air Force B-25s and B-26s attack bridges, viaducts, and rail lines servicing the battle area; XII TAC A-20s attack an ammunition dump; and XII TAC fighter-bombers provide support for advancing Allied ground forces, especially against roads and bridges.

YUGOSLAVIA: Fifteenth Air Force B-24s attack German Army troop concentrations around Niksic, and Fifteenth Air Force P-38s attack lines of communication in the Banjaluka-Bihac-Knin area.

May 29, 1944

AUSTRIA: Fifteenth Air Force heavy bombers attack various targets around Wiener-Neustadt: 104 B-24s attack the Bf-109 assembly plant, totally demolishing all that has survived previous attacks, and 126 B-24s attack the Bf-109 components factory at Atzgersdorf. Also, 300 B-17s and B-24s cause heavy damage at the Wollersdorf Airdrome, but 150 GAF fighters attack the bomber force, downing five heavy bombers. In all, 18 heavy bombers are lost. In the very heavy fighter engagements attending the bombing attacks, 31st and 52d Fighter group P-51 pilots down 31 Bf-109s and Bf-110s, and P-38 escort pilots are credited with two Bf-110s and a Ju-87.

BELGIUM: Ninth Air Force B-26s, A-20s, and P-47s attack marshalling yards, rail bridges, and airfields.

FRANCE: Ninth Air Force B-26s, A-20s, and P-47s attack marshalling yards, rail bridges, airfields, coastal batteries, and V-weapons sites.

GERMANY: Of 993 Eighth Air Force heavy bombers dispatched, 888 attack aircraft-industry targets at Cottbus, Krzesinski (Poland), Leipzig, Posen (Poznan Poland), and Sorau; an oil terminal at Politz; and Rendsburg and Tutow airdromes. Seventeen B-17s and 17 B-24s are lost.

Escort for the heavy bombers is provided by a record 1,265 VIII and IX Fighter command fighters, of which 12 are lost with ten pilots.

USAAF escort pilots down 41 GAF fighters over Germany between noon and 1500 hours. Of these, four Me-410s are downed by 2dLt Dale F. Spencer near Schwerin at about 1320 hours. 1stLt George A. Doersch, a P-51 pilot with the 359th Fighter Group's 370th Fighter Squadron, achieves ace status when he shares in the downing of two FW-190s near Stettin at 1215 hours; and 1stLt Glennon T. Moran, a P-51 pilot with the 352d Fighter Group's 487th Fighter Squadron, achieves ace status when he downs an FW-190 and a Bf-109, and shares in the downing of a second Bf-109, in the vicinity of Gustrow and Wolgast between 1210 and 1230 hours.

ITALY: Twelfth Air Force B-25s attack rail bridges at three locations; Twelfth Air Force B-26s attack the shipyard and a bridge at Voltri, a rail junction and marshalling yard, and several road bridges and viaducts; XII TAC A-20s attack supply dumps and bivouacs; and XII TAC fighter-bombers range against road targets in and behind the battle areas and around Rome.

XII Troop Carrier Command transports evacuate 400 Allied casualties from the Anzio beachhead.

YUGOSLAVIA: Fifteenth Air Force B-24s and their P-38 escorts attack numerous German Army troop concentrations and supply dumps.

May 30, 1944

AUSTRIA: Following an assessment of cumulative bomb damage throughout the Wiener-Neustadt aircraft-industry complex, Fifteenth Air Force planners become convinced that one more successful attack will force the Germans and Austrians to write it off. Thus, 299 B-24s attack five separate factories and mills around Wiener-Neustadt, of which several are demolished and one is missed altogether by misdropped bombs.

BELGIUM: Thirty-nine 3d Bombardment Division B-17s attack a marshalling yard in Brussels, and Ninth Air Force P-47 fighter-bombers attack numerous other targets.

ENGLAND: Loading begins of assault forces that will take part in the OVERLORD invasion of France.

FRANCE: Seventy-six 3d Bombardment Division B-17s attack V-weapons sites in the Pas-de-Calais area; 62 3d Bombardment Division B-17s attack a marshalling yards at Reims; and 60 3d Bombardment Division B-17s attack a marshalling yard at Troyes.

Thirty-seven VIII Fighter Command P-47 fighter-bombers attack a rail bridge at Longueil; 26 VIII Fighter Command P-47s bomb a rail bridge at Beaumont-sur-Oise; 23 VIII Fighter Command P-47s bomb a rail bridge at Canly-le-Jouque; and 12 VIII Fighter Command P-38s bomb a rail bridge at Creil.

IX Bomber Command B-26s attack Denain/Prouvy and Mantes/Limay airdromes, and highway bridges at Meulan and Rouen; and several hundred Ninth Air Force P-47 fighter-bombers attack scores of other targets.

GERMANY: Eighty-three 1st Bombardment Division B-17s attack aircraft-industry factories at Dessau; 107 1st Bombardment Division B-17s attack aircraft-industry factories at Halberstadt; 51 1st Bombardment Division B-17s attack aircraft-industry factories at Oschersleben; 135 2d Bombardment Division B-24s attack Oldenburg Airdrome; 147 2d Bombardment Division B-24s attack Rotenburg Airdrome; 71 2d Bombardment Division B-24s attack Zwischenahn Airdrome; 36 3d Bombardment Division B-24s attack Diepholz Airdrome; and 46 3d Bombardment Division B-24s attack Munster/Handorf Airdrome.

The 490th Heavy Bombardment Group, in B-24s, makes its combat debut with the 3d Bombardment Division's 93d Combat Bombardment Wing.

Escort for Eighth Air Force heavy-bomber missions to Germany, France, and

Belgium is provided by a total of 672 VIII Fighter Command fighters and 637 IX Fighter Command fighters—a new one-day total of 1,309 escort sorties. Of these, 12 fighters and their pilots are lost. Capt Fletcher E. Adams, a nine-victory P-51 ace with the 357th Fighter Group's 362d Fighter Squadron, is killed in action over Bernburg after sharing in the downing of an Me-410 at 1130 hours; and Capt Willard W. Millikan, a 13-victory P-51 ace with the 4th Fighter Group's 336th Fighter Squadron, is forced down and captured after colliding with another P-51.

The USAAF fighter pilots down 58 GAF fighters over Germany between 1100 and 1220 hours. Capt Robert H. Becker, a P-51 pilot with the 357th Fighter Group's 362d Fighter Squadron, achieves ace status when he downs three Bf-109s near Bernburg at 1115 hours; 1stLt Gilbert M. O'Brien, a P-51 pilot with the 357th Fighter Group's 362d Fighter Squadron, achieves ace status when he downs a Bf-109 and shares in the downing of an Me-410 near Bernburg between 1130 hours and noon; and Capt William R. O'Brien, a P-51 pilot with the 357th Fighter Group's 363d Fighter Squadron, achieves ace status when he downs two Bf-109s near Schenebeck at 1130 hours.

ITALY: Twelfth Air Force B-25s and B-26s attack many bridges and viaducts, damaging or destroying ten of them and thus adding further to the woes of the German Army forces attempting to stem the general Allied advance in central Italy. Also, XII TAC A-20s and fighter-bombers attack defended towns and gun emplacements in the battle area, and motor vehicles wherever they are encountered.

YUGOSLAVIA: Fifty-six Fifteenth Air Force B-17s attack a marshalling yard at Zagreb, and P-38 and P-51 escort fighters strafe numerous targets of opportunity.

May 31, 1944

BELGIUM: Unable to locate their primary target in France because of bad weather, 30 1st Bombardment Division B-17s attack Florennes/Juzaine Airdrome, and four B-17s attack a marshalling yard at Namur.
FRANCE: Thirty-six 1st Bombardment Division B-17s attack a marshalling yard at Luxeuil.

Four hundred ninety-one of the 495 2d and 3d Bombardment division B-24s dispatched to attack rail targets in France and Belgium are recalled due to heavy clouds in the target areas. Four B-24s attack bridges at Beaumont-sur-Oise and Melun.

Approximately 200 IX Bomber Command B-26s attack highway bridges at Bennecourt, Courcelles-sur-Seine, and Rouen.
GERMANY: As briefed, 88 3d Bombardment Division B-17s attack the marshalling yard at Osnabruck, and 54 3d Bombardment Division B-17s attack a marshalling yard at Schwerte. Also, after failing to locate their primary targets because of bad weather, 50 3d Bombardment Division B-17s attack a marshalling yard at Hamm and 52 B-17s attack a marshalling yard at Oeske.

Escort for the Eighth Air Force heavy-bomber missions to France and Germany is provided by 682 VIII Fighter Command fighters and 647 IX Fighter Command fighters—a new one-day record of 1,329 escort fighter sorties. Three VIII Fighter Command fighters and their pilots are lost. No GAF aircraft are downed by escort fighters.

Forty-three 56th Fighter Group P-47s and 35 353d Fighter Group P-47s attack Gutersloh Airdrome with 100-pound bombs. Also, 35 20th Fighter Group P-38s briefed to attack Lingen Airdrome get lost and attack Rheine/Hopstein Airdrome instead, also with 100-pound bombs. Five GAF FW-190s are downed over Gutersloh at about 1915 hours by 56th Fighter Group P-47 pilots, and the 20th Fighter Group claims five ground kills.
ITALY: Twelfth Air Force B-25s and B-26s and XII TAC A-20s and fighter-bombers provide direct support for Allied ground forces in the battle area south of

Rome by attacking several defended towns, troop concentrations, and road junctions. XII Troop Carrier Command transports continue to evacuate casualties from the Anzio beachhead.

NETHERLANDS: Unable to locate their primary target in France because of bad weather, 23 1st Bombardment Division B-17s attack Gilze-Rijen Airdrome, and 12 1st Bombardment Division B-17s attack a marshalling yard.

ROMANIA: Fifteenth Air Force B-17s and B-24s attack oil facilities at Ploesti. Fifteen heavy bombers are lost.

P-38 and P-51 escort pilots down 21 GAF and Romanian Air Force fighters between 1000 and 1050 hours. 1stLt John A. Maloney, a P-38 pilot with the 1st Fighter Group's 27th Fighter Squadron, achieves ace status when he downs a Bf-109 over Ploesti at 1045 hours.

JUNE 1944

June 1, 1944

FRANCE: Nearly 100 IX Bomber Command B-26s attack airdromes and coastal defense batteries from the Belgian frontier to the Cherbourg Peninsula.

ITALY: All Twelfth Air Force combat sorties are devoted to direct support of advancing Allied ground forces. Troop positions, lines of communication, rail and road targets, motor vehicles, and numerous other targets are bombed and strafed throughout the day.

June 2, 1944

ENGLAND: Ninth Air Force ground-air liaison officers (i.e., "forward air controllers") are briefed on the Normandy invasion plan by the 21st Army Group.

FRANCE: During the morning, 805 Eighth Air Force B-17s and B-24s attack 64 V-weapons sites without loss.

During the afternoon, 163 Eighth Air Force B-17s attack rail targets in the Paris area; a total of 62 B-17s divert from Paris and attack Beaumont-sur-Oise, Caen/ Carpiquet, and Conches airdromes; and a total of 74 B-24s attack Bretigny, Creil, and Villeneuve airdromes. Two B-17s and five B-24s are lost.

The 491st Heavy Bombardment Group, in B-24s, makes its combat debut with the 2d Bombardment Division's 95th Combat Bombardment Wing.

Throughout the day, nearly 350 IX Bomber Command B-26s and A-20s attack V-weapons sites and coastal-defense batteries along the English Channel coast. Also, Ninth Air Force P-38 and P-47 dive-bombers attack rail bridges and junctions, V-weapons sites, and fuel dumps.

HUNGARY: In the Fifteenth Air Force's inaugural mission of Operation FRANTIC, 130 B-17s from four groups of the 5th Heavy Bombardment Wing, escorted by 70 325th Fighter Group P-51s, leave their bases in Italy to attack strategic targets deep in central Europe (in this case, a marshalling yard at Debreczen, Hungary) and then fly on to land at USAAF-run bases (Eastern Command) in the southern Soviet Union—bombers at Mirgorod and Poltava airdromes, and fighters at Piryatin Airdrome. LtGen Ira C. Eaker participates in the mission as aerial commander.

Fifteenth Air Force B-24s attack marshalling yards at Miskolc and Szolnok and then return to their bases in Italy.

ITALY: Twelfth Air Force B-25s and B-26s attack rail and road bridges between the battle area and Rome; and XII TAC fighter-bombers attack German Army command posts, rail and road bridges, and motor transport throughout the battle area.

ROMANIA: Fifteenth Air Force B-17s attack a marshalling yard at Oradea, and B-24s attack marshalling yards at Cluj and Simeria.

June 3, 1944

FRANCE: During the morning, despite heavy cloud cover, 219 Eighth Air Force B-17s and 120 B-24s attack tactical targets, mostly coastal-defense positions, in the Pas-de-Calais area. Forty-five bombers are damaged by flak, but none is lost.

Specially equipped B-17s of the 492d Heavy Bombardment Group's 36th Heavy Bombardment Squadron mount the USAAF's first daylight radio-countermeasures sorties of the war. The objective is to jam or confound range-finding radars controlling GAF flak batteries.

More than 250 IX Bomber Command B-26s and A-20s attack airfields, coastal-defense batteries, and highway bridges in northern France; and, throughout the day, more than 400 Ninth Air Force P-38 and P-47 dive-bombers attack numerous targets in France and throughout northern Europe.

During the afternoon, 97 Eighth Air Force B-17s and 98 B-24s attack tactical targets, mostly coastal-defense positions, in the Pas-de-Calais area. Two B-17s are damaged and one P-51 escort fighter and its pilot are lost due to a mechanical failure.

ITALY: Twelfth Air Force B-25s and B-26s attack rail and road bridges throughout central Italy; XII TAC A-20s attack fuel and ammunition dumps; and XII TAC fighter-bombers provide direct and close support for the Allied ground forces along the battlefront.

YUGOSLAVIA: Most of the Fifteenth Air Force is grounded by bad weather, but 36 B-24s are able to attack military targets at Omis, and 38 B-24s attack the port and town areas at Split.

June 4, 1944

ENGLAND: A day after the loading of Allied assault troops has been completed, Gen Dwight D. Eisenhower postpones D day from June 5 to June 6 because of un-favorable weather forecasts.

All P-38 groups based in the U.K. stand down to be painted with black-and-white "invasion" stripe patterns for easy recognition by ground troops.

FRANCE: During the morning, 183 Eighth Air Force B-17s and 51 B-24s attack tactical targets, mostly coastal-defense positions, in the Pas-de-Calais area. Two GAF aircraft are downed, and two P-51 escorts are lost, but both pilots are saved.

More than 300 IX Bomber Command B-26s and A-20s attack coastal-defense batteries and highway bridges; and nearly 200 Ninth Air Force P-47 and P-51 dive-bombers attack bridges, locomotives and rail cars, rail junctions, and numerous targets of opportunity.

During the afternoon, 222 Eighth Air Force B-17s and 53 B-24s attack tactical targets, mostly coastal-defense positions, in the Pas-de-Calais area; 180 Eighth Air Force B-17s attack rail bridges at three inland locations; and 214 Eighth Air Force B-24s attack bridges across the Seine River at Melun, and the Avord, Bourges, Bretigny, and Romorantin/Prunieres airdromes.

One GAF advanced trainer and one Bf-109 are downed by USAAF fighter pilots during the late afternoon.

Fifteenth Air Force B-17s attack several rail bridges and viaducts in southern France.

ITALY: Fifteenth Air Force B-24s attack marshalling yards at Genoa, Novi Ligure, Savona, and Turin, as well as a number of rail bridges and viaducts along the German Army lines of supply and communication in northern Italy; Twelfth Air Force B-25s and B-26s attack rail bridges in north-central Italy; and XII TAC fighter-bombers mount an all-day effort against motor vehicles being used by the retreating German Army throughout the road network north of Rome. More than 600 motor vehicles are claimed as destroyed.

The city of Rome is liberated by Allied ground forces.

June 5, 1944

FRANCE: Four hundred twenty-three Eighth Air Force B-17s and 203 B-24s attack coastal defenses around Boulogne, Caen, Cherbourg, and Le Havre. Four B-17s, two B-24s, a P-47, and a P-51 are lost to ground fire.

While attacking coastal defenses near Wimereaux, the lead B-17 of the Eighth Air Force's 489th Heavy Bombardment Group is struck by fire that kills the pilot and nearly severs the right foot of the formation commander, LtCol Leon R. Vance. Despite his life-threatening injury, Vance takes control of the airplane and leads the entire group through a successful bombing run. Vance next flies the crippled B-17 to the English coast and orders the crew to bail out, which it does. However, erroneously believing that a wounded crewman has been unable to bail out, Vance ditches the crippled heavy bomber rather than bail out himself. LtCol Vance is rescued, his life is saved, and he is eventually awarded a Medal of Honor.

More than 100 IX Bomber Command B-26s and 100 P-47 dive-bombers attack coastal-defense batteries.

F-5 aircraft from the Ninth Air Force's 10th Photographic Reconnaissance Group are dispatched to Normandy to take final preinvasion photographs of the airborne landing and drop zones.

ITALY: Fifteenth Air Force B-24s attack marshalling yards at five locations in northern Italy; Fifteenth Air Force B-17s and B-24s attack six rail bridges in northern and north-central Italy; 53 Fifteenth Air Force escort P-38s strafe two airdromes; 40 Fifteenth Air Force P-38s dive-bomb and strafe two airdromes; Twelfth Air Force B-25s and B-26s attempt to slow retreating German Army forces by attacking road and highway bridges north of Rome; and XII TAC fighter-bombers continue their offensive against motor vehicles using the German Army's lines of retreat.

June 6, 1944

FRANCE: The 438th Troop Carrier Group's lead C-47, *Birmingham Belle,* takes off from its base in England at 2248 hours, June 5, with the lead elements of the U.S. 101st Airborne Division—and the invasion of France is on.

In all, 14 IX Troop Carrier Command C-47 and C-53 groups are to take part in delivering parachute and glider-borne elements of the U.S. 101st and 82d Airborne divisions to six drop zones and landing zones around the town of Ste.-Mere-Eglise.

First to go are six pathfinder "serials" (i.e., tactical groups) of three planes per serial, plus an extra plane in one serial—nineteen aircraft in all. The pathfinder teams aboard these transports will locate and mark drop zones and landing zones assigned to the main airborne assault forces.

The main airborne assault force is composed of 821 IX Troop Carrier Command C-47 and C-53 transports and 104 planes each towing a glider. The transports and towing planes, which depart in an exacting sequence from fourteen airfields—one plane every 11 seconds—are organized into twenty-eight serials. After the serials have organized into wings, specially trained pathfinder transport crews lead each formation along predetermined routes at various set altitudes. Airplane speed throughout the serial and wings is a uniform 140 miles per hour.

Light flak rises to meet formations passing the German-occupied Channel Islands, but losses are low. On approaching the French coast, the lead formations descend to 700 feet and reduce speed to 125 miles per hour. *Birmingham Belle* reaches its assigned drop zone at 0016 hours, June 6, and its entire complement of paratroopers leaves the airplane. The last planeful of paratroopers is dropped at 0404 hours.

Although many airborne pathfinder units do not land on or even near their assigned zones, and despite many of the by-then typical disorganizations and dislocations that attend night mass parachute drops, the airborne assault is a success of strategic magnitude. Of the 821 troop carriers and 104 towing planes dispatched, 805 troop carriers and 103 towing planes deliver troops and equipment to French soil. Twenty-one troop carriers and two towing planes are lost. Counting RAF aircraft delivering British airborne forces to Normandy, more than 1,400 C-47s, C-53s, and gliders are involved in the initial D-day airlanding operation—the largest airborne assault in history. Within hours, American, British, and Canadian infantry divisions fight their way ashore along the Normandy coast.

Also during the night of June 5–6—to help protect the troop-carrier groups—specially equipped B-17s of the 492d Heavy Bombardment Group's 36th Heavy Bombardment Squadron mount the USAAF's first night radio-countermeasures sorties of the war to jam or confound range-finding radars controlling GAF flak batteries.

Beginning before dawn, five Ninth Air Force fighter groups are assigned to attack specific targets, six groups are assigned for on-call support of U.S. Army ground forces, and five groups are to provide air cover against GAF attacks. Also, all four Eighth Air Force P-38 groups and the two Ninth Air Force P-38 groups are assigned to convoy-escort duties (because the distinctive twin-engine P-38s are less likely to be fired on by friendly naval forces than would be single-engine P-47s and P-51s).

Ninth Air Force tactical aircraft begin striking tactical targets along and near the UTAH invasion beach at first light. Fighter-bombers attack two coastal batteries, a rail embankment, and six bridges, each in squadron strength; and IX Bomber Command B-26s attack three coastal batteries, each in group strength. Results are classed as good to excellent by the ground forces. Thereafter, Ninth Air Force tactical aircraft are employed over both American invasion beaches, UTAH and OMAHA.

In all on D day, following months of intense efforts to deter the GAF from attacking the invasion fleet and forces, exactly two FW-190s manned by curious rather than attack-minded pilots overfly the invasion beaches. Both aircraft are chased away by P-38s from the convoy escort. From the standpoint of the air offensive leading up to D day, the invasion is a complete success.

Throughout the day, the Eighth Air Force dispatches a record 2,587 heavy-bomber sorties against targets within and around four of the five Normandy invasion beaches (OMAHA, GOLD, SWORD, and JUNO—American, British, British, and Canadian, respectively). In the end, despite confusion and poor visibility caused by clouds, haze, and the smoke from countless conflagrations, a total of 1,622 Eighth Air Force heavy bombers drop 4,852 tons of bombs on numerous targets between Cherbourg and Le Havre. Losses for the day are *one* heavy bomber downed by enemy fire, three heavy bombers crashed, and two written off due to operational accidents.

The 493d Heavy Bombardment Group, in B-24s, makes its combat debut with the 3d Bombardment Division's 93d Combat Bombardment Wing. It is the last of 40 heavy-bomber groups to serve with the Eighth Air Force.

Throughout the day, the Ninth Air Force dispatches 3,342 combat or escort sorties, and 3,050 aircraft complete their missions as follows: 823 sorties by B-26s and A-20s; 2,072 by fighters and fighter-bombers; and 155 by reconnaissance aircraft.

Every fighter group in the Eighth and Ninth air forces mounts at least one mission to France during the day. In all, while providing a *continuous* dawn-to-dusk fighter umbrella, VIII and IX Fighter command fighters mount 1,719 escort or patrol sorties—and an additional 466 fighter-bomber sorties, mostly against ground targets.

GAF opposition to the invasion does not begin until after noon. The first victory of the day is an FW-190 credited at 1225 hours over Dreux Airdrome to an F-6 pilot with the IX TAC's 10th Photographic Reconnaissance Group. Thereafter, the toll rises through the afternoon and early evening to 12 FW-190s, 12 Ju-87s, and one Bf-109. USAAF fighter losses for the day from all causes, including ground fire, are 25 fighters and 24 pilots, of which ten of each are from the 4th Fighter Group alone. Capt Bernard J. McGratten, an 8.5-victory P-51 ace with the 4th Fighter Group's 335th Fighter Squadron, is killed when his airplane is shot down in an air-to-air engagement near Rouen; and FO Evan D. McMinn, a five-victory P-47 ace with the 56th Fighter Group's 61st Fighter Squadron, is lost, apparently to flak, near Bernay.

Beginning with the delivery of follow-on airborne units and supplies between 2053 and 2250 hours, IX Troop Carrier Command aircraft begin a massive aerial resupply operation that involves nearly 1,000 sorties by the time airborne and infantry forces link up on the ground.

ITALY: The entire Twelfth Air Force is committed against lines of communication (i.e., lines of retreat) north of Rome.

ROMANIA: Flying from and returning to bases in the Soviet Union as part of Operation FRANTIC, 104 Fifteenth Air Force B-17s and 42 P-51s attack Galati Airdrome.

325th Fighter Group P-51 pilots down six GAF aircraft on the Galati mission between 0935 and 0950 hours. Achieving ace status are: 1stLt Cullen J. Hoffman, of the 325th Fighter Group's 317th Fighter Squadron, who downs a Ju-88 over Galati (the

first victory awarded to a USAAF pilot taking off from a base in the Soviet Union); 1stLt Robert M. Barkey, a P-51 pilot with the 325th Fighter Group's 319th Fighter Squadron, who downs a Bf-109 over Galati; and 1stLt Roy B. Hogg, of the 325th Fighter Group's 318th Fighter Squadron, who downs two FW-190s near Galati.

More than 570 Fifteenth Air Force B-24s dispatched from bases in Italy attack a canal at Turnu Severin, oil installations at Ploesti, and marshalling yards at Brasov and Pitesti. Two Axis fighters are downed by 31st Fighter Group P-51 pilots over Ploesti at about 0935 hours, and 1st and 52d Fighter group escort pilots down two Axis fighters over Brasov at about 1000 hours.

YUGOSLAVIA: Fifteenth Air Force B-17s based in Italy attack marshalling yards at Belgrade and various canals.

June 7, 1942

FRANCE: As the fighting and amphibious landings continue along the Normandy coast, an American glider-infantry regiment towed from bases in England by IX Troop Carrier Command C-47s is landed beyond the beachhead. In all, more than 400 IX Troop Carrier Command C-47s and C-53s take part in reinforcement and aerial resupply operations.

From the delivery of the first airborne pathfinders late on June 5, IX Troop Carrier Command aircraft and crews are dispatched on 1,662 combat sorties, including the delivery of 512 gliders. Five hundred three gliders are delivered, and 1,581 aircraft sorties are completed. Forty-one aircraft are lost, and 449 are damaged, mostly by enemy fire. In sum, the following was delivered by air transport: 13,215 troops, 223 artillery pieces, and 1,641,448 pounds of supplies and equipment. Gliders delivered the following: 4,047 troops, 110 artillery weapons, 281 light vehicles, and 412,477 pounds of supplies and equipment.

AEAF directs the various strategic and tactical air components operating out of the U.K. to deny German Army ground reinforcements access to the Normandy beachhead area. In their turn, the various target-selection departments pinpoint the many chokepoints leading to the beachhead area.

During the morning, 172 Eighth Air Force B-17s attack tactical targets at three inland locations, and 229 Eighth Air Force B-24s attack tactical targets at four inland locations. No bombers are lost. During the afternoon, 385 Eighth Air Force B-17s attack Kerlin/Bastard Airdrome and tactical targets in and around Nantes and Niort; and, although their primary target at Angers is obscured by clouds, 91 Eighth Air Force B-24s attack Laval Airdrome and tactical targets in and around Blain, Chateaubriant, Pouance, Tours, and Vitre. One B-17 and one B-24 are lost.

Throughout the day, more than 600 Ninth Air Force B-26 sorties successfully attack bridges, trestles, marshalling yards, rail and road junctions, and coastal-defense and field-artillery batteries in and around the Normandy beachhead.

Throughout the day, VIII Fighter Command fighters provide 820 patrol and escort sorties and 653 strafing sorties. Fourteen USAAF fighters and 12 pilots are lost.

Throughout the day, beginning at 0600 hours and ending at 2230 hours, fighter-bombers from IX Fighter Command's 365th, 366th, and 368th Fighter groups provide continuous on-call support in squadron strength for U.S. Army ground forces. In the course of 35 squadron-strength missions, 467 fighter-bombers from these groups attack targets of opportunity with 1,000-pound bombs or fragmentation cluster bombs. Other IX Fighter Command aircraft perform a host of other duties, from convoy and high cover to missions against specific targets.

VIII and IX Fighter command fighter and fighter-bomber pilots down 40 GAF fighters and one Ju-88 over France between 0511 and 2135 hours. 1stLt Robert J. Rankin, a P-47 ace with the 56th Fighter Group's 61st Fighter Squadron, brings his final personal tally to ten confirmed victories when he downs a Bf-109 near Senlis at 1825 hours.

Fifteenth Air Force heavy bombers attack the viaduct at Antheor and a bridge spanning the Var River.

ITALY: Fifteenth Air Force B-24s attack a marshalling yard, the rail junction at Savona, and the shipyard at Voltri; 42 Fifteenth Air Force P-38s bomb a viaduct; despite bad weather, Twelfth Air Force B-25s and B-26s attack rail and road bridges and viaducts in north-central Italy; and XII TAC fighter-bombers attack gun emplacements in the battle area and motor vehicles, troop concentrations, bridges, and rail cars north of Rome.

The Fifteenth Air Force reaches its full operational strength of 21 heavy-bomber groups and seven escort-fighter groups with the recommitment of the 332d Fighter Group to escort operations following its transition to P-47s.

June 8, 1944

ENGLAND: Gen Carl Spaatz directs USSTAF components to place Axis oil targets at the top of their priority target lists.

FRANCE: Once Allied ground forces are established ashore, it becomes the mission of Eighth Air Force heavy bombers, Ninth Air Force light and medium bombers, and numerous fighters and fighter-bombers from both air forces to seal the invasion area against German Army reinforcement and resupply efforts. With few exceptions, therefore, USAAF bomber missions are directed against bridges, rail lines, and other transportation targets, generally from the Loire River in the south to the Seine River in the east. Also, in addition to providing tactical support and cover within the invasion area, large numbers of fighters, fighter-bombers, and light and medium bombers are dispatched against fuel, ammunition, and supply dumps.

Of 1,178 Eighth Air Force heavy bombers dispatched on continuous missions throughout the day, 724 drop an aggregate of 1,876 tons of bombs on no fewer than twenty separate bridges, marshalling yards, airdromes, and other tactical targets in and around the beachhead area. The only Eighth Air Force heavy-bomber unit *not* to fly is the 34th Heavy Bombardment Group. One B-17 and two B-24s are lost.

Nearly 400 IX Bomber Command B-26 sorties are flown against marshalling yards, rail sidings, road and rail bridges and junctions, fuel and ammunition dumps, troop concentrations, and defended town areas. Also, a total of approximately 1,300 Ninth Air Force fighter and fighter-bomber sorties are flown as escort and support for the B-26s and to bomb and strafe bridges, artillery batteries, marshalling yards, rail lines, troop concentrations, motor vehicles, and defended town areas.

Every VIII Fighter Command group contributes to the day's total of 1,353 combat sorties to escort bombers, patrol the beachhead, sweep the general area, and attack ground targets, especially German Army lines of communication. In all, VIII Fighter Command losses are 22 fighters and 21 pilots, which is largely a testament to the dangers inherent in attacking ground targets at low level. 1stLt Robert J. Booth, an eight-victory P-51 ace with the 359th Fighter Group, is shot down by flak and taken prisoner at La Fleche.

Thirty-eight GAF aircraft are downed over France between 0530 and 1715 hours—31 by VIII Fighter Command pilots, and seven by IX Fighter Command pilots. VIII Fighter Command pilots also destroy 21 GAF aircraft on the ground. Maj Rockford V. Gray, the 371st Fighter Group operations officer, in a P-47, achieves ace status when he downs three FW-190s near Cabourg at 1715 hours.

ITALY: Twelfth Air Force B-25s and B-26s attack bridges; XII TAC A-20s attack a town; and XII TAC fighters and fighter-bombers attack numerous transportation targets.

YUGOSLAVIA: Although flight operations are limited by bad weather, 52

Fifteenth Air Force B-17s attack the submarine base at Pola.

June 9, 1944

ENGLAND: The entire Eighth and Ninth air forces are grounded by bad weather.

FRANCE: Allied naval forces down four USAAF reconnaissance aircraft during the late afternoon—all F-6s from the Ninth Air Force's 67th Tactical Reconnaissance Group. One pilot is rescued.

An advance detachment of the IX TAC's 70th Fighter Wing headquarters begins setting up a forward command post at Criqueville, in the Normandy beachhead.

GERMANY: Nearly 500 Fifteenth Air Force B-17s and B-24s attack an ordnance depot, aircraft-industry targets, and an airdrome in the Munich area. Thirteen heavy bombers are lost.

While escorting the heavy bombers, P-51 pilots of the 52d Fighter Group and P-47 pilots of the 332d Fighter Group (in their Fifteenth Air Force combat debut) down 19 GAF fighters between Udine (Italy) and Munich. Two P-51 pilots of the 52d Fighter Group's 2d Fighter Squadron achieve ace status on this mission: 2dLt Arthur G. Johnson, when he downs a Bf-109 over Traunstein at 1000 hours; and 2dLt James S. Varnell, when he downs a Bf-110 over Munich, also at 1000 hours.

ITALY: Fifteenth Air Force B-24s attack oil-industry targets at Porto Marghera; Twelfth Air Force B-25s and B-26s attack bridges; XII TAC A-20s attack targets of opportunity near the battle area; and XII TAC fighters and fighter-bombers attack motor transport and rail lines facilitating the retreat of German Army forces.

June 10, 1944

CORSICA: The XII Bomber Command, which has been moribund for months, is formally disbanded.

ENGLAND: The Ninth Air Force's 10th Photographic Reconnaissance Group (in F-5s) and 67th Tactical Reconnaissance Group (in F-6s) begin the exchange of two

squadrons apiece in order to make them balanced and equal. Over the next three days, the 12th and 15th Tactical Reconnaissance squadrons will move from the 10th to the 67th groups, and the 30th and 33d Photographic Reconnaissance squadrons will move from the 67th to the 10th groups.
FRANCE: Bad weather hampers heavy-bomber operations. Of 883 Eighth Air Force B-17s and B-24s dispatched throughout the day, 609 formed into small tactical formations (10 to 65 bombers) attack five GAF airdromes and numerous towns through which German Army lines of communication pass on the way to the Normandy battle area. One B-24 is lost.

VIII Fighter Command fighters mount 1,491 sorties while escorting the heavy bombers, patrolling the beachhead area, and attacking a wide variety of communications and tactical targets in the Normandy area. Twenty-four VIII Fighter Command fighters and their pilots are lost.

IX Bomber Command B-26s, A-20s, and fighter-bombers attack numerous transportation and tactical targets in the beachhead area.

VIII Fighter Command and Ninth Air Force fighter pilots down 29 GAF fighters and a Ju-52 over northwestern France between 1010 and 2150 hours. 1stLt Christopher J. Hanseman, a P-51 pilot with the 339th Fighter Group's 505th Fighter Squadron, achieves ace status when he downs a Bf-109 near Laigle at 1100 hours.

To better support U.S. First Army ground operations, IX TAC headquarters displaces from England to Au Guay. (This headquarters will continue to displace forward as the U.S. First Army advances across France, Belgium, and Germany.)
ITALY: Fifteenth Air Force B-17s and B-24s aircraft attack Ancona, the Ferrara Airdrome, a marshalling yard and oil-industry targets at Mestre, a marshalling yard at Porto Marghera, and oil-industry targets in Trieste; Twelfth Air Force B-25s and B-26s attack rail and road targets near Rome; XII TAC A-20s attack road targets;

and XII TAC fighters and fighter-bombers attack road targets and motor vehicles north of the battle area.
ROMANIA: Supported by 1st Fighter Group P-38s, 46 82d Fighter Group P-38s equipped as dive-bombers and fitted with one 1,000-pound bomb apiece, attack the Franco-Americano oil refinery at Ploesti. Thirty-six bombs are dropped, and an oil-cracking plant, oil tanks, and other facilities are damaged or destroyed, as are a variety of ground targets that are strafed by the fighters. Losses, however, are 14 1st Fighter Group P-38s and eight 82d Fighter Group P-38s.

1st and 82d Fighter group P-38 pilots down 33 Axis aircraft over Romania during the course of the mission. 2dLt Herbert B. Hatch, a P-38 pilot with the 1st Fighter Group's 71st Fighter Squadron, becomes an "instant ace" when he downs five (and probably a sixth) Romanian Air Force IAR.80 fighters over a Romanian Air Force airfield near Ploesti at 1130 hours. Also, 1stLt Armour C. Miller, a P-38 pilot with the 1st Fighter Group's 27th Fighter Squadron, achieves ace status when he downs a Bf-109.

June 11, 1942

FRANCE: Scheduled attacks on targets in Germany are canceled because of bad weather, but, of 1,055 Eighth Air Force B-17s and B-24s dispatched, a total of 606 formed into small tactical formations attack ten GAF airdromes and numerous rail targets in Brittany, the Loire River valley, and around Paris. Two B-17s and one B-24 are lost.

VIII Fighter Command fighters mount 914 effective sorties while escorting the heavy bombers, patrolling the beachhead area, and attacking a wide variety of communications targets in the Normandy area. Eight VIII Fighter Command fighters and seven pilots are lost.

During the morning, a total of 129 IX Bomber Command B-26s and A-20s, along with ten Ninth Air Force fighter-bomber groups, attack rail and road targets, oil tanks, gun emplacements, and defended town areas, but afternoon attacks are canceled because of bad weather.

356th Fighter Group P-47 pilots down two GAF fighters near Bernay at about 0700 hours, and 55th Fighter Group P-38 pilots down eight GAF fighters over northwestern France between 1500 and 1615 hours.
ITALY: All Twelfth Air Force bombers are grounded by bad weather, but a small number of XII TAC fighters and fighter-bombers attack rail and road targets and motor vehicles.
ROMANIA: While escorting Fifteenth Air Force B-24s on a mission against oil-industry targets at Constanta and Giurgiu, 14th Fighter Group P-38 pilots and 52d Fighter Group P-51 pilots down 18 Axis fighters over Romania between 0845 and 0935 hours.

Fifteenth Air Force B-17s returning from the inaugural FRANTIC mission to the Soviet Union attack the Axis airdrome at Foscani. One B-17 is lost. 325th Fighter Group P-51 escort pilots down three Bf-109s between 0940 and 1045 hours.
YUGOSLAVIA: Fifteenth Air Force B-17s attack oil-industry targets and a marshalling yard at Smederevo.

June 12, 1944

ENGLAND: During the night of June 12–13, the first V-1 pilotless "buzz bomb" strikes English soil.
FRANCE: Bad weather over Germany forces a cancellation of planned attacks there, so 1,277 Eighth Air Force B-17s and B-24s attack 16 GAF airdromes in northwest France and six rail bridges in the Rennes and St.-Nazaire areas. Six B-17s and two B-24s are lost in the largest GAF attacks on bomber formations since D day.

A battled-damaged 467th Heavy Bombardment Group B-24 becomes the first USAAF bomber to make a safe emergency landing on a U.S.-held airstrip in France.

Five hundred nine IX Bomber Command B-26s and A-20s attack rail and road targets, defended town areas, troop concentrations, and targets of opportunity in and around the battle area; and fifteen Ninth Air Force fighter-bomber groups attack rail lines, gun emplacements, defended areas and towns, troops and tanks, dumps, bridges, a radar installation, and numerous other tactical and transportation targets.

VIII Fighter Command fighters mount 988 sorties while escorting Eighth Air Force and Ninth Air Force bombers, patrolling the beachhead area, and attacking a wide variety of communications targets in the Normandy area, including two radar installations. Sixteen VIII Fighter Command fighters and 15 pilots are lost.

USAAF fighter pilots down 47 GAF fighters over the western France between 0550 to 1610 hours. FO Steven Gerick, a P-47 pilot with the 56th Fighter Group's 61st Fighter Squadron, achieves ace status when he downs two Bf-109s near Evreux at 1525 hours.
ITALY: Twelfth Air Force B-25s and B-26s attack bridges, viaducts, and rail targets north of the battle area; XII TAC A-20s attack a town; and, despite bad weather, XII TAC fighter-bombers attack bridges and roads along German Army lines of retreat.

June 13, 1944

AUSTRIA: A large force of Fifteenth Air Force B-24s and B-17s is dispatched against marshalling yards, an airdrome, and industrial areas in Munich. However, after fighting their way to Munich against determined GAF fighter opposition, the bomber formations are prevented from dropping their bombs because of solid man-made smoke cover throughout the area. Nearly all the bombers then fly through continuous and determined fighter opposition to bomb their alternate target, the marshalling yards at Innsbruck, Austria.

P-51 escort pilots of the 31st, 52d, and 325th Fighter groups down 20 GAF fighters over northern Italy, Austria, and southern Germany between 0933 and 1145 hours. 1stLt Murray D. McLaughlin, a P-51 pilot with the 31st Fighter Group's 309th Fighter Squadron, achieves ace status when he downs two Bf-109s near Munich at about 1015 hours; and three 52d Fighter Group P-51 pilots achieves ace status during this mission: 1stLt Robert L. Burnett, III, who downs a Bf-109; Capt Robert C. Curtis, of the 2d Fighter Squadron, who downs two Bf-109s; and 2dLt John B. Lawler, also of the 2d Fighter Squadron, who downs a Bf-109.

FRANCE: When bad weather forces a cancellation of scheduled missions to Germany, and despite heavy cloud cover that frustrates many bombing efforts, a total of 341 Eighth Air Force B-17s and B-24s, in morning and afternoon missions, attack five GAF airdromes, five bridges, and several towns. Two B-24s are lost.

Three hundred ninety-seven IX Bomber Command B-26s and A-20s attack rail and road targets, and fuel dumps; and Ninth Air Force fighter-bombers from nine tactical groups attack a powerhouse at Vire, as well as numerous tactical and transportation targets, also in the battle area.

Of 675 VIII Fighter Command fighters dispatched, a total of 416 escort Eighth and Ninth air force bombers, patrol the beachhead area, and attack tactical and transportation targets. Five VIII Fighter Command fighters and their pilots are lost.

VIII Fighter Command and Ninth Air Force fighter pilots down ten GAF fighters over central and northwestern France between 0615 and 2115 hours. LtCol Joseph J. Kruzel, the executive officer of the 361st Fighter Group, in a P-51, achieves ace status when he downs a Bf-109 near St.-Brieuc at 2050 hours. (Three of Kruzel's earlier victories were scored over Java in February 1942.)

ITALY: Fifteenth Air Force B-24s attack oil-industry targets at Porto Marghera; Twelfth Air Force B-25s and B-26s attack Axis shipping at Leghorn as well as numerous bridges and other transportation targets throughout north-central Italy; and XII TAC

fighter-bombers mount numerous attacks along the German Army lines of retreat.

June 14, 1944

BELGIUM: A total of 243 3d Bombardment Division B-17s and seven 2d Bombardment Division B-24s attack three airdromes and several other targets.

CZECHOSLOVAKIA: Fifteenth Air Force B-24s attack oil-industry targets at Pardubice.

FRANCE: Thwarted once again by bad weather over assigned targets in Germany, a total of 983 Eighth Air Force B-17s and B-24s attack nine GAF airfields, supply dumps, and several targets of opportunity. Twelve B-17s and two B-24s are lost.

More than 500 IX Bomber Command B-26 and A-20 sorties are mounted against rail lines southwest of Paris and German Army lines of communication south of the beachhead area. Many tactical targets of opportunity are also attacked.

One hundred sixty-eight VIII Fighter Command fighter-bombers attack the GAF headquarters at Chantilly as well as German Army tank columns encountered in the area, and 583 VIII Fighter Command fighters patrol the beachhead or sweep ahead of the Eighth Air Force heavy bombers. Seven VIII Fighter Command fighters and their pilots are lost. Also, fifteen Ninth Air Force fighter-bomber groups escort medium bombers and attack numerous tactical and transportation targets in the beachhead area and across central France.

USAAF fighter pilots down 15 GAF fighters over France between 0730 and 2020 hours. 1stLt Robert M. Shaw, a P-51 pilot with the 357th Fighter Group's 364th Fighter Squadron, achieves ace status when he downs an FW-190 near Paris at 0750 hours; and 1stLt Clayton K. Gross, a P-51 pilot with the 354th Fighter Group's 355th Fighter Squadron, achieves ace status when he downs a Bf-109 near Caen at 2020 hours.

GERMANY: Sixty-one 2d Bombardment Division B-24s attack an oil refinery at Emmerich.

HUNGARY: Fifteenth Air Force B-17s attack oil refineries at Budapest and Komarom.

P-38 pilots of the 14th Fighter Group's 49th Fighter Squadron down 15 Bf-109s over Petfurdo between 1100 and 1125 hours. 1stLt Louis Benne achieves ace status when he downs two Bf-109s near Petfurdo on his last scheduled mission before being rotated home. However, Benne is himself shot down and captured on this mission. 2dLt Jack Lenox, Jr., also achieves ace status when he downs three Bf-109s.

ITALY: Twelfth Air Force B-25s and B-26s attack viaducts and bridges in north-central Italy and ships in the harbor at Leghorn; XII TAC A-20s attack ammunition dumps; and XII TAC fighter-bombers attacks bridges and roads immediately to the north of the battle area.

NETHERLANDS: Sixty-three 2d Bombardment Division B-24s attack Eindhoven Airdrome.

YUGOSLAVIA: Fifteenth Air Force heavy bombers attack oil refineries at Osijek and Sisak, and Fifteenth Air Force P-38 dive-bombers attack Kecskemet Airdrome.

June 15, 1944

ENGLAND: During the night of June 15–16, nearly 300 V-1 pilotless bombs strike English soil.

FRANCE: Nearly 1,000 Eighth Air Force B-17s and B-24s attack rail bridges and via-ducts, marshalling yards, highway bridges, and airdromes. Two B-17s are lost.

IX Bomber Command B-26s and A-20s mount more than 550 sorties against rail and road targets, ammunition dumps, and a German armored division command post; and Ninth Air Force fighters and fighter-bombers mount more than 1,400 escort or tactical sorties.

Thirty-six VIII Fighter Command P-38 fighter-bombers attack a rail bridge at Etaples. One P-38 and its pilot are lost. Also, 177 VIII Fighter Command fighters mount sweeps ahead of the various heavy-bomber formations.

Nine GAF fighters are downed over northern France by VIII Fighter Command and Ninth Air Force pilots between 0705 and 2000 hours.

Fifteenth Air Force pilots of the 1st, 14th, 31st, 82d, and 325th Fighter groups involved in fighter sweeps over several GAF airdromes in southern France down five GAF fighters between 1155 and 1210 hours.

GERMANY: Nearly 200 Eighth Air Force B-17s attack an oil refinery at Hannover or nearby targets of opportunity.

ITALY: Fifteenth Air Force heavy bombers are grounded by bad weather; Twelfth Air Force B-25s and B-26s attack bridges around Florence and La Spezia; XII TAC A-20s attack ammunition dumps; and XII TAC fighters and fighter-bombers attack roads and bridges immediately north of the battle area.

June 16, 1944

AUSTRIA: Fifteenth Air Force heavy bombers attack a number of oil depots and refineries in the Vienna area through extremely heavy and determined opposition, including waves of rocket-firing Ju-88s. While covering the bombers during the penetration, target, and withdrawal phases of the mission, pilots of the 1st, 31st, 52d, 82d, and 325th Fighter groups down 40 GAF fighters between 0935 hours and noon.

CZECHOSLOVAKIA: Fifteenth Air Force heavy bombers attack oil-industry targets around Bratislava.

FRANCE: Many scheduled Eighth Air Force heavy-bomber missions are canceled because of bad weather, but 93 1st Bombardment Division B-17s attack the Juvincourt, Laon/Athies, and Laon/Couvron airdromes; 18 1st Bombardment Division B-17s attack various railway targets of opportunity; 56 2d Bombardment Division B-24s attack the Authe, Beauvais/Tille, and St.-Andre-de-L'Eure airdromes; and 156 2d Bombardment Division B-24s attack V-weapons sites at four locations. One B-17 is lost.

Six hundred twenty VIII Fighter

Command fighters escort Eighth Air Force heavy bombers or attack trains and troop concentrations. Making extensive use for the first time of a new fighter-bomber tactic, many fighters and fighter-bombers release their drop tanks against rail targets and set the fuel ablaze with incendiary machine-gun bullets. Of nearly 400 rail cars attacked in this manner, an estimated 200 are destroyed. Three VIII Fighter Command fighters and their pilots are lost.

All IX Bomber Command bombers are grounded by the bad weather, but more than 500 Ninth Air Force fighters and fighter-bombers bomb and strafe rail and road traffic and bridges in the Cherbourg area.

Just one GAF fighter is downed, a Bf-109 credited to a 56th Fighter Group P-47 pilot near Rouen at 1650 hours.

An advance echelon of P-51s from the Ninth Air Force's 354th Fighter Group (100th Fighter Wing, IX TAC), in P-51s, begins operating from Advance Landing Ground A-2, a wire-mesh–reinforced dirt fighter strip carved out by IX Engineer Command aviation engineers inside the Normandy beachhead near Criqueville. The P-51s immediately begin conducting low-level offensive missions against the German Army.

HUNGARY: 1stLt Richard S. Deakins, a P-51 pilot with the 325th Fighter Group's 318th Fighter Squadron achieves ace status when he downs a Bf-109 near Lake Balaton at 1000 hours.

ITALY: Twelfth Air Force B-25s and B-26s attack rail and road bridges; XII TAC A-20s attack several ammunition dumps; and XII TAC fighter-bombers continue to attack communications targets in and around the battle area.

June 17, 1944

FRANCE: During the morning, of 332 Eighth Air Force B-17s and B-24s dispatched against various GAF airdromes, 168 attack their assigned targets, 18 attack an unassigned airdrome, 31 attack an unassigned rail bridge, and 15 attack various other targets of opportunity. Two of the B-17s are lost.

Escort for the Eighth Air Force morning mission is provided by 427 VIII Fighter Command fighters, of which one is lost with its pilot. Also, 99 VIII Fighter Command P-38 fighter-bombers attack rail bridges at two locations. Four P-38s are lost with their pilots.

Two hundred sixty-five IX Bomber Command B-26s attack fuel dumps, a rail line, and a bridge; and Ninth Air Force fighters and fighter-bombers mount more than 1,300 tactical sorties against an array of ground targets in and around the Normandy battle area.

During the afternoon, 274 2d and 3d Bombardment division B-24s attack the Angers, Laval, and Tours airdromes as well as two auxiliary airfields. One B-24 is lost.

Two hundred seventy VIII Fighter Command P-47s and P-51s escort the Eighth Air Force B-24s; 49 P-38s and 39 P-47s attack rail bridges at two locations; and 47 P-47s escort the P-38 and P-47 fighter-bombers. Three VIII Fighter Command fighters and their pilots are lost.

During the course of numerous small engagements between 1345 and 1930 hours, VIII Fighter Command and Ninth Air Force fighters down 17 GAF fighters.

Operational control of all tactical missions—including tactical-bomber missions—in France is assumed by the IX TAC advance headquarters, which is in Normandy.

ITALY: All of the Fifteenth Air Force and most of the Twelfth Air Force are grounded by bad weather. However, Twelfth Air Force B-26s attack a bridge, A-20s attack an ammunition dump, and fighter-bombers attack several gun emplacements, a few bridges, and some coastal shipping. Support is also provided to an invasion of Elba Island by Free French Army forces.

June 18, 1944

FRANCE: Fifty-eight 2d Bombardment Division B-17s, escorted by 48 P-47s, attack V-weapons sites at Watten using GH radar, but a planned attack by VIII Fighter Command P-38 and P-47 fighter-bombers against rail bridges in the St. Quentin area is aborted because of bad weather.

During the morning, nearly 130 IX Bomber Command B-26s and A-20s attack marshalling yards at Meudon and Rennes, and fuel dumps at two locations.

During the afternoon, IX Bomber Command B-26s attack three V-weapons sites through heavy cloud cover.

Throughout the day, Ninth Air Force fighter-bombers attack transportation and tactical targets in the Cherbourg Peninsula.

The only victory credit of the day is awarded to 406th Fighter Group P-47 pilots who down a Bf-110 near Trouville-sur-Mer at 2045 hours.

An advance echelon of P-47s from the Ninth Air Force's 48th Fighter Group (100th Fighter Wing, IX Tactical Air Command) begins operating out of Advance Landing Ground A-4, at Deaux Jumeaux, in Normandy, to provide direct support for Allied ground forces in the beachhead area.
GERMANY: In the first large strategic mission since D day, 1,378 Eighth Air Force B-17s and B-24s are dispatched to attack oil refineries around Hamburg and Misburg (Hannover), and two GAF control centers. Bad weather encountered along the way results in more than 150 aborts, and many bomber formations must settle for secondary targets and targets of opportunity, especially the city of Hamburg, which receives the brunt of many piecemeal attacks. The city of Hannover and the Misburg refineries are also struck, as is the city of Bremen, several other towns and cities, and several GAF airdromes. Seven B-17s and four B-24s are lost. Among those killed is Col Ernest H. Lawson, commanding officer of the 1st Bombardment Division's 305th Heavy Bombardment Group.

Escort for the heavy bombers is provided by 537 VIII Fighter Command fighters. There are no losses and no victory claims.

ITALY: All Twelfth and Fifteenth air force bombers are grounded by bad weather, but XII TAC fighter-bombers are able attack several gun emplacements on Elba Islandand some coastal shipping near Piombino.

June 19, 1944

FRANCE: Despite heavy cloud cover that results in more than 200 aborts, a total of 261 Eighth Air Force B-17s attack the Bordeaux/Merignac, Cabanac, Cazaux, Cormes Ecluse, and Lanes-de-Bussac airdromes. Five B-17s are lost over Bordeaux/Merignac and two are interned in Spain. Escort for the bombers attacking the airdromes is provided by 88 P-38s and 261 P-51s, of which four P-38s and six P-51s are lost with their pilots.

Also during the morning, despite bad weather that results in nearly 400 aborts, two mixed formations aggregating 216 Eighth Air Force B-17s and 294 B-24s using GH radar attack V-weapons sites in and around the Pas-de-Calais area. Escort is provided by a total of 715 VIII Fighter Command fighters. There are no bombers or fighters lost. Following its escort assignment, one P-38 group dive-bombs and strafes several transportation targets.

There are no IX Bomber Command bombing missions, but nearly 200 Ninth Air Force fighters conduct patrols over France during the morning. During the afternoon, Ninth Air Force fighter-bombers attack six V-weapons sites.

The IX TAC's 368th Fighter Group becomes the first USAAF unit to be permanently assigned to a base in France—Advance Landing Ground A-3, at Cardonville, a crude wire-mesh runway that has been constructed by an engineer aviation battalion overseen by the IX Engineer Command.
ITALY: All Twelfth and Fifteenth air force bombers are grounded by bad weather, but fighters of the Twelfth Air Force's 87th Fighter Wing support Free French Army ground units on Elba Island during the afternoon; and XII TAC fighter-bombers

are able to attack gun emplacements, a factory, some coastal shipping, and several rail lines in north-central Italy, also during the afternoon.

June 20, 1944

FRANCE: During the morning, 126 2d Bombardment Division B-24s, escorted by 44 VIII Fighter Command P-47s, attack V-weapons sites in the Pas-de-Calais area. One B-24 and one P-47 are lost.

Approximately 370 IX Bomber Command B-26s and A-20s attack nine V-weapons sites and a coastal-defense battery.

During the afternoon, 196 Eighth Air Force B-17s and 33 B-24s, escorted by 72 VIII Fighter Command P-47s and 40 P-51s, attack V-weapons sites in the Pas-de-Calais area. One B-24 is lost.

Two hundred two VIII Fighter Command fighters and fighter-bombers bomb and strafe numerous targets across central France, especially in the Paris area. Two P-51s are lost with their pilots.

Throughout the day, Ninth Air Force fighters and fighter-bombers mount more than 1,000 tactical sorties against targets in the battle area as well as rail lines, bridges, and marshalling yards servicing the battle area.

USAAF fighter pilots down 16 GAF fighters over France between 0700 and 1944 hours.

The IX TAC's 366th Fighter Group moves into Advance Landing Ground A-1, at St.-Pierre-du-Mont.

GERMANY: Four hundred fifty-four 1st Bombardment Division B-17s attack oil and industrial targets at Hamburg; 316 2d Bombardment Division B-24s attack industrial targets at Politz and Ostermoor; 284 3d Bombardment Division B-17s attack industrial targets at Fallersleben, Konigsburg, and Magdeburg; 169 3d Bombardment Division B-24s attack oil targets at Hannover; and 26 heavy bombers attack various targets of opportunity. Losses are 13 B-17s and 35 B-24s, of which 20 2d Bombardment Division B-24s are interned in Sweden.

Escort for the heavy bombers is provided by 637 VIII Fighter Command fighters, of which five are lost with two pilots, and 81 IX Fighter Command P-51s, of which one is lost with its pilot. Maj James A. Goodson, a 14-victory ace with the 4th Fighter Group's 336th Fighter Squadron, is shot down by flak over Neubrandenburg Airdrome and taken prisoner.

In all, while escorting the various heavy-bomber formations to Germany, USAAF fighter pilots down 34 GAF fighters, two Ju-88s, and an Fi-156 between 0905 and 1030 hours. LtCol James A. Clark, Jr., of the 4th Fighter Group, brings his final personal tally to 10.5 confirmed victories when he downs an Me-410 near Anklam at 0930 hours.

ITALY: Despite bad weather, approximately 60 Twelfth Air Force medium bombers attack rail targets between Genoa and La Spezia; and XII TAC fighter-bombers attack rail and road bridges in and near the battle area, and damage an Italian Navy aircraft carrier tied up in Genoa harbor.

NETHERLANDS: Forty-eight VIII Fighter Command P-47 fighter-bombers bomb several airdromes.

June 21, 1944

ENGLAND: MajGen Earle E. Partridge, formerly Eighth Air Force deputy commanding general, succeeds MajGen Curtis E. LeMay as commanding general of the Eighth Air Force's 3d Bombardment Division when LeMay is reassigned to the USAAF B-29 bomber program.

FRANCE: More than 250 IX Bomber Command B-26s and A-20s attack 13 V-weapons sites in the Pas-de-Calais area.

Late in the afternoon, 70 2d Bombardment Division B-24s, escorted by 99 VIII Fighter Command P-47s, attack a total of 39 V-weapons sites at Siracourt and two German Army supply points. One B-24 is downed by flak. One escort fighter group strafes rail traffic and canal barges.

During the early evening, XIX TAC fighter-bomber pilots down a GAF fighter over Rouen and two GAF fighters near Paris.

GERMANY: Four hundred fifty-six 1st Bombardment Division B-17s, 103 3d Bombardment Division B-17s, and 47 2d Bombardment Division B-24s attack the city of Berlin; and 252 2d Bombardment Division B-24s, 85 3d Bombardment Division B-17s, and 12 1st Bombardment Division B-17s attack assigned industrial targets and several targets of opportunity, mostly in the Berlin area.

Escort for the Berlin-area heavy-bomber mission is provided by 958 VIII Fighter Command fighters and 441 IX Fighter Command fighters. Sixteen escort fighters are lost with 14 pilots.

In the second Operation FRANTIC mission of the war—the first from the U.K.—114 3d Bombardment Division B-17s, escorted by 70 4th and 352d Fighter group P-51s, attack oil targets around Ruhland (south of Berlin) and proceed on to bases in the Soviet Union. One B-17 is lost to unknown causes. Seventy P-51 escorts proceed with the B-17s all the way to the Soviet Union, and 162 escort fighters return to their bases in England.

USAAF escort fighters down 17 GAF fighters over Germany and seven GAF fighters over Poland. 1stLt John F. Thornell, Jr., a P-51 ace with the 352d Fighter Group's 328th Fighter Squadron, brings his final personal tally to 17.25 confirmed victories when he shares in the downing of an Me-410 near Dahmsdorf at 1005 hours; Capt George M. Lamb, a P-51 pilot with the 354th Fighter Group's 356th Fighter Squadron, achieves ace status when he downs two Me-410s near Berlin at 1130 hours; and two 4th Fighter Group P-51 pilots achieve ace status during the target withdrawal from Ruhland to Poltava, Soviet Union: 1stLt Joseph L. Lang, when he downs a Bf-109 near Warsaw at 1145 hours; and Capt Frank C. Jones, when he downs a Bf-109 near Kobrin, Poland, at 1300 hours.

ITALY: Twelfth Air Force B-25s and B-26s attack rail bridges in north and north-central Italy and shipping in Leghorn harbor; XII TAC A-20s attack ammunition dumps; and XII TAC fighter-bombers attack rail and road targets near the German Army's new Gothic Line.

SOVIET UNION: During the night of June 21-22, GAF bombers attack the USAAF base at Poltava Airdrome by flare light. Forty-seven of the 73 B-17s at the base are destroyed and many others are heavily damaged, as are a number of P-51s. Large supplies of fuel and munitions are also destroyed.

June 22, 1944

FRANCE: Mixed formations totaling 217 Eighth Air Force B-17s and B-24s attack V-weapons sites in the Pas-de-Calais area. One B-17 is lost. A small number of the 165 VIII Fighter Command P-47s and 97 P-51s providing escort for the heavy bombers also attack marshalling yards and GAF airdromes during their return to England. One fighter is lost with its pilot.

During the afternoon, numerous small formations amounting to 604 Eighth Air Force B-17s and B-24s attack more than 25 targets throughout northwestern France, including GAF airdromes, bridges, and marshalling yards. Seven heavy bombers are lost. Escort for the heavy bombers is provided by 372 VIII Fighter Command fighters, of which five are lost with their pilots.

One hundred one 3d Bombardment Division B-17s attack an oil depot in Paris. Two B-17s are lost. Escort for the Paris mission is provided by 78 VIII Fighter Command P-51s, of which three are lost with their pilots.

Throughout the day, IX Bomber Command B-26s and A-20s mount more than 600 sorties, and Ninth Air Force fighters and fighter-bombers mount more than 1,200 sorties. The bulk of the effort consists of a 55-minute rolling aerial bombardment in support of a morning assault by the U.S. First Army's VII Corps against the port of Cherbourg. This is by far the largest sustained ground-support effort to this point in the war, and it requires pinpoint accuracy combined with split-second timing as bombs are dropped just ahead of the advancing ground units. Later in the day, IX Bomber Command B-26s attack marshalling yards, fuel dumps, and a German Army headquarters; and fighter-bombers attack numerous tactical and transportation targets. One Ninth Air Force bomber and 24 Ninth Air Force fighters are lost.

During the afternoon and evening, USAAF fighter pilots down 20 GAF fighters and one Fi-156. 1stLt Clarence O. Johnson, a P-38 pilot with the 479th Fighter Group's 436th Fighter Squadron, achieves ace status when he downs an Fi-156 observation plane near Rheims at 1530 hours. (Johnson's four earlier victories were scored with the 82d Fighter Group in the MTO.) Also, Maj Randall O. Hendricks, the commanding officer of the 368th Fighter Group's 397th Fighter Squadron, in P-47s, achieves ace status when he downs a Bf-109 over France at 1420 hours.

ITALY: More than 600 Fifteenth Air Force B-17s and B-24s attack nine marshalling yards in northern Italy, a motor-transport factory in Turin, a motor-transport depot, an airdrome, three rail and road bridges, and oil tanks; Twelfth Air Force B-25s and B-26s attack several bridges and viaducts in northern Italy; XII TAC A-20s attack ammunition dumps; and XII TAC fighter-bombers attack rail lines between Bologna and Pistoia, as well as several rail and road bridges, mainly around Pisa

SOVIET UNION: During the night of June 22–23, GAF bombers attack the USAAF bases at Mirgorod and Piryatin. No Eighth Air Force airplanes are lost or damaged—they have been moved to Soviet Air Force bases much farther to the east—but fuel and munitions at both USAAF bases are destroyed.

June 23, 1944

FRANCE: One hundred ten 1st Bombardment Division B-17s and 102 2d Bombardment Division B-24s attack 12 V-weapons sites in the Pas-de-Calais area using GH radar. Escort is provided by 141 VIII Fighter Command P-51s, which strafe transportation targets in the Paris area following withdrawal by the bombers. One P-51 is lost with its pilot.

More than 90 3d Bombardment Division B-17s fail to complete their briefed mission against Nanteuil because of bad weather, but 13 B-17s are able to attack the target, and two B-17s attack targets of opportunity. One B-17 is lost. Also, 183 2d and 3d Bombardment division B-24s attack Coulommiers, Juvincourt, Laon/Athies, and Soissons airdromes. Six B-24s are lost. Escort for these heavy-bomber missions is provided by 155 VIII Fighter Command P-47s and 83 P-51s. Following the escort mission, P-47s bomb a marshalling yard at Givet.

One hundred sixty-nine VIII Fighter Command P-38 fighter-bombers attack bridges in the Paris area. Two P-38s are lost with their pilots.

IX Bomber Command B-26s and A-20s are grounded during the morning by bad weather, but during the afternoon 175 B-26s and A-20s attack seven V-weapons sites. Many of the 630 Ninth Air Force fighters escorting the bombers to France bomb and strafe communications centers and rail and road traffic.

IX TAC fighter and fighter-bomber pilots down five GAF fighters and one Fi-156 between 0700 and 1822 hours.

The IX TAC's 371st Fighter Group moves into Advance Landing Ground A-6, at Beauzeville, and the 354th Fighter Group makes a permanent move into Advance Landing Ground A-2, at Criqueville (from which it has been conducting some operations since June 16).

ITALY: Twelfth Air Force B-25s and B-26s are grounded by bad weather, but XII TAC A-20s attack ammunition dumps, and several P-47 groups that are able to get airborne attack rail targets near the battle area.

ROMANIA: As 139 Fifteenth Air Force heavy bombers attack targets throughout the

Ploesti oil complex with 283 tons of bombs, 2dLt David R. Kingsley, the bombardier of a severely crippled 97th Heavy Bombardment Group B-17, is killed in the crash of his airplane moments after giving his parachute to the seriously wounded tail gunner and helping the man bail out. For his selfless act, Kingsley is awarded a posthumous Medal of Honor. Altogether, six heavy bombers are lost in this attack.

Fifteenth Air Force B-24s also attack oil-industry targets around Giurgiu.

In all, 25 Axis fighters are downed along the bomber routes between 0940 and 1030 hours by fighter pilots of the 31st, 52d, and 325th Fighter groups. Four P-51 pilots achieve ace status while escorting the bombers on this mission: Capt James O. Tyler, of the 52d Fighter Group's 4th Fighter Squadron, when he downs an FW-190 and a G.50 fighter near Bucharest; 1stLt Daniel J. Zoerb, of the 52d Fighter Group's 2d Fighter Squadron, when he shares in the downing of an FW-190 and a Bf-109 near Bucharest; 1stLt Walter J. Goehausen, Jr., of the 31st Fighter Group's 308th Fighter Squadron, when he downs a Bf-109 near Bucharest; and 2dLt Cecil O. Dean, of the 325th Fighter Group's 317th Fighter Squadron, when he downs an FW-190 near Ploesti.

June 24, 1944

ENGLAND: The 422d Heavy Bombardment Squadron (the Eighth Air Force's independent night-leaflet squadron) is redesignated as the 406th Heavy Bombardment Squadron.

FRANCE: During the morning, 74 1st Bombardment Division B-17s and 265 2d and 3d Bombardment division B-24s attack airdromes, auxiliary fighter strips, and bridges in central and northwestern France. Two B-24s are lost. Also, 11 1st Bombardment Division B-17s unable to attack their targets in Germany attack the city of Rouen. One B-17 is lost. Three hundred seven VIII Fighter Command fighters provide escort for the morning heavy-bomber missions, and one fighter is lost with its pilot.

More than 430 IX Bomber Command B-26s and A-20s attack V-weapons sites, gun emplacements, fuel dumps, marshalling yards at two locations, and a rail bridge. Also, 11 Ninth Air Force fighter groups provide escort for the bombers and attack fuel dumps, bridges, and rail targets west of Paris.

During the afternoon, 57 1st Bombardment Division B-17s and 105 2d Bombardment Division B-24s attack two electrical and power stations, a marshalling yard at St.-Pol-sur-Mer, and V-weapons sites in the Pas-de-Calais area. Two B-24s are lost.

One hundred eighteen VIII Fighter Command fighters provide escort for the afternoon mission. Also, 25 VIII Fighter Command P-51s conducting a sweep through the Angers-Le Mans area destroy 25 GAF aircraft on the ground.

Ninth Air Force fighter and fighter-bomber pilots down four GAF fighters and one Ju-52 between 1245 and 1830 hours.

GERMANY: Two hundred thirteen Eighth Air Force B-17s attack oil-industry targets at Bremen, 40 B-17s attack the city of Bremen, and 53 B-17s unable to attack targets in Bremen attack an aircraft-industry site at Wesermunde. One B-17 is lost.

Two hundred fifty-one VIII Fighter Command P-38s and P-47s provide escort for the heavy-bomber mission to Bremen.

ITALY: Twelfth Air Force bombers are grounded by bad weather, and fighter-bomber operations are severely restricted, but some XII TAC P-47 groups are able to attack several bridges, rail lines, gun emplacements, and tactical targets in and around the battle area.

ROMANIA: Fifteenth Air Force B-24s attack oil-industry targets at Ploesti and the rail depot at Craiova, and Fifteenth Air Force B-17s attack a rail bridge.

Pilots of the 31st, 82d, and 325th Fighter groups down 14 Axis fighters over Bulgaria and Romania between 0850 and 1030 hours. 1stLt Wayne L. Lowry, a P-51 pilot with the 325th Fighter Group's 317th Fighter Squadron, achieves ace status when he downs a Bf-109 and an FW-190 near Bucharest between 0935 and 0945 hours.

June 25, 1944

FRANCE: During the day, a total of 500 Eighth Air Force B-17s and B-24s attack five airdromes, an oil dump, and numerous power and transformer stations. Five B-17s and two B-24s are lost.

VIII Fighter Command fighters mount a total of 430 escort sorties. Many of the escort fighter groups conduct strafing attacks after being released from escort duty. Two fighters and their pilots are lost. Also, 41 VIII Fighter Command P-47 fighter-bombers attack the Evreux/Fauville Airdrome.

More than 400 IX Bomber Command B-26s and A-20s attack rail bridges at four locations and fuel dumps at three locations; and fighter-bombers from 14 Ninth Air Force tactical groups escort the bombers or conduct dive-bombing attacks at Argentan, Chartes, Dreux, Orleans, and Tours.

VIII Fighter Command and Ninth Air Force fighter and fighter-bomber pilots down 49 GAF fighters between 0700 and 1940 hours.

The IX TAC's 50th Fighter Group moves into Advance Landing Ground A-10, at Carentan.

U.S. First Army ground forces capture Cherbourg/Maupertus Airdrome.

Fifteenth Air Force heavy bombers attack oil-industry targets and a marshalling yard at Sete, port facilities at Toulon, and a marshalling yard at Avignon.

1stLt Robert E. Riddle, a P-51 pilot with the 31st Fighter Group's 307th Fighter Squadron, achieves ace status when he downs a Bf-109 near Avignon at 0956 hours; and Col Charles M. McCorkle, the commanding officer of the 31st Fighter Group, brings his final personal tally to 11 confirmed victories when he downs a Bf-109 near Avignon at 0956 hours.

During the night of June 25–26, 320 3d Bombardment Division B-17s attack seven rail bridges in the Paris area, Paris/ Orly Airport, and a nearby marshalling yard; and 109 2d Bombardment Division B-24s attack three airdromes. Also, under cover of the bombing attacks, a number of 3d Bombardment Division B-17s drop supplies and a U.S. Office of Strategic Services (OSS) arms instructor to French partisans operating in the Paris area. One B-17 and five B-24s are lost.

ITALY: Twelfth Air Force B-25s and B-26s are grounded by bad weather; XII TAC A-20s attack ammunition dumps; XII TAC fighter-bombers attack towns and rail lines around the battle area; and a Fifteenth Air Force fighter group strafes all the traffic and other targets along the road linking Fiume, Italy, with Senje, Yugoslavia.

June 26, 1944

AUSTRIA: Six hundred seventy-seven Fifteenth Air Force B-17s and B-24s, escorted by 260 fighters, attack five of the seven oil refineries and an oil depot in the Vienna area. Thirty USAAF heavy bombers and fighters are downed during attacks by more than 150 Axis fighters during the target penetration phase.

82d Fighter Group P-38 pilots down 13 of the GAF fighters, mostly twin-engine Messerschmitts, over Bratislava, Czechoslovakia. 2dLt James D. Holloway, of the 82d Fighter Group's 95th Fighter Squadron, achieves ace status when he downs two Me-410s and a Bf-110. In all, along the bomber routes between 0855 and 1015 hours, pilots of the 1st, 31st, 52d, and 82d Fighter groups down 44 GAF aircraft, including a number of rocket-firing Ju-88s.

ENGLAND: Except for a few reconnaissance and fighter sorties over Normandy, the Eighth and Ninth air forces are grounded by bad weather.

FRANCE: Cherbourg falls to U.S. First Army ground forces.

ITALY: Twelfth Air Force bombers and most fighter-bombers are grounded by bad weather, but some XII TAC fighter-bombers manage to attack several rail and tactical targets near the Gothic Line.

POLAND: Seventy-two B-17s and 103 P-51 comprising the Eighth Air Force FRANTIC force leave the Soviet Union for USAAF bases in Italy. Along the way, they bomb the oil plant at Drohobycz, Poland. The Eighth Air Force formation is met along the withdrawal route by Fifteenth Air Force escort fighters.

June 27, 1944

FRANCE: Bad weather prevents 251 Eighth Air Force B-17s and B-24s from attacking V-weapons sites in the Pas-de-Calais area, but 218 of the heavy bombers scatter their bombs more or less throughout the target area, upon a canal lock, several supply dumps, and Creil Airdrome. Five B-24s are lost.

Among the airmen missing on this mission is BriGen A. W. Vanaman, the Eighth Air Force chief of intelligence, who is captured after bailing out of a B-24 plagued by a burning fuel leak. The B-24 returns to base with half its crew, BriGen Vanaman spends the rest of the war as a prisoner, and the Germans refuse to believe that he is not an intentional plant so do not use any of the information they manage to extract from him.

One hundred ninety-five VIII Fighter Command P-38s and P-51s provide escort for the heavy bombers, and many of the P-51s attack targets of opportunity while returning to England. Two P-51s are lost with their pilots.

During the afternoon, 46 VIII Fighter Command P-38s (of 193 dispatched) attack Connantre Airdrome; 36 VIII Fighter Command P-47s (of 158 dispatched) attack Villeneuve/Zertes Airdrome; and 32 VIII Fighter Command P-47s (of 49 dispatched) attack Coulommiers Airdrome after failing to locate their primary target. Three P-38s are lost. Also, 246 VIII Fighter Command fighters conduct sweeps against transportation targets of opportunity around Paris.

More than 700 Ninth Air Force fighters and fighter-bombers patrol over the Normandy battle area or attack rail, road,

and communications targets throughout France.

VIII Fighter Command fighters down 14 GAF fighters between 1935 and 2050 hours.

HUNGARY: Fifteenth Air Force B-17s attack marshalling yards at Budapest. Capt David "C" Wilhelm, a P-51 pilot with the 31st Fighter Group's 309th Fighter Squadron, achieves ace status when he downs an Me-210 at 1010 hours.

ITALY: Twelfth Air Force B-25s and B-26s are grounded by bad weather; XII TAC A-20s attack ammunition dumps; and XII TAC fighter-bombers attack bridges, rail and road targets, and tactical targets in or near the battle area.

POLAND: Fifteenth Air Force B-24s attack oil-industry targets at Drohobycz. While escorting the bombers over Hungary, pilots of the 31st, 52d, 82d, and 325th Fighter groups down 20 Axis aircraft between 0935 and 1035 hours.

YUGOSLAVIA: Fifteenth Air Force B-24s attack marshalling yards at Brod.

June 28, 1944

BELGIUM: Eleven 2d Bombardment Division B-24s that are unable to attack assigned targets at Saarbrucken, Germany, attack Florennes/Juzaine Airdrome.

ENGLAND: All Ninth Air Force bomber and fighter units based in the U.K. are grounded by bad weather.

FRANCE: Three hundred forty-one Eighth Air Force B-17s attack two bridges, an oil dump, and five airdromes. One B-17 is lost. More than 200 IX TAC fighter-bombers operating from advance landing grounds in Normandy attack bridges, rail facilities, ammunition and fuel dumps, gun emplacements, troop concentrations, motor vehicles, and many other tactical targets in and around the battle area.

Thirty VIII Fighter Command P-47s, of 50 dispatched, attack La Perthe Airdrome, and VIII Fighter Command pilots down two GAF fighters over France, and one over Belgium.

The IX TAC's 48th Fighter Group makes a permanent move into Advance Landing Ground A-4, at Deaux Jumeaux, from which elements have been operating since June 18.

GERMANY: Three hundred thirty-one 2d Bombardment Division B-24s attack marshalling yards at Saarbrucken. One B-24 is lost.

ITALY: All Twelfth Air Force bombers and most XII TAC fighter-bombers are grounded by bad weather, but some XII TAC fighter-bombers are able to attack rail lines servicing the Gothic Line.

ROMANIA: Fifteenth Air Force B-24s attack Karlova Airdrome and oil-industry targets around Bucharest, and 40 escort fighters conduct a sweep over Bucharest.

Pilots of the 31st, 52d, and 325th Fighter groups down 20 Axis fighters over and around Bucharest between 0958 and 1025 hours. 2dLt James W. Empey, a P-51 pilot with the 52d Fighter Group's 2d Fighter Squadron, achieves ace status when he downs a Bf-109.

June 29, 1944

FRANCE: Nearly 200 IX Bomber Command B-26s and A-20s attack gun emplacements, rail lines, and rail bridges; and Ninth Air Force fighters and fighter-bombers attack gun emplacements, rail and road traffic, bridges, and tactical targets.

Ninth Air Force fighter and fighter-bomber pilots down nine GAF fighters between 0705 and 1422 hours.

The IX TAC's 365th Fighter Group moves into Advance Landing Ground A-7, at Azeville.

GERMANY: Of 1,150 Eighth Air Force heavy bombers dispatched, more than 400 abort due to assembly problems in heavy clouds over England. However, 705 B-17s and B-24s attack ten aircraft-industry factories, a motor-vehicle factory, a synthetic oil plant, a ball-bearing factory, a marshalling yard, seven airdromes, and a military encampment, all in or around Leipzig. Six B-17s and nine B-24s are lost.

Escort for the Leipzig mission is provided by 674 VIII and IX Fighter command fighters, of which three are lost with their pilots. On the return flight, fighters from nine escort groups attack locomotives and rail cars, motor vehicles, barges, and German Army troops. The escort fighters also destroy 16 GAF aircraft on the ground.

USAAF escort fighter pilots down 35 GAF fighters over Germany between 0840 and 1012 hours. Three P-51 pilots with the 357th Fighter Group's 363d Fighter Squadron achieve ace status: Capt Donald H. Bockhay, when he downs a Bf-109 near Schoningen at 0905 hours; Capt James W. Browning, when he downs an Me-410 and shares in the downing of an FW-190 and another Me-410 near Leipzig between 0925 and 0955 hours; and Capt Robert W. Foy, when he downs an FW-190 and two Bf-109s near Leipzig at 0905 hours.

ITALY: Twelfth Air Force B-25s, B-26s, A-20s, and P-47s attack a large number of bridges, viaducts, rail lines, rail cars, locomotives, motor vehicles, landing grounds, ammunition dumps, and other targets in or near the Gothic Line.

NETHERLANDS: Four VIII Fighter Command P-38s attack Axis ships at sea off Ijmuiden.

June 30, 1944

BELGIUM: Twenty-four 1st Bombardment Division B-17s attack Le Culot Airdrome, and 11 1st Bombardment Division B-17s unable to locate their assigned target in France attack Coxyde/Furnes Airdrome.

ENGLAND: An Eighth Air Force Air-Sea Rescue Squadron P-47 pilot downs a V-1 rocket.

FRANCE: Thirty-nine 1st Bombardment Division B-17s attack Montdidier Airdromes, and 61 3d Bombardment Division B-24s attack Conches and Evreux/Fauville airdromes. GH radar is employed in all the attacks.

A total of 305 VIII Fighter Command fighters carry out bombing and strafing attacks against bridges, several marshalling yards, and transportation targets of opportunity. One P-38 and its pilot are lost.

Although 250 IX Bomber Command B-26s and A-20s are forced to abort in the face of bad weather, more than 125 others employ blind-bombing methods to attack several road junctions and fuel dumps through heavy cloud cover. More than 600 Ninth Air Force fighters escorting the bombers subsequently attack beach defenses, bridges near Paris and Evreux, marshalling yards at Chartres and another location, and several rail lines; and IX TAC fighter-bombers based in France attack numerous communications targets directly behind the Normandy battle lines.

VIII Fighter Command and Ninth Air Force fighter and fighter-bomber pilots down seven GAF fighters and one Ju-88 between 1045 and 2125 hours.

ITALY: Twelfth Air Force B-26s are grounded by bad weather, but B-25s attack a rail bridge, a viaduct, and a tunnel; and XII TAC fighter-bombers attack gun emplacements, bridges, rail targets, and motor vehicles along the battle line.

MTO: Fifteenth Air Force heavy bombers dispatched against targets at Blechhammer, Germany, are diverted by bad weather against a variety of targets of opportunity in Hungary and Yugoslavia.

JULY 1944

July 1, 1944

ENGLAND: The IX Air Defense Command is activated under the command of BriGen William L. Richardson to oversee air defense of areas behind friendly lines in France. (This new headquarters will displace to France by the end of the month.)

FRANCE: Of 323 2d and 3d Bombardment division heavy bombers dispatched against V-weapons sites, all but nine 486th Heavy Bombardment Group B-24s respond to a recall order based on bad-weather reports. The nine 486th Group B-24s attack the target with fewer than 20 tons of bombs. One B-24 is lost.

Of 531 VIII Fighter Command fighters dispatched, 206 complete missions escorting the heavy bombers or attacking rail and road targets. Three fighters and two pilots are lost against claims of eight GAF fighters downed between 1940 and 2040 hours, mostly in the St.-Quentin area.

Twenty IX Fighter Command fighter-bombers attack tactical ground targets around Vire.

The IX TAC's 100th Fighter Wing headquarters displaces from England to Criqueville, inside the Normandy beachhead, to oversee operations of several fighter groups engaged in close air-support operations for the U.S. First Army. Also, the IX TAC's 405th Fighter Group moves into Advance Landing Ground A-8, at Picauville.

ITALY: Twelfth Air Force B-25s, B-26s, and A-20s attack docks, fuel dumps, rail bridges, and viaducts in north-central Italy; P-47s attack road and rail bridges directly servicing the battle area and gun emplacements.

57th Fighter Group P-47 pilots down six Bf-109s near Reggio Emilia Airdrome.

July 2, 1944

ENGLAND: All IX Bomber Command bombers are grounded due to bad weather over France.

FRANCE: Two hundred eighty-two Eighth Air Force B-17s and B-24s use radar to attack V-weapons sites through heavy cloud cover. One B-24 is lost.

Seven Ninth Air Force tactical fighter

groups provide cover over the beachhead area and attack a German Army headquarters, fuel dumps, strongpoints, and rail lines alongside the Loire River.

IX TAC fighter pilots down two GAF fighters over France during the afternoon. One of them, LtCol Robert L. Coffey, Jr., the commanding officer of the Ninth Air Force's 365th Fighter Group, achieves ace status when he downs a Bf-109.

The IX TAC's 67th Tactical Reconnaissance Group moves into Advance Landing Ground A-9, at Le Molay, and the 362d Fighter Group moves into Advance Landing Ground A-12, at Lignerolles.

GERMANY: Fifteenth Air Force B-17s attack oil-industry targets at Blechhammer.

HUNGARY: Fifteenth Air Force B-24s attack marshalling yards, the airdrome, and oil-refining facilities at Budapest through intense antiaircraft fire and repeated fighter attacks; Fifteenth Air Force B-17s attack the oil facilities at Almasfuzito; and escort fighters mount sweeps over the Budapest area.

A total of 35 Bf-109s and FW-190s are downed by escort fighters of the 1st, 31st, 52d, 82d, 325th, and 332d Fighter groups—and eight additional Bf-109s are downed near Budapest by visiting P-51 pilots of the Eighth Air Force's 4th Fighter Group, which is transiting through Italy with Eighth Air Force heavy bombers returning to England from a FRANTIC shuttle mission to the Soviet Union. 1stLt Richard C. Lampe, a P-51 pilot with the 52d Fighter Group's 2d Fighter Squadron, achieves ace status when he downs 1.5 Bf-109s over Budapest at 1030 hours, during the target escort; 1stLt John J. Voll, a P-51 pilot with the 31st Fighter Group's 308th Fighter Squadron, achieves ace status when he downs a Bf-109 near Budapest at 1045 hours; Col Donald J. M. Blakeslee, the commanding officer of the visiting 4th Fighter Group, brings his final personal tally for the war to 14.5 victories when he downs a Bf-109 near Budapest at 1045 hours; and 1stLt Philip E. Tovrea, a P-38 pilot with

the 1st Fighter Group's 27th Fighter Squadron, achieves ace status when he downs an FW-190 near Pecs, Hungary, at noon, during withdrawal escort. Also, 2dLt Cecil O. Dean, a P-51 ace with the 325th Fighter Group, is taken prisoner following a mid-air collision near Budapest; and 2dLt Ralph K. Hofer, a 15-victory P-51 ace with the 4th Fighter Group's 334th Fighter Squadron, is shot down and killed in air-to-air combat near Mostar, Yugoslavia.

ITALY: Twelfth Air Force B-25s, B-26s, and A-20s attack several fuel dumps and German Army lines of communication north of the battle area; and XII TAC P-47s attack bridges and motor vehicles in the battle area.

YUGOSLAVIA: Fifteenth Air Force B-17s attack marshalling yards at Brod and Vinkovci.

July 3, 1944

FRANCE: Approximately 275 Ninth Air Force fighter-bombers attack tactical positions and lines of communication in the U.S. First Army battle area.

ITALY: Twelfth Air Force B-26s and A-20s attack German Army fuel dumps; Twelfth Air Force B-25s attack fuel storage facilities and various tunnels, bridges, and viaducts; and XII TAC P-47s support a new U.S. Fifth Army drive on Leghorn by attacking bridges, motor vehicles, a vehicle park, and an ammunition dump.

HUNGARY: Fifteenth Air Force heavy bombers attack a bridge at Szeged.

ROMANIA: Fifteenth Air Force B-17s and B-24s attack oil-industry targets at Giurgiu and Bucharest, repair shops at Arad, a rail bridge, and a marshalling yard.

31st and 325th Fighter group P-51 escort pilots down eight Axis fighters over Romania between 1140 and 1205 hours.

Fifty-five Eighth Air Force B-17s and 42 4th and 352d Fighter group P-51s transiting through Italy on return from their FRANTIC mission to Russia attack a marshalling yard at Arad and return to bases in Italy. One B-17 is lost.

YUGOSLAVIA: Eighty-four Fifteenth Air Force B-24s attack oil-industry targets at Belgrade.

July 4, 1944

FRANCE: Of 300 1st Bombardment Division B-17s dispatched against bridges and airfields in France, only 24 B-17s each attack primary targets at Dreux and Illiers L'Eveque airdromes, 13 attack Conches Airdrome (target of opportunity), and one attacks an unknown target of opportunity. All the other B-17s are thwarted by bad weather. One B-17 is lost.

One hundred ninety-two 2d and 3d Bombardment division B-24s, of 258 dispatched, attack Beaumont-le-Roger, Beaumont-sur-Oise, Conches, Creil, and Evreux airdromes. There are no losses.

Escort for the various heavy-bomber formations is provided by 569 VIII Fighter Command fighters, of which five are lost with their pilots. Also, 129 VIII Fighter Command P-47s attack several bridges and marshalling yards. Two fighter-bombers and their pilots are lost.

While on a bomber-escort mission against Conches Airdrome, P-47 pilots of the Eighth Air Force's 56th Fighter Group down 19 GAF fighters and thus raise their unit's total for confirmed victories to more than 500. Capt James R. Carter, a P-47 pilot with the 56th Fighter Group's 61st Fighter Squadron, achieves ace status when he downs a Bf-109 near Louviers at 1820 hours; and Capt Mark L. Moseley, a P-47 pilot with the 56th Fighter Group's 62d Fighter Squadron, achieves ace status when he downs a Bf-109 near Conches Airdrome at 1830 hours.

Although most IX Bomber Command bombers are grounded by bad weather over France, a total of 95 B-26s and A-20s using radar guidance are able to attack defended positions near Abbeville and a rail bridge at Oissel. Also, Ninth Air Force fighters and fighter-bombers mount more than 900 sorties to cover the beachhead and attack gun emplacements, troop concentra-

tions, marshalling yards, rail lines, highways, bridges, and a German Army command post.

IX TAC fighters down four GAF fighters over France during the afternoon.

ITALY: Twelfth Air Force bombers are grounded by bad weather, but a small numbers of fighters and fighter-bombers are able to mount attacks against gun emplacements, roads, bridges, and rail lines in the U.S. Fifth Army attack zone.

ROMANIA: Fifteenth Air Force B-24s attack a marshalling yard and rail bridge at Pitesti, and B-17s attack oil-industry targets at Brasov. Escort is provided by more than 350 fighters, which also conduct sweeps in the target areas. Ten Axis fighters and three Ju-52s are downed between 0950 and 1040 hours by 14th, 52d, and 82d Fighter group escort pilots.

July 5, 1944

BELGIUM: A total of 43 2d Bombardment Division B-24s attack Le Culot, Brussels/Melsbroek, and Tulemont airdromes.

FRANCE: A total of 101 2d Bombardment Division B-24s attack three V-weapons sites.

A total of 69 VIII Fighter Command P-47 fighter-bombers attack a number of bridges, towns, and communications targets in and around the Normandy battle area.

Nearly 180 IX Bomber Command B-26s and A-20s attack bridges and rail targets around Caen and four V-weapons headquarters sites. Many of the 600 Ninth Air Force fighters assigned to escort the light and medium bombers are released to conduct armed-reconnaissance sweeps against a wide variety of tactical and communications targets.

In all, VIII Fighter Command and IX TAC fighter pilots down 31 GAF aircraft over France between 0900 and 2025 hours. 1stLt Dale F. Spencer, a P-51 pilot with the 361st Fighter Group's 376th Fighter Squadron, achieves ace status when he downs two Bf-109s near Evreux between 0900 and 0910 hours; 1stLt Robert J. Keen, a P-47 pilot with the 56th Fighter Group's 61st Fighter Squadron, achieves ace status when he downs three Bf-109s over Evreux at 1555 hours; LtCol Francis S. Gabreski, operations officer of the 56th Fighter Group, brings his final personal tally to 28 confirmed victories when he downs a Bf-109 near Evreux at 1600 hours. (Gabreski will emerge from the war as the all-time high-scoring USAAF fighter pilot in the European Theater. He will also be credited with 6.5 victories in the Korean War.)

The IX TAC's 363d Fighter Group, in P-51s, moves into Cherbourg/Maupertus Airdrome (dubbed Advance Landing Ground A-15).

Fifteenth Air Force B-24s attack a marshalling yard at Beziers and the docks and submarine base at Toulon; Fifteenth Air Force B-17s attack a marshalling yard at Montpellier; and 70 B-17s of the Eighth Air Force's 3d Bombardment Division, escorted by a total of 228 VIII Fighter Command P-47s and P-51s, take part in the attack on the marshalling yard at Beziers on their way home from Russia via bases in Italy.

Six Bf-109s are downed over southern France between 1040 and 1115 hours by 52d and 325th Fighter group P-51 pilots.
ITALY: Twelfth Air Force B-25s attack a marshalling yard, a bridge, and several fuel dumps; XII TAC A-20s attack rail lines and a supply dump; and XII TAC fighter-bombers attack roads, bridges, rail lines, and tactical targets in support of the U.S. Fifth Army.

During the night of July 5–6, XII TAC A-20s attack an ammunition ship at La Spezia.
NETHERLANDS: A total of 77 1st Bombardment Division B-17s attack a factory and the Gilze-Rijen and Volkel airdromes; and 13 2d Bombardment Division B-24s attack Eindhoven Airdrome.

July 6, 1944

FRANCE: During the morning, 689 Eighth Air Force B-17s and B-24s attack 18 V-weapons sites in the Pas-de-Calais area; nearly 500 IX Bomber Command B-26s and A-20s attack bridges and rail lines throughout France; during the afternoon, 73 Eighth Air Force B-17s and 148 B-24s attack V-weapons sites in the Pas de Calais area and bridges south of Paris; and also during the afternoon, IX Bomber Command B-26s and A-20s attack V-weapons sites, bridges, fuel dumps, and rail lines.

A total of 1,027 VIII Fighter Command fighter sorties are flown throughout the day, escorting the various heavy-bomber attacks, and strafing and bombing various ground targets. In all, five fighters and four pilots are lost.

Throughout the day, Ninth Air Force fighters and fighter-bombers escort IX Bomber Command medium and light bombers, provide beachhead cover, conduct armed-reconnaissance sweeps, and attack troop concentrations, gun emplacements, numerous rail lines, bridges, tunnels, buildings, and a supply dump.

USAAF fighter pilots down 21 GAF aircraft over France between 0615 and 2020 hours. 1stLt George E. Bostwick, a P-47 pilot with the 56th Fighter Group's 62d Fighter Squadron, achieves ace status when he downs a Bf-109 near Beaumont at 0615 hours; and Maj Kenneth W. Gallup, the commanding officer of the 353d Fighter Group's 350th Fighter Squadron, in P-47s, achieves ace status when he downs a Bf-109 near Limay at 0630 hours.

The IX TAC's 404th Fighter Group moves into Advance Landing Ground A-5, at Chippelle.
GERMANY: Two hundred twenty-nine 2d Bombardment Division B-24s attack shipyards at Kiel. Three B-24s are lost.
ITALY: The Fifteenth Air Force mounts a total of 711 heavy-bomber sorties against marshalling yards at Verona, a viaduct, several oil- industry targets, oil- and fuel-storage areas, rail bridges, and the Bergamo steel works; Twelfth Air Force B-25s and B-26s attack lines of communication north of the battle area, warehouses, and German

Army headquarters; XII TAC A-20s attack fuel dumps; and XII TAC fighter-bombers attack rail lines and bridges just north of the battle area.

During the night of July 6–7, XII TAC A-20s attack the harbor at La Spezia and road targets in the La Spezia area.

July 7, 1944

CZECHOSLOVAKIA: Fifteenth Air Force B-24s attack an armaments factory at Dubnica.

FRANCE: More than 100 IX Bomber Command B-26s and A-20s attack rail bridges near Tours and targets of opportunity around Beauzeville and Lisieux. More than 500 Ninth Air Force fighters and fighter-bombers patrol the beachhead area and bomb and strafe a broad variety of tactical and communications targets in western France.

IX TAC fighter pilots down eight GAF fighters over France between 0930 and 2025 hours. Capt Felix M. Rogers, a P-51 pilot with the 354th Fighter Group's 353d Fighter Squadron, achieves ace status when he downs two FW-190s over Perdreauville at 2025 hours.

During the night of July 7–8, to help alleviate V-1 terror attacks on targets in England, 32 B-26s from the IX Bomber Command's 322d Medium Bombardment Group are dispatched to attack the V-weapons headquarters at Chateau de Ribeaucourt. Alerted by radar, GAF nightfighters, some using flares, down nine B-26s. Bomber gunners down a single-engine night-fighter and a Ju-88.

GERMANY: Nine hundred thirty-nine Eighth Air Force B-17s and B-24s, escorted by 656 VIII Fighter Command fighters, attack three synthetic-oil plants, eight aircraft-assembly plants, marshalling yards at two locations, an equipment depot, railway repair shops, a railroad station, and two airdromes in central Germany. Thirty-seven heavy bombers are lost and 390 are damaged. Also, 166 escort fighters strafe airfields and rail targets.

Six escort fighters and their pilots are lost. Capt James M. Morris, a P-38 ace with the 20th Fighter Group's 77th Fighter Squadron, brings his victory tally to 7.333 when he downs an Me-410 near Halle at 0935 hours, but Morris is then downed by another Me-410 and taken prisoner; and Col Glenn E. Duncan, the commanding officer of the 353d Fighter Group and a 19.5-victory P-47 ace, is downed by flak. Duncan (who is the third 353d group commander in a row to be shot down) evades capture and will continue to do so until April 22, 1945, when he returns to Allied hands.

VIII Fighter Command escort pilots down 77 GAF aircraft over Germany between 0830 and 1045 hours. LtCol Claiborne H. Kinnard, Jr., the 355th Fighter Group executive officer, in a P-51, achieves ace status when he downs two Me-410s and a Bf-109 near Lingen at about 0830 hours; Capt Frederick J. Christensen, Jr., a P-47 ace with the 56th Fighter Group's 62d Fighter Squadron, brings his final personal tally to 21.5 confirmed victories when he downs six Ju-52s near Gardlegen Airdrome at about 1045 hours; and 2dLt Billy G. Edens, a P-47 pilot with the 56th Fighter Group's 62d Fighter Squadron, achieves ace status when he downs three Ju-52s in the same engagement.

Fifteenth Air Force B-17s and B-24s attack two synthetic-fuel plants at Blechhammer, and B-24s also attack a synthetic-fuel plant and a coke plant at Odertal. Escort pilots from the 52d, 82d, and 325th Fighter groups down 13 Axis fighters along the bomber routes between 0950 and 1240 hours. Overall, 18 Fifteenth Air Force aircraft are lost on the day's various missions.

ITALY: Twelfth Air Force B-25s and B-26s attack rail bridges and a fuel dump; XII TAC A-20s attack several fuel dumps; and XII TAC fighter-bombers attack Ferrara Airdrome, a town, ammunition dumps, and various tactical and communications targets.

During the night of July 7–8, XII TAC A-20s attack several defended towns.

YUGOSLAVIA: Fifteenth Air Force B-24s attack the airdrome and marshalling yards at Zagreb.

July 8, 1944

AUSTRIA: Fifteenth Air Force heavy bombers attack targets in the Vienna area: the Markersdorf, Munchendorf, and Zwolfaxing airdromes; a marshalling yard; refineries at Korneuburg and Vosendorf; and the Floridsdorf oil storage facilities.

Escort pilots of the 52d, 82d, and 325th Fighter groups down 29 Axis fighters near Vienna, including many twin-engine bomber destroyers. Two 82d Fighter Group P-38 pilots achieve ace status on this mission: 1stLt Walter J. Carroll, Jr., of the 96th Fighter Squadron, when he downs three Me-410s near Vienna; and 1stLt Robert C. Griffith, of the 97th Fighter Squadron, when he downs one Bf-109 near Vienna. Maj Ralph J. Watson, the commanding officer of the 52d Fighter Group's 2d Fighter Squadron, in P-51s, also achieves ace status when he downs a Bf-109 at 1100 hours.

Altogether, 14 Fifteenth Air Force aircraft are lost.

FRANCE: Despite poor weather that results in more than 550 aborts, 462 Eighth Air Force B-17s and B-24s attack numerous tactical targets, including V-weapons sites, bridges, rail junctions, marshalling yards, and several airfields. Nine B-17s are lost.

Escort for the heavy bombers is provided by 588 VIII Fighter Command fighters, and 86 VIII Fighter Command P-47 fighter-bombers attack the St.-Andre-de-L'Eure Airdrome. VIII Fighter Command pilots claim the destruction of 15 locomotives during the day. One fighter and its pilot are lost.

Approximately 280 IX Bomber Command B-26s and A-20s attack the V-weapons headquarters at Chateau de Ribeaucourt as well as German Army strongpoints around Caen, fuel dumps, and road and rail bridges. Ninth Air Force escort fighters and IX TAC fighter-bombers conduct armed-reconnaissance missions over a broad area of France, but especially in the Normandy battle area, where numerous tactical targets are attacked.

Ninth Air Force fighter pilots down three GAF fighters over France during the morning.

HUNGARY: Fifteenth Air Force heavy bombers attack Veszprem Airdrome.

ITALY: Twelfth Air Force B-25s and B-26s attack a rail line near Parma, and several marshalling yards; XII TAC A-20s attack fuel dumps; and XII TAC fighter-bombers attack lines of communication north of the rather fluid U.S. Fifth Army battle area.

July 9, 1944

FRANCE: Despite bad weather over the target area that results in no attacks on assigned targets, 140 1st Bombardment Division B-17s attack several bridges and Chateaudun Airdrome during the morning.

Also during the morning, 60 of 250 IX Bomber Command B-26s and A-20s attack various lines-of-communication targets, but the remainder are thwarted by bad weather.

During the afternoon, 37 of the 104 3d Bombardment Division B-24s dispatched attack V-weapons launching sites, as assigned, and 15 of 77 3d Bombardment Division B-17s dispatched against V-weapon sites attack targets of oppor tunity, including St.-Omer/Longuenesse Airdrome.

Altogether during the day, 313 VIII Fighter Command fighters escort the heavy bombers, and, during the morning, 90 P-38s strafe ground targets.

VII Fighter Command pilots down six GAF aircraft over France between 0825 and 1400 hours. Capt William J. Maguire, a P-47 pilot with the 353d Fighter Group's 351st Fighter Squadron, achieves ace status when he downs a Bf-109 near Argentan at 1400 hours. Also, 2dLt Billy G. Edens, a 56th Fighter Group P-51 pilot who achieved ace status two days earlier, is downed by flak and captured near Trier, Germany.

Throughout the day, Ninth Air Force fighters and fighter-bombers cover the beachhead area and attack numerous on-call targets and targets of opportunity.

ITALY: Most scheduled Twelfth Air Force flight operations are canceled in the face of bad weather, but XII TAC fighter-bombers are able to attack several rail lines, German Army tanks and motor vehicles, and several gun emplacements.

ROMANIA: Fifteenth Air Force B-17s and B-24s, led for the first time by B-24s equipped with H2X radar, attack Ploesti's Xebia and Concordia-Vega refineries through an otherwise impenetrable smoke screen.

1stLt Donald R. Pucket, the pilot of a 98th Heavy Bombardment Group B-24 severely crippled by flak, administers first aid and words of encouragement to wounded crewmen while surveying the damage. Realizing that the bomber cannot possibly reach friendly territory, Pucket orders the crew to bail out, but he refuses to leave the descending bomber himself when he sees that three injured crewmen cannot do so. Pucket, who is killed with his three wounded comrades when the B-24 crashes into a mountainside, is awarded a posthumous Medal of Honor.

Pilots of the 1st, 52d, and 325th Fighter groups down 13 Axis fighters along the bomber route or over Ploesti between 1000 and 1115 hours. Two P-51 pilots of the 52d Fighter Group's 2d Fighter Squadron achieve ace status while escorting the bombers: Capt Fred F. Ohr and 1stLt James E. Hoffman, Jr., who each down a Bf-109 over Ploesti at 1020 hours.

Altogether, six Fifteenth Air Force aircraft are lost.

July 10, 1944

FRANCE: On a day otherwise marred by mission cancellations in the face of bad weather, Ninth Air Force fighters and fighter-bombers attack targets of opportunity and lines of communication in the battle area.

ITALY: Twelfth Air Force B-25s and B-26s attack bridges, viaducts, and marshalling yards in north-central Italy; and XII TAC fighter-bombers attack gun emplacements, rail lines, roads, and the Modena Airdrome.

July 11, 1944

FRANCE: IX Bomber Command B-26s and A-20s attack V-weapons sites, fuel dumps, and a rail bridge. Ninth Air Force fighters and fighter-bombers escort the bombers and attack rail targets, fuel dumps, gun emplacements, and various targets of opportunity around the battle area in France.

While attacking German Army pillboxes through driving rain in the vicinity of St.-Lo, in the Normandy beachhead area, P-47s of the Ninth Air Force's 366th Fighter Group discover a German Army tank column moving on an unsuspecting U.S. First Army ground unit. Despite the rain and intense flak, the group destroys the pillboxes against which it had been initially directed and severely damages many of the tanks from extremely low level, thus turning back the enemy attack on friendly forces. In fact, the group renews its attack on surviving tanks after landing at its base to rearm. Later, on their third mission of the day, 366th Fighter Group P-47s locate and defeat another German Army tank force. The group's activities during the day are considered "decisive" by U.S. Army ground forces in the area.

When bad weather prevents missions from going to other areas, 87 Fifteenth Air Force B-24s attack the port area at Toulon.

GERMANY: Guided by H2X radar, 1,047 Eighth Air Force B-17s and B-24s, escorted by 699 VIII Fighter Command fighters, attack marshalling yards, industrial targets, an airdrome, and several targets of opportunity in and around Munich. Sixteen B-24s, four B-17s, and four escort fighters are lost.

ITALY: Despite bad weather, a number of Twelfth Air Force medium bombers are able to mount attacks against several rail targets and bridges; and XII TAC fighter-bombers attack fuel dumps, gun emplacements, rail lines, Rimini Airdrome, and targets of opportunity in the battle area.

July 12, 1944

FRANCE: One hundred thirty-one 3d Bombardment B-24s and 131 RAF Spitfire escorts dispatched against ten V-weapons sites in the Pas-de-Calais area are thwarted by bad weather.

During morning and afternoon missions, more than 300 IX Bomber Command B-26 and A-20 sorties are flown against fuel dumps, troop concentrations, and road and rail targets. Also, Ninth Air Force fighters and fighter-bombers attack rail lines, bridges, motor vehicles, parked airplanes, and infantry and artillery emplacements in and around the battle area.

Ninth Air Force fighter pilots down six GAF fighters between 0955 and 1545 hours.

More than 420 Fifteenth Air Force B-24s attack marshalling yards at Miramas and Nimes, and bridges spanning the Var and Theoule rivers.

GERMANY: Unable to visually attack assigned targets in and around Munich, 1,124 Eighth Air Force B-17s and B-24s, escorted by 717 VIII Fighter Command fighters, employ radar to conduct an area attack on the city of Munich. Also, 27 heavy bombers attack other targets of opportunity. Twenty-four heavy bombers are lost, and 297 are damaged.

ITALY: Operation MALLORY MAJOR opens with attacks by Twelfth Air Force B-25s and B-26s against bridges spanning the Po River. Also, XII TAC A-20s attack ammunition dumps, and fighter-bombers attack small boats and barges on the Arno River as well as roads and rail lines, gun emplacements, ammunition dumps, and motor vehicles in and north of the battle area.

July 13, 1944

ENGLAND: All IX Bomber Command bombers are grounded by bad weather.
FRANCE: A limited number of Ninth Air

Force fighters and fighter-bombers attack road and rail traffic, warehouses, a barracks, and armored vehicles. IX TAC fighters also provide close air support for Allied ground troops and attack gun emplacements, vehicles, and troop concentrations.

GERMANY: Using H2X radar in the face of heavy cloud cover, 356 1st Bombardment Division B-17s and 139 3d Bombardment Division B-17s attack the city of Munich; 100 3d Bombardment Division B-17s attack aircraft-industry targets at Munich; 12 B-17s attack targets of opportunity; and 298 2d Bombardment Division B-24s attack a marshalling yard at Saarbrucken. Nine B-17s and one B-24 are lost.

Escort for the various heavy-bomber formations is provided by 543 VIII Fighter Command fighters, of which five airplanes and three pilots are lost. Escort pilots down two GAF fighters between 1045 and 1150 hours.

ITALY: Fifteenth Air Force B-24s attack the port at Fiume, oil storage facilities at Porto Marghera and Trieste, and marshalling yards at four locations; Fifteenth Air Force B-17s attack a marshalling yard and rail bridges at three locations; Twelfth Air Force medium bombers continue Operation MALLORY MAJOR with attacks on Po River bridges; XII TAC A-20s attack an ammunition plant; and XII TAC fighter-bombers concentrate on rail facilities servicing the battle area.

LUXEMBOURG: Two IX TAC P-47 pilots down four FW-190s over Luxembourg City at 1705 hours. One of them, Capt Edwin O. Fisher, of the 362d Fighter Group's 377th Fighter Squadron, achieves ace status.

July 14, 1944

FRANCE: Three hundred fifty-nine 3d Bombardment Division B-17s conducting a special operation (Operation CADILLAC) drop 3,700 arms containers from low altitude to French Resistance fighters around Limoges, St.-Lo, and Vercorse. Escort is provided by 499 P-51s.

Ninety-three 2d Bombardment Division B-24s attack Montdidier and Peronne airdromes.

Ninety-four VIII Fighter Command P-38 fighter-bombers attack rail targets around Paris. One P-38 and its pilot are lost.

Although bad weather severely curtails IX Bomber Command bomber operations, a total of 62 B-26s and A-20s attack two rail targets; Ninth Air Force fighters and fighter-bombers attack military transport and rail targets and troop concentrations across a wide area of France; and IX TAC ground controllers direct numerous close-air-support missions in the U.S. First Army zone of action.

VIII Fighter Command and IX TAC fighter pilots down 11 GAF fighters over France between 0930 and 2050 hours. Five Ninth Air Force fighters are lost in action with GAF fighters.

HUNGARY: More than 430 Fifteenth Air Force B-17s and B-24s attack four oil refineries at Budapest and Petfurdo. USAAF escort pilots down five Axis fighters.

ITALY: Fifteenth Air Force heavy bombers attack a marshalling yard at Mantua; Fifteenth Air Force P-38s dive-bomb Ghedi Airdrome and strafe trains north of La Spezia; Twelfth Air Force B-25s and B-26s continue to attack the Po River bridges (Operation MALLORY MAJOR); XII TAC A-20s attack supply dumps; and XII TAC fighter-bombers attack gun emplacements and lines of communication.

The XII Fighter Command headquarters is transferred from Algeria to Italy.

July 15, 1944

ENGLAND: Virtually all USAAF bomber operations are curtailed by bad weather.

FRANCE: Ninety-four VIII Fighter Command P-38s and 84 P-47s attack German military transport in the region southeast of Paris. Three fighter-bombers are lost with their pilots and one bombardier.

Because of bad weather, only four of 96 IX Bomber Command B-26s dispatched during the afternoon to attack a rail bridge

at L'Aigle are able to do so; the remainder of the B-26s abort.

A limited number of fighters and fighter-bombers under IX TAC control attack infantry, artillery, and rail targets during the day.

ITALY: Operation MALLORY MAJOR is deemed a success and is officially terminated, but Twelfth Air Force tactical bombers will continue to interdict bridge traffic attempting to cross the Po River. Twelfth Air Force fighter-bombers spend the day attacking gun emplacements, roads and road bridges, and targets of opportunity as well as providing on-call support for Allied ground forces.

ROMANIA: More than 600 Fifteenth Air Force B-17s and B-24s attack four oil refineries at Ploesti and the pumping station at Teleajenul. Fifteenth Air Force fighter pilots down four Axis fighters over Romania between 0950 and 1040 hours.

July 16, 1944

AUSTRIA: Nearly 300 Fifteenth Air Force B-17s and B-24s attack an aircraft-engine factory, oil storage facilities, an airdrome, and a marshalling yard in and around Vienna.

Between 1000 and 1040 hours, pilots of the 1st, 52d, 82d, 325th, and 332d Fighter groups down 23 Axis fighters, mostly over or near Vienna. 1stLt Dwaine R. Franklin, a P-51 pilot with the 52d Fighter Group's 2d Fighter Squadron, achieves ace status when he downs two Bf-110s (and probably downs another) near Vienna at about 1030 hours; and 1stLt William F. Hanes, Jr., of the 52d Fighter Group's 4th Fighter Squadron, achieves ace status when he downs a Ju-88 and shares in the downing of a Bf-110 near Vienna, also at 1030 hours.

BELGIUM: VIII Fighter Command fighters, on return from escort duty with heavy bombers bound for Germany, strafe Bruges Airdrome and rail targets of opportunity.

FRANCE: In separate morning and evening missions, a total of nearly 375 IX Bomber Command B-26 and A-20 sorties are mounted against ground targets in the St.-Lo area, bridges in the battle area, and bridges and a fuel dump at Rennes.

The IX TAC's 358th Fighter Group moves into Advance Landing Ground A-14, at Cretteville.

GERMANY: Despite heavy high-altitude cloud cover, 213 1st Bombardment Division B-17s attack an aircraft-engine factory in Munich and the Munich/Riem Airdrome; 52 1st Bombardment Division B-17s and 206 3d Bombardment Division B-17s attack the city of Stuttgart; 54 1st Bombardment Division B-17s attack the city of Augsburg; 52 B-17s attack several targets of opportunity; and 407 2d Bombardment Division B-24s attack a marshalling yard at Saarbrucken. Three B-17s and two B-24s are lost.

Escort for the heavy bombers is provided by 623 VIII Fighter Command fighters, of which three are lost with two pilots.

ITALY: Twelfth Air Force B-25s and B-26s attack several Po River bridges; and XII TAC fighter-bombers attack rail lines and road and rail bridges just north of the U.S. Fifth Army battlefront, which is nearing the Arno River.

MajGen Paul L. Williams, IX Troop Carrier Command commanding general, arrives in Italy to activate the Provisional Troop Carrier Division, which will oversee the airborne phase of the upcoming invasion of southern France.

July 17, 1944

FRANCE: Six hundred twenty Eighth Air Force B-17s and B-24s, escorted by 433 VIII Fighter Command fighters, attack numerous bridges spanning the Vire and Seine rivers, rail junctions, and other tactical targets, including many targets of opportunity. After completing their escort assignments, fighters from four groups strafe rail and road targets, claiming the destruction of 23 locomotives, 55 rail cars, and 18 motor vehicles. One B-17 and one P-47 are lost.

In a separate mission, 106 Eighth Air Force B-24s and 34 B-17s, escorted by 206

VIII Fighter Command fighters, attack 12 V-weapons sites in the Pas-de Calaisarea.

Despite bad weather, 69 IX Bomber Command B-26s are able to attack fuel dumps around Rennes, and 37 A-20s attack a marshalling yard and a fuel dump. Ninth Air Force fighters and fighter-bombers provide direct support for U.S. First Army units near Coutances and St.-Lo, and attack a marshalling yard at Nevers, Angers Airdrome, and a fuel dump.

For the first time in the war, IX TAC fighter-bombers attack ground targets with aerial rockets, which 12 P-47s (armed with four rockets apiece) employ with great success against a marshalling yard at Nevers. Also placed in use for the first time is napalm, which 14 370th Fighter Group P-38s employ against ground targets near Coutances.

VIII Fighter Command and IX TAC fighter pilots down 11 GAF fighters over France between 1000 and 2020 hours.

The IX TAC's 36th Fighter Group moves into Advance Landing Ground A-16, at Brucheville.

Fifteenth Air Force B-24s attack a marshalling yard at Avignon and rail bridges at Arles and Tarascon. 332d Fighter Group P-51 pilots down three Bf-109s near Toulon. **ITALY:** Twelfth Air Force B-25s and B-26s continue to attack the Po River bridges as well as bridges and viaducts servicing the battle area; and XII TAC fighter-bombers attack rail targets and bridges north of the battle area.

During the night of July 17–18, XII TAC A-20s attack several road junctions and the La Spezia area.

July 18, 1944

FRANCE: During the morning, 570 2d and 3d Bombardment Division B-24s attack several defended towns in the Caen area of Normandy in direct support of Allied ground forces. One B-24 is lost. Acting in conjunction with the heavy bombers, IX Bomber Command B-26s and A-20s also attack German-held towns in the Caen area.

During the afternoon, IX Bomber Command B-26s and A-20s attack rail and road bridges servicing the battle area.

Throughout the day, Ninth Air Force fighters and fighter-bombers strafe, bomb, and rocket gun emplacements and other military targets in the battle area and throughout northern and western France.

USAAF fighter pilots down 35 GAF fighters over France between 0915 and 1025 hours.

GERMANY: Using radar, a total of 216 3d Bombardment Division B-17s attack an oil refinery at Hemmingstedt, the city of Kiel, and the city of Cuxhaven (target of opportunity); 414 1st Bombardment Division B-17s visually attack the GAF experimental facilities and Peenemunde and Zinnowitz; and 20 B-17s that fail to locate their primary target attack a marshalling yard at Straslund. Three B-17s are lost.

A total of 419 VIII Fighter Command fighters provide escort for the B-17 formations over Germany. Three P-51s and two of their pilots are lost.

VIII Fighter Command escort pilots down ten Ju-88s and seven GAF fighters over Germany between 0900 and 0920, in the Rostock, Warnemunde, and Wismar areas.

More than 500 Fifteenth Air Force B-17s and B-24s attack a jet-aircraft factory at Manzell and the airdrome at Memmingen. In this attack, the 5th Heavy Bombardment Wing's 483d Heavy Bombardment Group loses 14 B-17s during massed attacks against its formation by an estimated 200 GAF fighters.

Between 0950 and 1105 hours, pilots of the 1st, 31st, 52d, and 332d Fighter groups down 39 Bf-109s and FW-190s between Udine, Italy, and southern Germany. 1stLt James L. Brooks, a P-51 pilot with the 31st Fighter Group's 307th Fighter Squadron, achieves ace status when he downs an Mc.205 at 1030 hours.

ITALY: Fifteenth Air Force B-17s and B-24s attack a rail bridge; Twelfth Air Force medium bombers are grounded by bad weather; and a limited number of XII TAC fighter-bombers are able to attack communications targets, gun emplacements, rail lines, and several bridges in or near the battle area.

July 19, 1944

BELGIUM: IX TAC fighter-bombers attack transportation targets in western Belgium, the farthest-ranging tactical strikes since D day.

FRANCE: During the afternoon, a total of 262 IX Bomber Command B-26s and A-20s attack bridges spanning the Loire and Seine rivers, and a fuel dump. Although hampered by bad weather, Ninth Air Force fighters and fighter bombers attack tactical targets, rail lines, and troop concentrations and positions.

Capt Joseph L. Egan, Jr., a five-victory P-47 ace with the 56th Fighter Group's 63d Fighter Squadron, is shot down and killed by flak near Nancy.

The IX TAC's 373d Fighter Group moves into Advance Landing Ground A-13, at Tour en Bessin.

GERMANY: 1,082 Eighth Air Force heavy bombers attack a broad array of industrial targets, a river dam, marshalling yards at six locations, and four airdromes throughout western and southwestern Germany, and even into Austria. Fourteen B-17s and three B-24s are lost, and three B-17s are interned in Switzerland.

Escort for the various heavy bomber formations is provided by a total of 670 VIII Fighter Command fighters, of which seven are lost with their pilots. Many fighters strafe ground targets following their release from escort duty. This is the first mission undertaken by the 55th Fighter Group since its transition from P-38s to P-51s.

VIII Fighter Command pilots down 15 GAF fighters over Germany between 0945 and 1020 hours. Capt William J. Hovde, a P-51 pilot with the 355th Fighter Group's 358th Fighter Squadron, achieves ace status when he downs a Bf-109 near Augsberg at 0945 hours.

Following by 90 minutes the Eighth Air Force heavy-bomber attacks in the same area, more than 400 Fifteenth Air Force B-17s and B-24s attack an aircraft factory, a motor factory, and an ordnance depot in and around Munich. Heavy flak opposition and weak fighter opposition account for 16 Fifteenth Air Force aircraft downed.

14th Fighter Group P-38 escort pilots down seven Bf-109s. 2dLt Michael Brezas, a P-38 pilot with the 14th Fighter Group's 48th Fighter Squadron, achieves ace status when he downs a Bf-109 near Munich.

ITALY: Twelfth Air Force bomber operations are severely restricted by bad weather, but B-26s are able to mount a late-afternoon attack against bridges at two locations, and B-25s attack a third bridge. Fighter-bomber operations are also severely limited by bad weather to several attacks on rail targets.

July 20, 1944

ALGERIA: The XII Air Force Training and Replacement Command is disbanded.
FRANCE: IX Bomber Command bombing missions are delayed by rain during the morning, but 62 B-26s and A-20s are able to mount an afternoon attack against a marshalling yard and a fuel dump. Ninth Air Force fighters and fighter-bombers attack gun emplacements, bridges, and rail lines.
GERMANY: On the day of the unsuccessful assassination attempt against Adolf Hitler, 1,077 Eighth Air Force B-17s and B-24s attack a broad array of oil-industry targets, ball-bearing plants, five airdromes, an arms factory, and an optical-instruments plant in western and central Germany. Nineteen heavy bombers are lost.

Escort for the heavy bombers is provided by 476 VIII Fighter Command fighters, of which eight are lost with seven pilots. One of the pilots who fails to return is LtCol Francis S. Gabreski, the USAAF's high-scoring fighter ace in the ETO, who is shot down by flak over Bassinheim Airdrome and taken prisoner.

VIII Fighter Command pilots down ten GAF fighters and a Do-217 over Germany between 1100 and 1140 hours. Capt Norman J. Fortier, a P-51 pilot with the 355th Fighter Group's 354th Fighter Squadron, achieves ace status when he downs a Bf-109 near Oschatz at 1115 hours.

This is the first mission undertaken by the 20th Fighter Group since its transition from P-38s to P-51s.

Fifteenth Air Force B-24s attack several aircraft factories around Friedrichshafen, and B-17s attack the airdrome at Memmingen .

Between 1045 and 1240 hours, pilots of the 1st, 14th, 31st, 82d, and 332d Fighter groups down 15 GAF fighters—over Memmingen during the bombing attack there and over northern Italy during both the penetration and withdrawal phases. 1stLt Robert J. Goebel, of the 31st Fighter Group's 308th Fighter Squadron, achieves ace status when he downs a Bf-109 over Villaorba, Italy, at 1210; and Maj Harry W. Dorris, Jr., commanding officer of the 31st Fighter Group's 308th Fighter Squadron, achieves ace status when he downs an Mc.202 near Villaorba at 1240 hours.
ITALY: Twelfth Air Force B-25s and B-26s continue to attack the Po River bridges, and XII TAC fighter-bombers concentrate on rail targets north of the battle area.

July 21, 1944

CZECHOSLOVAKIA: Fifteenth Air Force B-17s and B-24s attack a synthetic-fuel plant at Brux.

Escort pilots down four GAF fighters. 1stLt Ernest Shipman, a P-51 pilot with the 31st Fighter Group's 307th Fighter Squadron, achieves ace status when he downs a Bf-109 at 1230 hours.
ENGLAND: Virtually the entire Ninth Air Force is grounded by bad weather.
GERMANY: Nine hundred eighty Eighth Air Force B-17s and B-24s attack numerous aircraft-industry targets, ball-bearing plants, and airfields in southwestern Germany. Heavy opposition claims 31 heavy bombers.

Escort for the heavy bombers is provided by 706 VIII Fighter Command fighters, of which eight are lost with five pilots. Many fighters strafe ground targets, especially rail targets, after being released from escort assignments.

VIII Fighter Command escort pilots down seven GAF fighters over Germany between 1030 and 1120 hours.

Following the mission, the 3d Bombardment Division's 486th and 487th Heavy Bombardment groups are temporarily withdrawn from combat in order to transition from B-24s to B-17s, a program that will eventually involve all 3d Bombardment Division B-24 units.

ITALY: Fifteenth Air Force B-24s attack marshalling yards at Mestre; Twelfth Air Force medium bombers are grounded by bad weather; XII TAC A-20s attack a supply dump; and XII TAC fighter-bombers attack road and rail bridges in the Po River valley and near the battle area.

July 22, 1944

ENGLAND: Virtually the entire Eighth Air Force and most of the Ninth Air Force are grounded by bad weather.

FRANCE: Despite bad weather, two IX Bomber Command B-26 groups and one A-20 group attack a rail bridge and several fuel dumps. Escort for supply and evacuation aircraft and medium and light bombers is provided by the IX Fighter Command.

During the late evening, four IX Fighter Command fighter-bomber groups conduct rail-interdiction missions.

The IX TAC's 367th Fighter Group moves into Advance Landing Ground A-6, at Beauzeville.

GERMANY: In the only mission completed by Eighth Air Force aircraft, seven B-17s, escorted by 27 4th Fighter Group P-51s, drop leaflets over northwestern Germany. Two of the P-51s are lost in operational accidents, and one of the pilots is killed.

ITALY: Most Twelfth Air Force flight operations are canceled in the face of bad weather, but XII TAC A-20s are able to conduct several armed-reconnaissance missions and attacks on a munitions factory and motor vehicles; Twelfth Air Force B-25s are able to mount attacks on three bridges; and XII TAC fighter-bombers are able to strafe parked aircraft at Bergamo Airdrome and attack several gun emplacements, road and rail bridges, motor vehicles, and trains north of the battle area.

During the night of July 22–23, XII TAC A-20s strafe motor vehicles in the Po River valley.

ROMANIA: Four hundred fifty-eight Fifteenth Air Force B-17s and B-24s attack an oil refinery at Ploesti or alternate rail targets at Orsova, Verciorova, and Kragujevac (Yugoslavia).

On the Fifteenth Air Force's second (and first all-fighter) FRANTIC mission to the Soviet Union, 76 82d Fighter Group P-38s and 58 31st Fighter Group P-51s damage or destroy an estimated 41 Axis aircraft on the ground and a confirmed 20 Axis aircraft in the air while strafing the Buzau and Zilistea airdromes between 1015 and 1100 hours. Maj Victor E. Warford, the commanding officer of the 31st Fighter Group's 309th Fighter Squadron, achieves ace status when he downs a Bf-109 and an FW-190 near Buzau Airdrome at about 1030 hours. Also destroyed during the all-fighter mission are six locomotives and several trucks encountered along the way.

July 23, 1944

ALBANIA: Forty-two Fifteenth Air Force B-24s, escorted by 15 P-51s, attack oil-industry targets at Berat.

FRANCE: Employing GH radar guidance, 78 1st Bombardment Division B-17s attack Creil Airdrome; and a total of 166 2d Bombardment Division B-24s attack the Juvincourt, Laon/Athies, and Laon/Couvron airdromes. Escort for the heavy bombers is provided by 177 VIII Fighter Command fighters.

More than 330 IX Bomber Command B-26s and A-20s from all eleven IX Bomber

Command groups attack nine rail bridges and a fuel dump. Most of these attacks are carried out under cloudy conditions with the aid of pathfinders. IX TAC fighters and fighter-bombers attack strongpoints, bridges, and a supply dump in and around the battle area.

ITALY: Twelfth Air Force B-25s and B-26s attack bridges and bridge approaches in the Po River valley, and small flights of XII TAC fighter-bombers attack lines of communication in the battle area and throughout the Po River valley.

July 24, 1944

FRANCE: Operation COBRA, the scheduled air offensive leading up to an all-out push by the U.S. First Army to break out of the Normandy beachhead is delayed by poor flying conditions over the target area. Nevertheless, a total of 487 Eighth Air Force heavy bombers, escorted by 478 VIII Fighter Command fighters, attack alternate tactical targets in the Normandy area. Three VIII Fighter Command fighter groups strafe tactical targets in the battle zone. Three heavy bombers and five fighters are lost. Misdropped bombs kill 20 U.S. soldiers on the ground and wound approximately 60.

IX Bomber Command B-26s and A-20s originally scheduled to take part in the Operation COBRA missions are diverted against several ammunition and fuel dumps, and Ninth Air Force fighter-bombers attack bridges and supply dumps in the U.S. First Army battle area. The 344th Medium Bombardment Group, in B-26s, destroys part of a vital Loire River bridge near Tours.

USAAF fighter pilots down ten GAF fighters over France between 1300 and 1750 hours.

The IX TAC's 370th Fighter Group moves into Advance Landing Ground A-3, at Cardonville.

In southern France, Fifteenth Air Force B-24s attack Les Chanoines and Valence/La Tresorerie airdromes.

GERMANY: One hundred forty-three VIII Fighter Command P-51s conduct a sweep over Lechfeld and Leipheim airdromes. Three single-engine biplane trainers are downed by 359th Fighter Group P-51 pilots over Neu-Ulm at 1220 hours.

ITALY: Fifteenth Air Force B-24s attack the harbor at Genoa; Fifteenth Air Force B-17s attack a tank factory and ball-bearing plant at Turin; Twelfth Air Force B-25s and B-26s attack several bridges; XII TAC A-20s attack an ammunition dump; and XII TAC fighter-bombers attack rail lines in the Po River valley.

YUGOSLAVIA: Fifteenth Air Force heavy bombers attack troop concentrations at four locations, and escort fighters attack targets of opportunity.

July 25, 1944

AUSTRIA: Four hundred twenty Fifteenth Air Force B-17s and B-24s attack an armored-vehicle factory at Linz, the marshalling yard at Villach, and targets of opportunity elsewhere in Austria. A total of 21 bombers and escort fighters are downed when as many as 200 Axis fighters attack the bomber force.

Escort pilots of the 1st, 52d, and 325th Fighter groups down 13 Axis fighters over Austria between 1055 and 1220. Capt John B. Lawler, a P-51 pilot with the 52d Fighter Group's 2d Fighter Squadron, brings his final personal tally to 11 confirmed victories when he downs two Bf-109s at about 1115 hours.

BELGIUM: A scheduled late-afternoon attack by 106 3d Bombardment Division B-17s and 136 VIII Fighter Command fighters against the Brussels/Melsbroek Airdrome is recalled after encountering severe weather on the way to the target.

FRANCE: Operation COBRA begins when, between 0938 and 0957 hours, eight Ninth Air Force fighter groups, attacking at three-minute intervals in group and squadron columns, bomb and strafe an area 250 yards wide by 7,000 yards long just to the south of the St.-Lo–Periers road. When all Ninth Air Force fighters complete their attacks, 1,503 Eighth Air Force B-17s and B-24s, flying at right angles to the front lines, drop 3,300 tons of bombs in an area 1 mile wide by 5 miles long. Then, between 1100 and 1118 hours—immediately following the departure of the heavy bombers—seven Ninth Air Force fighter groups sweep the eastern and western extremities of the target area. Meanwhile, the U.S. First Army ground offensive jumps off right on schedule, at 1100 hours. Between 1132 and 1223 hours—as the last of the second wave of fighter-bombers depart—580 IX Bomber Command B-26s and A-20s from eleven groups saturate the target area with 260-pound fragmentation and 500-pound high-explosive bombs. In all, more than 4,000 tons of bombs are dropped from low level in an area occupied by just one German Army division. In addition, Eighth Air Force heavy bombers support Operation COBRA by attacking German troop concentrations around Montreuil. The German troops are rendered immobile and the ground assault is a success. Five heavy and one medium bombers—and *no* fighter-bombers—are lost. However, bombs dropped early by 42 B-26s from one group kill 102 and wound 380 U.S. soldiers.

Escort for the Eighth Air Force heavy bombers and IX Bomber Command medium and light bombers is provided by 483 VIII Fighter Command fighters, of which two are lost with their pilots.

Seventy-seven VIII Fighter Command P-47 fighter-bombers led by one droopsnoot P-38 attack a fuel dump at Fournival/Bois de Mont.

Between 1135 and 2104 hours, Ninth Air Force fighters and fighter-bombers, operating at group strength, aggressively patrol the COBRA battle area—as far as Amiens, Ghent, and Laval—attacking all manner of on-call targets and targets of opportunity. Also during the afternoon, four IX Bomber Command bomber groups attack bridges spanning the Loire and Seine rivers.

USAAF fighter pilots down 17 GAF fighters over France between 1115 and 2000

hours. Capt John F. Pugh, a P-51 pilot with the 357th Fighter Group's 362d Fighter Squadron, achieves ace status when he downs a Bf-109 near Versailles at noon.

ITALY: Twelfth Air Force B-25s and B-26s attack numerous bridges in northwestern Italy; XII TAC A-20s attack rail lines and a storage dump; and XII TAC fighter-bombers attack lines of communication through the Po River valley.

During the night of July 25–26, XII A-20s attack roads and motor vehicles.

POLAND: Thirty-three 82d Fighter Group P-38 fighter-bombers and 34 31st Fighter Group P-51 escort fighters taking part in the latest FRANTIC mission (beginning July 22) attack Mielec Airdrome, 120 miles west of Lwow, where they destroy 12 Axis fighters on the ground and down three in the air. While returning to bases in the Soviet Union, the P-51s destroy a German Army truck convoy and down 27 of 44 Ju-87 dive-bombers encountered along the way.

July 26, 1944

ALBANIA: Fifteenth Air Force heavy bombers attack an oil storage facility at Berat.

AUSTRIA: Fifteenth Air Force B-24s attack three Vienna-area airdromes, and Fifteenth Air Force B-17s attack an aircraft factory at Wiener-Neustadt.

Escort pilots from the 14th, 52d, 325th, and 332d Fighter groups down 20 Axis fighters and two Ju-52s over Austria and Hungary between 1055 and 1330 hours. Capt Richard W. Dunkin, a P-51 pilot with the 325th Fighter Group's 317th Fighter Squadron, achieves ace status when he downs a Bf-109 and an FW-190 near Wiener-Neustadt at about 1100 hours, during penetration escort; and 1stLt Arthur C. Fiedler, Jr., also a 317th Fighter Squadron P-51 pilot, scores his fourth victory of the war, an FW-190, over Vienna at 1115 hours and then, on the withdrawal, downs a Bf-109 near Lake Balaton, Hungary, at 1135 hours.

FRANCE: Many of the IX Bomber Command B-26s and A-20s on their way to support the U.S. First Army breakout abort in the face of bad weather, but 160 light and medium bombers manage to attack a fuel dump. Also, fighters and fighter-bombers respond to numerous close-air-support requests and fly aggressive armed-reconnaissance patrols around the battle area.

Forty VIII Fighter Command P-47 fighter-bombers attack a fuel dump, and 93 VIII Fighter Command P-47 fighter-bombers attack a marshalling yard after failing in the face of bad weather to locate their primary target, a fuel dump. One P-47 is lost.

In addition to one planned fighter-bomber mission, IX TAC fighters and fighter-bombers mount sixteen eight-plane "armed reconnaissance" missions in which the pilots are permitted to attack *any* authorized-type target anywhere within the mission area. On a day-to-day basis, armed-reconnaissance missions will shortly become the norm for most Ninth Air Force tactical fighter units.

Putting another new ground-support innovation to use for the first time in the war, a total of 70 four-plane flights of IX TAC fighter-bombers are attached to various U.S. Army armored units to provide "column cover." The aircraft are controlled by pilots on the ground with the tanks who have been specially trained to direct rocket, bombing, and strafing attacks on ground targets within their sight. Indeed, thanks to an innovation promulgated by the IX TAC's MajGen Elwood R. Quesada, air-force–type radios have been installed in selected armored vehicles for use by forward air controllers *and* ground-force commanders, who are also authorized to speak with and direct pilots of covering aircraft. Such covering operations are extremely profitable at the outset, resulting in higher German Army losses and swift advances by ground forces that might otherwise have been delayed or rebuffed. (Although such operations are far from being an American innovation, the evolution of the technique by American

forces from July 26, 1944, onward to the end of the war brings about a revolution in combined-arms maneuver warfare.)

IX TAC fighter pilots down 17 GAF fighters over France between 1430 and 1840 hours.

XII TAC fighter-bombers attack gun emplacements and destroy an estimated 20 parked aircraft at Valence Airdrome.

HUNGARY: Fifteenth Air Force heavy bombers attack Szombathely Airdrome.

ITALY: Twelfth Air Force B-25s and B-26 attack numerous road and rail bridges in northern Italy; XII TAC A-20s attack a fuel dump

P-47 pilots of the 79th Fighter Group's 86th Fighter Squadron down five Bf-109s near Brescia during an afternoon mission.

ROMANIA: Fifteenth Air Force P-38s and P-51 fighters returning to Italy from the Soviet Union strafe several targets around Bucharest and Ploesti, as do Fifteenth Air Force escort fighters released from duty with the heavy-bomber formations. In all, the Fifteenth Air Force fighter pilots down 18 Axis aircraft. Maj Claud E. Ford, the commanding officer of the 82d Fighter Group's 97th Fighter Squadron, achieves ace status in a P-38 when he downs a Bf-109 near Galati; Maj Warner F. Gardner, the commanding officer of the 82d Fighter Group's 95th Fighter Squadron, achieves ace status when he downs an He-111 over Manesti Airdrome; and Maj Samuel J. Brown, of the 31st Fighter Group's 307th Fighter Squadron, brings his final personal tally to 15.5 in under four months when he downs a Bf-109 at 1245 hours.

YUGOSLAVIA: Fifteenth Air Force fighters released from escort duty conduct aggressive sweeps between Brod and Zagreb.

July 27, 1944

BELGIUM: Thirty-four 3d Bombardment Division B-24s attack a signals depot in Brussels, and 12 B-24s attack several targets of opportunity, but 79 bombers dispatched on this mission return to base after being thwarted by low-lying haze.

FRANCE: Twenty 3d Bombardment Division B-24s attack the coastal batteries at Gravelines.

One hundred ninety-three VIII Fighter Command fighter-bombers attack rail targets and traffic south of Amiens and Rouen. Four fighters and their pilots are lost.

All IX Bomber Command B-26s and A-20s dispatched to attack bridges spanning the Loire and Seine rivers are recalled because of bad weather. However, Ninth Air Force fighters and fighter-bombers attack military installations, gun emplacements, and other tactical targets in and around the expanding battle area.

IX TAC fighter pilots down eight GAF fighters over France between 1220 and 2130 hours.

During the night of July 27–28, IX TAC fighter-bombers seed selected road junctions in the German Army area of operations with delayed-action bombs.

HUNGARY: Three hundred sixty-six Fifteenth Air Force B-17s and B-24s attack armaments factories in and around Budapest, and 24 B-24s attack a marshalling yard at Pecs. Fourteen Axis fighters are downed between 0933 and 1013 hours by pilots of the 52d, 325th, and 332d Fighter groups.

ITALY: During the night of July 27–28, XII TAC A-20s attack motor vehicles and lights encountered while on area patrol over northern Italy.

July 28, 1944

BELGIUM: Bad weather prevents attacks by 111 3d Bombardment Division B-24s against fuel dumps and a signals depot. All bombers are recalled.

ENGLAND: BriGen Ned Schramm assumes command of the IX Air Defense Command.

FRANCE: Bad weather prevents attacks by 180 2d Bombardment Division B-24s against rail bridges, fuel dumps, and V-weapons sites. All bombers are recalled.

IX Bomber Command B-26s, A-20s, and fighter-bombers respond to on-call requests from ground controllers with the U.S. First Army and also range afield against numerous rail bridges and dumps.

During the afternoon, 405th Fighter Group P-47 pilots on an armed reconnaissance locate a vast German Army road column bogged down by an immense traffic jam. Following continuous attack extending over six hours, the group claims the destruction of at least 400 motor vehicles, 12 tanks, and numerous other vehicles.

IX TAC fighter pilots down seven GAF fighters over France between 1615 and 2030 hours.

A small number of Twelfth Air Force fighter-bombers venture up the Rhone River valley to attack German Army road traffic.

During the night of July 28–29, IX TAC fighter-bombers seed selected road junctions in the German Army area of operations with delayed-action bombs.

GERMANY: Six hundred fifty-two Eighth Air Force B-17s attack the Leuna synthetic-oil plant at Merseburg; 36 B-17s attack the Taucha oil plant in Leipzig, and 26 B-17s attack targets of opportunity. Losses are seven B-17s. Among the airmen lost is Col Archibald Y. Smith, the 452d Heavy Bombardment Group commander, who is killed.

Bomber crewmen report the first sighting of the new Me-163 rocket-propelled fighter.

Escort is provided by 386 VIII Fighter Command fighters, of which two are lost during post-escort strafing attacks on rail and road traffic.

This is the first mission undertaken by the 364th Fighter Group since beginning its transition from P-38s to P-51s.

VIII Fighter Command escort pilots down three GAF fighters and a Ju-52 over Germany between 0930 and 1030 hours.

ITALY: Twelfth Air Force B-25s, B-26s, and fighter-bombers attack bridges throughout northwestern Italy, especially in the Po River valley.

ROMANIA: Three hundred forty-nine Fifteenth Air Force B-17s and B-24s attack two oil refineries at Ploesti and a marshalling yard at Florina with a total of 913 tons of bombs. Pilots of the 1st, 31st, and 325th Fighter groups down 11 Axis fighters over or near Ploesti between 1025 and 1035 hours, but 20 heavy bombers are lost to flak and fighter attacks.

July 29, 1944

ENGLAND: IX Bomber Command bombers are grounded by bad weather.

FRANCE: Thirty-eight 3d Bombardment Division B-24s attack the Juvincourt-et-Damary Airdrome, and 36 3d Bombardment Division B-24s attack the Laon/Couvron Airdrome. Escort is provided by 142 VIII Fighter Command P-51s.

Ninth Air Force fighters and fighter-bombers provide ground support and area coverage for the U.S. First Army.

GERMANY: Five hundred sixty-nine Eighth Air Force B-17s attack the Leuna synthetic-oil plant at Merseburg; 442 2d Bombardment Division B-24s attack an oil refinery at Bremen; and 34 B-17s and three B-24s attack various targets of opportunity. Fifteen B-17s and two B-24s are lost.

Escort is provided by a total of 535 VIII Fighter Command fighters. Two fighter groups strafe ground targets following completion of their escort duties. Seven fighters are lost with their pilots. 1stLt Christopher J. Hanseman, a P-51 ace with the 339th Fighter Group, is killed when his airplane hits the ground during a strafing attack at Naumberg.

VIII Fighter Command escort pilots down 23 GAF fighters—including the first reported downing of an Me-163 rocket-propelled fighter—over Germany between 1000 and 1145 hours. Capt Leonard K. Carson, a P-51 pilot with the 357th Fighter Group's 362d Fighter Squadron, achieves ace status when he downs a Bf-109 near Merseberg at 1010 hours. Also, in the 20th Fighter Group's first combat since transitioning to P-51s, 1stLt Rex E. Moncrief and 1stLt Louis W. Adams, Jr., attack a force of 50 GAF fighters at about 1050 hours, after becoming separated from

their squadron near Gutersloh. The pair downs three enemy fighters and is continuing its attack on the superior enemy force when forced to break off because of the arrival of 50 additional GAF fighters.

ITALY: All Twelfth and Fifteenth air force bombers are grounded by bad weather, but a small number of XII TAC fighter-bomber sorties are flown against rail lines, bridges, a defended town, several airdromes, and motor vehicles.

During the night of July 29–30, XII TAC A-20s attack Savona and the surrounding area.

July 30, 1944

ENGLAND: The VIII Air Force Composite Command formally takes administrative control of all Eighth Air Force independent, special, and provisional units.

FRANCE: More than 450 IX Bomber Command B-26s and A-20s attack defensive positions around Chaumont; and Ninth Air Force fighter-bombers attack numerous tactical and lines-of-communication targets, including German Army armored columns, while conducting aggressive armed-reconnaissance missions.

Two hundred thirty-seven VIII Fighter Command fighters conduct sweeps. One P-51 and its pilot are lost.

USAAF fighter pilots down 18 GAF fighters over France between 1430 and 1940 hours. Maj Richard E. Turner, the commanding officer of the 354th Fighter Group's 356th Fighter Squadron, in P-51s, brings his final personal tally to 11 confirmed victories when he downs a Bf-109 near Chaumont at 1620 hours.

HUNGARY: Fifteenth Air Force B-24s attack oil-industry targets at Lispe, and Fifteenth Air Force B-17s attack the Budapest/Duna Airdrome. Escort down four Axis fighters.

ITALY: Despite overcast that results in many aborts, Twelfth Air Force B-25s and B-26s continue their relentless attacks on bridges and other communications targets in the Po River valley. Also, XII TAC fighter-bombers attack shipping between Savona and Ventimiglia, and rail and road bridges throughout northern Italy. The P-47s account for eight German Army flak guns guarding a bridge at Ferrara.

YUGOSLAVIA: Fifteenth Air Force B-17s attack marshalling yards at Brod.

July 31, 1943

FRANCE: Thirty-six 3d Bombardment Division B-24s attack Creil Airdrome, and 47 3d Bombardment Division B-24s attack Laon/Athies Airdrome.

Approximately 500 IX Bomber Command B-26 and A-20 sorties are mounted against bridges spanning the Loire, Mayenne, Ruisseau la Forge, and Seine rivers, and a fuel dump.

Ninth Air Force fighters and fighter-bombers conduct armed-reconnaissance missions and dive-bomb tactical targets in the battle area.

IX TAC fighter pilots down three GAF fighters over France between 1230 and 1250 hours. Col Morton D. Magoffin, the commanding officer of the Ninth Air Force's 362d Fighter Group, in P-47s, achieves ace status when he downs an FW-190 near Beaumont-Hamel at 1250 hours.

The IX TAC's 406th Fighter Group moves into Advance Landing Ground A-13, at Tour en Bessin.

GERMANY: Five hundred sixty-seven Eighth Air Force B-17s attack industrial targets at Munich; 36 B-17s attack industrial targets at Allach; 43 B-17s attack industrial targets at Schleissheim; and 447 2d Bombardment Division B-24s attack a chemical plant at Ludwigshafen. Ten B-17s are lost over Munich and six B-24s are lost over Ludwigshafen.

Escort for the various heavy-bomber formations over Germany is provided by 574 VIII Fighter Command fighters, of which three are lost with their pilots.

ITALY: Twelfth Air Force bombers are grounded by bad weather, but XII TAC fighter-bombers attack bridges in the Po River valley, strafe airfields, and destroy an estimated 50 rail cars.

ROMANIA: More than 360 B-24s of the Fifteenth Air Force's 49th and 304th Heavy Bombardment wings attack Bucharest's Prahova oil refinery. Escort is provided by 96 P-51s of the 31st and 325th Fighter groups, whose pilots down 31 Axis fighters along the bomber route between 1103 and 1145 hours. On the way to Bucharest, Capt George C. Loving, a P-51 division leader with the 31st Fighter Group's 309th Fighter Squadron, achieves ace status when he downs two Bf-109s during an air battle over Rosiori-de-Vede, Romania, between 1100 and 1130 hours. Also achieving ace status on this mission, between 1100 and 1130 hours, are three P-51 pilots of the 325th Fighter Group's 318th Fighter Squadron: Capt Benjamin H. Emmert, Jr., who brings his final personal tally to seven confirmed victories when he downs three Bf-109s near Bucharest; 1stLt Harry A. Parker, who brings his final tally to eight confirmed victories when he downs four Bf-109s over Alexandria, Romania; and 2dLt Philip Sangermano, who downs three Bf-109s.

Fifteenth Air Force B-24s attack an oil storage facility at Targoviste, and Fifteenth Air Force B-17s attack oil refineries at Ploesti and Doicesti.

AUGUST 1944

August 1, 1944

ENGLAND: MajGen William E. Kepner succeeds MajGen James P. Hodges as commanding general of the Eighth Air Force's 2d Bombardment Division, and BriGen Murray C. Woodbury temporarily succeeds MajGen William E. Kepner as commanding general of the VIII Fighter Command.
FRANCE: Three hundred eighty-five 1st Bombardment Division B-17s attack a rail bridge and five airfields near Paris, and 15 1st Bombardment Division B-17s attack various targets of opportunity. Three B-17s are lost.

Two hundred fifty-seven 2d Bombardment Division B-24s attack an oil depot at Rouen, four bridges, and four airfields, and 33 B-24s attack various targets of opportunity. One B-24 is lost.

One hundred ninety-three 3d Bombardment Division B-17s undertake Operation BUICK—dropping 281 supply containers to French Resistance fighters at four locations in southeast France. Also, 76 3d Bombardment Division B-17s attack Tours Aerodrome. One B-17 is lost. This is the first combat mission undertaken by the 486th and 487th Heavy Bombardment groups since both units transitioned from B-24s to B-17s.

Sixty-one 3d Bombardment Division B-24s attack V-weapons sites at Pas-de-Calais, but nearly 50 others abort in the face of bad weather.

Escort for the various heavy-bomber missions is provided by a total of 397 VIII Fighter Command fighters, of which four and their pilots are lost in action and seven (and two pilots) are lost in operational accidents.

Approximately 250 IX Bomber Command B-26s and A-20s attack eight rail bridges spanning the Loire River, and Ninth Air Force fighter-bombers attack bridges and provide support for ground forces.

USAAF fighter pilots down four Bf-109s during the afternoon. 1stLt William "Y" Anderson, a P-51 pilot with the 354th Fighter Group's 353d Fighter Squadron, achieves ace status when he downs a Bf-109 near Tours at 1710 hours.

The Ninth Air Force's newly operational XIX Tactical Air Command (XIX TAC, commanded by MajGen Otto P. Weyland) begins providing direct support for the newly operational U.S. Third Army. For the moment, only three fighter groups are assigned to the XIX TAC.

ITALY: The Fifteenth Air Force is virtually grounded by bad weather; Twelfth Air Force B-25s and B-26s attack a marshalling yard and several bridges; and XII TAC fighter-bombers attack airfields, landing grounds, communications targets, and rail targets, especially in the Po River valley.

August 2, 1944

FRANCE: During the morning, 146 2d Bombardment Division B-24s and 149 3d Bombardment Division B-17s attack towns, a canal lock, a rail junction, a marshalling yard, a bridge, several airdromes, and targets of opportunity. Two B-17s are lost.

Escort for the Eighth Air Force morning missions is provided by 132 VIII Fighter Command P-51s, of which two are lost with their pilots.

In the late afternoon, 162 Eighth Air Force B-17s attack a road bridge, three rail bridges, and fifteen V-weapons sites; 182 Eighth Air Force B-24s attack V-weapons sites in the Pas-de-Calais area; and a total of 53 B-24s attack a road bridge, a rail bridge, Achiet Airdrome, and several targets of opportunity. Three B-17s are lost.

Escort for the Eighth Air Force afternoon mission is provided by 236 VIII Fighter Command fighters, of which five are lost with their pilots.

VIII Fighter Command P-38, P-47, and P-51 fighter-bombers attack road and rail targets in western France and around Brussels. Two fighters are lost with their pilots.

Nearly 300 IX Bomber Command B-26s and A-20s attack bridges spanning the Loire River, and ammunition dumps. However, at the request of the U.S. Third Army, the Ninth Air Force suspends attacks on bridges and fuel dumps in Brittany, except as specifically requested by ground

headquarters. (The Third Army wants to use the bridges and captured fuel supplies in its campaign to liberate the region.)

IX and XIX TAC fighters and fighter-bombers escort IX Bomber Command missions, fly armed-reconnaissance missions, and provide on-call support for the ground forces.

GAF opposition to the day's missions is virtually nil; just one GAF fighter is downed.

Fifteenth Air Force B-17s attack oil-industry targets, a torpedo factory, a marshalling yard, rail bridges, and oil storage facilities.

Twelfth Air Force medium-bomber groups based in Corsica conduct their first missions in support of the upcoming Operation ANVIL, the Allied invasion of southern France. The Twelfth Air Force mediums were to have begun sooner, but they have been tied up supporting Allied ground forces engaged in heavy fighting in Italy. So far, all three B-25s groups of the 57th Medium Bombardment Wing have been moved to Corsica to support the invasion, but the three B-26 groups of the 42d Medium Bombardment Wing remain in Sardinia. Having done so well in Italy earlier in the year, both medium-bomber wings are assigned to interdict the German Army lines of supply and communication in southern France, chiefly from Lyon to the sea and especially along the Rhone and Var rivers. Several Twelfth Air Force fighter-bomber missions are also directed against targets on both sides of the Franco-Italian frontier.

ITALY: Fifteenth Air Force B-24s attack the harbor at Genoa and marshalling yards, and XII TAC fighter-bombers attack ground targets in northern Italy.

August 3, 1944

BELGIUM: During the afternoon, 72 3d Bombardment Division B-24s and eight 2d Bombardment Division B-24s attack two oil refineries and a storage depot at Brussels and Ghent.

ENGLAND: BriGen Francis H. Griswold succeeds BriGen Murray C. Woodbury as commanding general of the VIII Fighter Command.

FRANCE: During the morning, 54 1st Bombardment Division B-17s attack a marshalling yard at Mulhouse; 68 1st Bombardment Division B-17s attack a marshalling yard at Strasbourg; 106 1st Bombardment Division B-17s attack an oil refinery at Merkwille; 16 1st Bombardment Division B-17s opt to attack Toul/Croix de Metz Airdrome; a total of 74 3d Bombardment Division B-17s attack bridges at two locations; and a total of 53 2d Bombardment Division B-24s (of 172 dispatched) divert from their cloud-obscured primaries (several bridges) to attack two airfields, a marshalling yard, and several other targets of opportunity. Six 1st Bombardment Division B-17s are lost.

Escort for the Eighth Air Force morning heavy-bomber missions to France and Germany is provided by 358 VIII Fighter Command fighters, of which six are lost with their pilots. Approximately half the P-51s involved in the escort later strafe ground targets, and 133 VIII Fighter Command P-38 and P-47 fighter-bombers attack rail traffic in the Metz, Strasbourg, and Saarbrucken areas. One P-47 is lost.

During the afternoon, 112 1st Bombardment Division B-17s and 139 2d Bombardment Division B-24s attack 20 V-weapons sites in the Pas-de-Calais area, and 97 2d Bombardment Division B-17s attack four oil storage sites. Two B-24s are lost in the Pas-de-Calais area.

Escort for the Eighth Air Force heavy-bomber afternoon missions to France and Belgium is provided by 166 VIII Fighter Command fighters.

More than 180 IX Bomber Command B-26s and A-20s attack road and rail targets and a fuel dump in northern France.

Eighth and Ninth air force fighter pilots down four GAF fighters over France between 1535 and 1900 hours.

GERMANY: During the morning, 62 1st Bombardment Division B-17s attack a marshalling yard at Saarbrucken, and 17 attack various targets of opportunity near Saarbrucken and along the Franco-German frontier.

VIII Fighter Command pilots down five GAF fighters over Germany between 1515 and 1520 hours. Capt Leslie D. Minchew, a P-51 pilot with the 355th Fighter Group's 354th Fighter Squadron, achieves ace status when he downs a Bf-109 near Baden Baden at 1515 hours.

Fifteenth Air Force B-17s and B-24s attack steel, chemical, and fabrics plants in the Friedrichshafen area, and B-17s also attack a marshalling yard at Immenstadt.

While escorting the Friedrichshafen mission, 325th Fighter Group P-51 pilots down 11 GAF fighters near Innsbruck, Austria, between 1040 and 1205 hours, during both the penetration and withdrawal phases. One of the 325th Group pilots, 2dLt Robert H. Brown, a member of the 318th Fighter Squadron, achieves ace status when he downs a Bf-109.

ITALY: Fifteenth Air Force B-24s attack bridges near Brenner Pass; Twelfth Air Force B-25s and B-26s attack bridges on both sides of the Franco-Italian frontier; and Twelfth Air Force fighter-bombers attack airfield and communications targets in northern Italy.

August 4, 1944

BELGIUM: During the morning, 22 3d Bombardment Division B-17s attack coastal defenses at Ostend.

ENGLAND: The Eighth Air Force's 7th Photographic Reconnaissance Group is placed under the operational control of the 325th Photographic Reconnaissance Wing (which has not yet arrived from the United States).

FRANCE: Ninety-five 1st Bombardment Division B-17s and 59 2d Bombardment Division B-24s, escorted by 35 VIII Fighter Command P-47s, are dispatched against V-weapons sites in the Pas-de-Calais area and two coastal batteries. All the primary targets are struck, but bad weather and faulty radar cause nearly 50 heavy-bomber aborts and the diversion of more than half the remaining bombers against targets of opportunity.

Sixty-seven VIII Fighter Command P-47 fighter-bombers attack Plantlunne Airdrome. One P-47 and its pilot are lost.

The first experimental attack undertaken under the auspices of Operation APHRODITE, four unmanned, television-controlled B-17 flying bombs are dispatched along with guidance and observation aircraft against four large V-weapons sites. No hits and only one near miss are scored. In fact, one drone bomb crashes in England.

Sixty-two IX Bomber Command B-26s and A-20s attack three rail bridges, a bivouac area, and an ammunition dump; and Ninth Air Force fighters and fighter-bombers attack fuel and ammunition dumps and provide support for Allied ground forces.

IX TAC fighter pilots down two Bf-109s over Nogent at 1830 hours.

Limited by bad weather, Twelfth Air Force medium-bomber and fighter-bomber missions along the Var River and the harbor at Nice achieve minimal results.

During the night of August 4–5, IX Bomber Command bombers attack the harbor at St.-Malo and a fuel dump.

GERMANY: Two hundred twenty-one 1st Bombardment Division B-17s attack the GAF experimental station at Peenemunde; 70 1st Bombardment Division B-17s attack an aircraft factory at Anklam; 110 1st Bombardment Division B-17s attack Anklam Airdrome; a total of 307 2d Bombardment Division B-24s attack aircraft-industry targets at Rostock, Schwerin, and Wismar; 34 2d Bombardment Division B-24s attack various targets of opportunity; 181 3d Bombardment Division B-17s attack an oil refinery at Hamburg; 50 3d Bombardment Division B-17s attack an oil refinery at Bremen; 23 3d Bombardment Division B-17s attack Nordhof Airdrome; seven 3d Bombardment Division B-17s attack several targets of opportunity; 89 2d Bom-

bardment Division B-24s attack the naval base at Kiel; 29 3d Bombardment Division B-24s attack an oil refinery at Hemmingstedt; and 39 3d Bombardment Division B-24s attack Husum Airdrome. Of a total of 1,186 effective heavy-bomber sorties, 11 B-17s and four B-24s are lost.

Escort for the Eighth Air Force heavy-bomber missions to Germany is provided by total of 666 VIII Fighter Command fighters, of which 14 are lost with their pilots.

VIII Fighter Command escort pilots down 37 GAF fighters over Germany and one over Denmark between 1300 and 1600 hours. Maj Donald A. Larson, the commanding officer of the 339th Fighter Group's 505th Fighter Squadron, achieves ace status when he downs two Bf-109s near Ulzen between 1315 and 1330 hours. However, Larson is killed a short time later in a midair collision with another P-51 while strafing ground targets. 1stLt James R. Starnes, a P-51 pilot with the 339th Fighter Group's 505th Fighter Squadron, achieves ace status when he downs a Bf-109 near Hamburg at 1330 hours; and 1stLt David F. Thwaites, a P-47 pilot with the 356th Fighter Group's 361st Fighter Squadron, achieves ace status when he downs a Bf-109 near Hamburg at 1345 hours.

ITALY: Most Twelfth Air Force missions are canceled in the face of bad weather, but several medium-bomber and fighter-bomber attacks are mounted against bridges, rail lines, gun emplacements, and airfields.

1stLt Marlow J. Leikness, a P-38 pilot with the 14th Fighter Group's 49th Fighter Squadron, achieves ace status when he downs a Bf-109 near Pizzo at 1715 hours.

During the night of August 4–5, XII TAC A-20s attack vehicles and light sources in the Po River valley.

ROMANIA: Responding to the first direct request of its kind from Soviet authorities, the Fifteenth Air Force mounts a new FRANTIC mission composed of 82d Fighter Group P-38 fighter-bombers escorted by 52d Fighter Group P-51s. After bombing and strafing the airdrome and town area at

Foscani, the more-than 70 USAAF fighters and fighter-bombers proceed to bases in the Soviet Union.

Capt James S. Varnell, a P-51 ace with the 52d Fighter Group's 2d Fighter Squadron, brings his final personal tally to 17 confirmed victories when he downs a Ju-52 over Romania at 1130 hours.

August 5, 1944

FRANCE: IX Bomber Command B-26s and A-20s attack a marshalling yard at Compiegne and six rail bridges spanning the Seine and Loire rivers.

During the afternoon, 38 1st Bombardment Division B-17s attack six V-weapons sites in the Pas-de-Calais area.

IX TAC fighter pilots down five GAF fighters over France during the day.

Headquarters, Ninth Air Force, moves from Uxbridge, England, to St.-Sauveur-Lendelin, France.

GERMANY: Due to bad weather, only 543 of 1,171 Eighth Air Force B-17s and B-24s dispatched are able to attack airfields, aircraft plants, and other strategic targets, primarily in and around Brunswick, Hannover, and Magdeburg. GAF fighter opposition is heavy, and 13 heavy bombers are lost.

Escort is provided by 573 VIII Fighter Command fighters, of which six are lost with their pilots.

VIII Fighter Command escort pilots down 27 GAF fighters over Germany between 1120 and 1430 hours. 1stLt Glennon T. Moran, a P-51 ace with the 352d Fighter Group's 487th Fighter Squadron, brings his final personal tally to 13 confirmed victories when he downs a Bf-109 near Hamburg at 1205 hours; and 1stLt Frederick W. Glover, a P-51 pilot with the 4th Fighter Group's 336th Fighter Squadron, achieves ace status when he downs a Bf-109 over Gardlegen at 1245 hours.

ITALY: Most of the Twelfth and Fifteenth air forces are grounded by bad weather.

August 6, 1944

ENGLAND: The 3d Bombardment Div-ision's 490th Heavy Bombardment Group is withdrawn from combat to transition from B-24s to B-17s.

FRANCE: Twenty-four 3d Bombardment Division B-24s, escorted by 24 P-47s, attack V-weapons sites in the Pas-de-Calais area.

An Eighth Air Force Operation APHRODITE test mission consisting of two drone B-17 flying bombs fails when both drones crash into the sea.

IX Bomber Command B-26s and A-20s attack fuel and ammunition dumps, a locomotive depot, and several bridges.

A historical first is scored when the XIX TAC assumes *primary* responsibility for guarding the extended and extending U.S. Third Army flank so that the available ground forces can concentrate their power on pursuing the fleeing German Army. Fortunately, the flank to be covered is shielded by the Loire River. Flank protection is in the form of aggressive armed-reconnaissance and tactical-reconnaissance missions.

IX TAC fighter pilots down two Bf-109s near Dreux at 1500 hours.

The IX TAC's 474th Fighter Group moves into Advance Landing Ground A-11, at St.-Lambert. The 474th is the last Ninth Air Force fighter unit to depart England for a new base on the Continent.

Fifteenth Air Force B-24s attack the submarine base at Toulon, as well as various rail bridges and oil storage depots in southern France. And Fifteenth Air Force B-17s attack a marshalling yard, oil-industry targets, and a rail bridge. Effective heavy-bomber sorties for the day total 1,069. Also, Fifteenth Air Force P-38s dive-bomb the Orange/Plan de Dieu and Valence airdromes.

Twelfth Air Force B-25s, B-26s, and fighter-bombers attack bridges in and around the Rhone and Var river valleys.

GERMANY: Eighth hundred thirty Eighth Air Force B-17s and B-24s mount highly successful visual bombing attacks against aircraft assembly plants and a munitions plant at Brandenburg, engine and diesel-engine plants at Berlin, six oil refineries at Hamburg, and several airdromes and other secondary targets in those regions. Twenty-four heavy bombers are lost.

Escort is provided by 535 VIII Fighter Command fighters, of which four are lost with their pilots.

VIII Fighter Command escort pilots down 30 GAF fighters and a Do-217 over Germany between 1100 and 1500 hours. Maj George E. Preddy, of the 352d Fighter Group, is credited with downing *six* Bf-109s in a running battle between Luneberg and Havelburg between 1110 and 1145 hours. This feat brings Preddy's personal tally to 22.833 enemy aircraft destroyed. Capt Bert W. Marshall, Jr., a P-51 pilot with the 355th Fighter Group's 354th Fighter Squadron, achieves ace status when he downs a Bf-109 near Hamburg at 1530 hours; and Capt Charles W. Lenfest, a P-51 pilot with the 355th Fighter Group's 354th Fighter Squadron, achieves ace status when he downs a Bf-109 near Hamburg, at 1530 hours.

ITALY: Twelfth Air Force fighter-bombers attack road and rail targets, airfields, several towns, and shipping in three German-held ports.

During the night of August 6–7, XII TAC A-20s attack shipping at three ports in northern Italy.

POLAND: Seventy-five Eighth Air Force B-17s of the 3d Bombardment Division's 95th and 390th Heavy Bombardment groups attack the Rahmel aircraft factory, near Gdynia, and proceed to USAAF bases in the Soviet Union. Escorting the bombers to Gdynia but returning to their own bases in the U.K. are 154 55th and 339th Fighter group P-51s, which are credited with the longest round-trip fighter mission so far of the war in Europe—1,592 miles. Four P-51s are lost with their pilots.

357th Fighter Group P-51 pilots, who join the FRANTIC bomber formation near Jutland, down a Ju-88 and a Bf-109 near Warsaw at 1345 hours.

ROMANIA: Sixty P-38 fighter-bombers of the Fifteenth Air Force's 82d Fighter Group attack rail targets in the Bucharest and Ploesti areas during their return to Italy from the August 4 FRANTIC mission to the Soviet Union.

August 7, 1944

FRANCE: In the first theater combat encounters of the new P-61 twin-engine, two-place night-fighter, two crews from the Ninth Air Force's newly committed 422d Night-Fighter Squadron score probable victories against a Ju-188 and a Do-217 between 0300 and 0310.

Four hundred eighty-three Eighth Air Force B-17s and B-24s, of 905 dispatched, attack numerous fuel dumps, bridges, airfields, and other tactical targets in northern France. One B-17 is lost.

Following its return from the mission to France, the 492d Heavy Bombardment Group is withdrawn from combat duties.

Escort and support for the heavy bombers are provided by 437 VIII Fighter Command fighters.

Two hundred seventy-one VIII Fighter Command P-47 and P-51 fighters and fighter-bombers attack marshalling yards and rail lines north and east of Paris. Eight fighters are lost with their pilots.

More than 380 IX Bomber Command B-26s and A-20s attack bridges spanning the Loire and Seine rivers.

Eighth and Ninth air force fighter pilots down 19 GAF fighters over France during the afternoon and early evening. 2dLt Loyd "J" Overfield, a P-51 pilot with the 354th Fighter Group's 353d Fighter Squadron, achieves ace status when he downs three Bf-109s over Mayenne at 1520 hours.

The IX and XIX TACs form mobile headquarters units to accompany the headquarters of the U.S. First and Third armies.

LtGen Lewis H. Brereton relinquishes command of the Ninth Air Force to assume command of the new First Allied Airborne Army.

As of August 7, the IX TAC consists of

the 70th Fighter Wing (48th, 367th, and 474th Fighter groups); the 71st Fighter Wing (366th 368th, and 370th Fighter groups); and the 84th Fighter Wing (50th, 365th, and 404th Fighter groups). The XIX TAC consists of the 100th Fighter Wing (354th, 362d, 363d, and 371st Fighter groups), and the 303d Fighter Wing (36th, 358th, 373d, 405th, and 406th Fighter groups). All of the wing and fighter-group assignments are considered temporary and will shift as required by operational needs. (In this regard, the TACs are *designed* to function simply as permanent headquarters controlling a constantly shifting roster of subordinate units. They are thus identical to army corps, with which they are on par in the overall American military command structure.)

Twelfth Air Force B-26s and A-20s attack bridges throughout southern France.

At 2330 hours, a P-61 crew from the Eighth Air Force's 422d Night-Fighter Squadron scores that unit's first confirmed victory, a Ju-88 downed over the Bay of Mont Michel. This is also the first P-61 victory in the ETO.

GERMANY: Three hundred sixty-five Fifteenth Air Force B-17s and B-24s attack two synthetic-oil refineries at Blechhammer.

Escort pilots from the 14th, 31st, and 325th Fighter groups down 21 GAF fighters and a twin-engine bomber between 1005 and 1230 hours along the bomber route through Hungary, Czechoslovakia, Poland, and Germany. 1stLt Robert D. Thompson, a P-51 pilot with the 31st Fighter Group's 309th Fighter Squadron, achieves ace status when he downs two Bf-109s near Lake Balaton, Hungary, between 1005 and 1035 hours; and 1stLt Wayne L. Lowry, a P-51 ace with the 325th Fighter Group's 317th Fighter Squadron, brings his final personal tally to 11 confirmed victories when he downs a Bf-109 near Ratibor, Poland, at 1150 hours.

ITALY: XII TAC fighter-bombers attack shipping at Imperia as well as several airfields.

POLAND: As part of Operation FRANTIC, 55 Eighth Air Force B-17s of the 95th and 390th Heavy Bombardment groups, operating from bases in the Soviet Union and escorted by 29 357th Fighter Group P-51s, attack oil refineries around Trzebinia with 134 tons of bombs and then return to the Soviet bases.

357th Fighter Group P-51 pilots down three GAF fighters over Poland between 1230 and 1330 hours. Maj John A. Storch, the commanding officer of the 357th Fighter Group's 364th Fighter Squadron, achieves ace status when he shares in the downing of a Bf-109 over Oswiecim at 1330 hours.

YUGOSLAVIA: A total of 76 Fifteenth Air Force B-24s attack oil-industry targets at Novi Sad and the airdrome at Alibunar.

August 8, 1944

ENGLAND: LtGen Hoyt S. Vandenburg, former USSTAF deputy commanding general, formally replaces LtGen Lewis H. Brereton as commanding general of the Ninth Air Force.

The VIII Fighter Command's 356th Fighter Group is reassigned to the 67th Fighter Wing, and the 361st Fighter Group is reassigned to the 65th Fighter Wing.

FRANCE: Three hundred fifty-nine Eighth Air Force B-24s, escorted by 265 VIII Fighter Command fighters, attack ten V-weapons sites in the Pas-de-Calais area; Bretigny, Clastres, La Perthe, Laon/Athies, and Romilly-sur-Seine airdromes; and several targets of opportunity, including two rail bridges. Also, two groups of escort fighters strafe numerous ground targets. One B-24 and two P-51s are lost.

In a separate action, 497 Eighth Air Force B-17s provide direct support for a ground operation undertaken by Canadian Army troops around Falaise. Targets are German Army troop concentrations and strongpoints. Counting RAF Bomber Command night attacks, this is the second-largest operation of its kind since the invasion, totaling more than 5,200 tons of bombs. Seven B-17s are lost, and bombs that are dropped short kill 25 Canadian Army soldiers and wound 131.

Escort for the B-17 ground-support mission is provided by 91 P-51s, of which three are lost with their pilots. At least one P-51 escort group strafes ground targets around Rouen.

One hundred seventy-five VIII Fighter Command P-38, P-47, and P-51 fighter-bombers attack rail lines around Amiens, Dijon, Paris, and St.-Quentin. Four fighters are lost with their pilots.

A total of 406 IX Bomber Command B-26s and A-20s attack tactical targets near St.-Malo, as well as radar installations, bridges, and rail embankments.

Eighth and Ninth air force fighter pilots down 12 GAF fighters over France during the afternoon and early evening.

Twelfth Air Force medium bombers attack bridges, rail lines, and other targets in the Rhone and Var river valleys, and at Avignon and Pont-Saint-Esprit.

During the night of August 8–9, XII TAC A-20s attack targets of opportunity along the road from Genoa, Italy, to Nice.

ITALY: The Fifteenth Air Force is grounded by bad weather; Twelfth Air Force medium bombers attack bridges and rail lines in the Po River valley; XII TAC A-20s attack a storage dump and the town area at Savigliano; and XII TAC fighter-bombers attack pontoon and rail bridges, various other bridges, a barge, and the causeway at Mantua.

NORWAY: Forty-one 4th Fighter Group P-51s escort an RAF Coastal Command anti-shipping strike to Norway. Three fighters are lost with their pilots.

ROMANIA: Seventy-three Eighth Air Force B-17s and 55 4th and 357th Fighter group P-51s on their way back to England from bases in the Soviet Union attack the Bizau and Zilistea airdromes, then land at Fifteenth Air Force bases in Italy. During the flight, Capt Frank C. Jones, a five-victory P-51 ace with the 4th Fighter Group's 335th Fighter Squadron, is shot down and killed by flak.

A 357th Fighter Group P-51 pilot downs a Bf-109 over Crocil at 1105 hours.

August 9, 1944

ENGLAND: The 325th Photographic Reconnaissance Wing headquarters is formally activated to oversee several Eighth Air Force reconnaissance groups; the 8th Provisional Photographic Reconnaissance Wing is deactivated; the Eighth Air Force's 802d Provisional Reconnaissance Group (B-17s and Mosquitoes) is redesignated the 25th Bombardment Reconnaissance Group and placed under the control of the 325th Photographic Reconnaissance Wing; and the former 802d Group's Provisional Light Weather Reconnaissance Squadron and Provisional Special Weather Reconnaissance Squadron are redesignated the 653d Light Bombardment Squadron and the 654th Special Bombardment Squadron.

FRANCE: A 422d Night-Fighter Squadron P-61 crew downs a Ju-88 near Caen at 0235 hours.

One hundred forty-nine VIII Fighter Command P-47 fighter-bombers, escorted by 40 P-51s, attack various lines-of-communication targets.

More than 400 IX Bomber Command B-26s and A-20s attack shipping at Brest, an ammunition dump, bridges, locomotives, and various other targets.

While attacking a heavily defended Seine River rail bridge, the leading 394th Medium Bombardment Group B-26, piloted by Capt Darrell R. Lindsey, is hit by flak, and the right engine bursts into flame. Capt Lindsey completes the bomb run and then orders the crew to bail out while he remains at the controls. When the bombardier offers to lower the nose wheel to aid in Lindsey's departure, Lindsey refuses because he feels the lowered wheel might induce a spin that will prevent the bombardier's escape. Lindsey, who then rides the flaming B-26 into the ground and is killed, is awarded a posthumous Medal of Honor.

Maj Don M. Beerbower, a 15.5-victory

ace and the newly promoted commanding officer of the 354th Fighter Group's 353d Fighter Squadron, is killed by flak while strafing Reims/Epernay Airdrome at tree-top height. Unbelievably, Beerbower's replacement as squadron commander, Maj Wallace N. Emmer, a 14-victory ace, is shot down by flak during an afternoon patrol mission near Rouen. Emmer is captured, but he will die in a German POW camp on February 15, 1945, from myocarditis.

IX TAC fighter pilots down a total of 14 GAF fighters over France in three separate actions, at 0935, 1330, and 1800 hours, respectively.

GERMANY: Of 824 Eighth Air Force B-17s and B-24s dispatched to attack tank factories, aircraft plants, fuel depots, and airfields in southeastern Germany, only 25 2d Bombardment Division B-24s are able to penetrate bad weather to attack their primary target. In all, 495 other heavy bombers attack several secondary targets and numerous targets of opportunity in Germany, the Netherlands, and Luxembourg. Eighteen heavy bombers are lost.

Escort for the heavy bombers is provided by 570 VIII Fighter Command fighters, of which three are lost with their pilots.

VIII Fighter Command escort pilots down 29 GAF fighters and a trainer over Germany between 1045 and 1135 hours. LtCol John B. Murphy, the commanding officer of the 359th Fighter Group's 370th Fighter Squadron, in P-51s, achieves ace status when he downs an FW-190 near Gunzberg at about 1120 hours.

HUNGARY: Fifteenth Air Force B-17s and B-24s attack two airdromes, an oil refinery at Budapest, and two factories at Gyor.

ITALY: Twelfth Air Force medium bombers are hampered by bad weather, but some B-25s are able to attack a rail line, and some B-26s are able to attack Bergamo/Orio al Serio Airdrome. Also XII TAC fighter-bombers attack rail targets throughout northwestern Italy and sink a vessel in the harbor at Imperia.

YUGOSLAVIA: Fifteenth Air Force B-17s attack an oil refinery and marshalling yard at Brod.

August 10, 1944

FRANCE: One hundred sixty-two 2d and 3d Bombardment division B-24s, escorted by 238 VIII Fighter Command P-51s, attack bridges and fuel dumps southeast of Paris. Escort fighters strafe rail and other transportation targets. One B-24 and three P-51s are lost.

Throughout the day, VIII Fighter Command fighters mount 298 effective sorties against numerous rail targets in eastern and central France. Eleven airplanes are lost with their pilots. Among the lost airmen is LtCol Kyle L. Riddle, the 479th Fighter Group commander, who evades capture and will resume his command on November 1, 1944.

Nearly 200 IX Bomber Command B-26s and A-20s attack rail embankments and bridges around Paris.

USAAF fighter pilots down 15 GAF fighters over northern France between 0806 and 1830 hours.

IX Troop Carrier Command C-47s parachute supplies to elements of the U.S. 30th Infantry Division that are encircled at Mortain.

Twelfth Air Force fighter-bombers attack coastal gun emplacements.

The first phase of the air campaign in long-term support of Operation DRAGOON (formerly ANVIL), which began on April 28, is officially terminated. In the course of the campaign, MAAF bombers and fighter-bombers have expended 12,500 tons of bombs. Phase II begins immediately against last-minute tactical targets such as radar installations, coast-defense batteries, troop concentrations, and highway and rail bridges. To help deceive the enemy, targets well out of the DRAGOON invasion area (i.e., the French Riviera) are also struck.

The Ninth Air Force's 362d Fighter Group displaces to Advance Landing Ground A-27, at Rennes.

MTO: Twelfth Air Force medium bombers are grounded and XII TAC fighter-bomber operations are severely limited by bad weather.

ROMANIA: More than 450 Fifteenth Air Force B-17s and B-24s attack six oil refineries in the Ploesti complex.

31st Fighter Group P-51 pilots down four Bf-109s in an engagement over Romania at 0955 hours. Capt Frederick J. Dorsch, Jr., a P-51 pilot with the 31st Fighter Group's 309th Fighter Squadron, achieves aces status when he downs two of the Bf-109s.

August 11, 1944

ENGLAND: The 492d Heavy Bombardment Group is effectively disbanded when most of its aircraft and personnel are transferred to other 2d Bombardment Division B-24 units. The unit's numerical designation is retained and transferred to the 801st Provisional Heavy Bombardment Group, the VIII Air Force Composite Command's secret special-operations unit engaged in parachuting agents and supplies into Occupied Europe and collecting agents and secret radio messages from German-held territory.

Personnel and B-24 aircraft from the former 492d Heavy Bombardment Group's 856th Heavy Bombardment Squadron are transferred to the Eighth Air Force's independent 36th Heavy Bombardment Squadron (Radio Counter Measures) and 406th Heavy Bombardment Squadron (night leaflets).

FRANCE: Forty-seven 2d Bombardment Division B-24s, 54 3d Bombardment Division B-24s, and 76 3d Bombardment Division B-17s attack four airfields; 136 2d Bombardment Division B-24s attack three fuel dumps; 152 3d Bombardment Division B-17s attack two marshalling yards; 125 2d Bombardment Division B-24s attack marshalling yards at Strasbourg, France, and Saarbrucken, Germany; and 11 B-24s attack several targets of opportunity. Four heavy bombers are lost.

Two hundred seventy-five 1st Bombardment Division B-17s attack barracks, troop concentrations, fuel dumps, gun emplacements, bunkers, and rail targets in the Brest Peninsula. One B-17 is lost, but its entire crew bails out safely into friendly hands.

Three hundred sixty-three VIII Fighter Command fighters provide escort for the various heavy-bomber missions, and 165 VIII Fighter Command fighters undertake a sweep in the Paris area. One P-51 is lost with its pilot.

Eighth Air Force fighter pilots down four Bf-109s near Paris at 1930 hours.

IX Bomber Command B-26s and A-20s attack gun emplacements, an ammunition dump, and bridges.

IX Troop Carrier Command C-47s and one IX TAC P-47 squadron drop supplies to elements of the U.S. 30th Infantry Division that are cut off at Mortain.

The Ninth Air Force's 10th Photographic Reconnaissance Group moves into Advance Landing Ground A-27, at Rennes; and the 354th Fighter Group displaces to Advance Landing Ground A-31, at Gael.

Twelfth Air Force B-25s, B-26s, and fighter-bombers attack gun emplacements along the Mediterranean coast from Genoa, Italy, to Nice.

ITALY: The main Operation DRAGOON invasion convoy leaves Naples.

August 12, 1944

ENGLAND: Lt Joseph P. Kennedy, Jr., USN, eldest son of the former U.S. ambassador to the U.K. and brother of the future U.S. president, is killed in the midair explosion of a U.S. Navy drone Liberator making a test flight over England.

The 467th Heavy Bombardment Group's 788th Heavy Bombardment Squadron and the 490th Heavy Bombardment Group's 850th Heavy Bombardment Squadron—which were transferred to the 801st Provisional Heavy Bombardment Group in May 1944—are reconstituted from personnel and airplanes from the disbanded 492d

Heavy Bombardment Group [see August 11, 1944].

FRANCE: Sixty-nine 1st Bombardment Division B-17s attack a marshalling yard at Metz, and 480 Eighth Air Force B-17s and B-24s attack eight airdromes in eastern and central France. Three B-24s are lost.

Sixty-nine 3d Bombardment Division B-17s returning from a FRANTIC mission to the Soviet Union via Italy attack the Toulouse/Francazal Airdrome on the final leg of the mission. Escort for the FRANTIC B-17s is provided by 58 P-51s that accompanied them to the Soviet Union and 42 VIII Fighter Command P-51s that meet them following the bombing attack. (Three B-17s, with four P-51 escorts, return to Italy due to mechanical problems.)

Altogether, 386 VIII Fighter Command P-47s and P-51s escort Eighth Air Force heavy bombers and IX Bomber Command medium bombers over France during the day. Several escort groups strafe ground targets. Three P-51s are lost with their pilots.

Throughout the day, the VIII Fighter Command mounts 706 fighter-bomber sorties against transportation targets in northeastern France and Belgium. Ten fighters are lost. Among the VIII Fighter Command pilots lost is Col Thomas J. J. Christian, Jr., the 361st Fighter Group commander, who is killed.

IX Bomber Command B-26s and A-20s attack a rail bridge spanning the Seine River (the last USAAF attack on a Seine River bridge), a refueling siding, and numerous targets along the highways in the Argentan area, through which large German Army forces are attempting to retreat. (The IX Bomber Command bombers attack forty chokepoints around Argentan between 1931 and 2051 hours.)

Eighth and Ninth air force fighter pilots down four Ju-88s and a Bf-109 over France between 0700 and 1450 hours.

Operating in support of the Operation DRAGOON preinvasion plan, 234 Fifteenth Air Force B-24s attack a variety of German Army gun positions in the invasion area and around Toulon; more than 100 Fifteenth Air Force P-51s attack radar installations and observation posts along the Mediterranean coast; and Twelfth Air Force medium bombers attack coastal gun emplacements.

During the night of August 12–13, 11 B-24s of the Fifteenth Air Force's 885th Special Heavy Bombardment Squadron conduct their unit's first operational mission of the war by dropping more than 33 tons of weapons, munitions, and other supplies from low level to several groups of partisan fighters of the French Forces of the Interior. To cover the true purpose of the mission, the bombers also scatter 225,000 leaflets.

Also during the night of August 12–13, XII TAC A-20s attack targets of opportunity along the Monaco-Toulon road.

ITALY: A total of 307 Fifteenth Air Force B-17s and B-24s attack German Army gun positions around Savona and Genoa, and Twelfth Air Force medium bombers attack gun emplacements in the U.S. Fifth Army battle area.

August 13, 1944

ENGLAND: The squadrons of the 492d Heavy Bombardment Group (formerly the 801st Provisional Heavy Bombardment Group) [see August 11, 1944] are redesignated as follows: the 850th Heavy Bombardment Squadron becomes the 857th Heavy Bombardment Squadron; and the 788th Heavy Bombardment Squadron becomes the 859th Heavy Bombardment Squadron. Also, the 856th and 858th Heavy Bombardment squadrons are reconstituted as new special-operations units.

FRANCE: As Allied ground forces race to capture tens of thousands of German Army soldiers in the Falaise Pocket, 1,206 Eighth Air Force B-17s and B-24s, escorted by 131 VIII Fighter Command P-51s, take part in efforts to close transportation chokepoints in the area between Paris and Le Havre. Several coastal batteries and targets of opportunity are also attacked. Thirteen heavy bombers are lost.

VIII Fighter Command fighter-bombers mount 844 effective sorties during the day against transportation targets, mostly in the vicinity of the Seine River. Fighter pilots claim the destruction of 776 motor vehicles, which is a credible count in light of the terrific road congestion caused by the German Army's collapse and headlong retreat in the Falaise area. Thirteen fighter-bombers are lost with their pilots.

In the first operational APHRODITE mission undertaken by the experimental unit attached to the 388th Heavy Bombardment Group, a drone B-17 equipped with a 2,000-pound television-guided bomb is directed against a target in Le Havre. The bomb, which misses its intended target, destroys a USAAF Mosquito support plane when it explodes.

More than 575 IX Bomber Command B-26 and A-20 sorties are mounted against several fuel storage facilities and, in the main, seventy transportation chokepoints in and around the Falaise pocket. Also, Ninth Air Force fighter-bombers attack numerous ground targets in and around the battle area. 397th Medium Bombardment Group B-26s attacking a marshalling yard at Corbiel score direct hits on an ammunition train, which in turn destroys three other military-supply trains and flattens neighboring war-goods factories.

In an exceptionally busy day, IX Troop Carrier Command C-47s mount at least 125 transportation and evacuation sorties.

XIX TAC fighter pilots down 12 GAF fighters over France between 0825 and 2015 hours.

Operating in support of the DRAGOON preinvasion plan, nearly 500 Fifteenth Air Force B-17s and B-24s, escorted by more than 180 fighters, attack a variety of German Army gun positions and bridges between Genoa, Italy, and Toulon; 31 Fifteenth Air Force P-38s dive-bomb Montelimar Airdrome; Twelfth Air Force B-25s and B-26s attack coastal defenses around Marseille; and Twelfth Air Force fighters and fighter-bombers attack six airdromes in southern France and one in northwestern Italy.

Capt Sylvan Feld, who shot down nine GAF aircraft while flying Spitfires with the 52d Fighter Group in North Africa and the Mediterranean, is himself shot down by flak near Argentan. (Feld survives and is taken prisoner, but he will be wounded by U.S. bombs on August 20 and will die of his injuries on August 21.)

During the night of August 13–14, IX Bomber Command B-26s attack an ammunition dump and troop bivouac.

ITALY: XII TAC A-20s attack ordnance dumps in the Arno River valley, targets of opportunity in the Po River valley, and a fuel dump in the northern Italy battle area.

YUGOSLAVIA: Twenty-eight Fifteenth Air Force B-17s attack targets around Pec.

August 14, 1944

BELGIUM: Thirty-three 1st Bombardment Division B-17s that are unable to attack assigned targets in Germany divert to attack Chievres and Florennes/Juzaine Airdromes.

ENGLAND: The 2d Bombardment Division's 95th Combat Bombardment Wing headquarters is disbanded. The 489th Heavy Bombardment Group is reassigned to the 20th Combat Bombardment Wing, and the 491st Heavy Bombardment Group is reassigned to the 14th Combat Bombardment Wing.

FRANCE: Seventy-two 1st Bombardment Division B-17s attack Metz/Frascati Airdrome; a total of 354 2d Bombardment Division B-24s, escorted by 92 VIII Fighter Command fighters, attack three airdromes, two bridges, and a rail junction; and 76 3d Bombardment Division B-24s, escorted by 40 fighters, attack two rail junctions.

One hundred thirty-six VIII Fighter Command P-38 and P-47 fighter-bombers attack transportation targets in the Paris area. Three fighter-bombers are lost with their pilots.

IX Bomber Command B-26s and A-20s attack rail bridges and sidings along

German Army lines of retreat, and IX and XIX TAC fighters and fighter-bombers aggressively support rapid advances by Allied ground forces seeking to encircle a large part of the German Army in France.

Eighth and Ninth air force fighter pilots down 16 GAF fighters over France between 0700 and 1645 hours. Maj Joseph H. Griffin, the commanding officer of the 367th Fighter Group's 392d Fighter Squadron, achieves ace status when he downs two FW-190s over Evreux at 1450 hours. (Griffin's first three victories were scored while he was flying P-40s in China.)

The Ninth Air Force's 358th Fighter Group displaces to Advance Landing Ground A-28, at Pontorson; and the Ninth Air Force's 36th Fighter Group displaces to Advance Landing Ground A-2, at Criqueville.

Now within 24 hours of the invasion of southern France, the Twelfth and Fifteenth air forces place the full weight of their attacks upon tactical targets in the beachhead area, chiefly coastal defenses, airfields, and radar stations. During the day, 144 57th Medium Bombardment Wing B-25s and 100 42d Medium Bombardment Wing B-26s demolish nine German Army artillery sites between Toulon and Nice, and 47th Light Bombardment Group A-20s attack three airfields. The XII TAC's six P-47 groups, all temporarily based in Corsica, attack radar installations in the Marseille area and a wide variety of tactical positions within the invasion area itself. Also, a total of 306 Fifteenth Air Force B-17s and B-24s attack 36 German Army gun positions between Genoa, Italy, and Toulon, putting 14 of the batteries out of action; and 145 Fifteenth Air Force P-38s and P-51s strafe radar installations along the invasion coast.

Beginning this day, USAAF pilots and crewman are forbidden to strafe human beings on the ground within the borders of France.

During the night of August 14–15, XII TAC A-20s attack three airdromes in southern France and targets of opportunity in the Rhone River valley.

GERMANY: Two hundred fifty 1st Bombardment Division B-17s and 330 3d Bombardment Division B-17s, escorted by 258 VIII Fighter Command fighters, attack aircraft-engine factories, synthetic-oil factories, and two airdromes at Ludwigshafen, Mannheim, Stuttgart, and several other locations. One fighter is lost with its pilot.

ITALY: A total of 205 Fifteenth Air Force B-17s and B-24s attack German Army coastal gun positions around Genoa and Savona.

August 15, 1944

BELGIUM: Fifty-nine 3d Bombardment Division B-24s attack Florennes/Juzaine Airdrome. One B-24 is lost.

Thirty-three VIII Fighter Command P-47 fighter-bombers attack rail targets at Braine-le-Comte. One P-47 is lost with its pilot.

FRANCE: Operation DRAGOON, the invasion of southern France, begins with an airborne drop of 5,100 British and American paratroopers from 396 Provisional Troop Carrier Division C-47s between 0423 and 0514 hours. Then, from 0550 hours onward, Allied fighters arrive over the beach to strafe targets of opportunity and protect scores of small formations of fighters and medium and heavy bombers dispatched against specific targets. At 0800 hours, by which time destruction of preliminary objectives has been undertaken by air and naval forces and the capture of preliminary objectives on the ground has been achieved by American and British paratroopers as a means to isolate the DRAGOON invasion area, three U.S. Army divisions of the U.S. Seventh Army land from the sea between Toulon and Nice. Finally, beginning at 0814 hours and ending at 1907 hours, three separate waves of towed gliders deliver 9,000 Allied airborne soldiers to the beachhead area along with 213 artillery pieces, 221 light vehicles (mostly jeeps), nearly 760,000 rounds of ammunition, nearly 1,300 gallons of gasoline, about 57,000 pounds of rations, and nearly 750,000 pounds of assorted other goods and supplies.

The DRAGOON airborne operation is virtually flawless, the best of the war. In 1,394 aircraft and glider sorties on D day, eleven troop carrier groups—four from the Twelfth Air Force and eight on loan from the Ninth Air Force—experience only two aborts due to mechanical failures, the premature release of only two paratroop loads and nine gliders, and missed drop zones by only 36 planeloads of paratroopers. In 746 glider landings, pilot losses are an extremely low eleven killed, four missing, and sixteen injured.

Twelfth Air Force medium bombers provide general support for the invasion by attacking coastal defenses, troop positions, artillery batteries, lines of communication, and numerous other targets throughout the invasion area. During the course of the day, from 0445 hours until 1618 hours, 42d Medium Bombardment Wing B-26s alone conduct 353 sorties, first against beach-defense positions and later against road and rail bridges west of Toulon. Also, XII TAC A-20s attack a German Army barracks in the invasion area, and Twelfth Air Force fighters and fighter-bombers patrol the invasion area and attack a broad range of ground targets.

While the Twelfth Air Force fighters and bombers see to close-in air support and interdiction, fighters of the Fifteenth Air Force's 306th Fighter Wing that are temporarily based in Sardinia support the DRAGOON landings at the beachhead and with farther-ranging attacks on German lines of supply in the Toulon area. Fifteenth Air Force B-17s and B-24s also take part in a variety of tactical-type missions aimed at cutting the German lines of supply and communication.

In northern France, more than 330 IX Bomber Command B-26s and A-20s attack coastal defenses at St.-Malo, rail bridges, a marshalling yard, fuel and ammunition dumps; and Ninth Air Force fighters and fighter-bombers provide direct support for U.S. Army divisions in the battle area.

XIX TAC fighters down 13 GAF fighters over France between 0735 and 1645 hours.

The Ninth Air Force's 365th Fighter Group displaces to Advance Landing Ground A-12, at Lignerolles; and the Ninth Air Force's 370th Fighter Group displaces to Advance Landing Ground A-19, at La Vielle.

During the night of August 15–16, XII TAC A-20s attack motor vehicles and light sources in the Rhone River valley north of the DRAGOON beachhead area.

GERMANY: Two hundred eleven 1st Bombardment Division B-17s and 312 2d Bombardment Division B-24s, escorted by a total of 175 VIII Fighter Command fighters, attack eight airdromes. Thirteen heavy bombers and five fighters are lost. Also, 184 3d Bombardment Division B-17s, escorted by 118 VIII Fighter Command P-51s, attack two airdromes.

VIII Fighter Command fighter pilots down ten GAF fighters over Germany between 0945 and 1245 hours.

NETHERLANDS: One hundred four 3d Bombardment Division B-17s attack Venlo Airdrome. Two B-17s are lost.

P-38 pilots of the 479th Fighter Group's 434th Fighter Squadron down three Bf-109s over Steenwijk Airdrome at 1315 hours.

August 16, 1944

FRANCE: Approximately 130 IX Bomber Command B-26s and A-20s attack five rail bridges and an ammunition dump.

IX TAC fighter pilots down 16 FW-190s over France during the afternoon and early evening. Fourteen of the victims are downed in a single action near Maintenon at 1640 hours by P-51 pilots of the 354th Fighter Group's 353d Fighter Squadron. Two 353d Fighter Squadron P-51 pilots achieve ace status: 1stLt Kenneth H. Dahlberg, when he downs three FW-190s, and 1stLt Charles W. Koenig, when he downs two FW-190s.

The Ninth Air Force's 50th Fighter Group displaces to Advance Landing Ground A-17, at Meutis.

The four B-26 groups of the 98th Combat Bombardment Wing begin to move from bases in England to bases in France.

In southern France, XII TAC A-20s and P-47s mount 1,250 direct-support sorties over the DRAGOON invasion area. Also, Fifteenth Air Force B-17s and B-24s conduct numerous attacks on rail and highway bridges throughout southern France, especially in the Rhone River valley.

MATAF C-47s, with a strong Fifteenth Air Force P-51 escort, drop supplies to Allied troops in the DRAGOON invasion area.

During the night of August 16–17, XII TAC A-20s attack motor vehicles in southern France.

GERMANY: A total of 976 Eighth Air Force B-17s and B-24s attack numerous aircraft factories, oil-industry targets, and several airdromes in central Germany. Twenty-three heavy bombers are lost.

Escort for the heavy bombers is provided by 612 VIII Fighter Command fighters, of which three are lost with their pilots.

Eighth Air Force escort pilots down 33 GAF fighters, including two Me-163 rocket fighters, between 0945 and 1100 hours. Maj John L. Elder, the commanding officer of the 355th Fighter Group's 357th Fighter Squadron, in P-51s, achieves ace status when he downs two Bf-109s near Hildesheim at 1030 hours.

Eighty-nine Fifteenth Air Force B-24s attack a chemical plant at Friedrichshafen.

August 17, 1944

BELGIUM: In the first attack of its kind by a USAAF fighter in the ETO, the 56th Fighter Group's deputy commander, LtCol David C. Schilling, fires six aerial rockets from his P-47 at rail cars in a rail yard at Braine-le-Comte. All six rockets hit targets, and four rail cars are left burning.

ENGLAND: All Eighth Air Force heavy bombers are grounded or forced to turn back while en route to their targets because of bad weather.

FRANCE: Three hundred ninety-seven VIII Fighter Command fighter-bombers attack communications and transportation targets throughout the region between Paris and Brussels. Seven aircraft are lost with their pilots.

An Operation APHRODITE television-guided B-17 flying bomb is successfully directed against a target at La Pallice.

More than 400 IX Bomber Command B-26s and A-20s attack seven road bridges and one rail bridge, and XIX TAC fighters attack a Gestapo headquarters near Chateauroux.

During the afternoon, XIX TAC fighter pilots down three GAF aircraft over France.

The Ninth Air Force's 406th Fighter Group displaces to Advance Landing Ground A-14, at Cretteville.

Approximately 100 Twelfth Air Force B-26s attack supply and communications targets and coastal defenses in and around Toulon, and XII TAC A-20s drop ammunition to Allied forces in the invasion area.

ROMANIA: Against no Axis fighter opposition whatever, approximately 250 Fifteenth Air Force B-24s attack three refineries and targets of opportunity around Ploesti.

August 18, 1944

BELGIUM: 1st Bombardment Division B-17s attack bridges at Liege and Namur.

FRANCE: Forty-three 3d Bombardment Division B-24s attack Roye/Amy Airdrome, and ten B-24s attack targets of opportunity. Escort is provided by 96 VIII Fighter Command P-51s. Two B-24s are lost.

Eighth Air Force B-17s and B-24s attack bridges, a marshalling yard, several airdromes, fuel dumps, and an aircraft-engine factory. Three escort fighter groups attack three airdromes during the return flight.

Three hundred twenty-three VIII Fighter Command fighter-bombers attack transportation targets along the Seine River and into Belgium. Losses are 13 fighter-bombers and ten of theirpilots.

Approximately 100 IX Bomber Command B-26s and A-20s attack rail lines, an important road junction on the German Army line of retreat, a fuel dump, and an ammunition dump.

IX and XIX TAC fighters and fighter-bombers mount more than 1,000 sorties in support of advancing Allied ground forces, especially in the Paris-Argentan area and along the Seine River.

Eighth and Ninth air force fighter pilots down 19 GAF fighters over France during the day.

When it is learned that the battleship *Strasbourg,* cruiser *La Gallissoniere,* and a former French Navy destroyer and submarine have been moved into a position in Toulon harbor from which they can sally against the DRAGOON invasion fleet and beachhead, 36 321st Medium Bombardment Group B-25s based in Corsica are ordered to conduct an immediate attack aimed at sinking the three warships. Arriving over the ships following a dead-reckoning approach, the B-25s attack from 13,000 feet through intense flak that damages 27 of the aircraft and wounds 12 crewmen, including the group commander. Nevertheless, bombs sink the *Strasbourg,* the *La Gallissoniere,* and the submarine at their anchors.

Twelfth Air Force fighters and fighter-bombers attack rail facilities and German Army defensive positions in the invasion area.

XII TAC headquarters is established ashore in the DRAGOON invasion area to oversee air operations in direct support of U.S. Seventh Army troops.

The Twelfth Air Force's 111th Tactical Reconnaissance Squadron is transferred from Corsica to an airfield in the DRAGOON beachhead.

NETHERLANDS: 1st Bombardment Division B-17s attack Eindhoven Airdrome and a bridge at Maastricht.

ROMANIA: Fifteenth Air Force heavy bombers conduct a particularly damaging raid against five refineries around Ploesti.

When a mere 35 Axis fighters attack the heavy bombers, 31st Fighter Group P-51 pilots down nine and drive the rest away. Capt Leland P. Molland, the commanding officer of the 31st Fighter Group's 308th Fighter Squadron, brings his final personal tally to 10.5 confirmed victories when he downs a Bf-109 near Ploesti at 1045 hours.

YUGOSLAVIA: Eighty-nine Fifteenth Air Force attack Alibunar Airdrome.

August 19, 1944

ENGLAND: The entire Eighth Air Force and all IX Bomber Command bombers are grounded by bad weather.

FRANCE: While covering Allied ground forces and mounting armed-reconnaissance missions over France, IX and XIX TAC fighter pilots down 11 GAF fighters during the morning.

The Ninth Air Force's 373d Fighter Group displaces to Advance Landing Ground A-29, at St.-James.

Twelfth Air Force B-25s and B-26s attack road and rail bridges; XII TAC A-20s attack several marshalling yards; and Twelfth Air Force fighters and fighter-bombers attack lines of communication and gun emplacements.

During the night of August 19–20, XII TAC A-20s attack motor vehicles and lights between the battle area and the Rhone River.

MTO: The 50th and 53d Troop Carrier wings are ordered to return to their bases in the U.K.

ROMANIA: Sixty-five Fifteenth Air Force B-17s conduct what turns out to be the final USAAF bombing mission against Ploesti.

August 20, 1944

CZECHOSLOVAKIA: Fifteenth Air Force B-24s attack oil refineries at Dubova.

ENGLAND: The entire Eighth Air Force is grounded by bad weather. The only flights during the day are undertaken by a weather-reconnaissance B-17 over the Atlantic Ocean and a weather-reconnaissance Mosquito that fails to return from a flight to Belgium.

FRANCE: Sixty-one IX Bomber Command B-26s attack German Army troops and equipment waiting to be ferried across the Seine River; IX and XIX TAC fighters and fighter-bombers mount numerous ground-support attacks; and more than 100 IX Troop Carrier Command transports fly resupply and evacuation missions.

IX and XIX TAC fighter pilots down seven GAF fighters over France during the afternoon and early evening.

Twelfth Air Force B-26s and fighter-bombers attack coastal-defense guns around Toulon, and B-25s attack bridges in the Rhone River valley and several airfields.

The Twelfth Air Force's 23d Photographic Reconnaissance Squadron is transferred from Corsica to southern France.

HUNGARY: Fifteenth Air Force B-24s attack the airdrome and a marshalling yard at Szolnok.

ITALY: During the night of August 20–21, XII TAC A-20s attack motor vehicles in the Po River valley.

POLAND: Fifteenth Air Force B-17s attack oil-industry targets at Czechowice and Oswiecim (Auschwitz).

August 21, 1944

ETO: The entire Eighth and Ninth air forces are grounded by bad weather. The only flights during the day are by several weather-reconnaissance aircraft and fewer than 20 transports.

FRANCE: Twelfth Air Force fighter-bombers attack gun emplacements and line-of-communication targets in and around the DRAGOON invasion area.

During the night of August 21–22, XII TAC A-20s attack motor vehicles near Nice.

HUNGARY: One hundred two Fifteenth Air Force B-24s and 46 P-51 fighter-bombers attack the airdrome at Hadju Boszormeny.

ITALY: Twelfth Air Force medium bomb-

ers attack bridges and roads throughout the Po River valley; XII TAC A-20s attack the barracks at Alessandria; and XII TAC fighter-bombers attack rail lines, a marshalling yard, and motor transport in northern Italy.

During the night of August 21–22, XII TAC A-20s attack motor vehicles near Alessandria.

YUGOSLAVIA: One hundred seventeen Fifteenth Air Force B-17s attack Nis Airdrome.

August 22, 1944

AUSTRIA: Fifteenth Air Force B-24s attack oil-industry targets around Vienna, including a run against the Lobau underground oil-storage facility by 39 484th Heavy Bombardment Group B-24s.

ENGLAND: The entire Eighth Air Force and all IX Bomber Command bombers are grounded by bad weather.

FRANCE: Ninth Air Force fighter-bombers provide support for U.S. Army ground forces and strafe many transportation and tactical targets.

IX and XIX TAC fighter pilots down 27 GAF fighters over France between 1230 and 1940 hours.

The IX Bomber Command's 387th Medium Bombardment Group displaces to Advance Landing Ground A-15, at Cherbourg/Maupertus Airdrome.

Despite bad weather that forces the cancellation of many other Twelfth Air Force missions, XII TAC A-20s attack several industrial targets, and XII TAC fighters and fighter-bombers attack motor vehicles.

The 79th Fighter Group, a Twelfth Air Force P-47 unit, is transferred from Corsica to a newly opened air base in southern France.

GERMANY: Fifteenth Air Force B-24s attack oil-industry targets at Blechhammer, and B-17s attack oil-industry targets at Odertal.

1stLt Barrie S. Davis, a P-51 pilot with the 325th Fighter Group's 317th Fighter

Squadron, achieves ace status when he downs an FW-190 and a Bf-109 near Lake Balaton, Hungary, at about 1340 hours.

ITALY: Twelfth Air Force B-26s attack bridges in the Po River valley.

August 23, 1944

AUSTRIA: Fifteenth Air Force Heavy B-17s and B-24s attack oil and other industrial targets in and around Vienna, as well as Markersdorf Airdrome.

P-51 escort pilots of the 52d, 325th, and 332d Fighter groups down 20 Axis fighters over Austria between 1205 and 1245 hours. 1stLt John M. Simmons, a P-51 pilot with the 325th Fighter Group's 317th Fighter Squadron, achieves ace status when he downs two FW-190s near Virdenburg at about 1220 hours; and Maj Robert C. Curtis, the commanding officer of the 52d Fighter Group's 2d Fighter Squadron, downs an FW-190, which brings his final personal tally to 14 confirmed victories. Maj Herschel H. Green, the commanding officer of the 325th Fighter Group's 317th Fighter Squadron, brings his final personal tally to 18 confirmed victories when he downs one FW-190 near Wiener-Neustadt at 1215 hours. For the time being, Green is the top-scoring ace in the MTO, and he will end the war as second top scorer in the theater.

ENGLAND: All Eighth Air Force bombers are grounded by bad weather.

FRANCE: One hundred forty-two VIII Fighter Command P-47 fighter-bombers from four groups sweep the region from St.-Omer to Reims.

Ninth Air Force fighter-bombers attack artillery batteries and provide support for Allied ground forces.

XIX TAC fighter pilots down five Bf-109s over France during the day.

More than 150 IX Troop Carrier Command transports mount supply and evacuation sorties.

The Ninth Air Force's 36th Fighter Group displaces to Advance Landing Ground A-35, at Le Mans; and the Ninth Air Force's 368th Fighter Group displaces to Advance Landing Ground A-40, at Chartres.

In southern France, Twelfth Air Force medium bombers attack bridges in the Rhone River valley, and XII TAC fighters and fighter-bombers attack tactical and lines-of-communication targets.

Free French Army combat units advancing from the DRAGOON beachhead enter Toulon and Marseille.

During the night of August 23–24, XII TAC A-20s attack targets of opportunity in the Rhone River valley.

GERMANY: More than 80 VIII Fighter Command fighter-bombers attack a marshalling yard at Hamm.

ITALY: Fifteenth Air Force B-24s attack a rail bridge near Ferrara, but all bombs go astray and hit a synthetic-rubber plant. Twelfth Air Force medium bombers attack rail and road bridges.

During the night of August 23–24, XII TAC A-20s attack targets of opportunity near Genoa, Milan, and Turin.

ROMANIA: Romania surrenders unconditionally as Soviet forces begin to overrun the nation.

August 24, 1944

CZECHOSLOVAKIA: One hundred thirty-nine Eighth Air Force B-17s attack oil refineries at Brux; Fifteenth Air Force B-17s attack the airdrome at Pardubice; and Fifteenth Air Force B-17s and B-24s attack three oil refineries at Kolin and Pardubice.

Fifteenth Air Force escort pilots down ten Axis fighters.

ENGLAND: IX Bomber Command bombers are grounded by bad weather.

FRANCE: Ninth Air Force fighters support U.S. Army ground forces and attack bridges spanning the Seine River. In daylong action, 474th Fighter Group P-38s conduct especially aggressive bombing attacks against German Army road columns attempting to reach and cross the Seine River—with the result that vast amounts of military stores are abandoned by the fleeing Germans.

IX Troop Carrier Command transports mount more than 275 supply and evacuation sorties.

The Ninth Air Force's 366th Fighter Group displaces to Advance Landing Ground A-41, at Dreux/Vermouillet Airdrome; and the Ninth Air Force's 10th Photographic Reconnaissance Group displaces to Advance Landing Ground A-39, at Chateaudun.

Twelfth Air Force medium bombers attack three bridges in southern France and gun emplacements near Marseille; and XII TAC fighter-bombers attack tactical targets, bridges, and motor vehicles.

During the night of August 24–25, XII TAC A-20s attack targets of opportunity in the Rhone River valley.

GERMANY: 1,074 Eighth Air Force B-17s and B-24s attack three aircraft factories, an armaments factory, an airdrome, five oil-industry targets, and various targets of opportunity, including five airdromes. Twenty-six heavy bombers are lost.

Escort for the heavy bombers is provided by 626 VIII Fighter Command fighters, of which four are lost with three pilots. Four escort groups strafe two airdromes and two marshalling yards. Capt John T. Godfrey, a P-51 ace with the 4th Fighter Group's 336th Fighter Squadron, is shot down by flak and captured.

VIII Fighter Command escort pilots down ten Bf-109s over Germany between 1112 and 1400 hours.

This is the last mission undertaken by 3d Bombardment Division B-24 units; upon return to their bases, the last groups are temporarily withdrawn from combat for conversion to B-17 aircraft.

Fifteenth Air Force B-17s and B-24s attack oil refineries in southern Germany.

HUNGARY: Fifteenth Air Force heavy bombers attack Szeged and a marshalling yard at Vinkovci.

ITALY: Fifteenth Air Force heavy bombers attack a rail bridge, and Twelfth Air Force medium bombers attack two bridges.

August 25, 1944

BELGIUM: During the afternoon, 31 1st Bombardment Division B-17s and 52 2d Bombardment Division B-24s, escorted by 152 VIII Fighter Command fighters, attack five ammonia and liquid-oxygen plants in Belgium and northern France.

CZECHOSLOVAKIA: More than 300 Fifteenth Air Force B-17s and B-24s attack aircraft factories at Brno and Kurim, and the airdromes at Brno and Prostejov.

Escort fighter pilots down 12 Axis fighters and an Fi-156 between 1030 and 1217 hours. 1stLt Michael Brezas, a P-38 ace with the 14th Fighter Group's 48th Fighter Squadron, downs two FW-190s at about 1140 hours, bringing his final personal tally to 12 confirmed victories.

FRANCE: Two hundred seventy-eight IX Bomber Command B-26s and A-20s (of 320 dispatched) and 157 XIX TAC fighter-bombers (undertaking 17 separate missions) attack German Army defensive positions in and around Brest; and Ninth Air Force fighter-bombers support the advances of U.S. Army ground forces and drop napalm on the reported headquarters of all German Army forces in France.

In the heaviest day of aerial combat over France since the invasion, IX and XIX TAC fighter pilots down 77 GAF fighters in a virtually unremitting series of engagements between 0810 and 1845 hours. Capt Maurice G. Long, a P-51 pilot with the 354th Fighter Group's 355th Fighter Squadron, achieves ace status during a morning mission when he downs two FW-190s and shares in the downing of a Bf-109 near Rethel. Two other 355th Fighter Squadron P-51 pilots also achieve ace status during a late-afternoon mission: Capt Warren S. Emerson, when he downs two FW-190s over Reims and a Bf-109 near Grandvillers, and 1stLt William B. King, when he downs three FW-190s over Reims.

After attacking GAF landing grounds in France all morning, the 367th Fighter Group, a Ninth Air Force P-38 unit, flies an 800-mile round-trip afternoon mission to strike a landing ground at Dijon and airdromes at Cognac and Bourges in southeastern France. During the second mission, Capt Laurence E. Blumer, of the group's 393d Fighter Squadron, becomes an "ace in a day" when he downs five FW-190s near St.-Quentin at 1240 hours.

In their own attacks against GAF landing grounds, 20th Fighter Group P-51 pilots destroy 20 German aircraft on the ground.

The German garrison commander surrenders the city of Paris to Free French Army armored units.

IX Bomber Command's 394th Medium Bombardment Group displaces to Advance Landing Ground A-13, at Tour en Bessin.

Twelfth Air Force B-25s and B-26s attack five bridges in the Rhone River valley and gun emplacements around Marseille; XII TAC A-20s attack ammunition dumps; and XII TAC fighter-bombers attack tactical targets in the battle area.

The Twelfth Air Force's 27th and 324th Fighter groups, in P-47s, are transferred from Corsica to bases in southern France.

During the night of August 25–26, XII TAC fighter-bombers attack motor vehicles and targets of opportunity in the Nice area.

GERMANY: 1,116 Eighth Air Force B-17s and B-24s attack airdromes at Anklam, Grossenbrode, Neubrandenburg, and Parow; GAF experimental facilities at Peenemunde and Rechlin; aircraft components factories at Lubeck, Rostock, Schwerin, and Wismar; an oil-industry target at Politz; and several targets of opportunity. Eighteen heavy bombers are lost.

Escort for the heavy bombers is provided by 629 VIII Fighter Command fighters, of which seven are lost with six pilots.

VIII Fighter Command escort pilots down 12 GAF fighters over Germany between 1130 and 1220 hours. Capt Robin Olds, a P-38 pilot with the 479th Fighter Group's 434th Fighter Squadron, achieves ace status when he downs three Bf-109s near Rostock between 1135 hours and noon.

ITALY: XII TAC fighter-bombers attack roads, bridges, and gun emplacements north of the Arno River.

NETHERLANDS: Ten 2d Bombardment Division B-24s, escorted by 36 VIII Fighter Command P-47s, attack the rail bridge at Moerdijk with Azon guided bombs, but no hits are scored.

August 26, 1944

ENGLAND: The IX Troop Carrier Command is formally transferred from the Ninth Air Force to the First Allied Airborne Army.

ETO: In an effort to slow the headlong retreat of German Army ground forces before fast-moving Allied spearheads, VIII Fighter Command fighter-bombers mount 389 effective sorties against transportation targets in eastern France, Belgium, and western Germany.

FRANCE: One hundred thirty-eight 3d Bombardment Division B-17s attack gun batteries and fortifications on the Brest Peninsula. Escort is provided by 48 VIII Fighter Command fighters, of which one is lost with its pilot.

IX Bomber Command B-26s and A-20s attack three fuel dumps, troop concentrations, and equipment storage areas.

The IX Bomber Command's 323d Medium Bombardment Group displaces to Advance Landing Ground A-20, at Lessay.

Although several missions fail in the face of bad weather, Twelfth Air Force B-25s and B-26s attack gun emplacements around Marseille, and XII TAC fighter-bombers attack ammunition dumps, rail lines, motor vehicles, gun emplacements, and other targets.

GERMANY: One hundred seventy-four 1st Bombardment Division B-17s attack two oil refineries at Gelsenkirchen (primaries) and several secondary targets; 95 2d Bombardment Division B-24s attack a chemical plant at Ludwigshafen (primary), marshalling yards at Ehrgang and Kons Karthaus (secondaries), and a target of opportunity; and a separate force of 116 2d Bombardment Division B-24s attacks oil refineries at

Emmerich and Salzbergen (primaries), and a fuel dump at Dulmen (primary). Ten heavy bombers are lost.

Escort for the various heavy-bomber missions to Germany is provided by 365 VIII Fighter Command fighters, of which two are lost with their pilots.

LtCol Frank E. Adkins, the commanding officer of the 50th Fighter Group's 313th Fighter Squadron, in P-47s, achieves ace status when he downs two Bf-109s near Elbauf at 1445 hours. Adkins's three previous victories were scored in the Pacific Theater.

ITALY: Fifteenth Air Force B-17s attack rail viaducts at Avisio, Latisana, and Venzone; and XII TAC fighter-bombers attack ammunition dumps in north-central Italy.

During the night of August 26–27, XII TAC A-20s attack targets of opportunity in the Po River valley.

NETHERLANDS: Thirty-six 2d Bombardment Division B-24s attack their secondary target, Eindhoven Airdrome, after failing to locate their primary target in Germany.

Nine 2d Bombardment Division B-24s, escorted by 32 VIII Fighter Command P-51s, are unable to attack the rail bridge at Moerdijk with Azon guided bombs because of heavy cloud cover.

An attempt to strike any of a variety of targets with a television-guided Operation Aphrodite B-17 flying bomb is thwarted by bad weather.

ROMANIA: As the German Army and GAF fight Romanians for control of Bucharest, 115 Fifteenth Air Force B-24s attack the city's Otopeni Airdrome and 114 B-24s attack the city's German Army barracks. Also, B-24s attack the ferry at Giurgiu.

YUGOSLAVIA: Fifteenth Air Force heavy bombers attack a viaduct at Borovnica.

August 27, 1944

FRANCE: Three hundred sixteen VIII Fighter Command P-47 fighter-bombers attack transportation targets in eastern France. One P-47 is lost with its pilot.

IX Bomber Command B-26s and A-20s attack a bridge and troop concentrations around Rouen, two fuel dumps, and a navigational station.

Twelfth Air Force medium bombers attack gun emplacements around Marseille.

GERMANY: An all-out effort against the city of Berlin and other targets in central and northern Germany by 1,203 Eighth Air Force heavy bombers is thwarted when extremely high clouds are encountered over northern Germany and Denmark. A total of 188 heavy bombers attack a variety of targets of opportunity, but the remainder abort or are recalled. Three heavy bombers are lost.

Escort for the heavy bombers is provided by 505 VIII Fighter Command fighters, of which ten are lost with their pilots. One of the downed pilots is LtCol Cy Wilson, the 20th Fighter Group commander, who is taken prisoner.

This is the first mission of the 3d Bombardment Division's 490th Heavy Bombardment Group since its transition from B-24s to B-17s.

Fifteenth Air Force B-17s and B-24s attack two oil refineries near Blechhammer.

ITALY: Fifteenth Air Force B-17s attack rail viaducts at Avisio and Venzone, and a rail bridge at Ferrara; Twelfth Air Force medium bombers attack bridges at Berceto; and XII TAC A-20s attack ammunition dumps.

During the night of August 27–28, XII TAC A-20s attack motor vehicles and targets of opportunity in the Po River valley.

YUGOSLAVIA: Fifteenth Air Force heavy bombers attack the viaduct at Borovnica.

August 28, 1944

AUSTRIA: Fifteenth Air Force B-17s attack an oil refinery and chemical plant at Moosbierbaum.

31st Fighter Group P-51 pilots down five GAF fighters and four Ju-52s near the target between 1115 and 1145 hours. 2dLt

Norman C. Skogstad, a P-51 pilot with the 31st Fighter Group's 307th Fighter Squadron, achieves ace status when he downs a Ju-52 near Vienna at 1145 hours; Capt Robert J. Goebel, a P-51 ace with the 31st Fighter Group's 308th Fighter Squadron and group leader this day, downs a Bf-109 near Vienna at 1115 hours, which brings his final personal tally to 11 confirmed victories; and Capt Walter J. Goehausen, Jr., another 308th Fighter Squadron ace, downs a Bf-109 near Vienna at 1120 hours, bringing his final personal tally to ten confirmed victories.

ETO: Despite bad weather that grounds all Eighth Air Force heavy bombers, hundreds of VIII Fighter Command fighters and fighter-bombers conduct an all-out effort against all manner of transportation targets in Belgium, France, western Germany, and the Netherlands. Sixteen fighters and all but one of their pilots are lost. Capt Albert L. Schlegel, an 8.5-victory P-51 ace with the 4th Fighter Group's 335th Fighter Squadron, fails to return from a mission.

Eighth and Ninth air force fighter pilots down 24 GAF aircraft and a glider in numerous actions during the day over Belgium, France, and Germany. Capt Robert W. Stephens, a P-51 ace with the 354th Fighter Group's 355th Fighter Squadron, brings his final personal tally to 13 confirmed victories when he downs a Bf-109 over Reims/Epernay Airdrome at 1155 hours.

FRANCE: IX Bomber Command B-26s and A-20s attack fuel and ammunition dumps; and Ninth Air Force fighters and fighter-bombers attack Bourges and Peronne airdromes and provide support for U.S. Army ground forces.

IX Troop Carrier Command transports mount approximately 400 supply and evacuation sorties.

Twelfth Air Force B-25s attack rail bridges around Lyon.

The German Army garrisons at Toulon and Marseille surrender to Free French Army combat units

GERMANY: IX Bomber Command bombers attack a fuel depot and an alcohol (i.e., fuel) distillery at Hamm.

HUNGARY: Fifteenth Air Force B-24s attack a marshalling yard at Miskolc, an oil refinery at Szony, and rail bridges and a viaduct at Szolnok.

ITALY: Fifteenth Air Force B-24s attack rail bridges and viaducts at three locations; Twelfth Air Force B-26s attack a bridge at Parma and the Villafranca di Verona Airdrome; XII TAC A-20s attack a German Army command post near Genoa; and XII TAC fighters and fighter-bombers attack shipping in the harbors at Imperia and Savona, and strafe and bomb roads and bridges in the battle area.

August 29, 1944

CZECHOSLOVAKIA: Fifteenth Air Force heavy bombers attack communications, oil, and industrial targets.

ETO: Bad weather grounds all Eighth Air Force heavy bombers and limits VIII Fighter Command to 104 effective P-38 and P-47 sorties against two airdromes and transportation targets in Belgium, France, and Germany. Three P-47s are lost with their pilots.

FRANCE: Although bad weather grounds most of the Ninth Air Force, a small number of IX Bomber Command B-26s are able to attack a fuel dump, and a small number of fighter-bombers mount sweeps over northwestern France.

The Ninth Air Force's 48th Fighter Group displaces to Advance Landing Ground A-42, at Villacoublay; the Ninth Air Force's 404th Fighter Group displaces to Advance Landing Ground A-48, at Bretigny; and the Ninth Air Force's 474th Fighter Group displaces to Advance Landing Ground A-43, at St.-Marceau.

XII TAC fighter-bombers attack numerous targets in the Rhone River valley.

HUNGARY: Fifteenth Air Force heavy bombers attack communications, oil, and industrial targets.

31st Fighter Group P-51 escort pilots

down five GAF fighters. 1stLt James L. Brooks, a P-51 ace with the 31st Fighter Group's 307th Fighter Squadron, brings his final personal tally to 13 confirmed victories when he downs two Bf-109s.

ITALY: Fifteenth Air Force heavy bombers attack communications targets in the Po River valley; the Fifteenth Air Force's 82d Fighter Group, in P-38 fighter-bombers led by a droopsnoot model, conduct a vertical-bombing attack against a rail bridge at Latisana; Twelfth Air Force B-25s and B-26s attack a viaduct and four bridges in northeastern Italy; XII TAC A-20s attack a fueling station; and XII TAC fighter-bombers support ground forces and attack roads and bridges.

During the night of August 29–30, XII TAC A-20s attack targets of opportunity in the Po River valley.

August 30, 1944

FRANCE: Using GH and H2X radar guidance, 107 Eighth Air Force B-17s and 108 B-24s, escorted by only 16 VIII Fighter Command P-51s, conduct an early-morning attack against eight V-weapons sites in the Pas-de-Calais area.

Although all Ninth Air Force fighter-bombers and most bombers are grounded by bad weather, approximately 75 B-26s and A-20s are able to attack a fuel dump and several gun emplacements.

The four B-26 groups of the IX Bomber Command's 98th Combat Bombardment Wing complete their moves to bases in France from bases in England.

XII TAC fighters and fighter-bombers attack rail and road targets in the Rhone River valley.

GERMANY: Using radar guidance, 282 Eighth Air Force B-17s attack the Kiel port area and U-boat base, and 327 B-17s attack the port area and an aircraft factory at Bremen. Escort is provided by 258 VIII Fighter Command P-51s.

ITALY: Twelfth Air Force medium bombers are grounded by bad weather; XII TAC A-20s attack fuel storage facilities; and XII

TAC and fighters and fighter-bombers attack rail and road targets in the Po River valley.

During the night of August 30–31, XII TAC A-20s attack targets of opportunity in the Po River valley.

ROMANIA: Fifteenth Air Force P-51s strafe Oradea Airdrome.

Two years and two months after the first daring low-level daylight bombing raid on the place by USAAF B-24s based in Egypt (June 12, 1942), Ploesti falls to Red Army ground troops.

YUGOSLAVIA: Fifteenth Air Force B-24s attack rail bridges at two locations; B-17s attack marshalling yards at Brod and Novi Sad; and P-51s strafe Kecskemet Airdrome.

August 31, 1944

ENGLAND: The Eighth Air Force conducts no combat operations and mounts only seven weather- and photo-reconnaissance sorties.

FRANCE: Ninety-nine IX Bomber Command B-26s and A-20s attack gun emplacements and an ammunition dump; and fighter-bombers provide direct support for U.S. Army ground forces.

During the month of August, on dates unknown (because of incomplete records), the Ninth Air Force's 363d Fighter Group displaced to Advance Landing Ground A-7, at Azeville, and the IX Bomber Command's 397th Medium Bombardment Group displaced to Advance Landing Ground A-26, at Gorges.

Twelfth Air Force fighter-bombers attack communications targets in support of the U.S. Seventh Army's drive on Lyon.

ITALY: Twelfth Air Force medium bombers attack rail bridges in the Po River valley; and XII TAC A-20s and fighter-bombers attack communications targets north of the Arno River.

During the night of August 31–September 1, XII TAC A-20s attack gun emplacements and targets of opportunity in the Po River valley.

ROMANIA: Thirty-eight Fifteenth Air

Force B-17s hastily modified to serve as transports inaugurate Operation REUNION by evacuating to Bari, Italy, more than 700 of the approximately 1,100 downed USAAF aircrewmen (and some other Allied servicemen) being held in prisoner-of-war camps in and around Bucharest, Romania. Operation REUNION is the brainchild of Romanian airmen and civilian humanitarians using the chaos of fighting in Bucharest between German and Red Army forces (and patriotic Romanians) to concentrate the Allied prisoners at a Romanian Air Force base while contacting Fifteenth Air Force headquarters (by flying a high-ranking USAAF prisoner to Bari, Italy, in a Romanian Air Force Bf-109!). Adding considerably to the general anxiety attending the hurried, makeshift operation is the requirement that the evacuation be kept as secret as possible from both German and Soviet forces.

Forty-eight 52d Fighter Group P-51s conduct a low-level approach and strafing attack against the crowded Axis landing ground at Reghin. An estimated 60 aircraft are destroyed on the ground, and seven are destroyed in the air between 1010 and 1055 hours. Also, Fifteenth Air Force P-51s strafe Oradea Airdrome.

Bucharest officially falls to the Red Army, but fighting continues to rage between and among German, Soviet, and various Romanian forces.

YUGOSLAVIA: Fifteenth Air Force B-17s attack a rail bridge at Novi Sad, and Fifteenth Air Force P-51s strafe Kecskemet Airdrome.

SEPTEMBER 1944

September 1, 1944

BALKANS: As German Army forces in Greece begin a withdrawal to avoid being cut off by Red Army forces advancing across southeastern Europe, the Fifteenth Air Force mounts a campaign to interdict rail lines and roads carrying German troops through the Balkans Peninsula, particularly the rail lines through Skoplje and Belgrade, Yugoslavia. B-24s attack bridges around Kraljevo and Mitrovica, Yugoslavia, and marshalling yards at Debreczen, Hungary, and B-17s attack the rail bridge at Moravia, Yugoslavia, and the airdrome at Nis, Yugoslavia.

BELGIUM: Maj Quince L. Brown, the commanding officer of the 78th Fighter Group's 84th Fighter Squadron, brings his final personal tally to 12.333 confirmed victories when he downs a Bf-109 near Liege at 2050 hours.

FRANCE: Two hundred sixty-five VIII Fighter Command fighter-bombers bomb and strafe rail targets in northern and northeastern France.

One hundred fifteen IX Bomber Command B-26s attack German Army fortifications in and around Brest.

While pursuing retreating German Army forces, 405th Fighter Group P-47 pilots destroy an estimated 200 motor vehicles and assorted other road targets in the course of six squadron-strength missions. Also, 36th Fighter Group P-47 pilots destroy more than 500 German Army vehicles in just four eight-plane undertaken missions throughout the day.

GERMANY: The Eighth Air Force main bombing attacks of the day—against targets in Germany—are recalled when the lead bombers encounter high clouds along the route over France. Just one of 973 heavy bombers drops its bombs. Three bombers are lost in operational accidents that take the lives of 30 crewmen.

ITALY: Fifteenth Air Force B-24s attack a rail bridge at Ferrara; Twelfth Air Force B-25s attack rail and road bridges north and northeast of Venice; and XII TAC fighter-bombers attack a German Army headquarters in the battle area near Florence.

During the night of September 1–2, XII

TAC A-20s attack pontoon bridges and targets of opportunity in the Po River valley.
NETHERLANDS: Twelve Eighth Air Force B-24s attack a rail bridge at Ravenstein using Azon bombs.

78th Fighter Group P-47 pilots down four Bf-110s over Gilze-Rijen Airdrome at 2030 hours.
ROMANIA: Sixteen Fifteenth Air Force B-17s complete the second Operation REUNION evacuation mission of USAAF airmen formerly held in prisoner-of-war camps around Ploesti and Bucharest.

September 2, 1944

BELGIUM: In the day's only Eighth Air Force operation, 56th Fighter Group P-47s strafe targets of opportunity in Belgium.
ENGLAND: Eighth Air Force and IX Bomber Command bombers are grounded by bad weather.
FRANCE: The IX TAC headquarters moves to Versailles.

Despite bad weather, XII TAC fighter-bombers attack rail lines and barracks in the Lyon area.

Lyon falls to the U.S. Seventh Army.
ITALY: Twelfth Air Force B-25s attack three bridges in the Po River valley; and XII TAC fighter-bombers attack gun emplacements, roads, and bridges in the Po River valley, dock facilities at Savona, and ships at sea.

A provisional XV Fighter Command is created, and BriGen Dean C. Strother is placed in command. At the same time, Strother's former command, the 306th Fighter Wing, is split into two parts. The 306th Wing retains control of the Fifteenth Air Force's four P-51 groups (31st, 52d, 325th, and 33d), and the 305th Provisional Fighter Wing is given control of the three P-38 groups (1st, 14th, and 82d).

During the night of September 2–3, XII TAC A-20s start fires in the Genoa port area.
YUGOSLAVIA: More than 380 Fifteenth Air Force B-24s attack a rail bridge at Kraljevo, a marshalling yard and bridge at Mitrovica, three marshalling yards at Nis, and a rail bridge at Supovac. Also, 27 Fifteenth Air Force P-38s bomb a road bridge at Cuprija, and 112 P-51s and 57 P-38s strafe roads and bridges in the Belgrade and Nis areas.

September 3, 1944

BELGIUM: One hundred twenty-five VIII Fighter Command P-47s strafe transportation targets.

55th Fighter Group P-51 pilots down seven FW-190s near Antwerp between 1300 and 1330 hours.
FRANCE: Three hundred ninety-three 3d Bombardment Division B-17s attack 16 German Army artillery batteries and other defensive positions in and around Brest; and 181 IX Bomber Command B-26s and A-20s attack defensive positions and bridges in the Brest area.

IX TAC fighters and fighter-bombers supporting the U.S. First Army's pursuit of German Army forces set a one-day record for the war when they destroy 919 motor vehicles, 757 horse-drawn vehicles, and 58 armored vehicles.

The Ninth Air Force's 365th Fighter Group displaces to Advance Landing Ground A-48, at Bretigny.

More than 50 "war-weary" Eighth Air Force B-24s transport supplies from bases in England to Orleans/Bricy Airdrome as part of an ongoing effort known as Operation TRUCKING.

Twelfth Air Force fighter-bombers harry German Army ground forces retreating up the Rhone River valley.
GERMANY: 325 1st Bombardment Division B-17s attack a synthetic-oil plant at Ludwigshafen.
HUNGARY: Fifteenth Air Force heavy bombers attack roads and supply lines south of Budapest.
ITALY: Fifteenth Air Force B-24s attack bridges throughout northern Italy, and Twelfth Air Force medium bombers attack bridges in the Po River valley.

During the night of September 3–4, XII

TAC A-20s attack motor vehicles around Milan and Turin.

ROMANIA: Three Fifteenth Air Force B-17s complete the third REUNION evacuation mission of USAAF airmen liberated from prisoner-of-war camps around Ploesti and Bucharest.

YUGOSLAVIA: Fifteenth Air Force heavy bombers and P-38 dive-bombers attack the ferry installation at Smederevo, heavy bombers attack numerous bridges, and P-51s strafe several airfields and numerous transportation targets.

September 4, 1944

BELGIUM: British Army ground forces liberate Brussels.

ETO: The Eighth and Ninth air forces are grounded by bad weather.

FRANCE: The Ninth Air Force's 50th Fighter Group displaces to Advance Landing Ground A-47, at Paris/Orly Airport; and the Ninth Air Force's 406th Fighter Group displaces to Advance Landing Ground A-35, at Le Mans.

The 363d Fighter Group is withdrawn from combat in order to be remanned, reequipped, and redesignated the 363d Tactical Reconnaissance Group.

ITALY: Fifteenth Air Force B-24s attack bridges and marshalling yards throughout northern Italy, and B-17s attack the port and submarines based at Genoa; Twelfth Air Force B-25s and B-26s attack bridges and a tunnel in the Po River valley; and XII TAC fighter-bombers attack numerous targets along and behind the German Army's Gothic Line.

During the night of September 4–5, XII TAC A-20s attack targets of opportunity around Genoa and Milan.

September 5, 1944

FRANCE: One hundred forty-three 3d Bombardment Division B-17s and 310 IX Bomber Command B-26s and A-20s attack targets in and around Brest.

Approximately 90 Eighth Air Force B-24s transport fuel to France.

GERMANY: Two hundred seventy-seven 1st Bombardment Division B-17s attack an oil refinery at Ludwigshafen; 183 2d Bombardment Division B-24s attack a marshalling yard at Karlsruhe; and 203 3d Bombardment Division B-17s attack an aircraft-engine factory at Stuttgart. Six heavy bombers are lost.

Two hundred seventeen VIII Fighter Command fighters strafe transportation targets in western Germany, and 67 VIII Fighter Command fighter-bombers attack targets around Hanau and Giessen.

VIII Fighter Command pilots down 25 GAF aircraft over Germany between 1110 and 1915 hours, and two GAF bombers are downed over the Netherlands. A Swiss Air Force Bf-109 is mistakenly shot down near the Swiss-German frontier. 1stLt William H. Allen and 1stLt William H. Lewis, P-51 pilots with the 55th Fighter Group's 343d Fighter Squadron, both achieve "ace-in-a-day" status when they each down five GAF trainers over Goppingen Airdrome at 1120 hours.

HUNGARY: To help impede the withdrawal of German Army forces from the Balkans, Fifteenth Air Force heavy bombers attack rail bridges at Budapest, Szob, and Szolnok.

ITALY: Fifteenth Air Force heavy bombers attack a rail bridge at Ferrara; Twelfth Air Force medium bombers attack bridges in the Po River valley; XII TAC A-20s attack ammunition storage areas; and XII TAC fighter-bombers attack rail lines south of the Po River.

During the night of September 5–6, XII TAC A-20s attack targets of opportunity around Milan and Savona.

September 6, 1944

FRANCE: Of 706 IX Bomber Command B-26s and A-20s dispatched, 545 attack a bridge and strongpoints in the Brest area; IX Bomber Command bombers also attack German Army batteries and defenses elsewhere in France; and Ninth Air Force fighter-bombers attack gun emplacements around Brest, an ammunition dump, and other targets in other battle areas.

Making their type's world combat debut during the Brest attack are Douglas A-26 Invader light bombers being combat-tested by special crews attached to the 386th Medium Bombardment Group's 553d Medium Bombardment Squadron. Special features of the A-26 are that it has the payload capacity of a medium bomber combined with the agility of a light bomber. The A-26 is also longer ranged than the latest A-20 model in service.

Seventy Eighth Air Force B-24s transport fuel to France.

The Ninth Air Force's 474th Fighter Group displaces to Advance Landing Ground A-72, at Peronne.

GERMANY: VIII Fighter Command fighters conduct sweeps in the Aachen and Koblenz areas.

Maj Quince L. Brown, a 12.333-victory P-47 ace and the commanding officer of the 78th Fighter Group's 84th Fighter Squadron, is murdered by an SS officer after he is shot down by flak and captured near Schleiden.

HUNGARY: Fifteenth Air Force heavy bombers attack two bridges over the Sebes Koros River, and a marshalling yard.

NETHERLANDS: VIII Fighter Command fighters conduct a sweep in the Rotterdam area.

ROMANIA: Fifteenth Air Force heavy bombers attack two marshalling yards at Oradea.

Two Fifteenth Air Force B-17s undertake the fourth Operation REUNION evacuation mission of USAAF airmen liberated from prisoner-of-war camps around Ploesti and Bucharest.

YUGOSLAVIA: Fifteenth Air Force B-24s attack a marshalling yard at Novi Sad, a marshalling yard and German Army troop and tank concentrations at Leskovac, and a bridge at Budapest.

September 7, 1944

ENGLAND: The entire Eighth Air Force and IX Bomber Command bombers are grounded by bad weather.

FRANCE: Ninth Air Force fighters are able to provide limited support for U.S. Army ground forces in France and Belgium. At about 1400 hours, while supporting elements of the U.S. Seventh Army in southern France, 36 P-47 pilots of the Ninth Air Force's 406th Fighter Group destroy an estimated 300 German Army vehicles along a 15-mile section of road. After rearming, the same P-47 pilots return to the scene and destroy approximately 200 additional vehicles.

MTO: The Twelfth and Fifteenth air forces are grounded by bad weather.

September 8, 1944

ENGLAND: IX Bomber Command bombers are grounded by bad weather, but fighters are able to support U.S. Army ground forces in France and Belgium.

ETO: The first German V-2 rocket launched operationally in the war strikes a Paris suburb, and the second V-2 strikes London within the hour.

FRANCE: More than 100 Eighth Air Force B-24s transport fuel to France.

The Ninth Air Force's 366th Fighter Group displaces to Advance Landing Ground A-70, at Laon/Couvron Airdrome; and the Ninth Air Force's 367th Fighter Group displaces to Advance Landing Ground A-71, at Clastres.

Twelfth Air Force fighters attack ten trains in the Belfort area and a horse-drawn convoy near Strasbourg.

XII TAC A-20s transport supplies to Lyon.

GERMANY: Three hundred forty-eight 1st Bombardment Division B-17s attack an oil-industry target at Ludwigshafen; 247 2d Bombardment Division B-24s attack a marshalling yard at Karlsruhe; 167 3d Bombardment Division B-17s attack an aircraft-industry target at Gustavsburg; and 166 3d Bombardment Division B-17s attack the oil depot at Kassel. Ten heavy bombers are lost.

One hundred sixty VIII Fighter Command fighter-bombers attack transportation targets east of the Rhine River, and 94 VIII Fighter Command fighters strafe targets of opportunity in western Germany.

ITALY: XII TAC fighter-bombers attack barges and two pontoon bridges along the Po River.

MTO: Twelfth Air Force medium bombers are grounded by bad weather.

ROMANIA: MATAF C-47s complete the fifth Operation REUNION evacuation mission of USAAF airmen liberated from prisoner-of-war camps around Bucharest.

YUGOSLAVIA: Fifteenth Air Force B-17s and B-24s attack bridges at Belgrade and Brod, and marshalling yards at Nis and Sarajevo. Also, 325th Fighter Group P-51s strafe Ecka Airdrome, destroying 58 GAF aircraft of all types on the ground; and 332d Fighter Group P-51s strafe the airdrome at Handza, destroying all of the 18 GAF aircraft parked there.

September 9, 1944

BELGIUM: VIII Fighter Command fighter-bombers attack targets of opportunity throughout Belgium.

IX Bomber Command bombers drop leaflets over large areas of Occupied Belgium.

One FW-190 is downed near Liege at 1905 hours by a IX TAC fighter pilot.

FRANCE: Sixty-eight 3d Bombardment Group B-17s drop supply containers to French Resistance fighters in southern France, near Besancon.

IX Bomber Command bombers drop leaflets over the remaining areas of Occupied France, and Ninth Air Force fighters attack bridges at Custines and Pompey.

IX Troop Carrier Command transports complete more than 700 supply and evacuation sorties.

GERMANY: Three hundred eighty-seven 1st Bombardment Division B-17s attack a marshalling yard at Mannheim; 265 2d Bombardment Division B-24s attack a marshalling yard at Mainz; 251 3d Bombard-

ment Division B-17s attack a munitions plant at Dusseldorf; and 69 heavy bombers attack various targets of opportunity.

Hundreds of VIII Fighter Command escort fighters attack ground targets throughout western Germany following their release from bomber-escort duties. Eight GAF aircraft are downed over Germany by VIII Fighter Command pilots between 1725 and 1800 hours.

ITALY: Twelfth Air Force B-25s attack supply points and troop concentrations near Bologna, and B-26s attack rail bridges spanning the Po River.

NETHERLANDS: VIII Fighter Command fighter-bombers attack shipping and shore targets in the Dutch islands. One Do-217 is downed by a 353d Fighter Group P-47 pilot at 1815 hours.

September 10, 1944

AUSTRIA: Three hundred forty-four Fifteenth Air Force B-17s and B-24s attack Horsching Airdrome, five ordnance depots, two oil refineries, and industrial areas around Vienna.

ETO: During the night of September 10–11, specially equipped, 474th Fighter Group P-38s mount night-intruder missions against German Army supply columns.

FRANCE: Approximately 340 IX Bomber Command B-26s and A-20s attack a rail bridge at Custines, a road bridge spanning the Moselle River, and several ammunition dumps and strongpoints.

The XIX TAC helps stem a violent German counterattack against U.S. Third Army units holding bridgeheads across the Moselle River near Arry.

IX Troop Carrier Command transports complete more than 800 supply and evacuation sorties.

The Ninth Air Force advance headquarters lays out a program for the interdiction of rail lines on both sides of the Rhine River through early October by IX and XIX TAC fighter-bomber groups.

Twelfth Air Force fighter-bombers attack rail lines around Belfort and Dijon.

Twenty-four Fifteenth Air Force B-24s transport supplies to Lyon.

GERMANY: A total of 1,063 Eighth Air Force B-17s attack marshalling yards at Heilbronn and Ulm, a tank factory at Nurnberg, an aircraft components factory at Furth, Giebelstadt Airdrome, an engine factory, a jet-engine factory, a motor-transport factory, and several targets of opportunity. Tested in combat for the first time on this mission is the GB-4 radio- and visually controlled guided bomb. Seven heavy bombers are lost.

One hundred twenty-one VIII Fighter Command P-47s strafe targets around Cologne, Frankfurt am Main, and Kassel.

Eighth and Ninth air force fighter pilots down eight GAF aircraft over Germany between 1115 and 1445 hours. 1stLt Ted E. Lines, a P-51 pilot with the 4th Fighter Group's 335th Fighter Squadron, achieves ace status with a total of seven confirmed victories when he downs three Bf-109s and a Ju-88 near Kaiserlautern at 1115 hours; and 1stLt Carl G. Bickel, a P-51 pilot with the 354th Fighter Group's 353d Fighter Squadron, achieves ace status when he downs an He-111 near Saarbrucken at 1445 hours.

ITALY: Eighty-eight Fifteenth Air Force B-24s attack the harbor at Trieste; Twelfth Air Force B-25s and B-26s attack bridges in the Po River valley and four supply and ammunition dumps; and XII TAC fighter-bombers support the Allied ground assault on the Gothic Line with attacks on lines of communication and various dumps.

LUXEMBOURG: Luxembourg City is liberated by elements of the U.S. First Army.

September 11, 1944

BELGIUM: The IX TAC headquarters displaces forward to Jamioulx from Versailles, France.

CANADA: President Franklin D. Roosevelt and Prime Minister Sir Winston S. Churchill meet in Quebec to discuss, among other matters, the final stages of the war in Europe.

FRANCE: A total of 358 IX Bomber Command B-26s and A-20s attack strongpoints and gun emplacements in and around Metz.

XIX TAC fighter-bombers continue to assist the U.S. Third Army in deflecting a German counterattack along the Moselle River.

The U.S. Seventh Army captures Dijon and links up with the U.S. Third Army, thereby forming a continuous Allied front line across France and Belgium, from the Mediterranean to the North Sea and from the English Channel to the Swiss frontier.

The Ninth Air Force's 368th Fighter Group displaces to Advance Landing Ground A-69, at Laon/Athies Airdrome; the Ninth Air Force's 36th Fighter Group displaces to Advance Landing Ground A-73, at Roye/Amy Airdrome; and the 9th Bombardment Division's 397th Medium Bombardment Group displaces to Advance Landing Ground A-41, at Dreux/Vermouillet Airdrome.

Fifty-four Fifteenth Air Force B-24s transport supplies to U.S. Army ground forces in France.

GERMANY: 1,016 Eighth Air Force heavy bombers, escorted by a total of 411 VIII Fighter Command fighters, attack synthetic-oil plants at eight locations, plus an ordnance depot at Magdeburg, an engineering plant at Hannover, and numerous targets of opportunity. More than 500 GAF fighters challenge the attacks, with the result that 40 heavy bombers and 17 USAAF fighters are downed in the first major aerial clash since May 28.

In the best one-day tally of the war so far, USAAF fighter pilots down 124 GAF aircraft—all fighters—over Germany between 1040 and 1530 hours. 1stLt Cyril W. Jones, Jr., a P-51 pilot with the 359th Fighter Group's 370th Fighter Squadron, achieves ace status when he downs four Bf-109s near Gotha between 1145 and 1215 hours; LtCol John L. McGinn, the commanding officer of the 55th Fighter Group's 338th Fighter Squadron, in P-51s, achieves ace status when he downs a Bf-109 near

Meiningen at 1150 hours (three of McGinn's earlier victories were scored in the South Pacific); Capt Benjamin H. King, a P-51 pilot with the 359th Fighter Group's 368th Fighter Squadron, achieves ace status when he downs two FW-190s and a Bf-109 near Eisleben at 1205 hours (King's three earlier victories were scored in the South Pacific); and 1stLt Francis R. Gerard, a P-51 pilot with the 339th Fighter Group's 503d Fighter Squadron, achieves ace status when he downs three Bf-109s and an FW-190 near Annaberg at about 1215 hours.

On the first leg of the third Eighth Air Force FRANTIC shuttle-bombing mission, 75 B-17s of the 96th and 452d Heavy Bombardment groups and 64 20th Fighter Group P-51s (included in the above statistics) attack a synthetic-oil plant at Chemnitz with 146 tons of bombs and land at bases in the Soviet Union. One P-51 is lost.

ITALY: The Fifteenth Air Force is grounded by bad weather; Twelfth Air Force B-25s attack supply stores and two rail bridges; Twelfth Air Force B-26s attack German Army positions along the Gothic Line; and XII TAC fighter-bombers attack bridges, gun emplacements, rail lines, railway guns, supply stores, and other targets in and around the battle area.

September 12, 1944

ETO: Ninth Air Force fighters and fighter-bombers support U.S. Army ground forces in the Franco-Belgian-German border areas, and IX Troop Carrier Command transports mount more than 400 supply and evacuation sorties.

IX TAC fighter pilots down six Bf-109s in the border area at 1430 hours.

During the night of September 12–13, specially equipped, bomb-armed 474th Fighter Group P-38s fly night-intruder missions against German Army supply columns.

FRANCE: IX Bomber Command bombers attack German Army fortifications at Nancy.

Twelfth Air Force fighter-bombers

attack rail lines at Belfort and on the French side of the Swiss frontier near Basel.

More than 50 Fifteenth Air Force B-24s transport supplies to U.S. Army ground forces in southern France.

GERMANY: Eight hundred thirteen Eighth Air Force heavy bombers, escorted by 579 VIII Fighter Command fighters, attack an aircraft-engine factory, two oil refineries, four synthetic-oil plants, an oil depot, and various targets of opportunity. Opposition by an estimated 400 to 450 GAF fighters results in the loss of 35 heavy bombers and 12 USAAF fighters. 1stLt Cyril W. Jones, Jr., a P-51 pilot with the 359th Fighter Group's 370th Fighter Squadron, who achieved ace status just one day earlier, is lost without a trace.

Eighth and Ninth air force fighter pilots down 96 GAF fighters over Germany between 1050 and 1615 hours. 2dLt William T. Kemp, a P-51 pilot with the 361st Fighter Group's 375th Fighter Squadron, achieves ace status when he downs three Bf-109s near Magdeburg at 1115 hours; 1stLt Henry J. Miklajcyk, a P-51 pilot with the 352d Fighter Group's 486th Fighter Squadron, achieves ace status when he downs an FW-190 and shares in the downing of another FW-190 over Kustrin (Poland) at 1130 hours; and 2dLt Robert Reynolds, a P-51 pilot with the 354th Fighter Group's 353d Fighter Squadron, achieves ace status with a total of seven confirmed victories when he downs three FW-190s near Frankfurt between 1300 and 1315 hours. However, Reynolds is himself shot down in air-to-air combat and taken prisoner.

IX Bomber Command bombers attack a German armored division as it entrains at Sankt Wendel, and fortifications along the West Wall (Siegfried Line).

Fifteenth Air Force B-24s attack an aircraft-engine factory and a jet-engine factory near Munich, and B-17s and B-24s attack the airdrome at Lechfeld.

In the Twelfth Air Force's first mission against a target on German soil, XII TAC fighter-bombers attack the rail line at Freiburg.

ITALY: Twelfth Air Force B-25s attack bridges spanning the Po River; and Twelfth Air Force B-25s, B-26s, and fighter-bombers attack strongpoints, gun emplacements, troop concentrations, flak batteries, and other tactical targets as the German Army falls back from the embattled Gothic Line.

MTO: BriGen Benjamin W. Chidlaw replaces BriGen Edward M. Morris as head of the XII Fighter Command.

September 13, 1944

CZECHOSLOVAKIA: Fifteenth Air Force heavy bombers attack a marshalling yard at Vrutky.

FRANCE: IX Bomber Command B-26s dispense leaflets over coastal areas of northern France and Belgium; XIX TAC fighter-bombers assist a French Army armored division in destroying 60 German tanks near Vittel; and other Ninth Air Force fighters and fighter-bombers mount numerous missions in direct support of U.S. Army ground forces around Brest, Metz, and Nancy.

The XIX TAC headquarters displaces forward with the U.S. Third Army headquarters to Chalons-sur-Marne; the Ninth Air Force's 404th Fighter Group displaces to Advance Landing Ground A-68, at Juvincourt; and the Ninth Air Force's 36th Fighter Group displaces to Advance Landing Ground A-64, at St.-Dizier/Robinson Airdrome.

In an effort to delay German Army efforts to establish a stronghold in the Rhone River valley near Belfort, P-47 fighter-bombers of the Twelfth Air Force's 27th Fighter Group, based in southern France, mount 58 sorties in 13 separate missions, in the course of which 107 vehicles, 12 locomotives, 30 horse-drawn artillery pieces, and several railroad guns are destroyed.

GERMANY: Of 1,026 Eighth Air Force heavy bombers dispatched against oil-industry targets in southern Germany, 790 complete attacks against five synthetic-oil plants and oil refineries, an airdrome, two munitions dumps, and numerous targets of opportunity. Several hundred escort fighters strafe ground targets of opportunity following release from escort duties. Fifteen heavy bombers and eight escort fighters are lost. Among the lost airmen is LtCol Cecil L. Wells, the 358th Fighter Group commander, who is killed.

VIII Fighter Command escort pilots down 33 Bf-109s over Germany between 1145 and 1245 hours.

As the XIX TAC opens its new rail-interdiction campaign, fighter-bombers mount numerous armed-reconnaissance missions in the Aachen, Cologne, Koblenz, Linz/Rhine, and Wahn areas.

Fifteenth Air Force B-24s attack an oil refinery at Odertal, and B-17s attack an oil refinery at Blechhammer.

HUNGARY: Seventy-three Eighth Air Force FRANTIC bombers and 63 P-51 escorts returning from the September 11 mission to the Soviet Union attack a steel plant at Diosgyoer with 263 tons of bombs on the way to England via Italy.

It is decided to discontinue Operation FRANTIC because the air bases allotted to the USAAF in the Soviet Union are so far behind the front lines *and* because of operational problems arising out of the Soviet government's blatant mistrust of the American airmen.

ITALY: Fifteenth Air Force B-24s attack a viaduct and several bridges; Twelfth Air Force B-25s cut the Milan-Verona rail line by destroying a bridge; B-25s and B-26s attack defensive positions and gun emplacements north of Florence; and XII TAC fighter-bombers attack bridges, rail lines, locomotives, and rolling stock throughout northern Italy.

POLAND: Fifteenth Air Force B-24s attack a rubber factory and oil refinery at Oswiecim (Auschwitz) and industrial targets at Crakow.

September 14, 1944

ENGLAND: The XXIX Tactical Air Com-

mand is established on a provisional basis under the command of BriGen Richard E. Nugent to oversee support for the new U.S. Ninth Army. The new command is placed under the temporary control of the IX TAC.
FRANCE: One hundred forty-four IX Bomber Command B-26s and A-20s attack fortifications and gun emplacements around Brest. This is the final IX Bomber Command strike against the Brest fortress.

The Ninth Air Force's 358th Fighter Group displaces to Advance Landing Ground A-67, at Vitry-le-François.

Most Twelfth Air Force fighter-bomber missions in southern France are canceled in the face of bad weather.
ITALY: Twelfth Air Force B-25s and B-26s attack numerous tactical targets along the remaining portions of the Gothic Line; and XII TAC fighter-bombers attack lines of communication in the Po River valley.

September 15, 1944

ENGLAND: The VIII Fighter Command's three fighter-wing headquarters and their fifteen escort-fighter groups are each transferred to the direct operational control of one of the three bombardment divisions: the 65th Fighter Wing to the 2d Bombardment Division, the 66th Fighter Wing to the 3d Bombardment Division, and the 67th Fighter Wing to the 1st Bombardment Division.
ETO: IX Bomber Command bombers are grounded by bad weather.
FRANCE: Headquarters, Ninth Air Force, displaces from Sunninghall Park, England, to Chantilly, France, to better control the operations of its tactical air commands and subunits.

The XII TAC passes to the direct operational control of the Ninth Air Force.

The Ninth Air Force's 48th Fighter Group displaces to Advance Landing Ground A-74, at Cambrai/Niergnies Airdrome; the Ninth Air Force's 50th Fighter Group displaces to Advance Landing Ground A-69, at Laon/Athies Airdrome; and the Ninth Air Force's 365th Fighter

Group displaces to Advance Landing Ground A-68, at Juvincourt.
GREECE: Fifteenth Air Force B-24s attack marshalling yards at Athens. Also, in an effort to halt or stall the evacuation of German Army troops and materiel by air, B-24s attack the Athens/Eleusis and Athens/Tatoi airdromes, and B-17s attack Athens/Kalamaki Airdrome. B-17s also attack the submarine base at Salamis.
MTO: All Twelfth Air Force medium bombers and most fighter-bombers are grounded by bad weather.

Twenty-four Fifteenth Air Force B-24s transport USAAF aircrewmen formerly imprisoned in Bulgaria to Bari, Italy, from their repatriation point in Cairo, Egypt.

The 87th Fighter Wing headquarters, 47th Light Bombardment Group (A-20s), 57th Fighter Group, and 86th Fighter Group are transferred from the XII TAC to the XII Fighter Command. Hereafter (until further changes are made), the XII TAC will support the U.S. Seventh Army in France, and the XII Fighter Command will support the U.S. Fifth Army in Italy.

September 16, 1944

FRANCE: XIX TAC fighters and fighter-bombers help the U.S. Third Army repel several German Army counterattacks in northeastern France.

Headquarters, Ninth Air Force, redesignates the IX Bomber Command as the 9th Bombardment Division (retroactively to August 30).

Citing incessant air attacks as the prime cause for his decision, a German Army general commanding 20,000 troops moving from southern to northern France formally surrenders his force to the new U.S. Ninth Army. Among the American general officers accepting the surrender is MajGen Otto P. Weyland, whose XIX TAC was instrumental in the surrender decision.
GERMANY: Two hundred ninety-five VIII Fighter Command P-47 and P-51 fighter-bombers attack Ahlhorn Airdrome and targets around Kaiserlautern and Mannheim.

IX TAC fighter pilots down 12 FW-190s over Aachen between 1630 and 1810 hours.

ITALY: The Fifteenth Air Force is grounded by bad weather; Twelfth Air Force B-25s and B-26s attack defensive positions and supply dumps around Bologna and Rimini; and XII Fighter Command fighter-bombers support the U.S. Fifth Army's continuing attacks on mountainous portions of the Gothic Line in which German Army forces are still holding out.

NETHERLANDS: One hundred fifty 9th Bombardment Division B-26s and A-20s attack a road and rail embankment at Arnemuiden and a dike at Bath.

September 17, 1944

CZECHOSLOVAKIA: Two Fifteenth Air Force B-17s transport wounded USAAF airmen from Czechoslovakia to Italy.

ENGLAND: 9th Bombardment Division bombers are grounded by bad weather.

Seventy-two Eighth Air Force B-17s and 59 P-51s return to England from Italy on the last leg of the third Eighth Air Force FRANTIC mission. No targets are attacked along the way.

Full-scale Eighth Air Force special-operations missions (agent and supply drops to partisan units) have been severely curtailed due to the recent liberation of most of the territory in northwestern Europe formerly under German domination. Therefore, most 492d Heavy Bombardment Group special-operations B-24s are committed to Operation TRUCKING. However, the group's 856th Heavy Bombardment Group is detached and placed under direct Eighth Air Force control to undertake agent and supply drops over Denmark, the Netherlands, and Norway.

ETO: During the night of September 17–18, specially equipped, bomb-armed 474th Fighter Group P-38s fly night-intruder missions against German Army supply columns.

FRANCE: XIX TAC fighter-bombers attack targets in the Brest area.

One hundred one Eighth Air Force B-24s transport fuel supplies to France.

The Ninth Air Force's 354th Fighter Group displaces to Advance Landing Ground A-66, at Orconte.

GERMANY: VIII Fighter Command pilots down seven GAF fighters over Germany at 1345 hours. 1stLt Ted E. Lines, a P-51 ace with the 4th Fighter Group's 335th Fighter Squadron, brings his final personal tally to ten confirmed victories when he downs three FW-190s near Bocholt at 1345 hours.

HUNGARY: More than 440 Fifteenth Air Force B-17s and B-24s attack four marshalling yards and two oil refineries at Budapest.

ITALY: Twelfth Air Force B-25s attack German Army troop concentrations near Rimini, in the British Eighth Army battle area; Twelfth Air Force B-25s and fighter-bombers attack rail bridges in the Po River valley; and XII Fighter Command fighter-bombers attack all manner of road and rail transportation targets.

NETHERLANDS: Operation MARKET-GARDEN begins with parachute and glider landings (MARKET) by one British and two American airborne divisions of the First Allied Airborne Army. IX Troop Carrier Command transports and tow planes are responsible for conveying many of the airborne troops to the targets.

In support of Operation MARKET, 821 Eighth Air Force B-17s and 503 VIII Fighter Command fighters and fighter-bombers attack flak batteries, airfields, and other military targets along the troop-carrier routes. Sixteen USAAF fighters are lost.

September 18, 1944

ENGLAND: 9th Bombardment Division bombers are grounded by bad weather.

ETO: Due to bad weather, fewer than 100 fighter sorties are mounted over northwestern Europe by the Ninth Air Force tactical air commands.

FRANCE: The 9th Bombardment Division headquarters displaces from England to Chartres; the Ninth Air Force's 36th Fighter

Group displaces to Advance Landing Ground A-65, at Perthes; and the 9th Bombardment Division's 387th Medium Bombardment Group displaces to Advance Landing Ground A-39, at Chateaudun.

GERMANY: Capt Michael J. Quirk, an 11-victory P-47 ace with the 56th Fighter Group's 62d Fighter Squadron, is shot down by flak and captured near Wurzburg/Seligenstadt Airdrome.

VIII Fighter Command and IX TAC pilots down 11 GAF aircraft over Germany between 1000 and 1715 hours. Four XI TAC P-47s are lost.

HUNGARY: Fifteenth Air Force heavy bombers attack a marshalling yard at Szeged, and rail bridges at Budapest and Szob; and Fifteenth Air Force fighters conduct an unchallenged patrol over the Budapest area.

ITALY: Despite bad weather, Twelfth Air Force B-25s attack gun emplacements and troop concentrations in the British Eighth Army zone, and B-26s and XII Fighter Command P-47s attack bridges and transportation targets in the Po River valley.

MTO: Fifteenth Air Force B-17s and B-24s attack bridges and marshalling yards throughout Hungary and Yugoslavia.

NETHERLANDS: The second airborne echelon (paratroop and glider-borne forces) of Operation MARKET-GARDEN is dropped or towed from England by IX Troop Carrier Command transports.

Two hundred forty-eight B-24s of the 2d Bombardment Division's 14th and 20th Combat Bombardment wings each drop 20 bundles of supplies from very low altitude to airborne troops already on the ground. Seven B-24s are lost to intense flak concentrations.

Escort for transports and support for the American and British airborne forces is provided by 12 VIII Fighter Command fighter groups; two fighter groups strafe rail and highway traffic; and 50 fighters bomb flak emplacements.

While aggressively supporting the reinforcement and resupply operations, the 56th Fighter Group loses 16 P-47s to enemy fire or operational accidents, the highest single-day loss sustained by any Eighth Air Force fighter group in the war. In all, 22 VIII Fighter Command fighters are lost while supporting the airborne operation.

357th Fighter Group P-51 pilots down 25 GAF fighters over the MARKET-GARDEN battle area between 1500 and 1520 hours, and other VIII Fighter Command pilots down three GAF aircraft over the Netherlands during the day. 1stLt Gerald E. Tyler, a P-51 pilot with the 357th Fighter Group's 364th Fighter Squadron, achieves ace status when he downs two Bf-109s and an FW-190 near Maastricht at 1510 hours.

POLAND: In response to desperate appeals from Polish Resistance fighters whose uprising in Warsaw is *not* being supported by nearby Red Army forces, 107 Eighth Air Force B-24s of the 13th Combat Bombardment Wing join an RAF resupply effort already under way over the besieged city. Although Operation FRANTIC has been terminated, the heavy bombers and their escorts—64 355th Fighter Group P-51s—fly on to bases in the Soviet Union. Future USAAF missions to Poland are canceled when Soviet Premier Josef Stalin refuses future landing rights. Two B-17s are lost.

355th Fighter Group P-51 escort pilots down three Bf-109s near Warsaw at about 1215 hours.

YUGOSLAVIA: Fifteenth Air Force heavy bombers attack a marshalling yard at Subotica and rail bridges at Belgrade and Novi Sad.

September 19, 1944

FRANCE: The Ninth Air Force's 362d Fighter Group displaces to Advance Landing Ground A-79, at Prosnes; the Ninth Air Force's 373d Fighter Group displaces to Advance Landing Ground A-62, at Reims; and the 9th Bombardment Division's 391st Medium Bombardment Group displaces to Advance Landing Ground A-73, at Roye/Amy Airdrome.

GERMANY: Six hundred seventy-nine Eighth Air Force B-17s, escorted by 240 VIII Fighter Command fighters, attack bridges, marshalling yards, rail lines, and ordnance depots throughout western Germany. Seven B-17s and one escort fighter are lost.

VIII Fighter Command pilots down ten GAF fighters over Germany between 1440 and 1730 hours. 1stLt Thomas D. Schank, a P-51 pilot with the 55th Fighter Group's 338th Fighter Squadron, achieves ace status when he downs a Bf-109 near Cologne at 1440 hours.

9th Bombardment Division bombers attack marshalling yards in and around Duren to prevent German Army reinforcements from reaching Aachen.

IX TAC fighter-bombers assist U.S. Army ground forces in beating back a German Army counterattack at Wallendorf.

HUNGARY: More than 90 Eighth Air Force Frantic B-17s attack the marshalling yard at Szolnok on their return leg to England via Italy.

ITALY: Twelfth Air Force fighter-bombers attack bridges in the Bologna area and defensive positions along the Gothic Line.

MTO: Twelfth Air Force medium bombers are grounded by bad weather.

NETHERLANDS: Deteriorating weather forces a sharp curtailment of air support and resupply missions for airborne forces taking part in Operation Market-Garden.

One hundred seventy-two VIII Fighter Command P-51s patrol over the Market battle area and support Allied airborne troops on the ground. Six P-51s are lost with their pilots.

VIII Fighter Command pilots down 22 of more than 100 GAF fighters encountered over the Market-Garden battle area between 1445 and 1728 hours. 1stLt Arval J. Roberson, a P-51 pilot with the 357th Fighter Group's 362d Fighter Squadron, achieves ace status when he downs two Bf-109s near Ijsselstein at 1705 hours; and Maj Edwin W. Hiro, the commanding officer of the 357th Fighter Group, achieves ace status when he downs a Bf-109 near Arnhem at 1720 hours. Unfortunately, Hiro is killed a short time later when his fighter is shot down over Vreden.

During the night, a GAF bombing raid against Eindhoven misses American troops near the city, but Dutch civilians and British Army troops in the city suffer many casualties.

YUGOSLAVIA: Ninety-six Fifteenth Air Force B-24s attack rail bridges at Kraljevo and Mitrovica.

September 20, 1944

CZECHOSLOVAKIA: Fifteenth Air Force B-24s attack oil-industry targets at Bratislava and Malacky Airdrome.

FRANCE: The Ninth Air Force advance headquarters moves with the U.S. 12th Army Group headquarters to Verdun.

GERMANY: To delay German Army reinforcements on their way to Aachen, approximately 40 9th Bombardment Division B-26s attack defensive positions at Herbach and a marshalling yard at Trier.

HUNGARY: Fifteenth Air Force B-17s and B-24s attack rail bridges at Budapest, a marshalling yard and aircraft-industry targets at Gyor, marshalling yards at Hatvan, and a rail bridge Szob.

MTO: The 27th and 79th Fighter groups are reassigned from the XII TAC to the XII Fighter Command (i.e., from the Ninth Air Force to the Twelfth Air Force).

Twelfth Air Force medium bombers and most fighters and fighter-bombers are grounded by bad weather.

NETHERLANDS: Six hundred forty-four VIII Fighter Command patrol sorties are mounted over the Market-Garden battle area. GAF light flak batteries down five fighters.

September 21, 1944

FRANCE: More than 80 Eighth Air Force B-24s transport fuel to France.

The Ninth Air Force's 406th Fighter Group displaces to Advance Landing Ground A-80, at Mourmelon-le-Grand; and the 9th Bombardment Division's 323d Medium Bombardment Group displaces to Advance Landing Ground A-40, at Chartres.

GERMANY: One hundred forty-one 1st Bombardment Division B-17s attack a marshalling yard at Mainz; 144 2d Bombardment Division B-24s attack a marshalling yard at Koblenz; and 147 3d Bombardment Division B-17s attack an oil-industry target at Ludwigshafen. Two B-24s are lost.

Seventy-nine 9th Bombardment Division B-26s and A-20s attack marshalling yards at three locations.

IX TAC fighter pilots cover the withdrawal of the U.S. V Corps from around Wallendorf and down ten GAF fighters over Germany between 1630 and 1645 hours.

HUNGARY: Fifteenth Air Force heavy bombers attack marshalling yards at two locations and bridges at three locations.

MTO: The entire Twelfth Air Force is grounded by bad weather.

NETHERLANDS: Ninety VIII Fighter Command fighters patrol over the MARKET-GARDEN battle area. Three fighters are lost.

VIII Fighter Command pilots down 19 GAF fighters over the MARKET-GARDEN battle area between 1500 and 1630 hours. Maj Boleslaw Gladych, a P-47 ace with the 56th Fighter Group's 61st Fighter Squadron, brings his final personal tally to 18.5 confirmed victories when he downs two FW-190s near Arnhem at 1515 hours. (Gladych, a Polish national and a former Polish Air Force pilot, scored his first 8.5 victories while he was flying Spitfires with the RAF's 303 "Polish" Squadron.)

YUGOSLAVIA: Fifteen Air Force heavy bombers attack a marshalling yard at Brod and a rail bridge at Novi Sad. Also, 42 Fifteenth Air Force P-38s dive-bomb a marshalling yard at Osijek.

Two C-47s evacuate downed Fifteenth Air Force airmen from Yugoslavia to bases in Italy.

September 22, 1944

ENGLAND: Eighty-four Eighth Air Force

FRANTIC B-27s and 51 P-51s return from Italy without attacking any targets along the way.

FRANCE: More than 100 Eighth Air Force B-24s transport fuel to France, as do 68 Fifteenth Air Force B-24s.

The XIX TAC headquarters displaces forward with the U.S. Third Army headquarters from Chalons-sur-Marne to Etain.

GERMANY: Six hundred eighteen Eighth Air Force B-17s and B-24s, escorted by 268 VIII Fighter Command P-51s, attack a motor-vehicle factory and an armored-vehicle plant at Kassel. Three heavy bombers and one P-51 are lost.

Ninth Air Force fighters and fighter-bombers attack ordnance depots, supply points, rail lines, strongpoints, and numerous targets of opportunity around Aachen, Bonn, Cologne, Dusseldorf, Koblenz, Mannheim, Strasbourg (France), and Trier.

Fifteenth Air Force B-24s attack Munich/Riem Airdrome, and B-17s attack aircraft-engine factories.

GREECE: Seventy-six Fifteenth Air Force B-17s attack a marshalling yard at Larissa.

ITALY: Twelfth Air Force medium bombers attack roads and rail bridges north of the battle area, and fighter-bombers support the U.S. Fifth Army and attack road, rail, and other transportation targets.

NETHERLANDS: Seventy-seven VIII Fighter Command P-47s patrol over the MARKET-GARDEN battle area. One P-47 is lost.

September 23, 1944

AUSTRIA: Fifteenth Air Force B-17s attack a marshalling yard at Wels.

CZECHOSLOVAKIA: Fifteenth Air Force B-17s attack a synthetic-oil plant at Brux.

ENGLAND: All Eighth Air Force heavy bombers are grounded by bad weather.

ETO: 9th Bombardment Division B-26s and A-20s dispatched against targets in Germany are recalled because of bad weather.

FRANCE: More than 150 Eighth Air Force B-24s transport fuel to France.

The Ninth Air Force's 36th Fighter Group displaces to Advance Landing Ground A-69, at Laon/Athies Airdrome.
GREECE: British Army troops land to begin liberating the country in the wake of withdrawing German forces.
ITALY: A total of 229 Fifteenth Air Force B-24s attack numerous rail bridges and viaducts throughout northern Italy.

Most Twelfth Air Force medium bombers are grounded or recalled on account of bad weather, but 24 B-25s of the Twelfth Air Force's 340th Medium Bombardment Group deliver a low-level attack against La Spezia harbor through intense antiaircraft fire and sink the Italian light cruiser *Taranto* before the ship can be scuttled so as to block the entrance to the strategically important harbor. Bombing is so accurate that the ship capsizes before aircraft in the final flight elements can release their bombs.

Twelfth Air Force fighter-bombers directly support the U.S. Fifth Army as it battles through the Gothic Line.
NETHERLANDS: IX Troop Carrier Command transports each release two gliders carrying reinforcements to the MARKET-GARDEN battle zone. Escort and support is provided by 519 VIII Fighter Command fighters and 40 IX Fighter Command P-38s. Fourteen VIII Fighter Command fighters are lost with their pilots. Capt Clarence O. Johnson, a seven-victory 352d Fighter Group P-38 and P-51 ace, is shot down and killed by a GAF fighter pilot over Almelo.

In engaging more than 150 GAF fighters, VIII Fighter Command pilots down 24 GAF fighters over the MARKET-GARDEN battle area and in running battles over both sides of the Dutch-German frontier between 1530 and 1745 hours.

September 24, 1944

ETO: The entire Eighth Air Force and 9th Bombardment Division are grounded by bad weather.
FRANCE: Called by ground controllers to directly support a unit of the U.S. Third Army, two P-47s squadrons of the Ninth Air Force's 405th Fighter Group repeatedly bomb and strafe German tank columns and truck convoys through severe weather and intense ground fire. Later in the day, the group's third squadron helps quell enemy opposition to ground attacks in the same area by bombing and strafing buildings, also in the face of bad weather and intense ground fire.

Forty-one Eighth Air Force B-24s transport fuel to France.
GREECE: In a final effort to halt or stall the German Army's evacuation of Greece by air and sea, 362 Fifteenth Air Force B-24s attack the Athens/Kalamaki and Athens/Tatoi airdromes, marshalling yard at Salonika, and the harbor at Skarmanga.
ITALY: Twelfth Air Force medium bombers are grounded by bad weather, but XII Fighter Command fighter-bombers provide on-call support for U.S. Army ground forces and attack a wide range of tactical targets in the battle zone.

September 25, 1944

FRANCE: Following a concerted 26-day aerial offensive by 9th Bombardment Division the XIX TAC, the German-held fortress at Brest falls into the hands of U.S. Ninth Army ground forces. During the Brest offensive, Ninth Air Force pilots and crews completed 1,573 bomber sorties (on only six mission days) and 3,698 fighter-bomber sorties (on 23 mission days). Only after the fall of the fortress, however, is it seen in high USAAF circles that the very heavy concentration of air power against the one static target has diverted the use of those same aircraft from more fruitful use against the German Army's frantic effort to withdraw from France and Belgium to positions along and behind Germany's West Wall. While the impressive weight of the Brest aerial campaign has reduced the large parts of the fortress to rubble, more has been lost than was gained by this uneconomical exploitation of air supremacy.

Nearly 125 Eighth Air Force B-24s transport fuel to France.

GERMANY: Four hundred ten 1st Bombardment Division B-17s attack industrial targets in and around Frankfurt am Main; 257 2d Bombardment Division B-24s attack two marshalling yards in Koblenz; and a total of 400 3d Bombardment Division B-17s attack a marshalling yard and an oil-industry target at Ludwigshafen. Two B-17s are lost.

IX TAC fighters and fighter-bombers support the U.S. First Army and dive-bomb rail lines in western Germany.

GREECE: Fifty-one Fifteenth Air Force B-24s attack harbor facilities at Piraeus, Salamis, and Skarmanga.

ITALY: Twelfth Air Force medium bombers are grounded by bad weather, but XII Fighter Command fighter-bombers are able to provide direct support for the U.S. Fifth Army and attack rail and road targets and barracks.

During the night of September 25–26, XII Fighter Command A-20s attack targets of opportunity in the Po River valley.

September 26, 1944

BELGIUM: The Ninth Air Force's 370th Fighter Group displaces to Advance Landing Ground A-78, at Florennes/Juzaine Airdrome.

FRANCE: XIX TAC aircraft attack fortified positions around Metz.

More than 160 Eighth Air Force B-24s transport fuel to France.

GERMANY: Three hundred eighty-three 1st Bombardment Division B-17s attack a steel plant and marshalling yard at Osnabruck; 274 2d Bombardment Division B-24s attack a marshalling yard at Hamm; 381 3d Bombardment Division B-17s attack a motor-vehicle factory at Bremen; and 32 heavy bombers attack various targets of opportunity. Nine heavy bombers and two of 405 VIII Fighter Command escorts are lost.

VIII Fighter Command pilots down 30 GAf fighters, and Ninth Air Force fighter pilots down six GAF fighters over Germany between 1400 and 1650 hours.

IX TAC aircraft cut rail lines west of the Rhine River.

ITALY: Twelfth Air Force B-25s and B-26s attack road and rail bridges in the Po River valley, and XII Fighter Command fighter-bombers attack supply points and road and rail targets.

During the night of September 26–27, XII Fighter Command A-20s attack motor vehicles in the Po River valley.

NETHERLANDS: Two hundred fifty-three VIII Fighter Command fighters and 67 IX Fighter Command P-38s provide support for the MARKET-GARDEN airborne force. One P-38 is lost.

September 27, 1944

FRANCE: More than 300 9th Bombardment Division B-26s and A-20s abort from their assigned mission due to bad weather.

One hundred sixty-three Eighth Air Force B-24s transport fuel to an Allied base in France.

The 9th Bombardment Division's 409th Light Bombardment Group displaces from England to Advance Landing Ground A-48, at Bretigny; the 9th Bombardment Division's 410th Light Bombardment Group displaces from England to Advance Landing Ground A-58, at Coulommiers; and the 9th Bombardment Division's 416th Light Bombardment Group displaces from England to Advance Landing Ground A-55, at Melun.

GERMANY: Four hundred twenty-one 1st Bombardment Division B-17s attack the city of Cologne; 248 2d Bombardment Division B-24s attack a motor-vehicle factory at Kassel; 214 3d Bombardment Division B-17s attack an oil-industry target at Ludwigshafen; and 49 heavy bombers attack various targets of opportunity. Heavy, aggressive GAF fighter opposition results in the loss of 28 heavy bombers, including 26 of the 37 B-24s in the 445th Heavy Bombardment Group formation. This, the largest loss by any single USAAF group on any single mission in the entire war, is the result mainly of the 445th's not having joined up with any larger formation, as is by then standard operating procedure.

Escort for the heavy bombers is provided by 640 VIII Fighter Command fighters, of which two are lost. The 479th Fighter Group completes its first all–P-51 mission since transitioning from P-38s.

VIII Fighter Command pilots down 31 GAF fighters, and Ninth Air Force fighter pilots down five GAF fighters over Germany between 0940 and 1655 hours. Capt Donald S. Bryan, a P-51 pilot with the 352d Fighter Group's 328th Fighter Squadron, achieves ace status when he downs two Bf-109s near Frankfurt at 1005 hours; and 1stLt William R. Beyer, a one-victory P-51 pilot with the 361st Fighter Group's 376th Fighter Squadron, achieves ace status when he downs five FW-190s near Eisenach between 1015 and 1045 hours.

ITALY: Twelfth Air Force medium bombers are grounded by bad weather, but XII Fighter Command fighter-bombers are able to mount a limited number of missions against troop concentrations, defensive emplacements, and rail and road targets.

September 28, 1944

FRANCE: Thirty-seven 9th Bombardment Division B-26s and A-20s attack German Army defenses; and Ninth Air Force P-47s attack three German fortresses near Metz with high-explosive bombs and napalm.

One hundred ninety-four Eighth Air Force B-24s transport fuel to France.

The 9th Bombardment Division's 394th Medium Bombardment Group displaces to Advance Landing Ground A-50, at Bricy; and the Ninth Air Force's 50th Fighter Group displaces to Advance Landing Ground Y-6, at Lyons/Bron Airdrome.

GERMANY: Only 23 of 417 1st Bombardment Division B-17s are able to locate and attack their primary target, an oil plant at Magdeburg, in bad weather; 359 others attack the city of Magdeburg, and 35 attack targets of opportunity. Also, 243 2d Bombardment Division B-24s attack a motor-vehicle plant at Kassel, and 301 3d

Bombardment Division B-17s attack an oil plant at Merseburg. Thirty-four heavy bombers are lost, of which 23 are 1st Bombardment Division B-17s downed in particularly violent GAF fighter attacks over Magdeburg.

Escort for the heavy bombers is provided by 646 VIII Fighter Command fighters, of which seven are lost with their pilots.

VIII Fighter Command fighters down 30 GAF aircraft over Germany between 1130 and 1750 hours. 1stLt George W. Gleason, a P-51 pilot with the 479th Fighter Group's 434th Fighter Squadron, achieves ace status when he downs a Bf-109 and an FW-190 near Halberstadt between 1115 and 1130 hours; 1stLt Robert H. Ammon, a P-51 pilot with the 339th Fighter Group's 503d Fighter Squadron, achieves ace status when he downs two FW-190s near Brunswick at 1145 hours; and 1stLt Ernest C. Fiebelkorn, a P-51 pilot with the 20th Fighter Group's 77th Fighter Squadron, achieves ace status when he downs three Bf-109s and an FW-190 near Magdeburg between 1140 hours and noon.

Ninth Air Force fighter-bombers attack rail lines west of the Rhine River.

ITALY: All Fifteenth Air Force and Twelfth Air Force bombers are grounded by bad weather, but some XII Fighter Command fighter-bombers are able to attack roads and rail lines in reduced strength.

September 29, 1944

ENGLAND: Most of the Eighth Air Force is grounded by bad weather.

ETO: During the day, Ninth Air Force fighters and fighter-bombers complete more than 1,500 effective combat sorties.

During the night of September 29–30, specially equipped, bomb-armed 474th Fighter Group P-38s fly night-intruder missions against German Army supply columns. However, the results of this and three previous night missions by the P-38s are deemed insignificant, and the P-38 night-intruder program is abandoned.

FRANCE: One hundred ninety Eighth Air Force B-24s transport fuel supplies to France.

The 9th Bombardment Division's 322d Medium Bombardment Group displaces to Advance Landing Ground A-61, at Beauvais/Tille Airdrome.

The 371st Fighter Group is formally transferred from the Ninth Air Force to the XII TAC.

GERMANY: More than 400 9th Bombardment Division B-26s and A-20s attack antitank barriers at Webenheim; marshalling yards and rail sidings at Bingen, Euskirchen, and Prum; and warehouses, barracks, rail sidings, and marshalling yards at Bitburg and Julich.

ITALY: Twelfth Air Force bombers are grounded by bad weather, and only 52 XII Fighter Command fighter-bomber sorties are flown against rail targets south of Milan.

An FW-190 downed over Pontevillo by a 350th Fighter Group P-47 pilot is the last of only 16 Axis aircraft downed in the entire theater during the month of September.

September 30, 1944

BELGIUM: On an unspecified date in September, the Ninth Air Force's 67th Tactical Reconnaissance Group displaces to Advance Landing Ground A-87, at Charleroi.

ETO: Ninth Air Force fighters and fighter-bombers attack rail targets in eastern France, Belgium, and western Germany.

More than 100 Eighth Air Force B-24s transport fuel to Allied bases in France and Belgium.

FRANCE: The 9th Bombardment Division's 344th Medium Bombardment Group displaces to Advance Landing Ground A-59, at Cormeilles-en-Vexin; and, on an unspecified date in September, the Ninth Air Advance Landing Ground A-64, at St.-Dizier/Robinson Airdrome.

GERMANY: Only 37 1st Bombardment Division B-17s attack their briefed primary targets, Munster/Handorf Airdrome and a marshalling yard at Munster; 239 1st Bombardment Division B-17s attack the city of Munster (target of opportunity); 206 2d Bombardment Division B-24s attack a marshalling yard at Hamm; 12 2d Bombardment Division B-24s attack the city of Munster; and 257 3d Bombardment Division B-17s attack a marshalling yard at Bielfeld. Eight heavy bombers are lost.

Escort for the heavy bombers is provided by 587 VIII Fighter Command fighters, and 86 VIII Fighter Command P-51s mount sweeps over northwestern Germany. No fighters are lost.

ITALY: Twelfth Air Force B-25s attack rail bridges in the Po River valley; Twelfth Air Force B-26s attack fuel dumps and three bridges; and XII Fighter Command fighter-bombers attack bridges and rail and road targets in the Po River valley.

NETHERLANDS: In the 9th Bombardment Division's only completed mission of the day, 14 B-26s attack a road bridge near Arnhem—and miss it.

OCTOBER 1944

October 1, 1944

BELGIUM: The Ninth Air Force's 474th Fighter Group displaces to Advance Landing Ground A-78, at Florennes/Juzaine Airdrome; and the Ninth Air Force's 404th Fighter Group displaces to Advance Landing Ground A-92, at St.-Trond Airdrome.
ENGLAND: The 36th Heavy Bombardment Squadron (Radio Counter Measures) is reassigned to the VIII Fighter Command.
ETO: The entire Eighth Air Force and all Ninth Air Force bombers are grounded by bad weather.
FRANCE: After operating since its inception under the direction of the XIX TAC, the new XXIX TAC becomes operationally independent under the Ninth Air Force, and its headquarters are established at Arlon.

The 363d Tactical Reconnaissance Group is placed under XXIX TAC control.

The Ninth Air Force's 36th Fighter Group displaces to Advance Landing Ground A-68, at Juvincourt; and the Ninth Air Force's 371st Fighter Group displaces to Advance Landing Ground Y-7, at Dole/Tavaux Airdrome.

ITALY: The Fifteenth Air Force is grounded by bad weather.

Twelfth Air Force B-25s and B-26s attack a factory, a barracks, fuel dumps, and bridges in the Po River valley; XII Fighter Command A-20s attack bivouacs and a fuel dump; and XII Fighter Command fighter-bombers attack lines of communication and gun emplacements.

The 5th Photographic Reconnaissance Group is assigned to the Fifteenth Air Force, which is now complete.

During the night of October 1–2, XII Fighter Command A-20s attack targets of opportunity in the Po River valley.
LUXEMBOURG: The Ninth Air Force's 363d Tactical Reconnaissance Group displaces to Advance Landing Ground A-97, at Luxembourg City.

October 2, 1944

BELGIUM: The IX TAC headquarters displaces forward to Verviers; and the Ninth Air Force's 368th Fighter Group displaces to Advance Landing Ground A-84, at Chievres Airdrome.
FRANCE: The 9th Bombardment Divi-

sion's 386th Medium Bombardment Group displaces from England to Advance Landing Ground A-60, at Beaumont-sur-Oise Airdrome.
GERMANY: Two hundred seventy-two 1st Bombardment Division B-17s and 384 3d Bombardment Division B-17s attack several industrial targets and an ordnance depot at Kassel and, because of bad weather and poor visibility, the city itself. Also, 110 1st Bombardment Division B-17s attack the Ford motor-transport factory at Cologne, and 70 B-17s attack assorted targets of opportunity. In a separate mission, 266 2d Bombardment Division B-24s attack a marshalling yard at Hamm, and 30 B-24s attack targets of opportunity. Two B-17s, two B-24s, and one of 712 VIII Fighter Command escort fighters are lost.

The VIII Fighter Command's 353d Fighter Group undertakes its first escort mission since transitioning from P-47s to P-51s. (It is the VIII Fighter Command plan to replace all P-47s and P-38s with P-51s.)

9th Bombardment Division B-26s and A-20s mount three separate attacks against defensive positions at Herbach and two separate missions against industrial targets at Ubach.

In the first known encounter between Allied fighters and a GAF Me-262 jet fighter, an Me-262 that has completely dominated a pair of 365th Fighter Group P-47 pilots in a chase and dogfight near Munster runs out of fuel and inadvertently crashes before either P-47 can fire a shot. Nevertheless, 1stLt Valmore J. Beaudreault is officially credited with the first USAAF jet kill in history.
ITALY: The Fifteenth Air Force and Twelfth Air Force medium bombers are grounded by bad weather, and XII Fighter Command fighters are unable to mount tactical ground-support missions.

October 3, 1944

GERMANY: One hundred ninety-eight 1st Bombardment Division B-17s attack a motor-transport factory at Nurnberg; 87 1st Bombardment Division B-17s attack the synthetic-oil plant at Wesseling; 37 1st Bombardment Division B-17s attack several targets of opportunity; 250 2d Bombardment Division B-24s attack industrial targets at Gaggenau and Lachen; 70 2d Bombardment Division B-24s attack secondary targets and targets of opportunity; due to bad weather, only 49 3d Bombardment Division B-17s attack the assigned primary, Giebelstadt Airdrome; 256 3d Bombardment Division B-17s attack the city of Nurnburg; and 48 3d Bombardment Division B-17s attack other targets of opportunity. Three B-17s and four of 699 VIII Fighter Command escort fighters are lost.

This is the last mission of the 479th Fighter Group in P-38s and the last use of the type by the Eighth Air Force.

Capt Henry W. Brown, a 14.2-victory P-51 ace with the 355th Fighter Group's 354th Fighter Squadron, is shot down by flak and taken prisoner at Nordlingen. And Capt Charles W. Lenfest, a five-victory ace with Brown's squadron, is also captured after he intentionally lands and becomes mired in mud while trying to rescue Brown.
ITALY: The Fifteenth Air Force is grounded by bad weather.

Twelfth Air Force B-25s and B-26s attack fuel dumps and bridges in the Po River valley; and XII Fighter Command A-20s and fighter-bombers attack transportation targets and fuel dumps, also in the Po River valley.
NETHERLANDS: More than 220 9th Bombardment Division B-26s and A-20s are recalled on their way to their targets because of bad weather.

October 4, 1944

BELGIUM: The Ninth Air Force's 365th Fighter Group displaces to Advance Landing Ground A-84, at Chievres Airdrome.
ENGLAND: The Eighth Air Force is grounded by bad weather.
GERMANY: Three hundred twenty-seven Fifteenth Air Force B-17s and B-24s attack the Munich/West marshalling yard.
GREECE: Thirty-nine Fifteenth Air Force

P-51s strafe Athens/Eleusis, Athens/Kalamaki, and Athens/Tatoi airdromes.

ITALY: Four hundred Fifteenth Air Force B-17s and B-24s attack Aviano Airdrome and roads and rail lines leading down to Italy from Brenner Pass; Twelfth Air Force medium bombers attack two bridges; and XII Fighter Command fighter-bombers attack communications targets and provide close on-call support for the U.S. Fifth Army.

During the night of October 4–5, XII Fighter Command A-20s attack targets of opportunity in the mountains south of Bologna. and around the Arno River valley.

October 5, 1944

GERMANY: The entire 1st Bombardment Division diverts to targets of opportunity: 248 1st Bombardment Division B-17s attack Cologne; 52 1st Bombardment Division B-17s attack Brechten, Koblenz, and Dortmund. Also, 175 2d Bombardment Division B-24s attack Lippstadt Airdrome; 107 2d Bombardment Division B-24s attack a marshalling yard at Rheine; 28 2d Bombardment Division B-24s attack Paderborn Airdrome; ten 2d Bombardment Division B-24s attack targets of opportunity; 235 3d Bombardment Division B-17s attack Munster/Loddenheide Airdrome; 68 3d Bombardment Division B-17s attack Munster/Handorf Airdrome; and 12 3d Bombardment Division B-17s attack targets of opportunity. Nine B-17s and five of 675 VIII Fighter Command escort fighters are lost.

Ninth Air Force fighter-bombers attack defensive emplacements along the West Wall and directly support the U.S. XV Corps.

ITALY: The Twelfth and Fifteenth Air forces are grounded by bad weather.

NETHERLANDS: More than 330 9th Bombardment Division B-26s and A-20s dispatched against targets in the Netherlands are recalled when they encounter bad weather.

October 6, 1944

FRANCE: The 9th Bombardment Division's 397th Medium Bombardment Group displaces to Advance Landing Ground A-72, at Peronne.

GERMANY: In the Eighth Air Force's largest mission to date, exactly 1,200 effective heavy-bomber sorties are mounted as follows: 199 1st Bombardment Division B-17s attack Stargard Airdrome; 12 1st Bombardment Division B-17s attack the city of Stettin; 73 1st Bombardment Division B-17s attack an aircraft-industry factory at Neubranden-burg; 100 1st Bombardment Division B-17s attack the city of Straslund; 38 1st Bombardment Division B-17s attack several targets of opportunity; 289 2d Bombardment Division B-24s attack two oil-industry targets and a munitions dump at Hamburg; 46 2d Bombardment Division B-24s attack an aircraft-industry target at Wenzendorf; 41 2d Bombardment Division B-24s attack various targets of opportunity; 144 3d Bombardment Division B-17s attack a munitions dump at Berlin; 138 3d Bombardment Division B-17s attack an aircraft factory at Berlin; 100 3d Bombardment Division B-17s attack an armored-vehicle factory at Berlin; and ten 3d Bombardment Division B-17s attack targets of opportunity. Nineteen heavy bombers and four of 699 VIII Fighter Command escort fighters are lost.

The 20th Fighter Group claims the destruction of 40 German seaplanes during strafing attacks against five seaplane bases between Stettin and Lubeck.

Ninth Air Force fighter-bombers support the U.S. Third and Seventh armies and attack rail lines around Dorsel. And 368th Fighter Group P-47s following GAF fighters to an airfield at Breitscheid down two Bf-109s in the landing pattern and destroy at least 22 Bf-109s on the ground during strafing attacks.

Altogether, in the first significant fighter actions of the month, Eighth and Ninth air force fighter pilots down 22 GAF fighters over Germany between 1100 and 1650 hours.

GREECE: Fifteenth Air Force P-38 and P-51 fighters strafe Athens/Eleusis, Athens/Kalamaki, Athens/Tatoi, Megalo Mikra, Megara, and Salonika/Sedhes airdromes.
ITALY: The entire Twelfth Air Force and Fifteenth Air Force bombers are grounded by bad weather.
NETHERLANDS: More than 300 9th Bombardment Division B-26s and A-20s attack an ammunition dump, barracks, and marshalling yards at Duren and Hengelo, and bridges at Aldenhoven and Arnhem.

October 7, 1944

AUSTRIA: More than 350 Fifteenth Air Force B-17s and B-24s attack oil-industry targets around Vienna.
GERMANY: On this record-setting day, the Eighth Air Force heavy bombers mount 1,401 effective combat sorties: 142 1st Bombardment Division B-17s attack an oil-industry target at Politz; 59 1st Bombardment Division B-17s attack an oil-industry target at Ruhland; 259 1st Bombardment Division B-17s attack various targets of opportunity; 129 2d Bombardment Division B-24s attack an oil-industry target at Merseburg; 88 2d Bombardment Division B-24s attack an oil-industry target at Lutzkendorf; 86 2d Bombardment Division B-24s attack an oil-industry target at Bohlen; 102 2d Bombardment Division B-24s attack various targets of opportunity; 122 3d Bombardment Division B-17s attack a motor-transport factory at Kassel; 88 3d Bombardment Division B-17s attack an armored-vehicle factory at Kassel; 87 3d Bombardment Division B-17s attack two oil-industry plants at Magdeburg; and 149 3d Bombardment Division B-17s attack various targets of opportunity. Due to extremely heavy and accurate flak coverage (which is now using H2X emissions to track the bombers), 40 heavy bombers are lost. Eleven of 521 VIII Fighter Command escort fighters are also lost. Among the lost airmen is Col James R. Luper, the 457th

Heavy Bombardment Group commander, who is taken prisoner.

9th Bombardment Division B-26s attack a supply depot at Euskirchen and bridges at two locations, and all three 9th Bombardment Division A-20 groups attack ten military-stores warehouses at a marshalling yard at Trier.

Eighth and Ninth Air Force fighter pilots down 38 GAF fighters over Germany between 1005 and 1640 hours. 1stLt Darrell S. Cramer, a P-51 pilot with the 55th Fighter Group's 338th Fighter Squadron, achieves ace status when he downs a Bf-109 over Leipzig at 1210 hours; Maj Arthur F. Jeffrey, the commanding officer of the 479th Fighter Group's 434th Fighter Squadron, in P-51s, achieves ace status when he downs a Bf-109 near Leipzig at 1215 hours; and 1stLt Urban L. Drew, a P-51 pilot with the 361st Fighter Group's 375th Fighter Squadron, achieves ace status when he downs two Me-262s over Achmer Airdrome at 1345 hours.

HUNGARY: Approximately 30 Fifteenth Air Force B-17s and B-24s attack targets of opportunity in Hungary, including the airdrome at Gyor.
ITALY: Twelfth Air Force medium bombers are grounded by bad weather, but fighter-bombers attack gun emplacements and defensive positions on the battle front and communications targets to the north.
NETHERLANDS: 9th Bombardment Division bombers attack a marshalling yard at Hengelo and bridges at Arnhem.

October 8, 1944

ETO: More than 300 9th Bombardment Division B-26s and A-20s and numerous Ninth Air Force fighter-bombers attack tactical targets in eastern France and western Germany, especially between Metz, France, and Aachen, Germany.
FRANCE: The 9th Bombardment Division's 394th Medium Bombardment Group moves to Advance Landing Ground A-74, at Cambrai/Niergnies Airdrome.
ITALY: The entire Fifteenth Air Force and

Twelfth Air Force medium bombers are grounded by bad weather, but XII Fighter Command fighter-bombers provide direct support for the U.S. Fifth Army.

October 9, 1944

GERMANY: Three hundred twenty-nine 1st Bombardment Division B-17s attack ball-bearing plants at Schweinfurt; 360 2d Bombardment Division B-24s attack marshalling yards at Koblenz; 210 3d Bombardment Division B-17s attack a marshalling yard at Mainz; and 148 3d Bombardment Division B-17s attack an aircraft-industry target at Gustavsburg. One B-24 is lost, but all 811 VIII Fighter Command and Ninth Air Force escort fighters return safely.

Thirty 9th Bombardment Division bombers attack a rail bridge at Euskirchen, but dive-bombers dispatched to attack airdromes in western Germany are recalled because of bad weather.

ITALY: The entire Fifteenth Air Force and Twelfth Air Force medium bombers are grounded by bad weather, but XII Fighter Command fighter-bombers attack rail crossings, roads, and transportation targets.

October 10, 1944

ETO: The Ninth Air Force is grounded by bad weather.

ITALY: Nearly 170 Fifteenth Air Force B-17s and B-24s attack rail bridges and four marshalling yards throughout northern Italy, but 350 other heavy bombers abort in the face of bad weather. Twelfth Air Force medium bombers and many fighter-bombers are grounded by bad weather, but XII Fighter Command fighter-bombers are able to provide direct support for elements of the U.S. Fifth Army.

October 11, 1944

AUSTRIA: Fifteenth Air Force B-17s and B-24s attack a motor factory and an ordnance depot in Vienna, a motor factory at Graz, a marshalling yard, and several towns.

CZECHOSLOVAKIA: Fifteenth Air Force escort fighters strafe Porstejov Airdrome, nearby targets of opportunity, and targets of opportunity at Bratislava.

FRANCE: Ninety-nine 9th Bombardment Division B-26s and A-20s on their way to attack a German Army military base are recalled when their pathfinding equipment malfunctions in bad weather.

GERMANY: Fifty-seven 1st Bombardment Division B-17s attack a synthetic-oil factory at Wesseling (primary), and 73 1st Bombardment Division B-17s attack a marshalling yard at Koblenz (secondary). Four B-17s and one of 135 VIII Fighter Command escorts are lost.

Ninth Air Force fighter-bombers attack rail lines and support U.S. Army ground forces around Aachen, Metz, and Saarlautern.

HUNGARY: Fifteenth Air Force escort fighters strafe the landing ground at Esztergom and targets of opportunity at Budapest.

ITALY: Fifteen Air Force heavy bombers attack the harbor at Trieste and road and rail bridges at Cesara; Twelfth Air Force medium bombers attack supply dumps and bridges; and XII Fighter Command fighter-bombers provide direct support for the U.S. Fifth Army and attack lines of communication.

YUGOSLAVIA: Fifteenth Air Force heavy bombers attack a rail bridge at Dravograd.

October 12, 1944

FRANCE: 9th Bombardment Division bombers attack the German Army military base at Camp-de-Bitche.

The Ninth Air Force is assigned direct administrative control over the XII TAC, which has been under USSTAF administration since it was transferred out of the Twelfth Air Force.

The XIX TAC headquarters displaces forward to Nancy.

GERMANY: Two hundred sixty-seven 2d Bombardment Division B-24s attack a marshalling yard at Osnabruck (secondary), and 238 3d Bombardment Division B-17s attack an aircraft-industry target at Bremen. Three heavy bombers and five of 483 VIII Fighter Command escorts are lost.

9th Bombardment Division bombers attack two defended towns and two rail bridges; and 368th Fighter Group P-47s repeatedly attack German Army armored vehicles and troops concentrating for an attack against a U.S. Army infantry division near Aachen. Later in the day, the 368th Fighter Group closely supports an attack by the same U.S. infantry division.

Eighth and Ninth Air Force fighter pilots down 28 GAF fighters over Germany between 1125 and 1520 hours. 1stLt Charles E. Yeager, a P-51 pilot with the 357th Fighter Group's 363d Fighter Squadron, achieves ace status with 6.5 victories when he downs five Bf-109s near Assen (Netherlands) at about 1100 hours.

HUNGARY: While conducting a series of afternoon fighter sweeps over Hungary, P-51 pilots of the 52d, 325th, and 332d Fighter groups down 18 Axis aircraft, the highest one-day total in the theater for the month.

ITALY: As part of Operation PANCAKE, 826 Fifteenth Air Force B-17s and B-24s attack troop concentrations, depots, and bivouacs in and around Bologna, and Twelfth Air Force medium bombers, fighters, and fighter-bombers provide direct support for the U.S. Fifth Army and attack supply dumps, bivouacs, barracks, lines of communication, gun emplacements, and troop concentrations throughout the battle area.

MTO: One hundred sixty Fifteenth Air Force P-51s strafe traffic on the Danube River in Austria and Hungary. Also attacked is Seregelyes Airdrome in Hungary.

NETHERLANDS: 9th Bombardment Division bombers attack Venraij.

October 13, 1944

AUSTRIA: Fifteenth Air Force B-24s attack various marshalling yards in Austria as well as a motor factory and other industrial targets in and around Vienna. Also, Fifteenth Air Force B-17s attack oil-industry targets around Vienna. Airfields are also attacked.

CZECHOSLOVAKIA: Fifteenth Air Force B-24s attack various marshalling yards around the country.

ETO: 9th Bombardment Division B-26s and A-20s attack bridges servicing German Army forces on various battlefronts in eastern France, the Netherlands, and western Germany; and Ninth Air Force fighters and fighter-bombers provide direct support for the U.S. First, Third, and Seventh armies along the various battlefronts.

FRANCE: The 9th Bombardment Division's 323d Medium Bombardment Group displaces to Advance Landing Ground A-69, at Laon/Athies Airdrome.

GERMANY: Eighth and Ninth Air Force fighter pilots down 17 GAF fighters over Germany between 1015 and 1550 hours.

Fifteenth Air Force B-17s attack oil-industry targets at Blechhammer.

GREECE: The Twelfth Air Force's 51st Troop Carrier Wing is committed to moving supplies and personnel in support of the British Army's occupation of southern Greece (Operation MANNA).

HUNGARY: Fifteenth Air Force B-24s attack various marshalling yards and airfields around the country.

ITALY: Many Twelfth Air Force medium bombers are grounded by bad weather, but a small number of attacks are completed against several bridges and supply dumps; and XII Fighter Command fighter-bombers undertake numerous missions against tactical targets, supply dumps, and lines of communication in the U.S. Fifth Army battle area.

October 14, 1944

CZECHOSLOVAKIA: Fifteenth Air Force heavy bombers attack marshalling yards at Bratislava and Nove Zamky.

ETO: The 9th Bombardment Division is grounded by bad weather, but Ninth Air Force fighters and fighter-bombers support U.S. Army ground forces along the various battlefronts.

GERMANY: On the day's first mission, 90 1st Bombardment Division B-17s attack the marshalling yard at Saarbrucken, and 117 2d Bombardment Division attack the city of Kaiserlautern. No bombers are lost but one of 253 VIII Fighter Command escorts is downed.

After downing two Bf-109s near St.-Dizier, France, at 1310 hours, Capt Joseph L. Lang, a P-51 ace with the 4th Fighter Group's 334th Fighter Squadron, is killed in air-to-air combat near Mannheim.

Three hundred twenty-six 1st Bombardment Division B-17s, 248 2d Bombardment Division B-24s, and 314 3d Bombardment Division B-17s attack industrial targets and marshalling yards in Cologne. Five heavy bombers are lost, but all 732 VIII Fighter Command escorts return safely.

Fifteenth Air Force B-24s attack oil-industry targets at Odertal, and Fifteenth Air Force B-17s attack oil-industry targets at Blechhammer.

GREECE: In the first of several Operation MANNA missions to be undertaken over several days, 55 Fifteenth Air Force P-38s escort C-47s carrying British airborne troops to an airdrome in Greece, in this case Megara.

HUNGARY: Fifteenth Air Force B-17s attack marshalling yards at two locations, an industrial area, and a military base. Escort fighters strafe two airdromes near Lake Balaton.

ITALY: Twelfth Air Force medium bombers are grounded by bad weather, but fighter-bombers attack tactical targets and lines of communication in support of the U.S. Fifth Army.

YUGOSLAVIA: Fifteenth Air Force B-24s attack the bridge at Maribor.

October 15, 1944

ETO: The 9th Bombardment Division is grounded by bad weather, but Ninth Air Force fighter-bombers are active along all fronts in eastern France, the Netherlands, and western Germany.

GERMANY: Three hundred seventy-nine 1st Bombardment Division B-17s, 185 2d Bombardment Division B-24s, and 339 3d Bombardment Division B-17s attack five marshalling yards at Cologne. Also, a total of 125 2d Bombardment Division B-24s attack oil-industry targets at Monheim and Reisholz, and 23 B-17s and 36 B-24s attack various secondary targets and targets of opportunity. Six B-17s and one B-24 are lost, but all 462 VIII Fighter Command escorts return safely.

Twenty-three Eighth Air Force B-17s attack the naval installation at Heligoland Island, and two APHRODITE drone B-17 flying bombs are directed against the same target (with negative results).

In the day's only fighter engagements, 78th Fighter Group P-47 pilots down five FW-190s at 0845 hours and an Me-262 at 1045 hours. Also, the Ninth Air Force's 48th Fighter Group routs a German Army counterattack in the zone of the U.S. XIX Corps.

ITALY: The Fifteenth Air Force is grounded by bad weather; Twelfth Air Force B-25s and B-26s attack bridges in the Po River valley; and XII Fighter Command fighter-bombers provide support for U.S. Army ground forces.

October 16, 1944

AUSTRIA: Fifteenth Air Force B-24s attack two tank factories and an aircraft-engine factory at Steyr, an ordnance depot and a benzol plant at Linz, and numerous targets of opportunity. Also, Fifteenth Air Force B-17s attack various marshalling yards throughout the country.

CZECHOSLOVAKIA: Fifteenth Air Force B-17s attack a synthetic-oil plant at Brux, and the Skoda arms complex at Pilsen.

Maj George T. Buck, Jr., commanding officer of the 31st Fighter Group's 309th Fighter Squadron, achieves ace status with a personal score of six confirmed victories when he downs three Bf-109s during withdrawal escort from Brux. Altogether, nine

Bf-109s are downed by pilots of Buck's squadron during a bounce on at least 75 GAF fighters at about 1215 hours.

ETO: All Eighth and Ninth air force flight operations are canceled because of bad weather.

GERMANY: P-51 pilots of the Fifteenth Air Force's 325th Fighter Group down eight GAF fighters east of Dresden in an engagement between 1220 and 1235 hours.

ITALY: Twelfth Air Force medium bombers are grounded by bad weather, but XII Fighter Command fighter-bombers are active in support of the U.S. Fifth Army.

During the night of October 16–17, XII Fighter Command A-20s attack targets of opportunity around Ravenna and in the Po River valley.

LUXEMBOURG: The Ninth Air Force advance headquarters displaces with the 12th Army Group headquarters to Luxembourg City.

October 17, 1944

AUSTRIA: Fifteenth Air Force B-24s attack marshalling yards at Vienna.

ENGLAND: Col Benjamin J. Webster succeeds BriGen Francis H. Griswold as head of the VIII Fighter Command.

FRANCE: The 9th Bombardment Division's 416th Light Bombardment Group is withdrawn from combat in order to transition completely from A-20s to new A-26s.

GERMANY: Four hundred one 1st Bombardment Division B-17s, 437 2d Bombardment Division B-24s, and 410 3d Bombardment Division B-17s attack four marshalling yards at Cologne. Four B-17s and one of 774 VIII Fighter Command escorts are lost.

Thirty-five 9th Bombardment Division B-26s attack a rail bridge at Euskirchen, and Ninth Air Force fighter-bombers attack rail targets in western Germany.

Fifteenth Air Force B-17s attack oil-industry targets at Blechhammer.

HUNGARY: Fifteenth Air Force heavy bombers unable to attack primary targets in Austria and Germany attack marshalling yards and rail bridges in Hungary and other targets scattered throughout the Balkans.

ITALY: All Twelfth Air Force medium bombers are grounded by bad weather, and XII Fighter Command fighter-bombers are able to undertake only limited ground-support operations.

October 18, 1944

ETO: With the exception of several groups attached to the IX TAC, Ninth Air Force combat units are grounded by bad weather.

GERMANY: Although several operations are canceled because of bad weather, 79 1st Bombardment Division B-17s attack the Ford plant at Cologne; 39 2d Bombardment Division B-24s attack an industrial plant at Leverkusen; 300 3d Bombardment Division B-17s attack Kassel; and 30 1st Bombardment Division B-17s and 30 2d Bombardment Division B-24s attack a marshalling yard at Cologne as a target of opportunity. Five heavy bombers and five of 565 VIII Fighter Command escorts are lost.

GREECE: The 51st Troop Carrier Wing is withdrawn from Operation MANNA, the British occupation of southern Greece.

ITALY: All but one of numerous Twelfth Air Force medium-bomber missions abort in the face of bad weather. B-26s attack rail bridges at Padua and a warehouse, and fighters and fighter-bombers provide limited support for the U.S. Fifth Army.

During the night of October 18–19, XII Fighter Command A-20s attack targets of opportunity around Bologna and Genoa.

YUGOSLAVIA: Thirty-eight Fifteenth Air Force P-38 dive-bombers attack Vinkovci.

October 19, 1944

ETO: 9th Bombardment Division bombers are grounded by bad weather, but Ninth Air Force fighter-bombers provide tactical support for U.S. Army ground forces, especially against a concentration of tanks near Luneville, France.

GERMANY: Only 25 of 374 1st Bombardment Division B-17s dispatched against an armored-vehicle factory at Mannheim attack the target, but 257 of the others bomb the city, and 82 attack various targets of opportunity; only 50 of 380 2d Bombardment Division B-24s dispatched against a diesel-engine plant at Gustavsburg attack the target, but 280 attack a marshalling yard at Mainz; and 217 of 267 3d Bombardment Division B-17s dispatched against an industrial target at Ludwigshafen attack the city of Mannheim, and 34 attack targets of opportunity. Six heavy bombers and two of 707 VIII Fighter Command escorts are lost.

ITALY: The entire Fifteenth Air Force is grounded by bad weather, but Twelfth Air Force B-25s attack three bridges near Milan; Twelfth Air Force B-26s attack a causeway at Mantua, a rail line, and two bridges; and XII Fighter Command fighter-bombers attack rail lines, bridges, and German Army forces massing for a ground attack. In the first opposition to Twelfth Air Force bombing operations in many months, GAF fighters down three B-26s, and B-26 gunners claim two GAF fighters.

The XII Fighter Command is formally redesignated XXII TAC.

October 20, 1944

AUSTRIA: Fifteenth Air Force B-24s attack a marshalling yard at Innsbruck.
CZECHOSLOVAKIA: Fifteenth Air Force B-17s attack an oil refinery at Brux.
FRANCE: In order to forestall a German plan to flood the Seille River valley, P-47 fighter-bombers of the XIX TAC's 362d Fighter Group breach a dam at Dieuze in order to release the waters of the Etang de Lindre.
GERMANY: Ninth Air Force fighter pilots down 20 GAF fighters over Germany in three separate air actions at about 0910, 1450, and 1540 hours.

Fifteenth Air Force B-17s and B-24s attack Bad Aibling Airdrome, an oil-storage facility at Regensburg, and a marshalling yard at Rosenheim.
ITALY: Fifteenth Air Force heavy bombers attack an armaments factory, a motor-

transport factory, and an ordnance plant at Milan.

Thanks to the first clear skies in many days, Twelfth Air Force B-25s and B-26s are able to mount a maximum effort against 12 bridges and railroad fills in the Po River valley. Also, XXII TAC P-47s attack communications targets, tactical targets, supply dumps, and troop concentrations in support of the U.S. Fifth Army's drive to take Bologna.

During the night of October 20–21, XXII TAC A-20s attack targets of opportunity north of the battle area.
NETHERLANDS: 9th Bombardment Division bombers attack two rail bridges, but other scheduled attacks are aborted in the face of bad weather.

October 21, 1944

ETO: 9th Bombardment Division bombers are grounded by bad weather, but Ninth Air Force fighter-bombers are able to support U.S. Army ground forces in northern Europe.
HUNGARY: One hundred four Fifteenth Air Force B-24s attack the airdromes and marshalling yards at Gyor and Szombathely, and nearly 100 escorting P-38s strafe Szombathely and Seregelyes airdromes and several rail lines near Lake Balaton.
ITALY: Despite bad weather that grounds all other Twelfth Air Force medium bombers, a number of B-26s are able to attack a rail bridge and causeway. Also, XXII TAC P-47s attack numerous targets in support of the U.S. Fifth Army.

October 22, 1944

BELGIUM: The Ninth Air Force's 373d Fighter Group displaces to Advance Landing Ground A-89, at Le Culot.
ENGLAND: MajGen Howard M. Turner succeeds MajGen Robert B. Williams as commanding general of the Eighth Air Force's 1st Bombardment Division.
ETO: The 9th Bombardment Division is grounded by bad weather.
GERMANY: One hundred seventy-one 1st

Bombardment Division B-17s attack an industrial target in Hannover; 148 1st Bombardment Division B-17s attack an industrial target in Brunswick; 353 2d Bombardment Division B-24s attack a marshalling yard at Hamm; and 352 3d Bombardment Division B-17s attack a marshalling yard at Munster. Two B-17s and one of 722 VIII Fighter Command escorts are lost.

Ninth Air Force fighter pilots down 24 GAF fighters between 1445 and 1825 hours. Twenty-one of the GAF fighters are credited to 365th Fighter Group P-47 pilots.

All but one squadron of the Eighth Air Force's 492d Heavy Bombardment Group is relieved of duties with Operation CARPETBAGGER. While the other squadrons undertake normal bombardment missions, the lone squadron will continue to undertake CARPETBAGGER partisan-resupply missions, especially in German, Norway, Denmark, and the occupied Netherlands.
ITALY: The entire Fifteenth Air Force and all Twelfth Air Force bombers are grounded by bad weather, and XXII TAC is able to provide only 20 support sorties throughout the day.
NETHERLANDS: The XXIX TAC headquarters displaces forward from Arlon, France, to Maastricht, along with the U.S. Ninth Army headquarters. Also, the 48th and 404th Fighter groups are reassigned to XXIX TAC control.

October 23, 1944

BELGIUM: The Ninth Air Force's 36th Fighter Group displaces to Advance Landing Ground A-89, at Le Culot; and the Ninth Air Force's 48th Fighter Group displaces to Advance Landing Ground A-92, at St.-Trond Airdrome.
CZECHOSLOVAKIA: Fifteenth Air Force B-17s attack the Skoda arms complex at Pilsen.
ETO: The entire Ninth Air Force is grounded by bad weather.
GERMANY: Fifteenth Air Force B-24s attack an arms factory at Plauen, and a marshalling yard and oil-industry targets at

Regensburg; and Fifteenth Air Force B-17s attack a marshalling yard at Rosenheim.
ITALY: Fifteenth Air Force B-24s attack rail lines around Brenner Pass and throughout northern Italy.

Twelfth Air Force medium bombers and most XXII TAC P-47s are grounded by bad weather, but some XXII TAC P-47s are able to attack many locomotives, rail cars, motor vehicles, and vessels around Genoa, Padua, Savona, and Turin.

During the night of October 23–24, XXII TAC A-20s attack targets of opportunity in the Po River valley.

October 24, 1944

ETO: Except for fighter patrols over friendly ground forces, the Ninth Air Force cancels its scheduled missions in the face of bad weather.
GERMANY: Three hundred seventy-nine VIII Fighter Command P-47 and P-51 fighter-bombers attack industrial targets in the Hannover and Kassel areas, and flak emplacements at Elburg. Seven aircraft are lost.
ITALY: The entire Fifteenth Air Force and all Twelfth Air Force medium bombers are grounded by bad weather, but XXII TAC mounts more than 300 P-47 sorties against communications targets in the Po River valley, shipping in the Genoa and Turin areas, and in support of the U.S. Fifth Army.

October 25, 1944

AUSTRIA: Fifteenth Air Force B-17s attack Klagenfurt Airdrome.
ETO: The 9th Bombardment Division is grounded by bad weather.

The provisional First Tactical Air Force is established on paper and is projected to be formally set up in mid-November. It will consist of XII TAC and the French First Air Army, and will support the U.S. Seventh Army and the French First Army (i.e., the 6th Army Group) on the Allied southern flank.
GERMANY: Two hundred eighty-five 1st Bombardment Division B-17s attack two oil

refineries at Hamburg; 100 1st Bombardment Division B-17s attack a marshalling yard at Hamm; 27 1st Bombardment Division B-17s attack a synthetic-oil plant at Gelsenkirchen; 216 2d Bombardment Division B-24s attack the airfield and an aircraft repair facility at Neumunster Airdrome; 91 2d Bombardment Division B-24s attack an industrial plant at Scholven; 37 2d Bombardment Division B-24s attack the city of Munster; 221 3d Bombardment Division B-17s attack an industrial target at Hamburg; and 214 3d Bombardment Division B-17s attack an oil refinery at Hamburg. Two B-17s and one of 475 VIII Fighter Command escorts are lost.

ITALY: Virtually the entire Fifteenth Air Force and all Twelfth Air Force medium bombers are grounded by bad weather, but XXII TAC P-47s are able to attack tactical targets and lines of communication south of Bologna. At least 20 locomotives are claimed as destroyed.

October 26, 1944

AUSTRIA: In the day's only offensive action in the MTO, seven Fifteenth Air Force B-17s attack marshalling yards at Innsbruck.

ETO: The 9th Bombardment Division is grounded by bad weather, but Ninth Air Force fighters attack tactical targets along and behind the various fronts.

GERMANY: One hundred fifty-five 1st Bombardment Division B-17s attack the city of Bielefeld (primary); 108 1st Bombardment Division B-17s attack an industrial plant at Munster; 87 1st Bombardment Division B-17s attack the city of Münster, and 25 1st Bombardment Division B-17s attack other targets of opportunity; 242 2d Bombardment Division B-24s attack the Mittelland Canal and an aqueduct at Minden; 65 2d Bombardment Division B-24s attack the synthetic-oil plant at Bottrop; 33 2d Bombardment Division B-24s attack the city of Munster; 155 3d Bombardment Division B-17s attack an industrial target at Hannover; 221 3d

Bombardment Division B-17s attack the city of Hannover, and 37 3d Bombardment Division B-17s attack other targets of opportunity. One of 626 VIII Fighter Command escorts is lost.

ITALY: The Twelfth and Fifteenth air forces are grounded by bad weather.

October 27, 1944

ETO: Except for limited XIX TAC fighter patrols and several aerial resupply missions, the entire Ninth Air Force is grounded by bad weather.

LtGen Robert C. Richardson assumes command of the IX Air Defense Command, which has been overseeing around-the-clock fighter cover and patrols over the U.S. Army battle zones in northern Europe.

ITALY: The entire Fifteenth Air Force and nearly the entire Twelfth Air Force are grounded by bad weather. A very small number of XXII TAC P-47s is able to mount armed-reconnaissance flights over the battle area.

October 28, 1944

AUSTRIA: Ten Fifteenth Air Force B-17s attack Klagenfurt Airdrome.

BELGIUM: Ninth Air Force fighter-bombers attack a tunnel and six bridges near the Belgian-German frontier.

FRANCE: The 9th Bombardment Division headquarters displaces to Reims.

The Ninth Air Force's 367th Fighter Group displaces to Advance Landing Ground A-68, at Juvincourt.

GERMANY: One hundred seventy-eight 1st Bombardment Division B-17s attack a marshalling yard at Munster, and 184 3d Bombardment Division B-17s attack a marshalling yard at Hamm. Three B-17s and two of 199 VIII Fighter Command escorts are downed.

Forty-five 9th Bombardment Division bombers attack Euskirchen Airdrome and rail bridges at three locations.

Ninth Air Force fighter pilots down seven GAF fighters in two separate engagements at 1150 and 1545 hours.

Eight Fifteenth Air Force B-17s attack a marshalling yard near Munich.

ITALY: Twelfth Air Force medium bombers are grounded by bad weather, and XXII TAC is able to mount only 65 P-47 sorties against lines-of-communication targets.

October 29, 1944

AUSTRIA: Thirty P-38s on escort duty with Fifteenth Air Force heavy bombers attack locomotives and other rail targets between Wels and Kienburg. Claims amount to 17 locomotives destroyed.

BELGIUM: The Ninth Air Force's 363d Tactical Reconnaissance Group displaces to Advance Landing Ground Y-10, at Le Culot Airdrome East.

ETO: Approximately 170 9th Bombardment Division B-26s and A-20s attack rail bridges at five locations in the Netherlands and western Germany, and Ninth Air Force fighters and fighter-bombers attack numerous bridges and rail targets in the areas directly behind the various battlefronts.

GERMANY: Ninth Air Force fighter pilots down 21 GAF fighters between 1145 and 1545 hours. Capt Harry E. Fisk, a P-51 pilot with the 354th Fighter Group's 356th Fighter Squadron, achieves ace status when he downs three Bf-109s near Karlsruhe at 1145 hours; and 2dLt Bruce W. Carr, a P-51 pilot with the 354th Fighter Group's 353d Fighter Squadron, achieves ace status when he downs two Bf-109s near Bockingen at 1145 hours.

Of 725 Fifteenth Air Force heavy bombers dispatched against several targets in southern Germany, only 35 B-24s attack a marshalling yard at Munich. The rest are thwarted by bad weather.

ITALY: Twelfth Air Force medium bombers are grounded by bad weather, and XXII TAC P-47s are able to mount only 15 sorties against rail lines in the Po River valley.

October 30, 1944

AUSTRIA: During the night of October 30–31, three Fifteenth Air Force B-24s attack Klagenfurt Airdrome.

ETO: All 9th Bombardment Division B-26s and A-20s dispatched against bridges and other targets in the battlefront areas are recalled because of bad weather.

FRANCE: The 9th Bombardment Division's 387th Medium Bombardment Group displaces to Advance Landing Ground A-71, at Clastres.

GERMANY: In what was to have been a major strike by more than 1,300 heavy bombers against German oil and oil-products production, bad weather forces the entire 3d Bombardment Division and many other Eighth Air Force heavy bombers to abort, and most of nearly 650 other heavy bombers to divert to numerous secondary targets and targets of opportunity. Nevertheless, 139 2d Bombardment Division B-24s manage to attack their primary targets, a pair of oil refineries at Hamburg. Two B-24s and five of 906 VIII Fighter Command escorts are lost.

Col Donald J. M. Blakeslee, the 4th Fighter Group commanding officer, flies the last of an estimated 350 combat sorties and is forcibly transferred to a desk job with the VIII Fighter Command's 65th Fighter Wing.

On what is scheduled to be his final combat sortie, Col Hubert Zemke, the legendary former commander of the 56th Fighter Group, current commander of the 479th Fighter Group, and a 17.75-victory ace, bails out over enemy territory and is captured when his P-51 is ripped apart in a thundercloud.

Twenty-six 3d Bombardment B-17s and two APHRODITE B-17 flying bombs attack the naval installation at Heligoland Island.

ITALY: Twelfth Air Force medium bombers are grounded by bad weather, and the XXII TAC is able to mount only 51 P-47 sorties against various targets in the Po River valley.

October 31, 1944

ETO: The 9th Bombardment Division is grounded, and Ninth Air Force fighter operations are sharply curtailed by bad weather. However, XII TAC fighters and fighter-bombers are able to support the U.S. Seventh Army around Metz.

ITALY: Twelfth Air Force B-26s attack a causeway and several bridges, and XXII TAC P-47s attack gun emplacements and defensive positions south of Bologna as well as shipping targets and lines of communication in the Po River valley.

YUGOSLAVIA: One hundred seventy-four Fifteenth Air Force B-24s dispatched against targets in Yugoslavia abort in the face of bad weather.

NOVEMBER 1944

November 1, 1944

AUSTRIA: Fifteenth Air Force heavy bombers attack a diesel-engine factory, an ordnance factory, and a marshalling yard at Vienna; marshalling yards at Graz; a marshalling yard at Gussing; a tank factory at Kapfenburg; and various communications targets.

ENGLAND: Col Kyle L. Riddle resumes command of the 479th Fighter Group. Riddle, who had commanded the unit until shot down on August 10, 1944, evaded capture and returned to the group as executive officer under Col Hubert Zemke (who was in turn captured on October 30, 1944).

ETO: 9th Bombardment Division bombers are grounded by bad weather, but Ninth Air Force fighters and fighter-bombers attack rail lines and bridges in and around the battle area.

The tactical organization of the IX Fighter Command on November 1, 1944, stands as follows: the IX TAC (70th Fighter Wing, consisting of the 365th, 366th, 367th, 368th, 370th, and 474th Fighter groups, the 67th Tactical Reconnaissance Group, and the 422d Night Fighter Squadron); the XIX TAC (100th Fighter Wing, consisting of the 354th, 358th, 362d, 405th, and 406th Fighter groups, the 10th Photographic Reconnaissance Group, and the 425th Night Fighter Squadron); and the XXIX TAC (84th and 303d Fighter wings, consisting of the 36th, 48th, 373d, and 404th Fighter groups, and the 363d Tactical Reconnaissance Group).

FRANCE: The Ninth Air Force's 50th Fighter Group and the XII TAC's 371st Fighter Group (formerly a Ninth Air Force unit) are formally transferred to the First Tactical Air Force.

GERMANY: One hundred thirteen 1st Bombardment Division B-17s and 143 2d Bombardment Division B-24s attack synthetic-oil plants at Gelsenkirchen, and a total of 60 1st and 3d Bombardment division B-17s attack a marshalling yard at Hamm, a rail bridge, and the city of Koblenz. One of 286 VIII Fighter Command escort fighters is downed. This is the first operational mission in which the Micro-H blind-bombing technique is used.

ITALY: Twelfth Air Force bombers are

grounded by bad weather, but limited numbers of XXII TAC P-47s are able to attack roads, bridges, and rail lines throughout northern Italy, and especially in the Po River valley.

YUGOSLAVIA: Fifteenth Air Force heavy bombers attack marshalling yards at Cakovec and Ljubljana.

November 2, 1944

AUSTRIA: Seven Fifteenth Air Force B-17s attack an oil refinery and airdrome at Moosbierbaum.

GERMANY: Two hundred ten 1st Bombardment Division B-17s attack a synthetic-oil plant at Merseburg; 107 1st Bombardment Division B-17s attack a synthetic-oil plant at Sterkrade; 172 2d Bombardment Division B-24s attack a bridge at Bielefeld; 131 2d Bombardment Division B-24s attack a synthetic-oil plant at Castrop; 383 3d Bombardment Division B-17s attack a synthetic-oil plant at Merseburg; and 78 B-17s and 24 B-24s attack secondary targets and targets of opportunity. In the heaviest air battles since September, the bomber force is attacked by an estimated 400 GAF fighters. Forty heavy bombers and 16 of 873 escort fighters are lost.

2dLt Robert E. Femoyer, the severely wounded navigator aboard a badly damaged 447th Heavy Bombardment Group B-17, refuses relief or even a sedative so that he can remain at his post for more than two hours in order to guide the crippled airplane home. Although the bomber lands safely at its home base, Femoyer soon dies of his wounds. He is awarded a posthumous Medal of Honor.

VIII Fighter Command fighter pilots down a record 136 GAF fighters over Germany between 1210 and 1415 hours. Capt Donald S. Bryan, a 6.333-victory P-51 ace with the 352d Fighter Group's 328th Fighter Squadron, downs five and damages two Bf-109s near Merseburg between 1230 and 1250 hours; and 1stLt James J. Pascoe, a P-51 pilot with the 364th Fighter Group's 385th Fighter Squadron, achieves ace

status when he downs two Bf-109s near Halle at 1235 hours.

1stLt Henry J. Miklajcyk, a 7.5-victory P-51 ace with the 352d Fighter Group's 486th Fighter Squadron, is lost near Halle.

The 352d Fighter Group's 487th Fighter Squadron becomes the only Eighth Air Force squadron to be awarded a Distinguished Unit Citation—for downing 38 GAF aircraft in one day, the second-highest squadron tally in the theater.

One hundred forty-seven 9th Bombardment Division bombers attack rail bridges at five locations in western Germany.

ITALY: The Twelfth and Fifteenth air forces are grounded by bad weather over their bases or potential targets.

November 3, 1944

AUSTRIA: Fewer than 50 unescorted Fifteenth Air Force B-17s and B-24s brave extremely bad weather conditions to mount individual attacks against an aircraft factory at Klagenfurt, an oil refinery at Moosbierbaum, an ordnance depot near Vienna, the cities of Graz and Innsbruck, a rail line near Graz, and a marshalling yard at Munich, Germany.

FRANCE: The 64th Fighter Wing headquarters is transferred from the Twelfth Air Force to the Ninth Air Force. It establishes a new command post at Ludres.

GERMANY: More than 140 9th Bombardment Division B-26s and A-20s attack rail bridges at four locations and a railway overpass.

ITALY: The Twelfth Air Force is grounded by bad weather.

November 4, 1944

AUSTRIA: Fifteenth Air Force B-24s attack a marshalling yard and a synthetic-oil plant at Linz.

GERMANY: Two hundred thirty-eight 1st Bombardment Division B-17s attack an oil-industry target at Hamburg; 91 1st Bombardment Division B-17s attack an oil-industry target at Bottrop; 210 2d Bombardment Division B-24s attack an oil-industry target at Hannover; 133 2d Bombardment Division B-24s attack an oil-industry target at Gelsenkirchen; 186 3d Bombardment Division B-17s attack an oil-industry target at Hamburg; 151 3d Bombardment Division B-17s attack an oil-industry target at Neunkirchen; and 87 B-17s attack various secondary targets (three marshalling yards) and targets of opportunity. Five heavy bombers and two of 768 VIII Fighter Command escorts are lost.

A total of 218 9th Bombardment Division B-26s and A-20s attack gun emplacements around Eschweiler, a depot at Baumholder, and an ordnance depot at Trier.

Ninth Air Force fighter-bombers attack bridges and rail lines, and support U.S. Army ground forces around Aachen.

Fifteenth Air Force B-17s and B-24s attack marshalling yards at Augsberg and Munich, and B-17s attack oil storage facilities at Regensburg.

ITALY: More than 200 Twelfth Air Force B-25s and B-26s attack road and rail bridges leading from Brenner Pass; more than 130 B-25s attack communications targets and bridges in the Po River valley; and XXII TAC P-47s attack trains and other communications targets in the Po River valley, and gun emplacements, rocket sites, and communications targets in and around the battle area. Four P-47s bomb a hotel in Milan at which Adolf Hitler is erroneously rumored to be staying.

YUGOSLAVIA: Fifteenth Air Force heavy bombers attack a German Army troop concentration at Podgorica.

November 5, 1944

AUSTRIA: In the Fifteenth Air Force's largest single mission of the entire war against a single target, 500 B-17s and B-24s, escorted by 337 fighters, attack the Vienna/Floridsdorf oil refinery with more than 1,100 tons of bombs. 52d and 325th Fighter group P-51 pilots escorting these bombers down ten Axis aircraft over Hungary between 1315 and 1435 hours.

FRANCE: The Ninth Air Force's 362d Fighter Group displaces to Advance Landing Ground A-82, at Rouvres.

GERMANY: Three hundred ninety-six 1st Bombardment Division B-17s attack a marshalling yard at Frankfurt am Main; 333 2d Bombardment Division B-24s attack a marshalling yard at Karlsruhe; 219 3d Bombardment Division B-17s attack a marshalling yard at Ludwigshafen; 177 3d Bombardment Division B-17s attack an oil-industry (secondary) target at Ludwigshafen; and 89 heavy bombers attack various targets of opportunity. Twelve heavy bombers and six of 626 VIII Fighter Command escorts are lost.

One hundred sixty 9th Bombardment Division B-26s and A-20s attack dumps in and around Hamburg.

Ninth Air Force fighters and fighter-bombers attack bridges and rail lines and support U.S. Army ground forces.

ITALY: Twelfth Air Force B-25s and B-26s mount more than 300 sorties against bridges leading down from the Brenner Pass and in the northeastern Po River valley.

YUGOSLAVIA: Twenty-four Fifteenth Air Force B-24s attack German Army troop concentrations around Mitrovica and a marshalling yard at Podgorica.

November 6, 1944

AUSTRIA: Fifteenth Air Force B-17s and B-24s attack a steel plant at Kapfenberg, an oil refinery at Moosbierbaum, an ordnance depot at Vienna, and several marshalling yards.

ETO: The 9th Bombardment Division is grounded by bad weather.

GERMANY: Two hundred eighty 1st Bombardment Division B-17s attack two oil refineries at Hamburg; 204 2d Bombardment Division B-24s attack the Mittelland Canal at Minden; 134 2d Bombardment Division B-24s attack a synthetic-oil target at Sterkrade; 23 3d Bombardment Division B-17s attack their primary target, an aircraft plant at Neumunster; 231 3d Bombardment Division B-17s attack their secondary target, a marshalling yard at Neumunster; 65 3d Bombardment Division B-17s attack a synthetic-oil plant at Duisburg; and 64 heavy bombers attack secondary targets and targets of opportunity. Five heavy bombers and five of 722 VIII Fighter Command escorts are lost.

Ninth Air Force fighters and fighter-bombers attack rail lines and bridges, and IX TAC fighter-bombers support U.S. Army ground forces near Schmidt.

ITALY: Fifteenth Air Force heavy bombers attack a railroad power station at Bolzano; Twelfth Air Force B-25s and B-26s attack roads and rail lines, including transformers and converters, in Brenner Pass; and XXII TAC P-47s attack communications targets north of the battle area and troop positions and gun emplacements in the battle area south of Bologna.

YUGOSLAVIA: Fifteenth Air Force B-17s and B-24s attack a marshalling yard at Maribor.

November 7, 1944

AUSTRIA: Fifteenth Air Force B-17s attack an oil-industry facility near Vienna.
ETO: 9th Bombardment Division bombers are grounded by bad weather, but Ninth Air Force fighters and fighter-bombers support the U.S. V Corps as it faces heavy counterattacks along the Kall River gorge.
ITALY: Fifteenth Air Force B-24s attack rail lines leading out of Brenner Pass and a marshalling yard; Twelfth Air Force B-25s and B-26s support the British Eighth Army and attack rail lines in northeastern Italy; and XXII TAC P-47s attack bridges and provide support for the U.S. Fifth Army.

Codifying changes that were made on October 19, 1944, the XII Fighter Command is formally and officially redesignated XXII TAC.
YUGOSLAVIA: Fifteenth Air Force heavy bombers attack marshalling yards at two locations and German Army troop concentrations at four locations. Also, 124 Fifteenth Air Force P-38s attack troop concentrations and roads and rail lines.

82d Fighter Group P-38s are mistakenly engaged by Soviet Air Force fighters, of which one is shot down, two are probably shot down, and one is damaged.

November 8, 1944

ENGLAND: The VIII Air Force Composite Command is disbanded and its personnel are transferred to the new provisional USSTAF Air Disarmament Command.
ETO: 9th Bombardment Division bombers are grounded or recalled because of bad weather; Ninth Air Force fighters and fighter-bombers attack bridges, rail targets, factories, and German Army command posts; and XIX TAC aircraft support the attacks by the U.S. Army at Metz as well as the withdrawal of the U.S. V Corps from its Kall River bridgehead.
FRANCE: Following numerous weather-related delays, the U.S. Third Army and the XIX TAC open Operation MADISON, an effort to break through the German-held Metz forts and close on the Rhine River. Throughout the day, XIX TAC fighter-bombers mount 389 effective sorties against defended buildings, rail lines, motor vehicles and other road targets, and bridges. Also, two German Army command posts are knocked out by the 405th Fighter Group. Thanks in large measure to air support, U.S. Third Army units cross the Seille River in three places.

Capt Edward E. Hunt, a P-51 ace with the 354th Fighter Group's 353d Fighter Squadron, is killed when, for unknown reasons, his airplane crasheses into the ground near Mericourt.

As a first step toward establishing a new VIII Air Force Service Command service center on the Continent, the Denain/Prouvy Airdrome is assigned to Eighth Air Force control.
GERMANY: One hundred ninety-three 1st Bombardment Division B-17s attack a synthetic-oil plant at Merseburg; 77 2d Bombardment Division B-24s attack a marshalling yard at Rheine; 19 heavy bombers attack targets of opportunity; and 266 3d

Bombardment Division B-17s bound for Merseburg are recalled on account of bad weather. Three B-17s and 11 of 788 VIII Fighter Command escorts are lost.

USAAF pilots down 12 GAF fighters over Germany between 1230 and 1500 hours. Capt Richard A. Peterson, a P-51 ace with the 357th Fighter Group's 364th Fighter Squadron, brings his final personal tally to 15.5 confirmed victories when he downs a Bf-109 over Neuhausen Airdrome at 1300 hours; and 1stLt Joseph Z. Matte, a P-47 pilot with the 362d Fighter Group's 378th Fighter Squadron, achieves ace status when he downs an FW-190 and probably downs two others near Saarbrucken between 1420 and 1500 hours.

ITALY: Twelfth Air Force B-25s and B-26s attack rail lines in Brenner Pass and throughout northern Italy. Also, XXII TAC P-47s attack communications targets around Bologna and bridges and rail lines in the Parma area.

YUGOSLAVIA: Thirty-four Fifteenth Air Force B-24s attack German Army troop concentrations at three locations, but 70 others that are dispatched abort in the face of bad weather.

November 9, 1944

FRANCE: Elements of the Eighth and Ninth air forces provide powerful air attacks to assist the U.S. Third Army's XX Corps in undertaking Operation MADISON, the battle to pierce the formidable German Army defenses around Metz. Three hundred forty-five 1st Bombardment Division B-17s and 385 2d Bombardment Division B-24s attack numerous tactical targets in and around the city of Metz, and 47 3d Bombardment Division B-17s attack tactical targets at Thionville. Four B-17s are lost, but there are no losses from among 476 VIII Fighter Command escorts.

After the rest of their crew bails out, 1stLt Donald J. Gott and 2dLt William E. Metzger, Jr., attempt to help a seriously wounded crewman leave a mortally damaged B-17 of the 3d Bombardment

Division's 452d Heavy Bombardment Group. Both officers and the wounded man are killed when the airplane explodes in midair. Gott and Metzger are subsequently awarded posthumous Medals of Honor.

Due to marginal weather conditions, a total of only 74 9th Bombardment Division bombers—of 514 dispatched through the day—attack barracks, arsenals, artillery bases, a storage depot, and road junctions in and near the Metz battle area along the Franco-German frontier.

Despite marginal weather conditions, XIX TAC P-47s mount 162 effective sorties against targets in the Metz area. Also in support of Operation MADISON, Ninth Air Force fighters and fighter-bombers attack the marshalling yard at Duren, Germany.

Advance elements of the Eighth Air Force's 7th Photographic Reconnaissance Squadron displace from England to Laon/Couvron Airdrome.

Thanks in large part to air support, elements of the U.S. Third Army cross the Moselle River in two places. Thereafter, for several weeks, German-held forts, towns, and villages comprising the Metz defensive area fall to the Third Army.

GERMANY: In conjunction with heavy-bomber attacks on tactical targets in and around Metz, France, 41 1st Bombardment Division B-17s, 15 2d Bombardment Division B-24s, and 276 3d Bombardment Division B-17s attack a marshalling yard at Saarbrucken (secondary); 28 1st Bombardment Division B-17s attack the city area at Koblenz; and 34 3d Bombardment Division B-17s attack the town area at Saarlautern.

One hundred thirty-nine VIII Fighter Command fighter-bombers attack targets of opportunity around Frankfurt am Main and Lannheim. Five fighter-bombers are lost.

ITALY: The Fifteenth Air Force is grounded by bad weather. Although severely limited by bad weather, Twelfth Air Force medium bombers attack bridges in the Po River valley, but XXII TAC P-47s complete fewer than 100 sorties against rail and road bridges near Bologna.

November 10, 1944

ENGLAND: The 2d Bombardment Division's 489th Heavy Bombardment Group is withdrawn from combat pending its return to the United States for retraining in B-29s.

ETO: More than 160 9th Bombardment Division bombers are recalled because of bad weather, but Ninth Air Force fighters and fighter-bombers are able to attack railroads and support the ground attacks against Metz.

FRANCE: The XII TAC headquarters, 64th Fighter Wing headquarters, 324th Fighter Group, 11th Tactical Reconnaissance Squadron, 415th Night Fighter Squadron, and several service units are formally transferred from the Twelfth Air Force to the First Tactical Air Force. (The 11th Tactical Reconnaissance Squadron is folded into a new First Tactical Air Force Provisional Reconnaissance Group along with two former Ninth Air Force reconnaissance units, the 34th Photographic Reconnaissance Squadron and the 162d Tactical Reconnaissance Squadron.)

GERMANY: One hundred ninety-three 1st Bombardment Division B-17s attack the Cologne/Butzweiler and Cologne/Ostheim airdromes; 229 2d Bombardment Division B-24s attack Hanau/Langendiebach Airdrome; 61 2d Bombardment Division B-24s attack a marshalling yard at Hanau (secondary); 105 3d Bombardment Division B-17s attack Wiesbaden Airdrome; and 73 3d Bombardment Division B-17s attack a chemical plant at Wiesbaden (secondary). Four heavy bombers are lost, but there are no losses among 757 VIII Fighter Command escort, support, and scout fighters.

ITALY: The Fifteenth Air Force is grounded by bad weather; Twelfth Air Force B-25s and B-26s attack rail targets in Brenner Pass, the rail ferry at Ostiglia, a number of dumps, and bridges spanning the Brenta and Po rivers; and XXII TAC P-47s attack gun emplacements and rail targets in the Po River valley.

During the night of November 10–11, XXII TAC A-20s attack Ghedi Airdrome and targets of opportunity in the Po River valley.

November 11, 1944

AUSTRIA: Although more than 400 Fifteenth Air Force B-17s and B-24s are recalled or abort in the face of bad weather, more than 100 heavy bombers are able to attack two bridges and marshalling yards at five locations.

CZECHOSLOVAKIA: Fifteenth Air Force B-17s and B-24s attack oil-industry targets at Brux.

FRANCE: XIX TAC fighters and fighter-bombers support U.S. Third Army ground forces battling in and around Metz and Thionville.

GERMANY: One hundred 1st Bombardment Division B-17s attack an oil refinery at Gelsenkirchen; 124 2d Bombardment Division B-24s attack a synthetic-oil plant at Bottrop; 146 3d Bombardment Division B-17s attack a marshalling yard at Oberlahnstein; and 50 heavy bombers attack secondary targets (marshalling yards at Koblenz and Rheine) and targets of opportunity. One B-24 and one of 308 VIII Fighter Command escorts and scouts are lost.

A total of 190 9th Bombardment Division B-26s and A-20s attack rail bridges at four locations and several strongpoints, and Ninth Air Force fighters and fighter-bombers support U.S. Army ground forces near Schmidt.

ITALY: Fifteenth Air Force B-17s and B-24s attack Aviano Airdrome and bridges at three locations; Twelfth Air Force B-25s and B-26s attack bridges at two locations; and XXII TAC P-47s support U.S. Army ground forces south of Bologna and attack Villafranca di Verona Airdrome and communications targets.

During the night of November 11–12, XXII TAC A-20s attack Bergamo Airdrome, road targets, and a Po River crossing point.

November 12, 1944

ENGLAND: The Eighth Air Force is grounded by bad weather.
ETO: 9th Bombardment Division bombers are grounded by bad weather, and fighter operations are severely restricted.
GERMANY: During the night of November 12–13, 14 Fifteenth Air Force B-17s and B-24s attack an oil-industry target at Blechhammer, and five other heavy bombers attack scattered targets along the route home from Germany.
ITALY: One hundred seven Fifteenth Air Force B-24s attack a viaduct and bridges at five locations in northern Italy; Twelfth Air Force medium bombers are grounded by bad weather; and XXII TAC P-47s attack rail targets in the Po River valley.

During the night of November 12–13, XXII TAC A-20s attack a pontoon bridge, several ammunition dumps, and targets of opportunity in the Po River valley.

November 13, 1944

ENGLAND: The Eighth Air Force is grounded by bad weather.
ETO: The Ninth Air Force is grounded by bad weather.
ITALY: The Fifteenth Air Force is grounded by bad weather, but despite thick fog that grounds many Twelfth Air Force medium bombers, one attack is completed against a rail bridge at Padua. Also, XXII TAC P-47s attack communications targets north of the battle area and an oil pipeline crossing the Po River at Ostiglia.

November 14, 1944

AUSTRIA: Fifteenth Air Force B-24s attack the benzol plant at Linz.
ENGLAND: The Eighth Air Force is grounded by bad weather.
ETO: Nearly the entire Ninth Air Force is grounded by bad weather.
ITALY: The Fifteenth Air Force and all Twelfth Air Force bombers are grounded by bad weather. Throughout the day, XXII TAC P-47s complete just 17 sorties against

roads and rail lines north of the battle area.

November 15, 1944

AUSTRIA: Fifteenth Air Force B-17s attack a marshalling yard at Innsbruck and a synthetic-fuel plant at Linz.
ENGLAND: The Eighth Air Force is grounded by bad weather.
ETO: The 9th Bombardment Division is grounded by bad weather, and Ninth Air Force fighter and fighter-bomber operations are severely restricted.

The 17th and 320th Medium Bombardment groups (in B-26s), one service group, and the headquarters of the 63d Fighter Wing and 42d Medium Bombardment Wing are formally transferred from the Twelfth Air Force to the First Tactical Air Force.

The 71st Fighter Wing headquarters, the 358th Fighter Group, two service groups, and an air-depot group are formally transferred from the Ninth Air Force to the First Tactical Air Force.
ITALY: The Twelfth Air Force is grounded by bad weather.
YUGOSLAVIA: Fifteenth Air Force B-24s attack German Army troop concentrations around Novi Pazar.

November 16, 1944

AUSTRIA: Fifteenth Air Force B-17s attack marshalling yards at Innsbruck.
GERMANY: To help soften up German Army defenses in the Aachen region prior to the start of Operation QUEEN, a ground offensive by the U.S. First and Ninth armies, 490 1st Bombardment Division B-17s and 228 2d Bombardment Division B-24s attack numerous tactical targets in and around Eschweiler, and 486 3d Bombardment Division B-17s attack numerous tactical targets in and around Duren. Also, 1,119 RAF heavy bombers attack Duren, Heunsburg, and Julich with 5,437 tons of bombs, and two VIII Fighter Command escort groups strafe transportation targets. One of 265 VIII Fighter Command escorts is downed.

Despite bad weather over their bases, 80 9th Bombardment Division B-26s (of

119 dispatched) support the U.S. First and Ninth armies with attacks against three defended towns, and 212 IX TAC and 137 XXIX TAC fighters and fighter-bombers attack numerous tactical targets throughout the QUEEN battle area.

Altogether, target saturation and coverage on the opening day of Operation QUEEN is greater than that provided for Operation COBRA, the Normandy breakout, in late July. However, only very limited initial breakthroughs are achieved on the ground. (The ground phase of Operation QUEEN will continue forward for four weeks, but it will be stopped in mid-December by a tenacious German Army defensive stand in the Huertgen Forest.)

Fifteenth Air Force B-17s and B-24s attack marshalling yards at Munich.

ITALY: Twelfth Air Force medium bombers mount more than 250 effective sorties against rail targets throughout northern Italy, especially in Brenner Pass; and XXII TAC P-47s attack ammunition dumps, gun emplacements, and tactical targets in support of the British Eighth Army as well as communications targets, a pontoon storage point, and two oil pipelines crossing the Po River.

Capt John J. Voll, a P-51 ace with the 31st Fighter Group's 308th Fighter Squadron, becomes the MTO's top-scoring ace with a final personal tally of 21 confirmed victories, when he downs a Ju-88, two FW-190s, and a Bf-109, near Aviano between 1100 and 1115 hours. In all, seven GAF aircraft are downed in this engagement by 31st and 332d Fighter group P-51 pilots.

YUGOSLAVIA: Fifteenth Air Force B-24s attack German Army troop concentrations around Visegrad.

November 17, 1944

AUSTRIA: Fifteenth Air Force B-24s attack a marshalling yard and oil and other industrial targets in Vienna, and marshalling yards at Graz. Fifteenth Air Force B-17s attack marshalling yards at Salzburg.

CZECHOSLOVAKIA: Fifteenth Air Force

B-17s attack oil-industry targets at Brux.

FRANCE: Despite bad weather that grounds or turns back the remainder of the 9th Bombardment Division, 30 416th Light Bombardment Group A-26s attack a stores depot at Haguenau. (This is the first fully operational A-26 mission undertaken in the war.)

GERMANY: Ninth Air Force fighters provide limited support—207 effective sorties—to U.S. Army ground forces near Aachen and Huertgen.

Fifteenth Air Force B-24s attack oil-industry targets at Blechhammer.

HUNGARY: Fifteenth Air Force B-24s attack a marshalling yard at Gyor.

ITALY: Twelfth Air Force medium bombers attack viaducts and rail bridges in northeastern Italy and Brenner Pass. XXII TAC fighter-bombers attack gun emplacements and other tactical targets as well as rail lines, rail yards, and ammunition and fuel dumps.

YUGOSLAVIA: Fifteenth Air Force B-24s attack marshalling yards at Maribor, and Twelfth Air Force medium bombers attack rail bridges along the Brod-Zagreb-Maribor lines.

November 18, 1944

AUSTRIA: Fifteenth Air Force B-17s and B-24s attack two oil refineries in the Vienna area.

GERMANY: More than 340 9th Bombardment Division B-26s and A-20s attack strongpoints and defended towns, barracks, and rail bridges and rail yards; and Ninth Air Force fighters support U.S. Army ground forces around Aachen and Sarreguemines, France.

Three hundred seventy-four VIII Fighter Command fighters attack two airdromes and two oil-storage depots. 4th and 353d Fighter group P-51s destroy 14 Me-262 jet fighters on the ground. During melees with an estimated 70 GAF fighters, 24 GAF fighters are downed between 1100 and 1545 hours, as are seven VIII Fighter Command fighters.

Capt Dale E. Shafer, Jr., a P-51 pilot

with the 339th Fighter Group's 503d Fighter Squadron, achieves ace status when he destroys a Bf-109 near Mannheim at 1235 hours. (Shafer's four earlier victories were scored in the MTO in 1943, when he was flying 31st Fighter Group Spitfires.) Capt Michael J. Jackson, a P-47 pilot with the 56th Fighter Group's 62d Fighter Squadron, achieves ace status when he downs an FW-190 near Hanau at 1240 hours; and Capt Evan M. Johnson, a P-51 pilot with the 339th Fighter Group's 505th Fighter Squadron, achieves ace status when he downs a Bf-109 over Heilbronn at 1245 hours.

ITALY: Fifteenth Air Force B-17s and B-24s attack four airdromes; Twelfth Air Force medium bombers attack bridges at six locations; and XXII TAC P-47s attack numerous dumps, gun emplacements, several pipelines, and rail lines. XXII TAC P-47 pilots claim the destruction of eight locomotives, more than 100 rail cars, and at least 75 motor vehicles.

During the night of November 18–19, XXII TAC A-20s attack Ghedi Airdrome and targets of opportunity around five northern Italian cities.

YUGOSLAVIA: Fifteenth Air Force B-17s, B-24s, and P-38 dive-bombers attack German Army troop concentrations at Visegrad, and Twelfth Air Force medium bombers attack a bridge.

November 19, 1944

AUSTRIA: Fifteenth Air Force B-17s and B-24s attack oil refineries and storage facilities in and around Linz and Vienna, an aircraft factory at Wiener-Neudorf, and Horsching Airdrome.

FRANCE: Ninth Air Force fighter-bombers attack numerous tactical targets near Metz and Sarreguemines.

GERMANY: More than 450 9th Bombardment Division B-26s, A-20s, and A-26s attack ordnance and storage depots, road and rail junctions, bridges, and defended areas at or near ten cities and towns.

Ninth Air Force fighter-bombers attack rail lines and numerous other types of targets throughout northwestern Germany.

Ninth Air Force fighter pilots down 11 GAF fighters over western Germany during the morning.

HUNGARY: Fifteenth Air Force heavy bombers attack a marshalling yard at Gyor, and 126 Fifteenth Air Force P-51s attack two airdromes and roads and rail lines.

ITALY: Fifteenth Air Force B-17s and B-24s attack various rail targets in northern Italy, but Twelfth Air Force medium bombers and most XXII TAC P-47s are grounded by fog and low clouds. Nevertheless, some XXII TAC P-47s are able to attack troop concentrations, motor vehicles, rail lines, gun emplacements, and other targets south of Bologna.

During the night of November 19–20, XXII TAC A-20s attack Po River crossing points and several airdromes.

YUGOSLAVIA: Fifteenth Air Force B-17s and B-24s attack a marshalling yard at Maribor, and Fifteenth Air Force P-38s dive-bomb troop concentrations at two locations.

November 20, 1944

CZECHOSLOVAKIA: Fifteenth Air Force B-17s and B-24s diverted by bad weather from attacking Blechhammer, Germany, attack a town and several marshalling yards during the return to Italy.

ETO: The 9th Bombardment Division is grounded by bad weather, but Ninth Air Force fighter-bombers are able to attack rail lines, buildings, and tactical targets in and around the battle area.

GERMANY: Sixty-one 1st Bombardment Division B-17s attack their primary, an oil-industry target at Gelsenkirchen, but 93 1st Bombardment Division B-17s divert to their secondary, a marshalling yard at Munster.

Three hundred ten VIII Fighter Command fighters strafe numerous targets of opportunity in western Germany, but eight fighters are lost.

Nearly 190 Fifteenth Air Force B-17s attack an oil refinery at Blechhammer.

HUNGARY: Fifteenth Air Force P-38s attack communications targets.

ITALY: Twelfth Air Force medium bombers are grounded by bad weather, but during the late morning fighter-bombers are able to attack two factories and several supply dumps.

YUGOSLAVIA: Ninety-two Fifteenth Air Force B-24s attack a marshalling yard at Sarajevo and three rail bridges. Also, Fifteenth Air Force P-38s attack a marshalling yard at Brod.

November 21, 1944

GERMANY: Two hundred 1st Bombardment Division B-17s attack a synthetic-oil plant at Merseburg; 349 2d Bombardment Division B-24s attack two synthetic-oil plants at Hamburg; 166 3d Bombardment Division B-17s divert to their secondary, a marshalling yard at Osnabruck; and 422 heavy bombers attack numerous targets of opportunity and targets of last resort. Twenty-five heavy bombers and 15 of 858 VIII Fighter Command escorts and scouts are lost in the face of heavy GAF fighter opposition.

9th Bombardment Division bombers attack ground defenses and rail bridges, and Ninth Air Force fighter-bombers support U.S. Army ground forces in western Germany and along the Franco-German frontier.

USAAF fighter pilots down 76 GAF fighters over Germany between 1125 and 1415 hours. 1stLt Claude J. Crenshaw, a P-51 pilot with the 359th Fighter Group's 369th Fighter Squadron, achieves ace status when he downs four FW-190s and probably downs another near Merseburg between 1135 and 1205 hours; and Capt William T. Whisner, a P-51 pilot with the 352d Fighter Group's 487th Fighter Squadron, achieves ace status with a total of 9.5 victories when he destroys five and probably destroys two FW-190s near Merseburg between 1230 and 1250 hours.

ITALY: Twelfth Air Force B-25s attack ground defenses and troop concentrations in the British Eighth Army battle area, and XXII TAC P-47s support the U.S. Fifth Army and attack supply dumps and the rail line through Brenner Pass.

YUGOSLAVIA: Twenty-five Fifteenth Air Force B-24s attack troop concentrations, highways, and rail lines, and 242 Fifteenth Air Force P-38s strafe or dive-bomb numerous road and rail targets throughout southern Yugoslavia.

November 22, 1944

AUSTRIA: Two hundred fourteen Fifteenth Air Force B-17s and B-24s dispatched against targets at Munich, Germany, are thwarted by bad weather, but many are able to attack marshalling yards at Linz, Salzburg, and Villach.

ENGLAND: The 3d Bombardment Division's 4th and 92d Combat Bombardment wings are incorporated into a new 4th Provisional Heavy Bombardment Wing.

ETO: 9th Bombardment Division bombers and all but 16 Ninth Air Force fighters are grounded by bad weather.

GERMANY: Two hundred five Fifteenth Air Force B-17s and B-24s attack two marshalling yards at Munich, but 214 others are thwarted by bad weather. A small number of the bombers divert to attack a marshalling yard at Regensburg.

ITALY: Eighty-eight Fifteenth Air Force B-24s attack a bridge at Ferrara and a rail line at Carbola; 39 Fifteenth Air Force P-38 fighter-bombers attack the motor-transport depot at Osoppo; Twelfth Air Force B-25s attack ground targets in the British Eighth Army battle area; and XXII TAC P-47s mount more than 350 effective sorties against   tactical targets in the U.S. Fifth Army battle area and rail lines in the Po River valley.

November 23, 1944

ETO: The Ninth Air Force is grounded by bad weather.

GERMANY: One hundred thirty-four 1st Bombardment Division B-17s attack a synthetic-oil plant at Gelsenkirchen. One of 83

VIII Fighter Command escorts and scouts is lost.

ITALY: Despite bad weather, Twelfth Air Force B-25s are able to provide limited support for the British Eighth Army, but only 16 XXII TAC P-47s are able to cut the rail lines south of Bologna in six places.

YUGOSLAVIA: Eighty-one Fifteenth Air Force B-24s attack several road and rail bridges; 13 Fifteenth Air Force B-17s and B-24s drop supplies to Yugoslav partisans; and 34 Fifteenth Air Force P-38s attack several road and rail bridges.

November 24, 1944

AUSTRIA: During the night of November 24–25, several dozen Fifteenth Air Force B-17s and B-24s attack a benzol plant at Linz and marshalling yards at Innsbruck and Klagenfurt.

ETO: The Ninth Air Force is grounded by bad weather.

GERMANY: During the night of November 24–25, a small number of Fifteenth Air Force heavy bombers attack two marshalling yards at Munich.

ITALY: Twelfth Air Force B-25s support the British Eighth Army, and XXII TAC P-47s complete two missions against a road bridge and a rail line near Modena.

November 25, 1944

FRANCE: Ninth Air Force fighter pilots down 12 GAF fighters over the Franco-German border area between 1530 and 1615 hours.

GERMANY: Three hundred fifty-six 1st Bombardment Division and 315 3d Bombardment Division B-17s attack the Leuna synthetic-oil plant at Merseburg through intense flak, and 254 2d Bombardment Division B-24s attack a marshalling yard at Bingen. Eight B-17s and six of 873 VIII Fighter Command escorts and scouts are lost.

The Eighth Air Force's 36th Heavy Bombardment Squadron mounts its first operational mission. The new unit is equipped to screen the bomber forces against German electronic countermeasures designed to jam or otherwise thwart communications, radar, and other guidance systems. The newly committed unit is also able to jam German radars, especially those upon which flak defenses are dependent. Elements of the 36th will take part in screening most Eighth Air Force bombing missions to the end of the war.

9th Bombardment Division bombers attack an ammunition dump at Neustadt and an arsenal and road junctions at Landau. And Ninth Air Force fighter-bombers support U.S. Army ground forces on both sides of the Franco-German frontier.

ITALY: Twelfth Air Force medium bombers are grounded by bad weather, but XXII TAC P-47s from three groups are able to mount 53 effective sorties against rail targets and targets of opportunity.

November 26, 1944

GERMANY: Two hundred forty-three 1st Bombardment Division B-17s attack an oil refinery at Misburg; 118 1st Bombardment Division B-17s attack a rail viaduct at Altenbeken; 240 2d Bombardment Division B-24s attack a rail viaduct at Bielefeld; 57 2d Bombardment Division B-24s attack an oil refinery at Misburg; 266 3d Bombardment Division B-17s attack a marshalling yard at Hamm; and 130 heavy bombers attack targets of opportunity (especially marshalling yards at Bielefeld, Gutersloh, Hannover, and Herford). Losses in the face of heavy flak and attacks by an estimated 500 GAF fighters are 34 heavy bombers and nine of 668 VIII Fighter Command escorts and scouts. GAF fighters down 21 491st Heavy Bombardment Group B-24s attacking an oil refinery at Misburg, but the remainder of the group completes the bombing mission, for which it is awarded a Distinguished Unit Citation.

One hundred seventy-three 9th Bombardment Division bombers attack storage areas and supply and ordnance depots at five locations in western Germany; and Ninth Air Force fighters and fighter-bombers support U.S. Army ground forces in action along the Franco-German frontier.

USAAF fighter pilots down 123 GAF aircraft over Germany between 1018 and 1600 hours (and an He-111 bomber at 2125 hours). Capt Frederick R. Haviland, Jr., a P-51 pilot with the 355th Fighter Group's 357th Fighter Squadron, achieves ace status when he downs an FW-190 and a Bf-109 near Gardlegen at 1210 hours; 1stLt Lester C. March, a P-51 pilot with the 339th Fighter Group's 503d Fighter Squadron, achieves ace status when he downs three FW-190s near Dummer Lake between 1235 and 1300 hours; 1stLt "J" "S" Daniell, a P-51 pilot with the 339th Fighter Group's 505th Fighter Squadron, achieves "ace-in-a-day" status when he downs five FW-190s near Hannover between 1245 and 1300 hours; and 1stLt Royce W. Priest, a P-51 pilot with the 355th Fighter Group's 354th Fighter Squadron, achieves ace status when he downs two FW-190s near Misburg between 1230 and 1250 hours.

During the night of November 26–27, 11 442d Night Fighter Squadron P-61s attack a V-weapons site, and then down two GAF aircraft on the return flight to their base.

HUNGARY: Thirty-nine Fifteenth Air Force P-38s attack Seregelyes Airdrome and nearby road traffic. In the first fighter engagement in the MTO in ten days, 14th Fighter Group P-38 pilots down six Ju-87s and two GAF fighters over Hungary between 1445 and 1505 hours.

ITALY: XXII TAC fighter-bombers provide support for the U.S. Fifth Army and attack rail lines at numerous points.

November 27, 1944

ETO: 9th Bombardment Division bombers are grounded by bad weather.
GERMANY: One hundred eighty-one 1st Bombardment Division B-17s and 144 2d Bombardment Division B-24s attack a marshalling yard at Offenburg; and 148 3d Bombardment Division B-17s attack a marshalling yard at Bingen. Three of 268 VIII

Fighter Command escorts and scouts are lost.

Four hundred sixty VIII Fighter Command fighter-bombers attack four oil-industry targets in northern and central Germany. Twelve fighter-bombers are lost.

Ninth Air Force fighters and fighter-bombers attack several bridges and support U.S. Army ground forces in western Germany.

USAAF fighter pilots down 94 GAF fighters and one He-111 bomber over Germany between 0240 and 1430 hours. Capt Walter E. Starck, a P-51 pilot with the 352d Fighter Group's 487th Fighter Squadron, achieves ace status with seven confirmed victories when he downs three Bf-109s near Hameln at noon. However, Starck is then shot down and captured. 1stLt Charles J. Cesky, a P-51 pilot with the 353d Fighter Group's 328th Fighter Squadron, achieves ace status when he downs a Bf-109 near Hannover at 1205 hours; 1stLt Frank L. Gailer, Jr., a P-51 pilot with the 357th Fighter Group's 363d Fighter Squadron, achieves ace status when he downs two FW-190s near Magdeburg at 1245 hours; and Capt Charles E. Yeager, a P-51 ace with the 357th Fighter Group's 363d Fighter Squadron, brings his final personal tally to 11.5 confirmed victories when he downs four FW-190s near Magdeburg at 1310 hours.

After the rest of the 359th Fighter Group, in P-51s, aborts due to weather, Capt Ray S. Wetmore and 1stLt Robert M. York press on over Germany. At about 1300 hours, the lone pair attack an estimated 200 GAF fighters without assistance. Before running out of ammunition and fleeing, Wetmore destroys three Bf-109s (bringing his score to date to 13.25), and York scores three victories and a probable.

Capt Edward H. Beavers, Jr., a P-51 pilot with the 339th Fighter Group's 503d Fighter Squadron, who achieved ace status one day earlier, is killed by flak over Belen.
ITALY: The Twelfth and Fifteenth air forces are grounded by bad weather.

November 28, 1944

GERMANY: 9th Bombardment Division bombers attack several defended towns, an ammunition dump, and a rail bridge; and Ninth Air Force fighters and fighter-bombers attack a bridge and support U.S. Army ground forces.

ITALY: The Fifteenth Air Force is grounded by bad weather; Twelfth Air Force B-25s attack the harbor at La Spezia and bridges at three locations; and XXII TAC P-47s attack rail lines at more than forty locations and support the U.S. Fifth Army.

During the night of November 28–29, XXII TAC A-20s attack several bridges and two airdromes with incendiary bombs.

November 29, 1944

AUSTRIA: During the night of November 29–30, 18 Fifteenth Air Force B-17s attack a benzol plant at Linz and marshalling yards at three locations.

ENGLAND: The 489th Heavy Bombardment Group air echelon departs for the United States, where the group will retrain in B-29s.

GERMANY: Three hundred ninety-one 1st Bombardment Division B-17s attack oil-industry targets at Misburg; 296 2d Bombardment Division B-24s attack rail viaducts at Altenbeken and Bielefeld; 294 3d Bombardment Division B-17s attack a marshalling yard at Hamm; and 47 heavy bombers attack various targets of opportunity. One heavy bomber is lost, but there are no losses among 849 VIII Fighter Command escorts and scouts.

9th Bombardment Division bombers attack depots and barracks, and Ninth Air Force fighters and fighter-bombers support U.S. Army ground forces.

ITALY: The entire Fifteenth Air Force and all Twelfth Air Force medium bombers are grounded by bad weather, but XXII TAC P-47s attack lines of communication throughout northern Italy.

November 30, 1944

AUSTRIA: Fifteenth Air Force B-24s

attack a marshalling yard at Innsbruck.

FRANCE: On an unspecified date in November, the Ninth Air Force's 10th Photographic Reconnaissance Group displaces to Advance Landing Ground A-94, at Conflans; and on an unspecified date in late November, the Eighth Air Force's 7th Photographic Reconnaissance Group displaces to Advance Landing Ground A-83, at Denain/Prouvy Airdrome.

GERMANY: Sixty-eight 1st Bombardment Division B-17s attack a synthetic-oil plant at Bohlen; 132 1st Bombardment Division B-17s attack an oil-industry target at Zeitz; 116 1st Bombardment Division B-17s divert to their secondary, the Leuna synthetic-oil plant at Merseburg; 284 2d Bombardment Division B-24s attack marshalling yards at Homburg and Neunkirchen; 301 3d Bombardment Division B-17s attack the Leuna synthetic-oil plant at Merseburg; 169 3d Bombardment Division B-17s attack an oil-industry target at Lutzkendorf; and 149 heavy bombers attack various targets of opportunity. Twenty-nine heavy bombers and three of 895 VIII Fighter Command escorts and scouts are lost, mostly to intense flak concentrations.

Two hundred eighty-eight 9th Bombardment Division bombers attack four defended villages, a marshalling yard, a military camp, a rail tunnel, and an armored-vehicle repair center; and Ninth Air Force fighters and fighter-bombers support U.S. Army ground forces.

LtCol Willie O. Jackson, Jr., the commanding officer of the 352d Fighter Group's 486th Fighter Squadron, in P-51s, achieves ace status when he downs a Bf-109 near Chemnitz at 1345 hours.

Fifteenth Air Force B-24s attack a marshalling yard at Munich.

ITALY: Twelfth Air Force B-25s attack two bridges, and XXII TAC P-47s attack communications targets, rail lines, and railroad equipment.

DECEMBER 1944

December 1, 1944

FRANCE: The Ninth Air Force's 354th Fighter Group displaces to Advance Landing Ground A-98, at Rosieres-en-Haye.

GERMANY: One hundred thirty-two 9th Bombardment Division bombers attack three defended towns in western Germany, and Ninth Air Force fighters and fighter-bombers support U.S. Army ground forces.

Ninth Air Force fighter pilots down four GAF fighters during the afternoon.

ITALY: Twelfth Air Force B-25s attack four rail bridges in the Po River Valley, and XXII TAC P-47s attack road and rail targets.

During the night of December 1–2, XXII TAC A-20s attack Ghedi Airdrome, rail lines, and targets of opportunity.

December 2, 1944

AUSTRIA: Fifteenth Air Force B-17s and B-24s attack an oil refinery at Vienna and an oil refinery at Strasshof.

CZECHOSLOVAKIA: Fifteenth Air Force heavy bombers attack a highway bridge.

GERMANY: One hundred twenty-nine 1st Bombardment Division B-17s attack a marshalling yard at Oberlahnstein; 135 2d Bombardment Division B-24s attack a marshalling yard at Bingen; and 160 3d Bombardment Division B-17s abort in the face of bad weather. Eleven B-24s are downed by GAF fighters west of the Rhine River, but there are no losses among 436 VIII Fighter Command escorts and scouts.

Two hundred ten 9th Bombardment Division bombers attack three defended towns in western Germany, and Ninth Air Force fighters and fighter-bombers attack marshalling yards and bridges, and support U.S. Army ground forces, especially U.S. First Army units battling in the Huertgen Forest area.

One hundred thirty-three VIII Fighter Command fighters sweep areas of western Germany. Four fighters are lost.

Eighth and Ninth Air Force fighter pilots down 36 GAF aircraft over Germany between 1135 and 1525 hours. Maj Paul A. Conger, the commanding officer of the 56th Fighter Group's 63d Fighter Squadron, achieves ace status when he downs two

Bf-109s near Marburg between 1230 and 1310 hours.

Fifteenth Air Force B-17s and B-24s attack oil-industry targets at Odertal and Blechhammer.

HUNGARY: Fifteenth Air Force heavy bombers attack a marshalling yard at Celldomolk.

ITALY: Twelfth Air Force medium bombers attack at least six bridges, and XXII TAC P-47s support U.S. Army ground forces.

During the night of December 2–3, XXII TAC A-20s attack light sources throughout the Po River valley.

December 3, 1944

AUSTRIA: A total of 85 Fifteenth Air Force B-17s and B-24s attack an industrial area in Linz; marshalling yards at Innsbruck, Klagenfurt, and Villach; and a goods depot at Vienna.

FRANCE: The 9th Bombardment Division is grounded by bad weather.

GERMANY: Ninth Air Force fighters and fighter-bombers are able to support U.S. Army ground forces in western Germany.

ITALY: Despite bad weather that turns back many formations, Twelfth Air Force medium bombers are able to attack a bridge near Mantua, and the 350th Fighter Group is able to mount 60 effective sorties in support of the U.S. Fifth Army.

YUGOSLAVIA: Fourteen Fifteenth Air Force heavy bombers drop supplies to partisan forces.

December 4, 1944

GERMANY: One hundred eighty-eight of 419 1st Bombardment Division B-17s dispatched attack marshalling yards Kassel and Soest; 199 2d Bombardment Division B-24s attack a marshalling yard at Bebra (primary); 99 2d Bombardment Division B-24s attack marshalling yards at Giessen and Koblenz (targets of opportunity); 221 3d Bombardment Division B-17s attack a marshalling yard at Mainz; 62 3d Bombardment Division B-17s attack a marshalling

yard at Giessen; 119 3d Bombardment Division B-17s attack a marshalling yard at Friedburg (target of opportunity); and 41 3d Bombardment Division B-17s attack various targets of opportunity. Three heavy bombers and three of 939 VIII Fighter Command escorts and scouts are lost.

The 9th Bombardment Division is grounded by bad weather, but Ninth Air Force fighters support U.S. Army ground forces in western Germany.

ITALY: Fifteenth Air Force bombers are grounded by bad weather; Twelfth Air Force B-25s attack an ammunition dump and two defended towns; and XXII TAC P-47s support the U.S. Fifth Army and attack lines of communication.

YUGOSLAVIA: Twenty-six Fifteenth Air Force P-38s bomb a rail bridge.

December 5, 1944

GERMANY: One hundred eighty-seven 1st Bombardment Division B-17s and 217 3d Bombardment Division B-17s attack the Berlin/Tegel tank factory and munitions works; 114 2d Bombardment Division B-24s attack a marshalling yard at Munster; and 23 heavy bombers attack targets of opportunity. Twelve heavy bombers and 17 of 796 VIII Fighter Command escorts and scouts are lost.

One hundred seventy-two 9th Bombardment Division bombers attack eight defended positions, a fuel dump, a road junction, and a marshalling yard; and Ninth Air Force fighters and fighter-bombers support U.S. Army ground forces.

Beginning with the downing of an He-111 by a 422d Night Fighter Squadron crew at 0040, USAAF pilots down 91 GAF aircraft over Germany through 1350 hours. Capt Merle M. Coons, a P-51 pilot with the 55th Fighter Group's 38th Fighter Squadron, achieves ace status when he downs an FW-190 and a Bf-109 near Berlin at 1045 hours; Capt Clarence E. Anderson, Jr., a P-51 ace with the 357th Fighter Group's 363d Fighter Squadron, brings his final personal tally to 16.25 confirmed victories when he downs two FW-190s near Berlin at 1050 hours; Maj William J. Hovde, a P-51 ace and the commanding officer of the 355th Fighter Group's 358th Fighter Squadron, brings his final personal tally for World War II to 10.5 victories when he downs a Bf-109 and four FW-190s, and shares in the downing of a fifth FW-190, over Berlin at about 1100 hours; Capt William F. Wilson, a P-51 pilot with the 364th Fighter Group's 385th Fighter Squadron, achieves ace status when he downs two FW-190s near Berlin at 1105 hours; Capt Wilbur R. Scheible, a flying staff officer with the 356th Fighter Group, in P-51s, achieves ace status when he downs two FW-190s near Eberswalde between 1105 and 1120 hours; Capt Donald J. Strait, a P-51 pilot with the 356th Fighter Group's 361st Fighter Squadron, achieves ace status when he downs two FW-190s near Eberswalde between 1105 and 1120 hours; Maj Howard D. Hively, a P-51 ace and the commanding officer of the 4th Fighter Group's 334th Fighter Squadron, brings his final personal tally to 12 confirmed victories when he downs an FW-190 near Nordhorn at 1115 hours; LtCol John H. Lowell, the commanding officer of the 364th Fighter Group's 384th Fighter Squadron, in P-51s, achieves ace status when he downs three FW-190s near Berlin at noon; and Capt William F. Tanner, a P-51 pilot with the 353d Fighter Group's 350th Fighter Squadron, achieves ace status when he downs an FW-190 near Steinhuder Lake at 1300 hours.

ITALY: Twelfth and Fifteenth Air Force bombers are grounded by bad weather, but XXII TAC P-47s are able to support the U.S. Fifth Army south of Bologna and attack rail targets in the Po River valley.

December 6, 1944

AUSTRIA: Fifteenth Air Force B-24s attack Graz Airdrome.
GERMANY: Two hundred forty-four 1st Bombardment Division B-17s and 202 3d Bombardment Division B-17s attack the Leuna synthetic-oil plant at Merseburg; 112

2d Bombardment Division B-24s attack a marshalling yard at Bielefeld; 140 2d Bombardment Division B-24s attack an aqueduct at Minden; and 64 heavy bombers attack various targets of opportunity. Four B-17s and one of 747 VIII Fighter Command escorts and scouts are lost.

One hundred fifty-four 9th Bombardment Division bombers attack four towns, and Ninth Air Force fighter-bombers attack gun emplacements and bridges, and support U.S. Army ground forces.
HUNGARY: Fifteenth Air Force B-24s attack marshalling yards at Sopron and Szombathely.
ITALY: Twelfth Air Force medium bombers are grounded by bad weather, but XXII TAC P-47s are able to mount nearly 100 effective sorties against communications targets.
YUGOSLAVIA: Fifteenth Air Force B-17s attack a rail bridge at Brod and the marshalling yard at Zagreb.

December 7, 1944

AUSTRIA: Before dawn, small numbers of Fifteenth Air Force B-24s attack an industrial area at Klagenfurt, and marshalling yards at Innsbruck and Salzburg. Also, Fifteenth Air Force B-17s attack marshalling yards at Klagenfurt and Salzburg.
ETO: The Eighth and Ninth air forces are grounded by bad weather.
GERMANY: Before dawn, several Fifteenth Air Force B-17s attack a benzol plant at Spittal.
GREECE: Fifteenth Air Force B-17s conduct a resupply mission to Athens.
ITALY: Twelfth Air Force medium bombers are grounded by bad weather, but XXII TAC P-47s attack numerous road and rail targets.

December 8, 1944

AUSTRIA: Before dawn, small numbers of Fifteenth Air Force B-17s and B-24s attack rail targets around Graz, Klagenfurt, Villach, and Volkermarkt, and an oil-industry target near Vienna.

GERMANY: Twenty-nine 9th Bombardment Division A-26s attack a rail bridge at Sinzig, and Ninth Air Force fighters support U.S. Army ground forces.

ITALY: The Twelfth Air Force is grounded by bad weather, but four XXII TAC P-47s on a weather-reconnaissance mission destroy four locomotives and an estimated 100 rail cars.

December 9, 1944

AUSTRIA: Fifteenth Air Force B-24s attack an industrial area at Linz, a marshalling yard at Villach, and oil-industry targets near Vienna.

CZECHOSLOVAKIA: Fifteenth Air Force B-24s attack an armaments plant at Pilsen.

GERMANY: Three hundred eighty-one 1st Bombardment Division B-17s, escorted by 247 VIII Fighter Command escorts and scouts, attack three marshalling yards at Stuttgart. One B-17 is lost. Also, VIII Fighter Command escort fighters strafe communications targets of opportunity.

Two hundred fifty-four 9th Bombardment Division bombers attack a barracks, several defended towns, depots, and several marshalling yards; and Ninth Air Force fighters and fighter-bombers support U.S. Army ground forces.

Fifteenth Air Force B-17s attack marshalling yards and oil-industry targets at Regensburg.

ITALY: Twelfth Air Force medium bombers are grounded by bad weather, but XXII TAC P-47s are able to attack lines of communication in the Po River valley.

December 10, 1944

GERMANY: One hundred seventy-three 2d Bombardment Division B-24s attack a marshalling yard at Bingen, and 277 3d Bombardment Division B-17s attack a marshalling yard at Koblenz. One of 535 VIII Fighter Command escorts and scouts is downed.

Nearly 130 9th Bombardment Division B-26s attack two defended towns, and Ninth Air Force fighters and fighter-bombers

attack numerous ground targets and support U.S. Army ground forces.

More than 550 Fifteenth Air Force heavy bombers on their way to attack oil-industry targets in Germany are recalled in the face of bad weather.

ITALY: Twelfth Air Force B-25s attack rail targets and a barracks, as well as defended positions in support of the British Eighth Army. Also, XXII TAC P-47s attack communications targets in the battle area.

During the night of December 10–11, XXII TAC A-20s attack rail lines, roads, and pontoon bridges in the Po River valley.

December 11, 1944

AUSTRIA: Fifteenth Air Force B-17s and B-24s attack oil-industry targets and a goods depot near Vienna.

GERMANY: Three hundred nineteen 1st Bombardment Division B-17s attack a marshalling yard at Frankfurt am Main; 171 1st Bombardment Division B-17s attack bridges in the Mannheim area; 297 2d Bombardment Division B-24s attack a marshalling yard at Hanau; 154 2d Bombardment Division B-24s attack a bridge; 353 3d Bombardment Division B-17s attack a marshalling yard at Giessen (primary); 135 3d Bombardment Division B-17s attack a marshalling yard at Giessen (secondary); and 38 heavy bombers attack secondary targets and targets of opportunity. Five heavy bombers and two of 777 VIII Fighter Command escorts and scouts are lost.

More than 200 9th Bombardment Division bombers on their way to Germany are recalled because of bad weather.

Ninth Air Force fighters and fighter-bombers attack several German cities and support U.S. Army ground forces.

ITALY: Twelfth Air Force medium bombers attack a bridge, and XXII TAC P-47s attack rail targets, defensive positions, towns, and gun emplacements.

December 12, 1944

CZECHOSLOVAKIA: Fifteenth Air Force heavy bombers attack Moravska-Ostrava.

GERMANY: Three hundred thirty-seven 1st Bombardment Division B-17s attack the Leuna synthetic-oil plant at Merseburg; 270 2d Bombardment Division B-24s attack a marshalling yard at Hanau; 69 2d Bombardment Division B-24s attack a marshalling yard at Aschaffenburg; 461 3d Bombardment Division B-17s attack a marshalling yard at Darmstadt; and 60 heavy bombers attack various secondary targets and targets of last resort. Four heavy bombers and seven of 831 VIII Fighter Command escorts and scouts are lost.

Ninety 9th Bombardment Division B-26s and A-20s attack nine defended villages and towns, and Ninth Air Force fighters and fighter-bombers support U.S. Army ground forces.

Ninth Air Force fighter pilots down 13 GAF fighters over western Germany between 1445 and 1600 hours.

Fifteenth Air Force B-17s and B-24s attack oil-industry targets around Blechham-mer.

ITALY: The Twelfth Air Force is grounded by bad weather.

December 13, 1944

ENGLAND: The day's Eighth Air Force heavy-bomber mission is canceled when all the escort fighters are grounded by bad weather.

GERMANY: Two hundred fifty 9th Bombardment Division bombers attack villages and towns, a dump, and a marshalling yard. Ninth Air Force fighters and fighter-bombers attack targets around Cologne and support U.S. Army ground forces.

ITALY: The entire Fifteenth Air Force is grounded by bad weather, and Twelfth Air Force medium bombers are grounded or abort because of bad weather, but XXII TAC P-47s are able to attack flak batteries and coastal batteries near La Spezia, communications targets in the Po River valley, and buildings in the battle area.

December 14, 1944

GERMANY: The 9th Bombardment Division is grounded by bad weather, but Ninth Air Force fighters are able to support U.S. Army ground forces.

ITALY: The Fifteenth Air Force is grounded by bad weather, but Twelfth Air Force medium bombers attack rail bridges, and XXII TAC P-47s attack rail lines and gun emplacements.

December 15, 1944

AUSTRIA: Fifteenth Air Force B-17s and B-24s attack various marshalling yards around the country.

FRANCE: On approximately this date, the 9th Bombardment Division's 409th Light Bombardment Group reenters combat after being withdrawn for a month to transition from A-20s to A-26s.

GERMANY: Three hundred eighteen 1st Bombardment Division B-17s attack a marshalling yard and a tank factory at Kassel, and 327 3d Bombardment Division B-17s attack a marshaling yard at Hannover. One B-17 and two of 528 VIII Fighter Command escorts and scouts are lost.

More than 300 9th Bombardment Division bombers attack oil stores, a military camp, and six defended areas; and Ninth Air Force fighters support U.S. Army ground forces and attack ammunition and supply dumps.

ITALY: Twelfth Air Force B-25s attack rail bridges and fuel and ammunition dumps, and XXII TAC P-47s support the U.S. Fifth Army and attack lines of communication.

December 16, 1944

AUSTRIA: Fifteenth Air Force B-17s and B-24s attack a benzol plant at Linz and marshalling yards at Innsbruck and Villach.

BELGIUM: Operation GREIF, the German Army's Ardennes counteroffensive (Battle of the Bulge) begins with an assault on the U.S. First Army's winter line by 18 divisions incorporating at least 500 tanks, 350 assault guns, and 1,300 artillery pieces—all supported by 1,350 GAF fighters and bombers. From the outset, Operation GREIF is amply protected from Allied air power by a virtually impenetrable wall of bad weather that effectively obviates air support for U.S. ground forces throughout the battle area. Deep breakthroughs are achieved all along the U.S. First Army front.

CZECHOSLOVAKIA: Fifteenth Air Force B-17s and B-24s attack an armaments factory at Pilsen and a synthetic-oil plant at Brux.

ETO: The 9th Bombardment Division is grounded by bad weather, but Ninth Air Force fighters and fighter-bombers support the U.S. First Army in the Ardennes region along the German-Belgian frontier.

During the night of December 16–17, despite horrendous weather conditions, P-61 crews of the IX TAC's 422d Night Fighter Squadron down five GAF aircraft over eastern Belgium and western Germany.

GERMANY: Of 236 3d Bombardment Division B-17s dispatched, 81 attack a marshalling yard at Stuttgart and 33 attack the town of Bietingheim. The rest abort in the face of bad weather. One B-17 is lost, but there are no losses among the 116 VIII Fighter Command escort and scouts.

ITALY: Twelfth Air Force medium bombers are grounded by bad weather, but XXII TAC P-47s are able to attack rail lines in Brenner Pass, gun emplacements, defended buildings, three vessels at La Spezia, and several rail bridges.

December 17, 1944

AUSTRIA: Fifteenth Air Force B-24s attack marshalling yards at Saak, Salzburg, Villach, and Wels.

CZECHOSLOVAKIA: Fifteenth Air Force heavy bombers attack a marshalling yard at Moravska-Ostrava.

ENGLAND: The 492d Heavy Bombardment Group's 857th Heavy Bombardment Squadron is transferred to Italy to conduct special-operations missions in support of Italian and Yugoslav partisan groups operating behind Axis lines. (The squadron will be formally transferred to the Fifteenth Air Force on January 23, 1945.)

ETO: The 9th Bombardment Division is grounded by bad weather.

IX and XIX TAC fighters and fighter-bombers mount 647 effective sorties, but few of them are over the weathered-in Ardennes battle area.

GERMANY: While completing a total of 647 effective sorties throughout the day—as against an estimated 650 GAF combat sorties—Ninth Air Force day-fighter pilots down 80 GAF aircraft between 0900 and 1555 hours. Capt John H. Hoefker, a F-6 pilot with the 10th Photographic Reconnaissance Group's 15th Reconnaissance Squadron, achieves ace status when he downs an FW-190 near Kirch Gons Airdrome at 1535 hours. The Ninth Air Force day fighters also account for several hundred German Army motor vehicles damaged or destroyed. Sixteen Ninth Air Force fighters are lost.

Fifteenth Air Force B-24s attack oil-industry targets at Blechhammer and Odertal, and a marshalling yard in southeastern Germany; and Fifteenth Air Force B-17s attack several oil refineries at Blechhammer.

In the most active day for Fifteenth Air Force fighters during the entire month, 23 GAF fighters are downed on both sides of the German-Polish frontier between 1145 and 1230 hours by pilots of the 14th, 31st, and 52d Fighter groups. Capt Robert A. Karr, a P-51 pilot with the 52d Fighter Group's 5th Fighter Squadron, achieves ace status when he downs three Bf-109s over Biata, Poland, at 1210 hours; and Capt Jack R. Smith, a P-51 pilot with the 31st Fighter Group's 308th Fighter Squadron, achieves ace status with he downs an FW-190 near Blechhammer at 1210 hours.

ITALY: Twelfth Air Force medium bombers are grounded by bad weather, but XXII TAC P-47s attack a marshalling yard at Trento and communications targets in the Po River valley.

December 18, 1944

AUSTRIA: Fifteenth Air Force B-17s attack Graz Airdrome, an oil refinery near

Vienna, a marshalling yard, and an industrial area.

BELGIUM: Despite total cloud cover and an extremely low ceiling, two 67th Tactical Reconnaissance Group F-6 pilots locate a key German Army combat column on a road near Stavelot, with the result that four-plane flights from the IX TAC's 365th and 368th Fighter groups continuously attack the German column until it is too dark to continue. In the course of seven four-plane missions flown between high hills and through heavy gunfire and flak, it is estimated that 32 of 60 tanks are destroyed along with at least 56 of 200 trucks.

CZECHOSLOVAKIA: Fifteenth Air Force heavy bombers attack an oil refinery at Moravska-Ostrava.

GERMANY: Thirty-two 1st Bombardment Division B-17s attack a marshalling yard at Cologne (primary); 102 1st Bombardment Division B-17s attack targets at Koblenz (secondary); 74 1st Bombardment Division B-17s attack Kaiserlautern (secondary); 11 1st Bombardment Division B-17s attack Bonn (target of last resort); 198 1st Bombardment Division B-17s abort in the face of bad weather; all 358 2d Bombardment Division B-24s dispatched abort in the face of bad weather; 157 3d Bombardment Division B-17s attack a marshalling yard at Mainz (primary); and 13 3d Bombardment Division B-17s attack targets of opportunity. There are no heavy-bomber losses, but two of 392 VIII Fighter Command escorts and scouts are lost.

Two hundred fifty-five VIII Fighter Command fighters sweep western Germany.

One hundred sixty-five 9th Bombardment Division bombers attack five defended towns in western Germany, and Ninth Air Force fighters and fighter-bombers complete approximately 500 sorties in support U.S. Army ground forces in the Ardennes region straddling the German-Belgian frontier.

In the face of a GAF aerial offensive amounting to more than 500 effective sorties, Ninth Air Force fighter pilots down 40 GAF fighters and VIII Fighter Command

fighter pilots down ten GAF fighters over western Germany between 0930 and 1530 hours.

Two P-38 pilots with the 474th Fighter Group's 429th Fighter Squadron achieve ace status near Cologne at noon: 1stLt Lenton F. Kirkland, Jr., when he downs two Bf-109s; and 1stLt Robert C. Milliken, when he downs one Bf-109. Two P-51 pilots with the 359th Fighter Group's 368th Fighter Squadron—1stLt David B. Archibald and 1stLt Paul E. Olson—achieve "ace-in-a-day" status when they *each* down five FW-190s over Wahn at about 1445 hours. Unfortunately, Olson is himself shot down and taken prisoner.

Fifteenth Air Force B-24s attack oil-industry targets at Blechhammer, and Fifteenth Air Force B-17s attack oil-industry targets at Odertal.

HUNGARY: Fifteenth Air Force heavy bombers attack a marshalling yard at Sopron.

ITALY: Twelfth Air Force medium bombers are grounded by bad weather, but XXII TAC P-47s support the U.S. Fifth Army south of Bologna and attack lines of communication in the Po River valley.

POLAND: Fifteenth Air Force B-24s attack oil-industry targets at Oswiecim (Auschwitz).

December 19, 1944

AUSTRIA: Fifteenth Air Force B-24s and B-17s attack various marshalling yards throughout the country.

BELGIUM: In anticipation of a possible emergency in the face of the German Army's Ardennes offensive, most of the XXIX TAC headquarters component is withdrawn from Maastricht, Netherlands, to St.-Trond.

CZECHOSLOVAKIA: Fifteenth Air Force heavy bombers attack an oil refinery at Moravska-Ostrava.

ETO: The 9th Bombardment Division and most Ninth Air Force fighter units are grounded by bad weather, but a small number of Ninth Air Force fighters and fighter-bombers are able to support U.S.

Army ground forces in Belgium, France, and Germany.

GERMANY: Unable to their attack assigned targets in Luxembourg, 24 1st Bombardment Division B-17s divert against a marshalling yard at Koblenz, and 82 2d Bombardment Division B-24s divert against a marshalling yard at Ehrgang.

Eighth and Ninth air force fighter pilots down 15 GAF fighters over western Germany and eastern Belgium between 1508 and 1535 hours.

Fifteenth Air Force B-24s attack various marshalling yards throughout the country, and B-17s attack oil-industry targets at Blechhammer.

HUNGARY: Fifteenth Air Force B-24s attack a marshalling yard at Sopron.

ITALY: Twelfth Air Force medium bombers are grounded by bad weather, but XXII TAC P-47s attack communications targets near the battle area and gun emplacements around La Spezia.

During the night of December 19–20, XXII TAC A-20s attack light sources in the Po River valley.

LUXEMBOURG: One hundred forty-four 1st Bombardment Division B-17s and 62 2d Bombardment Division B-24s attack tactical targets using GH blind-bombing equipment. These attacks are in support of U.S. Army ground forces involved in the Battle of the Bulge.

December 20, 1944

AUSTRIA: Fifteenth Air Force B-24s attack marshalling yards at Salzburg and Villach, and Fifteenth Air Force B-17s attack marshalling yards at Salzburg and Linz.

CZECHOSLOVAKIA: Fifteenth Air Force B-24s attack the Skoda arms complex at Pilsen, and Fifteenth Air Force B-17s attack oil-industry targets at Brux.

ETO: The Ninth Air Force is grounded by bad weather.

GERMANY: Fifteenth Air Force B-17s attack oil-industry targets at Regensburg.

ITALY: Twelfth Air Force medium bomb-

ers are grounded by bad weather, but XXII TAC P-47s mount limited attacks against targets of opportunity in the Po River valley and rail lines in Brenner Pass and around Trento.

During the night of December 20–21, XXII TAC A-20s attack roads and targets of opportunity in the Po River valley.

December 21, 1944

ETO: The entire Ninth Air Force is grounded by bad weather.

IX TAC and XXIX TAC are transferred to the operational control of the British Second Tactical Air Force for the duration of the Ardennes emergency. Along with RAF tactical units, they will operate against German Army forces in the northern Bulge.

GERMANY: Eighty-four Fifteenth Air Force B-24s attack marshalling yards at Rosenheim.

ITALY: Twelfth Air Force medium bombers are grounded by bad weather, but XXII TAC P-47s are able to mount a limited number of effective sorties against rail targets, Ghedi Airdrome, gun emplacements, and defended buildings.

During the night of December 21–22, XXII TAC A-20s attack targets in the Po River valley.

December 22, 1944

ETO: The 9th Bombardment Division is grounded by bad weather, and only a few Ninth Air Force fighters are able to undertake strafing missions in support of U.S. Army ground forces.

Three IX TAC fighter groups are temporarily transferred to XXIX TAC control to help support a counteroffensive by the U.S. Third Army against the southern Bulge.

GERMANY: 1stLt Eugene P. McGlauflin and 2dLt Roy L. Scales, P-51 pilots with the 31st Fighter Group's 308th Fighter Squadron, share in the downing of a Me-262 jet interceptor near Passau at about 1230 hours. This is the first GAF jet downed by Fifteenth Air Force fighter pilots.

ITALY: The Fifteenth Air Force is grounded by bad weather, but Twelfth Air Force medium bombers attack bridges at three locations, and XXII TAC P-47s attack numerous bridges and other rail targets as well as gun emplacements and road traffic.

During the night of December 22–23, XXII TAC A-20s attack crossing points and targets of opportunity in the Po River valley.

December 23, 1944

BELGIUM: Two hundred sixty IX Troop Carrier Command C-47s, escorted by three XIX TAC fighter groups, drop critically needed supplies to the U.S. 101st Airborne Division at Bastogne. Eight C-47s are downed by flak.

The 352d Fighter Group, a veteran VIII Fighter Command P-51 unit, moves from Bodney, England, to Advance Landing Ground A-84, at Chievres, Belgium, to temporarily bolster Ninth Air Force units waging the Battle of the Bulge.

1stLt Lenton F. Kirkland, Jr., a P-38 ace with the 474th Fighter Group's 429th Fighter Squadron, is downed by flak and killed near Liege.

ETO: On the first reasonably good weather day in a week, Ninth Air Force fighters and fighter-bombers mount 696 effective combat sorties, the bulk of them in support U.S. Army ground forces in and around the Bulge battle areas. Nineteen Ninth Air Force fighters are lost.

Eighth and Ninth air force fighter pilots down 133 GAF fighters and one Ju-88—of an estimated 800 GAF sorties—over western Germany and eastern Belgium between 0915 and 1600 hours. Col David C. Schilling, the commander of the P-47-equipped 56th Fighter Group, downs three Bf-109s and two FW-190s during a fighter sweep over Euskirchen Airdrome, between Bonn and Koblenz, at about 1145. These victories bring Schilling's final personal tally to 22.5 and cap a legendary fighting career that began for Schilling with the first

wartime mission of the 56th Fighter Group in April 1943. Also on this group fighter sweep, Maj Harold E. Comstock, an original member of the 56th Fighter Group and now the commanding officer of the 63d Fighter Squadron, achieves ace status when he downs two FW-190s near Bonn between 1145 and 1215 hours; and Capt Felix D. Williamson, a P-47 pilot with the 56th Fighter Group's 62d Fighter Squadron, achieves ace status when he downs a Bf-109 and an FW-190 over Euskirchen Airdrome between 1230 and 1245 hours.

1stLt James M. Fowle, a P-51 pilot with the 364th Fighter Group's 384th Fighter Squadron, achieves ace status when he downs four Bf-109s near Trier between 1210 and 1230 hours; Maj George F. Ceuleers, the commanding officer of the 364th Fighter Group's 383d Fighter Squadron, achieves ace status when he downs four Bf-109s near Trier at about 1220 hours; and 1stLt David L. King, a P-47 pilot with the 373d Fighter Group's 412th Fighter Squadron, achieves ace status when he downs two Bf-109s near Euskirchen between 1500 and 1530 hours.

GERMANY: Despite bad weather, 148 1st Bombardment Division B-17s, 106 2d Bombardment Division B-24s, and 143 3d Bombardment Division B-17s are able to attack communications centers, rail junctions, marshalling yards, and other transportation targets in western Germany; and 163 VIII Fighter Command fighters sweep the Bonn area. One heavy bomber and seven of 592 VIII Fighter Command fighters dispatched are lost.

During the morning, nearly 400 9th Bombardment Division B-26s, A-26s, and A-20s attack communications targets and villages in western Germany, directly to the rear of German Army forces engaged in the Ardennes offensive. Also, during the afternoon, approximately 200 9th Bombardment Division bombers return to the area to attack many of the same or similar targets. Thirty-five bombers are lost, the highest one-day bomber loss sustained by the Ninth

Air Force in the entire war. Of the aircraft lost, 16 391st Medium Bombardment Group B-26s are downed by GAF fighters during a bombing run against a rail viaduct at Ahrweiler. (Despite these losses, however, the 391st is able to mount a 21-plane afternoon mission.)

ITALY: The entire Fifteenth Air Force and all Twelfth Air Force medium bombers are grounded by bad weather, but XXII TAC P-47s attack rail targets in the Po River valley and an airfield near Milan.

December 24, 1944

ETO: As the weather continues to clear, Ninth Air Force fighters support U.S. Army ground forces throughout the Bulge battle areas of Luxembourg and eastern Belgium. 1,157 effective Ninth Air Force fighter and fighter-bomber sorties through the day result in the destruction of 736 motor vehicles, 167 rail cars, numerous tanks and artillery pieces, and the deaths of uncounted German Army soldiers.

Eighth and Ninth Air Force fighter pilots down 95 GAF aircraft over western Germany and eastern Belgium between 0148 and 1935 hours. 1stLt William J. Sykes, a P-51 pilot with the 364th Fighter Group's 376th Fighter Squadron, achieves ace status when he downs a Bf-109 and probably downs another Bf-109 near Wengerohr between 1350 and 1400 hours. Unfortunately, Sykes is himself shot down and captured during this engagement. 1stLt Russell C. Haworth, a P-51 pilot with the 55th Fighter Group's 338th Fighter Squadron, achieves ace status when he downs a Bf-109 over Vogelsburg at 1415 hours; 2dLt Otto D. Jenkins, a P-51 pilot with the 357th Fighter Group's 362d Fighter Squadron, achieves ace status, with a tally of 8.5 confirmed victories, when he downs four FW-190s near Fulda at 1425 hours; 1stLt John A. Kirla, also a P-51 pilot with the 357th Fighter Group's 362d Fighter Squadron, achieves ace status when he downs three FW-190s near Fulda at 1425 hours; and Capt William R. Hodges, a P-51 pilot

with the 359th Fighter Group's 370th Fighter Squadron, achieves ace status when he down an FW-190 near Bonn at about 1530 hours.

FRANCE: Ten 2d Bombardment Division B-24s attack coastal batteries at La Pallice.

The VIII Fighter Command's 361st Fighter Group, in P-51s, is temporarily reassigned to the XIX TAC to help with the Bulge emergency; it moves from its base in England to Advance Landing Ground A-64, at St.-Dizier/Robinson Airdrome.

GERMANY: Thanks to the arrival of a solid high-pressure system that finally clears the skies over northern Europe, a maximum effort by 1,874 Eighth Air Force heavy bombers and 800 RAF heavy bombers—the largest single heavy-bomber strike of World War II— results in attacks on a wide range of airfields and lines-of-communications centers throughout western Germany. USAAF losses are 12 heavy bombers and ten of 813 VIII Fighter Command escorts and scouts.

While filling in as co-pilot of the lead B-17 of the vanguard 3d Bombardment Division, BriGen Frederick W. Castle, commander of the 4th Combat Bombardment Wing, remains at the controls of the aircraft, fatally damaged by German fighters, until all the other crewmen except the pilot have bailed out. Unable to bail out himself, the wing commander perishes when the bomber explodes in flames at 12,000 feet. For this utterly selfless act, General Castle is awarded a posthumous Medal of Honor.

Three hundred seventy-six 9th Bombardment Division bombers attack communications centers and rail bridges in western Germany. Thanks to the disruption of GAF bases by Eighth Air Force and RAF heavy bombers, not a single 9th Bombardment Division bomber is lost.

ITALY: The entire Fifteenth Air Force and all Twelfth Air Force medium bombers are grounded by bad weather, but XXII TAC P-47s attack Thiene Airdrome and road and rail traffic.

December 25, 1944

AUSTRIA: Fifteenth Air Force B-24s attack flak concentrations at Innsbruck and marshalling yards at Graz, Hall, Innsbruck, Villach, and Wels.

BELGIUM: At 1233 hours, moments after shooting down two Bf-109s, Maj George E. Preddy, the commanding officer of the 352d Fighter Group's 328th Fighter Squadron and the Eighth Air Force's highest-scoring ace still flying in combat, is shot down and killed by friendly antiaircraft fire while chasing a GAF fighter at low level. Preddy's final tally is 26.833 confirmed victories, leaving him second only to LtCol Francis S. Gabreski.

CZECHOSLOVAKIA: Fifteenth Air Force B-17s attack a synthetic-oil plant at Brux.

ETO: Ninth Air Force fighters and fighter-bombers mounting 1,095 effective sorties in support of U.S. Army ground forces throughout the Bulge battle area are credited with destroying 813 motor vehicles and 99 armored vehicles. Twenty-four Ninth Air Force fighters are lost.

Eighth and Ninth Air Force fighter pilots down 80 GAF aircraft over western Germany and eastern Belgium between 0115 and 2300 hours. Capt William J. Stangel, a P-51 pilot with the 352d Fighter Group's 328th Fighter Squadron, achieves ace status near Koblenz during a morning mission; 1stLt Robert E. Welch, a P-51 pilot with the 55th Fighter Group's 343d Fighter Squadron, achieves ace status when he downs two Bf-109s near Koblenz at noon; Maj Pierce W. McKennon, a P-51 ace with the 4th Fighter Group's 335th Fighter Squadron, brings his final personal tally to 12 confirmed victories when he shares in the downing of an FW-190 near Bonn at 1215 hours; LtCol Donald A. Baccus, the executive officer of the 359th Fighter Group, in P-51s, achieves ace status when he downs a Bf-109 near Bonn at 1225 hours; and Maj Frederick W. Glover, a P-51 ace with the 4th Fighter Group's 336th Fighter Squadron, brings his final personal tally to 10.333

confirmed victories when he downs an FW-190 near Koblenz at 1230 hours.

Three IX TAC fighter groups on loan to the XIX TAC are returned to IX TAC control.

GERMANY: Two hundred thirty-two 2d Bombardment Division B-24s and 156 3d Bombardment Division B-24s attack numerous road and rail targets west of the Rhine River. Five heavy bombers and nine of 432 VIII Fighter Command escorts and scouts are lost.

Six hundred twenty-nine 9th Bombardment Division B-26s, A-26s, and A-20s attack communications centers and road and rail bridges over a wide area of western Germany. Three bombers are lost.

Fifteenth Air Force heavy bombers attack marshalling yards at Plattling and Rosswein.

ITALY: Twelfth Air Force medium bombers are grounded by bad weather, but XXII TAC P-47s are very active against rail lines in the Po River valley and leading to Brenner Pass.

During the night of December 25–26, XXII TAC A-20s attack Vicenza Airdrome and light sources, motor vehicles, and railroads in the Po River valley.

December 26, 1944

BELGIUM: As the German Army's Ardennes offensive runs out of steam west of the Maas River, 9th Bombardment Division bombers attack bridges and other communications and lines-of-supply targets along the Belgian-German frontier. Ninth Air Force fighters and fighter-bombers support U.S. Army ground forces throughout the Bulge battle area.

Gliders filled with supplies for surrounded elements of the U.S. 101st Airborne Divisionare are released over Bastogne, in the southern Bulge, by IX Troop Carrier Command C-47s.

Seventy VIII Fighter Command P-51s temporarily assigned to the Ninth Air Force attack tactical targets in eastern Belgium. Two of the P-51s are lost.

1stLt Duerr "H" Schuh, a P-51 pilot with the 352d Fighter Group's 487th Fighter Squadron, achieves ace status when he downs three Bf-109s over Belgium at 1515 hours; and 1stLt Paul A. Smith, a P-61 pilot with the Ninth Air Force's 422d Night-Fighter Squadron, achieves ace status when he downs two Ju-188s near St. Vith between 2210 and 2253 hours.

GERMANY: Despite bad weather, 71 2d Bombardment Division B-24s and 67 3d Bombardment Division B-17s, escorted by 249 VIII Fighter Command escorts, attack various rail targets in western Germany.

Eighth and Ninth Air Force fighter pilots down 63 GAF aircraft over western Germany and eastern Belgium between 0135 and 2253 hours. 1stLt George R. Vanden Heuval, a P-51 pilot with the 361st Fighter Group's 376th Fighter Squadron, achieves ace status when he downs an FW-190 and shares in the downing of another FW-190 near Merzig between 1140 hours and noon.

Fifteenth Air Force B-17s attack oil-industry targets at Blechhammer and Odertal.

ITALY: Fifteenth Air Force B-24s and Twelfth Air Force medium bombers attack lines of communication running through and south from Brenner Pass; Twelfth Air Force medium bombers also attack two dumps near Bologna; Fifteenth Air Force P-38s bomb a rail bridge at Latisana; and XXII TAC P-47s attack rail lines, shipping at Genoa and La Spezia, and numerous tactical targets in the U.S. Fifth Army battle area.

During the night of December 26–27, XXII TAC A-20s attack Turin Airdrome, pontoon bridges, road bridges at three locations, and roads in the Po River valley.

POLAND: Fifteenth Air Force B-24s attack oil-industry targets at Oswiecim (Auschwitz).

December 27, 1944

AUSTRIA: Fifteenth Air Force B-17s and B-24s attack marshalling yards at Bruck, Graz, Klagenfurt, Villach and Wiener-Neustadt; an oil refinery near Vienna; a rail junction at Feldbach; and an ordnance depot at Linz. Also, 29 Fifteenth Air Force P-51s strafe rail targets between Vienna and Linz.

ETO: 9th Bombardment Division bombers attack communication centers, bridges, and targets of opportunity in western Germany and eastern Belgium; and Ninth Air Force fighters and fighter-bombers support U.S. Army ground forces in the Bulge battle areas.

Eighth and Ninth air force fighter pilots down 73 GAF aircraft over western Germany and eastern Belgium between 0003 and 2115 hours. Capt Ernest E. Bankey, Jr., a flying staff officer with the 364th Fighter Group, in P-51s, achieves ace status with a tally of 7.5 confirmed victories when he downs four FW-190s and a Bf-109 and shares in the downing of a second Bf-109 near Bonn between 1055 and 1210 hours; 1stLt Earl R. Lazear, Jr., a P-51 pilot with the 352d Fighter Group's 486th Fighter Squadron achieves ace status when he downs a Bf-109 near Bonn at 1105 hours; 1stLt Raymond H. Littge, a P-51 pilot with the 352d Fighter Group's 487th Fighter Squadron, achieves ace status when he downs three FW-190s near Mauer at 1115 hours; Maj William T. Halton, the commanding officer of the 352d Fighter Group's 487th Fighter Squadron, in P-51s, also achieves ace status with a tally of 7.5 confirmed victories when he downs three Bf-109s and shares in the downing of a fourth near Bonn between 1100 and 1130 hours; and Capt Gilbert L. Jamison, a P-51 pilot with the 364th Fighter Group's 385th Fighter Squadron, achieves ace status with a tally of seven confirmed victories when he downs three FW-190s near Bonn at 1130 hours.

FRANCE: To balance fighter forces committed to the northern and southern Bulge areas in the wake of the wholesale transfer on December 21 of the IX and XXIX TACs to the British Second Tactical Air Force, the Ninth Air Force's 365th, 367th, and 368th Fighter groups are placed under the operational control of the XIX TAC (in the south). Two of the effected units must complete a physical move in order to comply with the transfer: the 365th Fighter Group displaces to Advance Landing Ground Y-34, at Metz/Frescati Airdrome; and the 368th Fighter Group displaces to Advance Landing Ground A-68, at Juvincourt. Also, to balance reconnaissance assets available to the various Ninth Air Force tactical air commands, the 363d Tactical Reconnaissance Group's 160th and 161st Tactical Reconnaissance squadrons are placed under IX TAC control, and must displace to Advance Landing Ground A-94, at Conflans.

GERMANY: Despite freezing fog in England that grounds many Eighth Air Force heavy bombers, 201 1st Bombardment Division B-17s, 172 2d Bombardment Division B-24s, and 202 3d Bombardment Division B-17s attack numerous rail targets in western Germany. Two heavy bombers and five of 193 VIII Fighter Command escorts and scouts are lost.

One hundred sixty-three VIII Fighter Command fighters mount a sweeping operation over western Germany.

ITALY: Fifteenth Air Force B-24s attack lines of communication in Brenner Pass and rail bridges in northern Italy; Twelfth Air Force medium bombers attack lines of communication in and around Brenner Pass and two supply dumps near Bologna; 44 Fifteenth Air Force P-38s bomb bridges; and XXII TAC P-47s help stem German Army counterattacks on the U.S. Fifth Army front and attack lines of communication in the Po River valley.

Twelfth Air Force C-47s drop supplies to Italian partisans in northern Italy.

During the night of December 27–28, XXII TAC A-20s attack motor vehicles and light sources in the Po River valley and Brenner Pass area.

YUGOSLAVIA: Fifteenth Air Force B-24s attack marshalling yards at Maribor.

December 28, 1944

AUSTRIA: Fifteenth Air Force B-17s attack marshalling yards at Salzburg and four other locations.

CZECHOSLOVAKIA: Fifteenth Air Force B-24s attack oil refineries at Pardubice and two other locations, and an oil storage depot.

ETO: The entire Ninth Air Force is grounded by bad weather.

GERMANY: Three hundred thirty 1st Bombardment Division B-17s, 284 2d Bombardment Division B-24s, and 510 3d Bombardment Division B-17s attack rail bridges and marshalling yards throughout western Germany. Two B-24s are lost, but there are no losses among 568 VIII Fighter Command escorts and scouts.

Fifteenth Air Force B-17s attack an oil depot and freight yard at Regensburg.

ITALY: Fifteenth Air Force B-24s attack lines of communication around Brenner Pass; Twelfth Air Force medium bombers attack a supply dump and a troop concentration; and XXII TAC P-47s support the U.S. Fifth Army and attack roads, bridges, and a motor-vehicle depot.

During the night of December 28–29, XXII TAC A-20s attack vehicles, road bridges, rail lines, ferry crossings, and targets of opportunity in the Po River valley.

December 29, 1944

AUSTRIA: Fifteenth Air Force B-17s and B-24s attack various marshalling yards throughout Austria.

BELGIUM: Only seven of more than 100 9th Bombardment Division bombers complete a mission against targets in the Bulge; the rest are recalled in the face of bad weather.

ETO: Despite deteriorating weather conditions, Ninth Air Force fighters and fighter-bombers complete several hundred sorties in support of U.S. Army ground forces in the Bulge.

GERMANY: Two hundred ninety-three 1st Bombardment Division B-17s, 241 2d

Bombardment Division B-24s, and 36 3d Bombardment Division B-17s attack bridges, marshalling yards, and communications centers in western Germany and eastern Belgium. Four heavy bombers and three of 587 VIII Fighter Command escorts and scouts are lost.

This is the first mission of the 78th Fighter Group since its transition from P-47s to P-51s. The only P-47 unit remaining in the Eighth Air Force is the 56th Fighter Group, which undertakes a sweep mission over western Germany.

Fifteenth Air Force B-24s attack various marshalling yards throughout southern Germany, and 14 Fifteenth Air Force P-38s attack a road bridge near Rosenheim.

ITALY: Fifteenth Air Force B-24s attack lines of communication around Brenner Pass; Fifteenth Air Force B-17s attack the locomotive repair facilities at Castelfranco and Udine; Twelfth Air Force medium bombers attack bridges and viaducts; and XXII TAC P-47s attack bridges, communications targets, motor vehicles, and trains.

During the night of December 29–30, XXII TAC A-20s attack Ghedi Airdrome and targets of opportunity.

December 30, 1944

CORSICA: The Twelfth Air Force's 319th Medium Bombardment Group, in B-26s, is ordered to cease combat operations and return to the United States. At this point, the only medium-bomber units remaining in the Twelfth Air Force are the 57th Medium Bombardment Wing's 310th, 321st, and 340th Medium Bombardment groups, which all are equipped with B-25s.

ETO: All 9th Bombardment Division bombers and IX TAC aircraft are grounded or recalled because of bad weather, but several hundred XIX TAC and XXIX TAC fighters and fighter-bombers are able to attack ground targets and support U.S. Army ground forces in western Germany, eastern Belgium, eastern France, and Luxembourg.

GERMANY: 393 1st Bombard Division

B-17s, 354 2d Bombardment Division B-24s, and 504 3d Bombardment Division B-17s attack rail bridges and marshalling yards throughout western Germany. Four B-17s and two of 528 VIII Fighter Command escorts and scouts are lost.

ITALY: Twelfth Air Force B-25s attack lines of communication in and around Brenner Pass, bridges, and an ammunition dump; and XXII TAC P-47s support the U.S. Fifth Army and attack bridges.

During the night of December 30–31, XXII TAC A-20s attack numerous targets in the Po River valley.

December 31, 1944

ETO: The 9th Bombardment Division is grounded by bad weather, but several hundred Ninth Air Force fighters and fighter-bombers are able to support U.S. Army ground forces in eastern Belgium and western Germany.

GERMANY: Four hundred ninety-two 1st Bombardment Division B-17s and 254 2d Bombardment Division B-24s attack numerous rail bridges, communications centers, and marshalling yards in western Germany, and 501 3d Bombardment Division B-17s attack industrial and oil-industry targets at six locations. Losses are 27 heavy bombers and ten of 721 VIII Fighter Command escorts and scouts.

Eighth and Ninth Air Force fighter pilots down 64 GAF fighters and one Ar-234 jet bomber over western Germany and eastern Belgium between 1045 and 2350 hours. Maj Samuel J. Wicker, the commanding officer of the 364th Fighter Group's 383d Fighter Squadron, achieves ace status with a total of seven victories when he downs four FW-190s near Hamburg between 1125 hours and noon; and 1stLt Charles D. Hauver, a P-51 pilot with the 355th Fighter Group's 354th Fighter Squadron, achieves ace status when he downs an FW-190 near Hamburg at 1210 hours.

ITALY: Twelfth Air Force B-25s attack a dump and several trains, and XXII TAC

P-47s attack rail bridges, rail lines, and trains.

During the night of December 31–January 1, XXII TAC A-20s attack a marshal-ling yard at Milan and a motor-vehicle park at Molinella.

YUGOSLAVIA: Twelfth Air Force medium bombers attack a bridge at Bodrez.

JANUARY 1945

January 1, 1945*

ENGLAND: The Eighth Air Force's independent 406th Heavy Bombardment Squadron (night leaflets) is administratively assigned to the 482d Heavy Bombardment Group (radar and pathfinding). Operationally, the 406th Squadron is transferred from VIII Fighter Command to the 1st Air Division.

ETO: At midnight, New Year's Eve, the 1st, 2d, 3d, and 9th Bombardment divisions are redesignated as *air* divisions.

More than 800 GAF tactical aircraft mount aggressive attacks against Allied airfields in Belgium, France, and the Netherlands (Operation HERMANN) between 0800

and 1000 hours. At least 30 USAAF aircraft are destroyed on the ground, and 62 are damaged. The British Second Tactical Air Force loses 162 aircraft destroyed and 62 damaged.

In all, USAAF fighters are credited with downing 69 GAF aircraft over Belgium and Germany between 0320 and 1230 hours, and RAF fighter pilots are credited with downing approximately 100 GAF aircraft—all at a cost of six Allied fighters downed.

One hundred ninety 9th Air Division bombers attack lines-of-communication targets and a German Army command post in Belgium and Germany.

BELGIUM: At approximately 0930 hours, as 12 P-51s of the 352d Fighter Group's 487th Fighter Squadron are taking off from their temporary base near Liege for an area patrol, the airdrome comes under attack and the P-51s are jumped by approximately 50 FW-190s and Bf-109s. Within minutes, the squadron routs the attack force and accounts for 20 of the GAF fighters destroyed without loss to itself. 1stLt Sanford K. Moats

---

* It may be assumed for the balance of hostilities that fighters and fighter-bombers controlled by the IX, XII, XIX, XXII, and XXIX TACs are supporting U.S. Army ground forces as a matter of course. Also, many VIII Fighter Command fighters are routinely flying sweeps and other nonescort missions over enemy territory.

achieves ace status in this battle when he downs four FW-90s; 1stLt Alexander F. Sears achieves ace status when he downs a Bf-109; Capt William T. Whisner brings his final personal World War II tally to 14.5 confirmed victories when he downs two Bf-109s and two FW-190s; and the 487th Fighter Squadron commander, LtCol John C. Meyer, brings his final World War II tally to 24 confirmed victories when he downs two FW-190s.

GERMANY: Only 11 of 428 1st Air Division B-17s dispatched against an oil-industry target at Magdeburg attack the primary; 292 1st Air Division B-17s attack a marshalling yard at Kassel (secondary); 26 1st Air Division B-17s attack a marshalling yard at Gottingen; 99 1st Air Division B-17s attack numerous targets of opportunity; 86 2d Air Division B-24s attack two rail bridges at Koblenz; 57 2d Air Division B-24s attack a rail bridge at Irlich; six 2d Air Division B-24s attack the rail bridge at Remagen; 42 2d Air Division B-24s attack several targets of opportunity; 54 3d Air Division B-17s attack an oil-industry target at Dollbergen; 24 3d Air Division B-17s attack an oil-industry target at Ehmen; and 21 3d Air Division B-17s attack several targets of opportunity. Eight Eighth Air Force heavy bombers (including five screening aircraft) and two of 626 VIII Fighter Command escorts and scouts are lost.

1stLt Robert M. York, a P-51 pilot with the 359th Fighter Group's 370th Fighter Squadron, achieves ace status when he downs an FW-190 near Luneberg at 1131 hours; and 1stLt Van E. Chandler, a P-51 pilot with the 4th Fighter Group's 336th Fighter Squadron, achieves ace status when he downs a Bf-109 over Uelzen at 1230 hours.

ITALY: The entire Fifteenth Air Force is grounded by bad weather, but Twelfth Air Force B-25s attack bridges at three locations, and XXII TAC P-47s attack a fuel dump at Parma and lines of communication.

January 2, 1945

BELGIUM: The VIII Air Force Service Command advance headquarters is established in Brussels.

ETO: One hundred thirty-five 9th Air Division bombers attack communications targets and rail bridges in Germany and Belgium.

GERMANY: Two hundred eighty-three 1st Air Division B-17s attack a marshalling yard and five communications centers in western Germany; 282 2d Air Division B-24s attack five rail bridges; 240 3d Air Division B-17s attack marshalling yards, rail bridges, and rail junctions; 128 3d Air Division B-17s attack German Army tank concentrations; and 23 heavy bombers attack targets of opportunity. Four heavy bombers and three of 492 VIII Fighter Command escorts and scouts are lost.

Eighth and Ninth air force fighter pilots down 14 GAF fighters over Germany between 0910 and 1615 hours.

ITALY: The entire Fifteenth Air Force and all Twelfth Air Force B-25s are grounded by bad weather, but XXII TAC P-47s attack rail lines and road and rail targets in the Po River valley and Brenner Pass as well as a marshalling yard at Milan.

During the night of January 2–3, XXII TAC A-20s attack Ghedi Airdrome, vehicles and pontoon bridges in the Po River valley.

January 3, 1945

BELGIUM: Ninety-eight 1st Air Division B-17s attack the German-held communications center at St.-Vith.

ETO: The 9th Air Division is grounded by bad weather.

GERMANY: One hundred forty-five 1st Air Division B-17s attack two marshalling yards and two rail junctions; 129 1st Air Division B-17s attack the city of Cologne (secondary); 311 2d Air Division B-24s attack five marshalling yards and a railhead; and 377 3d Air Division B-17s attack four marshalling yards and two communications centers. Four of 571 VIII Fighter Command scouts and escorts are lost.

ITALY: The Fifteenth Air Force is grounded by bad weather; Twelfth Air Force B-25s attack rail bridges at four locations; and XXII TAC P-47s attack numerous rail targets.

During the night of January 3–4, XXII TAC A-20s attack a bridge and a supply dump near Mestre and vehicles throughout northern Italy.

January 4, 1945

BELGIUM: VIII Fighter Command headquarters begins moving from Bushey Park, England, to Charleroi.

ETO: The Eighth and Ninth air forces are grounded by bad weather.

ITALY: More than 370 Fifteenth Air Force heavy bombers attack rail sidings and marshalling yards at seven locations; Twelfth Air Force B-25s attack two bridges; and XXII TAC P-47s attack communications targets in the Po River valley, and an ammunition dump.

During the night of January 4–5, XXII TAC A-20s attack targets of opportunity around Modena.

YUGOSLAVIA: Nine Fifteenth Air Force B-24s drop supplies to Yugoslav partisans.

January 5, 1945

BELGIUM: 9th Air Division bombers attack three communications centers, and Ninth Air Force fighters and fighter-bombers attack road traffic and other communications targets.

FRANCE: The Ninth Air Force's 368th Fighter Group displaces to Advance Landing Ground Y-34, at Metz/Frescati Airdrome.

GERMANY: Eight hundred ninety-three Eighth Air Force heavy bombers attack several airfields and numerous rail and other communications targets throughout western Germany. One B-17 and one of 537 VIII Fighter Command scouts and escorts are lost.

9th Air Division bombers attack rail

bridges at three locations, and Ninth Air Force fighters and fighter-bombers attack airfields, road traffic, and other communications targets.

ITALY: The Twelfth Air Force and most of the Fifteenth Air Force are grounded by bad weather.

LUXEMBOURG: 9th Air Division bombers attack the communications center at Massen.

YUGOSLAVIA: Fifteenth Air Force B-24s are recalled while on their way to attack Zagreb, but 33 Fifteenth Air Force P-38s bomb a rail bridge.

January 6, 1945

GERMANY: Seven hundred seventy-eight Eighth Air Force heavy bombers attack rail and other communications targets in western Germany, and one fighter-bomber group attacks a marshalling yard. One B-17 and two of 531 VIII Fighter Command escorts and scouts are lost.

Nearly the entire Ninth Air Force is grounded by bad weather, but 26 9th Air Division bombers are able to attack Prum.

ITALY: The entire Fifteenth Air Force and all Twelfth Air Force B-25s are grounded by bad weather, but XXII TAC P-47s attack rail lines and bridges between Genoa and La Spezia and ships in the harbors at Imperia and Genoa.

January 7, 1945

ETO: Except for several fighter groups involved in escorting Eighth Air Force heavy bombers, the Ninth Air Force is grounded by bad weather.

GERMANY: Nine hundred eighty-five Eighth Air Force heavy bombers attack marshalling yards, bridges, and other communications targets in western Germany. Three heavy bombers and one of 586 VIII Fighter Command escorts and scouts are lost.

ITALY: The entire Fifteenth Air Force and all Twelfth Air Force B-25s are grounded by bad weather, but XXII TAC P-47s attack rail targets throughout northern

Italy and ships in the harbors at San Remo and Savona.

During the night of January 7–8, XXII TAC A-20s attack targets of opportunity in the Po River valley.

January 8, 1945

AUSTRIA: More than 300 Fifteenth Air Force B-17s and B-24s attack the main railroad station and a marshalling yard at Linz and marshalling yards at Graz, Klagenfurt, Salzburg, and Villach.

ETO: The entire Ninth Air Force is grounded by bad weather.

GERMANY: Six hundred four Eighth Air Force heavy bombers attack marshalling yards, bridges, and other communications targets in western Germany. Two heavy bombers are lost.

ITALY: Of three Twelfth Air Force medium-bomber missions dispatched, only six B-25s are able to drop their bombs; the rest abort or are recalled because of bad weather. Fewer than 20 XXII TAC P-47 sorties are effective.

January 9, 1945

GERMANY: Fifteen 9th Air Division B-26s attack a rail bridge, but all other Ninth Air Force operations are canceled because of bad weather.

ITALY: The entire Fifteenth Air Force is grounded by bad weather, but Twelfth Air Force B-25s are able to attack bridges and an assembly area at four locations, and XXII TAC P-47s attack numerous communications and tactical targets throughout northern Italy.

January 10, 1945

ETO: All 9th Air Division bombers are grounded or forced to abort because of bad weather, but Ninth Air Force fighters and fighter-bombers are active against bridges and tactical targets in eastern Belgium and western Germany.

GERMANY: Nine hundred twelve Eighth Air Force heavy bombers attack airfields, marshalling yards, and bridges in western Germany. Ten heavy bombers are lost to dense flak concentrations.

ITALY: The entire Fifteenth Air Force and all Twelfth Air Force B-25s are grounded by bad weather, but XXII TAC P-47s attack numerous communications targets and dumps and sink a warship at Venice.

During the night of January 10–11, XXII TAC A-20s attack targets of opportunity in the Po River valley.

January 11, 1945

BELGIUM: 9th Air Division bombers attack communications centers.

GERMANY: 9th Air Division bombers attack communications centers, and Ninth Air Force fighters attack an ammunition dump at Mayen.

ITALY: The entire Fifteenth Air Force and all Twelfth Air Force B-25s are grounded by bad weather, but XXII TAC P-47s support U.S. Fifth Army ground forces and attack fuel and ammunition dumps, an alcohol refinery at Piacenza, and road and rail targets.

January 12, 1945

ENGLAND: The Eighth Air Force is grounded by bad weather.

ETO: The entire Ninth Air Force is grounded by bad weather.

ITALY: The entire Fifteenth Air Force and all Twelfth Air Force B-25s are grounded by bad weather, but XXII TAC P-47s attack road and rail targets in the Po River valley.

January 13, 1945

GERMANY: Nine hundred nine Eighth Air Force heavy bombers attack seven bridges spanning the Rhine River and several marshalling yards. Eight heavy bombers and one of 294 VIII Fighter Command escorts and scouts are lost.

9th Air Division bombers attack road and rail bridges at three locations.

ITALY: The entire Fifteenth Air Force and the entire Twelfth Air Force are grounded by bad weather.

January 14, 1945

ETO: More than 280 9th Air Division bombers attack German Army ground forces in the shrinking Ardennes (Bulge) salient and in nearby areas of Germany.

GERMANY: Eight hundred forty-seven Eighth Air Force heavy bombers attack oil-industry targets and highway bridges. Seven B-17s and eight of 645 VIII Fighter Command escorts and scouts are lost.

In the best one-day tally of World War II, USAAF fighter pilots down a record 174 GAF fighters over Germany and the Netherlands between 1010 and 1610 hours. Capt Leonard K. Carson, a P-51 ace with the 357th Fighter Group's 363d Fighter Squadron, attains a final personal tally of 18.5 confirmed victories when he downs two FW-190s and a Bf-109 near Berlin at about 1240 hours; Maj John B. England, the commanding officer of the 357th Fighter Group's 362d Fighter Squadron, brings his final personal tally to 17.5 confirmed victories when he downs a Bf-109 in the same action; 1stLt John "L" Sublett, a P-51 pilot with the 357th Fighter Group's 362d Fighter Squadron, achieves ace status when he downs two Bf-109s near Berlin at 1240 hours; LtCol Irwin H. Dregne, the 357th Fighter Group commanding officer, achieves ace status when he downs a Bf-109 near Brandenburg at 1245 hours; LtCol Andrew J. Evans, Jr., the 357th Fighter Group executive officer, achieves ace status when he downs two Bf-109s and two FW-190s near Brandenburg; Capt Chester K. Maxwell, a P-51 pilot with the 357th Fighter Group's 364th Fighter Squadron, achieves ace status when he downs three FW-190s near Berlin; 1stLt Charles E. Weaver, a P-51 pilot with the 357th Fighter Group's 364th Fighter Squadron, achieves ace status when he downs a Bf-109 and an FW-190 near Berlin; and 1stLt Harley L. Brown, a P-51 pilot with the 20th Fighter Group's 55th Fighter Squadron, achieves ace status when he downs two Bf-109s over Perleberg at 1245 hours.

The 357th Fighter Group's score of 56 victories is the highest tally by a single USAAF unit on a single mission.

ITALY: The entire Fifteenth Air Force and the entire Twelfth Air Force are grounded by bad weather.

During the night of January 14–15, XXII TAC A-20s attack crossing points in the Po River valley.

NETHERLANDS: 1stLt Ernest O. Bostrom, a P-51 pilot with the 352d Fighter Group's 486th Fighter Squadron, achieves ace status when he downs an FW-190 near Almelo at 1415 hours; and Maj Gordon M. Graham, the commanding officer of the 355th Fighter Group's 354th Fighter Squadron, in P-51s, achieves ace status when he downs two FW-190s near Meppel at 1430 hours.

January 15, 1945

AUSTRIA: Fifteenth Air Force heavy bombers attack marshalling yards and other rail targets near Vienna.

GERMANY: Six hundred nineteen Eighth Air Force B-17s and B-24s attack six marshalling yards and four towns in western Germany, and 62 VIII Fighter Command P-51 fighter-bombers bomb a marshalling yard. Two of 511 VIII Fighter Command escorts and scouts are lost.

Sixteen 9th Air Division bombers attack a bridge.

1stLt Robert P. Winks, a P-51 pilot with the 357th Fighter Group's 364th Fighter Squadron, achieves ace status when he downs an Me-262 over Schongau Airdrome at noon.

ITALY: Fifteenth Air Force heavy bombers attack a marshalling yard at Treviso; Twelfth Air Force B-25s mount nearly 150 effective sorties against six bridges

During the night of January 15–16, XII TAC A-20s attack road targets around Genoa and Milan.

January 16, 1945

ETO: Following a shift of fighter units to favor the most active U.S. field armies, the

Ninth Air Force's three tactical air commands are organized thusly: IX TAC—48th, 366th, 370th, 404th, and 474th Fighter groups; XIX TAC—354th, 362d, 365th, 367th, 368th, 405th, and 406th Fighter groups; and XXIX TAC—36th and 373d Fighter groups.

GERMANY: Sixty-one 2d Air Division B-24s attack an oil refinery at Magdeburg; 61 2d Air Division B-24s attack a munitions plant at Magdeburg (secondary); 67 2d Air Division B-24s attack an oil refinery at Ruhland; 138 2d Air Division B-24s attack a marshalling yard at Dresden (secondary); 146 3d Air Division B-17s attack a marshalling yard at Dessau (secondary); and 96 3d Air Division B-17s attack a chemical plant at Bitterfeld. Two B-24s and one of 586 VIII Fighter Command escorts and scouts are lost.

Three hundred eleven 9th Air Division bombers attack bridges, a motor-vehicle repair center, communications centers, and various other targets.

ITALY: The Fifteenth Air Force and most Twelfth Air Force aircraft are grounded by bad weather. Only 16 XXII TAC P-47 sorties are completed against communications targets in the Po River valley.

January 17, 1945

ETO: The 9th Air Division and most Ninth Air Force fighters are grounded by bad weather.

GERMANY: Three hundred ninety-seven 1st Air Division B-17s attack a marshalling yard at Paderborn; 37 1st Air Division B-17s attack a rail viaduct at Bielefeld; 78 2d Air Division B-24s attack an oil refinery at Harburg; 74 3d Air Division B-17s attack two oil refineries at Hamburg; and 73 3d Air Division B-17s attack the U-boat base at Hamburg. Nine heavy bombers and seven of 240 VIII Fighter Command escorts and scouts are lost.

ITALY: The Fifteenth Air Force is grounded by bad weather, but Twelfth Air Force B-25s and XXII TAC P-47s attack rail targets at numerous locations.

During the night of January 17-18, XXII TAC A-20s attack crossings in the Po River valley.

January 18, 1945

BELGIUM: The IX TAC rear headquarters moves to Charleroi from Verviers.

ETO: The Ninth Air Force is grounded by bad weather.

The IX TAC is returned to Ninth Air Force operational control after serving under the British Second Tactical Air Force.

GERMANY: Despite bad weather that grounds the rest of the Eighth Air Force bomber force, 114 3d Air Division B-17s attack a rail bridge at Kaiserlautern. Three of 109 VIII Fighter Command escorts and scouts are lost.

ITALY: The Fifteenth Air Force is grounded by bad weather, but Twelfth Air Force B-25s attack rail lines and XXII TAC P-47s attack numerous rail targets and supply and fuel dumps.

During the night of January 18–19, XXII TAC A-20s attack road and rail targets in the Po River valley.

January 19, 1945

ENGLAND: The Eighth Air Force is grounded by bad weather.

ETO: The 9th Air Division is grounded by bad weather.

ITALY: The Twelfth Air Force is grounded or unable to complete missions because of bad weather.

MTO: Due to unprecedented foul weather through the first weeks of the new year, Fifteenth Air Force P-38 and P-51 pilots have been unable to find GAF fighters over central and southern Europe. On this day, however, 325th Fighter Group P-51 pilots down two Ju-52 transports and three GAF fighters over Austria and Yugoslavia.

YUGOSLAVIA: More than 400 Fifteenth Air Force B-17s and B-24s attack a rail bridge, a highway bridge, and two marshalling yards at Brod, but 111 heavy bombers must abort in the face of bad weather on their way to Zagreb. Also, 46 Fifteenth Air

Force P-38s attack a rail bridge, and 59 P-51s sweep the area between Zagreb and Gyor, Hungary.

January 20, 1945

AUSTRIA: Fifteenth Air Force heavy bombers attack a station siding and two marshalling yards at Linz and a marshalling yard at Salzburg.

ETO: The 9th Air Division is grounded by bad weather.

GERMANY: Of 155 1st Air Division B-17s and 154 3d Air Division B-17s dispatched against the synthetic-oil plant at Sterkrade, only 24 and 12, respectively, are able to locate and attack the target. Of the remainder, 110 1st Air Division B-17s and 115 3d Air Division B-17s attack a marshalling yard at Rheine. Also, in other phases of the mission, 170 1st Air Division B-17s attack a rail bridge at Mannheim; 187 3d Air Division B-17s attack the marshalling yard at Pforzheim; and 35 B-17s attack various targets of opportunity. Four B-17s and one of 374 VIII Fighter Command escorts and scouts are lost.

Still three weeks short of his twentieth birthday, 1stLt Dale E. Karger, a P-51 pilot with the 357th Fighter Group's 364th Fighter Squadron, becomes the youngest USAAF ace in World War II when he downs an Me-262 near Munich at 1225 hours.

Fifteenth Air Force B-17s attack oil-industry targets at Regensburg and a marshalling yard at Rosenheim. This mission is carried out on one of only nine days this month on which MTO bombers are able to fly.

325th Fighter Group P-51 pilots are credited with four GAF fighters, of which three FW-190s are downed over Regensburg between 1300 and 1320 hours by the 317th Fighter Squadron's 2dLt Edward L. Miller. The five GAF aircraft downed on January 19 and the four downed on January 20 are the only enemy aircraft credited in the air to Fifteenth Air Force fighters during the entire month.

ITALY: Twelfth Air Force B-25s attack a marshalling yard at Trento and two bridges, and XXII TAC P-47s attack fuel and ammunition dumps and communications targets in the Po River valley.

During the night of January 20–21, XXII TAC A-20s attack communications targets in the Po River valley.

SOVIET UNION: A provisional Hungarian government signs a peace treaty with the United States, Great Britain, and the Soviet Union.

January 21, 1945

AUSTRIA: One hundred seventy Fifteenth Air Force B-17s attack two oil refineries at Vienna.

BELGIUM: The IX TAC main headquarters returns from Liege to Verviers.

GERMANY: Seven hundred fifty-three Eighth Air Force heavy bombers attack bridges, an oil plant, an armaments factory, six marshalling yards, two communications centers, and several targets of opportunity. Eight heavy bombers are lost.

One hundred sixty-six 9th Air Division bombers attack a marshalling yard and ground defenses at Mayen, and a bridge, rail junction, and marshalling yard at Euskirchen.

ITALY: Twelfth Air Force B-25s attack a supply dump, a railroad fill, and three bridges; XXII TAC P-47s attack ammunition and fuel dumps, numerous rail lines, vehicles, trains, and other communications targets; and 43 Fifteenth Air Force P-38s bomb an oil refinery at Fiume.

January 22, 1945

GERMANY: One hundred sixty-seven 1st Air Division B-17s attack a synthetic-oil plant at Sterkrade and 30 B-17s attack several targets of opportunity. Five B-17s are lost.

During the morning, as large components of the German Army withdraw into Germany from Belgium, 304 9th Bombardment Division bombers attack road and rail targets in eastern Belgium and western Germany. The 387th and 394th Medium

Bombardment groups, in 49 B-26s, destroy the bridge spanning the Our River at Dasburg, thus creating a traffic jam on the east bank amounting at the outset to an estimated 1,500 German Army vehicles. These vehicles are attacked through the remainder of the day by air-controlled U.S. Army artillery and IX and XIX TAC fighters and fighter-bombers, which destroy at least half of the trapped vehicles.

During the morning, pilots of the Ninth Air Force's 362d Fighter Group locate an estimated 1,500 German Army vehicles bogged down in an immense traffic jam near Prum. Here, as at Dasburg, IX and XIX TAC fighters and fighter-bombers destroy at least half of the vehicles during the course of continuous attacks.

Six IX TAC and seven XIX TAC fighters are lost during ground-attack missions at Dasburg and Prum.

ITALY: The Fifteenth Air Force is grounded by bad weather; Twelfth Air Force B-25s attack five bridges; and XXII TAC P-47s attack dumps and rail targets throughout northern Italy.

During the night of January 22–23, XXII TAC A-20s attack several airdromes as well as roads and river crossings at more than 50 locations in the Po River valley.

January 23, 1945

GERMANY: One hundred sixty-nine 1st and 3d Air division B-17s attack a marshalling yard at Neuss, and 12 B-17s attack a bridge at Neuss. One B-17 is lost. Among the airmen lost is Col Frank P. Hunter, the 398th Heavy Bombardment Group commander, who is killed.

Several very small formations of 9th Air Division A-26s mount low-level attacks against bridges and troop-and-vehicle concentrations at three locations. These are the first low-level attacks undertaken by USAAF bombers in northern Europe since the disastrous Ijmuiden raid of May 17, 1943.

Despite bad weather, IX and XIX TAC fighters mount nearly 600 effective sorties, mainly against the gutted German Army motor columns at Dasburg and Prum. More than 1,000 motor and horse-drawn vehicles, and some tanks and other armored vehicles, are destroyed at a cost of five IX TAC fighters. Also, XIX TAC mounts 159 effective sorties against locomotives and rail cars at Duren. At a cost of one fighter lost, the XXIX TAC airmen destroy six locomotives, 150 rail cars, 65 buildings, and a tank, as well as cutting rail lines and highways in nearly a dozen places.

ITALY: The entire Fifteenth Air Force and all Twelfth Air Force B-25s are grounded by bad weather, but XXII TAC P-47s attack gun emplacements, dumps, coastal shipping, and rail targets throughout northern Italy.

January 24, 1945

ENGLAND: The Eighth Air Force is grounded by bad weather.

GERMANY: Despite poor weather conditions, 25 9th Air Division bombers attack three communications centers, and Ninth Air Force fighters mount 312 effective sorties, mainly against the remains of the German Army motor vehicles trapped at Dasburg and Prum. At a cost of three fighters lost, IX TAC fighters and fighter-bombers destroy 12 tanks, 30 other armored vehicles, 359 motor vehicles, and 47 gun emplacements.

ITALY: The entire Fifteenth Air Force and virtually the entire Twelfth Air Force are grounded by bad weather.

During the night of January 24–25, XXII TAC A-20s attack road and rail targets.

January 25, 1945

ENGLAND: The Eighth Air Force is grounded by bad weather.

GERMANY: One hundred seventy 9th Air Division Bombers attack rail lines, bridges, and communications centers; and Ninth Air Force fighters mount 581 effective sorties, mainly against the concentrations at Dasburg and Prum. Due to deteriorating weather conditions, these are the last such attacks against those targets.

In all, during four days of intense strikes against withdrawing German Army forces at Dasburg, Prum, and other nearby locations, Ninth Air Force ground-attack aircraft are credited with the destruction of 61 tanks, 125 other armored vehicles, 3,627 motor vehicles, 149 gun emplacements, 35 locomotives, 1,157 rail cars, and an unknown number of horse-drawn vehicles.
ITALY: The entire Fifteenth Air Force and most of the Twelfth Air Force are grounded by bad weather. One medium-bomber mission is mounted against an ammunition dump at Cremona, and XXII TAC P-47s attack dumps and communications targets around Milan.

During the night of January 25–26, XXII TAC A-20s attack Ghedi Airdrome and crossing points in the Po River valley.

January 26, 1945

ENGLAND: The Eighth Air Force is grounded by bad weather.

The Eighth Air Force's air-sea rescue squadron—known officially as 65th Fighter Wing Detachment B—is redesignated the 5th Emergency Rescue Squadron.
GERMANY: Twenty-six 9th Air Division B-26s attack rail traffic around Euskirchen.
ITALY: The entire Fifteenth Air Force and the entire Twelfth Air Force are grounded by bad weather.

January 27, 1945

BELGIUM: The Ninth Air Force's 370th Fighter Group displaces to Advance Landing Ground Y-29, at Asche.
ENGLAND: The Eighth Air Force is grounded by bad weather.
ETO: The 9th Air Division and the XIX TAC are grounded by bad weather.
ITALY: The entire Fifteenth Air Force is grounded by bad weather, and all Twelfth Air Force B-25s dispatched on missions must abort in the face of bad weather. XXII TAC P-47s attack communications targets and destroy an oil plant.

January 28, 1945

GERMANY: Three hundred forty-two 1st Air Division B-17s attack two marshalling yards at Cologne; 41 1st Air Division B-17s attack several secondary targets and targets of opportunity; 115 2d Air Division B-24s attack a synthetic-oil plant at Kaiserstuhl; 58 2d Air Division B-24s attack a synthetic-oil plant at Gneisenau; 25 2d Air Division B-24s attack several targets of opportunity; 169 3d Air Division B-17s attack a marshalling yard at Hohenbudberg; 90 3d Air Division B-17s attack two bridges at Duisburg; and 15 3d Air Division B-17s attack several targets of opportunity. Seven B-24s and three B-17s are lost.

Ninety-five 9th Air Division bombers attack bridges and an overpass at four locations and a communications center at Mayen.
ITALY: The Fifteenth Air Force is grounded by bad weather; Twelfth Air Force B-25s attack two rail bridges; and XXII TAC P-47s attack numerous communications targets throughout northern Italy.

During the night of January 28–29, XXII TAC A-20s attack numerous light sources and several pontoon bridges in the Po River valley.

January 29, 1945

BELGIUM: The Ninth Air Force's 365th Fighter Group displaces to Advance Landing Ground A-78, at Florennes/Juzaine Airdrome.
ETO: Ninth Air Force fighter units are reorganized as follows: IX TAC—36th, 48th, 365th, 373d, 404th, and 474th Fighter groups; XIX TAC—354th, 362d, 367th, 368th, 405th, and 406th Fighter groups; and XXIX TAC—366th and 370th Fighter groups.
FRANCE: BriGen Glenn O. Barcus replaces BriGen Gordon P. Saville as commanding general of the XII TAC.
GERMANY: 1,001 Eighth Air Force B-17s and B-24s attack rail targets in

central Germany and 93 3d Air Division B-17s attack industrial targets at Kassel. One B-24 and two of 638 VIII Fighter Command escorts and scouts are lost.

Three hundred ninety-four 9th Air Division bombers attack supply stores, defended areas, rail bridges, and communication targets throughout western Germany. **ITALY:** The Fifteenth Air Force is grounded by bad weather; Twelfth Air Force B-25s are able to attack rail bridges at six locations and a railroad station; and XXII TAC P-47s attack numerous rail targets in the Po River valley.

During the night of January 29–30, XXII TAC A-20s attack scattered fuel dumps, the harbor at La Spezia, road and rail traffic around Milan, and several crossing points in the Po River valley. **YUGOSLAVIA:** During the night of January 29–30, 13 Fifteenth Air Force B-24s drop supplies to Yugoslav partisans.

January 30, 1945

ENGLAND: The Eighth Air Force is grounded by bad weather. **ETO:** The 9th Air Division is grounded by bad weather. **ITALY:** The Fifteenth Air Force is grounded by bad weather; Twelfth Air Force B-25s attack numerous points along the Brenner Pass rail line; and XXII TAC P-47s attack factories, bridges, and dumps in and around Parma.

During the night of January 30–31, Fifteenth Air Force B-24s drop supplies to partisans in northern Italy, and XXII TAC A-20s attack rail targets in the Po River valley.

January 31, 1945

AUSTRIA: Fifteenth Air Force B-17s and B-24s mount major attacks against an oil refinery near Vienna and a marshalling yard at Graz. **ETO:** The Ninth Air Force is grounded by bad weather. **GERMANY:** Four hundred three Eighth Air Force B-17s and B-24s dispatched against targets in Germany are recalled because of anticipated bad weather over their bases at the scheduled time of return. **ITALY:** Twelfth Air Force B-25s attack bridges at five locations and a marshalling yard; and XXII TAC P-47s attack bridges, rail lines, and road and rail traffic throughout northern Italy. **YUGOSLAVIA:** Fifteenth Air Force heavy bombers attack a marshalling yard at Maribor.

FEBRUARY 1945

February 1, 1945

AUSTRIA: More than 300 Fifteenth Air Force B-17s and B-24s attack marshalling yards at Furstenfeld, Graz, and Klagenfurt, and an oil refinery at Moosbierbaum.

BELGIUM: The 352d Fighter Group, in P-51s, is returned to Eighth Air Force control following temporary duty with the Ninth Air Force since December 23, 1944. The unit remains at Advance Landing Ground A-84, at Chievres Airdrome.

ENGLAND: The unit designation of the 493d Heavy Bombardment Group's 862d Heavy Bombardment Squadron is transferred to the Eighth Air Force's new 3d Scouting Force, but the squadron's aircraft and personnel are distributed to the other squadrons of the 493d Group.

ETO: The 361st Fighter Group, on loan to the XIX TAC since late December, is returned to VIII Fighter Command control. The unit moves from Advance Landing Ground A-64, at St.-Dizier/Robinson Airdrome, France, to Advance Landing Ground A-84, at Chievres Airdrome, Belgium.

FRANCE: The Ninth Air Force's 367th Fighter Group displaces to Advance Landing Ground A-64, at St.-Dizier/Robinson Airdrome.

GERMANY: Six hundred sixteen 1st and 3d Air division B-17s attack marshalling yards at Krefeld, Ludwigshafen, and Mannheim; highway and rail bridges at Mannheim; rail bridges at Wesel; and several targets of opportunity. Two B-17s are lost.

One hundred forty-six 9th Air Division bombers attack ground defenses and bridges between the Rhine and Moselle rivers.

During the night of February 1–2, the 9th Air Division's 410th Light Bombardment Group mounts its first effective night missions since being withdrawn from combat in early January to retrain and reequip as the Ninth Air Force's only dedicated night-bomber unit. Of 25 A-20s dispatched at 2050 hours, 22 receive a recall message (triggered by a report of bad weather), but the remaining three continue on to the target, a communications center at Hillesheim. Bombs are dropped at 2204 hours with the aid of GEE blind-bombing equipment, but results are unobserved. All planes return safely to their base by 2350 hours.

ITALY: Nearly the entire Twelfth Air Force is grounded by bad weather. Only 12 effective fighter-bomber sorties are completed.

February 2, 1945

FRANCE: The Ninth Air Force's 406th Fighter Group displaces to Advance Landing Ground Y-34, at Metz/Frescati Airdrome.

GERMANY: During the Eighth Air Force's only offensive mission of the day— a sweep by the 56th Fighter Group P-47s— Maj Paul A. Conger, the commanding officer of the 63d Fighter Squadron, brings his final personal tally to 11.5 confirmed victories when he downs at FW-190 and a Bf-109 near Berlin at 1040 hours.

More than 350 9th Air Division bombers attack road and rail bridges east of the Rhine River and defended areas in the battle zones in western Germany.

ITALY: Twelfth Air Force B-25s attack bridges at seven locations, but the Fifteenth Air Force and XXII TAC are grounded by bad weather over their bases.

February 3, 1945

GERMANY: Four hundred forty-three 1st Air Division B-17s and 494 3d Air Division B-17s attack the Tempelhof marshalling yard in Berlin; 116 2d Air Division B-24s attack a synthetic-oil plant at Magdeburg (primary); 246 2d Air Division B-24s attack marshalling yards at Magdeburg (targets of last resort); and 69 heavy bombers attack various targets of opportunity. Extremely heavy flak downs 23 B-17s over Berlin and two B-24s. Eight of 844 VIII Fighter Command escorts and scouts are also lost

VIII Fighter Command pilots down 21 GAF aircraft over Germany between 1040 and 1245 hours. Capt Cameron M. Hart, a P-47 pilot with the 56th Fighter Group's 63d Fighter Squadron, achieves ace status when he downs two Bf-109s near Berlin at

1040 hours; 1stLt Bernard H. Howes, a P-51 pilot with the 55th Fighter Group's 343d Fighter Squadron, achieves ace status when he downs an FW-190 and a "Mistel" (a manned FW-190 with an unmanned Ju-88 "flying bomb" attached) near Boizenburg at 1230 hours; and LtCol Elwyn G. Righetti, the commanding officer of the 55th Fighter Group, also achieves ace status when he downs one Mistel and probably downs another.

9th Air Division bombers attack a marshalling yard, a storage-and-repair depot, a communications center, and rail bridges at two locations.

During the night of February 3–4, 18 410th Light Bombardment Group A-20s attack a motor-transport depot at Mechernich (primary); and eight A-20s attack a rail junction (secondary).

ITALY: The Twelfth and Fifteenth air forces are grounded by bad weather.

February 4, 1945

GERMANY: 9th Air Division bombers attack a repair depot and a road-and-rail junction.

ITALY: The Fifteenth Air Force is grounded by bad weather; Twelfth Air Force B-25s attack rail bridges at five locations and a marshalling yard; and XXII TAC P-47s attack rail facilities and at least ten bridges.

During the night of February 4–5, XXII TAC A-20s attack road targets south of Bologna and in the Po River valley.

February 5, 1945

AUSTRIA: Fifteenth Air Force heavy bombers attack rail facilities at Salzburg and Villach.

ETO: All Ninth Air Force offensive operations are canceled in the face of bad weather.

GERMANY: Fifteenth Air Force heavy bombers attack an oil-storage facility at Regensburg and rail facilities at Rosenheim and Straubing.

ITALY: Twelfth Air Force B-25s attack bridges at three locations.

During the night of February 5–6, XXII TAC A-20s attack road traffic and lights in the Po River valley.

February 6, 1945

GERMANY: Of 1,383 Eighth Air Force heavy bombers dispatched to attack several oil-industry targets, 1,310 are forced by bad weather to divert against several secondary targets and nearly twenty targets of opportunity, mostly city and town areas. Five heavy bombers and four of 829 VIII Fighter Command escorts and scouts are lost.

Two hundred sixty-one 9th Air Division bombers attack a defended village, an ammunition dump, a motor-vehicle park, a communications center, and targets of opportunity.

ITALY: The Fifteenth Air Force is grounded by bad weather; Twelfth Air Force B-25s attack rail lines, a bridge, and marshalling yards; and XXII TAC P-47s attack numerous targets of opportunity.

During the night of February 6–7, XXII TAC A-20s attack lights and signs of movement throughout northern Italy.

February 7, 1945

AUSTRIA: Fifteenth Air Force heavy bombers attack at least six oil refineries in the Vienna area, and Zwolfaxing Airdrome.
GERMANY: Two hundred ninety-four 1st Air Division B-17s and all escorting fighters bound for Essen are recalled because of bad weather, but one B-17 attacks the target. Of all Eighth Air Force combat units, only the 364th Fighter Group gets into action, during a fighter sweep.

Although the Ninth Air Force is grounded by bad weather, 12 9th Air Division B-26s attack a rail siding at Lippe.
ITALY: Twelfth Air Force B-25s and XXII TAC P-47s attack bridges and rail lines, and XXII TAC P-47s attack several dumps and sugar refineries.

During the night of February 7–8, XXII TAC A-20s attack at least 58 targets in Brenner Pass and the Po River valley.
YUGOSLAVIA: Fifteenth Air Force heavy bombers attack a oil-storage facility at Pula and the town of Bratislava.

February 8, 1945

AUSTRIA: More than 500 Fifteenth Air Force B-17s and B-24s attack a marshalling yard at Graz and communications targets in and around Vienna.
BELGIUM: The Ninth Air Force's 406th Fighter Group displaces to Advance Landing Ground Y-29, at Asche.
ENGLAND: One hundred fifty Eighth Air Force B-17s and 254 B-24s are recalled on their way to Germany, most before leaving England.
ETO: Ninth Air Force fighter units are reorganized as follows: IX TAC—36th, 48th, 365th, 404th, and 474th Fighter groups; XIX TAC—354th, 362d, 367th, and 368th Fighter groups; and XXIX TAC—366th, 370th, 373d, 405th, and 406th Fighter groups.
GERMANY: In the Eighth Air Force's only offensive action of the day, 98 VIII Fighter Command P-51s based on the Continent mount a sweep against rail lines.

More than 320 9th Air Division bombers attack three defended areas, a marshalling yard, a road junction, and targets of opportunity.
ITALY: Twelfth Air Force B-25s attack bridges at three locations, and XXII TAC P-47s attack an oil dump and a rail bridge.

During the night of February 8–9, XXII TAC A-20s and A-26s (in their theater debut) attack communications targets throughout the Po River valley, and 11 Fifteenth Air Force heavy bombers drop supplies to partisan units in northern Italy.

February 9, 1945

AUSTRIA: Fifty-four Fifteenth Air Force heavy bombers attack an oil refinery at Moosbierbaum and marshalling yards at Graz and Bruck.
FRANCE: The Ninth Air Force's 323d Medium Bombardment Group displaces to Advance Landing Ground A-83, at Denain/ Prouvy Airdrome.

GERMANY: Two hundred thirty-three 1st Air Division B-17s attack an oil-industry target at Lutzkendorf; 147 1st Air Division B-17s attack rail viaducts at Arnsberg and Paderborn; ten 2d Air Division B-24s attack a synthetic-oil plant at Magdeburg (primary); 286 2d Air Division B-24s attack a marshalling yard at Magdeburg (secondary); 64 2d Air Division B-24s attack a rail viaduct at Bielefeld (primary); 198 3d Air Division B-17s attack a munitions plant at Weimar (secondary); 107 3d Air Division B-17s attack an oil-industry target at Dulmen (secondary); and 173 heavy bombers attack various targets of opportunity. Eight heavy bombers and five of 809 VIII Fighter Command escorts and scouts are lost.

VIII Fighter Command pilots down 22 GAF fighters over Germany between 1130 and 1350 hours. 1stLt William E. Whalen, a P-51 pilot with the Eighth Air Force's 2d Scouting Force, achieves ace status when he downs two Bf-109s and probably downs a third near Dessau at noon; Capt George W. Gleason, a P-51 ace with the 479th Fighter Group's 434th Fighter Squadron, brings his final personal tally to 12 confirmed victories when he downs a Bf-109 and an FW-190 near Magdeburg between 1211 and 1230 hours; and Capt James E. Duffy, Jr., a P-51 pilot with the 355th Fighter Group's 354th Fighter Squadron, achieves ace status when he downs an FW-190 near Berlin at 1310 hours.

Capt James W. Browning, a seven-victory P-51 ace with the 357th Fighter Group's 363d Fighter Squadron, is shot down and killed near Fulda.

Three hundred forty-seven 9th Air Division bombers attack marshalling yards, rail bridges, and communications centers.
ITALY: The Twelfth Air Force is grounded by bad weather.

During the night of February 9–10, XXII TAC A-20s and A-26s attack the dock area at La Spezia, and rail lines, light sources, and signs of movement in the Brenner Pass and Po River valley.

February 10, 1945

GERMANY: Unable to locate their primary target in the Netherlands, 140 1st Air Division B-17s attack an oil plant at Dulmen.

More than 320 9th Air Division bombers attack a rail bridge, communications centers at three locations, a vehicle depot, and targets of opportunity.
ITALY: Despite bad weather, that grounds the Fifteenth Air Force and many Twelfth Air Force units, Twelfth Air Force B-25s attack two bridges, and XXII TAC P-47s attack rail lines and a motor-vehicle park.

During the night of February 10–11, XXII TAC A-20s and A-26s attack bridges in the Po River valley, light sources and signs of movement throughout northern Italy, and Germany Army frontline defenses in the Apennine mountains.
NETHERLANDS: Of 164 Eighth Air Force B-17s dispatched against the U-boat base at Ijmuiden, only nine are able to locate and attack the target.

February 11, 1945

GERMANY: Unable to locate their primary target, 124 2d Air Division B-24s attack the oil plant at Dulmen.

Ninety-seven 9th Air Division bombers attack marshalling yards at Bingen and Modrath.
ITALY: The Fifteenth Air Force and all Twelfth Air Force B-25s are grounded by bad weather, but XXII TAC P-47s attack supply dumps, rail lines, and bridges.

During the night of February 11–12, XXII TAC A-20s and A-26s attack targets in Brenner Pass and the Po River valley.

February 12, 1945

ETO: The Ninth Air Force is grounded by bad weather.
ITALY: The entire Fifteenth Air Force and most of the Twelfth Air Force are grounded by bad weather, but some Twelfth Air Force B-25s are able to attack a bridge and a sugar refinery, and the XXII TAC's 57th Fighter Group, in P-47s, attacks gun

emplacements, a bridge, and rail lines in the Po River valley.

During the night of February 12–13, XXII TAC A-20s and A-26s attack troop movements in the Po River valley.

February 13, 1945

AUSTRIA: Fifteenth Air Force heavy bombers attack depots and railroad repair facilities around Vienna and marshalling yards at Graz and Matzleinsdorf.

GERMANY: More than 320 9th Air Division bombers attack two transportation depots, rail bridges at three locations, a defended town, and targets of opportunity; and Ninth Air Force fighter-bombers attack bridges at two locations.

ITALY: Twelfth Air Force B-25s attack bridges at four locations, and XXII TAC P-47s mount nearly 350 effective sorties against marshalling yards at three locations and communications targets throughout northern Italy.

During the night of February 13–14, XXII TAC A-20s and A-26s attack a bridge approach and targets of opportunity in the Po River valley.

MTO: Fifteenth Air Force fighter pilots are officially encouraged to attack rail targets, especially locomotives, following release from bomber-escort duty or during fighter sweeps over enemy territory.

YUGOSLAVIA: Fifteenth Air Force heavy bombers attack a railroad repair depot at Maribor; marshalling yards at Maribor, Sarvar, and Zagreb; and dock facilities at Pula.

February 14, 1945

AUSTRIA: Fifteenth Air Force heavy bombers attack oil refineries at four locations in and around Vienna and marshalling yards at four locations.

FRANCE: The Ninth Air Force's 410th Light Bombardment Group displaces to Advance Landing Ground A-68, at Juvincourt.

GERMANY: Three hundred eleven 1st Air Division B-17s attack a marshalling yard at Dresden; 340 2d Air Division B-24s attack a marshalling yard at Magdeburg (secondary); 294 3d Air Division B-17s attack a marshalling yard at Chemnitz; 37 3d Air Division B-17s attack a highway bridge at Wesel (primary); 35 3d Air Division B-17s attack an oil depot at Dulmen (secondary); and 277 heavy bombers attack various targets of opportunity, including the Czech cities of Brux, Pilsen, and Prague. Seven heavy bombers and seven of 837 VIII Fighter Command escorts and scouts are lost.

VIII Fighter Command pilots down 18 GAF fighters over eastern Germany between noon and 1235 hours. LtCol Arthur F. Jamison, the commanding officer of the 479th Fighter Group's 434th Fighter Squadron, in P-51s, brings his personal tally to 14 confirmed victories when he downs a Bf-109 near Berlin at about 1230 hours.

Capt Kenneth H. Dahlberg, a 14-victory P-51 ace with the 354th Fighter Group's 353d Fighter Squadron, is taken prisoner after being shot down by flak.

Throughout the day, 9th Air Division bombers mount 622 effective sorties against communications centers, marshalling yards, rail bridges, an ammunition dump, a vehicle depot, and targets of opportunity. Fourteen bombers are lost.

ITALY: Twelfth Air Force B-25s attack bridges and bridge approaches at three locations and several gun emplacements in the battle area; and XXII TAC P-47s attack communications targets in the Po River valley.

YUGOSLAVIA: Fifteenth Air Force heavy bombers attack marshalling yards at Celje, Maribor, and Zagreb.

February 15, 1945

AUSTRIA: Fifteenth Air Force heavy bombers attack an oil refinery, freight yards at five locations, a goods depot, and three marshalling yards, all in the Vienna area; as well as marshalling yards at Graz, Klagenfurt, and Wiener-Neustadt; an ordnance depot at Graz; and targets of opportunity.

FRANCE: The Ninth Air Force's 371st Fighter Group displaces to Advance Landing Ground Y-34, at Metz/Frescati Airdrome; the Ninth Air Force's 409th Light Bombardment Group displaces to Advance Landing Ground A-70, at Laon/Couvron Airdrome; and the Ninth Air Force's 416th Light Bombardment Group displaces to Advance Landing Ground A-69, at Laon/Athies Airdrome.

GERMANY: Two hundred ten 1st Air Division B-17s attack the city of Dresden (secondary); 353 2d Air Division B-24s attack a synthetic-oil plant at Magdeburg (secondary); 435 3d Air Division B-17s attack a marshalling yard at Cottbus (secondary); 58 3d Air Division B-17s attack a marshalling yard at Rheine (target of last resort); and 19 heavy bombers attack several targets of opportunity. Two heavy bombers and one of 433 VIII Fighter Command escorts and scouts are lost.

Approximately 90 9th Air Division B-26s attack marshalling yards at Mayen and Sinzig.

ITALY: Fifteenth Air Force heavy bombers attack the shipyard at Fiume.

Except for a limited mission against an ammunition dump, Twelfth Air Force B-25s are grounded by bad weather, but XXII TAC P-47s are able to attack rail targets in northeastern Italy and the Po River valley.

February 16, 1945

ENGLAND: The 3d Air Division's 4th Provisional Heavy Bombardment Wing is given official status as the 4th Heavy Bombardment Wing.

ETO: The 371st Fighter Group is transferred to the Ninth Air Force from the First Tactical Air Force and is assigned to the XIX TAC.

The Ninth Air Force's 367th Fighter Group returns to combat status following its transition from P-38s to P-47s; and the 354th Fighter Group is reequipped with P-51s following several months' service in P-47s.

GERMANY: One hundred ninety-four 1st Air Division B-17s attack oil-industry targets at Dortmund, Minster Stein, and Nordstern; 268 2d Air Division B-24s attack marshalling yards at Osnabruck and Rheine; 46 2d Air Division B-24s attack a marshalling yard at Munster; 208 3d Air Division B-17s attack a marshalling yard at Hamm; 63 3d Air Division B-17s attack a rail bridge at Wesel; and 102 heavy bombers attack various targets of opportunity. Eight heavy bombers are lost.

More than 300 9th Air Division bombers attack a communications center, a rail bridge, an ordnance depot, a jet-engine factory, and targets of opportunity, mostly in the Ruhr River valley; and Ninth Air Force fighters and fighter-bombers attack bridges and rail lines.

Two hundred sixty-three Fifteenth Air Force B-24s attack the Me-262 factory at Regensburg, where they destroy an estimated 20 jet interceptors on the ground and damage the manufacturing facility. Other B-24s attack the nearby jet airdrome at Neubiberg.

ITALY: Twelfth Air Force B-25s are grounded by bad weather, but XXII TAC P-47s attack rail lines and ammunition and fuel dumps.

MTO: Approximately 450 Fifteenth Air Force B-17s and B-24s dispatched against a variety of targets in central and southern Europe are forced by bad weather to return to their bases.

February 17, 1945

AUSTRIA: Fifteenth Air Force heavy bombers attack rail targets and a synthetic-oil plant at Linz, marshalling yards at four locations, a steel plant, and two tank factories.

ENGLAND: The 3d Air Division's 385th Heavy Bombardment Group is reassigned to the 93d Combat Bombardment Wing.

GERMANY: More than 550 1st and 2d Air division B-17s and B-24s are recalled in the face of bad weather, but 260 3d Air Division B-17s are able to attack their primary, a marshalling yard at Frankfurt am Main, and 71 3d Air Division B-17s are able to attack several targets of opportunity. Five heavy bombers and one of 167 VIII Fighter Command escorts and scouts are lost.

Thirty-one 9th Air Division B-26s attack a rail bridge at Mayen.

ITALY: Fifteenth Air Force heavy bombers attack harbor and shipyard facilities at Fiume and Trieste; Twelfth Air Force medium bombers attack bridges at four locations; and XXII TAC P-47s attack bridges, gun emplacements, and dumps over a wide area.

During the night of February 17–18, XXII TAC A-20s and A-26s attack towns and bridges in the Po River valley as well as Ghedi and Villafranca di Verona airdromes. Also, Fifteenth Air Force heavy bombers drop supplies to partisans in northern Italy.

YUGOSLAVIA: Fifteenth Air Force heavy bombers attack port facilities at Pula.

February 18, 1945

AUSTRIA: One hundred sixty Fifteenth Air Force B-17s attack a synthetic-fuel plant and rail facilities at Linz, but 290 B-24s bound for targets in Austria are recalled because of bad weather.

GERMANY: At the start of an air offensive to isolate the Ruhr region in anticipation of a major U.S. Army ground offensive, approximately 60 9th Air Division B-26s attack a rail bridge and several targets of opportunity.

ITALY: Nearly all the Twelfth Air Force B-25s dispatched on various missions abort in the face of bad weather, but one small attack is completed against a rail bridge at Ala. Also, fewer than 100 effective XXII TAC P-47 sorties are completed against rail bridges and ammunition dumps in the Po River valley.

February 19, 1945

AUSTRIA: Fifteenth Air Force heavy bombers attack rail targets in Vienna and marshalling yards at three locations.

GERMANY: Two hundred forty-six 1st Air Division B-17s attack oil-industry targets at four locations (primaries); 162 1st Air Division B-17s attack a marshalling yard at Münster (secondary); 86 2d Air Division B-24s attack a munitions plant; 97 2d Air Division B-24s attack an armaments factory; 94 2d Air Division B-24s attack a marshalling yard; 179 3d Air Division B-17s attack marshalling yards at Osnabruck (primary) and Münster (secondary); 131 3d Air Division B-17s attack a marshalling yard at Rheine; 68 3d Air Division B-17s attack a rail bridge at Wesel; and ten 3d Air Division B-17s attack targets of opportunity. One B-24 and seven of 358 VIII Fighter Command escorts and scouts are lost.

9th Air Division bombers attack rail bridges at three locations, an ordnance depot, a motor-vehicle depot, and targets of opportunity; and Ninth Air Force fighters and fighter-bombers attack bridges and rail lines.

ITALY: Twelfth Air Force B-25s are grounded by bad weather, but XXII TAC P-47s using radar-control techniques are able to mount limited attacks through heavy clouds against dumps and communications targets in the Po River valley and rail lines in Brenner Pass. Also, Fifteenth Air Force heavy bombers attack shipyard facilities at Fiume.

BriGen Edward M. Morris assumes command of the XII Air Force Service Command.

During the night of February 19–20, XXII TAC A-20s and A-26s attack more than 30 targets of opportunity in the Po River valley and marshalling yards and railway lines at ten locations.

MTO: Fifteenth Air Force P-38 and P-51 pilots are credited with the destruction of a record 31 locomotives during strafing attacks over enemy territory.

YUGOSLAVIA: Fifteenth Air Force heavy bombers attack a marshalling yard at Maribor and the harbor and military installations at Pula.

February 20, 1945

AUSTRIA: Fifteenth Air Force heavy bombers attack a marshalling yard and two oil refineries at Vienna, and a steel plant.
ETO: The 9th Air Division is grounded by bad weather.

The IX Engineer Command is transferred from Ninth Air Force control to USSTAF control.
GERMANY: Four hundred twenty-eight 1st Air Division B-17s and 403 3d Air Division B-17s attack rail targets at Nurnberg, but 360 2d Air Division B-24s abort in the face of bad weather along their route over Belgium. Five B-17s and 13 of 476 VIII Fighter Command escorts and scouts are lost.

VIII Fighter Command pilots down 16 GAF aircraft over Germany between noon and 1320 hours. 1stLt Clinton D. Burdick, a P-51 pilot with the 356th Fighter Group's 361st Fighter Squadron, achieves ace status when he downs two Fi-156s and shares in the downing of a third Fi-156 near Bayreuth at about 1240 hours; and Maj Donald J. Strait, the commanding officer of the 356th Fighter Group's 361st Fighter Squadron, brings his final personal tally to 13.5 confirmed victories when he downs three Fi-156s near Bayreuth between 1235 and 1245 hours.

Ninth Air Force fighters and fighter-bombers attack bridges and ground defenses.
ITALY: Fifteenth Air Force heavy bombers attack shipyards at Fiume and Trieste, and Twelfth Air Force B-25s attack bridges at four locations.

XXII TAC A-20s and night fighters attack supply dumps and communications targets in the Po River valley.
YUGOSLAVIA: Fifteenth Air Force heavy bombers attack port facilities at Pula.

February 21, 1945

AUSTRIA: Fifteenth Air Force B-17s and B-24s attack rail targets in and around Vienna as well as three marshalling yards.

ETO: The Ninth Air Force's 386th Medium Bombardment Group completes its transition from B-26s to A-26s, and flies its first all-A-26 combat mission.
GERMANY: 1,204 Eighth Air Force B-17s and B-24s attack the rail station and a marshalling yard at Nurnberg. Seven of 600 VIII Fighter Command escorts and scouts are lost.

Three hundred forty-eight 9th Air Division bombers attack an oil depot, marshalling yards, bridges, communications centers, and targets of opportunity; and Ninth Air Force fighters and fighter-bombers attack an airdrome and rail lines. One B-26 is downed by flak, and three B-26s are downed in a by-now rare attack by GAF piston fighters.
HUNGARY: Fifteenth Air Force heavy bombers attack marshalling yard at Sopron.
ITALY: Fifteenth Air Force heavy bombers attack shipyards at Fiume and Trieste; Twelfth Air Force B-25s attack bridges at three locations; and XXII TAC P-47s attack communications targets and frontline battle areas.

During the night of February 21–22, XXII TAC A-20s and A-26s attack light sources, an ammunition dump, rail lines, and rail bridges in the Po River valley.

February 22, 1945

AUSTRIA: Fifteenth Air Force heavy bombers attack various rail targets throughout Austria.
FRANCE: The 27th and 86th Fighter groups, both in P-47s, are transferred from the Twelfth Air Force's XXII TAC to the First Tactical Air Force and ordered to move from bases in Italy to bases in northeastern France.
GERMANY: The Eighth, Ninth, and Fifteenth Air forces inaugurate Operation CLARION, a general assault against the German transportation system.

1,372 Eighth Air Force B-17s and B-24s attack a vast array of primary targets and targets of opportunity. At targets without adequate flak defenses, the heavy-bomber formations attack from only 10,000 feet, about one-third their normal bombing altitude. Seven heavy bombers and 13 of 817 VIII Fighter Command escorts and scouts are lost.

More than 450 9th Air Division bombers attack a vast assortment of rail targets, including 46 rail bridges, 11 stations, and 12 marshalling yards. Many of the missions are conducted at low level, the first such Ninth Air Force bombing attacks since May 1943. Also, Ninth Air Force fighters mount 1,082 effective sorties. Ninth Air Force losses are three bombers and thirteen fighters.

Eighth and Ninth air force fighter pilots down 35 GAF fighters over Germany between 1210 and 1745 hours. Maj Wayne K. Blickenstaff, the commanding officer of the 353d Fighter Group's 350th Fighter Squadron, achieves ace status in a P-51 when he downs an Me-262 jet interceptor near Berlin at 1230 hours.

As part of Operation CLARION, Fifteenth Air Force heavy bombers attack numerous rail targets in southern Germany.

During the night of February 22–23, after A-26 and B-26 night pathfinders mark the target, 31 410th Light Bombardment Group A-20s attack the communications center at Blatzheim with good results.

ITALY: Fifteenth Air Force heavy bombers attack rail targets; Twelfth Air Force B-25s attack marshalling yards at three locations; and XXII TAC P-47s attack communications centers, road traffic, gun emplacements, and dumps, as well as bombing Bergamo and Ghedi airdromes.

During the night of February 22–23, XXII TAC A-20s and A-26s attack airdromes and marshalling yards throughout northern Italy.

February 23, 1945

AUSTRIA: Fifteenth Air Force heavy bombers attack marshalling yards and other rail targets at four locations.

GERMANY: At 0300 hours, the U.S. Ninth Army inaugurates Operation GRENADE, the

final drive to the Rhine River—and the nominal motive for Operation CLARION. Later in the day, the U.S. First Army inaugurates its delayed combat assault across the Roer River, also with the objective of reaching the Rhine.

Continuing Operation CLARION, 1,211 Eighth Air Force B-17s and B-24s attack numerous transportation targets, both primaries and targets of opportunity. One B-24 and five of 526 VIII Fighter Command escorts and scouts are lost.

9th Air Division bombers support the U.S. Army's crossing of the Roer River and projected drive on the Rhine River with attacks on communications centers east of the river; and Ninth Air Force fighters and fighter-bombers provide direct support to the three U.S. field armies, mainly against motor vehicles, locomotives, rail cars, and defended buildings.

Eighth and Ninth Air Force fighter pilots down 22 GAF fighters over Germany between 1330 and 1730 hours.

ITALY: Fifteenth Air Force heavy bombers attack rail facilities at Udine; Twelfth Air Force B-25s attack rail targets in and around Brenner Pass; and XXII TAC P-47s attack airdromes, rail lines, at least five rail bridges, and German Army troop movements.

During the night of February 23–24, XXII TAC A-20s and A-26s attack three airdromes and marshalling yards at four locations.

February 24, 1945

AUSTRIA: Fifteenth Air Force heavy bombers attack marshalling yards at Graz and Klagenfurt.

GERMANY: Three hundred forty-eight 1st Air Division B-17s attack two oil-industry targets at Hamburg; 104 2d Air Division B-24s attack an oil-industry target at Misburg; 61 2d Air Division B-24s attack a marshalling yard at Lehrte; 76 2d Air Division B-24s attack a marshalling yard at Bielefeld (secondary); 200 3d Air Division B-17s attack the U-boat yards at

Bremen; 134 3d Air Division B-17s attack a rail bridge at Bremen; 70 3d Air Division B-17s attack a rail bridge at Wesel; and 50 heavy bombers attack various targets of opportunity. Two heavy bombers and 11 of 514 VIII Fighter Command escorts and scouts are lost.

Approximately 500 9th Air Division bomber sorties are mounted against marshalling yards, communications centers, rail bridges, town areas, and targets of opportunity.

During the night of February 24–25, after A-26 and B-26 night pathfinders mark the target, 34 410th Light Bombardment Group A-20s attack the marshalling yard at Hillesheim with good results. Despite this and one other successful night missions— of four mounted—the night-bombing program is canceled because the recent swift Allied advances on the ground have obviated the need for a night-bombing effort over Germany. The 410th Light Bombardment Group is returned to day operations.

ITALY: Fifteenth Air Force heavy bombers attack a rail bridge at Ferrara and marshalling yards at Ferrara, Padua, Udine, and Verona; Twelfth Air Force B-25s attack bridge approaches, rail bridges, and rail lines at five locations and an industrial area; and XXII TAC P-47s attack airdromes, marshalling yards, rail bridges, and rail lines over a wide area.

During the night of February 24–25, XXII TAC A-20s and A-26s attack marshalling yards at five locations and two airdromes.

February 25, 1945

AUSTRIA: More than 600 Fifteenth Air Force B-17s and B-24s attack six marshalling yards at four locations, a synthetic-fuel plant at Linz, an ordnance depot, and targets of opportunity.

GERMANY: Two hundred forty-seven 1st Air Division B-17s attack rail targets at Munich; 63 1st Air Division B-17s attack a tank factory at Friedrichshafen; 51 1st Air Division B-17s attack a marshalling yard

at Ulm (secondary); 115 2d Air Division B-24s attack a marshalling yard at Aschaffenburg; 54 2d Air Division B-24s attack a tank factory at Aschaffenburg; 189 2d Air Division B-24s attack the Giebelstadt and Schwabisch Hall jet airdromes; 315 3d Air Division B-17s attack a marshalling yard at Munich; 88 3d Air Division B-17s attack the town of Neuberg; and 35 heavy bombers attack various targets of opportunity. Five B-17s and eight of 442 VIII Fighter Command escorts and scouts are lost.

9th Air Division bombers attack rail bridges, marshalling yards, communications centers, and targets of opportunity.

Altogether, Eighth and Ninth air force fighter pilots down 30 GAF aircraft over Germany between 0815 and 1115 hours. Capt Charles H. Cole, Jr., a P-51 pilot with the 20th Fighter Group's 55th Fighter Squadron, achieves ace status when he downs four FW-190s near Stendal at 1010 hours. 55th Fighter Group P-51 pilots down seven Me-262s in a running battle over northern Germany. This is a record score by one group in one day against the GAF jet fighters. Also credited to a pair of 364th Fighter Group P-51 pilots is the first Ar-234 twin-engine jet bomber known to be downed in the war.

Capt Kendall E. Carlson, a 4th Fighter Group six-victory ace, is captured after his P-51 hits the ground and crashes during an extremely low-level strafing run.

ITALY: Twelfth Air Force B-25s attack bridges at four locations and a rail fill, and XXII TAC P-47s attack rail targets, motor vehicles, and dumps.

During the night of February 25–26, XXII TAC A-20s and A-26s attack marshalling yards at two locations.

February 26, 1945

GERMANY: 1,066 Eighth Air Force B-17s and B-24s attack three railroad stations in Berlin, and 69 heavy bombers attack various secondary targets and targets of opportunity. Three B-17s and three of

687 VIII Fighter Command escorts and scouts are lost.

Two hundred thirty-five 9th Air Division bombers attack three towns, a communications center, road and rail junctions at two locations, and a dump. Due to bad weather, Ninth Air Force fighters (all from the XIX TAC) mount only 50 effective sorties.

ITALY: Twelfth Air Force B-25s attack rail bridges at four locations, and XXII TAC P-47s attack rail lines and other transportation targets at at least six locations, as well as Bergamo and Ghedi airdromes.

During the night of February 26–27, XXII TAC A-20s and A-26s attack German Army troop movements in the Po River valley, two airdromes, a defended town, and marshalling yards at two locations.

YUGOSLAVIA: One hundred two Fifteenth Air Force heavy bombers dispatched against tactical targets are recalled because of heavy cloud cover.

February 27, 1945

AUSTRIA: Fifteenth Air Force heavy bombers attack marshalling yards at three locations, and XXII TAC P-47s attack rail cars at Villach.

GERMANY: Three hundred sixty-three 1st Air Division B-17s and 378 3d Air Division B-17s attack rail and road targets at Leipzig; 314 2d Air Division B-24s attack a marshalling yard at Halle; and 31 heavy bombers attack targets of opportunity. Two B-24s and two of 690 VIII Fighter Command escorts and scouts are lost.

One hundred eighteen 9th Air Division bombers attack three communications centers, a rail bridge, and targets of opportunity, and Ninth Air Force fighter-bombers mount 235 effective sorties, including an attack against oil storage tanks at Frankfurt am Main.

Capt James N. McElroy, a P-51 pilot with the 355th Fighter Group's 358th Fighter Squadron, achieves ace status when

he downs a Do-217 near Plauen at 1340 hours.

Fifteenth Air Force heavy bombers attack a marshalling yard at Augsburg.

Elements of the U.S. First Army reach the outskirts of Cologne.

ITALY: Twelfth Air Force B-25s destroy two dumps and a railway diversion bridge, and attack other bridges and bridge approaches; and XXII TAC P-47s attack rail lines in the Brenner Pass and other areas of northeastern Italy.

During the night of February 27–28, XXII TAC A-20s and A-26s attack rail lines, several marshalling yards, and signs of movement.

February 28, 1945

AUSTRIA: Fifteenth Air Force heavy bombers attack a marshalling yard at Lienz, and 75 P-38 dive-bombers attack a marshalling yard and join other P-38s and P-51s in strafing rail lines over a wide area.

GERMANY: Nine hundred eighty-five Eighth Air Force B-17s and B-24s attack marshalling yards and rail bridges at seven locations; 79 2d Air Division B-24s attack a munitions plant at Meschede; and eight heavy bombers attack targets of opportunity. One B-17 and two of 381 VIII Fighter Command escorts and scouts are lost.

More than 340 9th Air Division bombers attack rail bridges at three locations, two marshalling yards, a road junction, an ordnance depot, and targets of opportunity.

ITALY: Fifteenth Air Force heavy bombers attack marshalling yards at nine locations and bridges at two locations; Twelfth Air Force B-25s attack bridges at five locations and a rail embankment; and XXII TAC P-47s attack Ghedi and Vicenza airdromes, an ammunition plant, ammunition dumps, and miscellaneous communications targets.

During the night of February 28–March 1, XXII TAC A-20s and A-26s attack numerous targets throughout northern Italy.

MARCH 1945

March 1, 1945

AUSTRIA: Fifteenth Air Force B-17s and B-24s attack marshalling yards at seven locations and an oil refinery at Moosbierbaum.

GERMANY: A total of 1,114 Eighth Air Force B-17s and B-24s attack marshalling yards at seven locations in southern and central Germany, and 95 B-17s and B-24s attack various secondary targets and targets of opportunity. Following the completion of their escort duties, fighters from seven escort groups strafe airfields and transportation targets of opportunity. Seven of 460 VIII Fighter Command escorts and scouts are lost.

More than 340 9th Air Division bombers attack communications centers at four locations, a rail bridge, a road bridge, an ordnance depot, and targets of opportunity.

Ninth Air Force fighter pilots down 17 GAF fighters over Germany between 0915 and 1330 hours.

HUNGARY: Pilots of the 14th, 52d, and 325th Fighter groups down seven Axis fighters over and near Lake Balaton between 1400 and 1430 hours.

ITALY: The Twelfth Air Force is grounded by bad weather.

NETHERLANDS: Elements of the U.S. Ninth Army capture Venlo.

YUGOSLAVIA: Fifteenth Air Force heavy bombers attack a marshalling yard at Maribor.

March 2, 1945

AUSTRIA: Fifteenth Air Force B-17s and B-24s attack marshalling yards at five locations.

GERMANY: Sixty 1st Air Division B-17s attack a synthetic-oil plant at Bohlen; 36 1st Air Division B-17s attack a gun battery, at Bohlen; 36 1st Air Division B-17s attack an oil refinery at Rositz; 255 1st Air Division B-17s attack the city of Chemnitz (secondary); 257 2d Air Division B-24s attack a tank factory at Magdeburg; 38 2d Air Division B-24s attack a synthetic-oil plant at Magdeburg; 24 3d Air Division B-17s attack a synthetic-oil plant at Ruhland; 406 3d Air Division B-17s attack the city of

Dresden (secondary); and 55 heavy bombers attack various targets of opportunity. Fourteen heavy bombers and 13 of 713 VIII Fighter Command escorts and scouts are lost.

9th Air Division bombers attack bridges at five locations, two communications centers, several city and town areas, three depots, and targets of opportunity. Ninth Air Force fighters and fighter-bombers mount more than 1,700 sorties, mostly in support of an offensive by the U.S. Third Army.

Eighth and Ninth Air Force fighter pilots down 71 GAF aircraft over Germany between 0450 and 1650 hours. 1stLt Herman E. Ernst, a P-61 pilot with the Ninth Air Force's 422d Night Fighter Squadron, achieves ace status when he downs two Ju-87s over the Rhine River between 0457 and 0506 hours. Guiding Ernst to all five victories, and thus an ace in his own right, has been radar operator 2dLt Edward H. Kopsel. Two P-51 pilots with the 357th Fighter Group's 364th Fighter Squadron achieve ace status when they each down a Bf-109 near Magdeburg at 1000 hours: 1stLt Raymond M. Bank and Capt Alva C. Murphy. Unfortunately, both of the new aces are shot down by flak. Bank is taken prisoner, and Murphy is killed. Capt Robert G. Schimanski, a P-51 pilot with the 357th Fighter Group's 352d Fighter Squadron, achieves ace status when he downs a Bf-109 and shares in the downing of a second Bf-109 near Magdeburg at 1000 hours; Maj William H. Julian, the commanding officer of the 78th Fighter Group's 83d Fighter Squadron, in P-51s, achieves ace status when he downs two Bf-109s over Burg Airdrome at 1010 hours; 1stLt Arthur C. Cundy, a P-51 pilot with the 353d Fighter Group's 352d Fighter Squadron, achieves ace status when he downs a Bf-109 and two FW-190s near Dessau between 1010 and 1030 hours; 1stLt Horace Q. Waggoner, a P-51 pilot with the 353d Fighter Group's 352d Fighter Squadron, achieves ace status when he downs two FW-190s and a Bf-109

over Ruhland at 1030 hours; and Capt Edwin L. Heller, a P-51 pilot with the 352d Fighter Group's 482d Fighter Squadron, achieves ace status when he downs an FW-190 near Leipzig at 1045 hours.

ITALY: Twelfth Air Force B-25s are grounded by bad weather; Fifteenth Air Force heavy bombers attack a marshalling yard at Brescia; and XXII TAC P-47s attack two sugar refineries, many dumps, gun emplacements, motor vehicles, buildings, and two airdromes.

During the night of March 2–3, XXII TAC A-20s and A-26s attack a marshalling yard, road traffic, and ammunition supply points in the Po River valley.

March 3, 1945

CZECHOSLOVAKIA: 1stLt Bernard H. Howes, a six-victory P-51 ace with the 55th Fighter Group's 343d Fighter Squadron, is shot down and taken prisoner.

GERMANY: Eighty-two 1st Air Division B-17s attack a tank factory at Hannover; 23 1st Air Division B-17s attack an oil refinery at Misburg; 24 1st Air Division B-17s attack a synthetic-oil plant at Ruhland; 166 1st Air Division B-17s attack the city of Chemnitz (secondary); 219 2d Air Division B-24s attack an oil refinery at Magdeburg; 41 2d Air Division B-24s attack a bridge at Nienburg; 48 2d Air Division B-24s attack a marshalling yard at Bielefeld (secondary); 191 3d Air Division B-17s attack a munitions plant and oil-industry targets at Brunswick; 53 3d Air Division B-17s attack an oil refinery at Dedenhausen; 37 3d Air Division B-17s attack an oil refinery at Dollbergen; 38 3d Air Division B-17s attack an industrial target at Hildesheim; and 50 heavy bombers attack various targets of opportunity. Nine heavy bombers and eight of 584 VIII Fighter Command escorts and scouts are lost.

9th Air Division bombers attack a communications center, two rail bridges, depots at five locations, an ammunition dump, a concentration of motor vehicles, a marshalling yard, and targets of opportunity.

ITALY: Fifteenth Air Force bombers are grounded by bad weather; Twelfth Air Force B-25s attack lines of communication in Brenner Pass and Po River valley bridges; and XXII TAC P-47s attack a sugar refinery, dumps, and lines of communication.

During the night of March 3–4, XXII TAC A-20s and A-26s attack a radar station, bridges and bridge approaches, light sources, and road traffic in the Po River valley.

March 4, 1945

AUSTRIA: Fifteenth Air Force heavy bombers attack marshalling yards at five locations.

GERMANY: Two hundred twenty-three 1st Air Division B-17s attack a munitions dump at Ulm; 59 1st Air Division B-17s attack a marshalling yard at Ulm (secondary); 69 1st Air Division B-17s attack an aircraft-industry plant at Schwabmunchen; and, unable to locate any primaries through thick cloud cover, 154 of 274 2d Air Division B-24s and 149 of 376 3d Air Division B-17s attack various secondaries and targets of opportunity.

Approximately 180 9th Air Division bombers attack rail targets and communications centers, but most Ninth Air Force fighters and fighter-bombers are grounded by bad weather.

HUNGARY: Fifteenth Air Force heavy bombers attack a marshalling yard at Szombathely, and two marshalling yards at Sopron.

ITALY: Twelfth Air Force B-25s attack rail bridges at seven locations, and XXII TAC P-47s attack bridges and roads.

During the night of March 4–5, XXII TAC A-20s and A-26s attack lines of communication in the Po River valley.

YUGOSLAVIA: Fifteenth Air Force heavy bombers attack a marshalling yard at Ljubljana and two marshalling yards at Zagreb.

March 5, 1945

GERMANY: More than 300 1st and 3d Air

division B-17s dispatched against a synthetic-oil plant at Ruhland are thwarted by bad weather, but 233 attack the city of Chemnitz, 34 attack a chemical plant at Plauen, and nine attack a chemical plant at Fulda. Also, 120 2d Air Division B-24s attack a synthetic-oil plant at Hamburg, as planned.

Five hundred sixty-five 9th Air Division bombers attack marshalling yards at six locations, a communications center, an ordnance depot, and targets of opportunity.

ITALY: The entire Fifteenth Air Force and Twelfth Air Force B-25s are grounded by bad weather, and only a few XXII TAC P-47 missions get airborne against bridges in the Po River valley.

During the night of March 5–6, XXII TAC A-20s and A-26s attack targets of opportunity in the Po River valley.

March 6, 1945

GERMANY: The IX and XIX TACs are grounded by bad weather, but more than 260 9th Air Division A-26s and B-26s attack marshalling yards at three locations, a storage depot, and targets of opportunity; and the XXIX TAC covers the first U.S. Army ground forces to reach the Rhine River (an element of the U.S. First Army, near Cologne).

ITALY: The entire Fifteenth Air Force is grounded by bad weather, but Twelfth Air Force B-25s attack targets in Brenner Pass and bridges at six locations.

During the night of March 6–7, XXII TAC A-20s and A-26s attack targets in the Brenner Pass area, a river crossing, and two bridges.

March 7, 1945

GERMANY: Eighty-six 1st Air Division B-17s attack two synthetic-oil plants at Dortmund; 211 1st Air Division B-17s attack marshalling yards at three locations (secondaries); 80 2d Air Division B-24s attack a water viaduct at Schildesche; 144 2d Air Division B-24s attack a marshalling yard at Soest; 173 3d Air Division B-17s attack two synthetic-oil plants at Datteln; 77 3d Air Division B-17s attack a synthetic-oil plant at Castrop; and 71 3d Air Division B-17s attack marshalling yards at two locations (secondaries). One of 274 VIII Fighter Command escorts and scouts is lost.

Except for the XXIX TAC, the Ninth Air Force is grounded by bad weather.

The U.S. First Army captures Cologne. Also, and of far greater strategic importance, elements of the U.S. First Army capture the Ludendorff rail bridge, which spans the Rhine River at Remagen. Immediately, as U.S. ground forces rush to protect the bridge and expand the bridgehead, the GAF mounts a steady stream of missions against the span itself—and IX TAC launches a virtually impermeable aerial umbrella to defend the bridge.

ITALY: The Fifteenth Air Force is grounded by bad weather; Twelfth Air Force B-25s attack rail and other communications targets; and XXII TAC P-47s attack dumps and communications targets in the Po River valley.

During the night of March 7–8, XXII TAC A-20s and A-26s attack Po River crossings at six locations, light sources, road traffic, and signs of movement in the Po River valley.

March 8, 1945

AUSTRIA: Fifteenth Air Force heavy bombers attack a steel works at Kapfenburg.
GERMANY: Three hundred thirty-seven 1st Air Division B-17s attack synthetic-oil plants at four locations; 109 1st Air Division B-17s attack a marshalling yard at Essen (target of opportunity); 257 2d Air Division B-24s attack marshalling yards at three locations; 272 3d Air Division B-17s attack three synthetic-oil plants at two locations; 122 3d Air Division B-17s attack a chemical plant; 77 3d Air Division B-17s attack marshalling yards at two locations (secondaries); and 33 heavy bombers attack various targets of opportunity.

Nearly all Ninth Air Force fighters and fighter-bombers are grounded by bad

weather, but 328 9th Air Division bombers attack two marshalling yards, communications centers at seven locations, an overpass, and a military transport depot.

The XXIX TAC operational headquarters displaces forward from Maastricht to Monchen-Gladbach.
HUNGARY: Fifteenth Air Force heavy bombers attack marshalling yards at two locations.
ITALY: Fifteenth Air Force heavy bombers attack a marshalling yard at Verona; Twelfth Air Force B-25s attack a marshalling yard, a bridge, and two rail fills; and XXII TAC P-47s attack supply dumps, a munitions factory, an industrial complex, and lines of communication.

During the night of March 8–9, XXII TAC A-20s and A-26s attack river crossings in the Po River valley.
YUGOSLAVIA: Fifteenth Air Force heavy bombers attack a locomotive depot at Maribor.

March 9, 1945

AUSTRIA: Fifteenth Air Force heavy bombers attack five marshalling yards at four locations and bridges along the Austro-Yugoslav border.
ETO: The Ninth Air Force's 370th Fighter Group flies its first operational missions following transitioning from P-38s to P-47s.
GERMANY: Three hundred eighteen 1st Air Division B-17s attack a munitions plant and a marshalling yard at Kassel; 277 2d Air Division B-24s attack marshalling yards at three locations; 372 3d Air Division B-17s attack two marshalling yards at Frankfurt am Main; and 38 3d Air Division B-17s attack a chemical plant at Frankfurt am Main. Seven heavy bombers are lost.

More than 600 9th Air Division bombers attack marshalling yards at six locations, a munitions plant, vehicle depots, storage depots, and targets of opportunity. In a rare show of force, GAF fighters attack three bomber formations over Wiesbaden and Niederhausen, and three B-26s are lost.

Ninth Air Force fighter pilots down 11

GAF fighters over Germany between 1157 and 1700 hours.

Elements of the U.S. First Army capture Bonn.

ITALY: Twelfth Air Force B-25s attack bridges at six locations, a bridge approach, and a marshalling yard; and XXII TAC P-47s attack supply dumps, parked airplanes, bridges, road and rail traffic, and buildings.

During the night of March 9–10, XXII TAC A-20s and A-26s attack communications targets in the Po River valley.

March 10, 1945

GERMANY: One hundred twenty-seven 1st Air Division B-17s attack rail centers at two locations; 293 1st Air Division B-17s attack marshalling yards at three locations; 129 2d Air Division B-24s attack a marshalling yard; 229 2d Air Division B-24s attack rail viaducts at two locations; 373 3d Air Division B-17s attack three marshalling yards at Dortmund; 138 3d Air Division B-17s attack a marshalling yard at Soest; and 43 heavy bombers attack several targets of opportunity. Two of 644 VIII Fighter Command escorts and scouts are lost.

Three hundred eighty-three 9th Air Division bombers attack two city areas, a communications center, marshalling yards at five locations, and targets of opportunity, all around Koblenz.

ITALY: One hundred ninety-one Fifteenth Air Force heavy bombers attack a key rail bridge near Verona.

Despite intense antiaircraft fire, 48 B-25s of the Twelfth Air Force's 310th Medium Bombardment Group successfully attack a rail bridge at Ora to cut a vital German supply line. This bombing mission cuts the last rail link between Germany and Italy by way of Brenner Pass. Four of the B-25s are shot down in flames by the thick flak, and ten others are barely able to return to the group's base in Corsica. Twelfth Air Force B-25s also attack two other bridges and a rail fill. Also, XXII TAC

P-47s attack bridges, ammunition dumps, and road traffic in the Po River valley.

During the night of March 10–11, XXII TAC A-20s and A-26s attack Ghedi and Pavia airdromes, and crossings and road junctions in the Po River valley.

NORTH SEA: 1stLt Arthur C. Cundy, a 353d Fighter Group P-51 pilot who achieved ace status on March 2, is killed when he ditches in the North Sea on return from the day's mission.

March 11, 1945

AUSTRIA: Twelfth Air Force B-25s attack a bridge at Drauberg.

GERMANY: Four hundred six 1st Air Division B-17s attack a U-boat yard at Bremen; 344 2d Air Division B-24s attack a U-boat yard at Kiel; and 469 3d Air Division B-17s attack an oil refinery at Hamburg. One B-17 and four of 766 VIII Fighter Command escorts and scouts are lost.

9th Air Division bombers mount 696 effective sorties against four airfields, two munitions plants, three communications centers, three city areas, and targets of opportunity.

ITALY: The Fifteenth Air Force is grounded by bad weather; Twelfth Air Force B-25s attack bridges and rail fills at three locations; and XXII TAC P-47s attack dumps and rail lines in the Po River valley.

During the night of March 11–12, XXII TAC A-20s and A-26s attack road and rail traffic, Po River crossings, and a sugar refinery.

NETHERLANDS: The Ninth Air Force's 373d Fighter Group and 363d Tactical Reconnaissance Group displace to Advance Landing Ground Y-55, at Venlo.

March 12, 1945

AUSTRIA: Seven hundred ninety Fifteenth Air Force B-17s and B-24s attack an oil refinery at Vienna, and marshalling yards at Graz, Wiener-Neustadt, and Zeltweg; and 98 Fifteenth Air Force P-38s bomb a rail bridge at Knittelfeld.

ENGLAND: The unit designation of the 492d Heavy Bombardment Group's 857th Heavy Bombardment Squadron is transferred to the Eighth Air Force's new 1st Scouting Force, but personnel and equipment are retained by the 492d Group.

GERMANY: Two hundred eighteen 1st Air Division B-17s, 220 2d Air Division B-24s, and 223 3d Air Division B-17s attack a marshalling yard at Swinemunde, and 653 Eighth Air Force heavy bombers attack marshalling yards at seven other locations. One B-17 and four of 734 VIII Fighter Command fighters are lost.

9th Air Division bombers attack a munitions plant, city areas, marshalling yards at eight locations, and targets of opportunity.

ITALY: Twelfth Air Force B-25s attack rail bridges and fills in Brenner Pass, in northeastern Italy, and on both sides of the Italian-Yugoslav border; and XXII TAC P-47s cut rail lines at 36 locations in northern Italy and Brenner Pass.

During the night of March 12–13, XXII TAC A-20s and A-26s attack dumps, crossings, and signs of movement in and around the Po River valley.

YUGOSLAVIA: XXII TAC P-47s attack a munitions plant near Zagreb.

March 13, 1945

ENGLAND: The Eighth Air Force is grounded by bad weather.

GERMANY: More than 450 9th Air Division bombers attack two airdromes, rail sidings, three marshalling yards, and targets of opportunity.

Ninth Air Force fighter pilots down 15 GAF fighters over Germany between 1245 and 1725 hours. Capt Joseph E. Miller, Jr., a P-38 pilot with the 474th Fighter Group's 429th Fighter Squadron, achieves ace status when he downs an FW-190 near Honnef at 1245 hours. (Miller's first four victories were scored in mid-1943, when he was flying with the 14th Fighter Group in the MTO.) Maj Lowell K. Brueland, the commanding officer of the 354th Fighter

Group's 355th Fighter Squadron, attains his final World War II tally of 12.5 confirmed victories when he downs a Bf-109 over Germany at 1725 hours.

Five hundred sixty-nine Fifteenth Air Force B-17s and B-24s attack a marshalling yard at Regensburg.

The XII TAC headquarters displaces from France to Germany.

ITALY: Twelfth Air Force B-25s attack rail bridges and fills at five locations, and XXII TAC P-47s attack flak emplacements, ammunition dumps, supply dumps, and rail lines throughout northern Italy.

During the night of March 13–14, XXII TAC A-20s and A-26s attack crossing points in the Po River valley.

March 14, 1945

AUSTRIA: Fifteenth Air Force heavy bombers attack marshalling yards at Graz, Knittelfeld, and Wiener-Neustadt.

CZECHOSLOVAKIA: Fifteenth Air Force heavy bombers attack a marshalling yard.

FRANCE: The Ninth Air Force's 367th Fighter Group displaces to Advance Landing Ground A-94, at Conflans.

GERMANY: Three hundred ninety 1st Air Division B-17s attack an industrial plant, two bridges, and a rail center; 267 2d Air Division B-24s attack marshalling yards at three locations; 404 3d Air Division B-17s attack a munitions factory, two oil refineries, two industrial plants, and a marshalling yard; and 143 heavy bombers attack secondary targets and targets of opportunity. Three B-17s and one of 605 VIII Fighter Command escorts and scouts are lost.

More than 350 9th Air Division bombers attack three airdromes, a rail junction, four rail bridges, five defended towns, and targets of opportunity.

Among numerous Ninth Air Force fighter missions, when 36th Fighter Group P-47 pilots locate more than 50 GAF bombers and escorts preparing to take off from Lippe Airdrome to attack the Remagen bridges, they destroy 23 Ju-87s and a

Bf-109 during the course of on-the-deck bomb, rocket, and strafing attacks. Minutes later, 12 404th Fighter Group P-47s destroy 21 of the remaining Ju-87s and Bf-109s. Two 404th Fighter Group P-47s are lost following a midair collision. Thereafter, GAF attacks against the Ludendorff bridge and several new engineer bridges at Remagen (amounting to 372 sorties between March 7 and March 14) drop off precipitously.

Eighth and Ninth air force fighter pilots down 26 GAF aircraft over Germany between 1330 and 1630 hours. Capt Donald S. Bryan, a P-51 ace with the 352d Fighter Group's 328th Fighter Squadron, brings his final personal tally to 13.333 confirmed victories when he downs an Ar-234 twin-engine jet bomber near Remagen at about 1545 hours; and LtCol Paul P. Douglas, Jr., the commanding officer of the 368th Fighter Group, achieves ace status when he downs three FW-190s near Frankfurt am Main at 1545 hours.

HUNGARY: Fifteenth Air Force heavy bombers attack oil refineries at two locations and a marshalling yard.

325th Fighter Group P-51 pilots down 20 FW-190s in a running fight near Lake Balaton between 1315 and 1410 hours. One of the P-51 pilots, 1stLt Gordon H. McDaniel, a member of the 318th Fighter Squadron, achieves ace status and brings his final personal tally to six confirmed victories when he downs five FW-190s near Budapest at about 1315 hours; and Capt Harry A. Parker, another member of the 318th Fighter Squadron, brings his final personal tally to 13 confirmed victories when he downs two FW-190s over Bicske, Hungary, between 1330 and 1345 hours.

ITALY: Twelfth Air Force B-25s attack bridges at four locations, and XXII TAC P-47s attack road and rail traffic and dumps.

During the night of March 14–15, XXII TAC A-20s and A-26s attack fills and crossings in the Po River valley.

YUGOSLAVIA: Fifteenth Air Force heavy bombers attack a marshalling yard at Zagreb.

March 15, 1945

AUSTRIA: More than 470 Fifteenth Air Force B-24s attack three oil refineries in or near Vienna, a bridge at Klagenfurt, and marshalling yards at six locations.

GERMANY: Two hundred seventy-six 1st Air Division B-17s and 308 2d Air Division B-24s attack a German Army head-quarters at Zossen, near Berlin; 145 1st Air Division B-17s and 467 3d Air Division B-17s attack a marshalling yard at Oranienburg; and 78 heavy bombers attack various targets of opportunity. Nine heavy bombers and four of 755 VIII Fighter Command escorts and scouts are lost.

Supporting the U.S. Seventh Army's Operation UNDERTONE (a ground attack aimed at breaking through the southern West Wall), the 9th Air Division mounts all 11 of its bomber groups against flak concentrations, two marshalling yards, two communications centers, and targets of opportunity.

Capt Ray S. Wetmore, a P-51 ace with the 359th Fighter Group's 370th Fighter Squadron, brings his final personal tally to 21.25 confirmed victories when he downs an Me-163 rocket fighter over Wittenberg at 1500 hours.

In the Fifteenth Air Force's deepest penetration into Germany of the war, 109 5th Heavy Bombardment Wing B-17s attack the synthetic-oil plant at Ruhland. Also, on the same mission, 103 5th Heavy Bombardment Wing B-17s attack a refinery at Kolin, Czechoslovakia (secondary).

The Ninth Air Force's 365th Fighter Group displaces to Advance Landing Ground Y-46, at Aachen.

ITALY: Twelfth Air Force B-25s attack rail fills and bridges at six locations; and XXII TAC P-47s attack rail targets throughout northern Italy as well as several ammunition and supply dumps.

During the night of March 15–16, XXII TAC A-20s and A-26s attack bridges and targets of opportunity in the Po River valley.

March 16, 1945

AUSTRIA: Fifteenth Air Force B-17s and B-24s attack oil refineries in and around Vienna and marshalling yards at three locations; and Twelfth Air Force B-25s attack a rail bridge at Brixlegg.

ETO: Eighth, Ninth, and First Tactical Air Force fighter pilots down ten GAF fighters over Germany and the Netherlands between 0915 and 1700 hours. 1stLt Ivan S. Hasek, a P-51 pilot with the 354th Fighter Group's 353d Fighter Squadron, achieves ace status when he downs four Bf-109s over Limburg at 1700 hours.

GERMANY: More than 280 9th Air Division bombers attack a barracks, seven defended towns, a communications center, and several rail and road targets.

Eighth, Ninth, and First Tactical air force fighter pilots down ten GAF fighters over Germany between 0915 and 1700 hours.

In its most intense single-day action of the war, the Ninth Air Force's 362d Fighter Group mounts 175 effective sorties, during which 403 motor vehicles, 40 horse-drawn vehicles, three tanks, six other armored vehicles, seven locomotives, 28 rail cars, six gun emplacements, and eight defended buildings are destroyed, and three GAF fighters are downed. One P-47 is lost.

ITALY: Twelfth Air Force B-25s attack a power plant and five bridges, and XXII TAC P-47s attack communications targets.

During the night of March 16–17, XXII TAC A-20s and A-26s attack light sources, signs of movement, and several crossing points in the Po River valley.

YUGOSLAVIA: Fifteenth Air Force heavy bombers attack marshalling yards at two locations.

March 17, 1945

GERMANY: One hundred fifty-two 1st Air Division B-17s attack a synthetic-oil plant at Bohlen; 127 1st Air Division B-17s attack a synthetic-oil plant and a power station at Molbis; 71 1st Air Division

B-17s attack an optics factory at Jena (secondary); 51 1st Air Division B-17s attack a marshalling yard at Erfurt; 146 2d Air Division B-24s attack a tank factory at Hannover; 170 2d Air Division B-24s attack a marshalling yard at Munster; 214 3d Air Division B-17s attack a synthetic-oil plant at Ruhland; 138 3d Air Division B-17s attack a synthetic-oil plant at Bitterfeld (secondary); 125 3d Air Division B-17s attack a munitions plant at Plauen; (target of last resort); and 81 heavy bombers attack various targets of opportunity. Five B-17s and two of 677 VIII Fighter Command escorts and scouts are lost.

9th Air Division bombers mount more than 650 effective sorties against marshalling yards, two communications centers, three city areas, an ordnance depot, and targets of opportunity.

The Ninth Air Force's 354th Fighter Group begins operating out of Y-64 Airfield, the former GAF Ober Olm Airdrome at Mainz. This is the first deployment of a USAAF tactical unit in Germany.

ITALY: Fifteenth Air Force heavy bombers are grounded by bad weather; Twelfth Air Force B-25s attack rail bridges and fills at eight locations; and XXII TAC P-47s hampered by bad weather mount a limited number of missions against dumps, rail targets, and bridges in the Po River valley.

During the night of March 17–18, XXII TAC A-20s and A-26s attack crossing points in the Po River valley.

YUGOSLAVIA: Nearly 100 Fifteenth Air Force P-38 dive-bombers attack bridges and marshalling yards.

March 18, 1945

GERMANY: Four hundred twenty-one 1st Air Division B-17s and 495 3d Air Division B-17s attack two rail stations, and 305 2d Air Division B-24s attack two tank factories. Also, 41 heavy bombers attack various targets of opportunity. Seven B-17s and downed by heavy flak concentrations, six B-17s are downed by Me-262s attacking en masse, and six of more than 425 VIII

Fighter Command escorts and scouts are downed.

Opening what will be a five-day preparation for three U.S. field armies (Third, Seventh, and Ninth) preparing to cross the Rhine River, the 9th Air Division mounts more than 660 effective sorties against marshalling yards, a communications center, and several towns.

While escorting heavy bombers over Berlin, the pilot of a 359th Fighter Group P-51 spots Soviet Air Force tactical aircraft nearby, the first known overlapping mission in northern Europe. Unfortunately, during the day, Soviet fighters shoot down a 353d Fighter Group P-51.

Eighth and Ninth air force fighter pilots down 22 GAF aircraft over Germany between 1045 and 1700 hours. Capt Ralph L. Cox, a P-51 pilot with the 359th Fighter Group's 369th Fighter Squadron, achieves ace status when he downs an FW-190 over Joachimsthal at 1135 hours.

ITALY: Fifteenth Air Force heavy bombers are grounded by bad weather; Twelfth Air Force B-25s attack a causeway at Mantua, two rail bridges, and a rail fill; and XXII TAC P-47s attack dumps.

During the night of March 18–19, XXII TAC A-20s and A-26s attack troop movements in the Po River valley.

MTO: Fifteenth Air Force fighters attack rail lines and airfields in Austria, Hungary, and Yugoslavia.

March 19, 1945

AUSTRIA: Fifteenth Air Force B-17s and B-24s drop more than 2,000 tons of bombs—their highest one-day total of the war—on a variety of transportation and oil-production targets in and around Vienna.

Twelfth Air Force B-25s attack a bridge at Muhldorf.

FRANCE: The 492d Heavy Bombardment Group's 856th and 858th Heavy Bombardment squadrons are transferred to Dijon, from which the two special-operations units will drop a total of 82 agents into Germany. Also, specially equipped Mosquitoes

assigned to the 856th Heavy Bombardment Squadron are to monitor and record radio messages from the agents.

GERMANY: Unable to locate their primaries because of thick clouds, 889 1st and 3d Air division B-17s attack various secondary targets—an optics factory at Jena, the city of Plauen, and a motor-transport factory at Zwickau—and numerous targets of opportunity. Also, as planned, 125 2d Air Division B-24s attack Neuberg Airdrome, 84 2d Air Division B-24s attack Leipheim Airdrome, and 126 2d Air Division B-24s attack an armored-vehicle factory at Baumenheim. Six heavy bombers and two of 623 VIII Fighter Command escorts and scouts are lost.

9th Air Division bombers attack five rail bridges, two communications centers, and targets of opportunity.

P-47s of the XIX TAC's 367th Fighter Group successfully bomb and strafe the headquarters of the German Command-in-Chief, West (OB West), at Ziegenburg, at very low level through mountainous terrain, a ground haze, and heavy antiaircraft fire.

Eighth and Ninth Air Force fighter pilots down 44 GAF aircraft over Germany between 0905 and 1715 hours. Maj Niven K. Cranfill, the commanding officer of the 359th Fighter Group's 369th Fighter Squadron, in P-51s, achieves ace status when he downs an Me-262 near Leipzig at about 1415 hours; 1stLt Joe W. Waits, an F-6 pilot with the 363d Tactical Reconnaissance Group's 162d Reconnaissance Squadron, achieves ace status when he downs a Bf-109 near Stuttgart at 1555 hours; and Maj Louis H. Norley, the commanding officer of the 4th Fighter Group's 334th Fighter Squadron, brings his final personal tally to 10.333 confirmed victories when he downs a Bf-109 near Frankfurt am Main at 1615 hours.

Elements of the U.S. Third Army capture Koblenz.

ITALY: Twelfth Air Force B-25s attack bridges and emergency fills at eight locations in northern Italy; and XXII TAC P-47s attack lines of communication, bridges, and dumps in northern Italy and the Po River valley.

During the night of March 19–20, XXII TAC A-20s and A-26s attack targets of opportunity in the Po River valley.

March 20, 1944

AUSTRIA: More than 760 Fifteenth Air Force B-17s and B-24s attack two oil refineries, a tank factory, and marshalling yards at five locations.
GERMANY: One hundred forty-nine 1st Air Division B-17s attack the port area at Hamburg (secondary); 114 2d Air Division B-24s attack an oil-industry target at Hemmingstedt; 13 3d Air Division B-17s attack a U-boat yard at Hamburg (primary); and 133 3d Air Division B-17s attack the port area at Hamburg (secondary). Four heavy bombers and one of 260 VIII Fighter Command escorts and scouts are lost.

More than 360 9th Air Division bombers attack a munitions plant, a marshalling yard, a town area, a rail bridge, and targets of opportunity.
ITALY: Twelfth Air Force B-25s attack four bridges on the line down from Brenner Pass and two bridges elsewhere in northeastern Italy; and XXII TAC P-47s attack fuel dumps near Mantua and communications targets in the Po River valley.

During the night of March 20–21, XXII TAC A-20s and A-26s attack crossing points in the Po River valley.

March 21, 1945

AUSTRIA: Fifteenth Air Force heavy bombers attack five marshalling yards at four locations, and a goods depot and three oil refineries in and around Vienna.
GERMANY: Three hundred sixty-four 1st Air Division B-17s, 496 2d Air Division B-24s, and 351 3d Air Division B-17s attack 11 GAF jet-fighter bases; 107 3d Air Division B-17s attack an armored-vehicle factory at Plauen; and 35 3d Air Division B-17s attack various targets of opportunity.

Seven B-17s and nine of 720 VIII Fighter Command escorts and scouts are lost.

The 9th Air Division mounts 582 effective sorties against a marshalling yard and six communications centers east of the Rhine River.

Eighth and Ninth air force fighter pilots down 18 GAF aircraft over Germany between 0105 and 1500 hours. 2dLt Robert F. Graham, a P-61 radar operator with the Ninth Air Force's 422d Night Fighter Squadron, becomes a "radar ace" when he guides the pilot of his airplane in the downing of an Do-217 near the Rhine River between 0045 and 0105 hours. 2dLt Dudley M. Amoss, a P-51 pilot with the 55th Fighter Group's 38th Fighter Squadron, achieves ace status when he downs three FW-190s near Münster at 1055 hours. However, Amoss is himself shot down by flak and taken prisoner.

Fifteenth Air Force B-24s effectively destroy the jet-aircraft factory and airdrome at Neuberg.

Elements of the U.S. Third Army reach the Rhine River.
ITALY: Twelfth Air Force B-25s attack two marshalling yards, a rail fill, bridge approaches, and two bridges; and XXII TAC P-47s attack rail targets and dumps in the Po River valley and near the battle areas.

During the night of March 21–22, XXII TAC A-20s and A-26s attack crossing points in the Po River valley.
YUGOSLAVIA: Fifteenth Air Force heavy bombers attack a marshalling yard.

March 22, 1945

AUSTRIA: Fifteenth Air Force heavy bombers attack two oil refineries and rail targets in Vienna, and marshalling yards at Graz, Klagenfurt, Wels, and Zeltweg.

Twelfth Air Force B-25s attack bridges at four locations.
CZECHOSLOVAKIA: Fifteenth Air Force heavy bombers attack an oil refinery and a marshalling yard.
GERMANY: Four hundred fifty 1st Air Division B-17s and 289 3d Air Division

B-17s attack ten German Army bases and encampments; 325 2d Air Division B-24s attack three GAF airdromes; 208 3d Air Division B-17s attack two GAF airdromes; and 21 heavy bombers attack secondary targets and targets of opportunity. One B-17 and three of 632 VIII Fighter Command escorts and scouts are lost.

Seven hundred ninety-eight 9th Air Division attack communications centers, a marshalling yard, flak concentrations, and seven towns; and Ninth Air Force fighters and fighter-bombers attack rail lines.

Eighth, Ninth, and First Tactical air force fighter pilots down 22 GAF fighters over Germany between 1230 and 1340 hours. LtCol Sidney S. Woods, the executive officer of the 4th Fighter Group, in P-51s, downs five FW-190s near Eggersdorf Airdrome between 1310 and 1340 hours. (Woods had earlier downed two Japanese airplanes while flying P-38s in the South Pacific.) 1stLt Franklin Rose, Jr., a P-51 pilot with the 354th Fighter Group's 353d Fighter Squadron, achieves ace status when he downs two FW-190s near Mannheim at 1340 hours.

One hundred thirty-six Fifteenth Air Force B-17s severely damage Germany's largest remaining synthetic-fuel factory, at Ruhland, and several attack an aluminum works at Lauta. Three B-17s are downed by GAF jet fighters, but pilots of the 1st, 14th, 31st, and 82d Fighter groups down five GAF aircraft over Ruhland and Papa Airdrome between 1225 and 1345. Capt William J. Dillard, a veteran 31st Fighter Group P-51 pilot, achieves ace status when he downs an Me-262 near Ruhland at 1255 hours.

The Ninth Air Force's 474th Fighter Group displaces to Advance Landing Ground Y-59, at Strassfeld.

ITALY: XXII TAC P-47s attack rail and communications targets.

During the night of March 22–23, XXII TAC A-20s and A-26s attack crossing points in the Po River valley.

March 23, 1945

AUSTRIA: Fifteenth Air Force heavy bombers attack an oil refinery at Vienna, marshalling yards at three locations, and a tank factory.

CZECHOSLOVAKIA: Fifteenth Air Force heavy bombers attack a marshalling yard.

GERMANY: As the main Allied ground assault across the Rhine begins, 1,206 Eighth Air Force B-17s and B-24s attack numerous rail targets in western and central Germany, and 38 heavy bombers attack various targets of opportunity. Seven heavy bombers are lost.

Eight hundred four 9th Air Division bombers attack several communications centers, flak concentrations, and a factory.

Ninth Air Force fighter pilots down 20 GAF aircraft over Germany between 0630 and 1445 hours. LtCol Jack T. Bradley, the commanding officer of the 354th Fighter Group's 353d Fighter Squadron, brings his final personal tally to 15 confirmed victories when he downs a Bf-109 near Frankfurt am Main at 0700 hours; and Capt George A. Doersch, a P-51 pilot with the 359th Fighter Group's 368th Fighter Squadron, brings his final personal tally to 10.5 confirmed victories when he shares in the downing of an Ar-96 advanced trainer near Salzwedel at 1445 hours.

Fifteenth Air Force heavy bombers attack an oil refinery at Ruhland.

ITALY: Twelfth Air Force B-25s attack eight bridges in and around the Brenner Pass, on both sides of the Austro-Italian border.

During the night of March 23–24, XXII TAC A-20s and A-26s attack crossing points, marshalling yards, bridges, and targets of opportunity in the Po River valley and across northeastern Italy.

March 24, 1945

AUSTRIA: Twelfth Air Force B-25s attack bridges at Muhlberg and Steinach.

CZECHOSLOVAKIA: Fifteenth Air Force

heavy bombers attack a marshalling yard. **GERMANY:** Throughout the day—in support of Operation VARSITY, the Anglo-American airborne assault across the Rhine River—1st Air Division B-17s mount 706 effective bombing sorties and 3d Air Division B-17s mount 625 effective bombing sorties against numerous GAF airfields and bases throughout northern and northwestern Germany. Also, VIII Fighter Command fighters mount 1,297 effective sorties throughout the day. Five B-17s and nine fighters are lost.

Beginning at 1000 hours—following intensive clearing attacks by USAAF fighters, including attacks on flak concentrations and airfields—paratroopers and glider-borne forces of the British 6th and U.S. 17th Airborne divisions taking part in Operation VARSITY are dropped into landing zones around Wesel by 2,029 IX Troop Carrier Command C-47s and gliders and 839 RAF aircraft and gliders. The landings are supported by low-level supply drops conducted by 240 2d Air Division B-24s and by an attack on nearby Nordhorn Airdrome by 58 466th Heavy Bombardment Group B-24s. Fourteen B-24s are lost, mostly to small-arms fire, while dropping supplies. Thirty-nine C-47s are downed by flak, one C-47 is lost in an accident, and six C-47s are lost to unknown causes.

9th Air Division bombers mount 688 effective sorties against flak concentrations, rail bridges, communications centers, and many tactical targets in and around the Operation VARSITY battle area. Throughout the day, Ninth Air Force fighters and fighter-bombers mount 2,039 effective sorties in direct support Allied ground forces and mount attacks to block access to the battle area by German reinforcements.

Eighth, Ninth, and First Tactical air force fighter pilots down a Ju-87 and 64 GAF fighters over Germany between 0244 and 1855 hours. Capt Clyde B. East, an F-6 pilot with the 10th Photographic Reconnaissance Group's 15th Reconnaissance Squadron, achieves ace status when he downs two Ju-87s near Eisenach at 0945 hours; LtCol John A. Storch, the commanding officer of the 357th Fighter Group's 364th Fighter Squadron, in P-51s, brings his final personal tally to 10.5 confirmed victories when he downs a Bf-109 near Gutersloh Airdrome at 1210 hours; Capt Paul R. Hatala, a P-51 pilot with the 357th Fighter Group's 364th Fighter Squadron, achieves ace status when he downs two Bf-109s over Gutersloh Airdrome at 1215 hours; Maj Robert W. Foy, the 357th Fighter Group operations officer, brings his final personal tally to 15 confirmed victories when he downs a Bf-109 near Gutersloh Airdrome at 1220 hours; Maj Robert A. Elder, the commanding officer of the 354th Fighter Group's 353d Fighter Squadron, in P-51s, becomes an "ace in a day" when he downs four FW-190s and a Bf-109 near Kassel between 1530 and 1600 hours; Capt Raymond E. Hartley, Jr., a P-51 pilot with the 353d Fighter Group's 350th Fighter Squadron, achieves ace status when he downs two FW-190s and a Bf-109 near Kassel between 1530 and 1600 hours (Hartley's two earlier victories were scored while he was serving with the Fifteenth Air Force); and in the same engagement, LtCol Wayne K. Blickenstaff, the commanding officer of the 350th Fighter Squadron, brings his final personal tally to ten confirmed victories when he downs three FW-190s and two Bf-109s.

Two hundred seventy-one Fifteenth Air Force B-24s destroy whatever remains of the Neuberg jet-aircraft factory as well as an estimated 20 jet aircraft parked on the adjacent airdrome.

More than 150 Fifteenth Air Force B-17s attack the Daimler-Benz tank-engine factory in Berlin. This is the Fifteenth's first mission to the German capital, a round trip exceeding 1,500 miles. On this mission, four B-17s are downed by flak near Brux, Czechoslovakia; a fifth is downed during the approach to the target when the bomber formation is attacked by 15 Me-262s; and a sixth is downed over the target by flak.

While defending the bombers over the target, Col William Daniel, the 31st Fighter Group commanding officer, achieves ace status when he downs one of the Me-262s and damages another. In all, eight of the GAF jets are downed between 1220 and 1250 by 31st and 332d Fighter group P-51 pilots. Fifteenth Air Force heavy bombers also attack airdromes at Erding, Munich, and Plattling.

ITALY: Fifteenth Air Force heavy bombers attack the airfield complex at Udine; Twelfth Air Force B-25s attack bridges and bridge approaches at six locations; and XXII TAC P-47s attack rail lines throughout northern Italy.

LtGen John K. Cannon replaces Gen Ira C. Eaker as commanding general of the Army Air Forces in the Mediterranean Theater of Operations (AAFMTO), and it is announced that he will be assuming command of MAAF.

During the night of March 24–25, XXII TAC A-20s and A-26s attack road and rail targets, and crossing points in the Po River valley.

March 25, 1945

CZECHOSLOVAKIA: Fifteenth Air Force B-17s and B-24s attack Cheb Airdrome, and a tank factory and two airfields in and around Prague.

1stLt Norman C. Skogstad, a P-51 ace with the 31st Fighter Group's 307th Fighter Squadron, brings his final personal tally to 12 confirmed victories when he downs four FW-190s near Olomouc at 1225 hours.

GERMANY: Two hundred forty-three 2d Air Division B-24s attack oil depots at three locations, but 737 1st and 3d Air division B-17s dispatched against other oil-industry targets and a tank factory are forced to abort in the face of bad weather during assembly over England. Four B-24s are lost.

Six hundred forty-one 9th Air Division bombers attack three marshalling yards, four communications centers, and flak concentrations.

Eighth, Ninth, and First Tactical air force fighter pilots down ten GAF fighters over Germany between 0700 and 1600 hours. Maj Glenn T. Eagleston, a P-51 ace and the commanding officer of the 354th Fighter Group's 353d Fighter Squadron, brings his final personal tally for World War II to 18.5 confirmed victories and thus becomes the Ninth Air Force's top-scoring ace of the war when he downs a Bf-109 near Neustadt at high noon.

The lead elements of the U.S. Third and Ninth armies cross the Rhine River.

ITALY: Twelfth Air Force medium-bomber missions against bridges on both sides of the Austro-Italian border are rendered ineffective by bad weather, but XXII TAC P-47s attack bridges and rail lines in the Po River valley and fuel dumps elsewhere in northern Italy.

During the night of March 25–26, XXII TAC A-20s and A-26s attack bridges at Cittadella and Verona.

March 26, 1945

AUSTRIA: Fifteenth Air Force heavy bombers attack marshalling yards at three locations.

CZECHOSLOVAKIA: Fifteenth Air Force heavy bombers attack a marshalling yard at Bratislava.

GERMANY: Due to bad weather, only 12 1st Air Division B-17s attack their primary, an oil-industry target at Zeitz, but 130 attack their secondary target, a tank factory at Plauen. Also, 139 3d Air Division B-17s attack their primary, the tank factory at Plauen, and 49 B-17s attack various targets of opportunity.

Approximately 300 9th Air Division bombers attack marshalling yards at three locations, and a defended town.

The Ninth Air Force's 48th Fighter Group displaces to Advance Landing Ground Y-54, at Kelz.

HUNGARY: Fifteenth Air Force heavy bombers attack a marshalling yard.

ITALY: Twelfth Air Force B-25s are grounded by bad weather, and XXII TAC

P-47s are able to mount only limited missions against rail targets in the Po River valley.

March 27, 1945

ENGLAND: The last V-1 rocket falls on English soil.
ETO: The 9th Air Division is grounded by bad weather.
ITALY: The Twelfth and Fifteenth air forces are grounded by bad weather.

March 28, 1945

GERMANY: Three hundred eighty-three 3d Air Division B-17s attack a munitions factory and an armaments factory in Berlin; 34 3d Air Division B-17s attack a tank factory at Hannover (primary); 431 3d Air Division B-17s attack a marshalling yard at Hannover (secondary); and 43 B-17s attack a secondary target and targets of opportunity.

Two hundred fifteen 9th Air Division bombers attack two oil-storage depots and numerous targets of opportunity.

The Ninth Air Force's 36th Fighter Group displaces to Advance Landing Ground Y-46, at Aachen.
ITALY: The entire Fifteenth Air Force, all Twelfth Air Force B-25s, and virtually all XXII TAC P-47s are grounded by bad weather.

During the night of March 28–29, XXII TAC A-20s and A-26s attack rail targets, road targets, bridges, a factory, and river crossings.

March 29, 1945

ETO: The Ninth Air Force is grounded by bad weather.
ITALY: The entire Fifteenth Air Force and all Twelfth Air Force B-25s are grounded by bad weather, but during the afternoon XXII TAC P-47s attack dumps, a viaduct, rail bridges and bridge approaches, and road and rail lines.

During the night of March 29–30, XXII TAC A-20s and A-26s attack lines of com-

munications, freight facilities, and crossing points in the Po River valley.

March 30, 1945

AUSTRIA: Approximately 60 Fifteenth Air Force B-17s and B-24s attack a tank factory and several widely separated rail targets.
GERMANY: Three hundred eighteen 1st Air Division B-17s attack the U-boat yard at Bremen; 109 1st Air Division B-17s attack a rail bridge at Bremen; 273 2d Air Division B-24s attack the U-boat yard at Wilhelmshaven; 85 2d Air Division B-24s attack the port area at Wilhelmshaven; 32 2d Air Division B-24s attack the U-boat yard at Farge using rocket-enhanced concrete-busting bombs; 169 3d Air Division B-17s attack an oil depot at Hamburg; 64 3d Air Division B-17s attack two U-boat yards at Hamburg; and 263 3d Air Division B-17s attack the port area at Hamburg (secondary). A total of five heavy bombers and four of VIII Fighter Command escorts and scouts are lost.

Three hundred thirty-seven 9th Air Division bombers attack an ordnance depot, a tank factory, an oil depot, and towns.

LtCol John D. Landers, an ace and the executive officer of the 78th Fighter Group, in P-51s, brings his final personal tally to 14.5 confirmed victories (including six in the Southwest Pacific) when he shares in the downing of an Me-262 near Rendsburg at 1345 hours.

The Ninth Air Force's 404th Fighter Group displaces to Advance Landing Ground Y-54, at Kelz.
ITALY: Twelfth Air Force B-25s attack bridges and bridge approaches at seven locations, and XXII TAC P-47s mount more than 400 effective sorties against dumps, rail lines, marshalling yards, bridges, and road and rail traffic.

During the night of March 30–31, XXII TAC A-20s and A-26s attack crossing points in the Po River valley, ammunition dumps, and rail facilities.

March 31, 1945

AUSTRIA: Fifteenth Air Force B-17s and B-24s attack the main rail station an at Linz, and a marshalling yard at Villach.

BELGIUM: The Ninth Air Force's 322d Medium Bombardment Group displaces to Advance Landing Ground A-89, at Le Culot.

GERMANY: Three hundred sixty-nine 1st Air Division B-17s attack a marshalling yard at Halle (secondary); 371 2d Air Division B-24s attack a marshalling yard at Halle; 265 3d Air Division B-17s attack the city of Brandenburg; 137 3d Air Division B-17s attack a synthetic-fuel plant at Zeitz; and 152 heavy bombers attack various secondary targets and targets of opportunity. Five heavy bombers and four of 847 VIII Fighter Command escorts and scouts are lost.

More than 550 9th Air Division bombers attack three storage depots, a defended town, and a marshalling yard.

Eighth and Ninth air force fighter pilots down 14 GAF fighters over Germany between 0715 and 1145 hours.

On unspecified dates in March, the Ninth Air Force's 10th Photographic Reconnaissance Group and 67th Tactical Reconnaissance Group displace to Advance Landing Ground Y-57, at Trier, and Advance Landing Ground Y-51, at Vogelsang, respectively.

ITALY: Fifteenth Air Force heavy bombers attack a marshalling yard at Treviso; despite bad weather, Twelfth Air Force B-25s attack rail bridges and a fill in the Brenner Pass area and the Po River valley; and XXII TAC P-47s attack dumps and lines of communication throughout northern Italy.

During the night of March 31–April 1, XXII TAC A-20s and A-26s attack road, rail, and other transportation targets in the Po River valley.

MTO: In their highest-scoring day of the entire year, Fifteenth Air Force P-38 and P-51 pilots of the 1st, 31st, and 332d Fighter groups down a total of 35 GAF fighters and one He-111 medium bomber over Austria, Czechoslovakia, and southern Germany.

APRIL 1945

April 1, 1945

AUSTRIA: Fifteenth Air Force heavy bombers attack marshalling yards at five locations and one rail bridge; and 82 Fifteenth Air Force P-38s attack a rail bridge.

While escorting a Fifteenth Air Force bombing mission, P-51 pilots of the 332d Fighter Group's 301st Fighter Squadron down 12 GAF fighters over Wels at about 1400 hours.

ETO: 9th Air Division bombers are grounded by bad weather.

GERMANY: Elements of the U.S. First Army capture Paderborn, and elements of the U.S. Third Army begin clearing Kassel.

ITALY: Fifteenth Air Force heavy bombers attack coastal batteries near Venice; Twelfth Air Force B-25s attack rail bridges at seven locations; and XXII TAC P-47s attack road and rail targets, especially bridges spanning the Po River.

During the night of April 1–2, XXII TAC A-20s and A-26s attack communications targets and crossing points in the Po River valley.

YUGOSLAVIA: Fifteenth Air Force heavy bombers attack a rail bridge at Maribor.

April 2, 1945

AUSTRIA: Nearly 600 Fifteenth Air Force B-17s and B-24s attack marshalling yards and rail bridges.

DENMARK: Due to bad weather, more than 700 Eighth Air Force B-17s and B-24s are recalled at the Danish coast while on their way to attack airfields in Denmark. One B-17 and one escort fighter are lost.

ETO: The 9th Air Division and XXIX TAC are grounded by bad weather.

GERMANY: XIX TAC fighter pilots down 17 GAF aircraft between 0715 and 1600 hours. 1stLt Henry S. Rudolph, a P-51 pilot with the 354th Fighter Group's 353d Fighter Squadron, achieves ace status when he downs two FW-190s near Bayreuth at 1600 hours.

The Ninth Air Force's 67th Tactical Reconnaissance Group displaces to Advance Landing Ground Y-83, at Limburg.

Advances on the ground by the First and Third U.S. armies bring about the formation of a German Army defensive locale known as the Ruhr Pocket.

ITALY: Twelfth Air Force B-25s attack rail bridges on both sides of the Austro-Italian border, and XXII TAC P-47s attack methane plants and lines of communication in the Po River valley.

In the last significant air-to-air engagement of the war in the MTO, P-47 pilots of the Twelfth Air Force's 350th Fighter Group down 13 Bf-109s in the Verona area between 1420 and 1430 hours.

MajGen Benjamin W. Chidlaw replaces LtGen John K. Cannon as commanding general of the Twelfth Air Force.

During the night of April 2-3, XXII TAC A-20s and A-26s attack a marshalling yard at Mantua and communications targets and crossing points in the Po River valley.

April 3, 1945

GERMANY: Two hundred eighteen 1st Air Division B-17s and 499 3d Air Division B-17s attack two U-boat yards at Kiel. Two B-17s and four of 636 VIII Fighter Command escorts and scouts are lost.

Approximately 230 9th Air Division bombers attack two marshalling yards and a defended town.

The XXIX TAC operational headquarters displaces forward to Haltern.

ITALY: Fifteenth Air Force heavy bombers and many Twelfth Air Force B-25s are grounded by bad weather, but some Twelfth Air Force B-25s are able to attack bridges at three locations; and XXII TAC P-47s attack methane plants, fuel dumps, communications targets, and road and rail targets throughout northern Italy.

April 4, 1945

GERMANY: One hundred ninety-nine 1st Air Division B-17s attack three GAF airfields (two of which are secondaries); 22 1st Air Division B-17s attack a U-boat yard at Hamburg; 159 2d Air Division B-24s of 438 dispatched attack three airfields (one of them a secondary); and 505 3d Air Divi-

sion B-17s attack a shipyard at Kiel. Ten heavy bombers and four of 812 VIII Fighter Command escorts and scouts are lost. One of the airmen lost is Col Troy W. Crawford, the 446th Heavy Bombardment Group commander, who is taken prisoner.

More than 330 9th Air Division bombers attack an oil depot, a supply depot, a marshalling yard, a barracks, a defended town, and a road and rail junction.

Eighth and Ninth air force fighter pilots down 34 GAF aircraft between 0800 and 1830 hours. LtCol George F. Ceuleers, the commanding officer of the 364th Fighter Group's 383d Fighter Squadron, brings his final personal tally to 10.5 confirmed victories when he downs an Me-262 over Leipzig at about 0940 hours; and 1stLt William J. Cullerton, a P-51 pilot with the 355th Fighter Group's 357th Fighter Squadron, achieves ace status when he downs an FW-190 near Halberstadt at 1020 hours.

P-51 pilots of the VIII Fighter Command's 339th Fighter Group claim 105 GAF aircraft destroyed on the ground during strafing attacks.

The XXIX TAC is returned from the operational control of the British Second Tactical Air Force to the operational control of the U.S. Ninth Air Force.

While escorting a Fifteenth Air Force bomber mission against targets around Munich, 325th Fighter Group P-51 pilots down five FW-190s over southern Germany between 1545 and 1635 hours.

ITALY: Fifteenth Air Force heavy bombers are grounded by bad weather; Twelfth Air Force B-25s attack bridges on both sides of Brenner Pass, and a methane plant at Merano; and XXII TAC P-47s attack rail lines, fuel and ammunition dumps, and German Army forces on the move in the Po River valley.

During the night of April 4-5, XXII TAC A-20s and A-26s attack bridges at seven locations.

April 5, 1945

BELGIUM: The Ninth Air Force's 344th

Medium Bombardment Group displaces to Advance Landing Ground A-78, at Florennes/Juzaine Airdrome.
ETO: The 9th Air Division is grounded by bad weather.
GERMANY: Three hundred five 1st Air Division B-17s attack two munitions dumps; 73 1st Air Division B-17s attack a marshalling yard at Bayreuth; 151 2d Air Division B-24s attack a marshalling yard at Plauen; 39 2d Air Division B-24s attack a munitions dump at Bayreuth; 59 3d Air Division B-17s attack an airdrome; 13 3d Air Division B-17s attack an electric plant; 54 3d Air Division B-17s attack a munitions dump at Furth; 37 3d Air Division B-17s attack a marshalling yard at Nurnberg; 271 3d Air Division B-17s attack the main railroad station at Nurnberg (secondary); and 33 heavy bombers attack targets of opportunity. Ten heavy bombers and one of 606 VIII Fighter Command escorts and scouts are lost.

Eighth and Ninth air force fighter pilots down 14 GAF aircraft between 0750 and 1700 hours.

The Ninth Air Force's 10th Photographic Reconnaissance Group displaces to Advance Landing Ground Y-64, at Mainz/Ober Olm Airdrome.

The U.S. Ninth Army crosses the Weser River.
ITALY: Fifteenth Air Force heavy bombers attack rail targets at Alessandria, Brescia, and Turin, and the airdrome complex at Udine; Twelfth Air Force B-25s attack gun emplacements at La Spezia and bridges in northern Italy and adjacent areas of Austria; and XXII TAC P-47s devote their entire effort to supporting the U.S. Fifth Army and attacking dumps and communications targets in the Po River valley.

During the night of April 5–6, XXII TAC A-20s and A-26s attack bridges and an assembly area in the Po River valley.
YUGOSLAVIA: Fifteenth Air Force heavy bombers attack a bridge, and 96 P-38s dive-bomb a rail bridge.

April 6, 1945

GERMANY: Two hundred fifteen 1st Air Division B-17s and 106 3d Air Division B-17s attack the main rail station at Leipzig (secondary); 183 2d Air Division B-25s attack a marshalling yard at Halle; and 33 heavy bombers attack several targets of opportunity. Four B-17s and one of 630 VIII Fighter Command escorts and scouts are lost.

Ninety-nine 9th Air Division bombers attack the city of Herzberg and marshalling yards at two other locations.

The U.S. First Army begins crossing the Weser River.
ITALY: Three hundred eighty-seven Fifteenth Air Force heavy bombers attack flak emplacements and an ordnance depot at Verona, and a marshalling yard and small-arms factory at Brescia, but 179 other heavy bombers are recalled because of bad weather over their targets; Twelfth Air Force B-25s are diverted by bad weather from attacking rail lines in the Brenner Pass area, but they are able to attack gun emplacements at La Spezia and six bridges in the Po River valley; and XXII TAC P-47s support the U.S. Fifth Army and attack lines of communication in the Po River valley.

BriGen Thomas C. Darcy assumes command of the XXII TAC.

During the night of April 6–7, XXII TAC A-20s and A-26s attack several crossing points in the Po River valley and bridges at four locations.

April 7, 1945

AUSTRIA: A small number of Fifteenth Air Force heavy bombers attack marshalling yards at three locations.
GERMANY: 1,261 Eighth Air Force B-17s and B-24s attack numerous airfields, ordnance depots, marshalling yards, and several industrial sites. In the last major effort by GAF fighters to stem a bombing attack over Germany, 17 heavy bombers are lost—including at least five 3d Air Division B-17s that are intentionally rammed

by aircraft from a special GAF unit—as are five of 830 VIII Fighter Command escorts and scouts. Among the airmen lost is Col John B. Herboth, Jr., the 389th Heavy Bombardment Group commander, who is killed.

Two hundred sixty-eight 9th Air Division bombers attack two marshalling yards and two defended towns.

Eighth and Ninth air force fighter pilots down 82 GAF aircraft between 0830 and 1900 hours. Maj Robin Olds, the commanding officer of the 479th Fighter Group's 434th Fighter Squadron and a P-38 and P-51 ace, brings his final personal World War II tally to 13 confirmed victories when he downs a Bf-109 near Bremen at 1220 hours; 1stLt Richard G. Candelaria, a P-51 pilot with the 479th Fighter Group's 435th Fighter Squadron, achieves ace status when he downs four Bf-109s and probably downs an Me-262 near Luneberg between 1225 and 1230 hours; Capt Gene E. Markham, a P-51 pilot with the 353d Fighter Group's 351st Fighter Squadron, achieves ace status when he downs a Bf-109 near Steinhuder Lake at 1235 hours; Capt Harrison B. Tordoff, a P-51 pilot with the 353d Fighter Group's 352d Fighter Squadron, achieves ace status when he downs a Bf-109 near Hamburg at 1250 hours; and Capt Donald M. Cummings, a P-51 pilot with the 55th Fighter Group's 38th Fighter Squadron, achieves ace status when he downs two Bf-109s over Celle at 1300 hours (Cummings's total of 6.5 victories includes two that he scored while flying A-36s in the MTO); and Capt Valentine S. Rader, an F-6 pilot with the 67th Tactical-Reconnaissance Group's 111th Reconnaissance Squadron, achieves ace status when he downs two Bf-109s near Stuttgart between 1710 and 1800 hours.

The Ninth Air Force's 371st Fighter Group displaces to Advance Landing Ground Y-74, at Frankfurt/Eschborn Airdrome.

ITALY: More than 500 Fifteenth Air Force heavy bombers dispatched against bridges and other targets in Austria and northern Italy are recalled because of bad weather, but a small number are able to attack two rail bridges and a road bridge in northern Italy; Twelfth Air Force B-25s are grounded by bad weather; and a small number of XXII TAC P-47s attack an oilfield at Montechino, ammunitions dumps, and communications targets.

During the night of April 7–8, XXII TAC A-20s and A-26s attack dumps and German Army command posts.

April 8, 1945

AUSTRIA: Fifteenth Air Force P-38s bomb a rail bridge at Rattenburg.
GERMANY: 1,103 Eighth Air Force B-17s and B-24s attack munitions plants, munitions dumps, marshalling yards, a jet factory, and several airdromes. Nine B-17s and one of 763 VIII Fighter Command escorts and scouts are lost.

Approximately 620 9th Air Division bombers attack an oil depot, an oil refinery, a communications center, a marshalling yard, and city areas at eight locations.

Eighth, Ninth, and First Tactical air force fighter pilots down 38 GAF aircraft between 0001 and 1900 hours. 2dLt Leland A. Larson, an F-6 pilot with the 10th Photographic-Reconnaissance Group's 15th Reconnaissance Squadron, achieves ace status when he downs a Ju-87 and shares in the downing of an He-111 near Dresden between 0800 and 0820 hours.

1stLt William J. Cullerton, a P-51 ace with the 355th Fighter Group's 357th Fighter Squadron, is shot down by flak and taken prisoner.

The IX TAC operational headquarters displaces forward from Bruhl to Marburg/Lahn; the Ninth Air Force's 36th Fighter Group displaces to Advance Landing Ground Y-62, at Neidermendig; the Ninth Air Force's 354th Fighter Group displaces to Advance Landing Ground Y-64, at Mainz/Ober Olm Airdrome; and the Ninth Air Force's 362d Fighter Group displaces to Advance Landing Ground Y-73, at Frankfurt/Rhein-Main Airdrome.

Fifteenth Air Force P-38s bomb a rail bridge at Garmisch and strafe rail traffic on the lines running from Munich to Salzburg and Linz.

ITALY: More than 500 Fifteenth Air Force B-17s and B-24s systematically attack lines of communication feeding into the Brenner Pass as well as an electrical-power dam and marshalling yards at 11 locations; despite bad weather, Twelfth Air Force B-25s attack rail bridges at four locations, a rail fill, a canal, and gun emplacements at La Spezia; and XXII TAC P-47s attack four bridges and lines of communication, all in Brenner Pass.

During the night of April 8–9, XXII TAC A-20s and A-26s attack bridges and targets of opportunity in the Po River valley and other areas of northern Italy.

April 9, 1945

BELGIUM: The Ninth Air Force's 386th Medium Bombardment Group displaces to Advance Landing Ground A-92, at St.-Trond Airdrome.

ENGLAND: The Eighth Air Force's 361st Fighter Group is returned to duty with the 65th Fighter Wing and transferred from a temporary base in Belgium to a permanent base in England.

GERMANY: 1,215 Eighth Air Force B-17s and B-24s attack ten airfields, an ordnance depot, and a marshalling yard. Seven heavy bombers and five of 812 VIII Fighter Command fighters are lost.

9th Air Division bombers mount more than 700 effective sorties against oil targets, ordnance depots, and marshalling yards, and Ninth Air Force fighters attack airfields and a fuel depot.

Eighth, Ninth, and First Tactical air force fighter pilots down 27 GAF fighters between 0001 and 1935 hours. LtCol Robert D. Johnston, the commanding officer of the 50th Fighter Group's 81st Fighter Squadron, in P-47s, achieves ace status when he downs two FW-190s near Crailsheim at 1900 hours.

ITALY: Eight hundred twenty-five Fif-

teenth Air Force B-17s and B-24s, Twelfth Air Force B-25s, and XXII TAC P-47s attack German Army headquarters, strongpoints, gun emplacements, and troop concentrations in support of a major offensive launched by the British Eighth Army. XXII TAC P-47s also attack a methane plant, ammunition and fuel dumps, and communications targets.

During the night of April 9–10, XXII TAC A-20s and A-26s attack gun emplacements along the British Eighth Army battle front, bridges in Brenner Pass, and crossing points in the Po River valley.

MTO: More than 150 Fifteenth Air Force P-38s bomb and strafe bridges and rail lines along the Austro-German border.

April 10, 1945

AUSTRIA: One hundred fifty-two Fifteenth Air Force P-38s bomb bridges, a tunnel, and a marshalling yard.

P-51 pilots of the 325th Fighter Group's 318th Fighter Squadron down five FW-190s and a Ju-88 near Linz between 1620 and 1640 hours. Maj Norman L. McDonald, the 318th Fighter Squadron commanding officer, brings his final personal tally to 11.5 confirmed victories when he downs one of the FW-190s; and 1stLt William E. Aron achieves ace status when he downs the Ju-88 near Linz at 1620 hours. Aron is the last Fifteenth Air Force fighter pilot to attain ace status in World War II.

GERMANY: Four hundred seventeen 1st Air Division B-17s attack a German Army headquarters, a munitions dump, an aircraft factory, and an airfield at Oranienburg; 262 2d Air Division B-24s attack two airfields at Rechlin; 492 3d Air Division B-17s attack four airfields; and 29 heavy bombers attack several targets of opportunity. Nineteen heavy bombers and eight of 868 escorts and scouts are lost.

Four hundred twenty-three 9th Air Division bombers attack oil and ordnance depots, a viaduct, a rail bridge, a marshalling yard, and an industrial area.

The 9th Air Division's 391st Medium

Bombardment Group flies its first mission since transitioning from B-26s to A-26s.

Eighth and Ninth air force fighter pilots down 43 GAF aircraft between 0001 and 1905 hours. Capt Gordon B. Compton, a P-51 pilot with the 353d Fighter Group's 351st Fighter Squadron, achieves ace status when he downs an Me-262 near Dessau at 1400 hours; and Capt Robert W. Abernathy, a P-51 pilot with the 353d Fighter Group's 350th Fighter Squadron, achieves ace status when he downs an Me-262 over Dessau at 1510 hours.

The Ninth Air Force's 67th Tactical Reconnaissance Group displaces to Advance Landing Ground R-11, at Eschwege Airdrome; and the Ninth Air Force's 367th Fighter Group displaces to Advance Landing Ground Y-74, at Frankfurt/Eschborn Airdrome.

ITALY: In their largest single-day effort to date, 648 Fifteenth Air Force B-17s and B-24s attack numerous tactical targets in direct support of the British Eighth Army offensive, as do Twelfth Air Force B-25s and XXII TAC P-47s. XXII TAC P-47s also attack lines of communication in the Po River valley and rail bridges on the line from the Brenner Pass.

During the night of April 10–11, XXII TAC A-20s and A-26s attack bridges at five locations and crossing points in the Po River valley.

April 11, 1945

FRANCE: Maj Gilbert F. Talbot, the commanding officer of the 354th Fighter Group's 355th Fighter Squadron, in P-51s, achieves ace status when he downs a Bf-109 near Muhlhausen at 0620 hours.

GERMANY: 1,270 Eighth Air Force heavy bombers attack two airfields, seven marshalling yards, a munitions factory, three munitions dumps, and two ordnance depots. One B-17 is lost.

9th Air Division bombers mount 689 effective sorties against marshalling yards at four locations, a truck plant, and an ordnance depot.

Ninth Air Force fighter pilots down 47 GAF aircraft over Germany between 0100 and 2340 hours. 1stLt Edward B. Edwards, Jr., a P-47 pilot with the 373d Fighter Group's 411th Fighter Squadron, achieves ace status when he downs four FW-190s over Sachau Airdrome at about 1745 hours.

1stLt Eugene D. Axtell, a P-61 pilot with the Ninth Air Force's 422d Night Fighter Squadron, achieves ace status when he downs a Ju-52 on each of two separate missions near Kassel, one at 0108 hours and the other at 2307 hours.

The Ninth Air Force's 366th Fighter Group displaces to Advance Landing Ground Y-94, at Munster/Handorf Airdrome.

The U.S. Ninth Army reaches the Elbe River near Magdeburg.

ITALY: Five hundred forty-four Fifteenth Air Force B-17s and B-24s continue their systematic interdiction of lines of supply and communication throughout northern Italy with attacks on bridges, marshalling yards, a fuel depot, and a vehicle repair facility.

In anticipation of the final Allied ground offensive of the war in Italy, the Twelfth Air Force opens an intense three-day operation aimed at blocking or snarling German Army lines of supply and communication. In addition to providing support for the ongoing British Eighth Army offensive, Twelfth Air Force B-25s attack four bridges in the Brenner Pass area and gun emplacements at La Spezia; and XXII TAC P-47s also attack the Brenner Pass rail line and ammunition and fuel dumps throughout northern Italy.

During the night of April 11–12, XXII TAC A-20s and A-26s attack crossing points in the Po River valley.

MTO: More than 100 Fifteenth Air Force P-38s and P-51s attack rail lines throughout Czechoslovakia, Germany, and Austria.

April 12, 1945

AUSTRIA: One hundred twenty-four Fifteenth Air Force P-38s bomb rail bridges at two locations.

GERMANY: Although more than 275 9th Air Division bombers abort in the face of bad weather, 167 bombers are able to attack an ordnance depot, a rail bridge, a marshalling yard, and several targets of opportunity. Of special note among numerous Ninth Air Force fighter missions, 11 36th Fighter Group P-47 pilots destroy 14 He-111s and three Do-217s on the ground at Schkeuditz Airdrome, and then discover more than 300 GAF aircraft on the ground at Leipzig/Mockau Airdrome. In the course of continuous strafing passes, the 11 P-47 pilots account for 16 Ju-88s, nine Fw-190s, eight Bf-109s, six He-111s, five Me-410s, ten assorted trainers, an Me-262, a Ju-87, and a captured P-47.

The Ninth Air Force's 404th Fighter Group displaces to Advance Landing Ground Y-86, at Fritzlar.

Erfurt falls to the U.S. Third Army.

ITALY: Although 128 B-24s abort in the face of bad weather, more than 400 Fifteenth Air Force B-17s and B-24s complete attacks on lines of communication on both sides of the Austro-Italian border and rail bridges at Padua; Twelfth Air Force B-25s attack the Brenner Pass rail line and support the British Eighth Army; and XXII TAC P-47s attack rail lines, communications targets, and dumps in the Po River valley.

UNITED STATES: President Franklin D. Roosevelt passes away in Warm Springs, Georgia.

YUGOSLAVIA: Twelfth Air Force B-25s attack a bridge at Maribor.

April 13, 1945

ETO: The 9th Air Division is grounded by bad weather.

GERMANY: Two hundred twelve 1st Air Division B-17s attack a marshalling yard at Neumunster (secondary). Two B-17s and eight of 372 VIII Fighter Command escorts and scouts are lost.

IX TAC P-47s mount a raid against the headquarters of the German Army Group B, in the Ruhr Pocket.

Capt Clyde B. East, an F-6 ace with

the 10th Photographic-Reconnaissance Group's 15th Reconnaissance Squadron, brings his final personal tally to 13 confirmed victories and secures his place as the USAAF's top-scoring F-6 ace when he downs a Bf-109 near Hof at 1500 hours.

1stLt Richard G. Candelaria, a P-51 ace with the 479th Fighter Group's 435th Fighter Squadron, is shot down by flak and taken prisoner.

The Ninth Air Force's 365th Fighter Group displaces to Advance Landing Ground Y-86, at Fritzlar.

The U.S. Ninth Army crosses the Elbe River.

ITALY: The Fifteenth Air Force is grounded by bad weather; Twelfth Air Force B-25s are able to mount only one mission, an attack on a road bridge; and XXII TAC P-47s attack gun emplacements at La Spezia and dumps and communications targets in the Po River valley.

During the night of April 13–14, XXII TAC A-20s and A-26s attack communications targets in the Po River valley.

April 14, 1945

AUSTRIA: Fifteenth Air Force heavy bombers attack a marshalling yard at Klagenfurt.

FRANCE: Preceding a clearing operation to be launched by French Army ground forces, 1,133 Eighth Air Force heavy bombers attack fortifications, strongpoints, gun emplacements, and flak positions at Bordeaux and other German defensive positions remaining along the French Atlantic coast. Four heavy bombers are lost.

1stLt Loyd "J" Overfield, a P-51 ace with the 354th Fighter Group's 353d Fighter Squadron, brings his final personal tally to 11 confirmed victories when he downs an Me-262 and an He-111 over Muhlhausen at 1530 hours.

GERMANY: Ninth and First Tactical air force fighter pilots down 14 GAF aircraft between 1330 and 1840 hours.

The XXIX TAC operational headquarters displaces forward to Gutersloh.

Advances by the First and Third U.S. armies split the Ruhr Pocket into two parts. **ITALY:** Fifteenth Air Force heavy bombers attack a motor-transport depot and four ammunition factories.

Although diverted by bad weather from primary targets in Brenner Pass, Twelfth Air Force B-25s attack gun emplacements at La Spezia, rail lines at three locations, and five defended areas along the British Eighth Army front.

Allied ground forces open what is being billed as the final ground offensive in Italy. The entire XXII TAC is committed to supporting the ground troops on a 24-hour-a-day on-call basis.

During the night of April 14–15, XXII TAC A-20s and A-26s attack crossing points and communications targets in the Po River valley.

April 15, 1945

FRANCE: 1,278 Eighth Air Force heavy bombers attack fortifications, strongpoints, gun emplacements, and flak positions at Bordeaux, Royan, and other German defensive positions remaining along the French Atlantic coast. One B-24 is lost. The Royan mission is of interest in that it involves the first and only operational use of napalm bombs by Eighth Air Force heavy-bomber units. The results are negligible, and plans to drop more napalm from heavy bombers are canceled.

GERMANY: Two hundred fifty-eight 9th Air Division bombers attack five marshalling yards and several targets of opportunity.

Ninth and First Tactical air force fighter pilots down ten GAF aircraft over Germany between 0745 and 1830 hours. Capt Richard W. Asbury, a P-51 pilot with the 354th Fighter Group's 356th Fighter Squadron, achieves ace status when he shares in the downing of an He-111 near Bayreuth at 0745 hours; 1stLt Bruce W. Carr, a P-51 ace with the 354th Fighter Group's 353d Fighter Squadron, brings his final personal tally to 15 confirmed victories when he

downs an He-111 over Gotha at 1400 hours; and Capt Gerald Brown, a P-51 pilot with the 55th Fighter Group's 38th Fighter Squadron, achieves ace status when he downs at FW-190 and an He-111 near Munster between 1430 and 1435 hours.

The Ninth Air Force's 368th Fighter Group displaces to Advance Landing Ground Y-73, at Frankfurt/Rhein-Main Airdrome; the Ninth Air Force's 406th Fighter Group displaces to Advance Landing Ground Y-94, at Munster/Handorf Airdrome; and the Ninth Air Force's 363d Tactical Reconnaissance Group displaces to Advance Landing Ground Y-99, at Gutersloh Airdrome.

ITALY: In its busiest day of the war, the Fifteenth Air Force mounts 1,235 heavy-bomber sorties and 586 fighter sorties in unremitting attacks against German Army troop concentrations, headquarters, gun positions, and supply points, especially in and around Bologna.

Twelfth Air Force B-25s and XXII TAC P-47s provide direct support for the U.S. Fifth and British Eighth armies.

During the night of April 15–16, XXII TAC A-20s and A-26s attack crossing points and three defended towns in the Po River valley.

MTO: Fifteenth Air Force fighters and fighter-bombers attack rail lines and other rail targets throughout Austria and southern Germany.

April 16, 1945

AUSTRIA: Five GAF aircraft are downed over or near Wels Airdrome between 1415 and 1450 hours by 52d Fighter Group P-51 pilots.

BELGIUM: The Ninth Air Force's 391st Medium Bombardment Group displaces to Advance Landing Ground Y-29, at Asche.

CZECHOSLOVAKIA: Pilots of the XIX TAC's 368th Fighter Group down three GAF fighters over Czechoslovakia at 1430.

ETO: VIII Fighter Command fighters from 15 groups claim the destruction of a record 747 GAF aircraft on the ground during

strafing missions against airfields throughout Germany and Czechoslovakia. 339th
Fighter Group P-51 pilots alone are credited with 118 of the ground kills—the first
and only USAAF group to destroy more
than a hundred enemy planes on the ground
on two occasions (the other being April 4,
1945). Thirty-four VIII Fighter Command
fighters are downed, mostly by light flak
and small arms.

LtCol Sidney S. Woods, the executive
officer of the 4th Fighter Group and a seven-
victory ace, is captured after his P-51 is shot
down by flak over Praha/Kbely Airdrome,
in Czechoslovakia.

FRANCE: During the morning, 485 3d Air
Division B-17s attack the defensive line and
antitank defenses around Bordeaux.

GERMANY: During the afternoon, 294 1st
Air Division B-17s attack a marshalling
yard and two rail bridges at Regensburg;
77 1st Air Division B-17s attack a marshalling yard at Plattling; 76 1st Air Division
B-17s attack a rail bridge at Straubing; and
273 2d Air Division B-24s attack a marshalling yard at Landshut. One B-24 is lost.

Approximately 450 9th Air Division
bombers attack an ordnance depot, two marshalling yards, a communications center,
and various gun emplacements. Throughout the day, Ninth Air Force fighters
destroy 215 GAF aircraft on the ground (and
damage 190 others), the best one-day tally
of its kinds in the war, and at a cost of just
one P-47 lost.

Ninth and First Tactical air force fighter
pilots down 30 GAF fighters over Germany
between 0745 and 1900 hours.

U.S. Army ground forces overrun the
eastern Ruhr Pocket, and the Red Army
begins its final drive on Berlin on a 200-
mile front along the Oder River.

ITALY: Although more than 700 Fifteenth
Air Force heavy-bomber sorties are aborted
in the face of bad weather, 98 B-24s are able
to attack defended positions near Bologna;
Twelfth Air Force B-25s attack bridges
spanning the Reno River and troop concentrations on the British Eighth Army front;

and XXII TAC P-47s mount 520 effective
ground-support sorties in support of the U.S.
Fifth Army.

The Fifteenth Air Force's 98th and
376th Heavy Bombardment groups, in
B-24s, are relieved of operational duties and
ordered to the United States to retrain in
B-29s for eventual deployment against
Japan.

During the night of April 16–17, XXII
TAC A-20s and A-26s attack crossing
points in the Po River valley and several
defended towns near Bologna.

April 17, 1945

AUSTRIA: One hundred forty-seven Fifteenth Air Force P-38 dive-bombers attack
two rail bridges.

CZECHOSLOVAKIA: Sixty-one 2d Air
Division B-24s attack rail targets at Beroun;
36 2d Air Division B-24s attack rail targets
at Kladno; and 115 3d Air Division B-17s
attack an ordnance depot and a marshalling yard at Roudnice.

Ninth Air Force fighters and fighter-
bombers attack two airfields.

GERMANY: Four hundred twenty-eight
1st Air Division B-17s attack a rail center
and marshalling yard at Dresden; 92 2d
Bombardment Division B-24s attack rail
targets at two locations near the Czech-
German border; 162 3d Air Division B-17s
attack rail targets in Dresden; and 87 3d
Air Division B-17s attack rail targets at
Aussig.

9th Air Division bombers attack the city
of Magdeburg and two marshalling yards
and three ordnance depots.

Ninth and First Tactical air force fighter
pilots down 28 GAF fighters over Germany
between 0700 and 1515 hours. 1stLt Donald
O. Scherer, a P-51 pilot with the 358th
Fighter Group's 366th Fighter Squadron,
achieves ace status when he downs an Me-
108 over Germany at 0825 hours; and Capt
Jack A. Warner, a P-51 pilot with the 354th
Fighter Group's 356th Fighter Squadron,
achieves ace status when he downs an
Me-262 near Karlsbad at 1345 hours.

The Ninth Air Force's 48th Fighter Bombardment Group displaces to Advance Landing Ground Y-96, at Kassel.

ITALY: Fifteenth Air Force B-17s and B-24s mount 751 effective sorties against supply dumps, gun emplacements, German Army headquarters, and troop concentrations in the U.S. Fifth Army zone south and southwest of Bologna; Twelfth Air Force B-25s provide direct support for the British Eighth Army, and attack four bridges across the Reno River, and bridges on both sides of the Austro-Italian border near the Brenner Pass; and XXII TAC P-47s provide support for the U.S. Fifth Army's drive on Bologna.

During the night of April 17–18, XXII TAC A-20s and A-26s attack lines of communication in the Po River valley and three defended towns on the U.S. Fifth Army front.

April 18, 1945

CZECHOSLOVAKIA: One hundred eighteen 3d Air Division B-17s attack marshalling yards at Kolin and Pilsen. One escort fighter is lost.

Maj Donald H. Bockhay, the commanding officer of the 357th Fighter Group's 363d Fighter Squadron, attains a final personal tally of 13.833 confirmed victories when he downs an Me-262 near Prague at 1300 hours.

GERMANY: One hundred forty-eight 1st Air Division B-17s attack a marshalling yard and an electric-transformer station at Rosenheim; 65 1st Air Division B-17s attack a marshalling yard and an electric-transformer station at Traunstein; 61 1st Air Division B-17s attack a marshalling yard at Freising (secondary); 194 2d Air Division B-24s attack rail targets at Passau; and 174 3d Air Division B-17s attack a marshalling yard at Straubing (secondary). Two B-17s and one escort fighter are lost.

Nearly 600 9th Air Division bombers attack an oil depot, two marshalling yards, and two rail junctions.

Eighth and Ninth air force fighter

pilots down 18 GAF aircraft over Germany between 0655 and 1330 hours. Maj James E. Hill, the commanding officer of the 365th Fighter Group's 388th Fighter Squadron, in P-47s, achieves ace status when he downs three Bf-109s near Juterborg at 1330 hours.

German Army forces trapped in the western Ruhr Pocket surrender.

ITALY: Four hundred seventy-three Fifteenth Air Force B-17s and B-24s attack defensive positions and communications targets in and around Bologna; 78 Fifteenth Air Force P-38s dive-bomb a bridge; Twelfth Air Force B-25s attack a bridge and two rail fills near the Brenner Pass and German Army troop concentrations near U.S. Fifth Army and British Eighth Army fronts; and XXII TAC P-47s support the U.S. Fifth Army.

During the night of April 18–19, XXII TAC A-20s and A-26s attack crossing points in the Po River valley as well as light sources, vehicles, and eight bridges around Bologna, Mantua, Milan, and Turin.

MTO: Eighty-seven Fifteenth Air Force P-38s attack two bridges near Kolbnitz, Austria, and Fifteenth Air Force P-51s attack communications targets around Augsburg, Germany; Linz, Austria; and Pilsen, Czechoslovakia.

April 19, 1945

CZECHOSLOVAKIA: VIII Fighter Command pilots down five Me-262s over Czechoslovakia between 1150 and 1300 hours.

GERMANY: Two hundred seventy-eight 1st Air Division B-17s attack marshalling yards at two locations, and 311 3d Air Division B-17s attack rail targets on both sides of the German-Czech border. Five B-17s and two of 532 VIII Fighter Command escorts and scouts are lost.

Despite bad weather, approximately 375 9th Air Division bombers attack three marshalling yards, the city of Donauworth, and various targets of opportunity.

The 9th Air Division's 387th Medium Bombardment Group flies what will turn out to be its last effective mission of the war.)

Eighth and Ninth air force fighter pilots down 16 GAF fighters over Germany between 0630 and 1545 hours.

LtCol Elwyn G. Righetti, the commanding officer of the 55th Fighter Group and a six-victory P-51 ace, is shot down by flak near Dresden. It is known that Righetti is alive and well after he crash-lands his P-51, but he is never heard from again.

Seventy-eight Fifteenth Air Force P-38 dive-bombers attack a marshalling yard at Welheim.

Elements of the U.S. First Army capture Halle and Leipzig.

ITALY: Twelfth Air Force B-25s support the U.S. Fifth Army and attack bridges in Brenner Pass.

Between 0001 hours, April 17, and 2359 hours, April 19, the XXII TAC mounts more than 1,500 effective sorties in support of Allied ground forces in northern Italy.

In what turns out to be their unit's final aerial engagement of the war, 325th Fighter Group P-51 pilots down six Bf-109s over Lake Garda.

During the night of April 19–20, XXII TAC A-20s and A-26s attack crossing points and signs of movement in the Po River valley.

MTO: Six hundred nineteen Fifteenth Air Force B-17s and B-24s attack bridges and viaducts in northern Italy, Austria, and southern Germany.

April 20, 1945

CZECHOSLOVAKIA: Fifty-four 2d Air Division B-24s attack rail targets at Klatovy.

1stLt Andrew J. Ritchey, a P-51 pilot with the 354th Fighter Group's 353d Fighter Squadron, achieves ace status when he downs two Bf-109s near Kladno at 1820 hours.

GERMANY: Seven hundred fifty-five Eighth Air Force B-17s and B-24s attack rail targets in the Berlin area. One B-17 is lost.

Five hundred sixty-four 9th Air Division bombers attack two oil depots, two ordnance depots, two marshalling yards, flak emplacements, and various targets of opportunity.

Aircraft from the 9th Air Division's 394th and 397th Medium Bombardment groups undertake what will turn out to be their units' last effective missions of the war. And the only 9th Air Division bomber lost during the day turns out to be the last Ninth Air Force bomber lost in World War II.

Maj Henry S. Bille, the commanding officer of the 355th Fighter Group's 357th Fighter Squadron, achieves ace status in a P-51 when he downs two Bf-109s over a GAF airdrome at 1200 hours; and 1stLt Melvyn R. Paisley, a P-47 pilot with the 366th Fighter Group's 390th Fighter Squadron, achieves ace status when he shares in the downing of an FW-190 near Potsdam during an afternoon mission.

The Ninth Air Force's 370th Fighter Group displaces to Advance Landing Ground Y-99, at Gutersloh Airdrome; and the Ninth Air Force's 373d Fighter Group displaces to Advance Landing Ground Y-98, at Lippstadt Airdrome.

ITALY: Twelfth Air Force B-25s attack four bridges on the Brenner Pass line, two bridges spanning the Reno River, and a German Army headquarters; and XXII TAC P-47s support the U.S. Fifth Army's drive down from the Apennine mountains to the Po River valley.

During the night of April 20–21, XXII TAC A-20s and A-26s attack crossing points in the Po River valley.

MTO: In attacks aimed at slowing German Army withdrawals from Italy and resupply efforts from Austria, Fifteenth Air Force B-17s and B-24s mount more than 700 effective sorties against numerous rail bridges, viaducts, road and fills, and marshalling yards on both sides of the Austro-Italian frontier. Also, 115 Fifteenth Air Force P-38 dive-bombers attack rail lines and marshalling yards throughout Austria.

April 21, 1945

AUSTRIA: Approximately 200 Fifteenth

Air Force heavy bombers attack marshalling yards at three locations. Also, 121 9th Air Division A-20s and A-26s attack a marshalling yard at Attnang-Pucheim, closing the line between Vienna and the area of southern Germany known as the Nazi (or Hitler) Redoubt.

CZECHOSLOVAKIA: Ninth Air Force fighters and fighter-bombers support the first U.S. Army ground units to cross from Germany into Czechoslovakia.

GERMANY: One hundred eleven 1st Air Division B-17s attack a marshalling yard at Munich; 186 2d Air Division B-24s abandon their attack on rail targets at Salzburg due to solid cloud cover; and 212 3d Air Division B-17s attack the town of Ingolstadt (target of last resort). One B-17, one B-24, and two of 408 VIII Fighter Command escorts and scouts are lost.

The 55th, 56th, and 339th Fighter groups are ordered to stand down after flying what turns out to be their last combat missions of the war. In coming days, as the war on the ground winds down, other veteran bomber and fighter groups will also be ordered to stand down.

BriGen Ralph F. Stearly assumes command of the IX Fighter Command and the IX TAC.

Fifteenth Air Force heavy bombers attack a marshalling yard at Rosenheim, and 138 Fifteenth Army Force P-38 divebombers attack rail lines and facilities in and around Munich, Rosenheim, and Rattenburg (Austria).

The Ninth Air Force's 36th Fighter Group displaces to Advance Landing Ground R-12, at Kassel/Rothwesten Airdrome.

ITALY: Despite bad weather that causes nearly 400 Twelfth Air Force B-25 sorties against communications targets in northern Italy to abort, B-25s are able to attack a bridge in Brenner Pass in the morning and a crossing point in the Po River valley in the afternoon. Also, despite being grounded by bad weather in the morning, XXII TAC A-26s, A-20s, and P-47s mount numerous afternoon missions in support of the U.S. Fifth Army drive through Bologna and on toward the Po River plain.

Bologna falls to the U.S. Fifth Army.

April 22, 1945

ETO: The 9th Air Division and the IX TAC are grounded by bad weather.

GERMANY: The XXIX TAC operational headquarters displaces forward to Brunswick; the Ninth Air Force's 363d Tactical Reconnaissance Group displaces to Advance Landing Ground R-37, at Brunswick; and the Ninth Air Force's 474th Fighter Group displaces to Advance Landing Ground R-2, at Langensalza.

The U.S. Third Army begins an advance along the Danube River, and the U.S. Seventh Army crosses the Danube at Billengen.

ITALY: The entire Twelfth Air Force is committed to slowing German Army forces retreating across the Po River: Twelfth Air Force B-25s mount 16 separate attacks on ferry lines and pontoon bridges; and XXII TAC A-20s, A-26s, and P-47s mount around-the-clock attacks on Po River crossings and troop movements throughout the Po River valley and on to the north. The XXII TAC claims the destruction of more than 900 motor and horse-drawn vehicles in a 24-hour period.

Fifteenth Air Force heavy bombers are grounded by bad weather, but 258 Fifteenth Air Force P-38s and P-51s attack airfields, road and rail traffic, marshalling yards, bridges, highways, and defended buildings throughout the day.

Capt Harry A. Parker, a 13-victory ace with the 325th Fighter Group's 318th Fighter Squadron, is killed in action.

During the night of April 22–23, XXII TAC A-20s, A-26s, and night fighters attack Po River crossing points, airfields, road and rail traffic, marshalling yards, and targets of opportunity.

April 23, 1945

ETO: The 9th Air Division, IX TAC, and

XXIX TAC are grounded by bad weather. During the morning, XIX TAC aircracraft are able to mount 158 effective combat sorties.

GERMANY: Red Army ground forces enter Berlin.

ITALY: Seven hundred nineteen Fifteenth Air Force B-17s and B-24s attack bridges spanning the Adige and Brenta rivers, and a supply dump; 165 Fifteenth Air Force P-38s and P-51s attack road and rail bridges and other communications targets throughout northeastern Italy; Twelfth Air Force B-25s attack bridges spanning the Brenta River and the Brenner Pass rail line; and XXII TAC P-47s attack road traffic, rail bridges, and numerous tactical targets along the U.S. Fifth Army front.

Elements of the U.S. Fifth Army cross the Po River.

During the night of April 23–24, XXII TAC A-20s and A-26s attack three airdromes, marshalling yards at three locations, and targets of opportunity throughout northern Italy.

April 24, 1945

GERMANY: One hundred seventy-two 9th Air Division bombers attack an oil depot and Landau Airdrome.

The 322d Medium Bombardment Group flies what turns out to be its last effective mission of World War II (its four hundred twenty-eighth).

ITALY: Fifteenth Air Force B-17s and B-24s attack seven rail bridges on both sides of the Austro-Italian frontier, three road bridges in Italy, and a supply dump; 79 Fifteenth Air Force P-38s and 90 P-51s attack targets of opportunity throughout the area north of the Po River; Twelfth Air Force B-25s attack six Po River crossing points and the Brenner Pass rail line at Trento and Verona; and XXII TAC P-47s attack road targets north of the Po River and around La Spezia and Parma.

During the night of April 24–25, XXII TAC A-20s and A-26s attack German Army forces in the northern Po River valley, and

night-fighters attack crossing points on the Adige and Po rivers, as well as marshalling yards at Brescia and Verona, and three airdromes.

April 25, 1945

AUSTRIA: Fifteenth Air Force heavy bombers attack several targets at the vital rail center at Linz and the marshalling yard at Wels.

CZECHOSLOVAKIA: Two hundred seventy-nine 1st Air Division B-17s attack the airfield and munitions factory at Pilsen. Six B-17s and one of 539 VIII Fighter Command escorts and scouts are lost to flak. The last unit to drop its bombs—and thus the last Eighth Air Force heavy-bomber unit to drop bombs in World War II—is the 41st Combat Bombardment Wing's 384th Heavy Bombardment Group.

78th Fighter Group P-51 pilots set the USAAF record for enemy aircraft destroyed on the ground by strafing: 135 in one day. (Other "firsts" by the venerable 78th have included the first VIII Fighter Command ace, the first Eighth Air Force triple victory, the first strafing run by a P-47 pilot, and the first Me-262 downed by an Eighth Air Force fighter.)

ENGLAND: At the conclusion of its missions to Germany and Czechoslovakia, the Eighth Air Force is ordered to stand down from combat operations.

GERMANY: Two hundred seventy-eight 2d Air Division B-24s attack three rail targets and an electric-transformer station in Bavaria.

1stLt Hilton O. Thompson, a 479th Fighter Group P-51, pilot downs what turns out to be the very last plane of World War II credited to an Eighth Air Force fighter pilot—an Ar-234 near Berchtesgaden that he downs at 1115 hours.

Two hundred ninety-six 9th Air Division bombers attack Erding Airdrome and an ordnance depot. This mission marks the last appearance of GAF jet fighters against Ninth Air Force bombers, and it turns out to be the last mission of the 323d and 344th

Medium Bombardment groups and the 410th Light Bombardment Group.

U.S. First Army and Red Army troops establish physical contact at Torgau, on the Elbe River.

ITALY: The entire Twelfth Air Force is committed to halting or slowing the retreat of German Army forces from northern Italy: Twelfth Air Force B-25s attack an Adige River crossing point, a marshalling yard, and five bridges and a rail fill on the Brenner Pass line on both sides of the Austro-Italian frontier; and XXII TAC P-47s and Fifteenth Air Force P-38s and P-51s attack a wide variety of tactical targets and lines of communication.

For the second day in a row, as Allied ground forces advance swiftly across the length and breadth of northern Italy, 1stLt Raymond L. Knight, a flight leader with the Twelfth Air Force's 350th Fighter Group, leads relentless attacks through intense flak to strafe Axis airdromes in northern Italy. Knight, whose P-47 is finally disabled and who must crash-land in the Apennine Mountains, is credited with 20 German aircraft destroyed on the ground, and he is awarded a Medal of Honor.

Verona and La Spezia fall to Allied ground forces.

During the night of April 25–26, XXII TAC A-20s, A-26s, and P-47s attack airfields, marshalling yards, road targets, and lines of communication in the northern Po River valley.

NETHERLANDS: The Ninth Air Force's 397th Medium Bombardment Group displaces to Advance Landing Ground Y-55, at Venlo.

April 26, 1945

AUSTRIA: Fifteenth Air Force B-24s, diverted by bad weather from their intended targets in northern Italy, are able to attack marshalling yards at four locations in southern Austria.

CZECHOSLOVAKIA: In the final air-to-air engagement of World War II undertaken by Fifteenth Air Force fighter pilots, three 332d Fighter Group P-51 pilots down four Bf-109s at about 1205 hours.

ETO: Ninth and First Tactical air force fighter pilots down 22 GAF aircraft over Austria and Germany between 0700 and 1945 hours. 2dLt Edward F. Bickford, a P-51 pilot with the 354th Fighter Group's 356th Fighter Squadron, achieves ace status when he downs two FW-190s near Passau, Germany, at 1945 hours. Bickford is the last USAAF pilot to achieve ace status in the war in Europe.

The 405th Fighter Group is transferred from the XXIX TAC to the XIX TAC.

GERMANY: One hundred twenty-five 9th Air Division A-26s attack Plattling Airdrome.

IX TAC headquarters moves from Marburg/Lahn to Weimar.

U.S. Army ground forces begin an assault crossing of the Danube River at Regensburg.

ITALY: Although nearly 320 Fifteenth Air Force B-17s and B-24s abort in the face of bad weather encountered on their way to targets in northern Italy, at least one formation of B-24s is able to attack a motor-transport depot at Tarvisio; also due to bad weather, Twelfth Air Force B-25s are able to complete only one of four assigned missions, an attack on a bridge. Roving XXII TAC P-47s claim the destruction of 150 motor vehicles during the afternoon, and Fifteenth Air Force P-38s and P-51s attack numerous targets of opportunity.

The last air-to-air victory credited to an MTO-based airman in World War II is scored at 1310 hours by 2dLt Roland E. Lee, a P-47 pilot with the 57th Fighter Group's 66th Fighter Squadron. This is the 3,764th victory scored by USAAF fighter pilots in the North African and Mediterranean theaters since 1stLt William J. Mount, also of the 57th Fighter Group, downed a Bf-109 over Egypt on October 9, 1942.

April 27, 1945

ETO: The 9th Air Division, IX TAC, and XXIX TAC are grounded by bad weather,

but the XIX TAC manages to mount 125 effective sorties.
GERMANY: Regensburg falls to U.S. Army ground forces.
ITALY: Fifteenth Air Force heavy bombers and Twelfth Air Force medium bombers are grounded by bad weather, which also severely limits fighter operations over northern Italy.

April 28, 1945

ETO: The Ninth Air Force is grounded by bad weather.

The 48th Fighter Group is transferred from the IX TAC to the XIX TAC.
GERMANY: The Ninth Air Force's 10th Photographic Reconnaissance Group displaces to Advance Landing Ground R-30, at Furth.
ITALY: Fifteenth Air Force heavy bombers and Twelfth Air Force medium bombers are grounded by bad weather, which also severely limits fighter operations over northern Italy.

Italian partisans apprehend and execute Benito Mussolini.

April 29, 1945

ETO: The 9th Air Division is grounded by bad weather, but Ninth Air Force fighters mount 387 effective sorties.

Ninth Air Force fighters destroy 191 motor vehicles, a tank, four locomotives, 52 rail cars, and 397 horse-drawn vehicles in territory still held by the German Army.
GERMANY: In the very last combat mission of the war by Eighth Air Force aircraft, two special 482d Heavy Bombardment Group heavy bombers—a B-17 and a B-24—are dispatched during the night to obtain radar photographs of Kiel harbor.

The Ninth Air Force's 48th Fighter Group displaces to Advance Landing Ground R-10, at Illesheim.
ITALY: Fifteenth Air Force heavy bombers and Twelfth Air Force B-25s are grounded by bad weather, but XXII TAC P-47s attack lines of communication, claim-

ing the destruction of more than 350 motor vehicles. Thirty-nine P-51s of the 52d and 325th Fighter groups conduct the last Fifteenth Air Force fighter sorties of the war when they bomb and strafe German Army troop positions and motor vehicles.

The commander-in-chief of all German Army forces remaining in Italy unconditionally surrenders to the Allies.

During the night of April 29–30, XXII TAC A-20s and A-26s attack motor vehicles near Lake Como and on several roads leading out of northern Italy.
NETHERLANDS: The Ninth Air Force's 387th Medium Bombardment Group displaces to the advance landing ground at Beek.

April 30, 1945

ETO: The 9th Air Division and XXIX TAC are grounded by bad weather.

The Ninth Air Force's 362d Fighter Group flies what will turn out to be its last missions of the war.
GERMANY: As the city of Berlin falls to the Red Army, Adolf Hitler commits suicide in his bunker. Also, Munich falls to the U.S. Seventh Army.

The Ninth Air Force's 354th Fighter Group displaces to Advance Landing Ground R-45, at Ansbach; the Ninth Air Force's 362d Fighter Group displaces to Advance Landing Ground R-30, at Furth; and the Ninth Air Force's 405th Fighter Group displaces to Advance Landing Ground R-6, at Kitzingen.
ITALY: Fifteenth Air Force heavy bombers and Twelfth Air Force B-25s are grounded by bad weather. XXII TAC P-47s and Fifteenth Air Force P-38s and P-51s undertaking armed-reconnaissance missions over northern Italy attack gun emplacements and motor vehicles.

During the night of April 30–May 1, XXII TAC A-20s and A-26s attack targets of opportunity in areas of northern Italy not yet occupied by Allied ground forces.

MAY 1945

May 1, 1945

AUSTRIA: In the Fifteenth Air Force's final bombing mission of the war, 27 B-17s brave bad weather to attack the railroad station and marshalling yard at Salzburg.

CZECHOSLOVAKIA: Nine 9th Air Division A-26s attack a munitions factory at Stod.

GERMANY: Ninth Air Force fighter-bombers dive-bomb the German state alternate headquarters at Berchtesgaden.

ITALY: Twelfth Air Force B-25s are grounded by bad weather, but XXII TAC P-47s attack motor vehicles and horse-drawn conveyances ahead of advancing U.S. Fifth Army elements.

Elements of the U.S. Fifth Army move toward Brenner Pass.

NETHERLANDS: Inaugurating a humanitarian effort that will continue beyond the end of hostilities in Europe, 392 3d Air Division B-17s drop 778 tons of food to needy Dutch civilians, in this case, in and around The Hague and Rotterdam.

YUGOSLAVIA: Elements of the British Eighth Army cross from northeastern Italy into Yugoslavia, where they link up with Yugoslav Army troops under the command of Marshal Josip Broz Tito.

May 2, 1945

ETO: The 9th Air Division is grounded by bad weather.

GERMANY: The Red Army announces that it is in complete control of the city of Berlin.

ITALY: The terms of surrender for German military forces become effective, ending hostilities in Italy.

Twelfth Air Force B-25s are grounded by bad weather, and XXII TAC P-47s fly uneventful combat patrols.

NETHERLANDS: The Ninth Air Force's 394th Medium Bombardment Group displaces to Advance Landing Ground Y-55, at Venlo.

May 3, 1945

CZECHOSLOVAKIA: In what turns out to be the 9th Air Division's final mission of World War II, 130 A-26s led by eight B-26 pathfinders attack the munitions factory at Stod. The final bombs are dropped at 1202 hours.

GERMANY: In the final combat missions undertaken by their units in the war, 14 366th Fighter Group P-47s attack ships and harbor facilities between Kiel and Lubeck, and 19 406th Fighter Group P-47s attack a large cargo vessel at Lubeck. These attacks turn out to be the last missions against specific targets undertaken by the Ninth Air Force in World War II.

MTO: The Fifteenth Air Force is grounded by bad weather, but Twelfth Air Force B-25s and P-47s drop leaflets to inform enemy soldiers and civilians in northern Italy and southwestern Austria that hostilities in the region have ended.

May 4, 1945

ETO: The 9th Air Division is ordered to stand down, but Ninth Air Force fighters fly armed-reconnaissance missions (amounting to 356 effective sorties) throughout regions of Germany, Austria, and Czechoslovakia not yet occupied by Allied ground forces. GAF aircraft on the ground are strafed (29 jet fighters are destroyed), and several ships (including two submarines) are bombed and strafed at sea near Kiel and Flensburg. Also, six GAF aircraft are downed during the day, including the last jet fighter (of 16) to be credited to the Ninth Air Force.

At 1820 hours, commanders of German military forces in the West sign the instrument of surrender.

ITALY: As U.S. Fifth Army ground units reach the Austro-Italian frontier by way of Brenner Pass, XXII TAC P-47s and a few Fifteenth Air Force fighters continue to fly armed-reconnaissance missions over German-occupied regions.

May 5, 1945

ETO: The surrender of German forces in the West becomes effective at 0800 hours.

The Ninth Air Force flight operations are limited to six reconnaissance missions.

GERMANY: XXII TAC fighters strafe many GAF aircraft located on the ground at an airdrome near Munich.

ITALY: XXII TAC P-47s continue to fly armed-reconnaissance missions over German-occupied regions.

May 6, 1945

GERMANY: Ninth Air Force P-47s (from the 373d Fighter Group) fly "demonstration" missions over the region around Klotze.

May 7, 1945

ETO: Ninth Air Force P-47s (from the 368th Fighter Group) sweep the area between Chemnitz, Germany, and Prague, Czechoslovakia. Also, Ninth Air Force F-6 reconnaissance aircraft are attacked at various times by four FW-190s, of which one is shot down near Prague.

The last airplane lost on a combat assignment in the war in Europe is a 95th Heavy Bombardment Group B-17 that goes down into the sea.

FRANCE: At proceedings conducted at Reims, the German high command unconditionally surrenders all land, sea, and air forces to the Allies, effective on May 9.

GERMANY: XIX TAC fighters fly "demonstration" missions over prisoner-of-war camps.

NETHERLANDS: In the very last wartime mission of its kind, 231 3d Air Division B-17s drop 426 tons of food supplies to needy civilians at five locations. One B-17 is damaged by fire from German troops on the ground. Also, one B-17 ditches due to an engine fire, and only two crewmen survive.

May 8, 1945

EUROPE: President Harry S Truman proclaims V-E day.

GERMANY: Fighter units mount the last USAAF operational combat missions of the war in Europe—amounting to several hundred effective sorties, mostly in the form of sweeps over territory still held by the

German Army. Nine German military airplanes and one Ninth Air Force F-6 are downed between 0715 and 2005 hours. 2dLt Leland A. Larson, a five-victory F-6 ace with the 10th Photographic Reconnaissance Group, becomes the last ace in the ETO to down a GAF combat airplane, an FW-190 Larson shoots down near Radnitz at 2000 hours. And the last official victory to be awarded to a USAAF pilot in the war against Germany is a staff plane downed at 2005 by 2dLt Kenneth L. Swift, of the 474th Fighter Group's 429th Fighter Squadron. This is the 7,504th victory awarded to a USAAF pilot in the ETO and the 11,268th Axis airplane downed by a USAAF pilot since 2dLt Samuel R. Junkin, of the 31st Fighter Group, downed an FW-190 over Dieppe, France, on August 19, 1942.

Twelve B-17s from the Eighth Air Force's 406th Heavy Bombardment Squadron drop surrender leaflets over Germany while 11 F-5 photo-reconnaissance aircraft of the 7th Reconnaissance Group conduct damage-assessment missions, also over Germany. At the end of the day, wartime air operations in the ETO are officially concluded. (The 406th Heavy Bombardment Squadron will continue to drop surrender leaflets until May 31, 1945.)

ITALY: The Fifteenth Air Force officially stands down.

May 9, 1945

EUROPE: All hostilities throughout the Continent of Europe are officially terminated at 0001 hours.

BIBLIOGRAPHY

Carter, Kit C., and Robert Mueller. *The Army Air Forces in World War II: Combat Chronology, 1941–1945*. Washington, D.C.: Office of Air Force History, 1973.

Copp, DeWitt S. *A Few Great Captains: The Men and Events that Shaped the Development of U.S. Air Power*. Garden City, NY: Doubleday, 1980.

———. *Forged in Fire: Strategy and Decisions in the Airwar Over Europe, 1940–1945*. Garden City, NY: Doubleday, 1982.

Freeman, Roger A. *The Mighty Eighth: A History of the Units, Men and Machines of the U.S. 8th Air Force*. Osceola, Wisconsin: Motorbooks International, 1991.

Freeman, Roger A., with Alan Crouchman and Vic Maslen. *The Mighty Eighth War Diary*. London: Arms & Armour, 1990.

Hammel, Eric. *Aces Against Germany,* Vol. II, *The American Aces Speak*. Novato, California: Presidio Press, 1993.

Maurer, Maurer (ed.). *Air Force Combat Units of World War II.* Washington, D.C.: Office of Air Force History, 1983.

McFarland, Stephen L., and Wesley Phillips Newton. *To Command the Sky: The Battle for Air Superiority Over Germany, 1942–1944.* Washington, D.C.: Smithsonian Institution Press, 1991.

Mets, David R. *Master of Airpower: General Carl A. Spaatz.* Novato, California: Presidio Press, 1988.

Mondey, David. *Concise Guide to American Aircraft of World War II.* London: Temple Press, 1982.

———. *Concise Guide to Axis Aircraft of World War II.* London: Temple Press, 1984.

———. *Concise Guide to British Aircraft of World War II.* London: Temple Press, 1982.

Morris, Danny. *Aces & Wingmen II,* Vol. I. Usk, Washington: Aviation–USK, 1989

Olmsted, Merle C. *The Yoxford Boys: The 357th Fighter Group on Escort Over Europe and Russia.* Fallbrook, California: Aero Publishers, Inc., 1971.

Olynyk, Frank J. *Victory List No. 5: USAAF (European Theater) Credits for the Destruction of Enemy Aircraft in Air-to-Air- Combat, World War 2.* Aurora, Ohio: Frank J. Olynyk, 1987.

———. *Victory List No. 6: USAAF (Mediterranean Theater) Credits for the Destruction of Enemy Aircraft in Air-to-Air Combat, World War 2.* Aurora, Ohio: Frank J. Olynyk, 1987.

Rust, Kenn C. *The 9th Air Force in World War II.* Fallbrook, California: Aero Publishers, Inc., 1967.

———. *Twelfth Air Force Story.* Terre Haute, Indiana: Sun Shine House, 1975

———. *Fifteenth Air Force Story.* Temple City, California: Historical Aviation Album, 1976.

Schaffer, Ronald. *Wings of Judgment: American Bombing in World War II.* New York: Oxford University Press, 1985.

Shores, Chris. "America's Spitfires," *Air Enthusiast,* August-November 1981.

Stanaway, John. *Peter Three Eight: The Pilots' Story.* Missoula, Montana: Pictorial Histories Publishing Company, 1986.

Toliver, Raymond F., and Trevor J. Constable. *Fighter Aces of the U.S.A.* Fallbrook, California: Aero Publishers, Inc., 1979.

339th Fighter Group Association. *The 339th Fighter Group.* Paducah, Kentucky: Turner Publishing, 1991.

Truluck, John H., Jr. *And So It Was: Memories of a World War II Fighter Pilot.* Walterboro, South Carolina: The Press and Standard, 1989.

U.S. Army Air Forces. *The AAF in Northwest Africa.* Washington, D.C.: U.S. Army Air Forces.

Williams, Mary H. *U.S. Army in World War II:* Special Studies, *Chronology: 1941–1945.* Washington, D.C.: Center of Military History, 1984.

INDEX I

U.S. Army Air Forces Numerical Unit Designations

The following index contains information relating only to U.S. Army Air Forces commands and units with *numerical* designations.

References are listed in the year-month-day format:
431020 = October 20, 1943

1st Air Defense Wing, 430130
1st Air Division, 450101, 450102, 450103, 450117, 450120, 450122, 450123, 450128, 450201, 450203, 450207, 450209, 450210, 450214, 450215, 450216, 450217, 450219, 450220, 450224, 450225, 450227, 450302, 450303, 450304, 450305, 450307, 450308, 450309, 450310, 450311, 450312, 450314, 450315, 450317, 450318, 450320, 450321, 450322, 450324, 450325, 450326, 450330, 450331, 450403, 450404, 450405, 450406, 450410, 450413, 450416, 450417, 450418, 450419, 450421, 450425
1st Bombardment Division, 430906, 430907, 430909, 430913, 430915, 430916, 430923, 430927, 431002, 431004, 431008, 431009, 431010, 431014, 431020, 431101, 431105, 431107, 431111, 431113, 431116, 431126, 431130, 431201, 431212, 431213, 431215, 431222, 440105, 440111, 440121, 440124, 440203, 440204, 440210, 440211, 440214, 440220, 440221, 440222, 440224, 440225, 440302, 440304, 440318, 440319, 440324, 440328, 440329, 440408, 440409, 440410, 440411, 440413, 440418, 440419, 440422, 440424, 440425, 440426, 440427, 440428, 440430, 440501, 440504, 440506, 440507, 440508, 440509,

450322, 450324, 450325, 450330,
450331, 450404, 450405, 450410,
450416, 450417, 450418, 450421,
450425
II Air Service Area Command, 431203,
440101
2d Bombardment Division, 430906, 430907,
430908, 430909, 430913, 430915,
431009, 431014, 431101, 431104,
431105, 431113, 431116, 431118,
431130, 431201, 431213, 431216,
431222, 440105, 440111, 440124,
440128, 440202, 440203, 440204,
440208, 440210, 440211, 440212,
440215, 440218, 440220, 440221,
440222, 440225, 440227, 440229,
440302, 440304, 440305, 440307,
440309, 440311, 440312, 440315,
440316, 440321, 440324, 440328,
440329, 440401, 440405, 440406,
440408, 440409, 440410, 440411,
440412, 440413, 440417, 440418,
440419, 440424, 440425, 440426,
440428, 440430, 440501, 440502,
440503, 440504, 440505, 440506,
440507, 440508, 440509, 440511,
440513, 440519, 440520, 440521,
440522, 440524, 440527, 440530,
440531, 440602, 440614, 440616,
440617, 440618, 440620, 440621,
440623, 440624, 440625, 440628,
440701, 440704, 440705, 440706,
440713, 440714, 440716, 440718,
440723, 440728, 440729, 440731,
440801, 440802, 440803, 440804,
440809, 440810, 440811, 440814,
440815, 440825, 440826, 440905,
440908, 440909, 440915, 440918,
440921, 440925, 440926, 440927,
440928, 440930, 441002, 441003,
441005, 441006, 441007, 441009,
441012, 441014, 441015, 441017,
441018, 441019, 441022, 441025,
441026, 441030, 441101, 441102,
441104, 441105, 441106, 441108,

441109, 441110, 441111, 441116,
441121, 441125, 441126, 441127,
441129, 441130, 441204, 441205,
441206, 441210, 441211, 441212,
441218, 441219, 441223, 441224,
441225, 441226, 441227, 441228,
441229, 441230, 441231
2d Combat Bombardment Wing, 430913,
431104
2d Heavy Bombardment Group, 430423,
431101, 431126, 431209, 440101,
440103, 440224
2d Heavy Bombardment Wing, 420727,
420907, 421010, 421206, 421220,
430317, 430325, 430416, 430514,
430517, 430529, 430613, 430628,
430702, 430902, 431008
2d Scouting Force, 450209
3d Air Defense Wing, 430223
3d Air Division, 450101, 450102, 450103,
450116, 450117, 450118, 450120,
450123, 450128, 450129, 450201,
450203, 450209, 450215, 450216,
450217, 450219, 450220, 450224,
450227, 450302, 450303, 450305,
450307, 450308, 450309, 450310,
450311, 450312, 450314, 450317,
450320, 450321, 450322, 450324,
450325, 450326, 450328, 450330,
450331, 450403, 450404, 450405,
450406, 450407, 450410, 450416,
450417, 450418, 450419, 450421,
450501, 450507
III Air Service Area Command, 440101
3d Bombardment Division, 430906, 430907,
430909, 430913, 430915, 430916,
430923, 430926, 430927, 431002,
431004, 431008, 431009, 431010,
431014, 431020, 431105, 431107,
431111, 431113, 431116, 431119,
431126, 431130, 431201, 431211,
431222, 431224, 440101, 440104,
440105, 440111, 440124, 440129,
440203, 440204, 440213, 440220,
440221, 440222, 440224, 440225,

430225, 430301, 430303, 430305,
430313, 430314, 430315, 430318,
430319, 430320, 430322, 430324,
430326, 430328, 430329, 430330,
430331, 430401, 430402, 430403,
430404, 430406, 430407, 430409,
430410, 430411, 430412, 430415,
430416, 430417, 430418, 430419,
430423, 430425, 430426, 430428,
430430, 430501, 430504, 430506,
430507, 430509, 430510, 430511,
430512, 430513, 430521, 430524,
430525, 430528, 430530, 430604,
430605, 430606, 430609, 430609,
430610, 430611, 430617, 430619,
430621, 430624, 430630, 430702,
430703, 430704, 430705, 430706,
430707, 430708, 430709, 430711,
430712, 430713, 430714, 430715,
430716, 430717, 430718, 430719,
430720, 430721, 430725, 430726,
430801, 430802, 430803, 430805,
430806, 430807, 430808, 430809,
430810, 430811, 430812, 430813,
430814, 430815, 430816, 430819,
430823, 430824, 430825, 430826,
430831, 430903, 430905, 430908,
430909, 430910, 430912, 430914,
430915, 430916, 430917, 430918,
430919, 430920, 430922, 431016,
431103, 431105, 431107, 431110,
431111, 431112, 431119, 431123,
431124, 431126, 431129, 431201,
431204, 431205, 431213, 431220,
431221, 431222, 431224, 431230,
431231, 440104, 440107, 440113,
440121, 440123, 440124, 440125,
440126, 440129, 440202, 440205,
440206, 440208, 440209, 440210,
440211, 440212, 440213, 440214,
440215, 440220, 440221, 440222,
440224, 440225, 440228, 440229,
440302, 440303, 440304, 440305,
440306, 440307, 440308, 440309,
440311, 440313, 440315, 440317,

440319, 440320, 440321, 440323,
440325, 440326, 440327, 440405,
440408, 440410, 440411, 440412,
440413, 440418, 440419, 440420,
440421, 440422, 440423, 440424,
440425, 440426, 440427, 440428,
440429, 440430, 440501, 440502,
440504, 440506, 440508, 440509,
440511, 440513, 440515, 440519,
440520, 440521, 440522, 440523,
440524, 440525, 440526, 440527,
440528, 440530, 440531, 440601,
440603, 440604, 440606, 440608,
440611, 440612, 440613, 440614,
440615, 440616, 440617, 440618,
440619, 440620, 440621, 440622,
440623, 440624, 440625, 440629,
440630, 440702, 440704, 440705,
440706, 440707, 440708, 440709,
440711, 440712, 440713, 440714,
440715, 440716, 440717, 440718,
440719, 440720, 440722, 440723,
440724, 440725, 440726, 440727,
440728, 440729, 440730, 440731,
440801, 440802, 440803, 440804,
440805, 440806, 440807, 440808,
440809, 440810, 440811, 440812,
440813, 440814, 440815, 440816,
440817, 440818, 440819, 440820,
440822, 440824, 440825, 440826,
440827, 440828, 440829, 440830,
440831, 440901, 440902, 440903,
440905, 440906, 440907, 440908,
440909, 440910, 440911, 440912,
440913, 440914, 440915, 440916
9th Bombardment Division, 440916, 440917,
440918, 440919, 440920, 440921,
440923, 440924, 440925, 440927,
440928, 440929, 440930, 441002,
441003, 441005, 441006, 441007,
441008, 441009, 441011, 441012,
441013, 441014, 441015, 441017,
441019, 441020, 441021, 441022,
441025, 441026, 441028, 441029,
441030, 441031, 441101, 441102,

Tenth Air Force, 420623, 420626, 440130, 440202
10th Photographic Reconnaissance Group, 440221, 440225, 440506, 440515, 440605, 440606, 440610, 440811, 440824, 441101, 441130, 441217, 450324, 450331, 450405, 450408, 450413, 450428, 450508
11th Combat Crew Replacement Command, 421021
Twelfth Air Force, 7, 8, 32, 420820, 420908, 420914, 420923, 421012, 421016, 421022, 421107, 421214, 430105, 430211, 430212, 430217, 430226, 430301, 430731, 430808, 430902, 430903, 430909, 430920, 430928, 431004, 431009, 431015, 431028, 431103, 431108, 431112, 431114, 431116, 431117, 431120, 431123, 431125, 431202, 431203, 431204, 431206, 431217, 431218, 431220, 431222, 431223, 431224, 431226, 431228, 431229, 440101, 440105, 440115, 440122, 440124, 440126, 440204, 440210, 440211, 440214, 440217, 440219, 440223, 440227, 440301, 440302, 440303, 440304, 440305, 440307, 440308, 440309, 440310, 440311, 440313, 440314, 440315, 440316, 440318, 440319, 440320, 440321, 440322, 440323, 440324, 440325, 440326, 440327, 440328, 440328, 440329, 440330, 440331, 440401, 440402, 440403, 440404, 440405, 440406, 440407, 440408, 440410, 440411, 440412, 440413, 440414, 440415, 440416, 440417, 440419, 440420, 440422, 440423, 440424, 440425, 440427, 440428, 440501, 440503, 440504, 440507, 440509, 440510, 440511, 440512, 440513, 440514, 440515, 440516, 440517, 440518, 440519, 440520, 440521, 440522, 440523, 440524, 440526, 440527, 440528, 440529, 440530, 440531, 440601, 440602, 440603, 440604, 440605, 440606, 440607, 440608, 440609, 440610, 440611, 440612, 440613, 440614, 440615, 440616, 440617, 440618, 440619, 440620, 440621, 440623, 440624, 440625, 440626, 440627, 440628, 440629, 440630, 440701, 440702, 440703, 440704, 440705, 440706, 440707, 440708, 440709, 440710, 440711, 440712, 440713, 440715, 440716, 440717, 440718, 440719, 440720, 440721, 440722, 440723, 440724, 440725, 440726, 440728, 440729, 440730, 440731, 440801, 440802, 440803, 440804, 440805, 440806, 440807, 440808, 440809, 440810, 440811, 440812, 440813, 440814, 440815, 440818, 440819, 440820, 440821, 440822, 440823, 440824, 440825, 440826, 440827, 440830, 440831, 440901, 440902, 440903, 440904, 440905, 440907, 440908, 440909, 440910, 440911, 440912, 440913, 440914, 440915, 440916, 440917, 440918, 440919, 440920, 440921, 440922, 440923, 440924, 440925, 440926, 440927, 440928, 440929, 440930, 441001, 441002, 441003, 441004, 441005, 441006, 441007, 441008, 441009, 441010, 441011, 441012, 441013, 441014, 441015, 441016, 441017, 441018, 441019, 441020, 441021, 441022, 441023, 441024, 441025, 441026, 441027, 441028, 441029, 441030, 441031, 441101, 441102, 441103, 441104, 441105, 441106, 441107, 441108, 441109, 441110, 441111, 441112, 441113, 441114, 441115, 441116, 441117, 441118, 441119, 441120, 441121, 441122, 441123, 441124, 441125, 441127, 441128, 441129, 441130, 441201, 441202, 441203,

440405, 440406, 440407, 440408,
440409, 440410, 440411, 440412,
440413, 440414, 440415

XII Bomber Command, 420902, 420912,
421116, 421122, 421123, 421124,
421128, 421204, 421205, 421206,
421207, 421211, 421212, 421214,
421215, 421217, 421218, 421221,
421222, 421223, 421226, 421227,
421228, 421229, 421230, 421231,
430101, 430102, 430104, 430105,
430106, 430107, 430108, 430109,
430110, 430111, 430112, 430113,
430114, 430115, 430116, 430117,
430118, 430119, 430120, 430121,
430122, 430123, 430124, 430126,
430127, 430128, 430129, 430130,
430131, 430201, 430202, 430203,
430204, 430205, 430206, 430207,
430208, 430210, 430213, 430214,
430215, 430216, 430217, 430218,
430222, 430226, 430301, 430404,
430822, 430901, 430902, 430904,
430905, 430906, 430907, 430908,
430909, 430910, 430911, 430912,
430913, 430914, 430915, 430916,
430917, 430918, 430920, 430921,
430922, 430923, 430924, 430925,
430929, 430930, 431001, 431003,
431004, 431005, 431006, 431008,
431009, 431010, 431011, 431012,
431013, 431014, 431015, 431016,
431017, 431016, 431019, 431020,
431021, 431022, 431023, 431024,
431026, 431027, 431029, 431030,
431031, 431101, 431127, 440101,
440102, 440103, 440104, 440106,
440107, 440108, 440109, 440110,
440111, 440112, 440113, 440114,
440115, 440116, 440117, 440118,
440119, 440121, 440123, 440125,
440127, 440128, 440129, 440130,
440201, 440202, 440203, 440205,
440206, 440207, 440208, 440209,
440213, 440214, 440215, 440216,

440218, 440219, 440220, 440221,
440222, 440224, 440228, 440229,
440610

Headquarters, 420831, 431101, 440301

XII Fighter Command, 420824, 420918,
420927, 421108, 421201, 421211,
421216, 421217, 421221, 421225,
421226, 421229, 421231, 430102,
430103, 430104, 430106, 430108,
430110, 430116, 430121, 430123,
430127, 430203, 430218, 430301,
430413, 430427, 430511, 430901,
431002, 431229, 440101, 440103,
440301, 440522, 440912, 440915,
440916, 440917, 440918, 440920,
440924, 440925, 440926, 440927,
440928, 440929, 440930, 441001,
441002, 441004, 441008, 441009,
441010, 441011, 441013, 441014,
441015, 441016, 441017, 441018,
441019, 441107

XII Ground Air Support Command, 420918,
420922, 420924

12th Medium Bombardment Group, 420714,
420716, 420731, 420816, 420817,
420822, 420825, 420829, 420831,
420901, 420902, 420903, 420904,
420913, 421009, 421014, 421022,
421024, 421025, 421026, 421027,
421028, 421029, 421030, 421031,
421102, 421103, 421104, 421105,
421107, 421120, 421205, 421213,
421215, 430102, 430118, 430203,
430222, 430320, 430403, 430415,
430601, 430602, 430802, 430805,
430822, 430904, 430910, 431102,
440101, 440130

XII Provisional Air Force Engineer
Command, 440101

XII Provisional Troop Carrier Command,
430909, 431209, 431222, 440301,
440305

XII Tactical Air Command (XII TAC),
440415, 440416, 440417, 440418,
440419, 440420, 440421, 440422,

440104, 440105, 440107, 440108,
440109, 440110, 440111, 440113,
440114, 440115, 440116, 440117,
440118, 440119, 440120, 440121,
440122, 440123, 440124, 440125,
440126, 440127, 440128, 440129,
440130, 440131, 440201, 440202,
440203, 440204, 440206, 440207,
440208, 440209, 440211, 440212,
440214, 440215, 440216, 440217,
440218, 440220, 440221, 440222,
440223, 440224, 440225, 440229,
440301, 440302, 440303, 440304,
440307, 440311, 440315, 440316,
440317, 440318, 440319, 440321,
440322, 440323, 440324, 440325,
440326, 440328, 440329, 440330,
440331, 440402, 440403, 440404,
440405, 440406, 440407, 440408,
440412, 440413, 440415, 440416,
440417, 440418, 440420, 440421,
440423, 440424, 440425, 440427,
440428, 440429, 440430, 440501,
440502, 440505, 440506, 440507,
440510, 440512, 440513, 440514,
440515, 440517, 440518, 440519,
440522, 440523, 440524, 440525,
440526, 440527, 440528, 440529,
440529, 440530, 440531, 440602,
440604, 440605, 440606, 440607,
440608, 440609, 440610, 440611,
440613, 440614, 440615, 440616,
440617, 440618, 440619, 440622,
440623, 440624, 440625, 440626,
440627, 440628, 440630, 440702,
440703, 440704, 440705, 440706,
440707, 440708, 440709, 440711,
440712, 440713, 440714, 440716,
440717, 440718, 440719, 440720,
440721, 440722, 440723, 440724,
440725, 440726, 440727, 440728,
440729, 440730, 440731, 440801,
440802, 440803, 440804, 440805,
440806, 440808, 440809, 440810,
440812, 440813, 440814, 440815,

440816, 440817, 440818, 440820,
440821, 440822, 440823, 440824,
440825, 440826, 440827, 440828,
440829, 440830, 440831, 440901,
440902, 440903, 440904, 440905,
440906, 440907, 440908, 440910,
440911, 440912, 440913, 440915,
440916, 440917, 440918, 440919,
440920, 440921, 440922, 440923,
440924, 440925, 440928, 441001,
441002, 441003, 441004, 441005,
441006, 441007, 441008, 441009,
441010, 441011, 441012, 441013,
441014, 441015, 441016, 441017,
441018, 441019, 441020, 441021,
441022, 441023, 441024, 441025,
441026, 441027, 441028, 441029,
441030, 441031, 441101, 441102,
441103, 441104, 441105, 441106,
441107, 441108, 441109, 441110,
441111, 441112, 441113, 441114,
441115, 441116, 441117, 441118,
441119, 441120, 441122, 441123,
441124, 441126, 441127, 441128,
441129, 441130, 441202, 441203,
441204, 441205, 441206, 441207,
441208, 441209, 441210, 441211,
441212, 441213, 441214, 441215,
441216, 441217, 441218, 441219,
441220, 441221, 441222, 441223,
441224, 441225, 441226, 441227,
441228, 441229, 450101, 450102,
450103, 450104, 450105, 450106,
450107, 450108, 450109, 450110,
450111, 450112, 450113, 450114,
450115, 450116, 450117, 450118,
450119, 450120, 450121, 450122,
450123, 450124, 450125, 450126,
450127, 450128, 450129, 450130,
450131, 450201, 450203, 450204,
450205, 450206, 450207, 450208,
450209, 450210, 450211, 450212,
450213, 450214, 450215, 450216,
450217, 450218, 450219, 450220,
450221, 450222, 450223, 450224,

450129, 450208, 450411, 450417, 450420, 450503

367th Fighter Group, 440509, 440722, 440807, 440814, 440825, 440908, 441028, 441101, 441227, 450116, 450129, 450201, 450208, 450314, 450319, 450410

368th Fighter Group, 440314, 440607, 440619, 440622, 440807, 440823, 440911, 441002, 441006, 441012, 441101, 441218, 441227, 450105, 450116, 450129, 450208, 450314, 450415, 450416, 450507

370th Fighter Group, 440212, 440501, 440717, 440724, 440807, 440815, 440926, 441101, 450116, 450127, 450129, 450208, 450309, 450420

371st Fighter Group, 440412, 440608, 440623, 440929, 441001, 441101, 450215, 450216, 450407

373d Fighter Group, 440404, 440508, 440719, 440819, 440919, 441022, 441101, 441223, 450116, 450129, 450208, 450311, 450411, 450420, 450506

376th Heavy Bombardment Group, 421031, 421102, 421107, 421108, 421109, 421110, 421118, 421121, 421127, 421215, 421223, 430102, 430204, 430222, 430412, 430613, 430628, 430920, 431101, 431111, 431117, 431126, 431228, 440101, 450416

379th Heavy Bombardment Group, 430415, 430519, 430913, 431010, 431020

381st Heavy Bombardment Group, 430515, 430622, 430623, 430714, 430913, 440408

384th Heavy Bombardment Group, 430525, 430622, 430913, 450425

385th Heavy Bombardment Group, 430626, 430717, 430728, 430913, 431020, 450217

386th Medium Bombardment Group, 430604, 430615, 430729, 430730, 430731, 430802, 430809, 430815, 430817, 430818, 430822, 430823,

430827, 430831, 430906, 430919, 431008, 431112, 431126, 440209, 440906, 441002, 450221, 450409

387th Medium Bombardment Group, 430625, 430731, 430802, 430815, 430816, 430817, 430819, 430825, 430831, 430904, 430918, 431009, 431112, 431126, 440822, 440918, 441030, 450122, 450419, 450429

388th Heavy Bombardment Group, 430623, 430717, 430913, 440813

389th Heavy Bombardment Group, 430613, 430628, 430702, 430703, 430709, 430801, 430826, 430907, 430908, 430913, 430919, 431003, 440215, 450407

390th Heavy Bombardment Group, 430713, 430812, 430913, 431010, 440806, 440807

391st Medium Bombardment Group, 440125, 440215, 440919, 441223, 450410, 450416

392d Heavy Bombardment Group, 430902, 430909, 430913, 431002

394th Medium Bombardment Group, 440311, 440323, 440809, 440825, 440928, 441008, 450122, 450420, 450502

397th Medium Bombardment Group, 440405, 440813, 440831, 440911, 441006, 450420, 450425

398th Heavy Bombardment Group, 440422, 440506, 450123

401st Heavy Bombardment Group, 431101, 431126, 431215

401st Heavy Bombardment Squadron, 430417

401st Provisional Combat Bombardment Wing, 430511, 430512, 430514, 430613, 430626, 430717

402d Provisional Combat Bombardment Wing, 430606, 430713

403d Provisional Combat Bombardment Wing, 430623, 430717

404th Fighter Group, 440404, 440501, 440518, 440519, 440706, 440807,

465th Heavy Bombardment Group, 440505
466th Heavy Bombardment Group, 440221,
    440322, 450324
467th Heavy Bombardment Group, 440212,
    440311, 440410, 440511, 440612,
    440812
474th Fighter Group, 33, 440312, 440425,
    440522, 440806, 440807, 440824,
    440829, 440906, 440909, 440912,
    440917, 440929, 441001, 441101,
    441218, 450116, 450129, 450208,
    450313, 450322, 450422, 450508
479th Antisubmarine Group, 430713,
    430820, 431111, 431204, 440328
479th Fighter Group, 440514, 440526,
    440622, 440810, 440815, 440825,
    440927, 440928, 441003, 441007,
    441030, 441101, 450209, 450214,
    450407, 450413, 450425
480th Fighter Squadron, 440401
482d Heavy Bombardment Group, 430820,
    450101, 450429
482d Heavy Pathfinder Bombardment
    Group, 430927, 431002, 431103,
    431111, 431204, 440214, 440227,
    440322
483d Heavy Bombardment Group, 440412,
    440718
484th Heavy Bombardment Group, 440429,
    440822
485th Heavy Bombardment Group, 440510
486th Heavy Bombardment Group, 440405,
    440507, 440701, 440721, 440801
487th Fighter Squadron, 441102
487th Heavy Bombardment Group, 440323,
    440405, 440507, 440721, 440801
489th Heavy Bombardment Group, 440403,
    440505, 440605, 440814, 441110,
    441129
490th Heavy Bombardment Group, 440412,
    440511, 440530, 440806, 440812,
    440827
491st Heavy Bombardment Group, 440421,
    440504, 440602, 440814, 441126
492d Heavy Bombardment Group, 440418,

440511, 440603, 440606, 440807,
    440811
492d Heavy Bombardment Group (Special
    Operations), 440811, 440812,
    440813, 440917, 441022, 441217,
    450312, 450319
493d Heavy Bombardment Group, 440501,
    450201
495th Fighter Training Group, 431026,
    431227
496th Fighter Training Group, 431227
553d Medium Bombardment Squadron,
    440906
652d Heavy Bombardment Squadron,
    430908, 440328
653d Light Bombardment Squadron, 440809
654th Special Bombardment Squadron,
    440809
689th Quartermaster Company, 420415
788th Heavy Bombardment Squadron,
    440511, 440812, 440813
801st Provisional Heavy Bombardment
    Group, 440328, 440511, 440811,
    440812, 440813
802d Provisional Reconnaissance Group,
    440422, 440809
803d Provisional Bombardment Squadron
    (Radio Counter Measures), 440119,
    440215, 440328
810th Medical Evacuation Squadron, 431222
850th Heavy Bombardment Squadron,
    440511, 440812, 440813
856th Heavy Bombardment Squadron,
    440811, 440813, 440917, 450319
857th Heavy Bombardment Squadron,
    440813, 441217, 450312
858th Heavy Bombardment Squadron,
    440813, 450319
859th Heavy Bombardment Squadron,
    440813
862d Heavy Bombardment Squadron,
    450201
885th Special Bombardment Squadron,
    440812
2906th Provisional Observation Training
    Group, 430816, 431026

INDEX II

Alphabetical Listings

The following alphabetical index contains a small number of *non-numerical* U.S. Army Air Forces command and unit designations (listed under "U.S. Army Air Forces"). For *Allied* air commands, see the listings under "Allied."

References are listed by date in the year-month-day format:
431020 = October 20, 1943

Bebra, Germany, 441204
Becker, Robert H., 440530
Beckham, Walter C., 431010, 440222
Bedja, Tunisia, 430228, 430301, 430302, 430303, 430311, 430423
Beek, Netherlands, 450429
Beerbower, Don M., 440220, 440809
Beeson, Duane W., 430728, 440405
Belandah landing ground, Libya, 421211
Belfort, France, 440511, 440908, 440910, 440912, 440913
Belgrade, Yugoslavia, 440416, 440417, 440424, 440507, 440518, 440606, 440703, 440901, 440902, 440906, 440908, 440918
Belgrade/Rogozarski Airdrome, Yugoslavia, 440417
Belvedere, Italy, 440318
Ben Gardane, Tunisia, 430112
Benedetto de Marsi, Italy, 440303
Benevento, Italy, 430820, 430827, 430911, 430912, 430916, 430921, 430927, 431001, 431003
Benghazi, Libya, 420621, 420623, 420704, 420705, 420708, 420711, 420713, 420715, 420717, 420719, 420723, 420810, 420912, 420913, 420916, 420922, 420925, 420927, 421006, 421008, 421009, 421010, 421016, 421021, 421023, 421025, 421104, 421106, 421110, 421114, 421118, 421120, 430626, 430702, 430719, 430801, 430813
Beni Khaled, Tunisia, 430508
Benne, Louis, 440614
Bennecourt, France, 440531
Bennett, Joseph H., 440308, 440525
Berat, Albania, 440723, 440726
Berat/Kocove Airdrome, Albania, 431105, 431112
Berceto, Italy, 440827
Berchtesgaden, Germany, 450501
Berck-sur-Mer Airdrome, France, 431123, 431124
Berck-sur-Mer, France, 440229, 440421

Bergamo Airdrome, Italy, 440722, 441111, 450222, 450226
Bergamo, Italy, 440706
Bergamo/Orio al Serio Airdrome, Italy, 440809
Bergen Op Zoom, Netherlands, 440410
Bergen/Alkmaar Airdrome, Netherlands, 420704, 430907, 440504
Berlin, Germany, 9, 26, 27, 440303, 440304, 440306, 440308, 440322, 440429, 440507, 440508, 440519, 440524, 440621, 440806, 441006, 441205, 450203, 450226, 450324, 450420, 450430, 450502
Bermuda, 421025
Bernay St.-Martin Airdrome, France, 430816
Bernay, France, 440611
Bernburg, Germany, 440222, 440411
Beroun, Czechoslovakia, 450417
Besa Matruh, Egypt, 420812
Besancon, France, 440909
Bettembourg, Germany, 440511
Beverley, George H., 431209, 431222
Beyer, William R., 440927
Beziers, France, 440705
Biancaville, Sicily, 430803, 430806
Bianco, Italy, 430303
Bickel, Carl G., 440910
Bickford, Edward F., 450426
Biel, Hipolitus T., 440411, 440424
Bielefeld, Germany, 440930, 441026, 441102, 441126, 441129, 441206, 450117, 450209, 450303
Bietingheim, Germany, 441216
Big Week, 24–27, 440220, 440222, 440224, 440225, 440229. *See also* Operation ARGUMENT
Bihac, Yugoslavia, 440402, 440517, 440525, 440526, 440528
Bille, Henry S., 450420
Billengen, Germany, 450422
Bingen, Germany, 440929, 441125, 441127, 441210, 450211

Brampton Grange, England, 420615

Brandenburg, Germany, 440418, 440508, 440806, 450331

Brasov, Romania, 440416, 440506, 440606, 440704

Bratislava, Czechoslovakia, 440616, 440920, 441011, 441014, 450326

Brazil, 420822

Brechten, Germany, 441005

Breitscheid, Germany, 441005

Bremen, Germany, 421119, 430226, 430417, 430613, 431008, 431113, 431126, 431129, 431213, 431216, 431220, 440624, 440729, 440804, 440830, 440926, 441012, 450224, 450311, 450330

Brenner Pass, Italy, 430902, 440513, 440803, 441004, 441023, 441104, 441105, 441106, 441107, 441108, 441110, 441116, 441117, 441121, 441216, 441220, 441226, 441227, 441228, 441229, 441230, 450102, 450130, 450207, 450209, 450211, 450219, 450223, 450227, 450303, 450306, 450310, 450312, 450320, 450323, 450331, 450404, 450406, 450408, 450409, 450410, 450411, 450412, 450417, 450418, 450419, 450420, 450421, 450423, 450424, 450425, 450501, 450504

Brenta River, Italy, 441110, 450423

Brereton, Lewis H., 26, 420623, 420626, 420628, 420630, 420810, 421022, 421112, 430131, 430313, 430808, 431014, 431015, 431016, 431125, 440410, 440807, 440808

Brescia, Italy, 450302, 450405, 450406, 450424

Breslau, Germany, 440304

Brest Peninsula, France, 430501, 430818, 440811, 440826

Brest, France, 421107, 430123, 430227, 430306, 430416, 440825, 440901, 440903, 440905, 440906, 440913, 440914, 440917, 440925

Bretigny Airdrome, France, 440602, 440604, 440808

Brezas, Michael, 440719, 440825

Brindisi Airdrome, Italy, 431118

British Army, 430505, 430612, 430710, 430803, 430909, 440606, 440904, 440923, 441013

First Army, 421115, 421117, 430225

1st Infantry Division, 430611

6th Airborne Division, 440315, 450324

Eighth Army, 420620, 420701, 420816, 421006, 421014, 421023, 421024, 421025, 421026, 421028, 421029, 421102, 421103, 421105, 421108, 421109, 421111, 421112, 421113, 421115, 421120, 421123, 421211, 421213, 421215, 421218, 421224, 430115, 430117, 430118, 430120, 430121, 430122, 430123, 430124, 430125, 430126, 430204, 430217, 430221, 430226, 430304, 430306, 430316, 430317, 430320, 430324, 430326, 430329, 430330, 430406, 430407, 430410, 430416, 430420, 430713, 430716, 430805, 430806, 430811, 430903, 430905, 430907, 430908, 430914, 430927, 431102, 431103, 431111, 431112, 431210, 431216, 431231, 440125, 440511, 440917, 440918, 441107, 441116, 441121, 441122, 441123, 441124, 441210, 450409, 450410, 450411, 450412, 450414, 450415, 450416, 450417, 450418, 450501

airborne forces, 421109, 421110, 421111, 421112, 421113, 421114, 421115, 421116, 421129, 430710, 430713, 440606, 440815, 440917, 441014

commandos, 421112

Brittany region, France, 440611, 440802

Brixlegg, Austria, 450316

Brno Airdrome, Czechoslovakia, 440825

Brno, Czechoslovakia, 440825

Broadhead, Joseph E., 440430

East, Clyde B., 450324, 450413
Eboli, Italy, 430916
Ecka Airdrome, Yugoslavia, 440908
Edens, Billy G., 440707, 440709
Edwards, Edward B., 450411
Egan, Joseph L., Jr., 440315, 440719
Ehmen, Germany, 450101
Ehrgang, Germany, 440511, 440826,
    441219
Eindhoven Airdrome, Netherlands, 440214,
    440330, 440614, 440705, 440818,
    440826
Eindhoven, Netherlands, 440131, 440919
Eisenach, Germany, 440224
Eisenhower, Dwight D., 20, 28, 420620,
    420624, 420628, 420718, 420721,
    420808, 420905, 421020, 421201,
    421224, 430204, 430726, 430727,
    430908, 430929, 431015, 431205,
    440116, 440118, 440120, 440214,
    440326, 440413, 440414, 440417,
    440508, 440604
El Adem Airdrome, Libya, 430204
El Agheila, Libya, 421123, 421205,
    421211, 421213, 421216
El Alamein, Egypt, 420628, 420701,
    420831, 420915, 421006, 421010,
    421019, 421020, 421021, 421022,
    421023, 421024, 421025, 421026,
    421028, 421029, 421030, 421101,
    421102, 421105, 421108
El Aouina Airdrome. *See* Tunis/El Aouina
    Airdrome
El Aouinet, Tunisia, 421230, 430130
El Bathan, Tunisia, 421206, 421207
El Daba landing ground, Egypt, 421009,
    421030, 421105
El Daba, Egypt, 421022
El Djem landing ground, Tunisia, 430401,
    430404, 430406, 430417
El Djem, Tunisia, 430102
El Fuka Airdrome, Egypt, 420814
El Guettar, Tunisia, 421230, 430130,
    430324
El Hamma, Tunisia, 430328

El Hammam, Egypt, 421022
El Haouaria Airdrome, Tunisia, 430602
El Kabrit Airdrome, Egypt, 421113,
    430131, 430310
Elba Island, 430921, 430922, 440412,
    440425, 440507, 440617, 440618,
    440619
Elbe River, Germany, 450411, 450413,
    450425
Elberfield, Germany, 440105
Elburg, Germany, 441024
Elder, John L., 440816
Elder, Robert A., 450324
Eleusis Airdrome, Greece. *See* Athens/
    Eleusis Airdrome
Elmas Airdrome, Sardinia, 421123,
    430206, 430207, 430217, 430218,
    430414, 430519
Emden, Germany, 14, 430127, 430204,
    430515, 430521, 430927, 431002,
    431008, 431211, 440203
Emerson, Warren S., 440825
Emmer, Wallace N., 440513, 440809
Emmerich, Germany, 440614, 440826
Emmert, Benjamin H., Jr., 440731
Emmons, Eugene H., 440406
Empey, James W., 440628
Enfidaville Airdrome, Tunisia, 430406
Enfidaville, Tunisia, 430123, 430312,
    430410, 430411, 430420, 430423,
    430424, 430425, 430427, 430428
England, John B., 440424, 450114
Enna Airdrome, Sicily, 430713
Enna, Sicily, 430714
Enschede Airdrome. *See* Twente/Enschede
    Airdrome
Ent, Uzal G., 430319, 430905
Eperlecques, France, 430830
Epinal, France, 440511, 440523
Erding Airdrome, Germany, 440424,
    450324, 450425
Erfurt, Germany, 450317, 450412
Erkner, Germany, 440303, 440308
Ernst, Herman E., 450302